10 ACTUAL, OFFICIAL LSAT **PREPTESTS** VOLUME VI™

A Publication of the Law School Admission Council,
Newtown, PA

FROM THE EDITOR

Although these PrepTests are presented to you in paper form, the LSAT® and LSAT Writing® are now delivered electronically. Please visit LSAC.org for the most up-to-date information about these tests.

ISBN: 978-0-9983397-8-8

Print number
12 11 10 9 8 7

TABLE OF CONTENTS

The 10 PrepTests in this book are disclosed Law School Admission Tests (LSATs) that were administered between June 2014 and June 2017. Each test in this volume includes actual Analytical Reasoning, Logical Reasoning, and Reading Comprehension items followed by the writing sample, score computation page, and answer key for that test. This publication is designed to be an inexpensive way for you to gain practice and better prepare yourself for taking the LSAT.

The LSAT is an integral part of law school admission in the United States, Canada, and a growing number of other countries. The LSAT is the only test accepted for admission purposes by all ABA-accredited law schools and Canadian common-law law schools. It consists of five 35-minute sections of multiple-choice questions. Four of the five sections contribute to the test taker's score. These sections include one Reading Comprehension section, one Analytical Reasoning section, and two Logical Reasoning sections. The unscored section, commonly referred to as the variable section, typically is used to pretest new test questions or to preequate new test forms. The placement of this section in the LSAT will vary. A 35-minute writing sample is also administered. The writing sample is not scored by LSAC, but copies are sent to all law schools to which you apply. The score scale for the LSAT is 120 to 180.

The LSAT is designed to measure skills considered essential for success in law school: the reading and comprehension of complex texts with accuracy and insight; the organization and management of information and the ability to draw reasonable inferences from it; the ability to think critically; and the analysis and evaluation of the reasoning and arguments of others.

The LSAT provides a standard measure of acquired reading and verbal reasoning skills that law schools can use as one of several factors in assessing applicants.

For up-to-date information about LSAC's services, go to our website, LSAC.org.

SCORING

Your LSAT score is based on the number of questions you answer correctly (the raw score). There is no deduction for incorrect answers, and all questions count equally. In other words, there is no penalty for guessing.

Test Score Accuracy—Reliability and Standard Error of Measurement

Candidates perform at different levels on different occasions for reasons quite unrelated to the characteristics of a test itself. The accuracy of test scores is best described by the use of two related statistical terms: reliability and standard error of measurement.

Reliability is a measure of how consistently a test measures the skills being assessed. The higher the reliability coefficient for a test, the more certain we can be that test takers would get very similar scores if they took the test again.

LSAC reports an internal consistency measure of reliability for every test form. Reliability can vary from 0.00 to 1.00, and a test with no measurement error would have a reliability coefficient of 1.00 (never attained in practice). Reliability coefficients for past LSAT forms have ranged from .90 to .95, indicating a high degree of consistency for these tests. LSAC expects the reliability of the LSAT to continue to fall within the same range.

LSAC also reports the amount of measurement error associated with each test form, a concept known as the *standard error of measurement* (SEM). The SEM, which is usually about 2.6 points, indicates how close a test taker's observed score is likely to be to his or her true score. True scores are theoretical scores that would be obtained from perfectly reliable tests with no measurement error—scores never known in practice.

Score bands, or ranges of scores that contain a test taker's true score a certain percentage of the time, can be derived using the SEM. LSAT score bands are constructed by adding and subtracting the (rounded) SEM to and from an actual LSAT score (e.g., the LSAT score, plus or minus 3 points). Scores near 120 or 180 have asymmetrical bands. Score bands constructed in this manner will contain an individual's true score approximately 68 percent of the time.

Measurement error also must be taken into account when comparing the LSAT scores of two test takers. It is likely that small differences in scores are due to measurement error rather than to meaningful differences in ability. The standard error of score differences provides some guidance as to the importance of differences between two scores. The standard error of score differences is approximately 1.4 times larger than the standard error of measurement for the individual scores.

Thus, a test score should be regarded as a useful but approximate measure of a test taker's abilities as measured by the test, not as an exact determination of his or her abilities. LSAC encourages law schools to examine the range of scores within the interval that probably contains the test taker's true score (e.g., the test taker's score band) rather than solely interpret the reported score alone.

Adjustments for Variation in Test Difficulty

All test forms of the LSAT reported on the same score scale are designed to measure the same abilities, but one test form may be slightly easier or more difficult than another. The scores from different test forms are made comparable through a statistical procedure known as equating. As a result of equating, a given scaled score earned on different test forms reflects the same level of ability.

Research on the LSAT

Summaries of LSAT validity studies and other LSAT research can be found in member law school libraries and at LSAC.org.

HOW THESE PREPTESTS DIFFER FROM AN ACTUAL LSAT

These PrepTests are made up of the scored sections and writing samples from the actual disclosed LSATs administered from June 2014 through June 2017. However, in the Analytical Reasoning section the questions are distributed over four pages rather than over eight pages as in more recent versions of the LSAT. Also, these PrepTests do not contain the extra, variable section that is used to pretest new test items of one of the three multiple-choice question types. The three multiple-choice question types may be in a different order in an actual LSAT than in these PrepTests. This is because the order of these question types is intentionally varied for each administration of the test.

THE THREE LSAT MULTIPLE-CHOICE QUESTION TYPES

The multiple-choice questions on the LSAT reflect a broad range of academic disciplines and are intended to give no advantage to candidates from a particular academic background.

The five sections of the test contain three different question types. The following material presents a general discussion of the nature of each question type and some strategies that can be used in answering them.

Analytical Reasoning Questions

Analytical Reasoning questions are designed to assess the ability to consider a group of facts and rules, and, given those facts and rules, determine what could or must be true. The specific scenarios associated with these questions are usually unrelated to law, since they are intended to be accessible to a wide range of test takers. However, the skills tested parallel those involved in determining what could or must be the case given a set of regulations, the terms of a contract, or the facts of a legal case in relation to the law. In Analytical Reasoning questions, you are asked to reason deductively from a set of statements and rules or principles that describe relationships among persons, things, or events.

Analytical Reasoning questions appear in sets, with each set based on a single passage. The passage used for each set of questions describes common ordering relationships or grouping relationships, or a combination of both types of relationships. Examples include scheduling employees for work shifts, assigning instructors to class sections, ordering tasks according to priority, and distributing grants for projects.

Analytical Reasoning questions test a range of deductive reasoning skills. These include:

- Comprehending the basic structure of a set of relationships by determining a complete solution to the problem posed (for example, an acceptable seating arrangement of all six diplomats around a table)

- Reasoning with conditional ("if-then") statements and recognizing logically equivalent formulations of such statements

- Inferring what could be true or must be true from given facts and rules

- Inferring what could be true or must be true from given facts and rules together with new information in the form of an additional or substitute fact or rule

- Recognizing when two statements are logically equivalent in context by identifying a condition or rule that could replace one of the original conditions while still resulting in the same possible outcomes

Analytical Reasoning questions reflect the kinds of detailed analyses of relationships and sets of constraints that a law student must perform in legal problem solving. For example, an Analytical Reasoning passage might describe six diplomats being seated around a table, following certain rules of protocol as to who can sit where. You, the test taker, must answer questions about the logical implications of given and new information. For example, you may be asked who can sit between diplomats X and Y, or who cannot sit next to X if W sits next to Y. Similarly, if you were a student in law school, you might be asked to analyze a scenario involving a set of particular circumstances and a set of governing rules in the form of constitutional provisions, statutes, administrative codes, or prior rulings that have been upheld. You might then be asked to determine the legal options in the scenario: what is required given the scenario, what is permissible given the scenario, and what is prohibited given the scenario. Or you might be asked to develop a "theory" for the case: when faced with an incomplete set of facts about the case, you must fill in the picture based on what is implied by the facts that are known. The problem could be elaborated by the addition of new information or hypotheticals.

No formal training in logic is required to answer these questions correctly. Analytical Reasoning questions are intended to be answered using knowledge, skills, and reasoning ability generally expected of college students and graduates.

Suggested Approach

Some people may prefer to answer first those questions about a passage that seem less difficult and then those that seem more difficult. In general, it is best to finish one passage before starting on another, because much time can be lost in returning to a passage and reestablishing familiarity with its relationships. However, if you are having great difficulty on one particular set of questions and are spending too much time on them, it may be to your advantage to skip that set of questions and go on to the next passage, returning to the problematic set of questions after you have finished the other questions in the section.

Do not assume that because the conditions for a set of questions look long or complicated, the questions based on those conditions will be especially difficult.

Read the passage carefully. Careful reading and analysis are necessary to determine the exact nature of the relationships involved in an Analytical Reasoning passage. Some relationships are fixed (for example, P and R must always work on the same project). Other relationships are variable (for example, Q must be assigned to either team 1 or team 3). Some relationships that are not stated explicitly in the conditions are implied by and can be deduced from those that are stated (for example, if one condition about paintings in a display specifies that Painting K must be to the left of Painting Y, and another specifies that Painting W must be to the left of Painting K, then it can be deduced that Painting W must be to the left of Painting Y).

In reading the conditions, do not introduce unwarranted assumptions. For instance, in a set of questions establishing relationships of height and weight among the members of a team, do not assume that a person who is taller than another person must weigh more than that person. As another example, suppose a set involves ordering and a question in the set asks what must be true if both X and Y must be earlier than Z; in this case, do not assume that X must be earlier than Y merely because X is mentioned before Y. All the information needed to answer each question is provided in the passage and the question itself.

The conditions are designed to be as clear as possible. Do not interpret the conditions as if they were intended to trick you. For example, if a question asks how many people could be eligible to serve on a committee, consider only those people named in the passage unless directed otherwise. When in doubt, read the conditions in their most obvious sense. Remember, however, that the language in the conditions is intended to be read for precise meaning. It is essential to pay particular attention to words that describe or limit relationships, such as "only," "exactly," "never," "always," "must be," "cannot be," and the like.

The result of this careful reading will be a clear picture of the structure of the relationships involved, including the kinds of relationships permitted, the participants in the relationships, and the range of possible actions or attributes for these participants.

Keep in mind question independence. Each question should be considered separately from the other questions in its set. No information, except what is given in the original conditions, should be carried over from one question to another.

In some cases a question will simply ask for conclusions to be drawn from the conditions as originally given. Some questions may, however, add information to the original conditions or temporarily suspend or replace one of the original conditions for the purpose of that question only. For example, if Question 1 adds the supposition "if P is sitting at table 2 ...," this supposition should NOT be carried over to any other question in the set.

Logical Reasoning Questions

Arguments are a fundamental part of the law, and analyzing arguments is a key element of legal analysis. Training in the law builds on a foundation of basic reasoning skills. Law students must draw on the skills of analyzing, evaluating, constructing, and refuting arguments. They need to be able to identify what information is relevant to an issue or argument and what impact further evidence might have. They need to be able to reconcile opposing positions and use arguments to persuade others.

Logical Reasoning questions evaluate the ability to analyze, critically evaluate, and complete arguments as they occur in ordinary language. The questions are based on short arguments drawn from a wide variety of sources, including newspapers, general interest magazines, scholarly publications, advertisements, and informal discourse. These arguments mirror legal reasoning in the types of arguments presented and in their complexity, though few of the arguments actually have law as a subject matter.

Each Logical Reasoning question requires you to read and comprehend a short passage, then answer one question (or, rarely, two questions) about it. The questions are designed to assess a wide range of skills involved in thinking critically, with an emphasis on skills that are central to legal reasoning. These skills include:

- Recognizing the parts of an argument and their relationships

- Recognizing similarities and differences between patterns of reasoning

- Drawing well-supported conclusions

- Reasoning by analogy

- Recognizing misunderstandings or points of disagreement

- Determining how additional evidence affects an argument

- Detecting assumptions made by particular arguments

- Identifying and applying principles or rules

- Identifying flaws in arguments

- Identifying explanations

The questions do not presuppose specialized knowledge of logical terminology. For example, you will not be expected to know the meaning of specialized terms such as "ad hominem" or "syllogism." On the other hand, you will be expected to understand and critique the reasoning contained in arguments. This requires that you possess a university-level understanding of widely used concepts such as argument, premise, assumption, and conclusion.

Suggested Approach

Read each question carefully. Make sure that you understand the meaning of each part of the question. Make sure that you understand the meaning of each answer choice and the ways in which it may or may not relate to the question posed.

Do not pick a response simply because it is a true statement. Although true, it may not answer the question posed.

Answer each question on the basis of the information that is given, even if you do not agree with it. Work within the context provided by the passage. LSAT questions do not involve any tricks or hidden meanings.

Reading Comprehension Questions

Both law school and the practice of law revolve around extensive reading of highly varied, dense, argumentative, and expository texts (for example, cases, codes, contracts, briefs, decisions, evidence). This reading must be exacting, distinguishing precisely what is said from what is not said. It involves comparison, analysis, synthesis, and application (for example, of principles and rules). It involves drawing appropriate inferences and applying ideas and arguments to new contexts. Law school reading also requires the ability to grasp unfamiliar subject matter and the ability to penetrate difficult and challenging material.

The purpose of LSAT Reading Comprehension questions is to measure the ability to read, with understanding and insight, examples of lengthy and complex materials similar to those commonly encountered in law school. The Reading Comprehension section of the LSAT contains four sets of reading questions, each set consisting of a selection of reading material followed by five to eight questions. The reading selection in three of the four sets consists of a single reading passage; the other set contains two related shorter passages. Sets with two passages are a variant of Reading Comprehension called Comparative Reading, which was introduced in June 2007.

Comparative Reading questions concern the relationships between the two passages, such as those of generalization/instance, principle/application, or point/counterpoint. Law school work often requires reading two or more texts in conjunction with each other and understanding their relationships. For example, a law student may read a trial court decision together with an appellate court decision that overturns it, or identify the fact pattern from a hypothetical suit together with the potentially controlling case law.

Reading selections for LSAT Reading Comprehension questions are drawn from a wide range of subjects in the humanities, the social sciences, the biological and physical sciences, and areas related to the law. Generally, the selections are densely written, use high-level vocabulary, and contain sophisticated argument or complex rhetorical structure (for example, multiple points of view). Reading Comprehension questions require you to read carefully and accurately, to determine the relationships among the various parts of the reading selection, and to draw reasonable inferences from the material in the selection. The questions may ask about the following characteristics of a passage or pair of passages:

- The main idea or primary purpose

- Information that is explicitly stated

- Information or ideas that can be inferred

- The meaning or purpose of words or phrases as used in context

- The organization or structure

- The application of information in the selection to a new context

- Principles that function in the selection

- Analogies to claims or arguments in the selection

- An author's attitude as revealed in the tone of a passage or the language used

- The impact of new information on claims or arguments in the selection

Suggested Approach

Since reading selections are drawn from many different disciplines and sources, you should not be discouraged if you encounter material with which you are not familiar. It is important to remember that questions are to be answered exclusively on the basis of the information provided in the selection. There is no particular knowledge that you are expected to bring to the test, and you should not make inferences based on any prior knowledge of a subject that you may have. You may, however, wish to defer working on a set of questions that seems particularly difficult or unfamiliar until after you have dealt with sets you find easier.

Strategies. One question that often arises in connection with Reading Comprehension has to do with the most effective and efficient order in which to read the selections and questions. Possible approaches include:

- reading the selection very closely and then answering the questions;

- reading the questions first, reading the selection closely, and then returning to the questions; or

- skimming the selection and questions very quickly, then rereading the selection closely and answering the questions.

Test takers are different, and the best strategy for one might not be the best strategy for another. In preparing for the test, therefore, you might want to experiment with the different strategies and decide what works most effectively for you. Remember that your strategy must be effective under timed conditions. For this reason, the first strategy—reading the selection very closely and then answering the questions—may be the most effective for you. Nonetheless, if you believe that one of the other strategies might be more effective for you, you should try it out and assess your performance using it.

Reading the selection. Whatever strategy you choose, you should give the passage or pair of passages at least one careful reading before answering the questions. Try to distinguish main ideas from supporting ideas, and opinions or attitudes from factual, objective information. Note transitions from one idea to the next and identify the relationships among the different ideas or parts of a passage, or between the two passages in Comparative Reading sets. Consider how and why an author makes points and draws conclusions. Be sensitive to implications of what the passages say.

You may find it helpful to mark key parts of passages. For example, you might underline main ideas or important arguments, and you might circle transitional words—"although," "nevertheless," "correspondingly," and the like—that will help you map the structure of a passage. Also, you might note descriptive words that will help you identify an author's attitude toward a particular idea or person.

Answering the Questions

- Always read all the answer choices before selecting the best answer. The best answer choice is the one that most accurately and completely answers the question being posed.

- Respond to the specific question being asked. Do not pick an answer choice simply because it is a true statement. For example, picking a true statement might yield an incorrect answer to a question in which you are asked to identify an author's position on an issue, since you are not being asked to evaluate the truth of the author's position but only to correctly identify what that position is.

- Answer the questions only on the basis of the information provided in the selection. Your own views, interpretations, or opinions, and those you have heard from others, may sometimes conflict with those expressed in a reading selection; however, you are expected to work within the context provided by the reading selection. You should not expect to agree with everything you encounter in Reading Comprehension passages.

THE WRITING SAMPLE*

You will be asked to write one sample essay. LSAC does not score the writing sample, but copies are sent to all law schools to which you apply. According to a 2015 LSAC survey of 129 United States and Canadian law schools, almost all use the writing sample in evaluating at least some applications for admission. Failure to respond to writing sample prompts and frivolous responses have been used by law schools as grounds for rejection of applications for admission.

In developing and implementing the writing sample portion of the LSAT, LSAC has operated on the following premises: First, law schools and the legal profession value highly the ability to communicate effectively in writing. Second, it is important to encourage potential law students to develop effective writing skills. Third, a sample of an applicant's writing, produced under controlled conditions, is a potentially useful indication of that person's writing ability. Fourth, the writing sample can serve as an independent check on other writing submitted by applicants as part of the admission process. Finally, writing samples may be useful for diagnostic purposes related to improving a candidate's writing.

The writing prompt presents a decision problem. You are asked to make a choice between two positions or courses of action. Both of the choices are defensible, and you are given criteria and facts on which to base your decision. There is no "right" or "wrong" position to take on the topic, so the quality of each test taker's response is a function not of which choice is made, but of how well or poorly the choice

---

*Note: The writing sample is now administered on a secure, proctored online platform at a time and place of your choosing. Visit LSAC.org for more details.

is supported and how well or poorly the other choice is criticized.

The LSAT writing prompt was designed and validated by legal education professionals. Since it involves writing based on fact sets and criteria, the writing sample gives applicants the opportunity to demonstrate the type of argumentative writing that is required in law school, although the topics are usually nonlegal.

You will have 35 minutes in which to plan and write an essay on the topic you receive. Read the topic and the accompanying directions carefully. You will probably find it best to spend a few minutes considering the topic and organizing your thoughts before you begin writing. In your essay, be sure to develop your ideas fully, leaving time, if possible, to review what you have written. Do not write on a topic other than the one specified. Writing on a topic of your own choice is not acceptable.

No special knowledge is required or expected for this writing exercise. Law schools are interested in the reasoning, clarity, organization, language usage, and writing mechanics displayed in your essay. How well you write is more important than how much you write.

TAKING THE PREPTESTS UNDER SIMULATED LSAT CONDITIONS

One important way to prepare for the LSAT is to simulate the day of the test by taking a practice test under actual time constraints. Taking a practice test under timed conditions helps you to estimate the amount of time you can afford to spend on each question in a section and to determine the question types on which you may need additional practice.

Since the LSAT is a timed test, it is important to use your allotted time wisely. During the test, you may work only on the section designated by the test supervisor. You cannot devote extra time to a difficult section and make up that time on a section you find easier. In pacing yourself, and checking your answers, you should think of each section of the test as a separate minitest.

Be sure that you answer every question on the test. When you do not know the correct answer to a question, first eliminate the responses that you know are incorrect, then make your best guess among the remaining choices. Do not be afraid to guess as there is no penalty for incorrect answers.

When you take a practice test, abide by all the requirements specified in the directions and keep strictly within the specified time limits. Work without a rest period. When you take an actual test, you will have a short break between two of the sections.

When taken under conditions as much like actual testing conditions as possible, a practice test provides very useful preparation for taking the LSAT.

Official directions for the four multiple-choice sections and the writing samples are included in these PrepTests so that you can approximate actual testing conditions as you practice.

To take the test:

- Set a timer for 35 minutes. Answer all the questions in Section I. Stop working on that section when the 35 minutes have elapsed.

- Repeat, allowing yourself 35 minutes each for Sections II, III, and IV.

- Set the timer again for 35 minutes, then prepare your response to the writing sample topic at the end of each PrepTest.

- Refer to the "Computing Your Score" section at the end of each PrepTest for instruction on evaluating your performance. An answer key is provided for that purpose.

THE OFFICIAL LSAT
PREPTEST®

- PrepTest 72
- Form 5LSN113

JUNE 2014

SECTION I

Time—35 minutes

27 Questions

Directions: Each set of questions in this section is based on a single passage or a pair of passages. The questions are to be answered on the basis of what is stated or implied in the passage or pair of passages. For some of the questions, more than one of the choices could conceivably answer the question. However, you are to choose the best answer; that is, the response that most accurately and completely answers the question, and blacken the corresponding space on your answer sheet.

In the last half-century, firefighters in North America have developed a powerful system for fighting wildfires using modern technology. But at the same time, foresters and ecologists are increasingly
(5) aware that too much firefighting can be worse than none at all. Over the millennia, many forest ecosystems have evolved in such a way that they are dependent on periodic fires for renewal and for limiting damage when fires do occur. Ancient ponderosa forests, for
(10) example, were stable in part because low-intensity fires maintained open forests with low levels of fuel for future fires. These fires burned lightly around the bases of mature trees, leaving these trees alive and clearing the understory of brush and young trees.
(15) Scientists can easily count the regular recurrence of fires in these forests over the centuries by examining the scars left on trunks; the typical interval between fires could be as short as 5 years and rarely extended beyond 25 years.
(20) If fires are kept out of forests, however, deadwood and other fuels build up; then, when fire is sparked by lightning or some other cause, what results is a fire so large that it leaves total devastation. Such fires often kill off wildlife that might escape low-intensity fires,
(25) and they also reach the crowns of centuries-old trees, destroying them and ultimately enabling rains to erode the unprotected topsoil. Because of the relative success of fire-suppression efforts, many forests, including ponderosa forests, have now been free of fire for
(30) 50 years or longer, leaving them vulnerable to these devastating crown fires. It is therefore increasingly necessary for land managers in North America to strive to manage rather than eliminate fires; land management policies should recognize the essential
(35) role that fire plays in many ecosystems.

Fire behavior depends on the complex interaction of three factors—topography, weather, and fuel—and since topography is fixed and weather is unpredictable, fuel is the only element that land managers can
(40) control. Land managers should therefore focus their efforts on fuel. A new kind of wildfire management that is designed to simulate the natural role of fire through a combination of selective harvesting and prescribed fires is the most promising method for
(45) controlling fuel. Selective timber harvesting focuses on smaller trees—markets for this smaller material do exist—leaving the larger, fire-tolerant trees on the land and thinning the forest, thereby re-creating the conditions that allow for low-intensity burns.
(50) Prescribed fire management includes both the intentional lighting of controlled burns and the policy

of allowing fires set by lightning to burn when the weather is damp enough to reduce the risk of extensive damage. Once fuels are reduced by these fires,
(55) maintenance burns at 15- to 20-year intervals will be needed. When wildfires inevitably occur, they will be more easily controlled and do much less damage.

1. The primary purpose of the passage is to

(A) claim that ideological dogma may be impeding the enactment of a fundamental and necessary policy change

(B) compare the actual effects that have resulted from two different policies designed to have the same effect

(C) contend that a recently implemented policy requires a substantial increase in funding

(D) recommend a fundamental policy change in light of evidence that current policy has created undesirable conditions

(E) argue that two seemingly contradictory goals of a policy are actually compatible in a fundamental way

2. By "maintenance burns" (line 55) the author most clearly refers to

(A) the low-intensity fires that regularly occurred in ancient forests

(B) fires that reduce the population density of mature trees

(C) the types of fires that are likely to occur in North American forest ecosystems today

(D) a type of fire that used to occur at intervals greater than 50 years

(E) naturally or intentionally set fires that are allowed to burn to eliminate fuel

GO ON TO THE NEXT PAGE.

3. Which one of the following sentences would most logically complete the last paragraph of the passage?

(A) However, if homes were not built in such close proximity to forests, the damage to developed property would be limited substantially.

(B) Unfortunately, until foresters recognize the dangers posed by excess fuel in forests, these proposals are likely to meet with resistance in the forestry community.

(C) But even with these policies, which require some years to achieve their intended effects, large, devastating fires will remain a threat in the near term.

(D) Yet, because smaller trees will likely yield less profit for timber companies, the ecological benefits of the new plans must be weighed carefully against their economic impact.

(E) But given the large financial resources needed to operate a prescribed fire management system, the chances of such policies being implemented are quite small.

4. The author cites the factors of topography, weather, and fuel in the last paragraph primarily as part of

(A) the support provided for the contention that land managers must focus on fuel to reduce the risk of crown fires

(B) an argument that, given the interaction among these factors, land managers' efforts to control wildfires will always be somewhat ineffective

(C) an attempt to provide a clearer understanding of why forest fires have become unnaturally devastating

(D) an argument that specific fuel types and forest densities are dependent on topographic and weather conditions

(E) the suggestion that fires started by lightning will continue to be a factor in wildfire suppression efforts

5. The passage provides the most support for inferring that which one of the following is true of ancient ponderosa forests?

(A) Ponderosas that thrived in these forests probably differed genetically from modern ponderosas in subtle, though significant, ways.

(B) The population density of trees in these forests was generally lower than it is in many ponderosa forests today.

(C) Weather patterns in these forests were substantially different from weather patterns in ponderosa forests today.

(D) The diversity of plant species was greater in these forests than it is in ponderosa forests today.

(E) In addition to clearing out excess fuel, periodic low-intensity fires helped to control wildlife populations in these forests.

6. It can be inferred from the passage that the author would be most likely to regard a policy in which all forest fires that were started by lightning were allowed to burn until they died out naturally as

(A) a viable means of restoring forests currently vulnerable to catastrophic fires to a cycle of periodic low-intensity fires

(B) an essential component of a new wildfire management plan that would also involve the regulation of timber harvests

(C) beneficial to forests that have centuries-old trees, though harmful to younger forests

(D) currently too extreme and likely to cause the destruction land managers are seeking to avoid

(E) politically infeasible given the public perception of the consequences of such fires

GO ON TO THE NEXT PAGE.

The government of Mali passed a law against excavating and exporting the wonderful terra-cotta sculptures from the old city of Djenne-jeno, but it could not enforce it. And it certainly could not afford
(5) to fund thousands of archaeological excavations. The result was that many fine Djenne-jeno terra-cotta sculptures were illicitly excavated in the 1980s and sold to foreign collectors who rightly admired them. Because these sites were looted, much of what we
(10) would most like to know about this culture—much that we could have learned had the sites been preserved by careful archaeology—may now never be known.

It has been natural to condemn such pillaging. And, through a number of declarations from UNESCO
(15) and other international bodies, a protective doctrine has evolved concerning the ownership of many forms of cultural property (the "UNESCO doctrine"). Essentially the doctrine provides that cultural artifacts should be regarded as the property of the culture. For
(20) an individual belonging to that culture, such works are, using UNESCO's terminology, part of an "artistic and cultural patrimony." Further, a number of countries have strengthened the UNESCO doctrine by declaring all antiquities that originate within their borders to be
(25) state property that cannot be freely exported.

Accordingly, it seems reasonable that the government of Mali, within whose borders the Djenne-jeno antiquities are buried, be the one to regulate excavating Djenne-jeno and to decide where
(30) the statues should go. Regrettably, and this is a painful irony, regulations prohibiting export and requiring repatriation can discourage recording and preserving information about cultural antiquities, one of the key reasons for the UNESCO regulations. For example, if
(35) someone in London sells a figure from Djenne-jeno with documentation that it came out of the ground there after the regulations were implemented, then the authorities committed to the restitution of objects taken illegally out of Mali have the very evidence
(40) they need to seize the figure.

Suppose that from the beginning, Mali had been helped by UNESCO to exercise its trusteeship of the Djenne-jeno terra-cotta sculptures by licensing excavations and educating people to recognize that
(45) such artifacts have greater value when they are removed carefully from the earth with accurate records of location. Suppose Mali had required that objects be recorded and registered before leaving the excavation site, and had imposed a tax on exported objects to
(50) fund acquisitions of important pieces for the national museum. The excavations encouraged by such a system may have been less well conducted and less informative than proper, professionally administered excavations by accredited archaeologists. Some people
(55) would still have avoided the rules. But would this not have been better than what actually happened?

7. Which one of the following most accurately expresses the main point of the passage?

(A) Declarations from UNESCO and other international bodies concerning the ownership of cultural artifacts gave rise to a doctrine based on the notion of artistic and cultural patrimony.

(B) Preserving cultural knowledge at sites like Djenne-jeno requires solutions that are more flexible than simply passing laws prohibiting the excavation and export of antiquities.

(C) Rather than acceding to the dictates of international bodies, countries like Mali must find their own unique solutions to problems concerning the preservation of cultural heritage.

(D) The government of Mali should have exercised its trusteeship of the Djenne-jeno terra-cotta sculptures by licensing only accredited archaeologists for the excavations.

(E) The idea that a culture's artistic and cultural patrimony is the property of the state does more harm than good in countries like Mali.

8. The passage indicates that some countries have made use of the UNESCO doctrine in which one of the following ways?

(A) requiring the origins of all antiquities sold to collectors to be fully documented

(B) restricting the export of antiquities and declaring all antiquities originating within the country's borders to be state property

(C) adopting plans to teach people to recognize that antiquities have greater value when they are removed carefully from the earth with accurate records of location

(D) encouraging trade in a particular ancient culture's artifacts among countries each of which contains within its boundaries a portion of that ancient culture's territory

(E) committing substantial resources to the restoration of antiquities taken illegally out of countries like Mali

9. The author asks the reader to suppose that Mali had imposed a tax on exported objects (lines 49–51) primarily in order to

(A) draw attention to the role of museums in preserving cultural patrimonies

(B) praise one of the Malian government's past policies concerning cultural antiquities

(C) present one part of a more pragmatic approach to regulating the trade in cultural antiquities

(D) suggest a means of giving people who excavate cultural antiquities incentive to keep careful records

(E) highlight a flaw in the UNESCO doctrine

GO ON TO THE NEXT PAGE.

10. The author of the passage would be most likely to agree with which one of the following statements about UNESCO?

(A) It can play an important role in stemming abuses that arise from the international trade in cultural artifacts.

(B) Its stance on cultural artifacts emerged for the most part in response to Mali's loss of terra-cotta sculptures from Djenne-jeno.

(C) It is more effective with initiatives that involve individual states than initiatives that involve several states.

(D) It pays too little attention to the concerns of countries like Mali.

(E) Its effectiveness in limiting the loss of cultural knowledge has been hampered by inadequate funding.

11. The author of the passage would be most likely to agree with which one of the following statements about regulations governing the trade in cultural antiquities in countries like Mali?

(A) Such regulations must be approved by archaeologists before being enacted.

(B) Such regulations must have as their goal maximizing the number of cultural antiquities that ultimately remain in these countries.

(C) Such regulations can be beneficial even if not all people strictly comply with them.

(D) Such regulations must be accompanied by very strict punishments for violators.

(E) Such regulations are most effective when they are very simple and easily understood.

12. The author of the passage would be most likely to agree with which one of the following statements about cultural antiquities?

(A) They must be owned and protected by a country's national museum.

(B) They must remain within the boundaries of the country in which they were found.

(C) They are too valuable to be owned exclusively by the state.

(D) They should be excavated by professional archaeologists when possible.

(E) They belong to whoever finds them and registers them with the state.

13. Which one of the following is an element of the author's attitude toward foreign collectors of terra-cotta sculptures from Djenne-jeno?

(A) appreciation of their efforts to preserve cultural artifacts

(B) approval of their aesthetic judgment

(C) dismay at their failure to take action against illegal exportation of cultural artifacts

(D) frustration with their lack of concern for the people of Mali

(E) sympathy with their motives

GO ON TO THE NEXT PAGE.

The following passage is based on an article published in 1987.

Medical practitioners are ethically required to prescribe the best available treatments. In ordinary patient-physician interactions, this obligation is unproblematic, but when physicians are clinical
(5) researchers in comparative studies of medical treatments, special issues arise. Comparative clinical trials involve withholding one or more of the treatments from at least one group of patients. Traditionally, most physicians and ethicists have agreed that in testing a
(10) new treatment on a patient population for which there exists a currently accepted treatment, the participating physicians should have no opinion as to which treatment is clinically superior—a state of mind usually termed "equipoise."
(15) Unfortunately, the conception of equipoise that is typically employed—which I will term "theoretical equipoise"—may be too strict. Theoretical equipoise exists only when the overall evidence for each of two treatment regimens is judged by each clinical
(20) researcher to be exactly balanced—an ideal hardly attainable in practice. Clinical researchers commonly have some preference for one of the treatments being tested, an intuitive preference perhaps, or one based on their interpretation and balancing of various sources
(25) of evidence. Even if researchers judged the evidence to be balanced at the start of a comparative clinical trial, such a balance would be extremely fragile, liable to be "tipped" by small accretions of evidence as the study progresses. Consequently, if the standard of
(30) theoretical equipoise is adhered to, few comparative clinical trials could commence and even fewer could proceed to completion.

These difficulties associated with theoretical equipoise suggest that a different notion of equipoise
(35) should be developed, one that I will label "clinical equipoise." Clinical equipoise would impose rigorous ethical standards on comparative clinical trials without unreasonably constricting them. One reason for conducting comparative clinical trials is to resolve a
(40) current or imminent conflict in the expert clinical community over what treatment is to be preferred for patients with a given illness. It could be that the standard treatment is A but new evidence suggests that B will be superior. Medical experts may be
(45) divided as to which treatment is better, with each side recognizing that opposing experts can differ honestly in their interpretation of the evidence.

The very absence of consensus within the expert clinical community is what makes clinical equipoise
(50) possible. One or more of a comparative clinical trial's researchers may have a decided treatment preference based on their assessments of the evidence. But that is no ethical bar to participation in the trial. The clinical researchers must simply each recognize that their less-
(55) favored treatment is preferred by a sizable constituency within the medical profession as a whole.

14. The author's primary purpose in the passage is to

(A) explain the difference between two conceptions of an ethical standard together with how these conceptions would affect comparative clinical trials

(B) argue for a more reasonable, less restrictive interpretation of an ethical requirement than the one traditionally given by ethicists and physicians

(C) demonstrate that a change in the standards governing comparative clinical trials will endanger the ability of researchers to derive valuable information from such trials

(D) demonstrate the need for clinical researchers to more closely examine the conceptions embodied in the ethical standards to which these researchers adhere

(E) argue for a change in the scientific methods used for gathering evidence in comparative clinical trials

15. The primary purpose of the second paragraph of the passage is to

(A) provide a view that contrasts with arguments in favor of clinical equipoise

(B) explore the factors underlying physicians' preferences regarding competing treatments

(C) undermine the moral principle that underlies the theory of theoretical equipoise

(D) state the main difficulty with adhering to the standards of theoretical equipoise

(E) illustrate the conflicts inherent in the general notion of equipoise

16. According to the passage, which one of the following is true?

(A) Comparative clinical trials that meet the standard of theoretical equipoise generally present no ethical problems.

(B) Clinical researchers are often forced to suspend comparative clinical trials prematurely because initial data from the trials strongly favors one treatment over another.

(C) A clinical trial comparing treatments is not rendered unethical merely because one of the participating physicians has come to favor one of the treatments over the other.

(D) A comparative clinical trial that meets the standard of clinical equipoise would therefore also meet the standard of theoretical equipoise.

(E) Medical researchers generally try to conduct comparative clinical trials in accordance with the standard of clinical equipoise.

17. Suppose two medical treatments are being compared in a clinical trial for their effectiveness in treating a condition. Based on the passage, which one of the following scenarios would be significantly more likely to jeopardize theoretical equipoise than clinical equipoise?

(A) The initial results of the trial so strikingly favored one treatment that they were published and widely disseminated before the study was even half over; as a result, most physicians who specialize in treating the condition came to favor the more effective treatment before the trial had ended.

(B) Preliminary results in the trial suggest that the two treatments are equally effective in treating the condition; but these results are not reported while the trial is underway and thus few in the expert clinical community are aware of them.

(C) Several of the physicians participating in the trial think that one treatment is more effective at treating the condition than the other; in this they agree with the consensus view within the expert clinical community.

(D) Initial results from the trial convince several of the participating physicians that one treatment more effectively treats the condition than the other does; this does not affect their recognition of the lack of consensus among experts in treating the disease.

(E) There is consensus among physicians participating in the trial that both treatments are equally effective at treating the condition; however, there is no consensus within the expert medical community as to the relative effectiveness of the treatments.

18. Which one of the following most accurately expresses the main point of the passage?

(A) The ethical requirement that physicians prescribe the best available treatment to their patients is jeopardized by an overly strict conception of equipoise.

(B) Medical research conducted through comparative clinical trials is able to achieve more if the ethical requirements it is bound by are not overly restrictive.

(C) It is sometimes ethically acceptable for a physician to participate in a clinical trial in which the physician has a decided treatment preference in favor of one of the treatments being tested.

(D) Clinical equipoise should be adopted because it is less likely to unreasonably constrict the conducting of comparative clinical trials than is theoretical equipoise.

(E) Even though comparative clinical trials often fail to meet the standard of theoretical equipoise, they should not, for that reason, be considered unethical.

19. As used in line 41 of the passage, the term "community" most nearly refers to a group of people

(A) who focus on a common set of problems using a shared body of knowledge

(B) who live and work in the same geographical area as one another

(C) who share opinions that differ significantly from those of other groups

(D) whose association with one another is based on their similar ethical values

(E) whose similar research methods are employed in unrelated disciplines

20. According to the passage, which one of the following is true?

(A) Most clinical trials that are conducted meet the appropriate ethical standards.

(B) Clinical trials would be conducted more often if there were a more reasonable ethical standard in place.

(C) Theoretical equipoise imposes an ethical standard on clinical trials that is rarely if ever met.

(D) Most physicians and ethicists believe that the currently accepted ethical requirements for comparative clinical trials are adequate.

(E) Most comparative clinical trials are undertaken to help resolve a conflict of opinion in the expert clinical community concerning the best available treatment.

21. The author's argument in the third and fourth paragraphs would be most weakened if which one of the following were true?

(A) In most comparative clinical trials, the main purpose is to prove definitively that a treatment considered best by a consensus of relevant experts is in fact superior to the alternative being tested.

(B) Physicians participating in comparative clinical trials rarely ask to leave the trials because early data favors one of the treatments being tested over another.

(C) The number of comparative clinical trials that are conducted annually is increasing rapidly, but the level of ethical oversight of these trials is decreasing.

(D) Medical ethicists are more inclined than are clinical researchers to favor an ethical requirement based on theoretical equipoise over one based on clinical equipoise.

(E) In clinical trials comparing two treatments, it rarely occurs that researchers who begin the trial with no preference for either of the treatments later develop a strong preference on the basis of data obtained early in the study.

GO ON TO THE NEXT PAGE.

Passage A

In 1994, Estonia became the first country to introduce a "flat tax" on personal and corporate income. Income is taxed at a single uniform rate of 26 percent: no schedule of rates, no deductions. So far eight
(5) countries have followed Estonia's example. An old idea that for decades elicited the response, "Fine in theory, just not practical in the real world," seems to be working as well in practice as it does on the blackboard.

Practical types who said that flat taxes cannot
(10) work offer a further instant objection, once they are shown such taxes working, namely, that they are unfair. Enlightened countries, it is argued, have "progressive" tax systems, requiring high-income earners to forfeit a bigger share of their incomes in tax than low-income
(15) earners have to pay. A flat tax seems to rule this out in principle.

Not so. A flat tax on personal incomes combines a threshold (that is, an exempt amount) with a single rate of tax on all income above it. The extent to which
(20) such a system is progressive can be varied within wide limits using just these two variables. Under the systems operating in most developed countries, the incentives for high-income earners to avoid tax (legally or otherwise) are enormous; and the opportunities to do
(25) so, which arise from the very complexity of the codes, are commensurately large. So it is unsurprising that high-income earners usually pay about as much tax under new flat-tax regimes as they would have paid under the previous codes.

Passage B

(30) A lot of people don't understand graduated, as opposed to "flat," taxes. They think that if you make more money you pay a higher rate on your entire earnings, which seems unfair. Actually, graduated progressive taxes treat all taxpayers equally.
(35) Every taxpayer pays the same rate on equivalent layers of income. People in higher brackets don't pay the higher rate on their entire income, only on the portion of income over a specified amount. People, not dollars, are treated equally.

(40) All people are created equal, but not all dollars are created equal. Earnings of the working poor go almost entirely for survival expenses such as food, shelter, and clothing. At that level, every dollar is critical; even a small difference causes tremendous
(45) changes in quality of life. Middle-income earners are still very conscious of expenses, but have much greater flexibility in absorbing small fluctuations in income.

Even some of the flat tax proposals recognize this, and want to exempt a primary layer from the tax
(50) system. So, since they recognize that survival dollars are different from discretionary dollars, why go suddenly from one extreme (paying no taxes) to the other (paying the top rate)? Since flat tax proposals are supposed to bring in the same total amount of tax
(55) revenue, if the working poor are going to pay less and the high-income earners are going to pay less, it is naturally going to fall on the middle class to make up the difference.

22. Both passages are concerned with answering which one of the following questions?

(A) Can a flat tax be implemented?
(B) Do graduated progressive taxes treat all taxpayers equally?
(C) Can a flat tax be fair to all taxpayers?
(D) What are some objections to progressive taxes?
(E) Do flat tax regimes reduce illegal tax avoidance?

23. Both passages seek to advance their arguments by means of which one of the following?

(A) accusing opponents of shifting their ground
(B) citing specific historical developments as evidence
(C) arguing on the basis of an analogy
(D) employing rhetorical questions
(E) correcting alleged misunderstandings

24. Which one of the following, if true of countries that have gone from a graduated progressive tax system to a flat tax, would most support the position of passage B over that of passage A?

(A) Revenues from taxation have remained the same as before.
(B) The tax codes in these countries have been greatly simplified.
(C) Most high-income taxpayers believe that they remain overtaxed.
(D) Middle-income taxpayers tend to pay higher taxes than before.
(E) Some legislators favor a return to a graduated progressive system.

25. Which one of the following is a conclusion for which passage A argues but that passage B does not address?

(A) that exempting a threshold amount enables a flat tax to avoid unfairness
(B) that flat tax proposals are not practical in the real world
(C) that higher taxes on high-income earners inhibit investment and economic growth
(D) that a flat tax decreases opportunities and incentives for high-income earners to avoid tax
(E) that a progressive tax is unfair to taxpayers who end up paying more

GO ON TO THE NEXT PAGE.

26. The authors of the two passages would be most likely to disagree over whether

(A) a flat tax system can be progressive

(B) high-income earners would pay less under a flat tax system than under a graduated progressive system

(C) flat tax systems are fine in theory but cannot be put into practice

(D) graduated progressive systems make higher-income taxpayers pay a higher rate on their entire earnings

(E) all of an individual's income should be subject to taxation

27. Which one of the following, if true, would be the most reasonable response for the author of passage B to make to the final argument of passage A?

(A) Even under a flat-tax regime, it will be possible for some with high incomes to avoid taxes by underreporting their incomes.

(B) Existing tax codes allow tax avoidance by those with high incomes mainly because they contain loopholes and special deductions, not because they are graduated.

(C) It is unfair to those with high incomes to single them out as tax avoiders, since people at all income levels have been known to try to avoid taxes, sometimes illegally.

(D) Most taxpayers prefer a system that affords them opportunities for avoiding taxes over one that does not afford such opportunities.

(E) The goal of reducing tax avoidance would be advanced by eliminating income taxes altogether in favor of taxes on consumption of goods and services.

S T O P

IF YOU FINISH BEFORE TIME IS CALLED, YOU MAY CHECK YOUR WORK ON THIS SECTION ONLY.
DO NOT WORK ON ANY OTHER SECTION IN THE TEST.

SECTION II

Time—35 minutes

26 Questions

<u>Directions:</u> The questions in this section are based on the reasoning contained in brief statements or passages. For some questions, more than one of the choices could conceivably answer the question. However, you are to choose the <u>best</u> answer; that is, the response that most accurately and completely answers the question. You should not make assumptions that are by commonsense standards implausible, superfluous, or incompatible with the passage. After you have chosen the best answer, blacken the corresponding space on your answer sheet.

1. Treat training consists of rewarding dogs with edible treats whenever they respond appropriately to commands. Most dogs will quickly learn what they need to do to receive a treat, so this appears to be an effective training method. However, most dogs who have been treat-trained will not obey commands unless they are shown a treat. Since you cannot always have treats on hand, you should instead use praise and verbal correction to train your dog.

    Which one of the following principles, if valid, most helps to justify the reasoning above?

    (A) The more quickly a dog learns to respond to a stimulus, the more likely it is that the owner will continue to use that stimulus.
    (B) The more often a dog is given a stimulus, the more likely it is that the dog will obey its owner's command even when the owner does not provide that stimulus.
    (C) A dog should be trained by the method that results in a high obedience rate in at least some circumstances.
    (D) A dog should be trained to respond to a stimulus that its owner can supply in all situations.
    (E) A dog should not be trained by a method that has not proven to be effective for any other dogs.

2. Archaeologist: For 2,000 years the ancient Sumerians depended on irrigation to sustain the agriculture that fed their civilization. But eventually irrigation built up in the soil toxic levels of the salts and other impurities left behind when water evaporates. When its soil became unable to support agriculture, Sumerian civilization collapsed. A similar fate is thus likely to befall modern civilizations that continue to rely heavily on irrigation for agriculture.

    Which one of the following, if true, most weakens the archaeologist's argument?

    (A) Most modern civilizations could not feed themselves through agriculture without relying heavily on irrigation.
    (B) Factors unrelated to the use of irrigation would probably have caused Sumerian civilization to collapse sooner or later.
    (C) Many modern farmers use irrigation techniques that avoid the buildup of salts and other toxic impurities in the soil.
    (D) Many modern civilizations do not rely to any significant extent on irrigation for agriculture.
    (E) The soil of ancient Sumeria already contained some toxic salts and other impurities before the Sumerians started using irrigation for agriculture.

3. Researcher: Dinosaur fossils come in various forms, including mineralized bones and tracks in dried mud flats. However, mineralized dinosaur bones and dinosaur tracks in dried mud flats are rarely found together. This isn't surprising, because creatures that scavenged dinosaur carcasses most likely frequented mud flats to find food.

    Which one of the following, if true, would most strengthen the researcher's argument?

    (A) Dinosaur tracks are also found in locations other than mud flats.
    (B) Scavengers commonly drag a carcass away from the site where it was found.
    (C) Researchers have found more fossil dinosaur tracks than fossil dinosaur bones.
    (D) Dinosaur fossils other than mineralized bone or tracks in dried mud flats are quite common.
    (E) It takes longer for bone to mineralize than it takes for tracks to dry in mud flats.

GO ON TO THE NEXT PAGE.

4. Electric stovetop burners would cause fewer fires if their highest temperature were limited to 350°C (662°F), which provides more than enough heat for efficient and effective cooking. The lowest temperature at which cooking oil and most common fibers ignite is 387°C, and electric burners on high go well above 700°C.

Which one of the following most accurately expresses the conclusion drawn in the argument?

(A) Electric stovetop burners would cause fewer fires if their highest temperature were limited to 350°C.

(B) A maximum temperature of 350°C provides more than enough heat for efficient and effective cooking.

(C) The lowest ignition temperature for cooking oil and most common fibers is 387°C.

(D) Electric burners on high go well above 700°C.

(E) Electric stovetop burners cause fires because they go well above 700°C when set on high.

5. Jenkins maintains that the movie *Firepower* was not intended to provoke antisocial behavior, arguing that, on the contrary, it is in the interest of *Firepower*'s director to prevent such behavior. Yet Jenkins's conclusion must be rejected, because the movie has clearly produced antisocial behavior among many of those who have seen it.

The reasoning in the argument is flawed in that it

(A) rejects an argument on the grounds that it was offered by a person who was biased

(B) concludes from a mere correlation between certain phenomena that those phenomena are causally related

(C) infers that something is true of a whole solely on the grounds that it is true of a part of the whole

(D) overlooks the possibility that people can act in a way that is contrary to their expressed interest

(E) concludes from the mere fact that an action had a certain effect that the effect was intended by the person who performed the action

6. The word "loophole" is a loaded, partisan word, one that implies wrongdoing and scandal. When "loophole" creeps into news stories, they start to read like editorials. So news reporters should not use the term "loophole" in their stories unless they provide evidence of wrongdoing.

Which one of the following principles, if valid, most helps to justify the reasoning in the argument?

(A) Making use of a loophole never constitutes wrongdoing or scandal.

(B) Editorials should meet the same journalistic standards as news stories.

(C) News stories need to give evidence to back up any suggestions of misconduct.

(D) Editorial writers should be free to use loaded, partisan words.

(E) News reporters should not report on wrongdoing and scandal that is not a matter of public interest.

7. Expert: Some people claim that, since food production has thus far increased faster than population has, there is no need to be concerned about widespread food shortages. These people fail to recognize that the planet's resources allow for food to be produced at only a few times the current amount, beyond which no increase in production will be possible. Thus, widespread food shortages are inevitable.

Which one of the following, if true, most strengthens the expert's reasoning?

(A) The world's food resources, though limited, are renewable.

(B) Food resources from the world's oceans will eventually be fully utilized.

(C) The world's population has recently remained fairly stable because of falling birth rates.

(D) Periodic regional food shortages have occurred at least briefly throughout history.

(E) Population will continue to grow at least briefly when food production has reached its maximum level.

GO ON TO THE NEXT PAGE.

8. In the earliest video games, the player typically controlled the movements of a simple icon on the screen. But in newer video games, players often control the movements of detailed human figures—a feature possible because of the greater technical sophistication of these games. It is hard for players to identify with these figures, since the players can see that the figures represent other people. Thus, in this respect the technical sophistication of the newer video games often makes them less compelling to players.

The conclusion of the argument can be properly drawn if which one of the following is assumed?

(A) There are no newer, more technically sophisticated video games in which the player controls the movements of a simple icon on the screen.

(B) Most early video games in which the player controlled a simple icon on the screen were in other respects less compelling to players than newer video games.

(C) The technical sophistication necessary for creating detailed human figures in video games cannot in itself make those video games fully compelling even to players who identify with those figures.

(D) When players cannot easily identify with the figure or icon whose movements they control in a video game, they usually find that game less compelling than it otherwise would be.

(E) If some aspect of a video game's technical sophistication makes it less compelling to players, then that video game contains a human figure with whom it is difficult for players to identify.

9. There are many agricultural regions in North America where the growing season is long enough to allow pumpkin production well into autumn with no risk of frost. Nonetheless, pumpkin production in North America is concentrated in regions with long, cold winters, where the growing season is delayed and pumpkin crops are exposed to risk of damage or destruction by early autumn frosts.

Which one of the following, if true, most helps to resolve the apparent discrepancy in the information above?

(A) Pumpkins are usually grown to reach maturity in autumn.

(B) Pumpkins depend on bees for pollination, and bees are active only in warm weather.

(C) More pumpkins are sold to consumers in regions of North America with long growing seasons than to those in regions with short growing seasons.

(D) Prolonged cold temperatures kill soil-borne fungus and other sources of disease that would kill or seriously damage pumpkins.

(E) Most of the pumpkin seed used by growers in North America is produced in areas where the growing season is long, and plants used for seed production are protected in greenhouses.

10. Council chair: The traditional code of parliamentary procedure contains a large number of obscure, unnecessary rules, which cause us to quibble interminably over procedural details and so to appear unworthy of public confidence. Admittedly, the code is entrenched and widely accepted. But success in our endeavors depends on the public's having confidence in our effectiveness. Therefore, it is imperative that we adopt the alternate code, which has been in successful use elsewhere for several years.

Which one of the following, if true, most seriously undermines the chair's conclusion?

(A) The council's use of the problematic rules in the traditional code is intermittent.

(B) Those who have adopted the alternate code sometimes attempt to use it to obscure their opponents' understanding of procedures.

(C) Revision of the traditional code is underway that will eliminate the problematic rules.

(D) It is not always reasonable to adopt a different code in order to maintain the public's confidence.

(E) The alternate code contains few provisions that have thus far been criticized as obscure or unnecessary.

GO ON TO THE NEXT PAGE.

11. Businesses frequently use customer surveys in an attempt to improve sales and increase profits. However, a recent study of the effectiveness of these surveys found that among a group of businesses that sold similar products, profits declined in most of the businesses that used surveys during the course of the study but not in most of the businesses that did not use any surveys during the course of the study.

Which one of the following, if true, most helps to explain why the profits of businesses that did not use customer surveys did not decline while the profits of those that used surveys did decline?

(A) When one business increases its profits, its competitors often report a decline in profits.

(B) Some businesses routinely use customer surveys.

(C) Most businesses of the kind included in the study generally administer customer surveys only as a response to complaints by customers.

(D) Customers who complete surveys do not always respond accurately to all the questions on the survey.

(E) Some of the businesses included in the study did not analyze the results of the customer surveys they conducted.

12. Humans' emotional tendencies are essentially unchanged from those of the earliest members of our species. Accordingly, although technology makes possible a wider range of individual and societal choices than in centuries past, humans are generally unable to choose more wisely.

The argument depends on assuming which one of the following?

(A) Humans have undergone no significant changes since the origin of the species.

(B) Humans who make wise choices are generally in control of their emotions.

(C) Human history cannot make humans any wiser unless humans are emotionally disposed to heed the lessons of history.

(D) Regardless of the range of choices available to humans, they choose on the basis of their emotions alone.

(E) Humans would now be able to make wiser choices than in centuries past only if an essential change had taken place in humans' emotional dispositions.

13. Some ornithologists believe that many species of songbirds are threatened by deforestation. Yet they also claim that, despite recent reforestation, matters continue to worsen, since it is fragmentation of forest rather than reduction of forest size that endangers songbird species. The introduction of open spaces and corridors in forests reduces the distance of songbird nests from unforested areas and thus reduces the songbirds' natural shield from predators.

The claim that there has recently been reforestation plays which one of the following roles in the ornithologists' argument?

(A) It is used as evidence that various species of songbirds will continue to be threatened with extinction.

(B) It is presented as a claim that is rejected by ornithologists who present declining songbird populations as evidence of deforestation.

(C) It is presented as a phenomenon that is compatible with the ornithologists' claim that the threat to songbirds continues to worsen.

(D) It is used as evidence that songbirds' predators will continue to have a habitat and so will continue to pose a threat to songbirds.

(E) It is presented as evidence for the claim that songbirds' predators are threatened by extinction unless they have open spaces and corridors that give them access to their prey.

14. Researchers recently studied the relationship between diet and mood, using a diverse sample of 1,000 adults. It was found that those who ate the most chocolate were the most likely to feel depressed. Therefore, by reducing excessive chocolate consumption, adults can almost certainly improve their mood.

The argument is most vulnerable to criticism on which one of the following grounds?

(A) It improperly infers from the fact that a substance causally contributes to a condition that a reduction in the consumption of the substance is likely to eliminate that condition.

(B) It draws a conclusion about the population as a whole on the basis of a sample that is unlikely to be representative of that population.

(C) It draws a conclusion about a causal relationship between two phenomena from evidence that merely suggests that there is a correlation between those phenomena.

(D) It confuses a condition that is necessary for establishing the truth of the conclusion with a condition that is sufficient for establishing the truth of the conclusion.

(E) Its conclusion is worded too vaguely to evaluate the degree to which the premises support the truth of the conclusion.

GO ON TO THE NEXT PAGE.

15. Among the many temptations of the digital age, manipulation of photographs has proved particularly troublesome for science. Recently, a journal of cellular biology began using a software tool to examine the digital images submitted along with articles for publication. It discovered that dozens of authors had submitted digital images that had been manipulated in ways that violated the journal's guidelines. Clearly, scientific fraud is a widespread problem among the authors submitting to that journal.

Which one of the following is an assumption required by the argument?

(A) The scientists who submitted manipulated images were aware that the journal used software to examine digital images for evidence of manipulation.

(B) The journal requires that all articles submitted for publication include digital images.

(C) Scientific fraud is possible in the field of cellular biology only if the research is documented with digital images.

(D) Many of the scientists who submitted articles with manipulated images did so in order to misrepresent the information conveyed by those images.

(E) Scientific fraud is a widespread problem only among scientists who submit articles to journals of cellular biology.

16. There are already more great artworks in the world than any human being could appreciate in a lifetime, works capable of satisfying virtually any taste imaginable. Thus, contemporary artists, all of whom believe that their works enable many people to feel more aesthetically fulfilled than they otherwise could, are mistaken.

The argument is most vulnerable to criticism on the grounds that it

(A) overlooks the possibility that not all contemporary artists believe that their works enable many people to feel more aesthetically fulfilled than they otherwise could

(B) presumes, without providing justification, that most human beings are inclined to take the time to appreciate many great artworks

(C) presumes, without providing justification, that the value of an artwork depends on the degree to which human beings appreciate it

(D) overlooks the possibility that the work of at least one contemporary artist is appreciated by many people whose access to the great majority of other artworks is severely restricted

(E) presumes, without providing justification, that the number and variety of great artworks already in the world affects the amount of aesthetic fulfillment derivable from any contemporary artwork

17. The government health service has said that it definitely will not pay for patients to take the influenza medicine Antinfia until the drug's manufacturer, PharmCo, provides detailed information about Antinfia's cost-effectiveness. PharmCo has responded that obtaining such information would require massive clinical trials. These trials cannot be performed until the drug is in widespread circulation, something that will happen only if the government health service pays for Antinfia.

If the statements of both the government health service and PharmCo are true, which one of the following is most likely to also be true?

(A) The government health service never pays for any medicine unless that medicine has been shown to be cost-effective.

(B) Antinfia will never be in widespread circulation.

(C) If the government health service does not pay for Antinfia, then many patients will pay for Antinfia themselves.

(D) The government health service should pay for patients to take Antinfia.

(E) Antinfia is not cost-effective.

18. Journalist: Scientists took blood samples from two large, diverse groups of volunteers. All the volunteers in one group reported that they enjoyed eating vegetables, whereas all those in the other group disliked vegetables. When the blood samples from the group that disliked vegetables were analyzed, it was discovered that all the volunteers in that group had a gene in common, the XRV2G gene. This strongly suggests that a dislike of vegetables is, at least in some cases, genetically determined.

The journalist's argument is most vulnerable to criticism on which one of the following grounds?

(A) It presumes that all human traits are genetically determined.

(B) It overlooks the possibility that the volunteers in one or both of the two groups may not have been representative of the human population as a whole in one or more respects.

(C) It overlooks the possibility that even when one phenomenon always produces another phenomenon, the latter phenomenon may often be present when the former is absent.

(D) It overlooks the possibility that even if a dislike of vegetables is genetically determined, it may be strongly influenced by genes other than the XRV2G gene.

(E) It takes for granted that the volunteers in the group that enjoyed eating vegetables did not also all have the XRV2G gene in common.

GO ON TO THE NEXT PAGE.

19. Ana: On libertarian principles, I oppose the proposed smoking ban. It is not the government's business to prevent people from doing things that harm only themselves.

Pankaj: But keep in mind that the ban would apply only to smoking in public places. People could still smoke all they want in private.

The dialogue provides the most support for the claim that Ana and Pankaj disagree over whether

(A) it is the government's business to prevent people from harming themselves

(B) government should be restrained by libertarian principles

(C) the proposed smoking ban is intended to prevent harm only to smokers themselves

(D) the proposed ban would prohibit smoking in public places

(E) there are cases in which government should attempt to regulate private behavior

20. Agricultural scientist: Wild apples are considerably smaller than cultivated apples found in supermarkets. In one particular region, archaeologists have looked for remains of cultivated apples dating from 5,000 years ago, around the time people first started cultivating fruit. But the only remains of apples that archaeologists have found from this period are from fruits the same size as the wild apples native to the region. So apples were probably not cultivated in this region 5,000 years ago.

The agricultural scientist's argument is most vulnerable to criticism on the grounds that the argument

(A) fails to consider that even if a plant was not cultivated in a given region at a specific time, it may have been cultivated in nearby regions at that time

(B) fails to consider that plants that have been cultivated for only a short time may tend to resemble their wild counterparts much more closely than plants that have been cultivated for a long time

(C) takes for granted that all apples are either the size of wild apples or the size of the cultivated apples now found in supermarkets

(D) employs a premise that is incompatible with the conclusion it is supposed to justify

(E) uses a claim that presupposes the truth of its main conclusion as part of the justification for that conclusion

21. Genuine happiness consists not in pleasurable feelings but instead in one's sense of approval of one's character and projects. Thus the happy life, in fact, tends to be the good life, where the good life is understood not—as it usually is these days—as a life of material well-being but rather as a morally virtuous life.

Which one of the following is an assumption required by the argument?

(A) A morally virtuous life requires the rejection of material well-being.

(B) People who approve of their own character and projects tend to lead morally virtuous lives.

(C) Approval of one's own character and projects tends not to result in pleasurable feelings.

(D) Attaining happiness is the real goal of people who strive for material well-being.

(E) Material well-being does not increase one's sense of approval of one's character and projects.

GO ON TO THE NEXT PAGE.

22. The return of organic wastes to the soil is a good solution to waste disposal problems only if the wastes are nontoxic and not too much energy is expended in transporting them. In small-scale organic farming, the wastes are nontoxic and not too much energy is expended in transporting them. Hence, returning organic wastes to the soil is a good way for small-scale organic farms to solve their waste disposal problems.

Which one of the following exhibits flawed reasoning most similar to the flawed reasoning exhibited by the argument above?

(A) Plants thrive if they get an abundance of moisture, light, and nutrients. In greenhouses, plants get an optimal combination of all three, which is why commercially produced plants are so healthy when you first buy them.

(B) When every country has equal access to markets, which will be the case 20 years from now, globalization of markets will provide a way for each country to optimize its use of resources. So, globalization of markets will show the desired results 20 years from now.

(C) To be viable, a business idea must be clear, cost-effective, practical, and responsive to a market demand. Your idea for a website information service has all these properties, so it is viable.

(D) Those competitors—and only those—who meet all of the following criteria are eligible for the award: they must be under 19 years of age, be in secondary school, and have played the sport for at least the two years immediately preceding the competition. You meet all the criteria, so you are eligible.

(E) A meal is nutritious only if it includes both carbohydrates and protein. Almost 80 percent of the calories in what I ate for lunch were from fat, so what I ate for lunch was not nutritious.

23. Scientist: Some colonies of bacteria produce antibiotic molecules called phenazines, which they use to fend off other bacteria. We hypothesize that phenazines also serve as molecular pipelines that give interior bacteria access to essential nutrients in the environment surrounding the colony.

Which one of the following, if true, provides the most support for the scientist's hypothesis?

(A) Bacteria colonies that do not produce phenazines form wrinkled surfaces, thus increasing the number of bacteria that are in direct contact with the surrounding environment.

(B) The rate at which a bacteria colony produces phenazines is determined by the number of foreign bacteria in the environment immediately surrounding the colony.

(C) When bacteria colonies that do not produce phenazines are buried in nutrient-rich soil, they grow as quickly as colonies that do produce phenazines.

(D) Bacteria colonies that produce phenazines are better able to fend off other bacteria than are bacteria colonies that do not produce phenazines.

(E) Within bacteria colonies that produce phenazines, interior bacteria are more likely to die than are bacteria along the edges.

24. Library preservationist: Due to the continual physical deterioration of the medieval manuscripts in our library's collection, we have decided to restore most of our medieval manuscripts that are of widely acknowledged cultural significance, though this means that some medieval manuscripts whose authenticity is suspect will be restored. However, only manuscripts whose safety can be ensured during the restoration process will be restored, and manuscripts that are not frequently consulted by researchers will not be restored.

If all of the library preservationist's statements are true, which one of the following must be true of the medieval manuscripts in the library's collection?

(A) Some of the medieval manuscripts whose authenticity is suspect are frequently consulted by researchers.

(B) All of the medieval manuscripts widely acknowledged to be of cultural significance are manuscripts whose safety can be ensured during the restoration process.

(C) All of the medieval manuscripts whose safety can be ensured during the restoration process are frequently consulted by researchers.

(D) The medieval manuscripts most susceptible to deterioration are those most frequently consulted by researchers.

(E) None of the medieval manuscripts that are rarely consulted by researchers is widely acknowledged to be of cultural significance.

GO ON TO THE NEXT PAGE.

25. Direct-mail advertising usually consists of advertisements for products to be purchased from the home, so the perception that it is bad for the environment is misguided. Because of direct-mail advertising, millions of people buy products by phone or online—products whose purchase would otherwise require the use of a car, thus adding pollutants to the air.

Which one of the following, if true, would most strengthen the argument?

(A) Although the primary intent of most direct-mail advertisers is to convince people to buy products from their homes, direct mail can also lead to increased sales in stores by customers who prefer to see a product prior to purchasing it.

(B) Most of the products purchased in response to direct-mail advertisements would be purchased even without the direct-mail advertisements.

(C) A person who receives and reads a direct-mail advertisement is more likely to purchase the product advertised than is a person who reads an advertisement for a product in a magazine that they subscribe to.

(D) Usually, a company that sends out direct-mail advertisements has good reason to think that the person to whom the advertisement is sent would be more interested in the product than would the average person.

(E) Products purchased as the result of direct-mail advertising comprise an increasingly large portion of the consumer products purchased each year.

26. The older a country is, the more likely it is to be ruled by a monarch. Thus, since most countries are not ruled by monarchs, if a country is particularly new it is probably not ruled by a monarch.

The pattern of reasoning in the argument above is most similar to that in which one of the following arguments?

(A) Most novels are not made into movies. However, the more popular a novel is, the more likely it is to be made into a movie. Thus, if a movie is quite unpopular, it was probably not based on a novel.

(B) Most novels are not made into movies. However, the more popular a movie is, the more likely it is that the movie was based on a novel. Thus, if a novel is particularly popular, it will probably be made into a movie.

(C) Most novels are not made into movies. Moreover, if a novel is particularly unpopular, it will probably not be made into a movie. Thus, the more popular a novel is, the more likely it is to be made into a movie.

(D) Most novels are not made into movies. However, the more popular a novel is, the more likely it is to be made into a movie. Thus, if a novel is quite unpopular, it will probably not be made into a movie.

(E) Most novels are not made into movies. Moreover, the more complex a novel's plot, the less likely the novel is to be made into a movie. Thus, if a novel has a particularly simple plot, it will probably be made into a movie.

S T O P

IF YOU FINISH BEFORE TIME IS CALLED, YOU MAY CHECK YOUR WORK ON THIS SECTION ONLY.
DO NOT WORK ON ANY OTHER SECTION IN THE TEST.

SECTION III

Time—35 minutes

25 Questions

Directions: The questions in this section are based on the reasoning contained in brief statements or passages. For some questions, more than one of the choices could conceivably answer the question. However, you are to choose the best answer; that is, the response that most accurately and completely answers the question. You should not make assumptions that are by commonsense standards implausible, superfluous, or incompatible with the passage. After you have chosen the best answer, blacken the corresponding space on your answer sheet.

1. Dentist: I recommend brushing one's teeth after every meal to remove sugars that facilitate the growth of certain bacteria; these bacteria produce acid that dissolves minerals in tooth enamel, resulting in cavities. And when brushing is not practical, I recommend chewing gum—even gum that contains sugar—to prevent the formation of cavities.

Which one of the following, if true, would most help to reconcile the dentist's apparently paradoxical recommendations?

(A) A piece of chewing gum that contains sugar contains far less sugar than does the average meal.

(B) Tooth decay can be stopped and reversed if it is caught before a cavity develops.

(C) Chewing gum stimulates the production of saliva, which reduces acidity in the mouth and helps remineralize tooth enamel.

(D) Sugars can be on teeth for as long as 24 hours before the teeth-damaging bacteria whose growth they facilitate begin to proliferate.

(E) Chewing gum exercises and relaxes the jaw muscles and so contributes to the overall health of the oral tract.

2. When the ancient fossils of a primitive land mammal were unearthed in New Zealand, they provided the first concrete evidence that the island country had once had indigenous land mammals. Until that discovery, New Zealand had no known native land mammals. The discovery thus falsifies the theory that New Zealand's rich and varied native bird population owes its existence to the lack of competition from mammals.

Which one of the following, if true, most seriously weakens the argument?

(A) The unearthed land mammal is only one of several ancient land mammals that were indigenous to New Zealand.

(B) The recently discovered land mammal became extinct long before the native bird population was established.

(C) The site at which the primitive land mammal was unearthed also contains the fossils of primitive reptile and insect species.

(D) Countries with rich and varied native land mammal populations do not have rich and varied native bird populations.

(E) Some other island countries that are believed to have no native land mammals in fact had indigenous land mammals at one time.

GO ON TO THE NEXT PAGE.

3. Restaurant owner: The newspaper reporter who panned my restaurant acknowledges having no special expertise about food and its preparation. His previous job was as a political reporter. He is a good writer, but he is not a true restaurant critic. A newspaper would never call someone a drama critic who had no special training in theater.

Which one of the following most accurately expresses the conclusion drawn in the restaurant owner's argument?

(A) The newspaper reporter who panned the restaurant acknowledges having no special expertise about food and its preparation.

(B) The previous job of the newspaper reporter who panned the restaurant was as a political reporter.

(C) The newspaper reporter who panned the restaurant is a good writer.

(D) The newspaper reporter who panned the restaurant is not a true restaurant critic.

(E) A newspaper would never call someone a drama critic who had no special training in theater.

4. It has been hypothesized that our solar system was formed from a cloud of gas and dust produced by a supernova—an especially powerful explosion of a star. Supernovas produce the isotope iron-60, so if this hypothesis were correct, then iron-60 would have been present in the early history of the solar system. But researchers have found no iron-60 in meteorites that formed early in the solar system's history, thereby disproving the hypothesis.

Which one of the following is an assumption required by the argument?

(A) If a meteorite is formed early in the solar system's history, it contains chemical elements that are unlikely to be found in gas and dust produced by a supernova.

(B) Other solar systems are not formed from clouds of gas and dust produced by supernovas.

(C) Supernovas do not produce significant quantities of any form of iron other than iron-60.

(D) Researchers have found iron-60 in meteorites that were formed relatively late in the solar system's history.

(E) If there had been iron-60 present in the early history of the solar system, it would be found in meteorites formed early in the solar system's history.

5. Safety expert: Tuna is often treated with carbon monoxide so that it will not turn brown as it ages. Treating tuna with carbon monoxide does not make it harmful in any way. Nonetheless, there is a danger that such treatment will result in more people getting sick from eating tuna.

Which one of the following, if true, most helps to resolve the apparent discrepancy in the safety expert's statements?

(A) Workers in fish processing plants can be sickened by exposure to carbon monoxide if the appropriate safety procedures are not followed at those plants.

(B) Over the last several years, tuna consumption has increased in most parts of the world.

(C) Tuna that is treated with carbon monoxide provides no visible indication when it has spoiled to the point that it can cause food poisoning.

(D) Treating tuna with carbon monoxide is the only way to keep it from turning brown as it ages.

(E) Most consumers strongly prefer tuna that is not brown because they believe that brown tuna is not fresh.

6. Astrophysicist: Gamma ray bursts (GRBs)—explosions of powerful radiation from deep space—have traditionally been classified as either "short" or "long," terms that reflect the explosion's relative duration. However, an unusual GRB has been sighted. Its duration was long, but in every other respect it had the properties of a short GRB. Clearly, the descriptive labels "short" and "long" have now outlived their usefulness.

The conclusion of the astrophysicist's argument is most strongly supported if which one of the following is assumed?

(A) No other GRBs with unusual properties have been sighted.

(B) The classification of GRBs can sometimes be made on the basis of duration alone.

(C) Properties other than duration are more important than duration in the proper classification of the unusual GRB.

(D) GRBs cannot be classified according to the different types of cosmic events that create them.

(E) Descriptive labels are easily replaced with nondescriptive labels such as "type I" and "type II."

GO ON TO THE NEXT PAGE.

7. In one study, hospital patients' immune systems grew stronger when the patients viewed comic videos. This indicates that laughter can aid recovery from illness. But much greater gains in immune system strength occurred in the patients whose tendency to laugh was greater to begin with. So hospital patients with a greater tendency to laugh are helped more in their recovery from illness even when they laugh a little than other patients are helped when they laugh a greater amount.

The argument is most vulnerable to criticism on the grounds that it

(A) overlooks the possibility that the patients whose tendency to laugh was greater to begin with laughed more at the comic videos than did the other patients

(B) fails to address adequately the possibility that the patients whose tendency to laugh was greatest to begin with already had stronger immune systems than the other patients

(C) presumes, without providing justification, that hospital patients have immune systems representative of those of the entire population

(D) takes for granted that the gains in immune system strength did not themselves influence the patients' tendency to laugh

(E) presumes, without providing justification, that the patients whose tendency to laugh was greatest to begin with recovered from their illnesses more rapidly than the other patients

8. A study of guppy fish shows that a male guppy will alter its courting patterns in response to feedback from a female guppy. Males with more orange on one side than the other were free to vary which side they showed to a female. Females were drawn to those males with more orange showing, and males tended to show the females their more orange side when courting.

Which one of the following, if true, provides the most support for the argument?

(A) When a model of a female guppy was substituted for the female guppy, male guppies still courted, but were not more likely to show their side with more orange.

(B) In many other species females show a preference for symmetry of coloring rather than quantity of coloring.

(C) No studies have been done on whether male guppies with more orange coloring father more offspring than those with less orange coloring.

(D) Female guppies have little if any orange coloring on their sides.

(E) The male and female guppies were kept in separate tanks so they could see each other but not otherwise directly interact.

9. Politician: Some proponents of unilateral nuclear arms reduction argue that it would encourage other countries to reduce their own nuclear arsenals, eventually leading to an international agreement on nuclear arms reduction. Our acting on the basis of this argument would be dangerous, because the argument ignores the countries presently on the verge of civil wars. These countries, many of which have nuclear capability, cannot be relied upon to conform to any international military policy.

Which one of the following most accurately expresses the conclusion of the politician's argument?

(A) Countries that are on the verge of civil wars are unlikely to agree to reduce either their nuclear arms or their conventional weapons.

(B) Unilateral nuclear arms reduction by the politician's country would encourage all countries to reduce their nuclear arsenals.

(C) Many countries cannot be relied upon to disclose the extent of their nuclear capability.

(D) It is unlikely that an international agreement on nuclear disarmament will ever be achieved.

(E) It is risky for the politician's country to unilaterally reduce nuclear arms in hopes of achieving an international agreement on arms reduction.

GO ON TO THE NEXT PAGE.

10. Advertisement: Auto accidents are the most common cause of whiplash injury, a kind of injury that is caused by a sudden sharp motion of the neck. However, many other types of accidents can produce a sudden sharp motion of the neck and thereby result in whiplash injury. A sudden sharp motion of the neck can be caused by a fall, a bump on the head, or even by being shoved from behind. That is why you should insist on receiving Lakeside Injury Clinic's complete course of treatment for whiplash after any accident that involves a fall or a bump on the head.

Which one of the following, if true, provides the strongest basis for criticizing the reasoning in the advertisement?

(A) Being shoved from behind rarely causes whiplash.
(B) Auto accidents often involve falling or being bumped on the head.
(C) Nonautomobile accidents other than those involving falls or bumps on the head also occasionally cause whiplash injuries.
(D) It is very uncommon for falling or being bumped on the head to result in a sudden sharp motion of the neck.
(E) The appropriate treatment for whiplash caused by a fall or a bump on the head is no different from that for whiplash caused by an auto accident.

11. A group of citizens opposes developing a nearby abandoned railroad grade into a hiking trail. Its members argue that trail users will likely litter the area with food wrappers and other debris. But this objection is groundless. Most trail users will be dedicated hikers who have great concern for the environment. Consequently, development of the trail should proceed.

The argument above is flawed in that it

(A) bases its conclusion mainly on a claim that an opposing argument is weak
(B) illicitly infers that because each member of a set has a certain property that set itself has the property
(C) illicitly assumes as one of its premises the contention it purports to show
(D) illicitly infers that an attribute of a few users of the proposed trail will characterize a majority of users of the trail
(E) attacks the citizens in the group rather than their objection to developing the trail

12. For years, university administrators, corporations, and government agencies have been predicting an imminent and catastrophic shortage of scientists and engineers. But since there is little noticeable upward pressure on the salaries of scientists and engineers, and unemployment is as high in these fields as any other, these doomsayers are turning out to be wrong.

Which one of the following would, if true, most strengthen the argument above?

(A) The proportion of all research in science and engineering being carried out by corporations is larger than it was five years ago.
(B) Most students choose fields of study that offer some prospect of financial success.
(C) The number of students in university programs in science and engineering has increased significantly in the last five years.
(D) Certain specializations in science and engineering have an oversupply of labor and others have shortages.
(E) The knowledge and skills acquired during university programs in science and engineering need to be kept current through periodic retraining and professional experience.

13. Rhonda: As long as the cost is not too great, you should use your time, energy, or money to help others. People who are active participants in charitable causes have richer lives than miserly hermits, however prosperous the hermits may be.

Brad: You should ignore the problems of complete strangers and focus your generosity on your immediate relatives and close friends, since these are the people who will remember your sacrifices and return the kindness when you yourself need help.

Which one of the following principles, if valid, would most help to justify both Rhonda's and Brad's arguments?

(A) One should always do what will produce the most benefit for the most people.
(B) One should treat others as one expects to be treated by them.
(C) One should act in ways that will benefit oneself.
(D) One should make sacrifices for others only if they will eventually return the favor.
(E) One should always act in a manner that one can reflect on with pride.

GO ON TO THE NEXT PAGE.

14. Columnist: Wildlife activists have proposed that the practice of stringing cable TV lines from the same poles that carry electric power lines should be banned because cable TV lines, while electrically neutral themselves, make it easier for animals to climb near electric power lines, risking electrocution. This particular argument for banning the practice fails, however, since some animals are electrocuted by power lines even where cable TV lines are all underground.

Which one of the following most accurately describes a flaw in the columnist's reasoning?

(A) It takes a sufficient condition for an argument's being inadequate to be a necessary condition for its being inadequate.

(B) It rejects an argument for a proposal merely on the grounds that the proposal would not completely eliminate the problem it is intended to address.

(C) It fails to consider the additional advantageous effects that a proposal to address a problem might have.

(D) It rejects an argument by criticizing the argument's proponents rather than by criticizing its substance.

(E) It rejects a proposal to address a problem merely on the grounds that other proposals to address the problem would also be effective.

15. The ancient reptile *Thrinaxodon*, an ancestor of mammals, had skull features suggesting that it had sensory whiskers. If *Thrinaxodon* had whiskers, it clearly also had hair on other parts of its body, which would have served as insulation that regulated body temperature. Therefore, *Thrinaxodon* was probably warm-blooded, for such insulation would be of little use to a cold-blooded animal.

Which one of the following most accurately describes the role played in the argument by the statement that if *Thrinaxodon* had whiskers, it clearly also had hair on other parts of its body, which would have served as insulation that regulated body temperature?

(A) It is a premise offered in support of the conclusion that insulation regulating body temperature would be of little use to a cold-blooded animal.

(B) It is a premise offered in support of the main conclusion drawn in the argument.

(C) It is a conclusion for which the claim that *Thrinaxodon* had skull features suggesting that it had sensory whiskers is offered as support.

(D) It is a statement of a hypothesis that the argument attempts to show is false.

(E) It is offered as an explanation of the phenomenon described by the argument's main conclusion, but it is not itself used to provide support for that conclusion.

16. Economist: Currently, many countries rely primarily on taxing income to fund government expenditures. But taxing income does nothing to promote savings and investment. Taxing consumption, on the other hand, would encourage savings. The most important challenge facing these countries is improving their economies, and the only way to accomplish this is to increase their savings rates. Hence, _____.

Which one of the following most logically completes the economist's argument?

(A) most governments should stop taxing savings and investment

(B) the economies of countries will rapidly improve if their governments adopt tax policies that encourage savings and investment

(C) in most countries taxes on consumption alone could raise adequate revenues to fund government expenditures

(D) the tax laws of many countries should be revised to focus on taxing consumption rather than income

(E) it is detrimental to the economic improvement of any country to continue to tax income

17. Meade: People who are injured as a result of their risky behaviors not only cause harm to themselves but, because we all have important ties to other people, inevitably impose emotional and financial costs on others. To protect the interests of others, therefore, governments are justified in outlawing behavior that puts one's own health at risk.

Which one of the following principles, if valid, most undermines the reasoning in Meade's argument?

(A) Endangering the social ties that one has to other people is itself a harm to oneself.

(B) People who have important ties to others have a personal obligation not to put their own health at risk.

(C) Governments are not justified in limiting an individual's behavior unless that behavior imposes emotional or financial costs on others.

(D) Preventing harm to others is not by itself a sufficient justification for laws that limit personal freedom.

(E) People's obligation to avoid harming others outweighs their obligation to avoid harming themselves.

GO ON TO THE NEXT PAGE.

18. Sanderson intentionally did not tell his cousin about overhearing someone say that the factory would close, knowing that if he withheld this information, his cousin would assume it would remain open. Clearly this was morally wrong. After all, lying is morally wrong. And making a statement with the intention of misleading someone is lying. True, it was Sanderson's failing to state something that misled his cousin. Yet there is no moral difference between stating and failing to state if they are done with the same intention.

Which one of the following is an assumption required by the argument?

(A) Sanderson believed that his cousin would not want to be informed about the factory closing.
(B) No one ever told Sanderson's cousin about the factory closing.
(C) Sanderson believed that the factory would in fact be closing.
(D) Sanderson would have lied to his cousin if his cousin had asked him whether the factory would be closing.
(E) Sanderson had something to gain by his cousin's continuing to believe that the factory would remain open.

19. After a judge has made the first ruling on a particular point of law, judges must follow that precedent if the original ruling is not contrary to the basic moral values of society. In the absence of precedent, when judges' own legal views do not contradict any widespread public opinion—and only then—they may abide by their own legal views in deciding a case.

Of the rulings described below, which one conforms most closely to the principles stated above?

(A) Judge Swoboda is confronted with a legal issue never before decided. Realizing that his own view on the issue contradicts what most people believe, he nonetheless issues a ruling that accords with his own legal views.
(B) Judge Valenzuela decides, in the absence of any precedent, whether children as young as twelve can be legally tried as adults. There is overwhelming public support for trying children twelve and older as adults, a practice that violates Judge Valenzuela's personal moral views. So Judge Valenzuela rules, in keeping with his own legal beliefs, against trying twelve-year-olds as adults.
(C) Judge Levinsky sets a legal precedent when she rules that the "starfish exception" applies to children. In deciding a later case concerning the starfish exception, Judge Wilson adheres to his own legal views rather than Judge Levinsky's ruling, even though he does not believe that Judge Levinsky's ruling opposes the basic moral values of society.
(D) Judge Watanabe must decide a case that depends on an issue for which no legal precedent exists. There is no widespread public opinion on the issue, so Judge Watanabe rules against the defendant because that conforms to her own legal view about the issue.
(E) Judge Balila rules against the defendant because doing so conforms to her own views about the legal issues involved. However, this ruling is contrary to relevant precedents, all of which conform to the basic moral values of society.

GO ON TO THE NEXT PAGE.

20. Neuroscientists subjected volunteers with amusia—difficulty telling different melodies apart and remembering simple tunes—to shifts in pitch comparable to those that occur when someone plays one piano key and then another. The volunteers were unable to discern a difference between the tones. But the volunteers were able to track timed sequences of musical tones and perceive slight changes in timing.

The statements above, if true, most strongly support which one of the following hypotheses?

(A) People who are unable to discern pitch compensate by developing a heightened perception of timing.

(B) Amusia results more from an inability to discern pitch than from an inability to discern timing.

(C) People who are unable to tell pitches apart in isolation are able to do so in the context of a melody by relying upon timing.

(D) The ability to tell melodies apart depends on the discernment of pitch alone and not at all on the perception of timing.

(E) Whereas perception of timing can apparently be learned, discernment of pitch is most likely innate.

21. Literary critic: There is little of social significance in contemporary novels, for readers cannot enter the internal world of the novelist's mind unless they experience that world from the moral perspective of the novel's characters. But in contemporary novels, the transgressions committed by some characters against others are sensationalistic spectacles whose only purpose is to make readers wonder what will happen next, rather than events whose purpose is to be seen as the injustices they are.

Which one of the following principles, if valid, would most help to justify the literary critic's argument?

(A) An artist who wants to engage the moral sensibilities of his or her audience should not assume that forms of artistic expression that previously served this purpose continue to do so.

(B) A novelist who wants to make a reader empathize with a victim of injustice should avoid sensationalistic spectacles whose only purpose is to make readers wonder what will happen next.

(C) A work of art is socially important only if it engages the moral sensibilities of its audience.

(D) If a novel allows a reader to understand injustice from the point of view of its victims, it will be socially significant.

(E) Novels have social significance only to the extent that they allow readers to enter the internal world of the novelist's mind.

22. A recent study revealed that people who follow precisely all the standard recommendations for avoidance of infection by pathogenic microorganisms in meat-based foods are more likely to contract diseases caused by these pathogens than are those who deviate considerably from the standard recommendations. Hence, the standard recommendations for avoidance of infection by these pathogens must be counterproductive.

The argument is most vulnerable to criticism on the grounds that it fails to take into account which one of the following possibilities?

(A) Pathogenic microorganisms can reproduce in foods that are not meat-based.

(B) Many people do follow precisely all the standard recommendations for avoidance of infection by pathogenic microorganisms in meat-based foods.

(C) Not all diseases caused by microorganisms have readily recognizable symptoms.

(D) Preventing infection by pathogenic microorganisms is simply a matter of following the appropriate set of recommendations.

(E) Those most concerned with avoiding pathogenic infections from meat-based foods are those most susceptible to them.

GO ON TO THE NEXT PAGE.

23. No nonfiction book published by Carriage Books has ever earned a profit. Since Carriage Books earned a profit on every book it published last year, it clearly did not publish a nonfiction book last year.

The pattern of reasoning in the argument above is most similar to that in which one of the following arguments?

(A) No actor represented by the talent agent Mira Roberts has ever won an important role in a major movie. Since every actor represented by Ms. Roberts had at least one important acting role last year, it is clear that none of those actors worked in a movie last year.

(B) No hotel owned by the Bidmore Group specializes in serving business travelers. Since the Cray Springs Hotel is owned by the Bidmore Group, it clearly does not specialize in serving business travelers.

(C) Pranwich Corporation has never given a bonus to an employee in its marketing division. Since Pranwich gave bonuses to every one of its systems analysts last year, it is clear that the company employed no systems analysts in its marketing division at that time.

(D) James Benson has never done business with the city of Waldville. Since Waldville only maintains business files on individuals that it does business with, it clearly does not have a business file on James Benson.

(E) Conway Flooring has never installed hardwood flooring for any customer in Woodridge. Since Conway Flooring has had a lot of customers in Woodridge, the company clearly does not install hardwood flooring.

24. All unemployed artists are sympathetic to social justice. And no employed artists are interested in the prospect of great personal fame.

If the claims made above are true, then which one of the following must be true?

(A) If there are artists interested in the prospect of great personal fame, they are sympathetic to social justice.

(B) All artists uninterested in the prospect of great personal fame are sympathetic to social justice.

(C) Every unemployed artist is interested in the prospect of great personal fame.

(D) If an artist is sympathetic to social justice, that artist is unemployed.

(E) All artists are either sympathetic to social justice or are interested in the prospect of great personal fame.

25. The police department has two suspects for the burglary that occurred last night, Schaeffer and Forster. Schaeffer has an ironclad alibi, so Forster must be the burglar.

Which one of the following arguments exhibits a flawed pattern of reasoning that is most similar to that exhibited by the argument above?

(A) It has been known for some time that the Wrightsburg Zoo might build a new primate house and that it might refurbish its polar bear exhibit. There is now good reason to believe the zoo will build a new primate house. Therefore, the zoo will not refurbish its polar bear exhibit.

(B) If Watson, a robbery suspect, had been picked out of a police lineup by the victim, then charging Watson with robbery would have been reasonable. But the victim did not pick Watson out of the lineup. So Watson should not be charged.

(C) If Iano Industries does not borrow money so that it can upgrade its factories, it will be unable to compete. While it is undesirable for Iano to take on more debt, being unable to compete would be even worse. So Iano should borrow the money needed to upgrade its factories.

(D) Baxim Corporation announced last year that it was considering moving its headquarters to Evansville and that it was also considering moving to Rivertown. But Baxim has now decided not to move to Evansville. Thus, we can be sure that Baxim will move to Rivertown.

(E) The only viable candidates in the mayoral race are Slater and Gonzales. Political analysts believe that Slater has little chance of winning. Therefore, it is likely that Gonzales will win the election.

S T O P

IF YOU FINISH BEFORE TIME IS CALLED, YOU MAY CHECK YOUR WORK ON THIS SECTION ONLY.
DO NOT WORK ON ANY OTHER SECTION IN THE TEST.

SECTION IV

Time—35 minutes

23 Questions

Directions: Each group of questions in this section is based on a set of conditions. In answering some of the questions, it may be useful to draw a rough diagram. Choose the response that most accurately and completely answers each question and blacken the corresponding space on your answer sheet.

Questions 1–6

A radio station airs hourly news updates every morning. Each update consists of exactly five reports—two of general interest: international and national; and three of local interest: sports, traffic, and weather. Each update must be structured as follows:

>   There are exactly two segments, the first segment containing three reports and the second segment containing two.
>
>   Within each segment, reports are ordered by length, from longest to shortest.
>
>   Each segment contains at least one report of local interest.
>
>   The national report is always the longest of the five reports.
>
>   The sports report is always the shortest of the five reports.
>
>   The international report is always longer than the weather report.

1. Which one of the following could be an accurate matching of reports to their segments, with the reports listed in order from earliest to latest?

(A)   first segment: international, national, sports
      second segment: traffic, weather

(B)   first segment: national, international, sports
      second segment: weather, traffic

(C)   first segment: national, international, weather
      second segment: sports, traffic

(D)   first segment: national, weather, international
      second segment: traffic, sports

(E)   first segment: traffic, weather, sports
      second segment: national, international

GO ON TO THE NEXT PAGE.

2. If the traffic report is the last report in the first segment, then which one of the following must be true?

   (A) The national report is the first report in the first segment.
   (B) The international report is the second report in the first segment.
   (C) The weather report is the second report in the first segment.
   (D) The national report is the first report in the second segment.
   (E) The sports report is the last report in the second segment.

3. If the national report is the first report in the second segment, then exactly how many of the reports are there any one of which could be the first report in the first segment?

   (A) one
   (B) two
   (C) three
   (D) four
   (E) five

4. Which one of the following CANNOT be true?

   (A) The international report is the first report in the first segment.
   (B) The national report is the first report in the first segment.
   (C) The national report is the first report in the second segment.
   (D) The weather report is the first report in the first segment.
   (E) The weather report is the last report in the second segment.

5. The order of the reports is fully determined if which one of the following is true?

   (A) The international report is the last report in the first segment.
   (B) The national report is the first report in the first segment.
   (C) The national report is the first report in the second segment.
   (D) The sports report is the last report in the second segment.
   (E) The weather report is the last report in the first segment.

6. If the traffic report is the first report in the first segment, then which one of the following could be true?

   (A) The international report is the first report in the second segment.
   (B) The national report is the second report in the first segment.
   (C) The weather report is the second report in the first segment.
   (D) The weather report is the first report in the second segment.
   (E) The weather report is the last report in the second segment.

GO ON TO THE NEXT PAGE.

Questions 7–12

On a single day, a realtor will show a client five houses, exactly one house in each of five neighborhoods—Quarry, Riverton, Shelburne, Townsend, and Valencia. Each house will be shown to the client exactly once. The order in which the houses are shown is subject to the following constraints:

The house in Riverton must be shown either first or second.
The house in Townsend must be shown either first or fifth.
The third house shown must be the house in Quarry or the house in Valencia.
The house in Quarry cannot be shown either immediately before or immediately after the house in Shelburne.

7. If the house in Quarry is shown fourth, which one of the following must be true?

(A) The house in Riverton is shown first.
(B) The house in Riverton is shown second.
(C) The house in Shelburne is shown second.
(D) The house in Townsend is shown first.
(E) The house in Valencia is shown third.

GO ON TO THE NEXT PAGE.

8. The order in which the houses are shown is fully determined if which one of the following is true?

 (A) The house in Quarry is shown third.
 (B) The house in Riverton is shown first.
 (C) The house in Shelburne is shown second.
 (D) The house in Townsend is shown fifth.
 (E) The house in Valencia is shown fourth.

9. If the house in Shelburne is shown earlier than the house in Quarry, which one of the following must be true?

 (A) The house in Quarry is shown fourth.
 (B) The house in Riverton is shown second.
 (C) The house in Shelburne is shown first.
 (D) The house in Townsend is shown fifth.
 (E) The house in Valencia is shown third.

10. Which one of the following could be true?

 (A) The house in Quarry is shown first.
 (B) The house in Quarry is shown fifth.
 (C) The house in Valencia is shown first.
 (D) The house in Valencia is shown second.
 (E) The house in Valencia is shown fifth.

11. If the house in Valencia is shown third, which one of the following must be true?

 (A) The house in Quarry is shown fourth.
 (B) The house in Riverton is shown second.
 (C) The house in Shelburne is shown first.
 (D) The house in Shelburne is shown fourth.
 (E) The house in Townsend is shown fifth.

12. Which one of the following, if substituted for the constraint that the house in Riverton must be shown either first or second, would have the same effect on the order in which the houses are shown?

 (A) The house in Riverton cannot be shown fourth.
 (B) The house in Riverton must be shown earlier than the house in Valencia.
 (C) The house in Valencia must be shown either third or fourth.
 (D) The house in Quarry must be shown either immediately before or immediately after the house in Riverton.
 (E) If the house in Townsend is not shown fifth, then it must be shown immediately before the house in Riverton.

GO ON TO THE NEXT PAGE.

Questions 13–18

Five artifacts—V, W, X, Y, and Z—recovered from a sunken ship are each known to have originated in Iceland, Norway, or Sweden. These artifacts, together with the surviving fragments of a cargo list, have enabled historians to determine the following:

W and Y originated in the same country.
X originated in Norway or Sweden.
More of the artifacts originated in Iceland than in Norway.
If V originated in Iceland, then Z originated in Sweden.

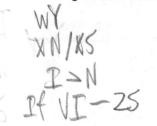

13. Which one of the following could be an accurate matching of the artifacts to their origins?

(A) Iceland: V, W
     Norway: X
     Sweden: Y, Z
(B) Iceland: W, Y
     Norway: none
     Sweden: V, X, Z
(C) Iceland: W, Y
     Norway: V, Z
     Sweden: X
(D) Iceland: V, W, Y
     Norway: Z
     Sweden: X
(E) Iceland: W, X, Y
     Norway: Z
     Sweden: V

GO ON TO THE NEXT PAGE.

14. If Y and Z originated in Iceland, then what is the minimum number of artifacts that originated in Sweden?

(A) zero
(B) one
(C) two
(D) three
(E) four

15. Which one of the following CANNOT be true?

(A) V and X both originated in Norway.
(B) V and Y both originated in Iceland.
(C) W and Z both originated in Iceland.
(D) W and Z both originated in Sweden.
(E) W and Y both originated in Norway.

16. If W and X originated in Sweden, then which one of the following must be true?

(A) None of the artifacts originated in Norway.
(B) None of the artifacts originated in Iceland.
(C) V originated in Sweden.
(D) Z originated in Iceland.
(E) Z originated in Sweden.

17. Exactly how many of the artifacts are there any one of which could have originated in Norway?

(A) one
(B) two
(C) three
(D) four
(E) five

18. Which one of the following CANNOT be true?

(A) Only V originated in Sweden.
(B) Only V and Z originated in Sweden.
(C) Only W and Y originated in Sweden.
(D) Only X and Z originated in Sweden.
(E) Only V, W, X, and Y originated in Sweden.

GO ON TO THE NEXT PAGE.

Questions 19–23

The employees of the Summit Company—J, K, L, and M—work a four-day workweek from Monday through Thursday. Every Monday, work begins on four raw workpieces, each of which is worked on for four consecutive days. On any given day, an employee works on exactly one workpiece. At the beginning of each workday after Monday, each workpiece is transferred from the employee who worked on it the previous day to another one of the employees, who will work on it that day. Workpieces cannot be transferred in any of the following ways:

From J to M
From K to J
From L to J

M   T   W   Th

19. Which one of the following describes four transfers of workpieces that could all occur together at the beginning of a particular workday?

(A)   From J to K; from K to L; from L to M; from M to J

(B)   From J to K; from K to M; from L to K; from M to J

(C)   From J to L; from K to M; from L to J; from M to K

(D)   From J to L; from K to J; from L to M; from M to K

(E)   From J to M; from K to L; from L to K; from M to J

K to L L to M M to J J to K

GO ON TO THE NEXT PAGE.

L to

L to M M to J J to L K to L

M to J J to K, J to L L to M

J to L, L to M M to K, K to J

J to L, L to K, K to M M to J

J to K, K to L L to M, M to J

20. Which one of the following transfers must occur at the beginning of any workday that is not a Monday?

   (A)   From J to K
   (B)   From J to L
   (C)   From K to L
   (D)   From L to M
   (E)   From M to J

21. If one workpiece is worked on by only two of the four employees in the course of an entire workweek, those two employees must be

   (A)   J and K
   (B)   J and L
   (C)   K and L
   (D)   K and M
   (E)   L and M

22. If L works on the same workpiece both on Tuesday and on Thursday, which one of the following must be true about that workpiece?

   (A)   J works on it on Monday.
   (B)   K works on it on Monday.
   (C)   M works on it on Monday.
   (D)   J works on it on Wednesday.
   (E)   K works on it on Wednesday.

23. Which one of the following could be true about Tuesday?

   (A)   Transfers from J to K and from K to M occur.
   (B)   Transfers from J to L and from L to M occur.
   (C)   Transfers from J to M and from M to J occur.
   (D)   Transfers from K to L and from L to K occur.
   (E)   Transfers from K to L and from L to M occur.

S T O P

IF YOU FINISH BEFORE TIME IS CALLED, YOU MAY CHECK YOUR WORK ON THIS SECTION ONLY.
DO NOT WORK ON ANY OTHER SECTION IN THE TEST.

Acknowledgment is made to the following sources from which material has been adapted for use in this test booklet:

Kwame Anthony Appiah, "Whose Culture Is It?" ©2006 by NYREV, Inc.

Bruce Bower, "Brain Roots of Music Depreciation." ©2004 by Science Service, Inc.

Benjamin Freedman, "Equipoise and the Ethics of Clinical Research." ©1987 by the Massachusetts Medical Society.

Michael Parfit, "The Essential Elements of Fire." ©1996 by the National Geographic Society.

Jack Shafer, "Shut Your Loophole." ©2007 by Washingtonpost. Newsweek Interactive Co. LLC.

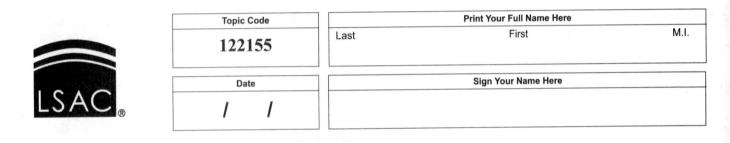

Scratch Paper
Do not write your essay in this space.

LSAT® Writing Sample Topic

Directions: The scenario presented below describes two choices, either one of which can be supported on the basis of the information given. Your essay should consider both choices and argue for one over the other, based on the two specified criteria and the facts provided. There is no "right" or "wrong" choice: a reasonable argument can be made for either.

A successful and politically active lawyer is deciding between two career moves: either to accept an appointment as a judge in the regional courts, or to run, with support from a major party, for a seat in the national legislature. Using the facts below, write an essay in which you argue for one choice over the other based on the following two criteria:

- The lawyer wants to have a significant impact on public policy and the future of the country.
- The lawyer wants to maintain a close-knit and prosperous family.

The judicial appointment is a permanent position. Regional judges are rarely removed from office. The regional courts decide at most one or two cases of wide significance in a year. A few regional judges advance to positions in the national courts where most significant cases are decided. Regional judges train law clerks, many of whom go on to important positions in public life. Judges work regular hours and are not required to travel. Judges have personal contact with important figures in government and business. Judges rarely have success in seeking other political office.

The legislative seat is in a highly competitive district and the holder faces frequent elections. New legislators seldom have much effect on legislation or government policy. Successful long-time legislators can greatly affect government policies and programs. The legislature is in session 36 weeks of the year. Legislators spend many hours campaigning and fundraising. They travel frequently between the national capital and their district. The national capital is a short flight from the lawyer's legislative district. Legislators are widely known in their districts and some eventually gain national recognition. A close and supportive family is a strong asset in politics.

WP-V122

Scratch Paper
Do not write your essay in this space.

COMPUTING YOUR SCORE

Directions:

1. Use the Answer Key on the next page to check your answers.

2. Use the Scoring Worksheet below to compute your raw score.

3. Use the Score Conversion Chart to convert your raw score into the 120–180 scale.

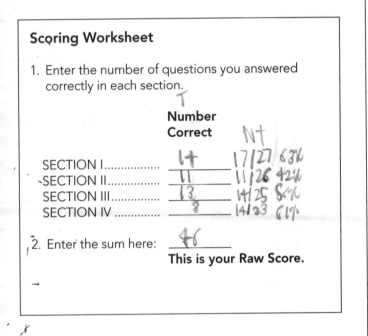

Scoring Worksheet

1. Enter the number of questions you answered correctly in each section.

	Number Correct	NT
SECTION I.................	14	17/27 63%
SECTION II...............	11	11/26 42%
SECTION III..............	13	14/25 84%
SECTION IV	8	14/23 61%

2. Enter the sum here: ___46___
This is your Raw Score.

Conversion Chart
For Converting Raw Score to the 120–180 LSAT
Scaled Score
LSAT Form 5LSN113

Reported Score	Raw Score Lowest	Raw Score Highest
180	99	101
179	98	98
178	97	97
177	96	96
176	95	95
175	94	94
174	93	93
173	92	92
172	90	91
171	89	89
170	88	88
169	87	87
168	85	86
167	84	84
166	82	83
165	81	81
164	79	80
163	77	78
162	76	76
161	74	75
160	72	73
159	71	71
158	69	70
157	67	68
156	65	66
155	64	64
154	62	63
153	60	61
152	58	59
151 NT	56	57
150	55	55
149	53	54
148	51	52
147	49	50
146	48	48
145 T	46	47
144	44	45
143	43	43
142	41	42
141	39	40
140	38	38
139	36	37
138	35	35
137	33	34
136	32	32
135	30	31
134	29	29
133	28	28
132	26	27
131	25	25
130	24	24
129	23	23
128	22	22
127	21	21
126	20	20
125	19	19
124	18	18
123	17	17
122	16	16
121	15	15
120	0	14

ANSWER KEY

SECTION I

1.	D	8.	B	15.	D	22.	C
2.	E	9.	C	16.	C	23.	E
3.	C	10.	A	17.	D	24.	D
4.	A	11.	C	18.	D	25.	D
5.	B	12.	D	19.	A	26.	B
6.	D	13.	B	20.	C	27.	B
7.	B	14.	B	21.	A		

SECTION II

1.	D	8.	D	15.	D	22.	C
2.	C	9.	D	16.	D	23.	A
3.	B	10.	C	17.	B	24.	A
4.	A	11.	C	18.	E	25.	B
5.	E	12.	E	19.	C	26.	D
6.	C	13.	C	20.	B		
7.	E	14.	C	21.	B		

SECTION III

1.	C	8.	A	15.	B	22.	E
2.	B	9.	E	16.	D	23.	C
3.	D	10.	D	17.	D	24.	A
4.	E	11.	A	18.	C	25.	D
5.	C	12.	C	19.	D		
6.	C	13.	C	20.	B		
7.	A	14.	B	21.	E		

SECTION IV

1.	B	8.	C	15.	E	22.	E
2.	E	9.	D	16.	A	23.	E
3.	B	10.	A	17.	C		
4.	D	11.	E	18.	C		
5.	A	12.	B	19.	A		
6.	E	13.	B	20.	E		
7.	E	14.	A	21.	C		

THE OFFICIAL LSAT
PREPTEST®

73

- PrepTest 73
- Form 4LSN110

SEPTEMBER 2014

SECTION I

Time—35 minutes

27 Questions

Directions: Each set of questions in this section is based on a single passage or a pair of passages. The questions are to be answered on the basis of what is <u>stated</u> or <u>implied</u> in the passage or pair of passages. For some of the questions, more than one of the choices could conceivably answer the question. However, you are to choose the <u>best</u> answer; that is, the response that most accurately and completely answers the question, and blacken the corresponding space on your answer sheet.

Charles Darwin objected to all attempts to reduce his theory of evolution to its doctrine of natural selection. "Natural selection has been the main but not the exclusive means of modification," he declared.

(5)   Nonetheless, a group of self-proclaimed strict constructionist Darwinians has recently risen to prominence by reducing Darwin's theory in just this way. These theorists use the mechanism of natural selection to explain all biological phenomena; they

(10)   assert that natural selection is responsible for every aspect of every species' form and behavior, and for the success or failure of species in general.

Natural selection is generally held to result in adaptation, the shaping of an organism's form and

(15)   behavior in response to environmental conditions to achieve enhanced reproductive success. If the strict constructionists are right, the persistence of every attribute and the survival of every species are due to such adaptation. But in fact, nature provides numerous

(20)   examples of attributes that are not adaptations for reproductive success and of species whose success or failure had little to do with their adaptations.

For example, while it is true that some random mutations of genetic material produce attributes that

(25)   enhance reproductive success and are thus favored by natural selection, and others produce harmful attributes that are weeded out, we now know from population genetics that most mutations fall into neither category. Research has revealed that neutral, nonadaptive

(30)   changes account to a large extent for the evolution of DNA. Most substitutions of one unit of DNA for another within a population have no effect on reproductive success. These alterations often change the attributes of species, but their persistence from

(35)   one generation to the next is not explainable by natural selection.

Additionally, the study of mass extinctions in paleontology has undermined the strict constructionist claim that natural selection can account for every

(40)   species' success or failure. The extinction of the dinosaurs some 65 million years ago was probably caused by the impact of an extraterrestrial body. Smaller animal species are generally better able to survive the catastrophic changes in climate that we

(45)   would expect to follow from such an impact, and mammals in the Cretaceous period were quite small because they could not compete on the large scale of the dominant dinosaurs. But while this scenario explains why dinosaurs died off and mammals fared

(50)   relatively well, it does not conform to the strict constructionist view of the adaptive reasons for the

success of species. For that view assumes that adaptations are a response to conditions that are already in place at the time the adaptations occur,

(55)   and mammals could not have adapted in advance to conditions caused by the impact. In a sense, their success was the result of dumb luck.

1. Which one of the following most accurately expresses the main point of the passage?

(A)   Evidence from two areas of science undermines the strict constructionist claim that natural selection is the only driving force behind evolution.

(B)   According to strict constructionist Darwinians, new evidence suggests that natural selection is responsible for the failure of most extinct species.

(C)   New evidence demonstrates that natural selection can produce nonadaptive as well as adaptive changes.

(D)   Strict constructionist followers of Darwin maintain that natural selection is responsible for all evolutionary change.

(E)   Evidence from the study of population genetics helps to disprove the claim that natural selection results in the survival of the fittest species.

2. According to the author, mammals were able to survive catastrophic environmental changes that occurred roughly 65 million years ago because they

(A)   had adapted previously to similar changes
(B)   were relatively small
(C)   were highly intelligent
(D)   lived in a wide range of environments
(E)   were able to reproduce quickly

GO ON TO THE NEXT PAGE.

3. The author asserts which one of the following regarding mutations of genetic material?

(A) The majority of such mutations are not passed on to subsequent generations.
(B) The majority of such mutations occur during periods when mass extinctions take place.
(C) The majority of such mutations change species' behavior rather than their appearance.
(D) The majority of such mutations have no effect on reproductive success.
(E) The majority of such mutations occur in larger rather than smaller species.

4. The author would be most likely to agree with which one of the following statements?

(A) Natural selection is responsible for almost none of the characteristics of existing species.
(B) The fact that a species flourishes in a certain environment is not proof of its adaptation to that environment.
(C) Only evolutionary changes that provide some advantage to a species are transmitted to subsequent generations.
(D) Large animal species are generally unable to survive in harsh environmental conditions.
(E) Natural selection is useful for explaining the form but not the behavior of most species.

5. The author's stance toward the arguments of the strict constructionist Darwinians can most accurately be described as one of

(A) emphatic disagreement
(B) mild disapproval
(C) open-minded neutrality
(D) conditional agreement
(E) unreserved endorsement

6. Which one of the following most accurately and completely describes the function of the second paragraph of the passage?

(A) It outlines the objections to traditional evolutionary theory raised by the strict constructionists mentioned in the first paragraph.
(B) It lists recent evidence suggesting that the strict constructionist claims described in the first paragraph are incorrect.
(C) It describes the strict constructionists' view of evolutionary theory in order to explain why the evidence described in subsequent paragraphs has recently gotten so much attention.
(D) It enumerates the arguments for the strict constructionist position that are rebutted in the paragraphs that follow.
(E) It explains the ramifications of the strict constructionists' claims and helps clarify the relevance of evidence offered in subsequent paragraphs.

7. The primary purpose of the passage is to

(A) argue in favor of a recently proposed hypothesis
(B) summarize a contemporary debate
(C) demonstrate that a particular view is incorrect
(D) criticize the proponents of a traditional theory
(E) explain why a particular theory is gaining popularity

GO ON TO THE NEXT PAGE.

From a critical discussion of the work of Victorian photographer Julia Margaret Cameron.

What Cameron called her "fancy-subject" pictures—photographs in which two or more costumed sitters enacted, under Cameron's direction, scenes from the Bible, mythology, Shakespeare, or Tennyson—
(5) bear unmistakable traces of the often comical conditions under which they were taken. In many respects they have more connection to the family album pictures of recalcitrant relatives who have been herded together for the obligatory group picture than they do to the
(10) masterpieces of Western painting. In Raphael and Giotto there are no infant Christs whose faces are blurred because they moved, or who are looking at the viewer with frank hatred. These traces, of course, are what give the photographs their life and charm. If
(15) Cameron had succeeded in her project of making seamless works of illustrative art, her work would be among the curiosities of Victorian photography—like Oscar Gustave Rejlander's extravagantly awful *The Two Ways of Life*—rather than among its most
(20) vital images.

It is precisely the camera's realism—its stubborn obsession with the surface of things—that has given Cameron's theatricality and artificiality its atmosphere of truth. It is the truth of the sitting, rather than the
(25) fiction which all the dressing up was in aid of, that wafts out of these wonderful and strange, not-quite-in-focus photographs. They are what they are: pictures of housemaids and nieces and husbands and village children who are dressed up as Mary Madonnas and
(30) infant Jesuses and John the Baptists and Lancelots and Guineveres and trying desperately hard to sit still. The way each sitter endures his or her ordeal is the collective action of the photograph, its "plot" so to speak. When we look at a narrative painting we can
(35) suspend our disbelief; when we look at a narrative photograph we cannot. We are always aware of the photograph's doubleness—of each figure's imaginary and real personas. Theater can transcend its doubleness, can make us believe (for at least some of the time) that
(40) we are seeing only Lear or Medea. Still photographs of theatrical scenes can never escape being pictures of actors.

What gives Cameron's pictures of actors their special quality—their status as treasures of photography
(45) of an unfathomably peculiar sort—is their singular combination of amateurism and artistry. In *The Passing of Arthur*, for example, the mast and oar of the makeshift boat representing a royal barge are obviously broomsticks and the water is white muslin
(50) drapery. But these details are insignificant. For once, the homely truth of the sitting gives right of place to the romantic fantasy of its director. The picture, a night scene, is magical and mysterious. While Cameron's fancy-subject pictures have been compared
(55) to poor amateur theatricals, *The Passing of Arthur* puts one in mind of good amateur theatricals one has seen, and recalls with shameless delight.

8. Which one of the following most accurately expresses the main point of the passage?

(A) The circumstances under which Cameron's fancy-subject pictures were taken render them unintentionally comical.

(B) The peculiar charm of Cameron's fancy-subject pictures derives from the viewer's simultaneous awareness of the fictional scene portrayed and the circumstances of its portrayal.

(C) The implicit claim of Cameron's fancy-subject pictures to comparison with the masterpieces of Western painting is undermined by the obtrusiveness of the sitters.

(D) The most successful of Cameron's fancy-subject pictures from an aesthetic point of view are those in which the viewer is completely unaware that the sitters are engaged in role playing.

(E) The interest of Cameron's fancy-subject pictures consists in what they tell us about the sitters and not in the imaginary scenes they portray.

9. The author mentions the props employed in *The Passing of Arthur* as

(A) examples of amateurish aspects of the work
(B) evidence of the transformative power of theater
(C) testimonies to Cameron's ingenuity
(D) indications that the work is intended ironically
(E) support for a negative appraisal of the work

10. Which one of the following, if true, would most help to explain the claim about suspension of disbelief in lines 34–36?

(A) Sitting for a painting typically takes much longer than sitting for a photograph.
(B) Paintings, unlike photographs, can depict obviously impossible situations.
(C) All of the sitters for a painting do not have to be present at the same time.
(D) A painter can suppress details about a sitter that are at odds with an imaginary persona.
(E) Paintings typically bear the stylistic imprint of an artist, school, or period.

GO ON TO THE NEXT PAGE.

11. Based on the passage, Cameron is most like which one of the following in relation to her fancy-subject pictures?

(A) a playwright who introduces incongruous elements to preserve an aesthetic distance between characters and audience

(B) a rap artist whose lyrics are designed to subvert the meaning of a song sampled in his recording

(C) a sculptor whose works possess a certain grandeur even though they are clearly constructed out of ordinary objects

(D) an architect whose buildings are designed to be as functional as possible

(E) a film director who employs ordinary people as actors in order to give the appearance of a documentary

12. Based on the passage, the author would agree with each of the following statements EXCEPT:

(A) A less realistic medium can be more conducive to suspension of disbelief than a more realistic medium.

(B) Amateurishness is a positive quality in some works of art.

(C) What might appear to be an incongruity in a narrative photograph can actually enhance its aesthetic value.

(D) We are sometimes aware of both the real and the imaginary persona of an actor in a drama.

(E) A work of art succeeds only to the extent that it realizes the artist's intentions.

13. The passage provides the most support for inferring that in Cameron's era

(A) there was little interest in photographs documenting contemporary life

(B) photography was practiced mainly by wealthy amateurs

(C) publicity stills of actors were coming into vogue

(D) there were no professional artist's models

(E) the time required to take a picture was substantial

14. The discussion of suspension of disbelief in the second paragraph serves which one of the following purposes?

(A) It is the main conclusion of the passage, for which the discussion of Cameron's fancy-subject pictures serves as a case study.

(B) It introduces a contrast the author uses in characterizing the peculiar nature of our response to Cameron's fancy-subject pictures.

(C) It is the key step in an argument supporting the author's negative appraisal of the project of narrative photography.

(D) It is used to explain a criticism of Cameron's fancy-subject pictures that the author shows to be conceptually confused.

(E) It draws a contrast between narrative painting and drama to support the author's conclusion that Cameron's fancy-subject pictures are more like the former.

15. The main purpose of the passage is

(A) to chronicle Cameron's artistic development as a photographer, which culminated in her masterpiece *The Passing of Arthur*

(B) to argue that the tension between Cameron's aims and the results she achieved in some of her works enhances the works' aesthetic value

(C) to show that Cameron's essentially theatrical vision accounts for both the strengths and the weaknesses of her photographic oeuvre

(D) to explain why Cameron's project of acquiring for photography the prestige accorded to painting was doomed to failure

(E) to defend Cameron's masterpiece *The Passing of Arthur* against its detractors by showing that it transcends the homely details of its setting

GO ON TO THE NEXT PAGE.

Some critics of advertising have assumed that the creation of false needs in consumers is the principal mechanism underlying what these critics regard as its manipulative and hegemonic power. Central to this
(5) type of critique are the writings of political theorist Herbert Marcuse, who maintained that modern people succumb to oppression by believing themselves satisfied in spite of their living in an objectively unsatisfying world. This process occurs because in
(10) mass market culture the powerful psychological techniques of advertising create "needs" that are false and whose satisfaction thus contributes, not to the genuine well-being of consumers, but rather to the profit—and thereby the disproportionate power—
(15) of corporations.

Marcuse supposed that we all have certain real needs, both physical and psychological. Advertising appropriates these needs for its own purposes, forging psychological associations between them and
(20) consumer items, e.g., between sex and perfume, thereby creating a false "need" for these items. Since the quest for fulfillment is thus displaced from its true objects to consumer items, the implicit promises of advertisements are never really fulfilled
(25) and the consumer remains at some level unsatisfied.

Unfortunately, the distinction between real and false needs upon which this critique depends is extremely problematic. If Marcusians are right, we cannot, with any assurance, separate our real needs
(30) from the alleged false needs we feel as a result of the manipulation of advertisers. For, in order to do so, it would be necessary to eliminate forces of persuasion that are so prevalent in society that they have come to inform our instinctive judgments about things.
(35) But, in fact, Marcusians make a major mistake in assuming that the majority of consumers who respond to advertising do not do so autonomously. Advertising techniques are unable to induce unwilling behavior in rational, informed adults, and regulations prohibit
(40) misinformation in advertising claims. Moreover, evidence suggests that most adults understand and recognize the techniques used and are not merely passive instruments. If there is a real need for emotional fulfillment, and if we can freely and
(45) authentically choose our means of obtaining it, then free, informed individuals may choose to obtain it through the purchase of commodities or even through the enjoyment occasionally provided by advertisements themselves. It is no doubt true that in many—perhaps
(50) even most—cases the use of an advertised product does not yield the precise sort of emotional dividend that advertisements seem to promise. This does not mean, however, that consumers do not freely and intentionally use the product as a means to another sort
(55) of fulfillment, or even that its genuine fulfillment of needs must be less than the advertisement suggests.

16. Which one of the following most accurately expresses the main point of the passage?

(A) Advertising has greater social value than Marcusians have supposed, because it is both an effective means of informing consumers and often an intrinsically entertaining medium of mass communication.

(B) Even if, as Marcusians have argued, there is a theoretical difference between real and false needs, that difference is obscured in practice by the relationship of consumers to the forces of persuasion in profit-motivated, consumer-oriented societies.

(C) Marcusian arguments regarding advertisers' creation of false needs are mistaken, because individuals are able to make autonomous decisions regarding their needs and are even able to use the elements of mass market culture to achieve genuine fulfillment.

(D) Critics of advertising typically focus on the development of false needs in the consumer and do not fully consider the ability of people to make independent choices by distinguishing their own real needs from the apparent needs that advertising induces.

(E) The problematic distinction that Marcusians have drawn between real and false needs provides an inadequate basis for their attacks on advertising, because the distinction overlooks consumers' physical and psychological needs.

17. The author states that Marcuse believed that advertisers

(A) base many of their manipulative strategies on psychological research findings

(B) appeal to people's real needs in order to create false needs

(C) are restricted to a degree by regulations prohibiting misinformation

(D) exaggerate the consumer's need for independent decision-making

(E) deny that the needs they create in people are less real than other needs

GO ON TO THE NEXT PAGE.

18. The main function of the first paragraph is to

(A)   summarize the political and economic context from which Marcusian critiques of advertising arise

(B)   outline the mechanisms by which false needs originate in mass market culture

(C)   evaluate the psychological processes by which the manipulative techniques of mass market advertising influence individuals

(D)   describe the prevailing views among contemporary critics of advertising and categorize Marcuse's theories in relation to those views

(E)   describe Marcusian views regarding mass market manipulation and indicate their role in certain criticisms of advertising

19. Which one of the following is a claim that the author attributes to Marcuse?

(A)   In modern society, advertising helps lead people to think that they are satisfied.

(B)   Modern societies differ from earlier societies in that they fail to satisfy basic physical needs.

(C)   It is impossible to draw any meaningful distinction between real and false psychological needs in modern society.

(D)   Advertising in modern society has sometimes become a tool of oppression working to the benefit of totalitarian political systems.

(E)   Advertising exploits basic human needs by deriving from them certain secondary needs which, though they become real needs, subtly work to the detriment of consumers.

20. By the term "forces of persuasion" (line 32), the author most probably refers to

(A)   intentionally dishonest claims that some theorists argue are common in advertising

(B)   innate, instinctual drives that some theorists say are fundamental to human behavior

(C)   emotional pressures that some theorists claim are exerted over individuals by society as a whole

(D)   subtle practices of social indoctrination that some theorists say are sponsored by the state

(E)   manipulative influences that some theorists say go unrecognized by those affected by them

21. Which one of the following sentences would most logically complete the passage?

(A)   Therefore, while in principle there might be grounds for holding that advertising is detrimental to society, the Marcusian critique does not provide such grounds.

(B)   Therefore, although Marcusian claims about advertising are rationally justified, the mistake of many recent critics of advertising is in their use of these claims for political gain.

(C)   Therefore, any shift in basic assumptions required to correct the abuses of advertising will require a change in the perception of human nature held by corporate leaders.

(D)   Therefore, while emphasizing only detrimental social aspects of advertising, Marcusians have failed to consider that such aspects are clearly outweighed by numerous social benefits.

(E)   Therefore, the Marcusian critique of advertising is mistaken except in its claim that advertisers exert economic power over those few people who are unable or unwilling to distinguish real from false needs.

GO ON TO THE NEXT PAGE.

Passage A

There are two principles that are fundamental to a theory of justice regarding property. The principle of justice in acquisition specifies the conditions under which someone can legitimately come to own
(5) something that was previously not owned by anyone. The principle of justice in transfer specifies the conditions under which the transfer of property from one person to another is justified.

Given such principles, if the world were wholly
(10) just, the following definition would exhaustively cover the subject of justice regarding property:

1. A person who acquires property in accordance with the principle of justice in acquisition is entitled to that property.
(15) 2. A person who acquires property in accordance with the principle of justice in transfer, from someone else who is entitled to the property, is entitled to the property.

3. No one is entitled to any property except by
(20) (repeated) applications of 1 and 2.

However, not all actual situations are generated in accordance with the principles of justice in acquisition and justice in transfer. Some people steal from others or defraud them, for example. The existence of past
(25) injustice raises the issue of the rectification of injustice. If past injustice has shaped present ownership in various ways, what, if anything, ought to be done to rectify that injustice? A principle of rectification would use historical information about previous
(30) situations and injustices done in them, and information about the actual course of events that flowed from these injustices, to produce a description of the property ownership that should have resulted. Actual ownership of property must then be brought
(35) into conformity with this description.

Passage B

In 1790, the United States Congress passed the Indian Nonintercourse Act, which requires that all transfers of lands from Native Americans to others be approved by the federal government. The law has not
(40) been changed in any relevant respect, and it remains in effect today. Its purpose is clear. It was meant to guarantee security to Native Americans against fraudulent acquisition by others of the Native Americans' land holdings. Several suits have been
(45) initiated by Native American tribes for recovery of lands held by them when the Nonintercourse Act took effect.

One natural (one might almost say obvious) way of reasoning about Native American claims to land in
(50) North America is this: Native Americans were the first human occupants of this land. Before the European invasion of North America, the land belonged to them. In the course of that invasion and its aftermath, the land was illicitly taken from them. The current owners
(55) lack a well-founded right to the land, which now lies illicitly in their hands. Ideally, the land should be restored to its rightful owners. This may be impractical; compromises might have to be made. But the original wrong can most easily be righted by returning the land
(60) to them—or by returning it wherever that is feasible.

22. Which one of the following most accurately describes the main purpose for which passage A was written and the main purpose for which passage B was written?

(A) Passage A: to propose a solution to a moral problem
Passage B: to criticize a proposed solution to a moral problem

(B) Passage A: to sketch a general outline of a branch of moral theory
Passage B: to give a particular moral analysis of a real case

(C) Passage A: to spell out the details of two fundamental principles
Passage B: to examine a case that exemplifies a moral ideal

(D) Passage A: to argue for a particular moral ideal
Passage B: to question the assumptions of a moral theory

(E) Passage A: to advocate the use of certain moral principles
Passage B: to provide a counterexample to some widely held moral principles

23. Both passages explicitly mention which one of the following?

(A) transfer of property from one owner to another
(B) a legal basis for recovery of property
(C) entitlement to property in a wholly just world
(D) practicability of rectification of past injustice
(E) injustice committed as part of an invasion

24. Which one of the following is true of the relationship between passage A and the second paragraph of passage B?

(A) The second paragraph of passage B attempts to develop a broader version of the theory presented in passage A.

(B) The second paragraph of passage B purports to state facts that bolster the argument made in passage A.

(C) The argument in the second paragraph of passage B is structurally parallel to the argument in passage A, but the subject matter of the two is different.

(D) Passage A presents a theory that tends to support the argument presented in the second paragraph of passage B.

(E) The second paragraph of passage B attempts to undermine the theory presented in passage A.

GO ON TO THE NEXT PAGE.

25. Based on what can be inferred from their titles, the relationship between which one of the following pairs of documents is most analogous to the relationship between passage A and passage B?

    (A) "Card Counting for Everyone: A Can't-Lose System for Beating the Dealer"
         "The Evils of Gambling"
    (B) "Mayor McConnell Is Unfit to Serve"
         "Why Mayor McConnell Should be Reelected"
    (C) "Pruning Fruit Trees: A Guide for the Novice"
         "Easy Recipes for Beginning Cooks"
    (D) "Notable Failures of the STORM Weather Forecasting Model"
         "Meteorologists' Best Tool Yet: The STORM Forecasting Model"
    (E) "Fundamentals of Building Construction and Repair"
         "Engineering Report: The Repairs Needed by the Thales Building"

26. The author of passage A would be most likely to characterize the purpose of the Indian Nonintercourse Act as which one of the following?

    (A) legitimization of actual property holdings during the eighteenth century
    (B) clarification of existing laws regarding transfer of property
    (C) assurance of conformity to the principle of justice in acquisition
    (D) prevention of violations of the principle of justice in transfer
    (E) implementation of a principle of rectification

27. Which one of the following most accurately describes the difference in approach taken by passage A as compared to passage B?

    (A) Passage A espouses a general view without providing details, while passage B sketches an argument that it does not necessarily endorse.
    (B) Passage A argues for the superiority of one view over competing views, while passage B considers only a single view.
    (C) Passage A invokes commonly held principles to support a policy recommendation, while passage B relies on the views of established authorities to support its claims.
    (D) Passage A briefly states a view and then provides an argument for it, while passage B provides a detailed statement of a view but no argument.
    (E) Passage A provides an argument in support of a view, while passage B attempts to undermine a view.

S T O P

IF YOU FINISH BEFORE TIME IS CALLED, YOU MAY CHECK YOUR WORK ON THIS SECTION ONLY.
DO NOT WORK ON ANY OTHER SECTION IN THE TEST.

SECTION II

Time—35 minutes

25 Questions

<u>Directions:</u> The questions in this section are based on the reasoning contained in brief statements or passages. For some questions, more than one of the choices could conceivably answer the question. However, you are to choose the <u>best</u> answer; that is, the response that most accurately and completely answers the question. You should not make assumptions that are by commonsense standards implausible, superfluous, or incompatible with the passage. After you have chosen the best answer, blacken the corresponding space on your answer sheet.

1. Editorial: The city has chosen a contractor to upgrade the heating systems in public buildings. Only 40 percent of the technicians employed by this contractor are certified by the Heating Technicians Association. So the city selected a contractor 60 percent of whose technicians are unqualified, which is an outrage.

Which one of the following is an assumption required by the argument in the editorial?

(A)   Certified technicians receive higher pay than uncertified technicians.
(B)   There are no contractors with fewer than 40 percent of their technicians certified.
(C)   Technicians who lack certification are not qualified technicians.
(D)   Qualified technicians installed the heating systems to be upgraded.
(E)   The contractor hired by the city has personal ties to city officials.

2. Jeneta: Increasingly, I've noticed that when a salesperson thanks a customer for making a purchase, the customer also says "Thank you" instead of saying "You're welcome." I've even started doing that myself. But when a friend thanks a friend for a favor, the response is always "You're welcome."

Which one of the following, if true, most helps to explain the discrepancy that Jeneta observes in people's responses?

(A)   Customers regard themselves as doing salespeople a favor by buying from them as opposed to someone else.
(B)   Salespeople are often instructed by their employers to thank customers, whereas customers are free to say what they want.
(C)   Salespeople do not regard customers who buy from them as doing them a favor.
(D)   The way that people respond to being thanked is generally determined by habit rather than by conscious decision.
(E)   In a commercial transaction, as opposed to a favor, the customer feels that the benefits are mutual.

3. Some video game makers have sold the movie rights for popular games. However, this move is rarely good from a business perspective. After all, StarQuanta sold the movie rights to its popular game *Nostroma*, but the poorly made film adaptation of the game was hated by critics and the public alike. Subsequent versions of the *Nostroma* video game, although better than the original, sold poorly.

The reasoning in the argument is most vulnerable to criticism in that the argument

(A)   draws a general conclusion on the basis of just one individual case
(B)   infers that a product will be disliked by the public merely from the claim that the product was disliked by critics
(C)   restates as a conclusion a claim earlier presented as evidence for that conclusion
(D)   takes for granted that products with similar content that are in different media will be of roughly equal popularity
(E)   treats a requirement for a product to be popular as something that ensures that a product will be popular

GO ON TO THE NEXT PAGE.

4. Principle: The executive in a given company whose compensation package is determined by advice of an external consultant is likely to be overcompensated if the consultant also has business interests with the company the executive manages.

Which one of the following judgments conforms most closely to the principle stated above?

(A) The president of the Troskco Corporation is definitely overpaid, since he receives in salary and benefits almost 40 times more than the average employee of Troskco receives.

(B) The president of the Troskco Corporation is probably overpaid, since his total annual compensation package was determined five years ago, when the company's profits were at an all-time high.

(C) The president of the Troskco Corporation is probably not overpaid, since his total compensation package was determined by the Troskco board of directors without retaining the services of an external compensation consultant.

(D) The president of Troskco Corporation is probably overpaid, since the Troskco board of directors determined his compensation by following the advice of an external consultant who has many other contracts with Troskco.

(E) The president of Troskco Corporation is definitely not overpaid, since the external consultant the board of directors retained to advise on executive salaries has no other contracts with Troskco.

5. Science writer: Lemaître argued that the universe began with the explosion of a "primeval atom," a singular point of infinite gravity in space and time. If this is correct, our current observations should reveal galaxies accelerating away from one another. This is precisely what we observe. Yet because there is another theory—the oscillating universe theory—that makes exactly this same prediction, Lemaître's theory must be considered inadequate.

Which one of the following most accurately describes a flaw in the science writer's reasoning?

(A) The conclusion is derived partly from assertions attributed to a purported expert whose credibility is not established.

(B) The conclusion is based on a shift in meaning of a key term from one part of the argument to another part.

(C) The science writer takes for granted the existence of a causal connection between observed phenomena.

(D) The science writer fails to see that one theory's correctly predicting observed data cannot itself constitute evidence against an alternative theory that also does this.

(E) The science writer presumes, without providing justification, that there are only two possible explanations for the phenomena in question.

6. Critic: The criticism of the popular film comedy *Quirks* for not being realistic is misguided. It is certainly true that the characters are too stylized to be real people. That could be problematic, but in this case the resulting film is funny. And that is the important thing for a comedy.

Which one of the following principles, if valid, most helps to justify the reasoning in the critic's argument?

(A) Films should be judged on how well they accurately capture the world.

(B) Films are successful as long as they are popular.

(C) Film comedies should find their humor in their stylistic portrayals.

(D) Films are successful if they succeed within their genre.

(E) Films should try to stay entirely within a single genre.

GO ON TO THE NEXT PAGE.

7. Party X has recently been accused by its opposition, Party Y, of accepting international campaign contributions, which is illegal. Such accusations are, however, ill founded. Three years ago, Party Y itself was involved in a scandal in which it was discovered that its national committee seriously violated campaign laws.

Which one of the following contains flawed reasoning most similar to the flawed reasoning in the argument above?

(A) The plaintiff accuses the defendant of violating campaign laws, but the accusations are ill founded. While the defendant's actions may violate certain laws, they are not immoral, because the laws in question are unjust.

(B) The plaintiff accuses the defendant of violating campaign laws, but these accusations show the plaintiff to be hypocritical, because the plaintiff has engaged in similar conduct.

(C) The plaintiff accuses the defendant of violating campaign laws, and, in the past, courts have declared such violations illegal. Nevertheless, because the plaintiff recently engaged in actions that were similar to those of the defendant, the plaintiff's accusations are ill founded.

(D) The plaintiff accuses the defendant of violating campaign laws, but these accusations are ill founded. They are clearly an attempt to stir up controversy, because they were made just two weeks before the election.

(E) The plaintiff accuses the defendant of voting only for campaign laws that would favor the defendant's party. This accusation is ill founded, however, because it attacks the defendant's motivations instead of addressing the arguments the defendant has put forth justifying these votes.

8. Biologist: Marine animals known as box jellyfish have eyes with well-formed lenses capable of producing sharp images that reveal fine detail. But the box jellyfish's retinas are too far forward to receive a clear image, so these jellyfish can receive only a blurry image that reveals prominent features of objects but not fine detail. This example shows that eyes are adapted only to an animal's needs rather than to some abstract sense of how a good eye would be designed.

The argument requires assuming which one of the following?

(A) Box jellyfish are the only kind of jellyfish with retinas that do not focus clearly.

(B) Box jellyfish have a need to detect prominent features of objects but not fine details.

(C) Box jellyfish would benefit from having retinas that allowed their eyes to focus more sharply.

(D) Box jellyfish developed from jellyfish whose retinas received clear images.

(E) Box jellyfish use vision as their main means of detecting prey.

9. Columnist: Research shows significant reductions in the number of people smoking, and especially in the number of first-time smokers in those countries that have imposed stringent restrictions on tobacco advertising. This provides substantial grounds for disputing tobacco companies' claims that advertising has no significant causal impact on the tendency to smoke.

Which one of the following, if true, most undermines the columnist's reasoning?

(A) People who smoke are unlikely to quit merely because they are no longer exposed to tobacco advertising.

(B) Broadcast media tend to have stricter restrictions on tobacco advertising than do print media.

(C) Restrictions on tobacco advertising are imposed only in countries where a negative attitude toward tobacco use is already widespread and increasing.

(D) Most people who begin smoking during adolescence continue to smoke throughout their lives.

(E) People who are largely unaffected by tobacco advertising tend to be unaffected by other kinds of advertising as well.

GO ON TO THE NEXT PAGE.

10. Actor: Bertolt Brecht's plays are not genuinely successful dramas. The roles in Brecht's plays express such incongruous motives and beliefs that audiences, as well as the actors playing the roles, invariably find it difficult, at best, to discern any of the characters' personalities. But, for a play to succeed as a drama, audiences must care what happens to at least some of its characters.

The conclusion of the actor's argument can be properly drawn if which one of the following is assumed?

(A) An audience that cannot readily discern a character's personality will not take any interest in that character.

(B) A character's personality is determined primarily by the motives and beliefs of that character.

(C) The extent to which a play succeeds as a drama is directly proportional to the extent to which the play's audiences care about its characters.

(D) If the personalities of a play's characters are not readily discernible by the actors playing the roles, then those personalities are not readily discernible by the play's audience.

(E) All plays that, unlike Brecht's plays, have characters with whom audiences empathize succeed as dramas.

11. Municipal legislator: The mayor proposes that the city accept a lighting company's gift of several high-tech streetlights. Surely there would be no problem in accepting these despite some people's fear that the company wants to influence the city's decision regarding park lighting contracts. The only ulterior motive I can find is the company's desire to have its products seen by mayors who will visit the city for an upcoming convention. In any case, favoritism in city contracts is prevented by our competitive-bidding procedure.

Which one of the following most accurately expresses the main conclusion of the municipal legislator's argument?

(A) Some people's fear that the company wants to influence the city's decision regarding park lighting contracts is unfounded.

(B) The mayor's proposal to accept the gift of streetlights should not be considered problematic.

(C) It is not appropriate that any company should have the unique opportunity to display its products to mayors attending the upcoming convention.

(D) The city's competitive-bidding procedure prevents favoritism in the dispensing of city contracts.

(E) The lighting company's desire to display its products to visiting mayors is the real motivation behind the suggested gift of streetlights.

12. The chairperson should not have released the Election Commission's report to the public, for the chairperson did not consult any other members of the commission about releasing the report before having it released.

The argument's conclusion can be properly inferred if which one of the following is assumed?

(A) It would have been permissible for the chairperson to release the commission's report to the public only if most other members of the commission had first given their consent.

(B) All of the members of the commission had signed the report prior to its release.

(C) The chairperson would not have been justified in releasing the commission's report if any members of the commission had serious reservations about the report's content.

(D) The chairperson would have been justified in releasing the report only if each of the commission's members would have agreed to its being released had they been consulted.

(E) Some members of the commission would have preferred that the report not be released to the public.

13. Reformer: A survey of police departments keeps track of the national crime rate, which is the annual number of crimes per 100,000 people. The survey shows no significant reduction in the crime rate in the past 20 years, but the percentage of the population in prison has increased substantially, and public expenditure on prisons has grown at an alarming rate. This demonstrates that putting more people in prison cannot help to reduce crime.

A flaw in the reformer's argument is that it

(A) infers without justification that because the national crime rate has increased, the number of crimes reported by each police department has increased

(B) ignores the possibility that the crime rate would have significantly increased if it had not been for the greater rate of imprisonment

(C) overlooks the possibility that the population has increased significantly over the past 20 years

(D) presumes, without providing warrant, that alternative measures for reducing crime would be more effective than imprisonment

(E) takes for granted that the number of prisoners must be proportional to the number of crimes committed

GO ON TO THE NEXT PAGE.

14. Inez: Space-exploration programs pay for themselves many times over, since such programs result in technological advances with everyday, practical applications. Space exploration is more than the search for knowledge for its own sake; investment in space exploration is such a productive investment in developing widely useful technology that we can't afford not to invest in space exploration.

    Winona: It is absurd to try to justify funding for space exploration merely by pointing out that such programs will lead to technological advances. If technology with practical applications is all that is desired, then it should be funded directly.

    Winona responds to Inez by

    (A) showing that there is no evidence that the outcome Inez anticipates will in fact be realized
    (B) suggesting that Inez has overlooked evidence that directly argues against the programs Inez supports
    (C) demonstrating that the pieces of evidence that Inez cites contradict each other
    (D) providing evidence that the beneficial effects that Inez desires can be achieved only at great expense
    (E) claiming that a goal that Inez mentions could be pursued without the programs Inez endorses

15. Marketing consultant: Last year I predicted that LRG's latest advertising campaign would be unpopular with customers and ineffective in promoting new products. But LRG ignored my predictions and took the advice of a competing consultant. This season's sales figures show that sales are down and LRG's new products are selling especially poorly. Thus, the advertising campaign was ill conceived.

    The marketing consultant's reasoning is most vulnerable to criticism on the grounds that

    (A) it takes for granted that LRG's sales would not have been lower still in the absence of the competitor's advertising campaign
    (B) it fails to consider that economic factors unrelated to the advertising campaign may have caused LRG's low sales figures
    (C) it takes for granted that in LRG's industry, new products should outsell established products
    (D) it takes for granted that the higher sales of established products are due to effective advertising
    (E) it confuses a condition necessary for increasing product sales with a condition that will ensure increased sales

16. The top prize in architecture, the Pritzker Prize, is awarded for individual achievement, like Nobel Prizes for science. But architects are judged by their buildings, and buildings are the result of teamwork. As achievements, buildings are not like scientific discoveries, but like movies, which compete for awards for best picture. Thus, it would be better if the top prize in architecture were awarded to the best building rather than the best architect.

    The argument proceeds by

    (A) reaching a conclusion about the way something should be done in one field on the basis of comparisons with corresponding practices in other fields
    (B) making a distinction between two different types of objects in order to conclude that one has more inherent value than the other
    (C) pointing to similarities between two practices as a basis for concluding that criticisms of one practice can rightly be applied to the other
    (D) arguing that because two different fields are disanalogous, the characteristics of one field are not relevant to justifying a conclusion about the other
    (E) contending that an action is inappropriate by presenting an argument that a corresponding action in an analogous case is inappropriate

GO ON TO THE NEXT PAGE.

17. If Suarez is not the most qualified of the candidates for sheriff, then Anderson is. Thus, if the most qualified candidate is elected and Suarez is not elected, then Anderson will be.

The reasoning in which one of the following is most similar to the reasoning in the argument above?

(A) If the excavation contract does not go to the lowest bidder, then it will go to Caldwell. So if Qiu gets the contract and Caldwell does not, then the contract will have been awarded to the lowest bidder.

(B) If the lowest bidder on the sanitation contract is not Dillon, then it is Ramsey. So if the contract goes to the lowest bidder and it does not go to Dillon, then it will go to Ramsey.

(C) If Kapshaw is not awarded the landscaping contract, then Johnson will be. So if the contract goes to the lowest bidder and it does not go to Johnson, then it will go to Kapshaw.

(D) If Holihan did not submit the lowest bid on the maintenance contract, then neither did Easton. So if the contract goes to the lowest bidder and it does not go to Easton, then it will not go to Holihan either.

(E) If Perez is not the lowest bidder on the catering contract, then Sullivan is. So if Sullivan does not get the contract and Perez does not get it either, then it will not be awarded to the lowest bidder.

18. Critic: An art historian argues that because fifteenth-century European paintings were generally more planimetric (that is, two-dimensional with no attempt at suggesting depth) than were sixteenth-century paintings, fifteenth-century painters had a greater mastery of painting than did sixteenth-century painters. However, this conclusion is wrong. Fifteenth-century European painters did not have a greater mastery of painting, for the degree to which a painting is planimetric is irrelevant to the painter's mastery.

The argument is flawed in that it

(A) rejects a position merely because the proponent of the position has other objectionable views

(B) illicitly relies on two different meanings of the term "mastery"

(C) takes a necessary condition for an argument's being inadequate to be a sufficient condition for an argument's being inadequate

(D) bases its conclusion on two claims that contradict each other

(E) rejects a position on the grounds that an inadequate argument has been made for it

19. A carved flint object depicting a stylized human head with an open mouth was found in a Stone Age tomb in Ireland. Some archaeologists believe that the object was a weapon—the head of a warrior's mace—but it is too small for that purpose. Because of its size and the fact that an open mouth symbolizes speaking, the object was probably the head of a speaking staff, a communal object passed around a small assembly to indicate who has the right to speak.

Which one of the following, if true, would most weaken the argument?

(A) The tomb in which the object was found did not contain any other objects that might have been weapons.

(B) Communal objects were normally passed from one generation to the next in Stone Age Ireland.

(C) The object was carved with an artistry that was rare in Stone Age Ireland.

(D) The tomb in which the object was found was that of a politically prominent person.

(E) A speaking staff with a stone head is thought to symbolize a warrior's mace.

20. The advent of chemical fertilizers led the farmers in a certain region to abandon the practice of periodically growing a "green-manure" crop, such as alfalfa, in a field to rejuvenate its soil. As a result, the soil structure in a typical farm field in the region is poor. So to significantly improve the soil structure, farmers will need to abandon the use of chemical fertilizers.

The argument relies on the assumption that

(A) most, if not all, farmers in the region who abandon the use of chemical fertilizers will periodically grow alfalfa

(B) applying chemical fertilizers to green-manure crops, such as alfalfa, has no positive effect on their growth

(C) the most important factor influencing the soil quality of a farm field is soil structure

(D) chemical fertilizers themselves have a destructive effect on the soil structure of farm fields

(E) many, if not all, farmers in the region will not grow green-manure crops unless they abandon the use of chemical fertilizers

GO ON TO THE NEXT PAGE.

21. Most of the students who took Spanish 101 at the university last semester attended every class session. However, each student who received a grade lower than B minus missed at least one class session.

Which one of the following statements about the students who took Spanish 101 at the university last semester can be properly inferred from the information above?

(A) At least some of the students who received a grade of A minus or higher attended every class session.

(B) Most, if not all, of the students who missed at least one class session received a grade lower than B minus.

(C) Most of the students received a grade higher than B minus.

(D) At least one student who received a grade of B minus or higher missed one or more class sessions.

(E) More than half of the students received a grade of B minus or higher.

22. Because the native salmon in Lake Clearwater had nearly disappeared, sockeye salmon were introduced in 1940. After being introduced, this genetically uniform group of sockeyes split into two distinct populations that do not interbreed, one inhabiting deep areas of the lake and the other inhabiting shallow areas. Since the two populations now differ genetically, some researchers hypothesize that each has adapted genetically to its distinct habitat.

Which of the following, if true, most strongly supports the researchers' hypothesis?

(A) Neither of the two populations of sockeyes has interbred with the native salmon.

(B) When the native salmon in Lake Clearwater were numerous, they comprised two distinct populations that did not interbreed.

(C) Most types of salmon that inhabit lakes spend part of the time in shallow water and part in deeper water.

(D) One of the populations of sockeyes is virtually identical genetically to the sockeyes originally introduced in 1940.

(E) The total number of sockeye salmon in the lake is not as large as the number of native salmon had been many years ago.

23. A developing country can substantially increase its economic growth if its businesspeople are willing to invest in modern industries that have not yet been pursued there. But being the first to invest in an industry is very risky. Moreover, businesspeople have little incentive to take this risk since if the business succeeds, many other people will invest in the same industry, and the competition will cut into their profits.

The statements above, if true, most strongly support which one of the following claims?

(A) Once a developing country has at least one business in a modern industry, further investment in that industry will not contribute to the country's economic growth.

(B) In developing countries, there is greater competition within modern industries than within traditional industries.

(C) A developing country can increase its prospects for economic growth by providing added incentive for investment in modern industries that have not yet been pursued there.

(D) A developing country will not experience economic growth unless its businesspeople invest in modern industries.

(E) Investments in a modern industry in a developing country carry little risk as long as the country has at least one other business in that industry.

GO ON TO THE NEXT PAGE.

24. A survey of a city's concertgoers found that almost all of them were dissatisfied with the local concert hall. A large majority of them expressed a strong preference for wider seats and better acoustics. And, even though the survey respondents were told that the existing concert hall cannot feasibly be modified to provide these features, most of them opposed the idea of tearing down the existing structure and replacing it with a concert hall with wider seats and better acoustics.

Which one of the following, if true, most helps to explain the apparent conflict in the concertgoers' views, as revealed by the survey?

(A) Before any of the survey questions were asked, the respondents were informed that the survey was sponsored by a group that advocates replacing the existing concert hall.

(B) Most of the people who live in the vicinity of the existing concert hall do not want it to be torn down.

(C) The city's construction industry will receive more economic benefit from the construction of a new concert hall than from renovations to the existing concert hall.

(D) A well-publicized plan is being considered by the city government that would convert the existing concert hall into a public auditorium and build a new concert hall nearby.

(E) Many popular singers and musicians who currently do not hold concerts in the city would begin to hold concerts there if a new concert hall were built.

25. Student: Before completing my research paper, I want to find the book from which I copied a passage to quote in the paper. Without the book, I will be unable to write an accurate citation, and without an accurate citation, I will be unable to include the quotation. Hence, since the completed paper will be much better with the quotation than without, _____.

Which one of the following most logically completes the student's argument?

(A) I will have to include an inaccurate citation

(B) I will be unable to complete my research paper

(C) if I do not find the book, my research paper will suffer

(D) if I do not find the book, I will include the quotation without an accurate citation

(E) if I do not find the book, I will be unable to complete my research paper

S T O P

IF YOU FINISH BEFORE TIME IS CALLED, YOU MAY CHECK YOUR WORK ON THIS SECTION ONLY.
DO NOT WORK ON ANY OTHER SECTION IN THE TEST.

SECTION III

Time—35 minutes

23 Questions

Directions: Each group of questions in this section is based on a set of conditions. In answering some of the questions, it may be useful to draw a rough diagram. Choose the response that most accurately and completely answers each question and blacken the corresponding space on your answer sheet.

Questions 1–7

A record producer is planning the contents of a CD consisting of a sequence of exactly five instrumental pieces—*Reciprocity, Salammbo, Trapezoid, Vancouver,* and *Wisteria.* To create and sustain certain moods, the sequence of pieces will satisfy the following constraints:

> *Salammbo* must be earlier than *Vancouver.*
> *Trapezoid* must either be earlier than both *Reciprocity* and *Salammbo* or later than both *Reciprocity* and *Salammbo.*
> *Wisteria* must either be earlier than both *Reciprocity* and *Trapezoid* or later than both *Reciprocity* and *Trapezoid.*

SV
T RS / RST
W RT / RT W

1. The five pieces could appear in which one of the following sequences on the CD, in order from first to last?

   (A) *Reciprocity, Trapezoid, Wisteria, Salammbo, Vancouver*

   (B) *Salammbo, Reciprocity, Trapezoid, Vancouver, Wisteria*

   (C) *Trapezoid, Wisteria, Salammbo, Vancouver, Reciprocity*

   (D) *Vancouver, Wisteria, Salammbo, Reciprocity, Trapezoid*

   (E) *Wisteria, Salammbo, Vancouver, Trapezoid, Reciprocity*

GO ON TO THE NEXT PAGE.

2. If *Salammbo* is the fourth piece on the CD, then which one of the following must be true?

(A)   *Reciprocity* is earlier on the CD than *Wisteria*.
(B)   *Salammbo* is earlier on the CD than *Trapezoid*.
(C)   *Trapezoid* is earlier on the CD than *Reciprocity*.
(D)   *Vancouver* is earlier on the CD than *Wisteria*.
(E)   *Wisteria* is earlier on the CD than *Trapezoid*.

3. If *Reciprocity* is the first piece on the CD, then which one of the following could be true?

(A)   *Trapezoid* is the second piece on the CD.
(B)   *Vancouver* is the third piece on the CD.
(C)   *Wisteria* is the third piece on the CD.
(D)   *Salammbo* is the fourth piece on the CD.
(E)   *Trapezoid* is the last piece on the CD.

4. If *Trapezoid* is the second piece on the CD, then which one of the following could be true?

(A)   *Salammbo* is the first piece on the CD.
(B)   *Reciprocity* is the first piece on the CD.
(C)   *Vancouver* is the third piece on the CD.
(D)   *Wisteria* is the fourth piece on the CD.
(E)   *Reciprocity* is the last piece on the CD.

5. The first and second pieces on the CD, listed in order, could be

(A)   *Reciprocity* and *Vancouver*
(B)   *Reciprocity* and *Wisteria*
(C)   *Salammbo* and *Trapezoid*
(D)   *Trapezoid* and *Wisteria*
(E)   *Wisteria* and *Salammbo*

6. If *Vancouver* is the second piece on the CD, then which one of the following could be true?

(A)   *Wisteria* is the first piece on the CD.
(B)   *Salammbo* is the third piece on the CD.
(C)   *Trapezoid* is the third piece on the CD.
(D)   *Reciprocity* is the fourth piece on the CD.
(E)   *Reciprocity* is the last piece on the CD.

7. If *Wisteria* is the first piece on the CD, then which one of the following CANNOT be true?

(A)   *Trapezoid* is the third piece on the CD.
(B)   *Vancouver* is the third piece on the CD.
(C)   *Salammbo* is the fourth piece on the CD.
(D)   *Vancouver* is the fourth piece on the CD.
(E)   *Trapezoid* is the last piece on the CD.

GO ON TO THE NEXT PAGE.

Questions 8–13

At a business symposium there will be exactly five speakers: Long, Molina, Xiao, Yoshida, and Zimmerman. Each speaker will give exactly one speech, in either the Gold Room or the Rose Room. In each room, there will be exactly one speech at 1 P.M. and one speech at 2 P.M. In one of the rooms, yet to be determined, there will also be a speech at 3 P.M. The schedule of speeches is constrained by the following:

Molina's speech must be earlier than Long's, and in the same room.

Neither Xiao's speech nor Yoshida's speech can be earlier than Zimmerman's.

If Long's speech is in the Gold Room, then Xiao's and Zimmerman's speeches must both be in the Rose Room.

8. Which one of the following could be the speeches given in each room, listed in the order in which they occur?

(A) Gold Room: Molina's, Long's
   Rose Room: Zimmerman's, Xiao's, Yoshida's

(B) Gold Room: Molina's, Yoshida's, Long's
   Rose Room: Xiao's, Zimmerman's

(C) Gold Room: Xiao's, Molina's, Long's
   Rose Room: Zimmerman's, Yoshida's

(D) Gold Room: Yoshida's, Long's, Molina's
   Rose Room: Zimmerman's, Xiao's

(E) Gold Room: Zimmerman's, Molina's
   Rose Room: Xiao's, Yoshida's, Long's

GO ON TO THE NEXT PAGE.

9. Which one of the following pairs of speeches CANNOT be given at the same time?

(A) Long's and Yoshida's
(B) Long's and Zimmerman's
(C) Molina's and Xiao's
(D) Xiao's and Yoshida's
(E) Yoshida's and Zimmerman's

10. If Xiao's speech is at 3 P.M., which one of the following CANNOT be true?

(A) Long's speech is in the same room as Yoshida's.
(B) Molina's speech is in the same room as Xiao's.
(C) Xiao's speech is in the same room as Yoshida's.
(D) Xiao's speech is in the same room as Zimmerman's.
(E) Yoshida's speech is in the same room as Zimmerman's.

11. Which one of the following could be a complete and accurate list of the speeches given in the Gold Room, in the order in which they occur?

(A) Long's, Molina's
(B) Molina's, Yoshida's
(C) Molina's, Yoshida's, Long's
(D) Yoshida's, Zimmerman's, Xiao's
(E) Zimmerman's, Molina's, Long's

12. If Yoshida's speech is at 1 P.M., which one of the following could be true?

(A) Long's speech is at 1 P.M. in the Gold Room.
(B) Long's speech is at 2 P.M. in the Rose Room.
(C) Molina's speech is at 2 P.M. in the Gold Room.
(D) Xiao's speech is at 3 P.M. in the Gold Room.
(E) Xiao's speech is at 1 P.M. in the Rose Room.

13. Which one of the following, if substituted for the constraint that neither Xiao's speech nor Yoshida's speech can be earlier than Zimmerman's, would have the same effect in determining the schedule of speeches with regard to rooms and times?

(A) Long's speech must be at 3 P.M.
(B) Molina's speech cannot be earlier than Zimmerman's.
(C) Either Xiao's speech or Yoshida's speech must be after Zimmerman's.
(D) Either Xiao's speech or Yoshida's speech or both must be at 2 P.M.
(E) Zimmerman's speech must be at 1 P.M.

GO ON TO THE NEXT PAGE.

Questions 14–18

During the seventeenth century, three families—the Trents, the Williamses, and the Yandells—owned the five buildings that constituted the center of their village—the forge, the granary, the inn, the mill, and the stable. Each family owned at least one of the buildings and each building was owned by exactly one of the families. The historical evidence establishes the following about the ownership of the buildings:

The Williamses owned more of the buildings than the Yandells owned.

Neither the inn nor the mill belonged to the owner of the forge.

Either the Trents owned the stable or the Yandells owned the inn, or both.

T, W, Y

F, G, I, M, S

W > Y

I M
F

T:S or Y:I or both T:S
Y:I

14. Which one of the following could be an accurate matching of each family to the building or buildings it owned?

(A) Trents: the granary, the stable
     Williamses: the inn, the mill
     Yandells: the forge
(B) Trents: the granary, the mill
     Williamses: the inn, the stable
     Yandells: the forge
(C) Trents: the forge, the mill
     Williamses: the granary, the stable
     Yandells: the inn
(D) Trents: the forge, the granary
     Williamses: the mill
     Yandells: the inn, the stable
(E) Trents: the stable
     Williamses: the inn, the mill
     Yandells: the forge, the granary

GO ON TO THE NEXT PAGE.

15. Which one of the following is a pair of buildings that CANNOT both have been owned by the Trents?

(A) the forge, the granary
(B) the granary, the mill
(C) the granary, the stable
(D) the inn, the mill
(E) the inn, the stable

16. If the Yandells owned the mill, which one of the following must be true?

(A) The Trents owned the forge.
(B) The Trents owned the inn.
(C) The Williamses owned the forge.
(D) The Williamses owned the granary.
(E) The Williamses owned the inn.

17. If one of the families owned both the granary and the inn, which one of the following could be true?

(A) The Trents owned the granary.
(B) The Trents owned the mill.
(C) The Williamses owned the forge.
(D) The Williamses owned the stable.
(E) The Yandells owned the inn.

18. If the Trents owned exactly one of the buildings, which one of the following is a complete and accurate list of the buildings any one of which could be the building that the Trents owned?

(A) the forge
(B) the forge, the mill
(C) the inn, the stable
(D) the forge, the granary, the mill
(E) the forge, the mill, the stable

GO ON TO THE NEXT PAGE.

Questions 19–23

A florist is filling a customer's order for three bouquets—bouquet 1, bouquet 2, and bouquet 3. Each of the bouquets is to be composed of one or more of five kinds of flowers—lilies, peonies, roses, snapdragons, and tulips—subject to the following conditions:

Bouquets 1 and 3 cannot have any kind of flower in common.

Bouquets 2 and 3 must have exactly two kinds of flowers in common.

Bouquet 3 must have snapdragons.

If a bouquet has lilies, that bouquet must also have roses but cannot have snapdragons.

If a bouquet has tulips, that bouquet must also have peonies.

19. Which one of the following could be a complete and accurate list of the kinds of flowers in each of the bouquets?

(A) bouquet 1: lilies, roses
bouquet 2: peonies, roses, tulips
bouquet 3: peonies, snapdragons, tulips

(B) bouquet 1: peonies, roses
bouquet 2: peonies, snapdragons
bouquet 3: peonies, snapdragons, tulips

(C) bouquet 1: peonies, tulips
bouquet 2: roses, snapdragons, tulips
bouquet 3: roses, snapdragons

(D) bouquet 1: roses
bouquet 2: peonies, snapdragons
bouquet 3: lilies, peonies, snapdragons

(E) bouquet 1: snapdragons
bouquet 2: lilies, roses
bouquet 3: lilies, roses

GO ON TO THE NEXT PAGE.

20. If lilies are in bouquet 1, which one of the following must be true?

(A) Lilies are in bouquet 2.
(B) Peonies are in bouquet 3.
(C) Roses are in bouquet 2.
(D) Tulips are in bouquet 2.
(E) Tulips are in bouquet 3.

21. If tulips are in bouquet 1, which one of the following could be a complete and accurate list of the kinds of flowers in bouquet 2?

(A) peonies, tulips
(B) peonies, snapdragons
(C) peonies, snapdragons, tulips
(D) peonies, roses, tulips
(E) peonies, roses, snapdragons, tulips

22. Which one of the following CANNOT be a complete and accurate list of the kinds of flowers in bouquet 2?

(A) lilies, roses
(B) peonies, tulips
(C) peonies, roses, snapdragons
(D) peonies, roses, tulips
(E) peonies, roses, snapdragons, tulips

23. Which one of the following CANNOT be true?

(A) Lilies and roses are the only kinds of flowers in bouquet 1.
(B) Peonies and tulips are the only kinds of flowers in bouquet 1.
(C) Lilies, peonies, and roses are the only kinds of flowers in bouquet 2.
(D) Peonies, roses, and snapdragons are the only kinds of flowers in bouquet 2.
(E) Peonies, snapdragons, and tulips are the only kinds of flowers in bouquet 3.

S T O P

IF YOU FINISH BEFORE TIME IS CALLED, YOU MAY CHECK YOUR WORK ON THIS SECTION ONLY.
DO NOT WORK ON ANY OTHER SECTION IN THE TEST.

SECTION IV

Time—35 minutes

26 Questions

Directions: The questions in this section are based on the reasoning contained in brief statements or passages. For some questions, more than one of the choices could conceivably answer the question. However, you are to choose the best answer; that is, the response that most accurately and completely answers the question. You should not make assumptions that are by commonsense standards implausible, superfluous, or incompatible with the passage. After you have chosen the best answer, blacken the corresponding space on your answer sheet.

1. In an experiment, ten people were asked to taste samples of coffee and rank them. Five of the people were given chocolate with the coffee, and this group subsequently reported that all the coffee samples tasted pretty much the same as one another. Five others tasted coffee only, and they were able to detect differences. Clearly, then, chocolate interferes with one's ability to taste coffee.

Which one of the following, if true, most undermines the conclusion drawn above?

(A) The ten people were randomly assigned to either the group that tasted only coffee or the group that was also given chocolate, although some people had asked to be in the group that received chocolate.

(B) Similar results were achieved when the experiment was repeated with a different, larger group of people.

(C) Chocolate is normally consumed as a solid, whereas coffee is normally consumed as a liquid.

(D) The five people who were originally given chocolate were asked a week later to taste coffee samples without chocolate, and they still detected no differences between the coffee samples.

(E) Some subjects who tasted just coffee reported only subtle differences between the coffee samples, while others thought the differences were considerable.

2. Residents of a coastal community are resisting the efforts of one family to build a large house on the family's land. Although the house would not violate any town codes, the land in question is depicted in a painting by a famous and beloved landscape painter who recently died. Residents argue that the house would alter the pristine landscape and hence damage the community's artistic and historic heritage.

Which one of the following principles, if valid, most helps to justify the reasoning of the residents opposed to building the house?

(A) Every possible effort should be made to preserve historic buildings that are well known and well loved.

(B) Communities that seek to preserve undeveloped areas of landscape or historic neighborhoods should purchase those properties for the public trust.

(C) Artists who choose to represent actual landscapes in their paintings have the right to demand that the owners of the land represented do not significantly alter the landscape.

(D) The right to build on one's own property is constrained by the artistic and historical interests of the community at large.

(E) In historic communities, the building and zoning regulations should prohibit construction that obstructs access to historic sites.

GO ON TO THE NEXT PAGE.

3. Moore: Sunscreen lotions, which are designed to block skin-cancer-causing ultraviolet radiation, do not do so effectively. Many scientific studies have shown that people who have consistently used these lotions develop, on average, as many skin cancers as those who have rarely, if ever, used them.

The reasoning in Moore's argument is most vulnerable to criticism on the grounds that the argument

(A) takes for granted that there are no other possible health benefits of using sunscreen lotions other than blocking skin-cancer-causing ultraviolet radiation

(B) fails to distinguish between the relative number of cases of skin cancer and the severity of those cases in measuring effectiveness at skin cancer prevention

(C) fails to consider the effectiveness of sunscreen lotions that are not specifically designed to block skin-cancer-causing ultraviolet radiation

(D) relies on evidence regarding the probability of people in different groups developing cancer that, in principle, would be impossible to challenge

(E) overlooks the possibility that people who consistently use sunscreen lotions spend more time in the sun, on average, than people who do not

4. Psychologist: Some have argued that Freudian psychotherapy is the most effective kind because it is so difficult and time consuming. But surely this does not follow. Similar reasoning—e.g., concluding that a car-repair chain has the most effective technique for repairing cars because the cars it services receive so much work and spend so much time in the shop—would never be accepted.

The reasoning technique employed by the psychologist is that of attempting to undermine an argument by

(A) introducing a principle that contradicts the one on which the argument is based

(B) questioning the truth of its premises

(C) presenting an analogous argument whose conclusion is thought to be obviously false

(D) claiming that the argument is based on a false analogy

(E) suggesting that a supposed cause of a phenomenon is actually an effect of that phenomenon

5. While biodiversity is indispensable to the survival of life on Earth, biodiversity does not require the survival of every currently existing species. For there to be life on Earth, various ecological niches must be filled; many niches, however, can be filled by more than one species.

Which one of the following statements most accurately expresses the conclusion drawn in the argument?

(A) Biodiversity does not require that all existing species continue to exist.

(B) There are various ecological niches that must be filled if there is to be life on Earth.

(C) The survival of life on Earth depends upon biodiversity.

(D) There are many ecological niches that can be filled by more than one species.

(E) The species most indispensable for biodiversity fill more than one ecological niche.

6. Clinician: Patients with immune system disorders are usually treated with a class of drugs that, unfortunately, increase the patient's risk of developing osteoporosis, a bone-loss disease. So these patients take another drug that helps to preserve existing bone. Since a drug that enhances the growth of new bone cells has now become available, these patients should take this new drug in addition to the drug that helps to preserve existing bone.

Which one of the following would be most useful to know in order to evaluate the clinician's argument?

(A) How large is the class of drugs that increase the risk of developing osteoporosis?

(B) Why are immune system disorders treated with drugs that increase the risk of developing osteoporosis?

(C) Is the new drug more expensive than the drug that helps to preserve existing bone?

(D) How long has the drug that helps to preserve existing bone been in use?

(E) To what extent does the new drug retain its efficacy when used in combination with the other drugs?

GO ON TO THE NEXT PAGE.

7. Critic: The perennial image of the "city on a hill" associates elevated locations with elevated purposes. The city's concert hall—its newest civic building—is located on a spectacular hilltop site. But because it is far from the center of the city, it cannot fulfill the purpose of a civic building. An example of a successful civic building is the art museum, which is situated in a densely populated downtown area. It encourages social cohesion and makes the city more alive.

The critic's reasoning most closely conforms to which one of the following principles?

(A) A civic building that is located in a downtown area should, if possible, be located on an elevated site.

(B) A city needs to have civic buildings if it is to have social cohesion.

(C) A civic building with an elevated purpose should be located on a spectacular site.

(D) The downtown area of a city should be designed in a way that complements the area's civic buildings.

(E) The purpose of a civic building is to encourage social cohesion and to make a city more alive.

8. Fluoride enters a region's groundwater when rain dissolves fluoride-bearing minerals in the soil. In a recent study, researchers found that when rainfall, concentrations of fluoride-bearing minerals, and other relevant variables are held constant, fluoride concentrations in groundwater are significantly higher in areas where the groundwater also contains a high concentration of sodium.

Which one of the following can most reasonably be concluded on the basis of the researchers' findings?

(A) Fluoride-bearing minerals are not the primary source of fluoride found in groundwater.

(B) Rainfall does not affect fluoride concentrations in groundwater.

(C) Sodium-bearing minerals dissolve at a faster rate than fluoride-bearing minerals.

(D) Sodium in groundwater increases the rate at which fluoride-bearing minerals dissolve.

(E) Soil that contains high concentrations of sodium-bearing minerals also contains high concentrations of fluoride-bearing minerals.

9. Fraenger's assertion that the artist Hieronymus Bosch belonged to the Brethren of the Free Spirit, a nonmainstream religious group, is unlikely to be correct. Fraenger's hypothesis explains much of Bosch's unusual subject matter. However, there is evidence that Bosch was a member of a mainstream church, and no evidence that he was a member of the Brethren.

The statement that there is no evidence that Bosch was a member of the Brethren figures in the argument in which one of the following ways?

(A) It is a premise that, when combined with the other premises, guarantees the falsity of Fraenger's assertion.

(B) It is used to support the claim that Bosch was a member of a mainstream church.

(C) It is used to dispute Fraenger's hypothesis by questioning Fraenger's credibility.

(D) It is intended to cast doubt on Fraenger's hypothesis by questioning the sufficiency of Fraenger's evidence.

(E) It is intended to help show that Bosch's choice of subject matter remains unexplained.

10. Vacuum cleaner salesperson: To prove that this Super XL vacuum cleaner is better than your old vacuum cleaner, I ran your old vacuum once over this dirty carpet. Then I ran the Super XL over the same area. All that dirt that the Super XL picked up is dirt your old vacuum left behind, proving the Super XL is the better vacuum.

The vacuum cleaner salesperson's argument is most vulnerable to the criticism that it

(A) ignores the possibility that dirt remained in the carpet even after the Super XL had been used in the test

(B) takes for granted that the Super XL will still perform better than the old vacuum cleaner when it is the same age as the old vacuum cleaner

(C) takes for granted that because the Super XL outperforms one vacuum cleaner it is the best vacuum cleaner available

(D) ignores the possibility that the amount of dirt removed in the test by the old vacuum cleaner is greater than the amount of dirt removed by the Super XL

(E) ignores the possibility that if the Super XL had been used first it would have left behind just as much dirt as did the old vacuum cleaner

GO ON TO THE NEXT PAGE.

11. Manager: This company's supply chain will develop significant weaknesses unless we make changes to our vendor contracts now. Some will argue that this problem is so far in the future that there is no need to address it today. But that is an irresponsible approach. Just imagine if a financial planner offered the same counsel to a 30-year-old client: "Don't worry, Jane, retirement is 35 years away; you don't need to save anything now." That planner would be guilty of gross malpractice.

Which one of the following most accurately expresses the overall conclusion drawn in the manager's argument?

(A) Some people argue that the supply-chain problem is so far in the future that there is no need to address it now.

(B) It would be irresponsible to postpone changes to the vendor contracts just because the supply chain will not develop weaknesses for a long time.

(C) If no changes are made to the vendor contracts, the supply chain will eventually develop significant weaknesses.

(D) In planning to meet its future obligations, a company should follow the same practices that are appropriate for an individual who is planning for retirement.

(E) Financial planners should advise their clients to save money for retirement only if retirement is many years away.

12. Worldwide, more books were sold last year than in any previous year. In particular, there were more cookbooks sold. For the first time ever, most of the cookbooks sold were not intended for beginners. Indeed, more cookbooks than ever were purchased by professional cooks. However, one of the few books available on every continent is a cookbook written for beginners, entitled *Problem-Free Cooking*.

Which one of the following is most strongly supported by the information above?

(A) Last year there were more cookbooks sold that were not intended for beginners than in any previous year.

(B) The best-selling cookbook last year was a cookbook that was intended for beginners.

(C) Sales of cookbooks intended for beginners were lower last year than in previous years.

(D) Most of the cookbooks purchased last year that were not intended for beginners were purchased by professional cooks.

(E) *Problem-Free Cooking* sold more copies last year than did any cookbook written for professional cooks.

13. In early 2003, scientists detected methane in the atmosphere of Mars. Methane is a fragile compound that falls apart when hit by the ultraviolet radiation in sunlight. So any methane in the Martian atmosphere must have been released into the atmosphere relatively recently.

The argument relies on the assumption that

(A) Mars had no methane in its atmosphere prior to 2003

(B) all methane in the Martian atmosphere is eventually exposed to sunlight

(C) methane cannot be detected until it has started to fall apart

(D) the methane that the scientists detected had been exposed to ultraviolet radiation

(E) methane in Earth's atmosphere does not fall apart as a result of exposure to ultraviolet radiation

14. Environmentalist: Pollution from gasoline burned by cars contributes to serious environmental problems. But the cost of these problems is not reflected in gasoline prices, and hence usually does not affect consumers' decisions about how much to drive. Heavier taxes on gasoline, however, would reflect this cost, and as a result consumers would pollute less.

The environmentalist's statements, if true, most strongly support which one of the following?

(A) The cost of pollution from driving should not be reflected in the price of gasoline unless the amount of pollution produced would be reduced as a result.

(B) Heavier taxes on gasoline would increase consumers' awareness of the kinds of environmental problems to which pollution from driving contributes.

(C) Consumers would purchase less gasoline, on average, if the cost of the environmental problems to which pollution from driving contributes were fully reflected in the price of gasoline.

(D) The only cost considered by most consumers when they are deciding how much to drive is the cost of gasoline.

(E) Pollution from gasoline burned by cars will be reduced only if consumers give more consideration to the cost of that pollution when deciding how much to drive.

GO ON TO THE NEXT PAGE.

15. Hine's emerald dragonflies are an endangered species that live in wetlands. The larvae of these dragonflies can survive only in the water, where they are subject to predation by several species including red devil crayfish. Surprisingly, the dragonfly populations are more likely to remain healthy in areas where red devil crayfish are present than in areas without red devil crayfish.

Which one of the following, if true, most helps to explain the surprising fact?

(A) Red devil crayfish dig chambers that remain filled with water even when the surrounding wetlands dry up.

(B) Red devil crayfish present no threat to adult Hine's emerald dragonflies.

(C) The varied diet of the red devil crayfish does not include any animal species that prey on dragonfly larvae.

(D) Red devil crayfish are found in many more locations than Hine's emerald dragonflies are.

(E) Populations of red devil crayfish in a wetland do not drop significantly if the local population of Hine's emerald dragonflies dies out.

16. Stress is a common cause of high blood pressure. By calming their minds and thereby reducing stress, some people can lower their blood pressure. And most people can calm their minds, in turn, by engaging in exercise.

Which one of the following is most strongly supported by the information above?

(A) For at least some people, having lower blood pressure has at least some tendency to cause their stress levels to be reduced.

(B) Most people with high blood pressure can lower their blood pressure by reducing their stress levels.

(C) Most people who do not exercise regularly have higher stress levels as a result.

(D) Engaging in exercise can directly lower one's blood pressure.

(E) For at least some people, engaging in exercise can cause their stress levels to be reduced.

17. A positive correlation has been found between the amount of soot in the atmosphere of cities and the frequency of a certain ailment among those cities' populations. However, the soot itself probably does not cause this ailment, since in cities where there are large amounts of soot in the air, there are usually also high concentrations of many other air pollutants.

Which one of the following statements, if true, most weakens the argument?

(A) In cities where there are high concentrations of many air pollutants but little if any soot in the air, the frequency of the ailment is just as high, on average, as it is in cities where there are large amounts of soot in the air.

(B) If the ailment rarely occurs except in cities in which there are large amounts of soot in the air, then the soot is probably the cause of the ailment.

(C) In each of the cities where there are large amounts of soot in the air but little other air pollution, the frequency of the ailment is at least as high as it is anywhere else.

(D) If high concentrations of many different pollutants in a city's air are correlated with a high frequency of the ailment among that city's population, then it is possible that two or more of those pollutants each causally contributes to the ailment.

(E) In cities in which there are high concentrations of many air pollutants, there are generally also high concentrations of other forms of pollution that are very likely to contribute causally to the ailment.

GO ON TO THE NEXT PAGE.

18. So far this summer there has been no rain in the valley. But usually a few inches of rain fall there each summer. Since only one week of summer is left, it will probably rain in the valley within the next week.

The flawed pattern of reasoning in the argument above is most similar to that in which one of the following arguments?

(A) Aisha has finished proofreading all but the last two pages of an issue of the journal *Periodos* and has encountered no errors. However, there are sometimes a few errors in an issue of the journal *Periodos*. So there may be errors in the pages that Aisha has not yet checked.

(B) There are generally few errors in an issue of the journal *Periodos*. Aisha has finished proofreading all but the last two pages of an issue of this journal but has encountered no errors. Hence, there are probably no errors in the pages that Aisha has not yet checked in this issue of the journal.

(C) On average, there are a few errors in an issue of the journal *Periodos*. Aisha has finished proofreading all but the last two pages of an issue of this journal but has encountered no errors. So there are probably errors in the pages she has not yet checked in this issue of the journal.

(D) Aisha has proofread several issues of the journal *Periodos* and has encountered no errors. But there are seldom any errors in an issue of this journal. So there will probably be no errors in the next issue of the journal *Periodos* that she proofreads.

(E) There usually are errors in each issue of the journal *Periodos*. Since Aisha has finished proofreading the latest issue of this journal and has detected no errors, Aisha has probably made a mistake in her proofreading.

19. Young people believe efforts to reduce pollution, poverty, and war are doomed to failure. This pessimism is probably harmful to humanity's future, because people lose motivation to work for goals they think are unrealizable. We must do what we can to prevent this loss of motivation and therefore must enable our children to believe that better futures are possible.

Which one of the following is an assumption on which the argument depends?

(A) Motivating people to work to solve humanity's problems will enable them to believe that the future can be better and will cause them to be less pessimistic.

(B) Enabling people to believe that better futures are possible will help prevent the loss of motivation that results from pessimistic beliefs about the future.

(C) Optimism about the future is better than pessimism, even if that optimism is based on an illusory vision of what is likely to occur.

(D) If future generations believe that the future can be better, then pollution, poverty, and war will be eliminated.

(E) The current prevalence of such problems as pollution and poverty stems from previous generations' inability to believe that futures can be better.

20. In a recent study of stroke patients, those who exhibited continuing deterioration of the nerve cells in the brain after the stroke also exhibited the highest levels of the protein glutamate in their blood. Glutamate, which functions within nerve cells as a neurotransmitter, can kill surrounding nerve cells if it leaks from damaged or oxygen-starved nerve cells. Thus glutamate leaking from damaged or oxygen-starved nerve cells is a cause of long-term brain damage resulting from strokes.

Which one of the following, if true, most strengthens the argument?

(A) Any neurotransmitter that leaks from a damaged or oxygen-starved nerve cell will damage surrounding nerve cells.

(B) Stroke patients exhibit a wide variety of abnormal chemical levels in their blood.

(C) Glutamate is the only neurotransmitter that leaks from oxygen-starved or physically damaged nerve cells.

(D) Leakage from damaged or oxygen-starved nerve cells is the only possible source of glutamate in the blood.

(E) Nerve cells can suffer enough damage to leak glutamate without being destroyed themselves.

GO ON TO THE NEXT PAGE.

A — 68 pc
pr ∠ 3c
b ∠ 3c

21. The only songs Amanda has ever written are blues songs and punk rock songs. Most punk rock songs involve no more than three chords. So if the next song Amanda writes is not a blues song, it probably will not involve more than three chords.

The reasoning in which one of the following arguments is most similar to that in the argument above?

(A) The only pets the Gupta family has ever owned are fish and parrots. Most parrots are very noisy. So if the next pet the Gupta family owns is a parrot, it will probably be very noisy.

(B) Most parrots are very noisy. The Gupta family has never owned any pets other than fish and parrots. So if the Gupta family has ever owned a noisy pet, it was probably a parrot.

(C) All the pets the Gupta family has ever owned have been fish and parrots. Most parrots are very noisy. So any pet the Gupta family ever owns that is not a fish will probably be very noisy.

(D) Every pet the Gupta family has ever owned has been a fish or a parrot. Most parrots are very noisy. So if the next pet the Gupta family owns is not a parrot, it will probably not be very noisy.

(E) The Gupta family has never owned any pets other than fish and parrots. Most parrots are very noisy. So the next pet the Gupta family owns will probably be very noisy if it is not a fish.

22. Advertising tends to have a greater influence on consumer preferences regarding brands of yogurt than it does on consumer preferences regarding brands of milk. Yet, since the LargeCo supermarket chain began advertising its store-brand products, sales of its store-brand milk increased more than sales of its store-brand yogurt.

Which one of the following, if true, most helps to resolve the apparent discrepancy described above?

(A) There has recently been increased demand at LargeCo stores for the chain's own brand of yogurt as well as for other brands of yogurt.

(B) The typical shopper going to LargeCo for the purpose of buying milk does not go with the intention of also buying yogurt.

(C) Shoppers at LargeCo tend to purchase the chain's own brand of dairy products more frequently than other brands of dairy products.

(D) Supermarkets throughout the entire nation have experienced a sharp decrease in sales of yogurt recently.

(E) Consumers tend to purchase store brands of yogurt, but purchase whichever brand of milk is least expensive.

23. Problem: If Shayna congratulates Daniel on his award, she will misrepresent her true feelings. However, if Shayna does not congratulate Daniel, she will hurt his feelings.

Principle: One should never be insincere about one's feelings, except possibly where one believes that the person with whom one is speaking would prefer kindness to honesty.

The principle, if valid, most helps to justify the reasoning in which one of the following arguments concerning the problem?

(A) If Shayna congratulates Daniel, she will avoid hurting his feelings, so she should congratulate him.

(B) Daniel might prefer for Shayna to congratulate him—even if insincerely—rather than for her to express her true feelings, and so Shayna would be doing nothing wrong in insincerely congratulating Daniel.

(C) Shayna believes that kindness should be preferred to dishonesty when speaking to others, so she should not tell Daniel her true feelings.

(D) Daniel's feelings would be hurt if he knew that congratulations from Shayna were insincere, so Shayna should not congratulate him.

(E) Shayna has no opinion about whether Daniel would prefer kindness to honesty, so she should not congratulate him.

24. Clearly, a democracy cannot thrive without effective news media. After all, a democracy cannot thrive without an electorate that is knowledgeable about important political issues, and an electorate can be knowledgeable in this way only if it has access to unbiased information about the government.

The argument's conclusion is properly inferred if which one of the following is assumed?

(A) All societies that have effective news media are thriving democracies.

(B) If an electorate has access to unbiased information about the government, then that electorate will be knowledgeable about important political issues.

(C) A democracy will thrive if its electorate is knowledgeable about important political issues.

(D) A democracy cannot thrive if the electorate is exposed to biased information about the government.

(E) Without effective news media, an electorate will not have access to unbiased information about the government.

GO ON TO THE NEXT PAGE.

25. Roberta is irritable only when she is tired, and loses things only when she is tired. Since she has been yawning all day, and has just lost her keys, she is almost certainly irritable.

The reasoning above is flawed in that it

(A) infers from a correlation between tiredness and yawning that tiredness causes yawning
(B) assumes the conclusion that it sets out to prove
(C) generalizes on the basis of a single instance
(D) takes a necessary condition for Roberta's losing things to be a sufficient condition
(E) takes a necessary condition for Roberta's being irritable to be a sufficient condition

26. Farmer: Crops genetically engineered to produce toxins that enable them to resist insect pests do not need to be sprayed with insecticides. Since excessive spraying of insecticides has harmed wildlife populations near croplands, using such genetically engineered crops more widely is likely to help wildlife populations to recover.

Which one of the following is an assumption the farmer's argument requires?

(A) Use of the crops that have been genetically engineered to resist insect pests in place of crops that have been sprayed with insecticides will cause less harm to wildlife populations.
(B) Wildlife populations that have been harmed by the excessive spraying of insecticides on croplands are likely to recover if the amount of insecticides sprayed on those croplands is reduced even slightly.
(C) Crops that have been genetically engineered to resist insect pests are never sprayed with insecticides that harm wildlife populations.
(D) Use of crops that have been genetically engineered to resist insect pests is no more costly to farmers than the use of insecticides on crops that are not genetically engineered.
(E) If a wider use of certain crops that have been genetically engineered to resist insect pests is likely to help at least some wildlife populations to recover, it is likely to have that effect only because its use will prevent excessive and ineffective spraying of insecticides on croplands.

S T O P

IF YOU FINISH BEFORE TIME IS CALLED, YOU MAY CHECK YOUR WORK ON THIS SECTION ONLY.
DO NOT WORK ON ANY OTHER SECTION IN THE TEST.

Wait for the supervisor's instructions before you open the page to the topic.
Please print and sign your name and write the date in the designated spaces below.

Time: 35 Minutes

General Directions

will have 35 minutes in which to plan and write an essay on the topic inside. Read the topic and the accompanying directions carefully.
will probably find it best to spend a few minutes considering the topic and organizing your thoughts before you begin writing. In your essay,
sure to develop your ideas fully, leaving time, if possible, to review what you have written. **Do not write on a topic other than the one
cified. Writing on a topic of your own choice is not acceptable.**

special knowledge is required or expected for this writing exercise. Law schools are interested in the reasoning, clarity, organization,
guage usage, and writing mechanics displayed in your essay. How well you write is more important than how much you write.

fine your essay to the blocked, lined area on the front and back of the separate Writing Sample Response Sheet. Only that area will be
roduced for law schools. Be sure that your writing is legible.

**Both this topic sheet and your response sheet must be turned in to the testing staff
before you leave the room.**

Topic Code	Print Your Full Name Here		
127250	Last	First	M.I.

Date	Sign Your Name Here
/ /	

Scratch Paper
Do not write your essay in this space.

LSAT® Writing Sample Topic

<u>Directions</u>: The scenario presented below describes two choices, either one of which can be supported on the basis of the information given. Your essay should consider both choices and argue for one over the other, based on the two specified criteria and the facts provided. There is no "right" or "wrong" choice: a reasonable argument can be made for either.

A medium-sized company is located in a technology park in a sparsely populated area outside a major city. It has had difficulty retaining employees because of the long and expensive commute between the city and work that nearly all of its employees face. Consequently, the company will implement a commuting assistance plan. It must decide between operating a free bus for employees and subsidizing employees' costs of using public transportation. Using the facts below, write an essay in which you argue for one plan over the other based on the following two criteria:

- The company wants to minimize its employees' commuting expenses and frustrations.
- The company wants reliability and flexibility in its employees' work schedules.

Under the first plan, the company would lease a bus and hire a driver. The bus would make several daily circuits between the company's location and a single downtown stop, accessible by public transportation and close to a large, inexpensive parking garage. The only riders on the bus would be the company's employees. The bus has reclining seats and free Wi-Fi. The average total commute time for an employee would be 75 minutes each way. A breakdown of the bus would be disruptive to the company's operations.

Under the second plan, the company would partially reimburse employees' cost of using public transportation to commute to work. The average savings for an employee would be about 80 percent. Most of the employees live within walking distance to a bus stop. Most employees would have to make one or two transfers. Buses are scheduled to arrive every half hour at a bus shelter in the technology park. Buses are sometimes late. None of them have Wi-Fi. The average total commute time for an employee would be 60 minutes each way. WP-V1:

Scratch Paper
Do not write your essay in this space.

Writing Sample Response Sheet

DO NOT WRITE IN THIS SPACE

**Begin your essay in the lined area below.
Continue on the back if you need more space.**

COMPUTING YOUR SCORE

Directions:

1. Use the Answer Key on the next page to check your answers.

2. Use the Scoring Worksheet below to compute your raw score.

3. Use the Score Conversion Chart to convert your raw score into the 120–180 scale.

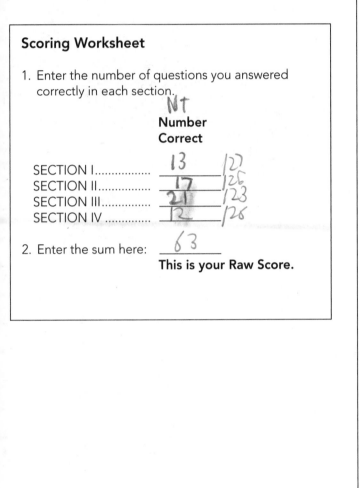

Scoring Worksheet

1. Enter the number of questions you answered correctly in each section.

NT

Number
Correct

SECTION I .... 13 |27
SECTION II .... 17 |26
SECTION III .... 21 |23
SECTION IV .... 12 |28

2. Enter the sum here: 63

This is your Raw Score.

Conversion Chart
For Converting Raw Score to the 120–180 LSAT Scaled Score
LSAT Form 4LSN110

Reported Score	Raw Score	
	Lowest	Highest
180	98	101
179	97	97
178	*	*
177	96	96
176	95	95
175	94	94
174	93	93
173	92	92
172	91	91
171	90	90
170	89	89
169	87	88
168	86	86
167	85	85
166	83	84
165	82	82
164	80	81
163	79	79
162	77	78
161	75	76
160	74	74
159	72	73
158	70	71
157	69	69
156	67	68
155	65	66
154 NT	63	64
153	61	62
152	60	60
151	58	59
150	56	57
149	54	55
148	53	53
147	51	52
146	49	50
145	47	48
144	46	46
143	44	45
142	43	43
141	41	42
140	39	40
139	38	38
138	37	37
137	35	36
136	34	34
135	32	33
134	31	31
133	30	30
132	29	29
131	27	28
130	26	26
129	25	25
128	24	24
127	23	23
126	22	22
125	21	21
124	20	20
123	19	19
122	18	18
121	17	17
120	0	16

*There is no raw score that will produce this scaled score for this form.

ANSWER KEY

SECTION I

1.	A	8.	B	15.	B	22.	B
2.	B	9.	A	16.	C	23.	A
3.	D	10.	D	17.	B	24.	D
4.	B	11.	C	18.	E	25.	E
5.	A	12.	E	19.	A	26.	D
6.	E	13.	E	20.	E	27.	A
7.	C	14.	B	21.	A		

SECTION II

1.	C	8.	B	15.	B	22.	A
2.	E	9.	C	16.	A	23.	C
3.	A	10.	A	17.	B	24.	D
4.	D	11.	B	18.	E	25.	C
5.	D	12.	A	19.	B		
6.	D	13.	B	20.	E		
7.	C	14.	E	21.	E		

SECTION III

1.	B	8.	A	15.	D	22.	A
2.	C	9.	B	16.	D	23.	C
3.	B	10.	A	17.	B		
4.	E	11.	C	18.	E		
5.	E	12.	C	19.	A		
6.	D	13.	E	20.	B		
7.	A	14.	A	21.	E		

SECTION IV

1.	D	8.	D	15.	A	22.	D
2.	D	9.	D	16.	E	23.	E
3.	E	10.	E	17.	C	24.	E
4.	C	11.	B	18.	C	25.	E
5.	A	12.	A	19.	B	26.	A
6.	E	13.	B	20.	D		
7.	E	14.	C	21.	E		

THE OFFICIAL LSAT
PREPTEST®

- PrepTest 74
- Form 4LSN111

DECEMBER 2014

Section I

Time—35 minutes

25 Questions

Directions: The questions in this section are based on the reasoning contained in brief statements or passages. For some questions, more than one of the choices could conceivably answer the question. However, you are to choose the best answer; that is, the response that most accurately and completely answers the question. You should not make assumptions that are by commonsense standards implausible, superfluous, or incompatible with the passage. After you have chosen the best answer, blacken the corresponding space on your answer sheet.

1. Children should be discouraged from reading Jones's books. Reading them is like eating candy, which provides intense, short-term sensory stimulation but leaves one poorly nourished and dulls one's taste for better fare. In other words, the problem with letting children read Jones's books is that _____.

Which one of the following most logically completes the argument above?

(A) it will lead them to develop a taste for candy and sweets
(B) too many children may become frustrated by their difficulty and stop reading altogether
(C) their doing so interferes with the development of appreciation for more challenging literature
(D) their message may undermine the positive teaching done by parents
(E) children may become so enthralled with books that they will want to spend all their time reading

2. Archaeologist: How did the Parthenon's stonemasons manage to carve columns that all bulged outward in the center in precisely the same way? One hypothesis is suggested by the discovery of a scale drawing of a column etched into the stone of a Greek temple at Didyma. The drawing is a profile view of a column surrounded by a grid, which makes it possible to determine the correct width at every height of the column. The stonemasons who carved the Parthenon's columns may have relied on a drawing like the one at Didyma.

Which one of the following, if true, adds the most support for the archaeologist's hypothesis?

(A) Modern attempts to recreate columns like those at the Parthenon have only been partially successful.
(B) The construction of the temple at Didyma was begun over a century after the Parthenon was constructed.
(C) Scale drawings were commonly used in many types of construction in ancient Greece.
(D) The surviving columns at Didyma are almost twice as tall as the columns at the Parthenon.
(E) The Parthenon's stonemasons had considerable experience carving columns before they started work on the Parthenon.

3. Editorial: The government should not fund any part of its health services with lottery revenue. These health services are essential to our community, but lottery revenue could decline at some time in the future, leaving the government scrambling to make up a budget shortfall.

The argument in the editorial most closely conforms to which one of the following principles?

(A) Governments should spend more of their revenue on essential services than on nonessential services.
(B) Essential government services must be funded from reliable sources of revenue.
(C) No government service should be entirely dependent on lottery revenue for its funding.
(D) Governments should consider all health services to be essential to the community.
(E) At least some lottery revenue must be set aside in case of budget shortfalls in the future.

GO ON TO THE NEXT PAGE.

4. Scientist: Rattlesnakes prey on young California ground squirrels. Protective adult squirrels harass a threatening rattlesnake by puffing up their tails and wagging them. New results show that the squirrel's tail also heats up when harassing a rattlesnake. Since rattlesnakes have an infrared sensing organ that detects body heat, the heating up of the squirrel's tail probably plays a role in repelling rattlesnakes.

Which one of the following, if true, most helps to support the scientist's hypothesis?

(A) Rattlesnakes do not have the ability to increase the temperature of their tails.

(B) Squirrels puff up their tails and wag them when they attempt to attract the attention of other squirrels.

(C) Rattlesnakes react much more defensively when confronted with a squirrel whose tail is heated up than when confronted with one whose tail is not.

(D) The rattlesnake is not the only predator of the California ground squirrel that causes it to engage in harassing behavior as a defensive mechanism.

(E) Mammals such as the California ground squirrel have no organ for sensing infrared energy.

5. Critic: Fillmore, an influential television executive, argues that watching television regularly is not detrimental to very young children. Fillmore bases this on the claim, which I grant, that children can learn much that is beneficial from television. But we should reject Fillmore's argument, because clearly it is to Fillmore's benefit to convince parents that television is not harmful to their children.

Which one of the following most accurately describes a flaw in the critic's reasoning?

(A) It takes a necessary condition for something's being harmful to be a sufficient condition for being harmful.

(B) It concludes that something is true merely on the grounds that there is no evidence to the contrary.

(C) It rejects an argument solely on the grounds that the argument could serve the interests of the person making that argument.

(D) It is based on an appeal to the views of someone with questionable authority on the subject matter.

(E) It bases its conclusion on claims that are inconsistent with one another.

6. While grapefruit juice is a healthy drink, it has been discovered that a chemical in the juice affects how certain medicines are absorbed, with the result that normal medicinal doses act like higher doses. Getting the wrong dose is dangerous. Since it is always desirable to take the lowest effective dose, the best medical approach would be to take lower doses of these medicines along with prescribed amounts of grapefruit juice.

Which one of the following, if true, most seriously weakens the argument?

(A) The amount of the chemical in grapefruit juice is highly unpredictable from glass to glass.

(B) Grapefruit juice is less expensive than most of the medicines with which it interacts.

(C) When scientists removed the chemical from grapefruit juice, the juice no longer affected how certain medicines were absorbed.

(D) The chemical in grapefruit juice works by inhibiting an enzyme in the body that affects how certain medicines are metabolized.

(E) Long before the chemical in grapefruit juice was identified, doctors were advising patients who took certain medicines to avoid grapefruit juice.

7. A landlord needed to replace the air-conditioning unit in a small rental home. The salesperson at the appliance store showed the landlord two air-conditioning units with identical prices. She told the landlord that the Sno-Queen was the most powerful unit for the price, but advised him to purchase the less powerful FreezAll unit, saying that the FreezAll was powerful enough for his needs.

The salesperson's advice to the landlord most closely conforms to which one of the following principles?

(A) When the prices of two different brands of a particular home appliance are identical, either of the products can satisfy the needs of the consumer.

(B) When a consumer is choosing between two different brands of a particular home appliance, the consumer should select the less powerful product only if it is also less expensive.

(C) A salesperson should always recommend that a customer buy the product that represents the best value.

(D) When advising customers about a purchase of a home appliance, a salesperson should direct the customer toward the product that yields the highest commission for the salesperson.

(E) When a consumer is choosing a home appliance, that consumer should choose the least powerful product that meets his or her needs.

GO ON TO THE NEXT PAGE.

8. Editorial: Our political discussions tend to focus largely on the flaws of our nation's leaders, but we need to remind ourselves that these leaders were chosen democratically. The real question that needs answering is how our nation's institutions and procedures enable such people to attain positions of power. Thus, to focus our attention on the flaws of our leaders is to indulge in a pointless distraction.

Which one of the following is an assumption that the argument requires?

(A) Examining an individual leader's personal flaws does not reveal anything about how the nation's institutions and procedures influence the selection of leaders.

(B) Political discussions that focus on the flaws of the nation's leaders will become even more common if the nation's institutions and procedures are not examined.

(C) The workings of the nation's current institutions and procedures ensure that only flawed individuals will attain positions of power.

(D) As yet, no one in the nation has made the effort to critically examine the details of the nation's institutions and procedures.

(E) Concentrating on the flaws of the nation's leaders creates greater dissatisfaction with those leaders.

9. Many calcium supplements contain lead, a potentially dangerous substance even in small amounts. The body can safely store in bones trace amounts of lead from food, but high levels of lead in the blood are a major public health concern, associated with anemia and nerve damage. Despite this, many doctors contend that for some people calcium supplements containing lead are preferable to no calcium supplements at all.

Which one of the following, if true, would most help to resolve the apparent discrepancy in the information above?

(A) Some fruits and vegetables contain trace amounts of lead derived from the soil in which they are grown.

(B) It is difficult to ensure that one has completely eliminated trace amounts of lead from one's diet.

(C) Lead is only one of the common public health concerns that are associated with anemia and nerve damage.

(D) A high-calcium diet decreases the amount of lead that the body is able to tolerate safely.

(E) When calcium intake is insufficient, the body draws calcium from bones, releasing stored lead into the bloodstream.

10. Principle: People should buy an expensive antique only if they can be confident of its authenticity and they find the piece desirable for its intrinsic qualities and not just for its value as an investment.

Application: Matilde should not buy the expensive antique vase offered for sale on the Internet.

Which one of the following, if true, most helps to justify the above application of the principle?

(A) While this style of vase is not currently sought after by other collectors, Matilde has acquired quite a few similar pieces and has developed significant expertise in identifying counterfeits.

(B) Although the seller is willing to take back the vase if Matilde cannot independently authenticate it, Matilde is not sure that the vase will appreciate much in value in the future.

(C) The seller of the vase has offered documentation of its age and origin, and Matilde is highly attracted to its shape and color; moreover, she suspects that it will be highly desirable to other collectors in the future.

(D) The asking price for the vase is significantly less than the amount Matilde thinks it is worth, and the vase is of a style that Matilde particularly likes.

(E) While Matilde likes the color and features of the vase, its particular style has frequently been reproduced for the mass market, and the vase cannot be examined closely or authenticated over the Internet.

GO ON TO THE NEXT PAGE.

11. Critic: In her presentation of important works of art in her art history textbook, Waverly claims to have presented only objective accounts: "I have sought neither to advocate nor to denigrate what I included." In writing about art, a pretense of objectivity never succeeds: clearly, Waverly writes much better about art she likes than about art to which she is indifferent.

The critic's statements, if true, most strongly support which one of the following?

(A)　Waverly believes that a historian of art should not prefer certain works of art to other works of art.

(B)　Waverly has only included works of art that she has strong opinions about in her textbook.

(C)　Waverly wrote her textbook with the intention of advocating the works of art that she likes best.

(D)　Waverly has not succeeded in her intended objectivity about works of art discussed in her textbook.

(E)　Waverly does not really believe that objectivity is a desirable trait in an art history textbook.

12. Archaeologists are discovering a great deal about the Sals culture. For example, recent excavations have unearthed smelting furnaces and tools of smelted copper and bronze. There were distinct Sals words for copper and for bronze, but none for iron. Thus, the Sals did not smelt iron.

The conclusion drawn above follows logically if which one of the following is assumed?

(A)　If a culture had a distinct word for a metal, then it smelted that metal.

(B)　If a culture was unfamiliar with a metal, then it did not have a distinct word for that metal.

(C)　If a culture smelted copper and bronze, then it had distinct words for copper and bronze.

(D)　If a culture did not smelt a metal, then it was unfamiliar with that metal.

(E)　If a culture smelted a metal, then it had a distinct word for that metal.

13. Community organizations wanting to enhance support for higher education programs need to convince the public that such programs benefit society as a whole. Taking this approach makes the public more receptive. It is much easier, for example, to get the public to support road building, which is seen as benefiting everyone, than it is to get them to support programs that are seen as benefiting only a relatively small segment of society.

Which one of the following most accurately expresses the overall conclusion drawn in the argument?

(A)　Community organizations seeking to encourage higher education programs must persuade the public that these programs benefit society as a whole.

(B)　It is easier to get the public to support programs that are seen as benefiting everyone than it is to get them to support programs that are seen as benefiting only a small segment of society.

(C)　It is easy to get the public to support road building, because road building is seen as benefiting society as a whole.

(D)　Convincing the public that higher education programs will benefit society as a whole makes the public more receptive to those programs.

(E)　Higher education is similar to road building in that both are beneficial to society as a whole.

14. Currently, no satellite orbiting Earth is at significant risk of colliding with other satellites or satellite fragments, but the risk of such a collision is likely to increase dramatically in the future. After all, once such a collision occurs, it will probably produce thousands of satellite fragments, each large enough to shatter other satellites. The resulting collisions will produce many more fragments, and so on, causing the space around Earth to become quite heavily cluttered with dangerous debris.

Which one of the following most accurately describes the role played in the argument by the claim that the risk of a satellite orbiting Earth colliding with other satellites or satellite fragments is likely to increase dramatically in the future?

(A)　It is an unsupported claim that is used to provide support for the argument's conclusion.

(B)　It is an unsupported claim that is used to support another claim that in turn supports the argument's conclusion.

(C)　It is a claim for which the argument provides some support, and which in turn is used to support the argument's conclusion.

(D)　It is a claim that serves as the argument's conclusion.

(E)　It is a claim that provides nonessential background information for the argument's conclusion.

GO ON TO THE NEXT PAGE.

15. Researcher: *Salmonella* bacteria are a major cause of illness in humans who consume poultry. Young chicks that underwent a new treatment exhibited a lower incidence of *Salmonella* infection than did untreated chicks, although one week after the treatment was administered the treated chicks had higher concentrations of a variety of bacteria than did untreated chicks.

Which one of the following, if true, most helps to explain the concentrations of bacteria one week after the treatment?

(A) The new treatment takes several weeks to administer.
(B) Levels of *Salmonella* bacteria in young chicks are generally not high to begin with.
(C) Most chicks develop resistance to many harmful bacteria by the time they reach adulthood.
(D) The untreated chicks experienced a higher incidence of illness from infection by bacteria other than *Salmonella* than did treated chicks.
(E) The bacteria found in the treated chicks were nonvirulent types whose growth is inhibited by *Salmonella* bacteria.

16. Debater: As a pedagogical practice, lecturing embodies hierarchy, since the lecturer is superior to the student in mastery of the subject. But people learn best from peer interaction. Thus, the hierarchy in lecturing is a great weakness.

Respondent: By definition, all teaching and learning are hierarchical, for all teaching and learning must proceed from simple to complex. In teaching mathematics, for example, arithmetic must precede calculus. Thus, the hierarchy in lecturing is a strength.

The respondent's reply to the debater's argument is most vulnerable to criticism on the grounds that the respondent

(A) concedes one of the major assumptions on which the debater's argument depends
(B) takes for granted that teaching methods that are effective in mathematics are also effective in other academic disciplines
(C) fails to consider the possibility that some characteristics of lecturing other than hierarchy are weaknesses
(D) applies a key concept to a different aspect of education than the aspect to which the debater applied it
(E) takes for granted that the conceptual structure of mathematics is sufficiently representative of the conceptual structure of at least some other academic disciplines

17. How the pigment known as Han purple was synthesized by the ancient Chinese of the Qin and Han dynasties has puzzled scientists. The Chinese chemists employed the same chemical ingredients used for Han purple in the production of a common type of white glass during that period. Both were produced in processes that involved subjecting the mixtures to high heat and mixing in lead to decrease the melting temperature. Thus, Han purple was probably discovered by fortuitous accident during glass production.

Which one of the following, if true, would most strengthen the argument?

(A) Chemical analysis shows that most of the known fragments of both Han purple and the white glass were produced within a small geographical radius.
(B) Han purple was used for luxury and ceremonial items, whereas the white glass was used to make certain household items.
(C) The technique used for producing Han purple was known to very few people during the Qin and Han dynasties.
(D) The ingredients used in producing both Han purple and the white glass were easily obtainable during the Qin and Han dynasties.
(E) The white glass is found in more surviving artifacts from the Qin and Han dynasties than Han purple is.

GO ON TO THE NEXT PAGE.

18. Medical researcher: A survey of more than 1 million adults found that there was a greater frequency of illness among people who regularly slept at least 8 hours a night than among people who slept significantly less. This shows that mild sleep deprivation is not unhealthy and, in fact, probably bolsters the body's defenses against illness.

The reasoning in the medical researcher's argument is most vulnerable to criticism on the grounds that the argument

(A) fails to address the possibility that an observed correlation between two phenomena is due to another factor that causally contributes to both phenomena

(B) fails to consider that even if a given factor causally contributes to the occurrence of a given phenomenon, it may not be the only factor affecting the occurrence of that phenomenon

(C) concludes, from the claim that a certain phenomenon occurs and the claim that a certain condition is sufficient for that phenomenon to occur, that the condition also exists

(D) takes for granted that there will be an observable correlation between two phenomena if either of those phenomena causally contributes to the other

(E) fails to consider that even if a specific negative consequence is not associated with a given phenomenon, that phenomenon may have other negative consequences

19. If temperatures had dropped below freezing when I was gone last week, the impatiens in my garden would have died. If the impatiens had died, they obviously could not continue to bloom. However, since the impatiens in my garden are still in bloom today, temperatures did not drop below freezing last week.

The pattern of reasoning in which one of the following arguments most closely parallels that in the argument above?

(A) If a species is highly adaptable, it will thrive when introduced into a new environment. If a species thrives in its new environment, it will have an adverse effect on species already existing in that environment. But, since this species has not had an adverse effect on any species already existing in its new environment, it is not highly adaptable.

(B) If a species thrives in a new environment, that species is adaptable. Species that adapt to new environments adversely affect some species already existing in those environments. So, if a species does not adversely affect any species already existing in its new environment, it has not adapted to it.

(C) If a species is introduced into a new environment, it adversely affects some species already existing in that environment, but only if it adapts well to it. Therefore, if a species does not adapt well to a new environment, it will not adversely affect any species already existing in it.

(D) If the introduction of a new species would adversely affect some species already existing in an environment, that species should not be introduced into it. Therefore, since the introduction of species into new environments will result in some species in those environments being adversely affected, species should probably not be introduced into new environments.

(E) If a new species would damage an environment, that species should not be introduced into it. If a new species is introduced, the risk can be reduced by controlling its population. Therefore, because the introduction of species into new environments is likely to happen, their populations should be controlled.

GO ON TO THE NEXT PAGE.

20. If the city builds the proposed convention center, several national professional organizations will hold conventions there. And if several large conventions are held in the city, the total number of visitors will of course increase. Tax revenues will certainly increase if the number of visitors increases. Thus, building the convention center will increase the city's tax revenues.

The conclusion of the argument follows logically if which one of the following is assumed?

(A) If the number of visitors to the city does not increase, then the city's tax revenues will not increase.

(B) If the number of visitors to the city increases, then the amount of money spent by visitors will increase.

(C) The city's tax revenues will not increase unless the convention center is built.

(D) People who are now regular visitors to the city will continue to visit the city if the new convention center is built.

(E) If several national professional organizations hold their conventions in the convention center, those conventions will be large.

21. In a study, pairs of trained dogs were placed side by side and given a command such as "sit." After both obeyed the command, one dog was given a treat while its partner was given no reward at all. Over time, the dogs who went unrewarded began to disobey the command. This shows that dogs have an aversion to being treated unfairly.

Which one of the following would be most useful to know in order to evaluate the argument?

(A) Were dogs who were accustomed to receiving regular rewards prior to the study more inclined to obey the command?

(B) Is there a decline in obedience if rewards are withheld from both dogs in the pair?

(C) Were dogs who received treats in one trial ever used as dogs that did not receive treats in other trials?

(D) Were there any cases in which the dog who was given a reward became more inclined to obey the command?

(E) How many repetitions were required before the unrewarded dogs began to disobey the command?

22. A study of 20,000 20- to 64-year-olds found that people's satisfaction with their incomes is not strongly correlated with the amount they make. People tend to live in neighborhoods of people from their same economic class, and the study shows that people's satisfaction with their incomes depends largely on how favorably their incomes compare with those of their neighbors.

The statements above, if true, most strongly support which one of the following hypotheses?

(A) People with high incomes are consistently more satisfied with their incomes than are people in the middle class.

(B) Older people are generally more satisfied with their incomes than are younger people.

(C) Satisfaction with income is strongly correlated with neighborhood.

(D) In general, people's income levels have little effect on their level of satisfaction with life as a whole.

(E) An increase in everyone's incomes is not likely to greatly increase people's levels of satisfaction with their own incomes.

23. Geologist: The dominant view that petroleum formed from the fossilized remains of plants and animals deep in the earth's crust has been challenged by scientists who hold that it formed, not from living material, but from deep carbon deposits dating from the formation of the earth. But their theory is refuted by the presence in petroleum of biomarkers, molecules indicating the past or present existence of a living organism.

Which one of the following, if true, most weakens the geologist's argument?

(A) Fossils have been discovered that are devoid of biomarkers.

(B) Living organisms only emerged long after the earth's formation.

(C) It would take many millions of years for organisms to become petroleum.

(D) Certain strains of bacteria thrive deep inside the earth's crust.

(E) Some carbon deposits were formed from the fossilized remains of plants.

GO ON TO THE NEXT PAGE.

24. Any driver involved in an accident leading to personal injury or property damage exceeding $500 is legally required to report the accident to the department of motor vehicles, unless the driver is incapable of doing so. Ted is not required to report the accident in which he was involved as a driver.

Which one of the following can be properly inferred from the statements above?

(A) If Ted is incapable of reporting the accident, then the accident did not lead to property damage exceeding $500.

(B) If Ted's car was damaged in excess of $500 in the accident, then he is incapable of reporting the accident to the department of motor vehicles.

(C) Someone other than Ted is legally required to report the accident to the department of motor vehicles.

(D) If Ted is incapable of reporting the accident to the department of motor vehicles, then he was injured in the accident.

(E) Either no one was injured in the accident or the accident did not lead to property damage exceeding $500.

25. Student: If a person has an immunity to infection by a microorganism, then that microorganism does not cause them to develop harmful symptoms. Since many people are exposed to staphylococcus without developing any harmful symptoms, it follows that they have an immunity to infection by this microorganism.

The student's argument is most similar in its flawed pattern of reasoning to which one of the following?

(A) Everything morally right is just, but some actions that best serve the interests of everyone are not just. Thus, some morally right actions do not serve the interests of everyone.

(B) Advertisers try to persuade people that certain claims are true. Since writers of fiction are not advertisers, they probably never try to persuade people that certain claims are true.

(C) Isabel said that she would take the medication. Obviously, though, she did not do so, because medication either cures disease or alleviates its symptoms, and Isabel is still quite ill.

(D) When business owners are subjected to excessive taxation, they become less willing to expand their businesses. The recent decline in business expansions thus shows that their taxes are too high.

(E) Studies show that doctors tend to wash their hands less often than any other health care professionals. This shows that the procedure cannot be of much value in preventing disease.

S T O P

IF YOU FINISH BEFORE TIME IS CALLED, YOU MAY CHECK YOUR WORK ON THIS SECTION ONLY.
DO NOT WORK ON ANY OTHER SECTION IN THE TEST.

Section II

Time—35 minutes

23 Questions

Directions: Each group of questions in this section is based on a set of conditions. In answering some of the questions, it may be useful to draw a rough diagram. Choose the response that most accurately and completely answers each question and blacken the corresponding space on your answer sheet.

Questions 1–5

A concert is given by a six-member band—guitarist, keyboard player, percussionist, saxophonist, trumpeter, violinist. During the concert, each member performs exactly one solo. The following restrictions apply:

The guitarist does not perform the fourth solo.

The percussionist performs a solo at some time before the keyboard player does.

The keyboard player performs a solo at some time after the violinist does and at some time before the guitarist does.

The saxophonist performs a solo at some time after either the percussionist does or the trumpeter does, but not both.

1. Which one of the following is an acceptable ordering of solos from first to last?

(A) violinist, percussionist, saxophonist, guitarist, trumpeter, keyboard player

(B) percussionist, violinist, keyboard player, trumpeter, saxophonist, guitarist

(C) violinist, trumpeter, saxophonist, percussionist, keyboard player, guitarist

(D) keyboard player, trumpeter, violinist, saxophonist, guitarist, percussionist

(E) guitarist, violinist, keyboard player, percussionist, saxophonist, trumpeter

GO ON TO THE NEXT PAGE.

2. If the percussionist performs a solo at some time before the saxophonist does, then which one of the following must be true?

(A) The percussionist performs the first solo.
(B) The percussionist performs the second solo.
(C) The violinist performs a solo at some time before the saxophonist does.
(D) The percussionist performs a solo at some time before the trumpeter does.
(E) The saxophonist performs a solo at some time before the keyboard player does.

3. Each of the following must be false EXCEPT:

(A) The keyboard player performs the first solo.
(B) The guitarist performs the second solo.
(C) The guitarist performs a solo at some time before the saxophonist does.
(D) The guitarist performs a solo at some time before the percussionist does.
(E) The keyboard player performs a solo at some time before the saxophonist does.

4. Which one of the following CANNOT perform the third solo?

(A) guitarist
(B) keyboard player
(C) saxophonist
(D) trumpeter
(E) violinist

5. If the violinist performs the fourth solo, then each of the following must be true EXCEPT:

(A) The percussionist performs a solo at some time before the violinist does.
(B) The trumpeter performs a solo at some time before the violinist does.
(C) The trumpeter performs a solo at some time before the guitarist does.
(D) The saxophonist performs a solo at some time before the violinist does.
(E) The trumpeter performs a solo at some time before the saxophonist does.

GO ON TO THE NEXT PAGE.

Questions 6–10

Four art historians—Farley, Garcia, Holden, and Jiang—will give a series of four public lectures, each lecture on a different topic—lithographs, oil paintings, sculptures, and watercolors. The lectures will be given one at a time, with each art historian giving a lecture on a different one of the topics. The schedule of the lectures is subject to the following constraints:

> The oil paintings lecture and the watercolors lecture must both be earlier than the lithographs lecture.
> Farley's lecture must be earlier than the oil paintings lecture.
> Holden's lecture must be earlier than both Garcia's lecture and Jiang's lecture.

6. Which one of the following is an acceptable ordering of the lectures, from first to fourth?

(A) Farley: sculptures; Holden: lithographs; Garcia: oil paintings; Jiang: watercolors
(B) Farley: watercolors; Jiang: oil paintings; Holden: sculptures; Garcia: lithographs
(C) Garcia: sculptures; Farley: watercolors; Holden: oil paintings; Jiang: lithographs
(D) Holden: oil paintings; Jiang: watercolors; Farley: lithographs; Garcia: sculptures
(E) Holden: sculptures; Farley: watercolors; Jiang: oil paintings; Garcia: lithographs

GO ON TO THE NEXT PAGE.

7. Which one of the following must be true?

(A) Farley's lecture is earlier than the sculptures lecture.
(B) Holden's lecture is earlier than the lithographs lecture.
(C) The sculptures lecture is earlier than Garcia's lecture.
(D) The sculptures lecture is earlier than Jiang's lecture.
(E) The watercolors lecture is earlier than Garcia's lecture.

8. If the watercolors lecture is third, which one of the following could be true?

(A) Farley gives the watercolors lecture.
(B) Garcia gives the oil paintings lecture.
(C) Garcia gives the sculptures lecture.
(D) Holden gives the sculptures lecture.
(E) Jiang gives the lithographs lecture.

9. Which one of the following CANNOT be true?

(A) Farley gives the lithographs lecture.
(B) Garcia gives the sculptures lecture.
(C) Garcia gives the watercolors lecture.
(D) Holden gives the oil paintings lecture.
(E) Jiang gives the watercolors lecture.

10. If Garcia gives the sculptures lecture, which one of the following could be true?

(A) The lithographs lecture is third.
(B) The oil paintings lecture is third.
(C) The sculptures lecture is first.
(D) The sculptures lecture is second.
(E) The watercolors lecture is second.

GO ON TO THE NEXT PAGE.

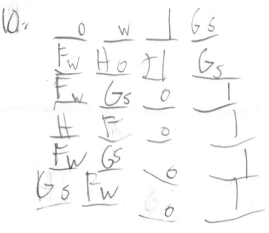

Questions 11–16

Three rugs will be woven out of colored thread. Six colors of thread are available—forest, olive, peach, turquoise, white, and yellow—exactly five of which will be used to weave the rugs. Each color that is used will be used in only one of the rugs. The rugs are either solid—woven in a single color—or multicolored. The rugs must be woven according to the following rules:

In any rug in which white is used, two other colors are also used.

In any rug in which olive is used, peach is also used.

Forest and turquoise are not used together in a rug.

Peach and turquoise are not used together in a rug.

Peach and yellow are not used together in a rug.

11. Which one of the following could be the colors of the three rugs?

(A) forest only;
turquoise only;
olive, peach, and white

(B) forest only;
turquoise only;
olive, peach, and yellow

(C) peach only;
turquoise only;
forest, olive, and white

(D) yellow only;
forest and turquoise;
olive and peach

(E) yellow only;
olive and peach;
turquoise and white

GO ON TO THE NEXT PAGE.

12. Which one of the following must be true?

(A) There are no multicolored rugs in which forest is used.
(B) There are no multicolored rugs in which turquoise is used.
(C) Peach is used in one of the rugs.
(D) Turquoise is used in one of the rugs.
(E) Yellow is used in one of the rugs.

13. If one of the rugs is solid peach, which one of the following must be true?

(A) One of the rugs is solid forest.
(B) One of the rugs is solid turquoise.
(C) One of the rugs is solid yellow.
(D) Forest and white are used together in a rug.
(E) White and yellow are used together in a rug.

14. If there are exactly two solid rugs, then the colors of those two rugs CANNOT be

(A) forest and peach
(B) forest and yellow
(C) peach and turquoise
(D) peach and yellow
(E) turquoise and yellow

15. If forest and peach are used together in a rug, which one of the following could be true?

(A) There is exactly one solid rug.
(B) White is not used in any of the rugs.
(C) Yellow is not used in any of the rugs.
(D) Turquoise and white are used together in a rug.
(E) Turquoise and yellow are used together in a rug.

16. If one of the rugs is solid yellow, then any of the following could be true EXCEPT:

(A) There is exactly one solid color rug.
(B) One of the rugs is solid forest.
(C) Turquoise is not used in any of the rugs.
(D) Forest and olive are used together in a rug.
(E) Peach and white are used together in a rug.

GO ON TO THE NEXT PAGE.

Questions 17–23

The manager of a photography business must assign at least two photographers to each of two graduation ceremonies—one at Silva University and the other at Thorne University. Exactly six photographers are available—Frost, Gonzalez, Heideck, Knutson, Lai, and Mays—but not all have to be assigned. No photographer can be assigned to both ceremonies. The following constraints apply:

Frost must be assigned together with Heideck to one of the graduation ceremonies.

If Lai and Mays are both assigned, it must be to different ceremonies.

If Gonzalez is assigned to the Silva University ceremony, then Lai must be assigned to the Thorne University ceremony.

If Knutson is not assigned to the Thorne University ceremony, then both Heideck and Mays must be assigned to it.

17. Which one of the following is an acceptable assignment of photographers to the two graduation ceremonies?

(A) Silva University: Gonzalez, Lai
     Thorne University: Frost, Heideck, Mays
(B) Silva University: Gonzalez, Mays
     Thorne University: Knutson, Lai
(C) Silva University: Frost, Gonzalez, Heideck
     Thorne University: Knutson, Lai, Mays
(D) Silva University: Frost, Heideck, Mays
     Thorne University: Gonzalez, Lai
(E) Silva University: Frost, Heideck, Mays
     Thorne University: Gonzalez, Knutson, Lai

GO ON TO THE NEXT PAGE.

18. If Heideck is assigned to the same graduation ceremony as Lai, then which one of the following must be true?

   (A) Frost is assigned to the Thorne University ceremony.
   (B) Gonzalez is assigned to the Silva University ceremony.
   (C) Gonzalez is assigned to neither graduation ceremony.
   (D) Knutson is assigned to the Thorne University ceremony.
   (E) Lai is assigned to the Thorne University ceremony.

19. Which one of the following could be the complete assignment of photographers to the Silva University ceremony?

   (A) Frost, Gonzalez, Heideck, Knutson
   (B) Frost, Gonzalez, Heideck
   (C) Gonzalez, Knutson
   (D) Heideck, Lai
   (E) Knutson, Mays

20. Which one of the following is a complete and accurate list of all of the photographers who must be assigned?

   (A) Frost, Heideck
   (B) Frost, Heideck, Knutson
   (C) Frost, Heideck, Knutson, Lai
   (D) Frost, Gonzalez, Heideck
   (E) Frost, Gonzalez, Heideck, Mays

21. If exactly four of the photographers are assigned to the graduation ceremonies, then which one of the following must be assigned to the Silva University ceremony?

   (A) Frost
   (B) Gonzalez
   (C) Knutson
   (D) Lai
   (E) Mays

22. Which one of the following CANNOT be the complete assignment of photographers to the Thorne University ceremony?

   (A) Frost, Gonzalez, Heideck, Mays
   (B) Frost, Heideck, Knutson, Mays
   (C) Gonzalez, Knutson, Lai
   (D) Gonzalez, Knutson, Mays
   (E) Knutson, Mays

23. Which one of the following, if substituted for the constraint that if Knutson is not assigned to the Thorne University ceremony, then both Heideck and Mays must be assigned to it, would have the same effect in determining the assignment of photographers to the graduation ceremonies?

   (A) If Knutson is assigned to the Silva University ceremony, then Heideck and Mays cannot both be assigned to that ceremony.
   (B) If Knutson is assigned to the Silva University ceremony, then Lai must also be assigned to that ceremony.
   (C) Unless Knutson is assigned to the Thorne University ceremony, both Frost and Mays must be assigned to that ceremony.
   (D) Unless Knutson is assigned to the Thorne University ceremony, Heideck cannot be assigned to the same ceremony as Lai.
   (E) Unless either Heideck or Mays is assigned to the Thorne University ceremony, Knutson must be assigned to that ceremony.

S T O P

IF YOU FINISH BEFORE TIME IS CALLED, YOU MAY CHECK YOUR WORK ON THIS SECTION ONLY.
DO NOT WORK ON ANY OTHER SECTION IN THE TEST.

Section III

Time—35 minutes

27 Questions

Directions: Each set of questions in this section is based on a single passage or a pair of passages. The questions are to be answered on the basis of what is stated or implied in the passage or pair of passages. For some of the questions, more than one of the choices could conceivably answer the question. However, you are to choose the best answer; that is, the response that most accurately and completely answers the question, and blacken the corresponding space on your answer sheet.

Given the amount of time and effort that curators, collectors, dealers, scholars, and critics spend on formulating judgments of taste in relation to oil paintings, it seems odd that so few are prepared to
(5) apply some of the same skills in exploring works of art that stimulate another sense altogether: that of smell. Why is great perfume not taken more seriously? While art professionals are very serious about many branches of literature, architecture, and music, I have
(10) yet to find a curatorial colleague who regularly beats a path to the fragrance counter in search of, say, *Joy Parfum*, the 1930 masterpiece by Henri Alméras.

And yet, the parallels between what ought to be regarded as sister arts are undeniable. Painters
(15) combine natural and, these days, synthetic pigments with media such as oils and resins, much as the perfumer carefully formulates natural and synthetic chemical compounds. The Old Masters deployed oil paint across the color spectrum, and applied layers on
(20) a determining ground and various kinds of underpainting, slowly building up to the surface, completing their work with thin glazes on top. Thus various types of mashed-up earth and vegetable suspended in linseed or poppy oil are brushed over a
(25) stretch of woven fabric. They begin to dry, and a picture is born. Its appearance changes over time, because the tendency of oil paint is to become gradually more transparent.

So, too, talented "noses" experiment with
(30) complex configurations of olfactory elements and produce in symphonic combination many small sensations, at times discordant, sweet, bitter, melancholy, or happy, as the case may be. These combinations change and develop in sequence or in
(35) unison as the substance and its constituents evaporate at different rates, some quickly, others slowly, thanks to the warmth of our skin. A brilliant perfumer may thus devise an imaginary world no less powerful, or intimate, than that of a great composer or painter, and
(40) in calling on our capacity to discover there some memory of childhood or of a long-forgotten experience, perfumers are in the same business as the artist who creates the illusion of life on canvas.

Perhaps one reason that truly great smells are so
(45) often undervalued is that perfumes are today made and distributed under the not particularly watchful gaze of a few large corporations. The cynical bean counters in Paris and Zurich do not hesitate to tamper with old formulas, insisting on the substitution of cheap
(50) chemical compounds that approximately resemble rarer, better ingredients in an effort to increase profits.

They do not tell their customers when or how they do this; indeed, they presume their customers won't notice the difference. Consequently, fine perfume is
(55) now hopelessly entangled with the international cosmetic dollar, and ill-served by marketing and public relations.

1. Which one of the following most accurately expresses the main point of the passage?

(A) Despite their pursuit of profit, corporations that produce and market perfumes value artistic skill.

(B) A masterpiece perfume evokes reactions that are no less powerful than those evoked by a masterpiece in music or painting.

(C) The corporate nature of the perfume business is the reason that so few truly great perfumes are now produced.

(D) Great perfumes are works of art and deserve respect and attention as such.

(E) Perfume-making and oil painting should be regarded as sister arts, both of which involve the skilled application of complex configurations of ingredients.

2. In which one of the following circumstances would the author of the passage be most likely to believe that a perfume manufacturer is justified in altering the formula of a classic perfume?

(A) The alteration makes the perfume more closely resemble *Joy Parfum*.

(B) The alteration is done to replace an ingredient that is currently very costly.

(C) The alteration replaces a synthetic chemical compound with a natural chemical compound.

(D) The alteration is done to make the perfume popular with a wider variety of customers.

(E) The alteration takes a previously altered perfume closer to its creator's original formula.

GO ON TO THE NEXT PAGE.

3. The word "noses" (line 29) refers to

 (A) perfumers
 (B) perfume collectors
 (C) particular perfumes
 (D) people with expertise in marketing perfumes
 (E) people with expertise in pricing perfumes

4. The passage provides the most support for which one of the following statements about art?

 (A) A work of art can bring about an aesthetic experience through the memories that it evokes.
 (B) In any work of art, one can detect the harmonious combination of many small sensations.
 (C) A work of art will inevitably fail if it is created for the sake of commercial success.
 (D) The best works of art improve with age.
 (E) Some forms of art are superior to others.

5. The author would be most likely to hold which one of the following opinions about *Joy Parfum* by Henri Alméras?

 (A) As time goes on, its artistry is appreciated more and more.
 (B) As a work of art, it is no less important than a great piece of sculpture.
 (C) It was the foremost accomplishment of its time in perfume making.
 (D) It is a fragrance that is appreciated only by people with refined taste.
 (E) Its original formula is similar to many other perfumes of the 1930s.

6. Which one of the following is most analogous to what the author calls the "cynical bean counters" (line 47)?

 (A) an art museum curator who caters to popular tastes in choosing works for an exhibition
 (B) a movie studio executive who imposes cost-saving production restrictions on a film's director
 (C) a director of an art institute who cuts the annual budget because of projections of declining revenues
 (D) a business executive who convinces her company to invest in art merely for the sake of tax benefits
 (E) an art school dean who slashes the budget of one project in order to increase the budget of his pet project

7. The last paragraph most strongly supports which one of the following statements?

 (A) The names of the world's best perfumes are not known to most customers.
 (B) The profitability of a particular perfume is not a good indicator of its quality.
 (C) Companies that sell perfume pay little attention to what their customers want.
 (D) Perfume makers of the past would never tamper with established formulas.
 (E) Companies that sell perfume make most of their profits on perfumes in the least expensive price ranges.

8. Which one of the following most accurately describes the organization of the passage?

 (A) The first paragraph makes an observation, the middle paragraphs elaborate on that observation while considering one possible explanation for it, and the final paragraph delivers an alternative explanation.
 (B) The first paragraph advances a thesis, the middle paragraphs present a case for that thesis, and the final paragraph considers and rejects one particular challenge to that thesis.
 (C) The first paragraph sets out a challenge to received wisdom, the middle paragraphs present a response to that challenge, and the final paragraph presents a concrete example that supports the response.
 (D) The first paragraph poses a question, the middle paragraphs present a case that helps to justify the posing of that question, and the final paragraph presents a possible answer to the question.
 (E) The first paragraph outlines a problem, the middle paragraphs present two consequences of that problem, and the final paragraph attempts to identify the parties that are responsible for the problem.

GO ON TO THE NEXT PAGE.

"Stealing thunder" is a courtroom strategy that consists in a lawyer's revealing negative information about a client before that information is revealed or elicited by an opposing lawyer. While there is no point
(5) in revealing a weakness that is unknown to one's opponents or that would not be exploited by them, many lawyers believe that if the weakness is likely to be revealed in opposing testimony, it should be volunteered; otherwise, the hostile revelation would
(10) be more damaging.

Although no empirical research has directly tested the effectiveness of stealing thunder in actual trials, studies involving simulated trial situations have suggested that the technique is, in fact, effective, at
(15) least within a reasonably broad range of applications. Lawyers' commonly held belief in the value of stealing thunder is not only corroborated by those experimental findings; it is also supported by several psychological explanations of why the technique
(20) should work. For one thing, volunteering damaging information early may create an image of credibility. Psychological research suggests that people who reveal information that appears to be against their own best interest are likely to be perceived as more credible
(25) and thus may be more persuasive. Stealing thunder may also provide juries with an impetus for critical assessment by previewing, and thus alerting them to, testimony that the opposition plans to present. In psychological experiments, audiences that were
(30) previously warned of an upcoming attempt at persuasion became more resistant to the persuasive attempt, forming counterarguments based on the warning. Also, the value placed on a persuasive message is probably much like the value placed on any
(35) commodity; the scarcer the commodity, the more valuable it is. A persuasive message will thus increase in value and effectiveness to the extent that it is seen as scarce. In the courtroom, a piece of evidence brought by both the prosecution and the defense, as
(40) when thunder is stolen, may be seen as less scarce—becoming "old news." Thus, unless that evidence is of overriding consequence, it should carry less weight than if it had been included only in hostile testimony.

Finally, stealing thunder may work because the
(45) lawyer can frame the evidence in his or her own terms and downplay its significance, just as politicians sometimes seek to put their "spin" on potentially damaging information. However, it may therefore be effective only when the negative information can be
(50) framed positively. Jurors, who often initially have little information about a case, are usually eager to solidify their position regarding the case. They can therefore be expected to use the early positive framing to guide their subsequent analysis of the trial information. But
(55) this also suggests limitations on the use of the technique: when information is very damaging, stealing thunder may create an early negative impression that forms a cognitive framework for jurors, who then filter subsequent information through this schema.

9. Which one of the following most accurately expresses the main point of the passage?

(A) Although there are limits to the usefulness of stealing thunder, its effectiveness in actual trials has been demonstrated through research conducted by psychologists and legal scholars.

(B) The commonly practiced courtroom strategy of stealing thunder can have unintended consequences if the lawyers using it do not accurately predict jurors' attitudes.

(C) Lawyers' commonly held belief in the value of stealing thunder is supported by several psychological explanations of how that strategy may influence jurors.

(D) The risks involved in stealing thunder can outweigh the probable benefits when the information to be revealed is too readily available or too negative in its impact.

(E) Research designed to confirm the usefulness of stealing thunder has vindicated lawyers' belief in the value of the technique and has identified the general limitations of the strategy's effectiveness.

10. It can be most reasonably inferred from the passage that which one of the following is an example of stealing thunder?

(A) warning jurors that a client on the opposing side has a serious conflict of interest and cannot be trusted

(B) disclosing in opening statements of a defense against copyright infringement that one's client has in the past been guilty of plagiarism

(C) responding to the opposition's revelation that one's client has a minor criminal background by conceding that this is the case

(D) pointing out to jurors during opening statements the mistaken reasoning in the opposition's case

(E) stressing that one's client, while technically guilty, is believable and that mitigating circumstances should be considered

11. Which one of the following does the author mention as a factor that in some instances probably contributes to the success of stealing thunder?

(A) careful timing of the thunder-stealing message to precede the opposition's similar message by only a short time

(B) some lawyers' superior skill in assessing jurors' probable reactions to a message

(C) the willingness of some lawyers' clients to testify in person about their own past mistakes

(D) jurors' desire to arrive at a firm view regarding the case they are hearing

(E) lawyers' careful screening of prospective jurors prior to the beginning of courtroom proceedings

GO ON TO THE NEXT PAGE.

12. The author discusses the "cognitive framework" that jurors create (line 58) primarily to

(A) indicate that at least some information mentioned early in a trial can influence the way jurors evaluate information presented later in the trial

(B) indicate that jurors bring into court with them certain attitudes and biases that at least in part inform their opinions during trials

(C) suggest that damaging evidence that is framed positively early in a trial will have a greater impact than damaging evidence presented later in a trial

(D) theorize that stealing thunder is best done as early as possible in a case, before the opposition has an opportunity to solidify jurors' opinions

(E) speculate that creating credibility in some cases is probably more effective than positively framing very harmful information

13. The author's attitude regarding stealing thunder can most accurately be described as

(A) concerned that the technique may become so common that lawyers will fail to recognize its drawbacks

(B) favorable toward its use by lawyers during the opening statements of a case but skeptical of its value otherwise

(C) concerned that research results supporting it may omit crucial anecdotal evidence indicating pitfalls in its use

(D) approving of its use on the grounds that its success is experimentally supported and can be psychologically explained

(E) skeptical of its suitability for use by lawyers without lengthy experience in courtroom strategies

14. The author's characterization of stealing thunder in the passage is based at least partly on both

(A) informal surveys of lawyers' clients' reactions to stealing thunder and controlled research based on simulated trial situations

(B) statistical surveys of lawyers who steal thunder and observations of lawyers' tactics in trials

(C) records of judges' decisions in court cases and the results of studies involving simulated courtroom situations

(D) informal observations of nontrial uses of techniques analogous to stealing thunder and controlled studies of lawyers' courtroom behavior

(E) research that was not directly concerned with legal proceedings and research in which subjects participated in simulated trial situations

15. By saying that certain studies have suggested that in some applications, "the technique is, in fact, effective" (line 14), the author most likely means that those studies have given evidence that the technique in question

(A) inclines juries to regard the clients of those using the technique more favorably than would be the case if the negative information about them were first divulged by the opposition

(B) is a reliable means, in courtroom settings, of introducing a set of counterarguments that jurors will be able to use in resisting the opposition's subsequent attempts at persuasion

(C) invariably results in cases being decided in favor of the clients of those using the technique rather than in favor of parties opposing those clients, if it is used broadly

(D) appears generally to succeed as a means of forcefully capturing jurors' attention and thus leading them to focus more attentively than they would otherwise on the lawyer's message

(E) more often than not achieves its goal of timing a negative revelation so as to dramatically precede the opposition's revelation of the same information

16. The passage most strongly implies that many lawyers believe which one of the following concerning decisions about whether to steal thunder?

(A) A lawyer should be concerned with how readily the negative information can be positively framed, especially if the information is very negative.

(B) A lawyer should take into account, among other things, whether or not the jurors are already familiar with some of the relevant facts of the case prior to the trial.

(C) The decision should be based on careful deliberations that anticipate both positive and negative reactions of jurors and opposing lawyers.

(D) The decision should depend on how probable it is that the opposition will try to derive an advantage from mentioning the negative information in question.

(E) The decision should be based at least partly on a lawyer's knowledge of relevant psychological research findings and legal statistics.

GO ON TO THE NEXT PAGE.

Passage A

To a neuroscientist, you are your brain; nothing causes your behavior other than the operations of your brain. This viewpoint, together with recent findings in neuroscience, radically changes the way we think

(5) about the law. The official line in the law is that all that matters is whether you are rational, but you can have someone who is totally rational even though their strings are being pulled by something beyond their control. Indeed, people who believe themselves to be

(10) making a free and rational moral choice may really be deluding themselves—a brain scan might show that such a choice correlates with activity in emotional centers in the brain rather than in the region of the brain associated with deliberative problem solving.

(15) This insight suggests that the criminal-justice system should abandon the idea of retribution—the idea that bad people should be punished because of their freely chosen immoral acts—which is now dominant as a justification of punishment. Instead, the law should

(20) focus on deterring future harms. In some cases, this might mean lighter punishments. If it is really true that we do not get any prevention bang from our punishment buck when we punish some person, then it is not worth punishing that person.

Passage B

(25) Neuroscience constantly produces new mechanistic descriptions of how the physical brain causes behavior, adding fuel to the deterministic view that all human action is causally necessitated by events that are independent of the will. It has long been

(30) argued, however, that the concept of free will can coexist with determinism.

In 1954 English philosopher Alfred J. Ayer put forth a theory of "soft determinism." He argued, as the philosopher David Hume had two centuries earlier,

(35) that even in a deterministic world, a person can still act freely. Ayer distinguished between free actions and constrained actions. Free actions are those that are caused by internal sources, by one's own will (unless one is suffering from a disorder). Constrained actions

(40) are those that are caused by external sources, for example, by someone or something forcing you physically or mentally to perform an action, as in hypnosis or in mental disorders such as kleptomania. When someone performs a free action to do A, he or

(45) she could have done B instead, since no external source precluded doing so. When someone performs a constrained action to do A, he or she could have done only A.

Ayer argued that actions are free as long as they

(50) are not constrained. It is not the existence of a cause but the source of the cause that determines whether an action is free. Although Ayer did not explicitly discuss the brain's role, one could make the analogy that those actions—and indeed those wills—that originate from

(55) a disease-free brain are not constrained, and are therefore free, even though they may be determined.

---

17. Both passages are concerned with answering which one of the following questions?

(A) Should people be punished for actions that are outside of their control?

(B) Does scientific research into the brain have implications regarding freedom of the will?

(C) Can actions that are not free be effectively deterred by the threat of punishment?

(D) Is the view that retribution is a legitimate justification for punishment compatible with the findings of neuroscience?

(E) Can an action be free if someone else physically forced the actor to perform it?

18. Which one of the following concepts plays a role in the argument of passage B but not in that of passage A?

(A) mental disorder

(B) free choice

(C) causality

(D) self-delusion

(E) moral responsibility

19. One purpose of the reference by the author of passage B to David Hume (line 34) is to

(A) characterize Ayer as someone who is not an original thinker

(B) add credence to the theory of soft determinism

(C) suggest that the theory of soft determinism is primarily of historical importance

(D) suggest that the theory of soft determinism has been in existence as long as mechanistic descriptions of the brain have

(E) add intellectual respectability to the view that the brain should not be described mechanistically

GO ON TO THE NEXT PAGE.

20. Passage B differs from passage A in that passage B displays an attitude toward the ideas it discusses that is more

(A) engaged
(B) dismissive
(C) detached
(D) ironic
(E) skeptical

21. Which one of the following arguments is most analogous to the argument advanced in passage A?

(A) Many word processors are packed with nonessential features that only confuse most users and get in the way of important functions. Word processors with fewer features thus enhance productivity.

(B) Economic models generally presume that actors in an economy are entirely rational. But psychological studies have documented many ways in which people make irrational choices. Thus, economic models, in theory, should not be able to predict human behavior.

(C) The existing program for teaching mathematics in elementary schools is based on mistaken notions about what sorts of mathematical concepts children can grasp, and it should therefore be replaced.

(D) Civil disobedience is justified only in those cases in which civil law conflicts with one's sincere moral or religious convictions. Any attempt to justify civil disobedience on something other than moral or religious grounds is therefore illegitimate.

(E) Being autonomous does not imply having full control over one's behavior. After all, addicted smokers are unable to exercise control over some behaviors but are nevertheless autonomous in the general sense.

GO ON TO THE NEXT PAGE.

This passage is adapted from a review of a 1991 book.

In a recent study, Mario García argues that in the United States between 1930 and 1960 the group of political activists he calls the "Mexican American Generation" was more radical and politically diverse
(5) than earlier historians have recognized. Through analysis of the work of some of the era's most important scholars, García does provide persuasive evidence that in the 1930s and 1940s these activists anticipated many of the reforms proposed by the more
(10) militant Chicanos of the 1960s and 1970s. His study, however, suffers from two flaws.

First, García's analysis of the evidence he provides to demonstrate the Mexican American Generation's political diversity is not entirely
(15) consistent. Indeed, he undermines his primary thesis by emphasizing an underlying consensus among various groups that tends to conceal the full significance of their differences. Groups such as the League of United Latin American Citizens, an
(20) organization that encouraged Mexican Americans to pursue a civil rights strategy of assimilation into the United States political and cultural mainstream, were often diametrically opposed to organizations such as the Congress of Spanish-Speaking People, a coalition
(25) group that advocated bilingual education and equal rights for resident aliens in the United States. García acknowledges these differences but dismisses them as insignificant, given that the goals of groups as disparate as these centered on liberal reform, not
(30) revolution. But one need only note the fierce controversies that occurred during the period over United States immigration policies and the question of assimilation versus cultural maintenance to recognize that Mexican American political history since 1930
(35) has been characterized not by consensus but by intense and lively debate.

Second, García may be exaggerating the degree to which the views of these activists were representative of the ethnic Mexican population residing in the
(40) United States during this period. Noting that by 1930 the proportion of the Mexican American population that had been born in the United States had significantly increased, García argues that between 1930 and 1960 a new generation of Mexican American
(45) leaders appeared, one that was more acculturated and hence more politically active than its predecessor. Influenced by their experience of discrimination and by the inclusive rhetoric of World War II slogans, these leaders, according to García, were determined to
(50) achieve full civil rights for all United States residents of Mexican descent. However, it is not clear how far this outlook extended beyond these activists. Without a better understanding of the political implications of important variables such as patterns of bilingualism
(55) and rates of Mexican immigration and naturalization, and the variations in ethnic consciousness these variables help to create, one cannot assume that an increase in the proportion of Mexican Americans born in the United States necessarily resulted in an increase
(60) in the ethnic Mexican population's political activism.

22. According to the passage, the League of United Latin American Citizens differed from the Congress of Spanish-Speaking People in that the League of United Latin American Citizens

(A) sought the political goals most popular with other United States citizens

(B) fought for equal rights for resident aliens in the United States

(C) favored a more liberal United States immigration policy

(D) encouraged Mexican Americans to speak Spanish rather than English

(E) encouraged Mexican Americans to adopt the culture of the United States

23. It can be inferred from the passage that García would most probably agree with which one of the following statements about the Mexican American political activists of the 1930s and 1940s?

(A) Some of their concerns were similar to those of the Mexican American activists of the 1960s and 1970s.

(B) They were more politically diverse than the Mexican American activists of the 1960s and 1970s.

(C) They were as militant as the Mexican American activists of the 1960s and 1970s.

(D) Most of them advocated bilingual education and equal rights for resident aliens in the United States.

(E) Most of them were more interested in revolution than in liberal reform.

GO ON TO THE NEXT PAGE.

24. The passage suggests that García assumes which one of the following to have been true of Mexican Americans between 1930 and 1960?

(A) Increased ethnic consciousness among Mexican Americans accounted for an increase in political activity among them.

(B) Increased familiarity among Mexican Americans with United States culture accounted for an increase in political activity among them.

(C) The assimilation of many Mexican Americans into United States culture accounted for Mexican Americans' lack of interest in political activity.

(D) Many Mexican Americans were moved to political militancy as a means of achieving full civil rights for all United States residents of Mexican descent.

(E) Many Mexican Americans were moved to political protest by their experience of discrimination and the patronizing rhetoric of World War II slogans.

25. It can be inferred that the author of the passage believes which one of the following about the Mexican American political activists of the 1930s and 1940s?

(A) Their common goal of liberal reform made them less militant than the Mexican American activists of the 1960s and 1970s.

(B) Their common goal of liberal reform did not outweigh their political differences.

(C) Their common goal of liberal reform helped them reach a consensus in spite of their political differences.

(D) They were more or less evenly divided between those favoring assimilation and those favoring cultural maintenance.

(E) They did not succeed in fully achieving their political goals because of their disparate political views.

26. The author of the passage expresses uncertainty with regard to which one of the following?

(A) whether or not one can assume that the increase in the number of Mexican Americans born in the United States led to an increase in Mexican American political activism

(B) whether or not historians preceding García were correct in their assumptions about Mexican Americans who were politically active between 1930 and 1960

(C) whether or not there was general consensus among Mexican American political activists between 1930 and 1960

(D) the extent to which the views of Mexican American activists were shared by the ethnic Mexican population in the United States

(E) the nature of the relationship between the League of United Latin American Citizens and the Congress of Spanish-Speaking People

27. The passage supports which one of the following statements about ethnic consciousness among Mexican Americans?

(A) Ethnic consciousness increases when rates of Mexican immigration and naturalization increase.

(B) Ethnic consciousness increases when the number of Mexican Americans born in the United States increases.

(C) Ethnic consciousness decreases when the number of Mexican Americans assimilating into the culture of the United States increases.

(D) Variations in the influence of Mexican American leaders over the Mexican American population at large account in part for variations in ethnic consciousness.

(E) Variations in rates of Mexican immigration and naturalization account in part for variations in ethnic consciousness.

S T O P

IF YOU FINISH BEFORE TIME IS CALLED, YOU MAY CHECK YOUR WORK ON THIS SECTION ONLY.
DO NOT WORK ON ANY OTHER SECTION IN THE TEST.

Section IV

Time—35 minutes

26 Questions

<u>Directions:</u> The questions in this section are based on the reasoning contained in brief statements or passages. For some questions, more than one of the choices could conceivably answer the question. However, you are to choose the <u>best</u> answer; that is, the response that most accurately and completely answers the question. You should not make assumptions that are by commonsense standards implausible, superfluous, or incompatible with the passage. After you have chosen the best answer, blacken the corresponding space on your answer sheet.

1. Ming: Since trans fat is particularly unhealthy, it's fortunate for the consumer that so many cookie manufacturers have completely eliminated it from their products.

   Carol: Why do you say that? Even without trans fat, desserts do not make for healthy eating.

   Carol's response indicates that she interpreted Ming's remarks to mean that

   (A)   the more trans fat a cookie contains, the more unhealthy it is
   (B)   food that doesn't contain trans fat is healthy food
   (C)   if a food is not healthy, then it is unhealthy
   (D)   a cookie containing any amount of trans fat is unhealthy
   (E)   consumers should purchase cookies only if they do not contain trans fat

2. Historian: During the Industrial Revolution, for the first time in history, the productivity of the economy grew at a faster rate than the population and thus dramatically improved living standards. An economist theorizes that this growth was made possible by the spread of values such as hard work and thrift. But successful explanations need to be based on facts, so no one should accept this explanation until historical evidence demonstrates that a change in values occurred prior to the Industrial Revolution.

   The overall conclusion of the historian's argument is that

   (A)   during the Industrial Revolution the productivity of the economy grew at a faster rate than the population
   (B)   the fact that the productivity of the economy grew at a faster rate than the population during the Industrial Revolution led to a dramatic improvement in living standards
   (C)   no one should accept the economist's explanation until historical evidence demonstrates that a change in values occurred prior to the Industrial Revolution
   (D)   the improvement in living standards that occurred during the Industrial Revolution was not due to the spread of a change in values
   (E)   values such as hard work and thrift did not become widespread prior to the Industrial Revolution

3. The master plan for the new park calls for the planting of trees of any species native to this area, except for those native trees that grow to be very large, such as the cottonwood. The trees that the community group donated were purchased at Three Rivers Nursery, which sells mostly native trees and shrubs. Thus, the donated trees are probably consistent with the master plan.

   Which one of the following, if true, most strengthens the argument?

   (A)   Some tree species that grow to be very large are consistent with the master plan.
   (B)   Three Rivers Nursery sells cottonwood trees.
   (C)   Many of the native species that Three Rivers Nursery sells are shrubs, not trees.
   (D)   Tree species that are not native to this area and that are consistent with the master plan are rare and hard to find.
   (E)   Three Rivers Nursery does not sell any tree species that grow to be very large.

GO ON TO THE NEXT PAGE.

4. Paleontologists had long supposed that the dinosaur *Diplodocus* browsed for high-growing vegetation such as treetop leaves by raising its very long neck. But now computer models have shown that the structure of *Diplodocus*'s neck bones would have prevented such movement. The neck could, however, bend downward and even extend below ground level, allowing *Diplodocus* to access underwater vegetation from dry land. Thus, *Diplodocus* must have fed on plants on or near the ground, or underwater.

Which one of the following is an assumption required by the argument?

(A) The same type of neck structure is found in modern ground-feeding animals.

(B) *Diplodocus* was not able to see in front of itself unless its head was angled steeply downward.

(C) It would be impossible for a large animal such as *Diplodocus* to supply blood to an elevated brain.

(D) *Diplodocus* had no other way of accessing high-growing vegetation, such as by rising up on its hind legs.

(E) *Diplodocus* was not able to browse for underwater vegetation by kneeling beside bodies of water or by walking into them.

5. Government official: Although the determination of local residents to rebuild hiking trails recently devastated by a landslide indicates that they are strongly committed to their community, the government should not assist them in rebuilding. The reason is clear: there is a strong likelihood of future landslides in that location that could cause serious injury or worse.

Which one of the following principles, if valid, most helps to justify the reasoning in the government official's argument?

(A) Residents should not be allowed to rebuild trails unless the government assists them in rebuilding.

(B) The determination of residents to rebuild hiking trails devastated by landslides should be what determines government support for the project.

(C) Government agencies should not assist people with projects unless those people are strongly committed to their community.

(D) The government should not assist in projects that are very likely to result in circumstances that could lead to serious injury.

(E) Residents should be discouraged from rebuilding in any area that has had an extensive history of landslides.

6. Scientist: There is a lot of concern that human behavior may be responsible for large-scale climate change. But this should be seen as more of an opportunity than a problem. If human behavior is responsible for climate change, then we can control future climate change to make it less extreme than previous climate shifts.

The scientist's argument requires assuming which one of the following?

(A) The same degree of climate change produces less damage if it is caused by human behavior than if it has a purely natural cause.

(B) Human beings can control the aspects of their behavior that have an impact on climate change.

(C) At least some previous large-scale climate changes have been caused by human behavior.

(D) Large-scale climate change poses a greater danger to human beings than to other species.

(E) It is easier to identify the human behaviors that cause climate change than it is to change those behaviors.

7. In a study of heart patients awaiting treatment for reduced blood flow to the heart, those still waiting to find out whether they would need surgery were less likely to experience pain from the condition than were those who knew what type of treatment they would receive. Assuming that this uncertainty is more stressful than knowing what one's future holds, then it is reasonable to conclude that _____.

Which one of the following most logically completes the argument?

(A) stress sometimes reduces the amount of pain a heart patient experiences

(B) the pain experienced by heart patients is to some extent beneficial

(C) the severity of a heart patient's condition is usually worsened by withholding information from the patient about the treatment that that patient will receive

(D) stress is probably an effect rather than a cause of reduced blood flow to the heart

(E) heart patients suffering from reduced blood flow to the heart who are experiencing pain from the condition are more likely to require surgery than are such patients who are not experiencing pain

GO ON TO THE NEXT PAGE.

8. Given the shape of the hip and foot bones of the Kodiak bear, it has been determined that standing and walking upright is completely natural behavior for these bears. Thus, walking on hind legs is instinctive and not a learned behavior of the Kodiak.

To which one of the following criticisms is the argument most vulnerable?

(A) The argument incorrectly generalizes from the behavior of a few bears in support of its conclusion.

(B) The argument fails to consider the possibility that walking on hind legs is the result of both learning and an innate capacity.

(C) The word "behavior" illicitly changes meaning during the course of the argument.

(D) The argument presumes, without giving justification, that all behavior can be explained in one or both of only two ways.

(E) The argument incorrectly appeals to the authority of science in order to support its conclusion.

9. People are usually interested in, and often even moved by, anecdotes about individuals, whereas they rarely even pay attention to statistical information, much less change their beliefs in response to it. However, although anecdotes are generally misleading in that they are about unrepresentative cases, people tend to have fairly accurate beliefs about society.

Which one of the following, if true, would most help to explain why people tend to have accurate beliefs about society despite the facts described above?

(A) Statistical information tends to obscure the characteristics of individuals.

(B) Most people recognize that anecdotes tend to be about unrepresentative cases.

(C) The more emotionally compelling an anecdote is, the more likely it is to change a person's beliefs.

(D) Statistical information is made more comprehensible when illustrated by anecdotes.

(E) People tend to base their beliefs about other people on their emotional response to those people.

10. In 2005, paleontologist Mary Schweitzer made headlines when she reported finding preserved soft tissue in the bones of a *Tyrannosaurus rex* dinosaur. Analysis of the collagen proteins from the *T. rex* showed them to be similar to the collagen proteins in modern-day chickens. Schweitzer's discovery therefore adds to the mountain of evidence that dinosaurs are closely related to birds.

The answer to which one of the following questions would be most useful to know in order to evaluate the argument?

(A) How rare is it to find preserved soft tissue in the bones of a dinosaur?

(B) Is there any evidence at all against the claim that dinosaurs are closely related to birds?

(C) How likely is it for animals that are not closely related to each other to have similar collagen proteins?

(D) Is it possible that *T. rex* is more closely related to modern-day chickens than to certain other types of dinosaurs?

(E) Before Schweitzer's discovery, did researchers suppose that the collagen proteins in *T. rex* and chickens might be similar?

11. A university professor researching sleep disorders occasionally taught class after spending whole nights working in a laboratory. She found lecturing after such nights difficult: she reported that she felt worn out and humorless, and she had difficulty concentrating and finding the appropriate words. After several weeks of lectures, she asked her students to guess which lectures had been given after nights without sleep. Interestingly, very few students were able to correctly identify them.

Which one of the following statements is most strongly supported by the information above?

(A) The subjective effects of occasional sleep deprivation are more pronounced than are its effects on overt behavior.

(B) No one can assess the overall effects of sleep deprivation on a particular person as well as that sleep-deprived person can.

(C) Sleep deprivation has less effect on professors' job performance than it does on the job performance of others.

(D) Occasional sleep deprivation is not as debilitating as extended sleep deprivation.

(E) University students in a lecture audience tend to be astute observers of human behavior.

GO ON TO THE NEXT PAGE.

12. Prime minister: Our nation's government should give priority to satisfying the needs of our nation's people over satisfying the needs of people of any other nation. This is despite the fact that the people of other nations are equal in worth to the people of our nation, which means that it is objectively no more important to satisfy the needs of our nation's people than to satisfy those of other nations' people.

Which one of the following principles, if valid, most helps to reconcile the apparent conflict among the prime minister's claims?

(A) A nation's government should not attempt to satisfy the needs of a group of people unless the satisfaction of those people's needs is objectively more important than that of any other group's needs.

(B) A nation's government should give priority to satisfying the needs of its own people over satisfying the needs of another nation's people only if its own people are more worthy than the other nation's people.

(C) The priority a nation's government should place on satisfying the needs of a group of people depends mainly on how objectively important it is for the needs of those people to be satisfied.

(D) When the people of two nations are equally worthy, the needs of the people of each of those nations should be satisfied primarily by the people's own governments.

(E) A nation's government should give priority to the satisfaction of the needs of a group of people if, but only if, there is no other way for that group's needs to be satisfied.

13. Mayor: To keep our neighborhoods clean, every street in town will be swept at least once a month. If a neighborhood needs more frequent sweepings, due to excessive dirt from major construction for example, that neighborhood will be qualified for interim sweepings. All requests for interim sweepings from qualified neighborhoods will be satisfied immediately.

If all of the mayor's statements are true, then which one of the following must also be true?

(A) All neighborhoods in which construction is under way are qualified neighborhoods.

(B) All qualified neighborhoods will get their streets swept more than once a month.

(C) No street will be swept more than once a month unless it is located in a qualified neighborhood.

(D) A qualified neighborhood that requests an interim sweeping will have its streets swept more than once a month.

(E) No street in an unqualified neighborhood will be swept more than once a month even if the neighborhood requests it.

14. Journalist: It is unethical for journalists to lie—to say something untrue with the purpose of deceiving the listener—to get a story. However, journalists commonly withhold relevant information in interviews in order to elicit new information. Some argue that this, like lying, is intentional deception and therefore unethical. However, this argument fails to recognize the distinction between failing to prevent a false belief and actively encouraging one. Lying is unethical because it actively encourages a false belief.

The journalist argues by

(A) pointing out a difference between the two cases being compared in order to show that a conclusion based on their similarities should not be drawn

(B) defending what the journalist considers a controversial distinction by offering an example of a clear instance of it

(C) defining a concept and then showing that under this definition the concept applies to all of the cases under discussion

(D) appealing to a counterexample to undermine an ethical principle that supports an argument the journalist is trying to refute

(E) clarifying and defending a moral principle by comparing a case in which it applies to one in which it does not apply

15. Economist: Many of my colleagues are arguing that interest rates should be further lowered in order to stimulate economic growth. However, no such stimulation is needed: the economy is already growing at a sustainable rate. So, currently there is no reason to lower interest rates further.

The reasoning in the economist's argument is questionable in that the argument

(A) relies solely on the testimony of experts

(B) confuses economic growth with what stimulates it

(C) presumes that a need to stimulate economic growth is the only possible reason to lower interest rates now

(D) takes what is merely one way of stimulating economic growth to be the only way of stimulating economic growth

(E) concludes that a further reduction of interest rates would lead to unsustainable economic growth merely from the fact that the economy is already growing at a sustainable rate

GO ON TO THE NEXT PAGE.

16. Most commentators on Baroque painting consider Caravaggio an early practitioner of that style, believing that his realism and novel use of the interplay of light and shadow broke sharply with current styles of Caravaggio's time and significantly influenced seventeenth-century Baroque painting. One must therefore either abandon the opinion of this majority of commentators or reject Mather's definition of Baroque painting, which says that for any painting to be considered Baroque, it must display opulence, heroic sweep, and extravagance.

The conclusion of the argument can be properly drawn if which one of the following is assumed?

(A) Paintings that belong to a single historical period typically share many of the same stylistic features.

(B) A painter who makes use of the interplay of light and shadow need not for that reason be considered a nonrealistic painter.

(C) Realism was not widely used by painters prior to the seventeenth century.

(D) A realistic painting usually does not depict the world as opulent, heroic, or extravagant.

(E) Opulence, heroic sweep, and extravagance are not present in Caravaggio's paintings.

17. Under the legal doctrine of jury nullification, a jury may legitimately acquit a defendant it believes violated a law if the jury believes that law to be unjust. Proponents argue that this practice is legitimate because it helps shield against injustice. But the doctrine relies excessively on jurors' objectivity. When juries are empowered to acquit on grounds of their perceptions of unfairness, they too often make serious mistakes.

The argument uses which one of the following techniques in its attempt to undermine the position that it attributes to the proponents of jury nullification?

(A) attacking the motives of the proponents of the doctrine

(B) identifying an inconsistency within the reasoning used to support the position

(C) attempting to show that a premise put forward in support of the position is false

(D) presenting a purported counterexample to a general claim made by the doctrine's proponents

(E) arguing that the application of the doctrine has undesirable consequences

18. Pharmacist: A large study of people aged 65–81 and suffering from insomnia showed that most of insomnia's symptoms are substantially alleviated by ingesting melatonin, a hormone produced by the pineal gland, which plays a role in the regulation of the body's biological clock. Thus, the recent claims made by manufacturers of melatonin supplements that the pineal gland produces less melatonin as it ages are evidently correct.

The pharmacist's argument is flawed in that it

(A) infers from the effect of an action that the action is intended to produce that effect

(B) relies on the opinions of individuals who are likely to be biased

(C) depends on using two different meanings for the same term to draw its conclusion

(D) confuses an effect of a phenomenon with its cause

(E) relies on a sample that is unrepresentative

GO ON TO THE NEXT PAGE.

19. The recent concert was probably not properly promoted. Wells, who is quite knowledgeable about the concert business, was certain that it would sell out unless it was poorly promoted. But the concert did not sell out.

The pattern of reasoning in which one of the following is most similar to that in the argument above?

(A)   Dr. Smith, a well-trained cardiologist, said the patient would probably survive the heart transplant if it were performed by a highly skilled surgeon. Thus, since the patient did not survive the surgery, it probably was not properly performed.

(B)   Professor Willis, who is quite knowledgeable about organic chemistry, said that the sample probably did not contain any organic compounds. So, the sample probably is not labeled correctly, for if it were, it would contain organic compounds.

(C)   My neighbor, who is an experienced home renovator, said the damage to the wall would not be noticeable if it were properly repaired. Thus, the repair to the wall probably was not properly done, since one can still notice the damage.

(D)   The builder said that the school's roof would not require repairs for years, unless it is damaged in a storm. The roof is already leaking. Thus, since there have been no major storms, the builder was probably wrong.

(E)   Professor Yanakita, who is an expert on the subject, said that the tests would find lead in the soil if they were properly conducted. So, since the tests did find lead in the soil, they probably were properly conducted.

20. Economist: Global recessions can never be prevented, for they could be prevented only if they were predictable. Yet economists, using the best techniques at their disposal, consistently fail to accurately predict global recessions.

The economist's argument is most vulnerable to the criticism that it

(A)   presupposes in a premise the conclusion that it purports to establish

(B)   fails to establish that economists claim to be able to accurately predict global recessions

(C)   treats the predictability of an event, which is required for the event to be preventable, as a characteristic that assures its prevention

(D)   fails to address the possibility that the techniques available to economists for the prediction of global recessions will significantly improve

(E)   implicitly bases an inference that something will not occur solely on the information that its occurrence is not predictable

21. Letter to the editor: When your newspaper reported the (admittedly extraordinary) claim by Mr. Hanlon that he saw an alien spaceship, the tone of your article was very skeptical despite the fact that Hanlon has over the years proved to be a trusted member of the community. If Hanlon claimed to have observed a rare natural phenomenon like a large meteor, your article would not have been skeptical. So your newspaper exhibits an unjustified bias.

The argument in the letter conflicts with which one of the following principles?

(A)   If a claim is extraordinary, it should not be presented uncritically unless it is backed by evidence of an extraordinarily high standard.

(B)   One should be skeptical of claims that are based upon testimonial evidence that is acquired only through an intermediary source.

(C)   If a media outlet has trusted a source in the past and the source has a good reputation, the outlet should continue to trust that source.

(D)   People who think they observe supernatural phenomena should not publicize that fact unless they can present corroborating evidence.

(E)   A newspaper should not publish a report unless it is confirmed by an independent source.

22. Fish with teeth specialized for scraping algae occur in both Flower Lake and Blue Lake. Some biologists argue that because such specialized characteristics are rare, fish species that have them should be expected to be closely related. If they are closely related, then the algae-scraping specialization evolved only once. But genetic tests show that the two algae-scraping species, although possibly related, are not closely related. Thus, the algae-scraping specialization evolved more than once.

The reasoning in the argument is flawed in that it

(A)   infers a cause merely from a correlation

(B)   infers that just because the evidence for a particular claim has not yet been confirmed, that claim is false

(C)   takes a sufficient condition as a necessary one

(D)   infers merely because something was likely to occur that it did occur

(E)   appeals to the authority of biologists who may not be representative of all biologists with expertise in the relevant area

GO ON TO THE NEXT PAGE.

23. The constitution of Country F requires that whenever the government sells a state-owned entity, it must sell that entity for the highest price it can command on the open market. The constitution also requires that whenever the government sells a state-owned entity, it must ensure that citizens of Country F will have majority ownership of the resulting company for at least one year after the sale.

The government of Country F must violate at least one of the constitutional requirements described above if it is faced with which one of the following situations?

(A) The government will sell StateAir, a state-owned airline. The highest bid received was from a corporation that was owned entirely by citizens of Country F when the bid was received. Shortly after the bid was received, however, noncitizens purchased a minority share in the corporation.

(B) The government has agreed to sell National Silver, a state-owned mine, to a corporation. Although citizens of Country F have majority ownership of the corporation, most of the corporation's operations and sales take place in other countries.

(C) The government will sell PetroNat, a state-owned oil company. World Oil Company has made one of the highest offers for PetroNat, but World Oil's ownership structure is so complex that the government cannot determine whether citizens of Country F have majority ownership.

(D) The government will sell National Telephone, a state-owned utility. The highest bid received was from a company in which citizens of Country F have majority ownership but noncitizens own a minority share. However, the second-highest bid, from a consortium of investors all of whom are citizens of Country F, was almost as high as the highest bid.

(E) The government will sell StateRail, a state-owned railway. The government must place significant restrictions on who can purchase StateRail to ensure that citizens of Country F will gain majority ownership. However, any such restrictions will reduce the price the government receives for StateRail.

24. The makers of Activite, a natural dietary supplement, claim that it promotes energy and mental alertness. To back up their claim, they offer a month's supply of Activite free to new customers. Clearly, Activite must be effective, since otherwise it would not be in the company's interest to make such an offer.

Which one of the following, if true, most weakens the argument?

(A) The nutrients in Activite can all be obtained from a sufficiently varied and well-balanced diet.

(B) There are less expensive dietary supplements on the market that are just as effective as Activite.

(C) A month is not a sufficient length of time for most dietary supplements to be fully effective.

(D) The makers of Activite charge a handling fee that is considerably more than what it costs them to pack and ship their product.

(E) The mere fact that a dietary supplement contains only natural ingredients does not insure that it has no harmful side effects.

GO ON TO THE NEXT PAGE.

25. Of the citizens who disapprove of the prime minister's overall job performance, most disapprove because of the prime minister's support for increasing the income tax. However, Theresa believes that the income tax should be increased. So Theresa probably approves of the prime minister's overall job performance.

Which one of the following arguments exhibits flawed reasoning that is most parallel to that in the argument above?

(A) Of the people who support allowing limited logging in the Grizzly National Forest, most support it because they think it will reduce the risk of fire in the forest. Andy thinks that limited logging will not reduce the risk of fire in the forest, so he probably opposes allowing limited logging there.

(B) Of the people who expect the population in the area to increase over the next ten years, most think that an expected population increase is a good reason to build a new school. Bonita does not expect the population to increase over the next ten years, so she probably does not favor building a new school.

(C) Of the people who believe that the overall economy has improved, most believe it because they believe that their own financial situation has improved. Chung believes that the economy has worsened, so he probably believes that his own financial situation has worsened.

(D) Of the people who oppose funding a study to determine the feasibility of building a light rail line in the Loffoch Valley, most also believe that the Valley Freeway should be built. Donna opposes increasing funding for a study, so she probably supports building the Valley Freeway.

(E) Of the people who believe that there will be a blizzard tomorrow, most believe it because of the weather report on the Channel 9 news. Eduardo believes that there will be a blizzard tomorrow, so he probably saw the weather report on the Channel 9 news.

26. Bird watcher: The decrease in the mourning-dove population in this area is probably a result of the loss of nesting habitat. Many mourning doves had formerly nested in the nearby orchards, but after overhead sprinklers were installed in the orchards last year, the doves ceased building nests there.

Which one of the following, if true, most strengthens the argument?

(A) Mourning doves were recently designated a migratory game species, meaning that they can be legally hunted.

(B) The trees in the nearby orchards were the only type of trees in the area attractive to nesting mourning doves.

(C) Blue jays that had nested in the orchards also ceased doing so after the sprinklers were installed.

(D) Many residents of the area fill their bird feeders with canola or wheat, which are appropriate seeds for attracting mourning doves.

(E) Mourning doves often nest in fruit trees.

S T O P

IF YOU FINISH BEFORE TIME IS CALLED, YOU MAY CHECK YOUR WORK ON THIS SECTION ONLY.
DO NOT WORK ON ANY OTHER SECTION IN THE TEST.

Acknowledgment is made to the following sources from which material has been adapted for use in this test booklet:

Michael S. Gazzaniga and Megan S. Steven, "Neuroscience and the Law." ©2007 by Scientific American, Inc.
http://www.sciammind.com/article.cfm?articleID=00053249-43D1-123A-822283414B7F4945.

Jeffrey Rosen, "The Brain on the Stand." ©2007 by The New York Times Company.
http://www.nytimes.com/2007/03/11/magazine/11Neurolaw.t.html?_r=2&oref=slogin&oref=slogin.

Angus Trumble, "Smelly Masterpieces." ©2008 by Times Newspapers Ltd.

Kipling D. Williams, Martin J. Bourgeois, and Robert T. Croyle, "The Effects of Stealing Thunder in Criminal and Civil Trials." ©1993 by Plenum Publishing Corporation.

Topic Code	Print Your Full Name Here		
126351	Last	First	M.I.

Date	Sign Your Name Here
/ /	

LSAC®

Scratch Paper
Do not write your essay in this space.

LSAT® Writing Sample Topic

> <u>Directions</u>: The scenario presented below describes two choices, either one of which can be supported on the basis of the information given. Your essay should consider both choices and argue for one over the other, based on the two specified criteria and the facts provided. There is no "right" or "wrong" choice: a reasonable argument can be made for either.

A brother and sister, Hector and Teresa, are deciding whether to spend the upcoming summer recording music and playing in cafes and bars together, or to continue in the summer along their original career paths. Using the facts below, write an essay in which you argue for one option over the other based on the following two criteria:

- They want the risks they take in their lives to reflect the potential rewards.
- They want to be responsible with respect to their educational preparation and the choices they have already made.

Hector and Teresa each have extensive musical training. They are talented enough that if they spend the summer on music, there is a good chance that they will become popular enough to get steady work performing and selling albums. It is unlikely that they will have another occasion to spend so much time together. Spending the summer on music could allow them to develop their sibling relationship, which has not been very close because of their five-year age difference. Spending so much time together could reveal personality clashes.

Teresa is pursuing her PhD in economics. She completed all the coursework and general examinations four years ago. Spending the summer on music might delay finishing her dissertation. This could further jeopardize her job prospects in a field where the opportunities have been diminishing. Hector has been working in a medical laboratory since receiving his undergraduate degree five years ago. To advance in his field, he is scheduled to begin a difficult master's program in biochemistry early in the fall. Hector and Teresa each might have to go into debt as a consequence of spending the summer on music.

WP-V1

Scratch Paper
Do not write your essay in this space.

COMPUTING YOUR SCORE

Directions:

1. Use the Answer Key on the next page to check your answers.

2. Use the Scoring Worksheet below to compute your raw score.

3. Use the Score Conversion Chart to convert your raw score into the 120–180 scale.

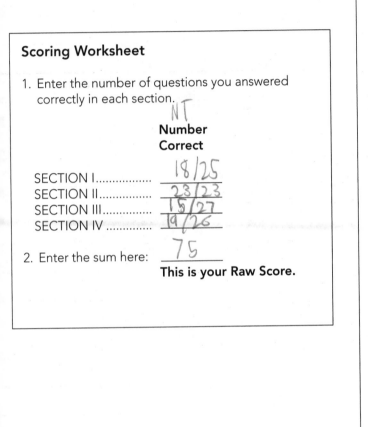

Scoring Worksheet

1. Enter the number of questions you answered correctly in each section.

   Number Correct

   SECTION I................. 18/25
   SECTION II................ 23/23
   SECTION III.............. 15/27
   SECTION IV 19/26

2. Enter the sum here: 75

   This is your Raw Score.

Conversion Chart
For Converting Raw Score to the 120–180 LSAT Scaled Score
LSAT Form 4LSN111

Reported Score	Raw Score Lowest	Raw Score Highest
180	99	101
179	98	98
178	97	97
177	96	96
176	95	95
175	*	*
174	94	94
173	93	93
172	92	92
171	90	91
170	89	89
169	88	88
168	86	87
167	85	85
166	84	84
165	82	83
164	80	81
163	79	79
162	77	78
161	75	76
160	74	74
159	72	73
158	70	71
157	68	69
156	67	67
155	65	66
154	63	64
153	61	62
152	59	60
151	58	58
150	56	57
149	54	55
148	53	53
147	51	52
146	49	50
145	48	48
144	46	47
143	44	45
142	43	43
141	41	42
140	40	40
139	38	39
138	36	37
137	35	35
136	33	34
135	32	32
134	31	31
133	29	30
132	28	28
131	27	27
130	25	26
129	24	24
128	23	23
127	22	22
126	21	21
125	20	20
124	19	19
123	18	18
122	17	17
121	16	16
120	0	15

*There is no raw score that will produce this scaled score for this form.

ANSWER KEY

SECTION I

1.	C	8.	A	15.	E	22.	E
2.	C	9.	E	16.	D	23.	D
3.	B	10.	E	17.	A	24.	B
4.	C	11.	D	18.	A	25.	D
5.	C	12.	E	19.	A		
6.	A	13.	A	20.	E		
7.	E	14.	D	21.	B		

SECTION II

1.	C	8.	E	15.	B	22.	B
2.	D	9.	A	16.	A	23.	C
3.	E	10.	A	17.	E		
4.	A	11.	A	18.	D		
5.	E	12.	C	19.	B		
6.	E	13.	E	20.	B		
7.	B	14.	D	21.	A		

SECTION III

1.	D	8.	D	15.	A	22.	E
2.	E	9.	C	16.	D	23.	A
3.	A	10.	B	17.	B	24.	B
4.	A	11.	D	18.	A	25.	B
5.	B	12.	A	19.	B	26.	D
6.	B	13.	D	20.	C	27.	E
7.	B	14.	E	21.	C		

SECTION IV

1.	B	8.	B	15.	C	22.	C
2.	C	9.	B	16.	E	23.	E
3.	E	10.	C	17.	E	24.	D
4.	D	11.	A	18.	E	25.	A
5.	D	12.	D	19.	C	26.	B
6.	B	13.	D	20.	D		
7.	A	14.	A	21.	A		

THE OFFICIAL LSAT
PREPTEST®

75

- PrepTest 75
- Form 6LSN117

JUNE 2015

SECTION I

Time—35 minutes

25 Questions

Directions: The questions in this section are based on the reasoning contained in brief statements or passages. For some questions, more than one of the choices could conceivably answer the question. However, you are to choose the best answer; that is, the response that most accurately and completely answers the question. You should not make assumptions that are by commonsense standards implausible, superfluous, or incompatible with the passage. After you have chosen the best answer, blacken the corresponding space on your answer sheet.

1. Pundit: Our city made a mistake when it sold a private company the rights to assess and collect parking fees. The private company raised parking fees and so has been able to reap profits far greater than what it paid for the rights to assess and collect the fees. If the city had not sold the rights, then that money would have gone to the city.

   The pundit's argument requires the assumption that

   (A)   other private companies would have been willing to pay for the rights to assess and collect parking fees
   (B)   the city could have raised parking fees had it not sold the rights
   (C)   municipal functions like assessing and collecting parking fees should always be handled directly by the municipality in question
   (D)   the revenue from parking fees is not the only factor that cities need to consider in setting the rates for parking fees
   (E)   private companies assess and collect parking fees more efficiently than cities do

2. Popular science publications that explain new developments in science face a dilemma. In order to reach a wide audience, these publications must rely heavily on metaphorical writing, which usually fails to convey the science accurately. If the writing is more rigorous, they get the science right but fail to reach a wide audience. These publications should therefore give up trying to explain new developments in science to a wide audience.

   Which one of the following principles, if valid, most helps to justify the reasoning in the argument?

   (A)   Science publications should balance the use of metaphors with more rigorous writing.
   (B)   The more recent a scientific development is, the harder it is to explain it accurately to a wide audience.
   (C)   In reporting scientific developments, it is better to fail to reach a wide audience than to be inaccurate.
   (D)   In reporting scientific developments, it is better to reach a wide audience than to be accurate.
   (E)   Even the most rigorous explanations of some scientific concepts must still contain metaphors.

GO ON TO THE NEXT PAGE.

3. Critic: Rock music is musically bankrupt and socially destructive, but at least the album covers of rock LPs from the 1960s and 1970s often featured innovative visual art. But now, since the success of digital music has almost ended the production of LPs, rock music has nothing going for it.

Which one of the following is an assumption on which the critic's argument relies?

(A) Digital music is not distributed with accompanying innovative visual art.
(B) Although very few LPs are produced today, most of these are rock LPs.
(C) In the 1960s and 1970s, only rock LPs featured innovative album cover art.
(D) The LPs being produced today have innovative album cover art.
(E) Rock music is less sophisticated musically and more destructive socially now than it was in the 1960s and 1970s.

4. Scientist: In testing whether a baby's babbling is a linguistic task or just random sounds, researchers videotaped the mouths of babies as they babbled. They discovered that babbling babies open the right sides of their mouths wider than the left. Past studies have established that during nonlinguistic vocalizations people generally open the left side of the mouth wider. So babbling turns out to be a linguistic task.

Which one of the following most accurately describes how the scientist's argument proceeds?

(A) It describes an argument for a given conclusion and presents a counterargument to suggest that its conclusion is incorrect.
(B) It questions the adequacy of a generally accepted principle by providing evidence to undermine that principle, and offers a different principle in its place.
(C) It raises a question, describes a potential experimental test, and argues that the test is necessary to answer the question.
(D) It describes an explanation for some facts, counters assertions that the explanation is unlikely to be correct, and concludes that it is correct after all.
(E) It presents two possible interpretations of a phenomenon and provides evidence in support of one interpretation and against the other.

5. Environment minister: Because of our concern about global warming, this country has committed itself to reducing its emissions of carbon dioxide substantially over the next ten years. Since trees absorb carbon dioxide, planting large numbers of trees will help us fulfill our commitment.

Which one of the following, if true, would most weaken the environment minister's argument?

(A) Owners of large tracts of private land are usually unwilling to plant trees unless they are given a financial incentive for doing so.
(B) Over the last ten years the proportion of land that is deforested annually has not increased as much as has the proportion of carbon dioxide in the atmosphere.
(C) When ground is disturbed in the course of planting trees, more carbon dioxide is released into the atmosphere by rotting organic matter in the soil than the new trees will absorb in ten years.
(D) Many climate researchers believe that global warming is such an urgent problem that carbon dioxide emissions should be substantially reduced in less than ten years.
(E) Gases other than carbon dioxide contribute to global warming, and trees do not absorb any of these other gases.

6. Sport utility vehicles (SUVs) are, because of their weight, extremely expensive to operate but, for the same reason, in an accident they are safer for their occupants than smaller vehicles are. Nonetheless, an analysis of recent traffic fatality statistics has led auto safety experts to conclude that the increasing popularity of SUVs is an alarming trend.

Which one of the following, if true, most helps to account for the response of auto safety experts to the popularity of SUVs?

(A) Vehicles with a reputation for being safer than others tend to be driven more carefully than other vehicles.
(B) Vehicles with a high average fuel consumption have fuel tanks with larger capacities.
(C) Recent statistics suggest that large vehicles such as SUVs tend to carry more passengers than smaller vehicles do.
(D) Recent statistics suggest that the average number of fatalities in collisions between SUVs and smaller vehicles is higher than for other collisions.
(E) Recent statistics suggest that SUVs are as likely to be involved in collisions as smaller vehicles are.

7. Political advertisement: Sherwood campaigns as an opponent of higher taxes. But is anybody fooled? For the last 10 years, while Sherwood served on the city council, the council consistently increased taxes year after year. Break the cycle of higher and higher taxes: reject Sherwood's bid for reelection to city council.

The argument in the political advertisement is most vulnerable to criticism on the grounds that it

(A) bases a crucial generalization on a very limited sample

(B) fails to consider the possibility that something that is unavoidable might nonetheless be undesirable

(C) mistakes something that is sufficient to bring about a result for something that is necessary to bring about that result

(D) makes a personal attack on someone who holds a certain view rather than addressing the reasonableness of that view

(E) takes for granted that a characteristic of a group as a whole is shared by an individual member of that group

8. Client: The owners of the catering company we use decided to raise their rates. They argued that the increase was necessary to allow them to hire and train new staff to accommodate their expanding client base. They should reconsider that decision and not raise their rates. After all, the mission of the company is to provide low-cost gourmet catering, and this mission will be jeopardized if they raise rates.

Which one of the following most accurately expresses the main conclusion of the client's argument?

(A) The owners of the catering company decided to raise their rates.

(B) The catering company needs to increase its rates to accommodate its expanding client base.

(C) The catering company's rates should not be raised.

(D) The catering company's mission is to provide low-cost gourmet catering.

(E) The catering company's mission will be jeopardized if its rates are increased.

9. Red admiral butterflies fly in a highly irregular fashion, constantly varying their speed, wing strokes, and flight path. While predators avoid poisonous butterfly species, nonpoisonous butterflies like the red admiral need to elude predators to survive. Scientists therefore hypothesize that the red admiral's flight style, which is clearly not energy efficient, evolved as a means of avoiding predators.

Which one of the following, if true, most strengthens the support for the scientists' hypothesis?

(A) No species of poisonous butterfly has an irregular flight style like that of the red admiral.

(B) Attacks from predators are not the most common cause of death for butterflies.

(C) Many other types of butterfly have flight styles similar to that of the red admiral.

(D) It is much more energy efficient for butterflies to fly in an irregular fashion than it is for heavier varieties of insects.

(E) All of the predators that prey on the red admiral also prey on other species of nonpoisonous butterflies.

10. Copyright statutes benefit society by providing incentive to produce original works, so some kind of copyright statute is ultimately justified. But these statutes also represent a significant cost to society because they create protected monopolies. In many countries, copyright statutes grant copyright protection for the life of the author plus several decades. This is too long, since the societal benefit from the additional years of copyright is more than offset by the societal cost.

Which one of the following principles, if valid, most strongly supports the reasoning in the argument?

(A) A statute should be written in a way that eliminates any appearance of its being inconsistent in its aims.

(B) A statute should be repealed if the conditions that originally justified enacting the statute no longer hold true.

(C) A statute that is justified in one country is justified in every country.

(D) A statute should not limit rights unless it can be shown that it thereby enhances other rights.

(E) If a statute is to be justified by its benefit to society, it should be designed so that its societal benefit always exceeds its societal cost.

GO ON TO THE NEXT PAGE.

11. Police chief: During my tenure as chief, crime in this city has fallen by 20 percent. This is clearly the result of my policing strategy, which uses real-time crime data and focuses police resources on the areas with the most crime.

Which one of the following, if true, most calls into question the police chief's explanation for the drop in crime?

(A) The crime rate in the police chief's city is still significantly higher than in many other cities.

(B) The crime rate in the police chief's city is higher now than it was several decades before the chief's tenure began.

(C) The crime rate in the police chief's city fell significantly during the first few years of the chief's tenure, then it leveled off.

(D) The crime rate in the country as a whole fell by about 30 percent during the police chief's tenure.

(E) The variation in crime rates between different areas of the city is smaller in the police chief's city than in many other cities.

12. Commentator: The Duke of Acredia argued long ago that only virtuous Acredian rulers concerned with the well-being of the people will be able to rule successfully. Since then, when Acredian governments have fallen, their falls have always been during the rule of one who viciously disregards the people's needs. The Duke, then, was right about at least one thing: Concern for the welfare of the people is necessary for the successful governance of Acredia.

The reasoning in the commentator's argument is most vulnerable to criticism on the grounds that the argument

(A) ignores the possibility that the conditions that are necessary for the welfare of the people are likely to change over time

(B) infers the necessity of a certain condition for success from the fact that its absence has always led to failure

(C) appeals to evidence from sources that are likely to be in some way biased or unreliable

(D) infers that a certain condition is required for success from the fact that the lack of that condition is associated with failure

(E) presumes, without providing justification, that the character of past rulers can be assessed in some completely objective way

13. Dr. Khan: Professor Burns recognizes that recent observations fail to confirm earlier ones that apparently showed a comet reservoir far out in our solar system. She claims this nonconfirmation is enough to show that the earlier observations are incorrect. But the recent observations occurred under poor conditions.

Which one of the following is most supported by Dr. Khan's statements?

(A) If the recent observations had been made under good conditions, they would have provided conclusive evidence of a comet reservoir far out in our solar system.

(B) Contrary to Professor Burns's view, the recent observations confirm the earlier ones.

(C) Professor Burns's claim about the implications of the recent observations is incorrect.

(D) The recent observations, even if they had been made under good conditions, would not have been enough to suggest that the earlier ones are incorrect.

(E) The poor conditions present during recent observations render them worthless.

14. If people refrained from being impolite to one another the condition of society would be greatly improved. But society would not be better off if the government enacted laws requiring people to be polite to each other. Enforcing such laws would create even more problems than does impoliteness.

Which one of the following most accurately describes the role played in the argument by the claim that society would not be better off if the government enacted laws requiring people to be polite to each other?

(A) It is the conclusion drawn by the argument as a whole.

(B) It is cited as evidence for the generalization that is the argument's overall conclusion.

(C) It is cited as evidence for the assertion used to support the argument's overall conclusion.

(D) It is cited as an illustration of a generalization that serves as the main premise of the argument.

(E) It describes a phenomenon that the conclusion of the argument purports to explain.

GO ON TO THE NEXT PAGE.

15. Astronomer: In most cases in which a planet has been detected orbiting a distant star, the planet's orbit is distinctly oval, whereas the orbits of Earth and several other planets around our sun are approximately circular. However, many comets orbiting our sun have been thrown into oval orbits by close encounters with planets orbiting our sun. So some of the planets in oval orbits around distant stars were probably thrown into those orbits by close encounters with other planets orbiting the same stars.

Which one of the following, if true, would most strengthen the astronomer's argument?

(A) When two planets or other large objects in orbit have a close encounter, usually the smaller of the two is the more greatly affected.

(B) There is no indication that the orbit of any planet orbiting our sun has been affected by a close encounter with another planet orbiting our sun.

(C) In most cases in which planets have been discovered orbiting a distant star, more than one planet has been found orbiting the star.

(D) Most comets with an oval orbit around our sun were thrown into that orbit by a close encounter with some other object.

(E) For each distant star that has been found to have a planet, no other object large enough to affect the planet's orbit has been found orbiting the star.

16. It is possible to grow agricultural crops that can thrive when irrigated with seawater. Such farming, if undertaken near oceans, would actually be cheaper than most other irrigated agriculture, since the water would not have to be pumped far. The greatest expense in irrigated agriculture is in pumping the water, and the pumping costs increase with the distance the water is pumped.

Which one of the following most accurately describes the role played in the argument by the claim that the greatest expense in irrigated agriculture is in pumping the water?

(A) It is a claim that the argument shows to be false.

(B) It is a hypothesis that, if proven, would undermine the argument's conclusion.

(C) It is evidence provided to support the argument's conclusion.

(D) It is the argument's conclusion.

(E) It is a claim for which the argument provides evidence, but which is not the argument's conclusion.

17. Critics worry that pessimistic news reports about the economy harm it by causing people to lose confidence in the economy, of which everyone has direct experience every day. Journalists respond that to do their jobs well they cannot worry about the effects of their work. Also, studies show that people do not defer to journalists except on matters of which they have no direct experience.

The statements above, if true, most strongly support which one of the following?

(A) Critics who think that the economy is affected by the extent of people's confidence in it are wrong.

(B) Pessimistic news reports about such matters as foreign policy, of which people do not have experience every day, are likely to have a negative impact.

(C) Pessimistic news reports about the state of the economy are likely to harm the economy.

(D) News reports about the economy are unlikely to have a significant effect on people's opinions about the state of the economy.

(E) Journalists need not be deeply concerned about their reporting's effects on the well-being of the average citizen.

18. Police captain: The chief of police has indicated that gifts of cash or objects valued at more than $100 count as graft. However, I know with certainty that no officer in my precinct has ever taken such gifts, so the recent accusations of graft in my precinct are unfounded.

The reasoning in the police captain's argument is most vulnerable to criticism on the grounds that the argument

(A) bases a rebuttal of accusations of graft on knowledge about only a limited sample of officers

(B) fails to consider that there may be other instances of graft besides those indicated by the chief of police

(C) bases a claim about the actions of individuals on an appeal to the character of those individuals

(D) takes for granted that if the accusations of graft are unfounded, so is any accusation of corruption

(E) relies on a premise that contradicts the conclusion drawn in the argument

GO ON TO THE NEXT PAGE.

19. Economist: Although average hourly wages vary considerably between different regions of this country, in each region, the average hourly wage for full-time jobs increased last year. Paradoxically, however, in the country as a whole, the average hourly wage for full-time jobs decreased last year.

Which one of the following, if true of the economist's country, most helps to resolve the apparent paradox in the economist's statements?

(A) In the country as a whole, the average hourly wage for full-time jobs has decreased slightly for each of the last three years.

(B) Last year, to reduce costs, employers moved many full-time jobs from regions with relatively high hourly wages to regions where those jobs typically pay much less.

(C) The year before last, the unemployment rate reached a ten-year low; last year, however, the unemployment rate increased slightly.

(D) Last year, the rate at which the average hourly wage for full-time jobs increased varied considerably between different regions of the country.

(E) Last year, hourly wages for most full-time jobs in the manufacturing sector declined while those for most full-time jobs in the service sector increased.

20. Researchers compared the brains of recently deceased people who had schizophrenia with those of recently deceased people who did not have schizophrenia. They found that 35 percent of the former and none of the latter showed evidence of damage to a structure of nerve cells called the subplate. They knew that this damage must have occurred prior to the second fetal trimester, when the subplate controls the development of the connections between the different parts of the brain.

Which one of the following conclusions is most strongly supported by the information above?

(A) Roughly 35 percent of people with abnormal brain subplates will eventually have schizophrenia.

(B) A promising treatment in some cases of schizophrenia is repair of the damaged connections between the different parts of the brain.

(C) Some people developed schizophrenia because of damage to the brain subplate after the second fetal trimester.

(D) Schizophrenia is determined by genetic factors.

(E) There may be a cause of schizophrenia that predates birth.

21. A new device uses the global positioning system to determine a cow's location and, when a cow strays outside of its pasture, makes noises in the cow's ears to steer it back to its home range. Outfitting all of the cattle in a herd with this device is far more expensive than other means of keeping cattle in their pastures, such as fences. The device's maker nevertheless predicts that ranchers will purchase the device at its current price.

Which one of the following, if true, does the most to support the prediction made by the device's maker?

(A) The price of the device will come down appreciably if the device's maker is able to produce it in large quantities.

(B) As they graze, cattle in a herd follow the lead of the same few members of the herd.

(C) The device has been shown not to cause significant stress to cattle.

(D) The device has been shown to be as effective as fences at keeping cattle in their pastures.

(E) The device's maker offers significant discounts to purchasers who buy in bulk.

GO ON TO THE NEXT PAGE.

22. Food co-ops are a type of consumer cooperative. Consumer cooperatives offer the same products as other stores but usually more cheaply. It is therefore more economical to shop at a food co-op than at a supermarket.

Which one of the following is most appropriate as an analogy demonstrating that the reasoning in the argument above is flawed?

(A) By that line of reasoning, we could conclude that people who own sports cars use much more gasoline in their cars than people who own other types of cars, since sports cars use more gasoline per mile than most other cars.

(B) By that line of reasoning, we could conclude that it is better to buy frozen vegetables than fresh vegetables, since fresh vegetables are more expensive than frozen vegetables and spoil more quickly.

(C) By that line of reasoning, we could conclude that a person who rides a bicycle causes more pollution per mile traveled than one who rides a public bus, since bicycling is a private means of transportation and private means of transportation tend to generate more pollution per mile traveled than do public means.

(D) By that line of reasoning, we could conclude that more people must be shopping at health food stores than ever before, since people tend to choose healthful food over unhealthful food as long as the healthful food tastes at least as good, and healthful food today is better tasting than ever.

(E) By that line of reasoning, we could conclude that the best way to lose weight is to increase one's consumption of artificially sweetened foods, since artificially sweetened foods have fewer calories than foods sweetened with sugar, and excessive calorie intake contributes to weight gain.

23. Editorial: The gates at most railroad crossings, while they give clear warning of oncoming trains, are not large enough to prevent automobile drivers from going around them onto the tracks. Some people claim that the ensuing accidents are partly the fault of the railroad company, but this is a mistake. Granted, if one has a small child in the house, then one ought to block access to stairs completely; but a licensed driver is a capable adult who should know better.

The editorial's conclusion follows logically if which one of the following is assumed?

(A) The gates could be made larger, yet irresponsible drivers might still be able to go around them onto the tracks.

(B) Capable adults have a responsibility to take some measures to ensure their own safety.

(C) When the warnings of companies are disregarded by capable adults, the adults are fully responsible for any resulting accidents.

(D) Small children are not involved in accidents resulting from drivers going around the gates.

(E) Any company's responsibility to promote public safety is not unlimited.

GO ON TO THE NEXT PAGE.

24. Researcher: People who participate in opinion surveys often give answers they believe the opinion surveyor expects to hear, and it is for this reason that some opinion surveys do not reflect the actual views of those being surveyed. However, in well-constructed surveys, the questions are worded so as to provide respondents with no indication of which answers the surveyor might expect. So if a survey is well constructed, survey respondents' desire to meet surveyors' expectations has no effect on the survey's results.

The reasoning in the researcher's argument is questionable in that the argument overlooks the possibility that

(A) an opinion survey that disguises the surveyor's expectations may be flawed in a number of ways, some of which have nothing to do with the surveyor's expectations

(B) when people who respond to opinion surveys hold strong opinions, their answers are unlikely to be influenced by other people's expectations

(C) many opinion surveyors have no expectations whatsoever regarding the answers of people who respond to surveys

(D) some people who know what answers an opinion surveyor expects to hear will purposefully try to thwart the surveyor's expectations

(E) the answers of opinion-survey respondents can be influenced by beliefs about the surveyor's expectations even if those beliefs are unfounded

25. The availability of television reduces the amount of reading children do. When television is made unavailable, a nearly universal increase in reading, both by parents and by children, is reported. When television is available again, the level of reading by both parents and children relapses to its previous level.

The reasoning in which one of the following is most similar to the reasoning above?

(A) Whenever the money supply in an economy fluctuates, interest rates tend to fluctuate. When the money supply remains constant, interest rates tend to remain stable. Thus, the money supply's remaining constant stabilizes interest rates.

(B) The consumption of candy between meals disrupts a child's appetite at mealtimes. When candy is not consumed, blood sugar declines until mealtime, so the child feels hungry. A child who eats healthy meals feels less desire for candy.

(C) Global warming is caused by increased carbon dioxide in the atmosphere. Furthermore, industrial pollution causes increased carbon dioxide in the atmosphere. So industrial pollution causes global warming.

(D) Voting behavior is affected by factors other than political candidates' records of political achievement. For example, a candidate who projects confidence will gain votes as a result, whereas a candidate with a supercilious facial expression will lose votes.

(E) Adults read less than they once did because there are so many other activities to divert them. This can be seen from the fact that the more time they spend on such other activities, the less they read. Conversely, the less they read, the more time they spend on such other activities.

S T O P

IF YOU FINISH BEFORE TIME IS CALLED, YOU MAY CHECK YOUR WORK ON THIS SECTION ONLY.
DO NOT WORK ON ANY OTHER SECTION IN THE TEST.

SECTION II

Time—35 minutes

27 Questions

Directions: Each set of questions in this section is based on a single passage or a pair of passages. The questions are to be answered on the basis of what is stated or implied in the passage or pair of passages. For some of the questions, more than one of the choices could conceivably answer the question. However, you are to choose the best answer; that is, the response that most accurately and completely answers the question, and blacken the corresponding space on your answer sheet.

Having spent several decades trying to eliminate the unself-conscious "colonial gaze" characteristic of so many early ethnographic films, visual anthropologists from the industrialized West who study indigenous
(5) cultures are presently struggling with an even more profound transformation of their discipline. Because inexpensive video equipment is now available throughout the world, many indigenous peoples who were once examined by the Western ethnographer's
(10) camera have begun to document their own cultures. Reaction to this phenomenon within Western anthropological circles is sharply divided.

One faction, led by anthropologist James Weiner, sees the proliferation of video and television as the
(15) final assault of Western values on indigenous cultures. Weiner argues that the spread of video represents "a devaluation of the different," culminating in the replacement of genuine historical, linguistic, social, and cultural difference with superficial difference
(20) among electronic images. He believes that video technologies inevitably purvey a Western ontology, one based on realism, immediacy, and self-expression. Thus, Weiner concludes, using video technology costs indigenous peoples the very cultural identity they seek
(25) to record. Moreover, he maintains that anthropologists who attribute a paramount truth value to these films simply because they are made by indigenous peoples are theoretically naive.

But Weiner's opponents contend that his views
(30) betray a certain nostalgia for the idea of the "noble savage." One such opponent, anthropologist Faye Ginsburg, concedes that no Western object that has entered cultural circulation since the fifteenth century has been neutral, but she considers it
(35) little more than boilerplate technological determinism to argue that using a video camera makes one unwittingly Western. Unlike Weiner, Ginsburg maintains that non-Western indigenous peoples can use Western media without adopting the conventions of Western
(40) culture. In fact, Ginsburg and many other anthropologists believe that video affords societies—especially oral ones—an invaluable opportunity to strengthen native languages and traditions threatened by Western exposure.

The Brazilian fieldwork of anthropologist
(45) Terence Turner, who studies the relationship between traditional Kayapo culture and Kayapo videotapes, lends credence to Ginsburg's position. Primarily an oral society, the Kayapo use video to document both ceremonial performances and transactions with
(50) representatives of the Brazilian government (this latter use is intended to provide legally binding records of

the transactions). In contrast to Weiner's argument that video foists a Western ontology onto its users, Turner has found that the representations of Kayapo
(55) ceremonies, including everything from the camerawork to the editing, conform to the same principle of beauty embodied in the ceremonies themselves, one rooted in a complex pattern of repetition and sequential organization. The videos aesthetically mirror the
(60) ceremonies. The camera is not so at odds with Kayapo culture, it seems, that it transforms any Kayapo who uses it into a Westerner.

1. Which one of the following most accurately and completely summarizes the passage?

(A) Some anthropologists argue that the proliferation of video technology has been harmful to indigenous peoples because it encourages the adoption of a Western ontology based on immediacy and self-expression.

(B) By making video technology available to indigenous peoples throughout the world, anthropologists have succeeded in eliminating the "colonial gaze" that many early ethnographic films exhibited.

(C) Anthropologists are divided in their assessments of the impact of video technology on indigenous peoples, but there is some evidence that video technology is compatible with the preservation of indigenous cultures.

(D) Some anthropologists argue that the proliferation of video technology has actually strengthened indigenous cultures threatened by Western influences, but the long-term impact of video technology on indigenous cultures is still unknown.

(E) The Kayapo people's use of video technology validates the position of one faction in the debate in anthropological circles regarding the effect of the proliferation of Western video technology on indigenous cultures.

GO ON TO THE NEXT PAGE.

2. Based on the passage, which one of the following most accurately describes Faye Ginsburg's stance toward the position attributed to James Weiner?

(A) fundamental rejection
(B) reluctant censure
(C) mild disapproval
(D) diplomatic neutrality
(E) supportive interest

3. Which one of the following is most analogous to the Kayapo's use of video to document ceremonial performances, as that use is described in the last paragraph?

(A) As various groups have emigrated to North America, they have brought their culinary traditions with them and thereby altered the culinary practices of North America.
(B) In the 1940s, Latin American composers incorporated African American inspired jazz instrumentation and harmonies into their music but remained faithful to the traditions of Latin American music.
(C) Some writers are predicting that the interactive nature of the Internet will fundamentally reshape fiction, and they are already producing narratives that take advantage of this capacity.
(D) In the late 1980s, some fashion designers produced lines of various articles of clothing that imitated fashions that were current in the 1920s and 1930s.
(E) Early in the twentieth century, some experimental European artists rejected the representational traditions of Western painting and began to produce works inspired by surrealist literature.

4. According to the passage, Weiner claims that an essential characteristic of Western ontology is

(A) a pattern of sequential organization
(B) paramount truth value
(C) self-expression
(D) the "colonial gaze"
(E) theoretical naivete

5. The passage provides information that is most helpful in answering which one of the following questions?

(A) Why do the Kayapo use video technology to create legal records?
(B) What is the origin of the idea of the "noble savage"?
(C) Which indigenous cultures have not yet adopted Western video technologies?
(D) Which Western technologies entered cultural circulation in the fifteenth century?
(E) What factors have made video equipment as inexpensive as it now is?

6. Terence Turner would be most likely to agree with which one of the following assessments of Weiner's position regarding the spread of video?

(A) Weiner fails to recognize the vast diversity of traditional practices among the world's indigenous peoples.
(B) Weiner overestimates the extent to which video technology has become available throughout the world.
(C) Weiner does not fully recognize the value of preserving the traditional practices of indigenous peoples.
(D) Weiner underestimates indigenous peoples' capacity for adapting the products of alien cultures to fit their own cultural values.
(E) Weiner ignores the fact that, even before the spread of video, many Western technologies had already been adapted by indigenous cultures.

7. In using the phrase "technological determinism" (line 35), the author refers to the idea that

(A) technology is exchanged in ways that appear to be predestined
(B) the technologies used by field anthropologists influence their views of the cultures they study
(C) cultures generally evolve in the direction of greater dependence on technology
(D) a culture's ethical values determine its reaction to new technologies
(E) cultures are shaped in fundamental ways by the technologies they use

GO ON TO THE NEXT PAGE.

The current approach to recusal and disqualification of judges heavily emphasizes appearance-based analysis. Professional codes of conduct for judges typically focus on the avoidance of both impropriety

(5) and the appearance of impropriety. Judges are expected to recuse (i.e., remove) themselves from any case in which their impartiality might reasonably be questioned. In some jurisdictions, statutes allow a party to a court proceeding to request disqualification of a judge for

(10) bias. In other jurisdictions, the responsibility for recusal falls upon the judge alone.

The rules provide vague guidance at best, making disqualification dependent on whether the judge's impartiality "might reasonably be questioned,"

(15) without giving any idea of whose perspective to take or how to interpret the facts. It is a mistake for rules governing judicial ethics to focus on the appearance of justice rather than on the elimination of bias that renders a judge cognitively incapable of properly

(20) reaching a just outcome because of a too-close personal involvement in the matter before the court. Focusing on appearances may cause sources of actual bias that are not apparent to outside observers, or even to judges themselves, to be overlooked.

(25) The function of the law is the settlement of normative disputes. Such settlement will work only if it is well reasoned. The achievement of actual justice by the use of legal reasoning is the primary function of judges. Therefore, the best way to address concerns

(30) about judicial impartiality is to require judges to make their reasoning transparent. Accordingly, we should eliminate disqualification motions alleging bias, whether actual or apparent. This unreliable mechanism should be replaced by the requirement of a written

(35) explanation of either the reasons for a judge's decision to recuse, or if the judge decides against recusal, the legal basis for the judgment reached, based on the merits of the case. That is, judges should not be required to explain why they did not recuse themselves,

(40) but rather they should be required to show the legal reasoning on the basis of which their ultimate judgments were made.

A potential objection is that the reasoning given by the judge, however legally adequate, may not be

(45) the judge's real reasoning, thus allowing for the presence of undetected bias. However, as long as a knowledgeable observer cannot find any fault with the legal reasoning provided, then there are no grounds for complaint. Under the law, a right of recourse arises only if harm

(50) accrues. If a judge who had no improper considerations in mind could have reached the same conclusion for the reasons stated by a judge who had hidden reasons in mind, then there is no harm on which to base a complaint.

8. According to the passage, a weakness of current rules regarding recusal and disqualification is that they

(A) interfere with judges' reasoning about the cases that they hear

(B) fail to specify whose perspective is relevant to determining apparent bias

(C) exaggerate the importance of transparency in judicial reasoning

(D) place responsibility for recusal entirely on judges

(E) ignore the importance of the appearance of propriety

9. Which one of the following most accurately expresses the primary purpose of the second paragraph?

(A) to state the author's objections to the approach described in the first paragraph

(B) to present a solution that is rejected in the third paragraph

(C) to provide concrete examples of the problems discussed in the first paragraph

(D) to explore the history that led to the situation described in the first paragraph

(E) to state the thesis to be defended in the rest of the passage

10. The author of the passage regards the legal principle that "a right of recourse arises only if harm accrues" (lines 49–50) as

(A) an established principle of law

(B) part of the definition of the function of the law

(C) a tool for judges to disguise their real reasoning

(D) unfair to parties to legal proceedings

(E) central to the current means of addressing judicial bias

GO ON TO THE NEXT PAGE.

11. It can be inferred from the passage that the author would be most likely to consider which one of the following to be a weakness of statutes that allow parties to court proceedings to request disqualification of judges for bias?

(A) The guidelines for applying such statutes are excessively rigid.

(B) Such statutes are incompatible with a requirement that judges make their reasoning transparent.

(C) Such statutes can fail to eliminate actual bias because parties to court proceedings are not always aware of judges' prejudices.

(D) Such statutes conflict with professional codes of conduct that require judges to recuse themselves if they believe that they are biased.

(E) There is no guarantee that all requests for disqualification of judges will be granted.

12. The passage suggests that if judges are required to provide written explanations for the legal reasoning underlying their decisions about cases, then

(A) judicial bias will be almost completely eliminated

(B) any faulty reasoning employed by judges can in principle be detected

(C) judges' written explanations will usually conceal their real reasoning

(D) the public perception of the impartiality of the judiciary will improve

(E) judges will be motivated to recuse themselves when there is an appearance of bias

13. Which one of the following would be an example of the kind of "real reasoning" referred to in the first sentence of the last paragraph of the passage?

(A) the reasoning leading to a judge's decision against recusal

(B) an argument that is too technical to be understood by someone without formal legal training

(C) reasoning that is motivated by the judge's personal animus against a defendant

(D) reasoning that a knowledgeable observer cannot find any fault with

(E) a central legal principle referred to in a judge's written explanation

14. The author would be most likely to consider which one of the following to be an accurate description of the effects of the current approach to recusal and disqualification of judges?

(A) The standards in place fail to assure the general public that the legal system is adequately protected against judicial bias.

(B) The professional codes of conduct for judges are considered meddlesome and ineffective by many judges.

(C) Judges are rarely removed from cases for bias when they are not actually biased, but they are allowed to sit on many cases even though they are biased.

(D) Judges are rarely allowed to sit on cases when they are biased, but judges are removed from many cases for bias even though they are not actually biased.

(E) Judges are sometimes removed from cases for bias even though they are not actually biased, while some instances of judicial bias occur and are never detected.

GO ON TO THE NEXT PAGE.

Passage A

Saint Augustine wrote that to proceed against lies by lying would be like countering robbery with robbery. To respond to wrongdoing by emulating it is certainly at times to accept lower standards.

(5) And yet it has seemed to many that there is indeed some justification for repaying lies with lies. Such views go back as far as the kind of justice that demands an eye for an eye. They appeal to our sense of fairness: to lie to liars is to give them what they deserve, to
(10) restore an equilibrium they themselves have upset. Just as bullies forfeit the right not to be interfered with by others, so liars forfeit the right to be dealt with honestly.

Two separate moral questions are involved in
(15) this debate. The first asks whether a liar has the same claim to be told the truth as an honest person. The second asks whether one is more justified in lying to a liar than to others.

In order to see this distinction clearly, consider a
(20) person known by all to be a pathological liar but quite harmless. Surely, as the idea of forfeiture suggests, the liar would have no cause for complaint if lied to. But his tall tales would not constitute sufficient reason to lie to him. For the harm to self, others, and general
(25) trust that can come from the practice of lying has to be taken into account in weighing how to deal with him, not merely his personal characteristics.

Passage B

A view derived from Immanuel Kant holds that when rational beings act immorally toward others,
(30) then, by virtue of their status as rational beings, they implicitly authorize similar actions as punishment aimed toward themselves. That is, acting rationally, one always acts as one would have others act toward oneself. Consequently, to act toward a person as that
(35) person has acted toward others is to treat that person as a rational being, that is, as if that person's act is the product of a rational decision.

From this it might be concluded that we have a duty to do to offenders what they have done, since
(40) this amounts to according them the respect due rational beings. But the assertion of a duty to punish seems excessive, since if this duty to others is necessary to accord them the respect due rational beings, then we would have a duty to do to all rational
(45) persons everything—good, bad, or indifferent—that they do to others. The point is rather that by your acts and by virtue of your status as a rational being, you authorize others to do the same to you; you do not compel them to do so. The Kantian argument leads to
(50) a right rather than a duty. Rational beings cannot validly object to being treated in the way in which they treated others. Where there is no valid complaint, there is no injustice, and where there is no injustice, others have acted within their rights.

15. Both passages are concerned with answering which one of the following questions?

(A) Can immoral actions be harmless?
(B) Should the same rules apply in evaluating moral wrongs and criminal wrongs?
(C) Is it right to respond to a person's wrongdoing with an action of the same kind?
(D) What is the difference between a duty and a right?
(E) Is it just to treat all wrongdoers as rational beings?

16. Which one of the following considerations is introduced in passage A but not in passage B?

(A) the harm that may result as a consequence of treating people as they treat others
(B) the consequences of not reciprocating another's wrongdoing
(C) the properties an action must have to count as rational
(D) the extent to which people who break moral rules are due respect
(E) instances in which people have been wronged by being treated as they treated others

17. The passages are alike in that each seeks to advance its main argument by

(A) anticipating and refuting the most probable objections to a theory
(B) using an analogy to support its overall claim
(C) focusing on a specific case to illustrate a generalization
(D) suggesting that a view can have unreasonable consequences
(E) offering and defending a new definition for a commonly used term

GO ON TO THE NEXT PAGE.

18. The author of passage A would be most likely to agree with which one of the following statements?

  (A) Maintaining a policy of reciprocating wrongdoing fails to accord rational beings the respect that they are due.

  (B) People have a duty to respond to even the morally neutral actions of others with actions of the same kind.

  (C) It can be unjustified to treat a person in a certain way even though that person has forfeited the right not to be treated in that way.

  (D) There is no circumstance in which there is sufficient reason to counter a wrong with a wrong of the same kind.

  (E) To restore moral equilibrium, justice will occasionally require that an innocent person forfeit the right to be treated in a certain way.

19. Which one of the following most accurately characterizes the difference between the kind of right referred to in passage A (lines 11–13) and the kind of right referred to in passage B (line 50)?

  (A) In passage A, the kind of right referred to is a legal right, whereas in passage B the kind of right referred to is a moral right.

  (B) In passage A, the kind of right referred to involves benefits granted by society, whereas in passage B the kind of right referred to involves benefits granted by an individual in a position of authority.

  (C) In passage A, the kind of right referred to is an entitlement held by groups of people, whereas in passage B the kind of right referred to is an entitlement held only by individuals.

  (D) In passage A, the kind of right referred to is something that cannot be given up, whereas in passage B the kind of right referred to is something that can be lost because of certain actions.

  (E) In passage A, the kind of right referred to involves behavior that one is entitled to from others, whereas in passage B the kind of right referred to involves behavior that one is licensed to engage in.

20. Which one of the following, if true, would most help to make the suggestion in passage A that a harmless pathological liar's tall tales would not constitute sufficient reason to lie to him (lines 23–24) compatible with the Kantian argument laid out in the first paragraph of passage B?

  (A) Responding to pathological behavior with pathological behavior is irrational.

  (B) Rationality cannot be reasonably attributed to pathological behavior.

  (C) Pathological liars, if harmless, deserve to be treated as rational beings by others.

  (D) Having the right to lie to a pathological liar is not equivalent to having a duty to do so.

  (E) To model one's behavior on that of a pathological liar is to lower one's own standards.

GO ON TO THE NEXT PAGE.

To glass researchers it seems somewhat strange that many people throughout the world share the persistent belief that window glass flows slowly downward like a very viscous liquid. Repeated in

(5) reference books, in science classes, and elsewhere, the idea has often been invoked to explain ripply windows in old houses. The origins of the myth are unclear, but the confusion probably arose partly from a misunderstanding of the fact that the atoms in glass

(10) are not arranged in a fixed crystal structure. In this respect, the structure of liquid glass and the structure of solid glass are very similar, but thermodynamically they are not the same. Glass does not have a precise freezing point; rather, it has what is known as a glass

(15) transition temperature, typically a range of a few hundred degrees Celsius. Cooled below the lower end of this range, molten glass retains an amorphous atomic structure, but it takes on the physical properties of a solid.

(20) However, a new study debunks the persistent belief that stained glass windows in medieval cathedrals are noticeably thicker at the bottom because the glass flows downward. Under the force of gravity, certain solid materials including glass can, in fact, flow

(25) slightly. But Brazilian researcher Edgar Dutra Zanotto has calculated the time needed for viscous flow to change the thickness of different types of glass by a noticeable amount, and, according to his calculations, medieval cathedral glass would require a period well

(30) beyond the age of the universe.

The chemical composition of the glass determines the rate of flow. Even germanium oxide glass, which flows more easily than other types, would take many trillions of years to sag noticeably, Zanotto calculates.

(35) Medieval stained glass contains impurities that could lower the viscosity and speed the flow to some degree, but even a significant difference in this regard would not alter the conclusion, since the cathedrals are only several hundred years old. The study demonstrates

(40) dramatically what many scientists had reasoned earlier based on information such as the fact that for glass to have more than a negligible ability to flow, it would have to be heated to at least 350 degrees Celsius.

The difference in thickness sometimes observed

(45) in antique windows probably results instead from glass manufacturing methods. Until the nineteenth century, the only way to make window glass was to blow molten glass into a large globe and then flatten it into a disk. Whirling the disk introduced ripples and

(50) thickened the edges. To achieve structural stability, it would have made sense to install these panes in such a way that the thick portions were at the bottom. Later, glass was drawn into sheets by pulling it from the melt on a rod, a method that made windows more

(55) uniform. Today, most window glass is made by floating liquid glass on molten tin. This process makes the surface extremely flat.

21. Which one of the following most accurately states the main point of the passage?

(A) Zanotto's research has proven that the amount of time required for viscous flow to change the thickness of medieval cathedral glass would be greater than the age of the universe.

(B) The technology of window-glass production has progressed substantially from medieval stained-glass techniques to today's production of very flat and very uniform panes.

(C) After years of investigation motivated partly by a common misunderstanding about the structure of glass, scientists have developed ways of precisely calculating even extremely slow rates of gravity-induced flow in solids such as glass.

(D) Recent research provides evidence that although solid glass flows slightly under the influence of gravity, such flow is only one of several factors that have contributed to noticeable differences in thickness between the top and the bottom of some old windows.

(E) Contrary to a commonly held belief, noticeable differences in thickness between the top and the bottom of some old glass windows are not due to the flowing of solid glass, but probably result instead from old glassworking techniques.

22. The passage most helps to answer which one of the following questions?

(A) What is one way in which seventeenth-century windowpane manufacturing techniques differ from those commonly used in medieval times?

(B) What is one way in which nineteenth-century windowpane manufacturing techniques differ from those commonly used today?

(C) Was glass ever used in windows prior to medieval times?

(D) Are unevenly thick stained-glass windowpanes ever made of germanium oxide glass?

(E) How did there come to be impurities in medieval stained glass?

GO ON TO THE NEXT PAGE.

23. Which one of the following best summarizes the author's view of the results of Zanotto's study?

(A) They provide some important quantitative data to support a view that was already held by many scientists.

(B) They have stimulated important new research regarding an issue that scientists previously thought had been settled.

(C) They offer a highly plausible explanation of how a mistaken hypothesis came to be widely believed.

(D) They provide a conceptual basis for reconciling two scientific views that were previously thought to be incompatible.

(E) They suggest that neither of two hypotheses adequately explains a puzzling phenomenon.

24. The passage suggests that the atomic structure of glass is such that glass will

(A) behave as a liquid even though it has certain properties of solids

(B) be noticeably deformed by the force of its own weight over a period of a few millennia

(C) behave as a solid even when it has reached its glass transition temperature

(D) flow downward under its own weight if it is heated to its glass transition temperature

(E) stop flowing only if the atoms are arranged in a fixed crystalline structure

25. The author of the passage attributes the belief that window glass flows noticeably downward over time to the erroneous assumption that

(A) the atomic structure of solid glass is crystalline rather than amorphous

(B) the amorphous atomic structure of glass causes it to behave like a very viscous liquid even in its solid form

(C) methods of glass making in medieval times were similar to the methods used in modern times

(D) the transition temperature of the glass used in medieval windows is the same as that of the glass used in modern windows

(E) liquid glass and solid glass are thermodynamically dissimilar

26. Which one of the following is most analogous to the persistent belief about glass described in the passage?

(A) Most people believe that the tendency of certain fabrics to become wrinkled cannot be corrected during the manufacturing process.

(B) Most people believe that certain flaws in early pottery were caused by the material used rather than the process used in manufacturing the pottery.

(C) Most people believe that inadequate knowledge of manufacturing techniques shortens the life span of major appliances.

(D) Most people believe that modern furniture made on an assembly line is inferior to individually crafted furniture.

(E) Most people believe that modern buildings are able to withstand earthquakes because they are made from more durable materials than were older buildings.

27. The passage suggests that which one of the following statements accurately characterizes the transition temperature of glass?

(A) It is higher for medieval glass than for modern glass.

(B) It has only recently been calculated with precision.

(C) Its upper extreme is well above 350 degrees Celsius.

(D) It does not affect the tendency of some kinds of glass to flow downward.

(E) For some types of glass, it is a specific temperature well below 350 degrees Celsius.

S T O P

IF YOU FINISH BEFORE TIME IS CALLED, YOU MAY CHECK YOUR WORK ON THIS SECTION ONLY.
DO NOT WORK ON ANY OTHER SECTION IN THE TEST.

SECTION III

Time—35 minutes

25 Questions

Directions: The questions in this section are based on the reasoning contained in brief statements or passages. For some questions, more than one of the choices could conceivably answer the question. However, you are to choose the best answer; that is, the response that most accurately and completely answers the question. You should not make assumptions that are by commonsense standards implausible, superfluous, or incompatible with the passage. After you have chosen the best answer, blacken the corresponding space on your answer sheet.

1. When industries rapidly apply new technology, people who possess the skills and knowledge to master it prosper, while many others lose their jobs. But firms that resist technological innovations will eventually be superseded by those that do not, resulting in the loss of all their employees' jobs. Obviously, then, resisting the application of new technology in industry _____.

   Which one of the following most logically completes the argument?

   (A) is less likely to dislocate workers than it is to create job security for them
   (B) will affect only those who possess technical skills
   (C) cannot prevent job loss in the long run
   (D) eventually creates more jobs than it destroys
   (E) must take priority over any attempt to promote new industries

2. While sales of other highly fuel-efficient automobiles are in decline, sales of the Hydro are rising. The Hydro's manufacturers attribute its success to the Hydro's price and very low fuel consumption. However, the Hydro is comparable in price and fuel efficiency to its competitors, so it is more likely that its success is due to the fact that people want to appear environmentally conscious to their neighbors.

   Which one of the following is an assumption required by the argument?

   (A) The Hydro is the most popular highly fuel-efficient automobile available.
   (B) The Hydro is recognizable as environmentally friendly in a way that its competitors are not.
   (C) The Hydro has a better safety record than its competitors.
   (D) Hydro buyers are more likely to have neighbors who also drive Hydros.
   (E) Hydro buyers have less interest in environmental causes than buyers of other highly fuel-efficient automobiles.

3. Louise McBride, a homeowner, filed a complaint against a nearby nightclub through the Licensing Bureau, a government agency. Although regulations clearly state that Form 283 is to be used for formal complaints, Bureau staff gave McBride Form 5, which she used with the intention of filing a formal complaint. The nightclub argues that the complaint should be dismissed because the incorrect form was used. But that would be unfair.

   Which one of the following principles, if valid, most helps to justify the judgment that dismissing the complaint would be unfair?

   (A) People who wish to file complaints through the Licensing Bureau should be informed of all relevant regulations.
   (B) Government agencies should make their forms straightforward enough that completing them will not be unduly burdensome for the average person.
   (C) It is unfair for someone's complaint to be dismissed because of an incorrect action on the part of a government agency.
   (D) A government agency should not make its procedures so complex that even the agency's employees cannot understand the procedures.
   (E) It is unfair for a business to be subject to a formal complaint unless the complaint is made in a way that provides the business with an opportunity to defend itself.

4. The size of the spleen is a good indicator of how healthy a bird is: sickly birds generally have significantly smaller spleens than healthy birds. Researchers found that, in general, birds that had been killed by predators had substantially smaller spleens than birds killed accidentally.

   Which one of the following is most strongly supported by the information above?

   (A) Predators are unable to kill healthy birds.
   (B) Most birds with smaller than average spleens are killed by predators.
   (C) Predators can sense whether a bird is sick.
   (D) Sickly birds are more likely than healthy birds to be killed by predators.
   (E) Small spleen size is one of the main causes of sickness in birds.

GO ON TO THE NEXT PAGE.

5. Home ownership is a sign of economic prosperity. This makes it somewhat surprising that across the various regions of Europe and North America, high levels of home ownership correspond with high levels of unemployment.

Which one of the following, if true, helps to resolve the apparent conflict described above?

(A) Home ownership makes it more difficult to move to a place where jobs are more plentiful.
(B) Over the last few decades jobs have been moving from centralized areas to locations that are closer to homeowners.
(C) The correspondence between high levels of home ownership and high levels of unemployment holds across countries with widely different social systems.
(D) People who own homes are more likely than those who rent to form support networks that help them to learn of local jobs.
(E) People are more likely to buy homes when they are feeling economically secure.

6. If newly hatched tobacco hornworms in nature first feed on plants from the nightshade family, they will not eat leaves from any other plants thereafter. However, tobacco hornworms will feed on other sorts of plants if they feed on plants other than nightshades just after hatching. To explain this behavior, scientists hypothesize that when a hornworm's first meal is from a nightshade, its taste receptors become habituated to the chemical indioside D, which is found only in nightshades, and after this habituation nothing without indioside D tastes good.

Which one of the following, if true, adds the most support for the hypothesis?

(A) Tobacco hornworms that first fed on nightshade leaves show no preference for any one variety of nightshade plant over any other.
(B) If taste receptors are removed from tobacco hornworms that first fed on nightshade leaves, those hornworms will subsequently feed on other leaves.
(C) Tobacco hornworm eggs are most commonly laid on nightshade plants.
(D) Indioside D is not the only chemical that occurs only in nightshade plants.
(E) The taste receptors of the tobacco hornworm have physiological reactions to several naturally occurring chemicals.

7. Employee: My boss says that my presentation to our accounting team should have included more detail about profit projections. But people's attention tends to wander when they are presented with too much detail. So, clearly my boss is incorrect.

The reasoning in the employee's argument is flawed because the argument

(A) takes for granted that the boss's assessments of employee presentations are generally not accurate
(B) fails to distinguish between more of something and too much of it
(C) fails to consider that an audience's attention might wander for reasons other than being presented with too much detail
(D) infers a generalization based only on a single case
(E) confuses two distinct meanings of the key term "detail"

8. The local news media have long heralded Clemens as an honest politician. They were proven wrong when Clemens was caught up in a corruption scandal. This demonstrates how the local media show too much deference toward public figures. Even the editor of the local newspaper admitted that her reporters neglected to follow leads that might have exposed the scandal far earlier.

Which one of the following most accurately expresses the overall conclusion drawn in the argument?

(A) Clemens has long been portrayed as an honest politician by the local news media.
(B) The local news media were wrong to herald Clemens as an honest politician.
(C) The local news media show too much deference toward public figures.
(D) Reporters from the local newspaper neglected to follow leads that might have exposed the scandal much earlier.
(E) The local newspaper's treatment of Clemens is indicative of its treatment of public figures in general.

GO ON TO THE NEXT PAGE.

9. We know that if life ever existed on the Moon, there would be signs of life there. But numerous excursions to the Moon have failed to provide us with any sign of life. So there has never been life on the Moon.

The pattern of reasoning in the argument above is most similar to that in which one of the following?

(A) We know that the spy is a traitor. We do not know that the general is a traitor. So the general is not a spy.

(B) If we have any mayonnaise, it would be in the refrigerator. But the refrigerator is almost empty. So it is unlikely that we have mayonnaise.

(C) Hendricks will win the election only if voters are concerned primarily with fighting crime. Hendricks is in favor of tougher criminal penalties. So voters will probably go with Hendricks.

(D) If rodents are responsible for the lost grain from last year's harvest, we would find signs of rodents in the warehouses. And we have found signs of rodents there. So rodents are responsible for the lost grain.

(E) If their army is planning an attack, there would either be troop movements along the border or a transfer of weapons. But intelligence reports show no indication of either. So their army is not planning an attack.

10. Television host: While it's true that the defendant presented a strong alibi and considerable exculpatory evidence and was quickly acquitted by the jury, I still believe that there must be good reason to think that the defendant is not completely innocent in the case. Otherwise, the prosecutor would not have brought charges in the first place.

The reasoning in the television host's argument is flawed in that the argument

(A) takes lack of evidence for a view as grounds for concluding that the view is false

(B) presupposes as evidence the conclusion that it is trying to establish

(C) places undue reliance on the judgments of an authority figure

(D) confuses legal standards for guilt with moral standards for guilt

(E) concludes that a judgment is suspicious merely on the grounds that it was reached quickly

11. Literature professor: Critics charge that the work of C. F. Providence's best-known follower, S. N. Sauk, lacks aesthetic merit because it employs Providence's own uniquely potent system of symbolic motifs in the service of a political ideal that Providence—and, significantly, some of these critics as well—would reject. Granting that Sauk is more imitator than innovator, and that he maintained political views very different from those Providence maintained, it has yet to be shown that these facts make his writings any less subtly or powerfully crafted than those of his more esteemed mentor. So the critics' argument should be rejected.

The literature professor argues that the conclusion drawn by the critics has not really been established, on the grounds that

(A) the claims made in support of this conclusion are inaccurate

(B) Sauk's work has aesthetic merit

(C) these critics are motivated by antipathy toward Sauk's political ideas

(D) the claims made in support of this conclusion have not been shown to be correct

(E) the claims made in support of this conclusion have not been shown to be relevant to it

12. Policy: The factory's safety inspector should not approve a new manufacturing process unless it has been used safely for more than a year at another factory or it will demonstrably increase safety at the factory.

Application: The safety inspector should not approve the proposed new welding process, for it cannot be shown to increase safety at the factory.

Which one of the following, if true, justifies the above application of the policy?

(A) The factory at which the new welding process was first introduced has had several problems associated with the process.

(B) The proposed new welding process has not been used in any other factory.

(C) Some of the manufacturing processes currently in use at the factory are not demonstrably safer than the new welding process.

(D) The safety inspector will not approve any new process that has not been used extensively elsewhere.

(E) The proposed new welding process has been used in only one other factory.

GO ON TO THE NEXT PAGE.

13. University administrator: Graduate students incorrectly claim that teaching assistants should be considered university employees and thus entitled to the usual employee benefits. Granted, teaching assistants teach classes, for which they receive financial compensation. However, the sole purpose of having teaching assistants perform services for the university is to enable them to fund their education. If they were not pursuing degrees here or if they could otherwise fund their education, they would not hold their teaching posts at all.

Which one of the following, if true, most seriously weakens the administrator's argument?

(A) The administrator is cognizant of the extra costs involved in granting employee benefits to teaching assistants.

(B) The university employs adjunct instructors who receive compensation similar to that of its teaching assistants.

(C) The university has proposed that in the interest of economy, 10 percent of the faculty be replaced with teaching assistants.

(D) Most teaching assistants earn stipends that exceed their cost of tuition.

(E) Teaching assistants work as much and as hard as do other university employees.

14. Branson: Most of the air pollution in this country comes from our largest cities. These cities would pollute less if they were less populated. So if many people in these cities were to move to rural areas, air pollution in the country as a whole would be reduced.

Which one of the following demonstrates most effectively by parallel reasoning that Branson's argument is flawed?

(A) Similarly, we could conclude that Monique spends most of her salary on housing. After all, people are bound to spend more on housing if they live in a city where the cost of housing is high, and Monique recently moved to a city where the cost of housing is very high.

(B) Similarly, we could conclude that Karen's family would have more living space if they moved from an apartment to a single-family home. After all, single-family homes are typically larger than apartments.

(C) Similarly, we could conclude that most of Ward's farm is planted with corn. After all, in Ward's county most of the fields that used to be planted with other crops are now planted with corn.

(D) Similarly, we could conclude that Javier could consume fewer calories by eating for breakfast, lunch, and dinner only a portion of what he now eats, and eating the remainder as snacks. After all, breakfast, lunch, and dinner together account for most of the calories Javier consumes.

(E) Similarly, we could conclude that most of this city's air pollution would be eliminated if this city built a public transportation system. After all, public transportation produces much less pollution per passenger, and all automobile trips could be replaced by trips on public transportation.

GO ON TO THE NEXT PAGE.

15. Ninety percent of recent car buyers say safety was an important factor in their purchase. Yet of these car buyers, only half consulted objective sources of vehicle safety information before making their purchase; the others relied on advertisements and promotional materials. Thus, these other buyers were mistaken in saying that safety was important to them.

The argument's conclusion follows logically if which one of the following is assumed?

(A)   Someone who claims that safety was an important factor in a buying decision does not necessarily mean that safety was the most important factor.

(B)   Advertisements and promotional materials sometimes provide incomplete vehicle safety information.

(C)   Recent car buyers do not necessarily tell the truth when asked about the factors that contributed to their vehicle purchases.

(D)   Most consumers are aware that advertisements and promotional materials are not objective sources of vehicle safety information.

(E)   Anyone to whom safety is an important factor in purchasing a car will consult an objective source of vehicle safety information before buying.

16. Theorist: To be capable of planned locomotion, an organism must be able both to form an internal representation of its environment and to send messages to its muscles to control movements. Such an organism must therefore have a central nervous system. Thus, an organism incapable of planned locomotion does not have a central nervous system.

The theorist's argument is flawed in that it

(A)   confuses a necessary condition for an organism's possessing a capacity with a sufficient one

(B)   takes for granted that organisms capable of sending messages from their central nervous systems to their muscles are also capable of locomotion

(C)   presumes, without providing justification, that planned locomotion is the only biologically useful purpose for an organism's forming an internal representation of its environment

(D)   takes for granted that adaptations that serve a biologically useful purpose originally came about for that purpose

(E)   presumes, without providing justification, that an internal representation of its environment can be formed by an organism with even a rudimentary nervous system

17. Rocket engines are most effective when exhaust gases escape from their nozzles at the same pressure as the surrounding atmosphere. At low altitudes, where atmospheric pressure is high, this effect is best produced by a short nozzle, but when the rocket passes through the thin upper atmosphere, a long nozzle becomes more effective. Thus, to work most effectively throughout their ascents, all rockets must have both short nozzles and long nozzles on their engines.

Which one of the following is an assumption the argument requires?

(A)   Equipping a rocket's engines with both short and long nozzles is not significantly more difficult than equipping them with nozzles of equal lengths.

(B)   At some point during their ascents, all rockets will pass through the thin upper atmosphere.

(C)   A rocket with only short nozzles on its engines cannot reach high altitudes.

(D)   For a rocket to work effectively, its engines' exhaust gases must leave the nozzles at the same pressure as the surrounding atmosphere throughout the rocket's ascent.

(E)   For a rocket to work most effectively at both low and high atmospheric pressures, it must have at least one engine that has both a short nozzle and a long nozzle.

GO ON TO THE NEXT PAGE.

18. Consumer advocate: Manufacturers of children's toys often place warnings on their products that overstate the dangers their products pose. Product-warning labels should overstate dangers only if doing so reduces injuries. In fact, however, manufacturers overstate their products' dangers merely for the purpose of protecting themselves from lawsuits brought by parents of injured children. Therefore, manufacturers of children's toys should not overstate the dangers their products pose.

Which one of the following most accurately describes a reasoning flaw in the consumer advocate's argument?

(A) The argument confuses a necessary condition for reducing the number of injuries caused by a product with a sufficient condition.

(B) The argument overlooks the possibility that warnings that do not overstate the dangers that their products pose do not always reduce injuries.

(C) The argument relies on a sample that is unlikely to be representative.

(D) The argument presumes, without providing justification, that if a warning overstates a danger, then the warning will fail to prevent injuries.

(E) The argument relies on the unjustified assumption that an action has an effect only if it was performed in order to bring about that effect.

19. A recent study showed that the immune system blood cells of the study's participants who drank tea but no coffee took half as long to respond to germs as did the blood cells of participants who drank coffee but no tea. Thus, drinking tea boosted the participants' immune system defenses.

Which one of the following is an assumption on which the argument depends?

(A) All of the participants in the study drank either tea or coffee, and none drank both.

(B) Coffee has no health benefits that are as valuable as the boost that tea purportedly gives to the body's immune system.

(C) In the study, drinking coffee did not cause the blood cell response time to double.

(D) Coffee drinkers in general are no more likely to exercise and eat healthily than are tea drinkers.

(E) Coffee and tea do not have in common any chemicals that fight disease in the human body.

20. Engineer: Semiplaning monohulls are a new kind of ship that can attain twice the speed of conventional ships. Due to increased fuel needs, transportation will be much more expensive on semiplaning monohulls than on conventional ships. Similarly, travel on jet airplanes was more expensive than travel on other planes at first, but jet airplanes still attracted enough passengers to be profitable, because they offered greater speed and reliability. Semiplaning monohulls offer the same advantages over traditional ships. Thus they will probably be profitable as well.

Which one of the following most accurately describes the role played in the engineer's argument by the statement that transportation will be much more expensive on semiplaning monohulls than on traditional ships?

(A) It serves as one of two analogies drawn between semiplaning monohulls and jet airplanes, which function together to support the argument's main conclusion.

(B) It draws an analogy between semiplaning monohulls and conventional ships that constitutes an objection to the argument's main conclusion, one that is subsequently rejected by appeal to another analogy.

(C) It draws a distinction between characteristics of semiplaning monohulls and characteristics of conventional ships that independently provides support for the argument's main conclusion.

(D) It constitutes a potential objection to the argument's main conclusion, but is subsequently countered by an analogy drawn between ships and airplanes.

(E) It draws a distinction between characteristics of semiplaning monohulls and characteristics of conventional ships that the argument's main conclusion compares to a distinction between types of airplanes.

GO ON TO THE NEXT PAGE.

21. Maté is a beverage found in much of South America. While it is uncertain where maté was first made, there are more varieties of it found in Paraguay than anywhere else. Also, maté is used more widely there than anywhere else. Therefore, Paraguay is likely the place where maté originated.

Which one of the following, if true, would most strengthen the argument?

(A) It is rare for there to be a great variety of types of a beverage in a place where the beverage has not been in use for a very long time.

(B) Many Paraguayans believe that maté became popular at a time when people from other areas of South America were first migrating to Paraguay.

(C) Many Paraguayans believe that the best maté is found in Paraguay.

(D) There are few places outside of South America where maté is regularly consumed.

(E) Typically, the longer a beverage has been in use in a particular place, the more widely that beverage is used there.

22. From 1996 to 2004, the average family income in a certain country decreased by 10 percent, after adjustments for inflation. Opponents of the political party that ruled during this time claim that this was due to mismanagement of the economy by that party.

Each of the following rejoinders, if true, directly counters the opponents' explanation of the decrease in average family income EXCEPT:

(A) There had been a rise in family income in 1996, after adjustments for inflation.

(B) For noneconomic reasons, fewer families had multiple incomes at the end of the period than at the beginning.

(C) During the period, international events beyond the control of the country's government had a negative effect on family incomes in the country.

(D) Younger wage earners usually earn less than older ones, and the average age of household wage earners fell during most years in the past several decades.

(E) The biggest decreases in family income resulted from policies enacted before the ruling party came to power in 1996.

23. Amateur gardeners who plant based on the phases of the moon tend to get better results than those who do not. This seems surprising since the phases of the moon do not affect how plants grow. An alternative practice often found among amateur gardeners is to plant during the first warm spell of spring, which leads to problems when a frost follows. So, amateur gardeners who use the phases of the moon are less likely to lose plants to a frost.

The argument requires assuming which one of the following?

(A) Using the phases of the moon usually leads amateur gardeners to plant later in the spring than those planting at the first warm spell.

(B) The phases of the moon affect whether a frost follows the first warm spell of spring.

(C) Amateur gardeners who use the phases of the moon tend to plant different types of plants than do other amateur gardeners.

(D) Amateur gardeners cannot improve their results unless they understand why their methods work as they do.

(E) Professional gardeners only rarely plant at the first warm spell of spring.

GO ON TO THE NEXT PAGE.

24. Columnist: On average, about 70 percent of the profit from tourism in developing countries goes to foreign owners of tourist businesses. In general, as a country becomes a more established tourist destination, the proportion of revenues exported in this way increases. However, tourists can counteract this effect by obtaining accommodations and other services directly from local people.

Which one of the following is most strongly supported by the statements made by the columnist?

(A) Tourists in a developing nation should obtain accommodations and other services directly from local people if most of the profits from tourism in that nation go to foreign owners of tourist businesses.

(B) In at least some of the developing countries that are most established as tourist destinations, most of the profits from tourism go to foreign owners of tourist businesses.

(C) In at least some developing countries, tourists obtain most of their accommodations and other services directly from local people.

(D) In general, as a developing country becomes a more established tourist destination, local people become progressively poorer.

(E) Tourists who obtain accommodations and other services directly from local people do not contribute in any way to the profits of foreign owners of tourist businesses.

25. The populations of certain species of amphibians have declined dramatically in recent years, an effect many scientists attribute to industrial pollution. However, most amphibian species' populations vary greatly from year to year because of natural variations in the weather. It is therefore impossible to be sure that the recent decline in those amphibian populations is due to industrial pollution.

The argument depends on assuming which one of the following?

(A) The amphibian species whose population declines have been attributed by many scientists to industrial pollution are not known to be among those species whose populations do not vary greatly as a result of natural variations in the weather.

(B) The variations in amphibian species' populations that result from natural variations in the weather are not always as large as the amphibian population declines that scientists have attributed to industrial pollution.

(C) Either industrial pollution or natural variations in the weather, but not both, caused the amphibian population declines that scientists have attributed to industrial pollution.

(D) If industrial pollution were reduced, the decline in certain amphibian populations would be reversed, and if industrial pollution increases, the decline in certain amphibian populations will be exacerbated.

(E) If industrial pollution is severe, it can create more variations in the weather than would occur naturally.

S T O P

IF YOU FINISH BEFORE TIME IS CALLED, YOU MAY CHECK YOUR WORK ON THIS SECTION ONLY.
DO NOT WORK ON ANY OTHER SECTION IN THE TEST.

SECTION IV

Time—35 minutes

23 Questions

Directions: Each group of questions in this section is based on a set of conditions. In answering some of the questions, it may be useful to draw a rough diagram. Choose the response that most accurately and completely answers each question and blacken the corresponding space on your answer sheet.

Questions 1–6

A corporation's Human Resources department must determine annual bonuses for seven employees—Kimura, Lopez, Meng, and Peterson, who work in the Finance department; and Vaughan, Xavier, and Zane, who work in the Graphics department. Each employee will receive either a $1,000 bonus, a $3,000 bonus, or a $5,000 bonus, in accordance with the following:

  No one in the Graphics department receives a $1,000 bonus.

  Any employee who was rated Highly Effective receives a larger bonus than anyone in his or her department who was not rated Highly Effective.

  Only Lopez, Meng, and Xavier were rated Highly Effective.

1. Which one of the following is an allowable distribution of bonuses to the seven employees?

(A) [Finance] Kimura: $1,000; Lopez: $5,000; Meng: $5,000; Peterson: $1,000
[Graphics] Vaughan: $3,000; Xavier: $3,000; Zane: $3,000

(B) [Finance] Kimura: $1,000; Lopez: $5,000; Meng: $5,000; Peterson: $3,000
[Graphics] Vaughan: $3,000; Xavier: $5,000; Zane: $1,000

(C) [Finance] Kimura: $1,000; Lopez: $5,000; Meng: $5,000; Peterson: $3,000
[Graphics] Vaughan: $3,000; Xavier: $5,000; Zane: $3,000

(D) [Finance] Kimura: $3,000; Lopez: $5,000; Meng: $3,000; Peterson: $1,000
[Graphics] Vaughan: $3,000; Xavier: $5,000; Zane: $3,000

(E) [Finance] Kimura: $3,000; Lopez: $5,000; Meng: $5,000; Peterson: $1,000
[Graphics] Vaughan: $1,000; Xavier: $5,000; Zane: $3,000

GO ON TO THE NEXT PAGE.

2. If Lopez does not receive the same bonus as Meng, which one of the following could be true?

(A) Kimura receives a $3,000 bonus.
(B) Lopez receives a $3,000 bonus.
(C) Peterson receives a $3,000 bonus.
(D) Kimura receives the same bonus as Vaughan.
(E) Peterson receives a larger bonus than Kimura.

3. If only one of the employees receives a $1,000 bonus, which one of the following must be true?

(A) Meng receives a $5,000 bonus.
(B) Peterson receives a $3,000 bonus.
(C) Meng receives a $3,000 bonus.
(D) The employee who receives a $1,000 bonus is Peterson.
(E) The employee who receives a $1,000 bonus is Kimura.

4. Which one of the following must be true?

(A) At least one of the employees receives a $1,000 bonus.
(B) At least three of the employees receive $3,000 bonuses.
(C) At most three of the employees receive $3,000 bonuses.
(D) At least two of the employees receive $5,000 bonuses.
(E) At most three of the employees receive $5,000 bonuses.

5. If exactly two of the employees receive $5,000 bonuses, which one of the following must be true?

(A) Lopez receives a $3,000 bonus.
(B) Meng receives a $3,000 bonus.
(C) Meng is one of the employees who receives a $5,000 bonus.
(D) Peterson receives a $1,000 bonus.
(E) Peterson receives a $3,000 bonus.

6. Any of the following could be true of the seven employees EXCEPT:

(A) The same number receive $1,000 bonuses as receive $3,000 bonuses.
(B) More receive $1,000 bonuses than receive $3,000 bonuses.
(C) The same number receive $1,000 bonuses as receive $5,000 bonuses.
(D) More receive $1,000 bonuses than receive $5,000 bonuses.
(E) More receive $3,000 bonuses than receive $5,000 bonuses.

GO ON TO THE NEXT PAGE.

Questions 7–11

A landscaper will plant exactly seven trees today—a hickory, a larch, a maple, an oak, a plum, a sycamore, and a walnut. Each tree must be planted on exactly one of three lots—1, 2, or 3—in conformity with the following requirements:

The trees planted on one lot are the hickory, the oak, and exactly one other tree.

The maple is not planted on the same lot as the walnut.

Either the larch or the walnut, but not both, is planted on lot 1.

Either the maple or the oak, but not both, is planted on lot 2.

More trees are planted on lot 3 than on lot 1.

7. Which one of the following could be the list of the trees that the landscaper plants on each of the lots today?

(A) lot 1: the larch, the maple
   lot 2: the hickory, the oak
   lot 3: the plum, the sycamore, the walnut

(B) lot 1: the larch, the maple
   lot 2: the hickory, the oak, the walnut
   lot 3: the plum, the sycamore

(C) lot 1: the maple
   lot 2: the hickory, the larch, the oak
   lot 3: the plum, the sycamore, the walnut

(D) lot 1: the sycamore, the walnut
   lot 2: the larch, the maple
   lot 3: the hickory, the oak, the plum

(E) lot 1: the walnut
   lot 2: the plum, the sycamore
   lot 3: the hickory, the maple, the oak

GO ON TO THE NEXT PAGE.

8. If the hickory is planted on lot 2, then which one of the following trees must be planted on lot 3?

   (A) the larch
   (B) the maple
   (C) the plum
   (D) the sycamore
   (E) the walnut

9. Which one of the following is a complete and accurate list of the trees any of which could be planted on lot 1?

   (A) the hickory, the plum, the sycamore, the walnut
   (B) the hickory, the sycamore, the walnut
   (C) the larch, the plum, the sycamore, the walnut
   (D) the larch, the plum, the walnut
   (E) the plum, the sycamore, the walnut

10. If the walnut is planted on lot 3, then which one of the following could be true?

    (A) The sycamore is planted on lot 1.
    (B) The hickory is planted on lot 2.
    (C) The larch is planted on lot 2.
    (D) The plum is planted on lot 3.
    (E) The sycamore is planted on lot 3.

11. Where each of the trees is planted is completely determined if which one of the following trees is planted on lot 2?

    (A) the walnut
    (B) the sycamore
    (C) the plum
    (D) the maple
    (E) the larch

GO ON TO THE NEXT PAGE.

Questions 12–18

Seven librarians—Flynn, Gomez, Hill, Kitson, Leung, Moore, and Zahn—are being scheduled for desk duty for one week—Monday through Saturday. The librarians will be on duty exactly one day each. On each day except Saturday, there will be exactly one librarian on duty, with two on duty on Saturday, subject to the following constraints:

Hill must be on desk duty earlier in the week than Leung.
Both Hill and Moore must be on desk duty earlier in the week than Gomez.
Flynn must be on desk duty earlier in the week than both Kitson and Moore.
Kitson must be on desk duty earlier in the week than Zahn.
Unless Leung is on desk duty on Saturday, Leung must be on desk duty earlier in the week than Flynn.

F, G, H, K, L, M Z

M – F:1
S:2

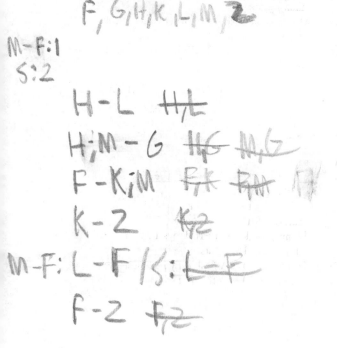

H – L   H↓L
H;M – G   H↓G   M↓G
F – K;M   F↓K   F↓M   ↑
K – Z   K↓Z
M – F: L – F / S: L – F
F – Z   F↓Z

12. Which one of the following is an acceptable schedule for the librarians, listed in order from Monday through Saturday?

(A) Flynn; Hill; Moore; Kitson; Zahn; Gomez and Leung

(B) Flynn; Moore; Hill; Leung; Kitson; Gomez and Zahn

(C) Hill; Kitson; Moore; Flynn; Gomez; Leung and Zahn

(D) Hill; Leung; Flynn; Moore; Zahn; Gomez and Kitson

(E) Leung; Flynn; Kitson; Moore; Hill; Gomez and Zahn

GO ON TO THE NEXT PAGE.

13. ___ | E |

14. K – M   K – G
    M – G
    G – K

15. F | K | M | Z | H | L   G
    H   L   F   Z
    F | M | K | Z | H | L, G

16. E | M | _ | _ | _ | L _

17. F – H
    F – L
    F – G

    | E | _ | _ | _ | _ | L _

13. Which one of the following CANNOT be on desk duty on Tuesday?

    (A) Flynn
    (B) Hill
    (C) Kitson
    (D) Moore
    (E) Zahn

14. If Kitson is on desk duty earlier in the week than Moore, which one of the following CANNOT be true?

    (A) Flynn is on desk duty earlier in the week than Leung.
    (B) Gomez is on desk duty earlier in the week than Kitson.
    (C) Gomez is on desk duty earlier in the week than Zahn.
    (D) Hill is on desk duty earlier in the week than Kitson.
    (E) Zahn is on desk duty earlier in the week than Moore.

15. If Zahn is on desk duty on Thursday, which one of the following must be true?

    (A) Flynn is on desk duty earlier in the week than Leung.
    (B) Hill is on desk duty earlier in the week than Flynn.
    (C) Hill is on desk duty earlier in the week than Moore.
    (D) Hill is on desk duty earlier in the week than Zahn.
    (E) Kitson is on desk duty earlier in the week than Moore.

16. If Moore is on desk duty on Tuesday, which one of the following must be true?

    (A) Hill is on desk duty on Thursday.
    (B) Kitson is on desk duty on Thursday.
    (C) Leung is on desk duty on Saturday.
    (D) Zahn is on desk duty on Friday.
    (E) Zahn is on desk duty on Saturday.

17. If Flynn is on desk duty earlier in the week than Hill, which one of the following must be true?

    (A) Hill is on desk duty earlier in the week than Kitson.
    (B) Hill is on desk duty earlier in the week than Zahn.
    (C) Kitson is on desk duty earlier in the week than Moore.
    (D) Moore is on desk duty earlier in the week than Leung.
    (E) Moore is on desk duty earlier in the week than Zahn.

18. Which one of the following, if substituted for the constraint that Flynn must be on desk duty earlier in the week than both Kitson and Moore, would have the same effect in determining the schedule for the librarians?

    (A) Flynn cannot be on desk duty on Thursday.
    (B) Only Flynn or Hill can be on desk duty on Monday.
    (C) Only Hill and Leung can be on desk duty earlier than Flynn.
    (D) Flynn must be on desk duty earlier in the week than both Gomez and Kitson.
    (E) Flynn must be on desk duty earlier in the week than both Moore and Zahn.

GO ON TO THE NEXT PAGE.

Questions 19–23

Each issue of a business newsletter has five slots, numbered 1 through 5. The policy of the newsletter requires that there are at least three features per issue, with each feature completely occupying one or more of the slots. Each feature can be one of four types—finance, industry, marketing, or technology. Any slot not containing a feature contains a graphic. The newsletter's policy further requires that each issue be structured as follows:

   Any feature occupying more than one slot must occupy consecutively numbered slots.
   If an issue has any finance or technology feature, then a finance or technology feature must occupy slot 1.
   An issue can have at most one industry feature.

1-5

f i m t

g

19. Which one of the following is an allowable structure for an issue of the newsletter?

(A)   slot 1: a finance feature; slot 2: an industry feature; slot 3: a second industry feature; slot 4: a graphic; slot 5: a graphic

(B)   slot 1: a graphic; slot 2: a technology feature; slot 3: a second technology feature; slot 4: a graphic; slot 5: a third technology feature

(C)   slots 1 and 2: a single industry feature; slots 3 and 4: a single marketing feature; slot 5: a finance feature

(D)   slot 1: a technology feature; slots 2 and 3: a single industry feature; slot 4: a finance feature; slot 5: a graphic

(E)   slot 1: a technology feature; slots 2 and 4: a single marketing feature; slot 3: an industry feature; slot 5: a graphic

GO ON TO THE NEXT PAGE.

20. If an issue of the newsletter has no technology feature and if there is a finance feature that occupies both slots 4 and 5, then which one of the following is required for that issue?

(A) A finance feature occupies slot 1.
(B) A finance feature occupies slot 2 or slot 3 or both.
(C) A marketing feature occupies slot 2.
(D) An industry feature or a marketing feature occupies slot 2.
(E) An industry feature or a marketing feature occupies slot 3.

21. Which one of the following is NOT allowed for an issue of the newsletter?

(A) There is exactly one industry feature, and it occupies slot 1.
(B) There is exactly one finance feature, and it occupies slot 2.
(C) There is exactly one technology feature, and it occupies slot 3.
(D) Each feature except the feature occupying slot 1 is either a finance feature or a marketing feature.
(E) Each feature except the feature occupying slot 5 is either an industry feature or a marketing feature.

22. If, in a particular issue of the newsletter, slot 1 is occupied by the only industry feature in that issue, then which one of the following is required for that issue?

(A) There is an industry feature that occupies slots 1 and 2, and only those slots.
(B) There is an industry feature that occupies slots 1, 2, and 3, and only those slots.
(C) There is a marketing feature that occupies slot 2 or slot 3 or both.
(D) There is a marketing feature that occupies one or more of slots 2, 3, and 4.
(E) There is a marketing feature that occupies slot 3 or slot 5 or both.

23. Any of the following is allowed for an issue of the newsletter EXCEPT:

(A) There is exactly one finance feature and no industry or marketing feature.
(B) There is exactly one industry feature and no finance or marketing feature.
(C) There is exactly one industry feature and no marketing or technology feature.
(D) There is exactly one marketing feature and no finance or technology feature.
(E) There is exactly one marketing feature and no industry or technology feature.

S T O P

IF YOU FINISH BEFORE TIME IS CALLED, YOU MAY CHECK YOUR WORK ON THIS SECTION ONLY.
DO NOT WORK ON ANY OTHER SECTION IN THE TEST.

Acknowledgment is made to the following sources from which material has been adapted for use in this test booklet:

Sissela Bok, *Lying: Moral Choice in Public and Private Life.* ©1978 by Sissela Bok.

Sarah M. R. Cravens, "In Pursuit of Actual Justice" in *Alabama Law Review.* ©2007 by Alabama Law Review.

John Palattella, "Pictures of Us." ©1998 by Lingua Franca.

Jeffrey Reiman, "Justice, Civilization, and the Death Penalty." ©1985 by Princeton University Press.

C. Wu, "Analysis Shatters Cathedral Glass Myth." ©1998 by Science Service.

Topic Code	Print Your Full Name Here		
135161	Last	First	M.I.

Date	Sign Your Name Here
/ /	

LSAC®

LSAT® Writing Sample Topic

Directions: The scenario presented below describes two choices, either one of which can be supported on the basis of the information give
Your essay should consider both choices and argue for one over the other, based on the two specified criteria and the facts provided. There
is no "right" or "wrong" choice: a reasonable argument can be made for either.

History professor Talia Cordero has just finished a history book manuscript. Two different companies have offered to publish the manuscript, and Cordero must decide which offer to accept. Using the facts below, write an essay in which you argue for one offer over the other based on the following two criteria:

- Cordero wants to maximize the influence her book's ideas have on the study of history.
- Cordero wants to retain as many rights as possible over future use of the book's content.

Penwright Publishing is a major generalized academic press. The principal history journals frequently review Penwright's new history publications. These reviews often influence historians' decisions about what to read. Penwright has been slow to embrace electronic publish Their contract would give them exclusive publishing rights to Cordero's manuscript for 25 years. During that time, neither Cordero nor Penwright could allow more than a few paragraphs of the book to be used in other publications without first obtaining the other's permission.

Woodville Press is an up-and-coming academic press focusing on humanities publications. Woodville will soon market a new series of books as being on important topics in history. Cordero's book would be the first publication in the series. To promote the series, Woodville's website would initially offer both electronic and paper copies of the book at a significant discount. Woodville's contract would give them exclusive publishing rights to Cordero's manuscript for 15 years. Throughout that period, other publications authored by Cordero could each include up to one chapter from the book. Woodville would have sole authority over all other publication decisions concerning the book's content.

WP-W135

Scratch Paper
Do not write your essay in this space.

COMPUTING YOUR SCORE

Directions:

1. Use the Answer Key on the next page to check your answers.

2. Use the Scoring Worksheet below to compute your raw score.

3. Use the Score Conversion Chart to convert your raw score into the 120–180 scale.

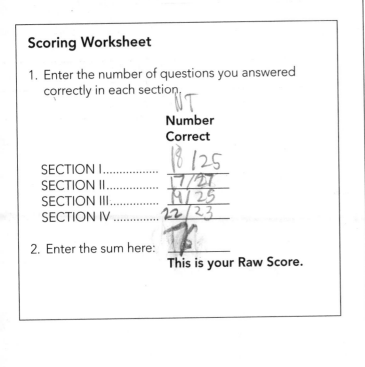

Scoring Worksheet

1. Enter the number of questions you answered correctly in each section.

   Number Correct

   SECTION I 18/25
   SECTION II 17/27
   SECTION III 14/25
   SECTION IV 22/23

2. Enter the sum here: _____
   This is your Raw Score.

Conversion Chart
For Converting Raw Score to the 120–180 LSAT Scaled Score
LSAT Form 6LSN117

Reported Score	Raw Score Lowest	Raw Score Highest
180	98	100
179	*	*
178	97	97
177	96	96
176	95	95
175	*	*
174	94	94
173	93	93
172	92	92
171	91	91
170	90	90
169	88	89
168	87	87
167	86	86
166	84	85
165	83	83
164	81	82
163	79	80
162	78	78
161	76	77
160	74	75
159	72	73
158	70	71
157	69	69
156	67	68
155	65	66
154	63	64
153	61	62
152	59	60
151	57	58
150	56	56
149	54	55
148	52	53
147	50	51
146	48	49
145	47	47
144	45	46
143	43	44
142	42	42
141	40	41
140	38	39
139	37	37
138	35	36
137	34	34
136	33	33
135	31	32
134	30	30
133	29	29
132	27	28
131	26	26
130	25	25
129	24	24
128	23	23
127	22	22
126	21	21
125	20	20
124	19	19
123	18	18
122	*	*
121	17	17
120	0	16

*There is no raw score that will produce this scaled score for this form.

ANSWER KEY

SECTION I

1.	B	8.	C	15.	C	22.	C
2.	C	9.	A	16.	C	23.	C
3.	A	10.	E	17.	D	24.	E
4.	E	11.	D	18.	B	25.	A
5.	C	12.	D	19.	B		
6.	D	13.	C	20.	E		
7.	E	14.	A	21.	B		

SECTION II

1.	C	8.	B	15.	C	22.	B
2.	A	9.	A	16.	A	23.	A
3.	B	10.	A	17.	D	24.	D
4.	C	11.	C	18.	C	25.	B
5.	A	12.	B	19.	E	26.	B
6.	D	13.	C	20.	B	27.	C
7.	E	14.	E	21.	E		

SECTION III

1.	C	8.	C	15.	E	22.	A
2.	B	9.	E	16.	A	23.	A
3.	C	10.	C	17.	B	24.	B
4.	D	11.	E	18.	E	25.	A
5.	A	12.	B	19.	C		
6.	B	13.	C	20.	D		
7.	B	14.	D	21.	E		

SECTION IV

1.	C	8.	B	15.	A	22.	D
2.	B	9.	C	16.	C	23.	D
3.	A	10.	A	17.	D		
4.	E	11.	A	18.	C		
5.	D	12.	A	19.	D		
6.	B	13.	E	20.	A		
7.	D	14.	B	21.	E		

THE OFFICIAL LSAT
PREPTEST®

76

- PrepTest 76
- Form 5LSN115

OCTOBER 2015

1

SECTION I

Time—35 minutes

27 Questions

__Directions:__ Each set of questions in this section is based on a single passage or a pair of passages. The questions are to be answered on the basis of what is __stated__ or __implied__ in the passage or pair of passages. For some of the questions, more than one of the choices could conceivably answer the question. However, you are to choose the __best__ answer; that is, the response that most accurately and completely answers the question, and blacken the corresponding space on your answer sheet.

"Never was anything as incoherent, shrill, chaotic and ear-splitting produced in music. The most piercing dissonances clash in a really atrocious harmony, and a few puny ideas only increase the disagreeable and
(5) deafening effect."

This remark aptly characterizes the reaction of many listeners to the music of Arnold Schoenberg. But this particular criticism comes from the pen of the dramatist August von Kotzebue, writing in 1806 about
(10) the overture to Beethoven's opera *Fidelio*.

Both Beethoven and Schoenberg stirred controversy because of the way they altered the language and extended the expressive range of music. Beethoven, of course, has stood as a cultural icon for
(15) more than a century, but that didn't happen overnight. His most challenging works did not become popular until well into the twentieth century and, significantly, after the invention of the phonograph, which made repeated listening possible.

(20) Like Beethoven, Schoenberg worked in a constantly changing and evolving musical style that acknowledged tradition while simultaneously lighting out for new territory. This is true of the three different musical styles through which Schoenberg's music
(25) evolved. He began in the late-Romantic manner— music charged with shifting chromatic harmonies— that was pervasive in his youth. People who enjoy the music of Brahms ought to love Schoenberg's *Verklaerte Nacht*, and they usually do, once they
(30) get past the fact that they are listening to a piece by Schoenberg.

Schoenberg later pushed those unstable harmonies until they no longer had a tonal basis. He did this in part because in his view it was the next inevitable step
(35) in the historical development of music, and he felt he was a man of destiny; he also did it because he needed to in order to express what he was compelled to express.

Finally, he developed the 12-tone technique as a
(40) means of bringing a new system of order to nontonal music and stabilizing it. In all three styles, Schoenberg operated at an awe-inspiring level of technical mastery. As his career progressed, his music became more condensed, more violent in its contrasts, and therefore
(45) more difficult to follow.

But the real issue for any piece of music is not how it is made, but what it has to say. If Schoenberg hadn't existed, it would have been necessary to invent him, and not because of the 12-tone system, the seeds
(50) of which appear in Mozart. What makes Schoenberg's music essential is that he precisely delineated

recognizable and sometimes disquieting emotional states that music had not recorded before. Some of his work remains disturbing not because it is incoherent,
(55) shrill, and ear-splitting, but because it unflinchingly faces difficult truths.

1. Which one of the following most accurately expresses the main point of the passage?

   (A) Though Schoenberg's music is more widely appreciated today than when he was alive, it is still regarded by many as shrill and incoherent.

   (B) Because of his accomplishments as a composer, Schoenberg deserves to be as highly regarded as Beethoven.

   (C) Though Schoenberg's music has not always been well received by listeners, it is worthy of admiration for both its expressive range and its technical innovations.

   (D) Schoenberg is most important for his invention of the 12-tone technique of musical composition.

   (E) Despite the fact that he wrote at a time when recordings of his compositions were possible, Schoenberg has not been accepted as quickly as Beethoven.

2. Which one of the following could be said to be disturbing in a way that is most analogous to the way that Schoenberg's music is said to be disturbing in line 54?

   (A) a comedian whose material relies heavily upon vulgar humor

   (B) a comedian whose humor shines a light on aspects of human nature many people would prefer to ignore

   (C) a comedian whose material is composed primarily of material already made famous by other comedians

   (D) a comedian whose material expresses an extreme political philosophy

   (E) a comedian whose style of humor is unfamiliar to the audience

GO ON TO THE NEXT PAGE.

3. The author begins with the quote from Kotzebue primarily in order to

(A) give an accurate account of the music of Beethoven

(B) give an accurate account of the music of Schoenberg

(C) suggest that even Beethoven composed works of uneven quality

(D) suggest that music that is at first seen as alienating need not seem alienating later

(E) suggest that one critic can sometimes be out of step with the general critical consensus

4. All of the following are similarities between Beethoven and Schoenberg that the author alludes to EXCEPT:

(A) They worked for a time in the late-Romantic style.

(B) Their music has been regarded by some listeners as incoherent, shrill, and chaotic.

(C) Their compositions stirred controversy.

(D) They worked in changing and evolving musical styles.

(E) They altered the language and expressive range of music.

5. Which one of the following aspects of Schoenberg's music does the author appear to value most highly?

(A) the technical mastery of his compositions

(B) the use of shifting chromatic harmonies

(C) the use of the 12-tone system of musical composition

(D) the depiction of emotional states that had never been captured in music before

(E) the progression through three different styles of composition seen over the course of his career

6. It can be inferred from the passage that the author would be most likely to agree with which one of the following statements about the relationships between the three styles in which Schoenberg wrote?

(A) Each successive style represents a natural progression from the previous one.

(B) Each successive style represents an inexplicable departure from the previous one.

(C) The second style represents a natural progression from the first, but the third style represents an inexplicable departure from the second.

(D) The second style represents an inexplicable departure from the first, but the third style represents a natural progression from the second.

(E) The second style represents an inexplicable departure from the first, but the third style represents a natural progression from the first.

GO ON TO THE NEXT PAGE.

The following passage was adapted from a law journal article published in 1998.

Industries that use biotechnology are convinced that intellectual property protection should be allowable for discoveries that stem from research and have commercial potential. Biotechnology researchers

(5) in academic institutions increasingly share this view because of their reliance on research funding that is in part conditional on the patentability of their results. However, questions about the extent to which biotechnology patenting is hindering basic research

(10) have recently come to the fore, and the patenting and commercialization of biotechnology inventions are now the focus of increased scrutiny by scientists and policy makers.

The perceived threat to basic research relates to

(15) restrictions on access to research materials, such as genetic sequences, cell lines, and genetically altered animals. These restrictions are seen as arising either from enforcement of a patent right or through operation of a contractual agreement. Some researchers

(20) fear that patenting biological materials will result in the patent holder's attempting or threatening to enjoin further research through a legal action for patent infringement. In other instances, a patent holder or the owner of biological materials may refuse to make such

(25) materials available to scientists conducting basic research unless a costly materials-transfer agreement or license agreement is undertaken. For example, the holder of a patent on unique biological materials may want to receive a benefit or compensation for the costs

(30) invested in the creation of the material. Academic researchers who oppose biotechnology patents fear that corporate patent holders will charge prohibitively high fees for the right to conduct basic research involving the use of patented materials.

(35) While it is true that the communal tradition of freely sharing research materials has shifted to a market model, it is also undoubtedly true that even in the early days of biotechnology, some researchers took measures to prevent competitors from gaining access

(40) to materials they had created. Scientists who resist the idea of patenting biotechnology seem to be confusing patent rights with control of access to biological materials. They mistakenly assume that granting a patent implies granting the right to deny access. In

(45) reality, whether a patent could or would be enforced against a researcher, particularly one conducting basic and noncommercial research, is questionable. First, patent litigation is an expensive endeavor and one usually initiated only to protect a market position

(50) occupied by the patent holder or an exclusive patent licensee. Second, there has been a tradition among judges deciding patent cases to respect a completely noncommercial research exception to patent infringement. Moreover, it is likely that patents will

(55) actually spur rather than hinder basic research, because patents provide scientists with a compelling incentive to innovate. Researchers know that patents bring economic rewards as well as a degree of licensing control over the use of their discoveries.

7. Which one of the following most accurately expresses the main point of the passage?

(A) By commercializing the research enterprise, biotechnology patents threaten the progress of basic research in the biological sciences.

(B) The recent shift away from a communal tradition and toward a market-driven approach to basic scientific research has caused controversy among scientists.

(C) The current system of patent protection for intellectual property unfairly penalizes both academic researchers and commercial interests.

(D) Concerns expressed by academic researchers that biotechnology patents will negatively affect their ability to conduct basic research are largely misguided.

(E) Patent litigation is so expensive that biotechnology patent holders are unlikely to bring patent-infringement lawsuits against scientists engaged in basic research.

8. The academic researchers mentioned in lines 30–31 would be most likely to subscribe to which one of the following principles?

(A) The competitive dynamics of the market should be allowed to determine the course of basic scientific research.

(B) The inventor of a biological material should not be allowed to charge fees that would prevent its use in basic research.

(C) Academic researchers should take measures to prevent their competitors from gaining access to materials they have created.

(D) Universities should take aggressive legal action to protect their intellectual property.

(E) Funding for scientific research projects should depend at least in part on the commercial potential of those projects.

GO ON TO THE NEXT PAGE.

9. According to the passage, why do university researchers increasingly believe that patents should be granted for commercially promising biotechnology discoveries?

(A) Researchers' prospects for academic advancement depend on both the quality and the quantity of their research.

(B) Researchers' funding is often contingent on whether they can produce a patentable product.

(C) Researchers see no incompatibility between unfettered basic research and the granting of biotechnology patents.

(D) Researchers increasingly believe their intellectual labor is being unfairly exploited by universities that partner with for-profit corporations.

(E) Most researchers prefer a competitive model of scientific research to a communal model.

10. With which one of the following statements would the author be most likely to agree?

(A) In the early days of biotechnology research, scientists freely shared research materials because they were not entitled to intellectual property protection for their inventions.

(B) Corporate patent holders typically charge excessive fees for the right to conduct research involving their patented materials.

(C) The cost of patent litigation is an effective check on patent holders who might otherwise try to prevent researchers engaged in basic research from using patented materials.

(D) Biotechnology researchers in academic institutions rely too heavily on funding that is partially contingent on the patentability of their results.

(E) Scientists who oppose the idea of patenting biotechnology do so because their work is not sufficiently innovative to qualify for patent protection.

11. The author refers to the early days of biotechnology (line 38) primarily in order to

(A) furnish a brief account of the evolution of academic biotechnology research

(B) establish that present competitive practices in biotechnology research are not entirely unprecedented

(C) express nostalgia for a time when biotechnology research was untainted by commercial motives

(D) argue that biotechnology research is considerably more sophisticated today than it was in the past

(E) provide a historical justification for opposition to biotechnology patents

12. The passage provides the strongest support for inferring which one of the following?

(A) Policy makers are no less likely than academic researchers to favor new restrictions on biotechnology patents.

(B) Most biotechnology patent holders believe that the pursuit of basic research in academic institutions threatens their market position.

(C) Biotechnology researchers who work in academic institutions and oppose biotechnology patents are generally unable to obtain funding for their work.

(D) Suing for patent infringement is not the only way in which patent holders can assert legal control over the use of their patented materials.

(E) Rapid commercialization in the field of biotechnology has led to a dearth of highly educated biologists willing to teach in academic institutions.

13. Suppose a university researcher wants to conduct basic, noncommercial research involving cell lines patented by a for-profit biotechnology corporation. The author would be most likely to make which one of the following predictions about the researcher's prospects?

(A) The researcher will probably be unable to use the cell lines because the corporation holding the patent will demand a prohibitively high payment for their use.

(B) The corporation holding the patent will probably successfully sue the researcher for patent infringement if she conducts the research without permission.

(C) The university that employs the researcher will likely prohibit the research in an effort to avoid being sued by the corporation holding the patent.

(D) The researcher has a good chance of not being held liable for patent infringement if she conducts the research and is subsequently sued.

(E) The corporation will probably offer to fund the research if granted exclusive rights to any resulting marketable product.

GO ON TO THE NEXT PAGE.

Before contact with Europeans, the Haudenosaune, a group of nations in northeastern North America also known as the Iroquois, had been developing a form of communication, primarily for political purposes, that

(5) used wampum, a bead carved from seashell. Most historians have insisted that wampum was primarily a form of money. While wampum certainly did become a medium of exchange among Europeans and Haudenosaune alike, this was due to the Europeans,

(10) who misinterpreted the significance of wampum and used it solely to purchase goods from the Haudenosaune. However, the true significance of wampum for the Haudenosaune lies in its gradual development from objects with religious significance into a method for

(15) maintaining permanent peace among distinct nations. Over time wampum came to be used to record and convey key sociopolitical messages.

Wampum came in two colors, white and deep purple. Loose beads constituted the simplest and oldest

(20) form of wampum. Even in the form of loose beads, wampum could represent certain basic ideas. For example, white was associated with the sky-yearning spirit, Sapling, whose terrestrial creations, such as trees, were often beneficial to humanity; deep purple

(25) was associated with Sapling's twin brother, Flint, the earth-loving spirit whose frequent mischievous vandalism (e.g., in the form of storms) often severely disrupted human life. Legend indicates, for example, that ancient Haudenosaune anglers threw the beads

(30) into the water in which they fished to communicate with Sapling or Flint (differing versions of the Haudenosaune cosmology attribute the creation of fish to one or the other of these spirits). Later, loose beads were strung together forming string wampum. It is

(35) thought that string wampum was used to send simple political messages such as truce requests.

It was, however, the formation of the Haudenosaune Confederacy from a group of warring tribes, believed by some to have occurred around 1451, that supplied

(40) the major impetus for making wampum a deliberate system of both arbitrary and pictorially derived symbols designed primarily for political purposes. This is evident in the invention of wampum belts to encode the provisions of the Haudenosaune

(45) Confederacy's constitution. These belts combined string wampum to form icons that could be deciphered by those knowing the significance of the stylized symbols. For example, longhouses, depicted in front-view outline, usually meant a particular nation

(50) of the confederacy. Council fires, possibly indicating talks in progress, were diamond outlines that could appear alone or within trees or longhouses. Lines between humanlike figures seem to have indicated the current state of relations between peoples; belts

(55) containing such images were often used as safe-conduct passes. The arrangements of the two colors also directed interpretation of the symbols. Thus, the belts served to record, store, and make publicly available items of governmental business.

(60) Although the wampum symbol system had a limited lexicon, it served to effectively frame and enforce the law of the confederacy for hundreds of years.

14. Which one of the following most accurately expresses the main point of the passage?

(A) The Haudenosaune's use of wampum originated with combinations of strings of beads with religious significance, but the need for communication between nations led to more complex uses of wampum including the transmission of political messages.

(B) For the Haudenosaune, wampum did not originally serve as a form of money but as an evolving form of communication that, through the use of colors and symbols, conveyed information and that eventually encoded the provisions of the Haudenosaune Confederacy's constitution.

(C) Wampum's significance for the Haudenosaune— as a form of communication linking their traditions with the need for the sharing of information within the confederacy—was changed through European contact so that it became exclusively a medium of commercial exchange.

(D) There is substantial evidence that the Haudenosaune's use of wampum as a medium of communication based on color combinations had its origin in the political events surrounding the establishment of the Haudenosaune Confederacy.

(E) Because of the role played by wampum in relations between the Haudenosaune and Europeans, many historians have overlooked the communicative role that bead combinations played in Haudenosaune culture prior to contact with Europeans.

15. The fishing practice mentioned in the second paragraph is offered primarily as an instance of

(A) a type of knowledge that was encoded and passed on through the use of wampum

(B) a traditional practice that was altered by contact with Europeans

(C) an activity that was regulated by the laws of the Haudenosaune Confederacy

(D) a practice that many historians learned of by studying wampum

(E) a traditional practice that reflects a stage in the evolution of wampum's uses

GO ON TO THE NEXT PAGE.

16. The last paragraph of the passage serves primarily to

(A) detail how wampum belts evolved from other forms of wampum
(B) distinguish between wampum belts and less complex forms of string wampum
(C) illustrate how wampum functioned as a system of symbolic representation
(D) outline the Haudenosaune Confederacy's constitution as it was encoded using wampum
(E) give evidence of wampum's effectiveness as a means of ensuring compliance with the law of the Haudenosaune Confederacy

17. It can be inferred from the passage that the author would be most likely to agree with which one of the following?

(A) Even if the evolution of wampum had not been altered by the arrival of Europeans, wampum would likely have become a form of currency because of its compactness.
(B) The use of colors in wampum to express meaning arose in response to the formation of the Haudenosaune Confederacy.
(C) The ancient associations of colors with spirits were important precursors to, and foundations of, later wampum representations that did not depend directly on these associations for their meaning.
(D) Because the associations with certain colors shifted over time, the same color beads acquired different meanings on belt wampum as opposed to string wampum.
(E) If the Europeans who first began trading with the Haudenosaune had been aware that wampum was used as a means of communication, they would not have used wampum as a medium of exchange.

18. The passage provides the most support for inferring which one of the following?

(A) Wampum was probably used on occasion as a medium of economic exchange long before the Haudenosaune had contact with Europeans.
(B) The formation of the Haudenosaune Confederacy called for a more complex method of communication than wampum as used until then had provided.
(C) Once wampum came to be used as currency in trade with Europeans, the constitution of the Haudenosaune Confederacy had to be recodified using other methods of representation.
(D) Prior to Haudenosaune contact with Europeans, wampum served primarily as a means of promulgating official edicts and policies of the Haudenosaune Confederacy.
(E) As belt wampum superseded string wampum as a method of communication, wampum beads acquired subtler shadings in the colors used to represent abstract ideas.

19. It can be inferred from the passage that the author would be most likely to agree with which one of the following?

(A) There is evidence that objects similar to wampum were used for symbolic representation by other peoples in addition to the Haudenosaune.
(B) The Europeans who first came in contact with the Haudenosaune insisted on using wampum as a form of currency in spite of their awareness of its true significance.
(C) There is evidence that Europeans who came in contact with the Haudenosaune adopted some long-standing Haudenosaune uses of wampum.
(D) A long-term peaceful association among the groups that formed the Haudenosaune Confederacy was an important precondition for the use of wampum as a means of communication.
(E) Present day interpretations of the significance of some of the symbols used in wampum belts are not conclusive.

GO ON TO THE NEXT PAGE.

Passage A

Karl Popper's main contribution to the philosophy of science concerns the power of negative evidence. The fundamental point is simple: No number of white swans, for example, can ever prove that all swans are
(5) white, but a single black swan disproves the hypothesis. Popper gives this logical asymmetry between positive and negative evidence hyperbolic application, maintaining that positive evidence has no value as evidence and that negative evidence is tantamount to
(10) disproof. Moreover, Popper takes the search for negative evidence to be at the heart of scientific research; that is, for Popper, scientific research involves not only generating bold theories, but also searching for evidence that would disprove them.
(15) Indeed, for him, a theory counts as scientific only if it makes predictions that are testable in this way.

However, Popper's use of the logical asymmetry does not adequately capture the actual situation scientists face. If a theory deductively entails a false
(20) prediction, then the theory must be false as well. But a scientific theory rarely entails predictions on its own. When scientists actually derive a theory's predictions, they almost always need diverse additional "auxiliary" premises, which appeal to other theories, to the correct
(25) functioning of instrumentation, to the absence of disturbing forces, etc. When a prediction fails, logic indicates that at least one of the premises must be false, but it does not indicate which one. When an experiment does not work out as predicted, there is
(30) usually more than one possible explanation. Positive evidence is never conclusive. But negative evidence rarely is either.

Passage B

When the planet Uranus was discovered, astronomers attempted to predict its orbit. They based
(35) their predictions on Newton's laws and auxiliary assumptions about the mass of the sun and the masses, orbits, and velocities of other planets. One of the auxiliary assumptions was that no planets existed in the vicinity of Uranus. When the astronomers made
(40) their observations, they found that the orbit they had predicted for Uranus was incorrect. One possible explanation for the failure of their prediction was that Newton's laws were incorrect. Another was that there was an error in the auxiliary assumptions. The
(45) astronomers changed their assumptions about the existence of other planets, concluding that there must be another planet close enough to Uranus to produce the observed orbit. Not long afterward, scientists discovered the planet Neptune in the precise place it
(50) would have to be to bring their calculations into alignment with their observations.

Later astronomers, again using Newton's laws, predicted the orbit of Mercury. Once again, the predictions were not borne out. They hypothesized the
(55) existence of another planet in the vicinity, which they called Vulcan. However, Vulcan was never found, and some scientists began to think that perhaps Newton's laws were in error. Finally, when Einstein's general theory of relativity was introduced, astronomers

(60) discovered that calculations based on that theory and the old auxiliary assumptions predicted the observed orbit of Mercury, leading to the rejection of Newton's theory of gravity and to increased confidence in Einstein's theory.

20. Which one of the following is a central topic of both passages?

(A) the logical asymmetry of positive and negative evidence
(B) the role of auxiliary assumptions in predicting planetary orbits
(C) the role of negative evidence in scientific research
(D) the proper technique for confirming a scientific theory
(E) the irrelevance of experimentation for disproving a scientific theory

21. Which one of the following is mentioned in passage A and illustrated in passage B?

(A) repudiating an experimental result
(B) revising a theory
(C) disproving a theory
(D) predicting a planet's orbit
(E) theories that are not testable by experiment

22. In passage B, which one of the following most clearly illustrates a disturbing force, as described in passage A (line 26)?

(A) Uranus
(B) the sun
(C) Neptune
(D) Mercury
(E) the moon

23. In saying that Popper gives a certain idea "hyperbolic application" (line 7), the author of passage A means to suggest that Popper

(A) extends the idea to cases in which it does not apply
(B) underestimates the significance of the idea
(C) commits a logical fallacy in reasoning about the idea
(D) draws too radical a conclusion from the idea
(E) exaggerates the idea's relevance to a particular theory

GO ON TO THE NEXT PAGE.

24. The author of passage A would be most likely to take which one of the following results mentioned in passage B as support for the claim made in the last sentence of passage A?

(A) the discovery of Uranus
(B) the initial failure of Newton's laws to correctly predict Uranus's orbit
(C) the ultimate failure of Newton's laws to correctly predict Mercury's orbit
(D) the failure to find Vulcan
(E) the success of Einstein's general theory of relativity at predicting Mercury's orbit

25. In passage B's description of the developments leading to the rejection of Newton's theory of gravity, which one of the following astronomical bodies plays a role most analogous to the black swan discussed in passage A?

(A) Mercury
(B) Uranus
(C) Neptune
(D) Venus
(E) the sun

26. It can be inferred that the author of passage B would be likely to be most skeptical of which one of the following ideas mentioned in passage A?

(A) Popper's main contribution to the philosophy of science concerned the power of negative evidence.
(B) Positive evidence plays no role in supporting a theory.
(C) Auxiliary premises are usually needed in order to derive predictions from a scientific theory.
(D) There is a logical asymmetry between positive and negative evidence.
(E) Scientific research involves generating bold theories and attempting to refute them.

27. Which one of the following scientific episodes is most analogous to the discovery of Neptune, as that episode is described in passage B?

(A) Galileo proposed that ocean tides are the result of Earth's motion in its orbit around the sun. But Galileo's theory of tides falsely predicted that there is only one high tide per day, when in fact there are two.

(B) By observing "variable stars"—stars that vary in brightness—in Andromeda, Edwin Hubble discovered that Andromeda is actually a galaxy in its own right. This enabled him to settle the debate about whether the Milky Way constitutes the entirety of the universe.

(C) Walter Alvarez postulated that an asteroid impact caused the extinction of the dinosaurs. He based this on observing high levels of the mineral iridium in certain rock core samples. Later evidence of a large impact crater was discovered in the Yucatan Peninsula that dates to the time of the dinosaur extinction.

(D) Bernard Brunhes discovered rocks that were magnetized in a direction opposite to that of the present-day magnetic field. He concluded that Earth's magnetic field must have been reversed at some point in the past.

(E) When a neutron decays into a proton and an electron, the combined energies of the two particles is less than the energy of the original neutron, in apparent contradiction of the law of conservation of energy. Wolfgang Pauli postulated that a third undetected particle is also created during the decay. The particle's existence was later confirmed.

S T O P

IF YOU FINISH BEFORE TIME IS CALLED, YOU MAY CHECK YOUR WORK ON THIS SECTION ONLY.
DO NOT WORK ON ANY OTHER SECTION IN THE TEST.

SECTION II

Time—35 minutes

26 Questions

<u>Directions:</u> The questions in this section are based on the reasoning contained in brief statements or passages. For some questions, more than one of the choices could conceivably answer the question. However, you are to choose the <u>best</u> answer; that is, the response that most accurately and completely answers the question. You should not make assumptions that are by commonsense standards implausible, superfluous, or incompatible with the passage. After you have chosen the best answer, blacken the corresponding space on your answer sheet.

1. In the bodies of reptiles, some industrial by-products cause elevated hormonal activity. Hormones govern the development of certain body parts, and in reptiles abnormal development of these parts occurs only with elevated hormonal activity. Recently, several alligators with the telltale developmental abnormalities were discovered in a swamp. So, apparently, industrial by-products have entered the swamp's ecosystem.

   The reasoning in the argument is most vulnerable to criticism on the grounds that the argument

   (A) provides no explanation for developmental abnormalities that do not result from elevated hormonal activity
   (B) fails to consider whether elevated hormonal activity can result from factors other than the presence of industrial by-products
   (C) fails to address the possibility that industrial by-products were contained in food the alligators ate
   (D) fails to say whether reptiles other than alligators were examined for the same developmental abnormalities that were discovered in the alligators
   (E) uses evidence drawn from a sample of alligators that is unlikely to be representative of alligators in general

2. Government official: Residents who are foreign citizens can serve as public servants at most levels, but not as cabinet secretaries. This is wise, since cabinet secretaries perform some duties that should be performed only by citizens, and no one should be appointed to a position if it involves duties that person should not perform. Moreover, a cabinet undersecretary is expected to serve as cabinet secretary when the actual secretary is unavailable. So, _____.

   Which one of the following most logically completes the government official's statement?

   (A) foreign citizens who serve as public servants should be granted citizenship in the country they serve
   (B) foreign citizens should not be appointed as cabinet undersecretaries
   (C) only former cabinet undersecretaries should be appointed as cabinet secretaries
   (D) foreign citizens should be eligible to serve as cabinet secretaries
   (E) cabinet undersecretaries should not be expected to stand in for cabinet secretaries

GO ON TO THE NEXT PAGE.

3. Doris: I've noticed that everyone involved in student government is outspoken. So if we want students to be more outspoken, we should encourage them to become involved in student government.

   Zack: Those who are in student government became involved precisely because they are outspoken in the first place. Encouraging others to become involved will do nothing to make them more outspoken.

   Doris and Zack disagree over whether

   (A) students should be more outspoken
   (B) students should be encouraged to become involved in student government
   (C) becoming involved in student government makes students more outspoken
   (D) all students who are involved in student government are outspoken
   (E) students will not become more outspoken unless they become involved in student government

4. Biologist: A careful study of the behavior of six individual chameleons concluded that lizards such as chameleons bask in the sun not only for warmth but also to regulate their production of vitamin D. Critics of the study—although correct in observing that its sample size was very small—are wrong to doubt its results. After all, the study's author is well regarded professionally and has been doing excellent work for years.

   The reasoning in the biologist's argument is most vulnerable to criticism on the grounds that the argument

   (A) takes the behavior of chameleons to be generalizable to lizards as a whole
   (B) fails to explain how chameleons regulate their vitamin D production by basking in the sun
   (C) focuses its attention on the study's author rather than on the study itself
   (D) fails to demonstrate that the study's critics have relevant expertise
   (E) holds the study's author to a higher standard than it holds the study's critics

5. Political scientist: Some analysts point to the government's acceptance of the recent protest rally as proof that the government supports freedom of popular expression. But the government supports no such thing. Supporting freedom of popular expression means accepting the expression of ideas that the government opposes as well as the expression of ideas that the government supports. The message of the protest rally was one that the government entirely supports.

   Which one of the following is an assumption that is required by the political scientist's argument?

   (A) The government helped to organize the recent protest rally.
   (B) The message of the recent protest rally did not concern any function of the government.
   (C) The government would not have accepted a protest rally whose message it opposed.
   (D) There are groups that are inhibited from staging a protest rally out of a fear of government response.
   (E) The government feared a backlash if it did not show acceptance of the recent protest rally.

6. Lawyer: In addition to any other penalties, convicted criminals must now pay a "victim surcharge" of $30. The surcharge is used to fund services for victims of violent crimes, but this penalty is unfair to nonviolent criminals since the surcharge applies to all crimes, even nonviolent ones like petty theft.

   Which one of the following principles, if valid, would most help to justify the reasoning in the lawyer's argument?

   (A) The penalties for a crime should be severe enough to deter most people who would commit the crime if there were no penalties.
   (B) The overall penalty for a violent crime should be more severe than the overall penalty for any nonviolent crime.
   (C) A surcharge intended to provide services to victims is justified only if all proceeds of the surcharge are used to provide services.
   (D) A criminal should not be required to pay for services provided to victims of crimes that are more serious than the type of crime the criminal has been convicted of.
   (E) Convicted thieves should be fined an amount at least as great as the value of the property stolen.

GO ON TO THE NEXT PAGE.

7. Economist: Owing to global economic forces since 1945, our country's economy is increasingly a service economy, in which manufacturing employs an ever smaller fraction of the workforce. Hence, we have engaged in less and less international trade.

Which one of the following, if true, would most help to explain the decreasing engagement in international trade by the economist's country?

(A) International trade agreements have usually covered both trade in manufactured goods and trade in services.

(B) Employment in the service sector tends to require as many specialized skills as does employment in manufacturing.

(C) Because services are usually delivered in person, markets for services tend to be local.

(D) Many manufacturing jobs have been rendered obsolete by advances in factory automation.

(E) Some services can be procured less expensively from providers in other countries than from providers in the economist's country.

8. Merton: A study showed that people who live on very busy streets have higher rates of heart disease than average. I conclude that this elevated rate of heart disease is caused by air pollution from automobile exhaust.

Ortiz: Are you sure? Do we know whether people living on busy streets have other lifestyle factors that are especially conducive to heart disease?

Ortiz criticizes Merton's argument by

(A) raising a question about the validity of the study that Merton cites

(B) contending that Merton needs to take into account other effects of air pollution

(C) claiming that Merton misunderstands a crucial aspect of the study's findings

(D) raising a counterexample to the general conclusion that Merton draws

(E) suggesting that alternative explanations for the study's findings need to be ruled out

9. Two lakes in the Pawpaw mountains, Quapaw and Highwater, were suffering from serious declines in their fish populations ten years ago. Since that time, there has been a moratorium on fishing at Quapaw Lake, and the fish population there has recovered. At Highwater Lake, no such moratorium has been imposed, and the fish population has continued to decline. Thus, the ban on fishing is probably responsible for the rebound in the fish population at Quapaw Lake.

Which one of the following, if true, most seriously weakens the argument above?

(A) Highwater Lake is in an area of the mountains that is highly susceptible to acid rain.

(B) Prior to the ban, there was practically no fishing at Quapaw Lake.

(C) Highwater Lake is much larger than Quapaw Lake.

(D) Several other lakes in the Pawpaw mountains have recently had increases in their fish populations.

(E) There used to be a greater variety of fish species in Highwater Lake than in Quapaw Lake, but there no longer is.

10. The Asian elephant walks with at least two, and sometimes three, feet on the ground at all times. Even though it can accelerate, it does so merely by taking quicker and longer steps. So the Asian elephant does not actually run.

The conclusion drawn above follows logically if which one of the following is assumed?

(A) If an animal cannot accelerate, then it cannot run.

(B) To run, an animal must have all of its feet off the ground at once.

(C) The Asian elephant can walk as quickly as some animals run.

(D) It is unusual for a four-legged animal to keep three feet on the ground while walking.

(E) All four-legged animals walk with at least two feet on the ground at all times.

GO ON TO THE NEXT PAGE.

11. A hardware store generally sells roughly equal numbers of Maxlast brand hammers and Styron brand hammers. Last week, all of the Maxlast hammers were put on sale and placed in a display case just inside the store entrance while the Styron hammers retained their usual price and location. Surprisingly, the Styron hammers slightly outsold the Maxlast hammers.

Which one of the following, if true, does most to explain the surprising result?

(A) For the first several seconds after shoppers enter a store, they do not take detailed notice of the store's merchandise.

(B) Most of the hardware store's customers are attracted by quality and service rather than low prices.

(C) Customers who bought the Maxlast hammers last week commonly mentioned the sale as their reason for buying a hammer at that time.

(D) The hardware store circulated flyers that publicized the sale prices on Maxlast hammers.

(E) In general, a single item that is on sale will not motivate shoppers to make a special trip to a store.

12. In an experiment, two groups of mice—one whose diet included ginkgo extract and one that had a normal diet—were taught to navigate a maze. The mice whose diet included ginkgo were more likely to remember how to navigate the maze the next day than were the other mice. However, the ginkgo may not have directly enhanced memory. Other studies have found that ginkgo reduces stress in mice, and lowering very high stress levels is known to improve recall.

Which one of the following, if true, would most weaken the argument?

(A) The doses of ginkgo in the diet of the mice in the experiment were significantly higher than the doses that have been shown to reduce stress in mice.

(B) Neither the mice who received the ginkgo nor the other mice in the experiment exhibited physiological signs of higher-than-normal stress.

(C) Some chemical substances that reduce stress in mice also at least temporarily impair their memory.

(D) Scientists have not yet determined which substances in ginkgo are responsible for reducing stress in mice.

(E) The mice who received the ginkgo took just as long as the other mice to learn to navigate the maze.

13. Some of the politicians who strongly supported free trade among Canada, the United States, and Mexico are now refusing to support publicly the idea that free trade should be extended to other Latin American countries.

If the statement above is true, which one of the following must also be true?

(A) Some of the politicians who now publicly support extending free trade to other Latin American countries did not support free trade among Canada, the United States, and Mexico.

(B) Not all politicians who now publicly support extending free trade to other Latin American countries strongly supported free trade among Canada, the United States, and Mexico.

(C) Some of the politicians who strongly supported free trade among Canada, the United States, and Mexico have changed their position on free trade.

(D) Not all politicians who strongly supported free trade among Canada, the United States, and Mexico now publicly support extending free trade to other Latin American countries.

(E) Some of the politicians who strongly supported free trade among Canada, the United States, and Mexico now publicly oppose extending free trade to other Latin American countries.

GO ON TO THE NEXT PAGE.

14. Principle: Any person or business knowingly aiding someone's infringement on a copyright is also guilty of copyright infringement.

Application: Grandview Department Store, which features a self-service photo-printing kiosk, is guilty of copyright infringement since a customer using the kiosk infringed on a wedding photographer's copyright by printing photographs whose copyright is held by the photographer.

Which one of the following, if assumed, most helps to justify the application of the principle?

(A) The operator of a business has the same legal obligations to customers who use self-service facilities as it has to customers who use full-service facilities.

(B) The management of a business that is open to the public is obligated to report to the authorities any illegal activity that it witnesses on its property.

(C) The owner of a self-service printing kiosk should post a notice advising customers that copyrighted material should not be printed at the kiosk without the permission of the copyright holder.

(D) Owners of self-service facilities should monitor those facilities in order to ensure that they are not used for illegal or unethical purposes.

(E) A person or business providing a service that can be expected to be used to infringe on a copyright should be considered to knowingly aid any copyright infringer using the service.

15. Journalism's purpose is to inform people about matters relevant to the choices they must make. Yet, clearly, people often buy newspapers or watch television news programs precisely because they contain sensationalistic gossip about people whom they will never meet and whose business is of little relevance to their lives. Obviously, then, the sensationalistic gossip contained in newspapers and television news programs _____.

Which one of the following most logically completes the argument?

(A) is at least sometimes included for nonjournalistic reasons

(B) prevents those news media from achieving their purpose

(C) is more relevant to people's lives now than it used to be

(D) should not be thought of as a way of keeping an audience entertained

(E) is of no value to people who are interested in journalism

16. When surveyed about which party they would like to see in the legislature, 40 percent of respondents said Conservative, 20 percent said Moderate, and 40 percent said Liberal. If the survey results are reliable, we can conclude that most citizens would like to see a legislature that is roughly 40 percent Conservative, 20 percent Moderate, and 40 percent Liberal.

Which one of the following most accurately describes a flaw in the reasoning of the argument?

(A) The argument uses premises about the actual state of affairs to draw a conclusion about how matters should be.

(B) The argument draws a conclusion that merely restates a premise presented in favor of it.

(C) The argument takes for granted that the preferences of a group as a whole are the preferences of most individual members of the group.

(D) The argument fails to consider that the survey results might have been influenced by the political biases of the researchers who conducted the survey.

(E) The argument uses evidence that supports only rough estimates to draw a precisely quantified conclusion.

GO ON TO THE NEXT PAGE.

17. City leader: If our city adopts the new tourism plan, the amount of money that tourists spend here annually will increase by at least $2 billion, creating as many jobs as a new automobile manufacturing plant would. It would be reasonable for the city to spend the amount of money necessary to convince an automobile manufacturer to build a plant here, but adopting the tourism plan would cost less.

The city leader's statements, if true, provide the most support for which one of the following?

(A) The city should implement the least expensive job creation measures available.

(B) In general, it is reasonable for the city to spend money to try to convince manufacturing companies to build plants in the city.

(C) The city cannot afford both to spend money to convince an automobile manufacturer to build a plant in the city and to adopt the new tourism plan.

(D) It would be reasonable for the city to adopt the new tourism plan.

(E) The only way the city can create jobs is by increasing tourism.

18. An article claims that many medical patients have an instinctual ability to predict sudden changes in their medical status. But the evidence given is anecdotal and should not be trusted. The case is analogous to empirically disproven reports that babies are born in disproportionately high numbers during full moons. Once that rumor became popular, maternity room staff were more likely to remember busy nights with full moons than busy nights without them.

The argument requires the assumption that

(A) the article claiming that medical patients can instinctually predict sudden changes in their medical status will soon be empirically disproven

(B) patients' predictions of sudden changes in their medical status are less likely to be remembered by medical staff if no such change actually occurs

(C) the patients in the article were not being serious when they predicted sudden changes in their medical status

(D) babies are less likely to be born during a night with a full moon than during a night without a full moon

(E) the idea that medical patients have an instinctual ability to predict sudden changes in their medical status is not a widely held belief

19. Politician: Union leaders argue that increases in multinational control of manufacturing have shifted labor to nations without strong worker protections, resulting in a corresponding global decrease in workers' average wages. Given that these leaders have a vested interest in seeing wages remain high, they would naturally want to convince legislators to oppose multinational control. Thus, legislators should reject this argument.

The reasoning in the politician's argument is flawed in that the argument

(A) treats the mere fact that certain people are union members as sufficient to cast doubt on all of the viewpoints expressed by those people

(B) presumes, without providing justification, that anyone whose political motivations are clearly discernible is an unreliable source of information to legislators

(C) treats circumstances potentially affecting the union leaders' argument as sufficient to discredit those leaders' argument

(D) presumes, without providing justification, that the argument it cites is the union leaders' only argument for their view

(E) presumes, without providing evidence, that leaders of all unions argue against increases in multinational control of manufacturing

20. Professor: The number of new university students who enter as chemistry majors has not changed in the last ten years, and job prospects for graduates with chemistry degrees are better than ever. Despite this, there has been a significant decline over the past decade in the number of people earning chemistry degrees.

Which one of the following, if true, most helps to explain the decline?

(A) Many students enter universities without the academic background that is necessary for majoring in chemistry.

(B) There has been a significant decline in the number of undergraduate degrees earned in the natural sciences as a whole.

(C) Many students are very unsure of their choice when they pick a major upon entering universities.

(D) Job prospects for graduates with chemistry degrees are no better than prospects for graduates with certain other science degrees.

(E) Over the years, first-year chemistry has come to be taught in a more routinely methodical fashion, which dampens its intellectual appeal.

GO ON TO THE NEXT PAGE.

21. Although the first humans came to Australia 56,000 years ago and undoubtedly brought new diseases with them, human-borne diseases probably did not cause the mass extinction of large land animals and birds that took place over the following 10,000 years. After all, more than 55 different species disappeared at about the same time, and no one disease, however virulent, could be fatal to animals across that many different species.

Which one of the following arguments exhibits flawed reasoning that is most parallel to that in the argument above?

(A) Even though high interest rates can lead to an economic downturn, high interest rates probably did not cause the current economic downturn. It is true that rates have been on the rise, but high interest rates are not always economically harmful.

(B) Even though I can fix some things and you can fix some things, the two of us will be unable to repair our apartment without outside help. The apartment has both a broken window and a broken bedroom door, and neither of us is able to fix both doors and windows.

(C) Even though Lena, Jen, and Mark would like to go out to dinner together after the movie tonight, they will probably go straight home after the show. Of the five restaurants that are in the immediate vicinity of the theater, there is not a single one that all three of them like.

(D) Even though this painting is highly regarded by critics, it cannot legitimately be deemed great art. Most art that was produced in the last hundred years is not great art, and this painting, beautiful though it is, was probably painted only 40 years ago.

(E) Even though the influenza vaccine does not always prevent influenza, it sometimes reduces the severity of its symptoms. Therefore it is incorrect to say that some people who receive the vaccine derive no benefit from it.

22. A tax preparation company automatically adds the following disclaimer to every e-mail message sent to its clients: "Any tax advice in this e-mail should not be construed as advocating any violation of the provisions of the tax code." The only purpose this disclaimer could serve is to provide legal protection for the company. But if the e-mail elsewhere suggests that the client do something illegal, then the disclaimer offers no legal protection. So the disclaimer serves no purpose.

The argument's conclusion can be properly drawn if which one of the following is assumed?

(A) If the e-mail does not elsewhere suggest that the client do anything illegal, then the company does not need legal protection.

(B) If e-mail messages sent by the tax preparation company do elsewhere suggest that the recipient do something illegal, then the company could be subject to substantial penalties.

(C) A disclaimer that is included in every e-mail message sent by a company will tend to be ignored by recipients who have already received many e-mails from that company.

(D) At least some of the recipients of the company's e-mails will follow the advice contained in the body of at least some of the e-mails they receive.

(E) Some of the tax preparation company's clients would try to illegally evade penalties if they knew how to do so.

23. Well-intentioned people sometimes attempt to resolve the marital problems of their friends. But these attempts are usually ineffectual and thereby foster resentment among all parties. Thus, even well-intentioned attempts to resolve the marital problems of friends are usually unjustified.

Which one of the following principles, if valid, most strongly supports the reasoning above?

(A) One should get involved in other people's problems only with the intention of producing the best overall consequences.

(B) Interpersonal relations should be conducted in accordance with doing whatever is right, regardless of the consequences.

(C) Good intentions are the only legitimate grounds on which to attempt to resolve the marital problems of friends.

(D) The intentions of an action are irrelevant to whether or not that action is justified.

(E) No actions based on good intentions are justified unless they also result in success.

GO ON TO THE NEXT PAGE.

24. It has been said that authors who write in order to give pleasure cannot impart to their readers the truth of their subject matter. That claim cannot be true. If it were, one could determine the truthfulness of a book simply by looking at its sales figures. If the book were very popular, one could reasonably conclude that it gave people pleasure and therefore that at least some of what is written in the book is not true.

Which one of the following is an assumption required by the argument?

(A) When people choose to read a book, they generally do not already know whether reading it will give them pleasure.

(B) Even when an author writes with the goal of giving people pleasure, that goal will not necessarily be achieved.

(C) In many cases, a book's readers are unconcerned about the truth of the book's contents.

(D) A book will not give its readers pleasure unless it was intended by its author to have that effect.

(E) A book can be popular for reasons other than its ability to give readers pleasure.

25. It is likely that most of the new television programs Wilke & Wilke produce for this season will be canceled. Most of the new shows they produced last season were canceled due to insufficient viewership. Furthermore, their new shows are all police dramas, and few police dramas have been popular in recent years.

Which one of the following, if true, most helps to strengthen the argument?

(A) Wilke & Wilke have produced more new shows for this season than they produced last season.

(B) Most of the shows that Wilke & Wilke produced last year were police dramas.

(C) None of the shows that Wilke & Wilke produced last year that were not canceled were police dramas.

(D) All of the new shows that Wilke & Wilke produced last year that were canceled were police dramas.

(E) None of the most popular television shows last year were police dramas.

26. If a corporation obtains funds fraudulently, then the penalty should take into account the corporation's use of those funds during the time it held them. In such cases, the penalty should completely offset any profit the corporation made in using the funds.

Which one of the following conforms most closely to the principle illustrated above?

(A) If a driver causes an accident because the automobile being driven was not properly maintained, that driver should be required from then on to regularly demonstrate that his or her automobile is being properly maintained.

(B) If a factory is found to have been recklessly violating pollution laws, that factory should be required to make the expenditures necessary to bring it into compliance with those laws to the satisfaction of the regulators.

(C) If someone is sentenced to perform community service, the court has a responsibility to ensure that the community at large rather than a private group benefits from that service.

(D) If an athlete is found to have used banned performance-enhancing substances, that athlete should be prohibited from participating in all future athletic competitions.

(E) If a convicted criminal writes a memoir describing the details of that criminal's crime, any proceeds of the book should be donated to a charity chosen by a third party.

S T O P

IF YOU FINISH BEFORE TIME IS CALLED, YOU MAY CHECK YOUR WORK ON THIS SECTION ONLY.
DO NOT WORK ON ANY OTHER SECTION IN THE TEST.

SECTION III

Time—35 minutes

23 Questions

Directions: Each group of questions in this section is based on a set of conditions. In answering some of the questions, it may be useful to draw a rough diagram. Choose the response that most accurately and completely answers each question and blacken the corresponding space on your answer sheet.

Questions 1–6

A detective is trying to determine the order in which a criminal recruited seven accomplices—Peters, Quinn, Rovero, Stanton, Tao, Villas, and White. In addition to discovering that the suspect recruited the accomplices one at a time, the detective has established the following:

Stanton was recruited neither immediately before nor immediately after Tao.

Quinn was recruited earlier than Rovero.

Villas was recruited immediately before White.

Peters was recruited fourth.

1. Which one of the following could be the order in which the accomplices were recruited, from first to last?

(A) Quinn, Tao, Stanton, Peters, Villas, White, Rovero

(B) Quinn, White, Rovero, Peters, Stanton, Villas, Tao

(C) Villas, White, Quinn, Stanton, Peters, Tao, Rovero

(D) Villas, White, Stanton, Peters, Quinn, Tao, Rovero

(E) Villas, White, Stanton, Peters, Rovero, Tao, Quinn

GO ON TO THE NEXT PAGE.

2. Which one of the following could be the list of the middle five accomplices, in the order in which they were recruited, from second to sixth?

    (A) Quinn, Stanton, Peters, Tao, Villas
    (B) Quinn, Stanton, Peters, Tao, White
    (C) Villas, White, Peters, Quinn, Stanton
    (D) Villas, White, Peters, Rovero, Stanton
    (E) Villas, White, Quinn, Rovero, Stanton

3. If Tao was recruited second, which one of the following could be true?

    (A) Quinn was recruited third.
    (B) Rovero was recruited fifth.
    (C) Stanton was recruited sixth.
    (D) Villas was recruited sixth.
    (E) White was recruited third.

4. If Quinn was recruited immediately before Rovero, then Stanton CANNOT have been recruited

    (A) first
    (B) second
    (C) third
    (D) fifth
    (E) seventh

5. If White was recruited earlier than Rovero and if Rovero was recruited earlier than Tao, then which one of the following could be true?

    (A) Quinn was recruited first.
    (B) Rovero was recruited third.
    (C) Stanton was recruited second.
    (D) Tao was recruited sixth.
    (E) Villas was recruited sixth.

6. If White was recruited immediately before Quinn, which one of the following must have been recruited sixth?

    (A) Quinn
    (B) Rovero
    (C) Stanton
    (D) Villas
    (E) White

GO ON TO THE NEXT PAGE.

Questions 7–13

In the Lifestyle, Metro, and Sports sections of tomorrow's newspaper, a total of six different photographs are to appear, exactly two photographs per section. Each of the available photographs was taken by one of three photographers: Fuentes, Gagnon, and Hue. Selection of the photographs is constrained by the following conditions:

For each photographer, at least one but no more than three of that photographer's photographs must appear.

At least one photograph in the Lifestyle section must be by a photographer who has at least one photograph in the Metro section.

The number of Hue's photographs in the Lifestyle section must be the same as the number of Fuentes' photographs in the Sports section.

None of Gagnon's photographs can be in the Sports section.

L: __ __   F G H

M: __ __

S: __ __ *6*

7. Which one of the following could be an acceptable selection of the photographs to appear?

(A) Lifestyle: both photographs by Fuentes
     Metro: one photograph by Fuentes and one by Hue
     Sports: one photograph by Gagnon and one by Hue

(B) Lifestyle: one photograph by Fuentes and one by Gagnon
     Metro: one photograph by Fuentes and one by Gagnon
     Sports: both photographs by Hue

(C) Lifestyle: both photographs by Fuentes
     Metro: both photographs by Gagnon
     Sports: both photographs by Hue

(D) Lifestyle: both photographs by Gagnon
     Metro: one photograph by Fuentes and one by Gagnon
     Sports: one photograph by Fuentes and one by Hue

(E) Lifestyle: one photograph by Gagnon and one by Hue
     Metro: both photographs by Hue
     Sports: one photograph by Fuentes and one by Hue

GO ON TO THE NEXT PAGE.

9. L: G H
   M: G H
   6 S: F H

10. L: H H | H G | F H
    M: F G | F F | F G
    S: F F | F H | F H

11. L: F H
    M: G F H
    S: F H

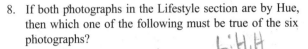

8. If both photographs in the Lifestyle section are by Hue, then which one of the following must be true of the six photographs?

L: H,H
M: H, G
S: F, F

(A) Exactly one is by Fuentes.
(B) Exactly three are by Fuentes.
(C) Exactly one is by Gagnon.
(D) Exactly two are by Gagnon.
(E) Exactly two are by Hue.

9. If one photograph in the Lifestyle section is by Gagnon and one is by Hue, then which one of the following must be true?

(A) Exactly one photograph in the Metro section is by Fuentes.
(B) Exactly one photograph in the Metro section is by Gagnon.
(C) Both photographs in the Metro section are by Gagnon.
(D) Exactly one photograph in the Sports section is by Hue.
(E) Both photographs in the Sports section are by Hue.

10. Which one of the following could be true of the photographs by Fuentes appearing in tomorrow's paper?

(A) One is in the Lifestyle section, one is in the Metro section, and one is in the Sports section.
(B) One is in the Lifestyle section, and two are in the Sports section.
(C) Two are in the Lifestyle section, and one is in the Sports section.
(D) One is in the Metro section, and two are in the Sports section.
(E) Two are in the Metro section, and one is in the Sports section.

11. If one photograph in the Lifestyle section is by Fuentes and one is by Hue, then which one of the following could be true?

(A) Both photographs in the Metro section are by Fuentes.
(B) Both photographs in the Metro section are by Gagnon.
(C) Exactly one photograph in the Metro section is by Hue.
(D) Both photographs in the Sports section are by Hue.
(E) Neither photograph in the Sports section is by Hue.

12. If both photographs in one of the three sections are by Gagnon, then which one of the following could be true?

(A) Both photographs in the Lifestyle section are by Hue.
(B) One photograph in the Lifestyle section is by Fuentes and one is by Hue.
(C) Both photographs in the Metro section are by Fuentes.
(D) One photograph in the Metro section is by Gagnon and one is by Hue.
(E) Both photographs in the Sports section are by Hue.

13. If one photograph in the Metro section is by Fuentes and one is by Hue, then which one of the following could be true?

(A) Both photographs in the Lifestyle section are by Fuentes.
(B) Both photographs in the Lifestyle section are by Gagnon.
(C) One photograph in the Lifestyle section is by Gagnon and one is by Hue.
(D) Both photographs in the Lifestyle section are by Hue.
(E) Both photographs in the Sports section are by Fuentes.

GO ON TO THE NEXT PAGE.

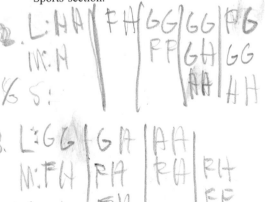

Questions 14–18

Exactly five students—Grecia, Hakeem, Joe, Katya, and Louise—are to work at a campus art gallery during a special exhibit that runs for exactly five days, Monday through Friday. Each day is divided into two nonoverlapping shifts—first and second—with each student working exactly two shifts. Each shift is worked by exactly one of the students according to the following scheduling restrictions:

No student works both shifts of any day.
On two consecutive days, Louise works the second shift.
On two nonconsecutive days, Grecia works the first shift.
Katya works on Tuesday and Friday.
Hakeem and Joe work on the same day as each other at least once.
Grecia and Louise never work on the same day as each other.

14. Which one of the following could be the list of the students who work the second shifts at the gallery, in order from Monday through Friday?

(A)   Hakeem, Louise, Louise, Hakeem, Katya
(B)   Joe, Hakeem, Grecia, Louise, Louise
(C)   Joe, Katya, Hakeem, Louise, Katya
(D)   Louise, Katya, Joe, Louise, Katya
(E)   Louise, Louise, Hakeem, Joe, Joe

GO ON TO THE NEXT PAGE.

15. Which one of the following must be true?

    (A) Grecia does not work at the gallery on Tuesday.
    (B) Hakeem does not work at the gallery on Wednesday.
    (C) Joe does not work at the gallery on Tuesday.
    (D) Joe does not work at the gallery on Thursday.
    (E) Louise does not work at the gallery on Tuesday.

16. If Hakeem works at the gallery on Wednesday, then Joe must work at the gallery on which one of the following pairs of days?

    (A) Monday and Wednesday
    (B) Monday and Thursday
    (C) Tuesday and Wednesday
    (D) Tuesday and Thursday
    (E) Wednesday and Thursday

17. If there is at least one day on which Grecia and Joe both work at the gallery, then which one of the following could be true?

    (A) Grecia works the first shift on Tuesday.
    (B) Hakeem works the second shift on Monday.
    (C) Hakeem works the second shift on Wednesday.
    (D) Joe works the first shift on Wednesday.
    (E) Joe works the first shift on Thursday.

18. If Katya works the second shift on Tuesday at the gallery, then which one of the following could be true?

    (A) Grecia works the first shift on Monday.
    (B) Hakeem works the first shift on Monday.
    (C) Hakeem works the second shift on Wednesday.
    (D) Joe works the second shift on Thursday.
    (E) Louise works the second shift on Monday.

GO ON TO THE NEXT PAGE.

<u>Questions 19–23</u>

A publisher is planning to publish six cookbooks—K, L, M, N, O, and P—over the course of the next year. Each cookbook will be published in one of two seasons—fall or spring—subject to the following conditions:

  M and P cannot be published in the same season as each other.
  K and N must be published in the same season as each other.
  If K is published in the fall, O must also be published in the fall.
  If M is published in the fall, N must be published in the spring.

19. Which one of the following is an acceptable schedule for the publication of the cookbooks?

  (A) fall: K, L, M, and O
      spring: N and P
  (B) fall: K, L, N, and O
      spring: M and P
  (C) fall: K, L, N, and P
      spring: M and O
  (D) fall: K, M, N, and O
      spring: L and P
  (E) fall: M and O
      spring: K, L, N, and P

GO ON TO THE NEXT PAGE.

20. If M is published in the fall, which one of the following is a pair of cookbooks that could both be published in the fall along with M?

   (A) K and O
   (B) L and N
   (C) L and O
   (D) N and P
   (E) O and P

21. If N is published in the fall, which one of the following could be true?

   (A) K is published in the spring.
   (B) L is published in the fall.
   (C) M is published in the fall.
   (D) O is published in the spring.
   (E) P is published in the spring.

F- N, K, O, M
S- M, L

22. The schedule for the publication of the cookbooks is fully determined if which one of the following is true?

   (A) K is published in the fall and L is published in the spring.
   (B) O is published in the fall and P is published in the spring.
   (C) P is published in the fall and L is published in the spring.
   (D) Both K and L are published in the spring.
   (E) Both M and L are published in the fall.

23. Which one of the following, if substituted for the condition that if M is published in the fall, N must be published in the spring, would have the same effect in determining the schedule for the publication of the cookbooks?

   (A) If L is published in the fall, M must be published in the spring.
   (B) If N is published in the fall, P must also be published in the fall.
   (C) If M is published in the spring, P must be published in the fall.
   (D) If N is published in the spring, M must also be published in the spring.
   (E) If O is published in the spring, N must also be published in the spring.

S T O P

IF YOU FINISH BEFORE TIME IS CALLED, YOU MAY CHECK YOUR WORK ON THIS SECTION ONLY.
DO NOT WORK ON ANY OTHER SECTION IN THE TEST.

SECTION IV

Time—35 minutes

25 Questions

Directions: The questions in this section are based on the reasoning contained in brief statements or passages. For some questions, more than one of the choices could conceivably answer the question. However, you are to choose the best answer; that is, the response that most accurately and completely answers the question. You should not make assumptions that are by commonsense standards implausible, superfluous, or incompatible with the passage. After you have chosen the best answer, blacken the corresponding space on your answer sheet.

1. Aisha: Vadim is going to be laid off. Vadim's work as a programmer has been exemplary since joining the firm. But management has already made the decision to lay off a programmer. And this firm strictly follows a policy of laying off the most recently hired programmer in such cases.

   Aisha's conclusion follows logically if which one of the following is assumed?

   (A) The firm values experience in its programmers more highly than any other quality.
   (B) When Vadim was hired, the policy of laying off the most recently hired programmer was clearly explained.
   (C) Vadim is the most recently hired programmer at the firm.
   (D) Every other programmer at the firm has done better work than Vadim.
   (E) It is bad policy that the firm always lays off the most recently hired programmer.

2. Wanda: It is common sense that one cannot create visual art without visual stimuli in one's work area, just as a writer needs written stimuli. A stark, empty work area would hinder my creativity. This is why there are so many things in my studio.

   Vernon: But a writer needs to read good writing, not supermarket tabloids. Are you inspired by the piles of laundry and empty soda bottles in your studio?

   Which one of the following most accurately expresses the principle underlying Vernon's response to Wanda?

   (A) It is unhealthy to work in a cluttered work area.
   (B) The quality of the stimuli in an artist's environment matters.
   (C) Supermarket tabloids should not be considered stimulating.
   (D) Messiness impairs artistic creativity.
   (E) One should be able to be creative even in a stark, empty work area.

3. The official listing of an animal species as endangered triggers the enforcement of legal safeguards designed to protect endangered species, such as tighter animal export and trade restrictions and stronger antipoaching laws. Nevertheless, there have been many cases in which the decline in the wild population of a species was more rapid after that species was listed as endangered than before it was so listed.

   Which one of the following, if true, does most to account for the increase in the rate of population decline described above?

   (A) The process of officially listing a species as endangered can take many years.
   (B) Public campaigns to save endangered animal species often focus only on those species that garner the public's affection.
   (C) The number of animal species listed as endangered has recently increased dramatically.
   (D) Animals are more desirable to collectors when they are perceived to be rare.
   (E) Poachers find it progressively more difficult to locate animals of a particular species as that species' population declines.

4. Annette: To persuade the town council to adopt your development plan, you should take them on a trip to visit other towns that have successfully implemented plans like yours.

   Sefu: But I have a vested interest in their votes. If council members were to accept a trip from me, it would give the appearance of undue influence.

   The dialogue provides the most support for the claim that Annette and Sefu disagree over whether

   (A) the council should adopt Sefu's development plan
   (B) Sefu should take the council on a trip to visit other towns
   (C) Sefu has a vested interest in the council's votes
   (D) other towns have successfully implemented similar development plans
   (E) the appearance of undue influence should be avoided

GO ON TO THE NEXT PAGE.

5. Scholar: Recently, some religions have updated the language of their traditional texts and replaced traditional rituals with more contemporary ones. These changes have been followed by increases in attendance at places of worship affiliated with these religions. This shows that any such modernization will result in increased numbers of worshipers.

The scholar's reasoning is flawed because the scholar presumes without giving sufficient justification that

(A) not every religion can update its texts and replace its traditional rituals

(B) modernization of religious texts and rituals will not involve an alteration of their messages

(C) the modernization of the texts and rituals of some religions was the cause of their increases in attendance

(D) making texts and rituals more modern is the only way in which a religion could bring about an increase in attendance at places of worship

(E) the growth in attendance at places of worship affiliated with religions that made their texts and rituals more modern is irreversible

6. If one is to participate in the regional band, one must practice very hard or be very talented. Therefore, Lily, who is first trombonist in the regional band and is very talented, does not practice hard.

The flawed reasoning in which one of the following arguments most closely resembles the flawed reasoning in the argument above?

(A) In order to have a chance to meet its objectives, the army needs good weather as a precondition for retaining its mobility. The weather is good today, so the army will meet its objectives.

(B) If Lois were on vacation, she would be visiting her brother in Chicago or seeing friends in Toronto. Since she is not on vacation, she is in neither Chicago nor Toronto.

(C) If Johnson is to win the local election, then neither Horan nor Jacobs can enter the race. Since neither of them plans to run, Johnson will win the race.

(D) To stay informed about current events, one must read a major newspaper or watch national TV news every day. So Julie, who is informed about current events and reads a major newspaper every day, does not watch TV news.

(E) If Wayne is to get a ride home from the library, either Yvette or Marty must be there. Yvette is not at the library, so Marty must be there.

7. Dietitian: Eating fish can lower one's cholesterol level. In a study of cholesterol levels and diet, two groups were studied. The first group ate a balanced diet including two servings of fish per week. The second group ate a very similar diet, but ate no fish. The first group showed lower cholesterol levels, on average, than the second group. The two groups had displayed similar average cholesterol levels prior to the study.

Which one of the following most accurately describes the role played in the dietitian's argument by the claim that the two groups had displayed similar average cholesterol levels prior to the study?

(A) It is offered as an objection to the main conclusion of the argument.

(B) It expresses the main conclusion of the argument.

(C) It rules out an alternative explanation of the data collected in the study.

(D) It provides background information on the purpose of the study.

(E) It introduces an alternative explanation of the phenomenon described in the main conclusion.

8. Satellite navigation systems (satnavs) for cars, in which computer voices announce directions as you drive, save fuel and promote safety. Studies show that, when assigned to novel destinations, drivers using satnavs took, on average, 7 percent fewer miles per journey than drivers using paper maps. Fewer miles driven means, on average, less fuel consumed. Also, the drivers who used satnavs drove more carefully in that they were not taking their eyes off the road to check paper maps.

Which one of the following, if true, most strengthens the argument?

(A) People who are often required to drive to novel destinations are more likely to use satnavs than people who are rarely required to drive to novel destinations.

(B) The more fuel a vehicle consumes, the more motivation a driver has to find the shortest route to his or her destination.

(C) Drivers who do not routinely need to drive to an unfamiliar location are more likely to plan out their route carefully prior to departure.

(D) Drivers who own satnavs usually prefer to drive to their accustomed destinations by using their customary routes rather than by following the directions given by the satnavs.

(E) Drivers who are given directions as needed are less likely to change course suddenly or make other risky maneuvers.

GO ON TO THE NEXT PAGE.

9. A manager cannot extract the best performance from employees by threatening them with termination or offering financial rewards for high productivity. Rather, employees must come to want to do a good job for its own sake. One of the best ways for a manager to achieve this is to delegate responsibility to them, especially for decisions that previously had to be made by the manager.

Which one of the following propositions is best illustrated by the situation described in the passage?

(A) Increased responsibility can improve a person's sense of how power should be used.

(B) It is often the case that the desire for prestige is more powerful than the desire for job security.

(C) In some cases one's effectiveness in a particular role can be enhanced by a partial relinquishing of control.

(D) People who carry out decisions are in the best position to determine what those decisions should be.

(E) Business works best by harnessing the self-interest of individuals to benefit the company as a whole.

10. Richard: Because it fails to meet the fundamental requirement of art—that it represent—abstract art will eventually be seen as an aberration.

Jung-Su: Although artists, like musicians, may reject literal representation, makers of abstract art choose to represent the purely formal features of objects, which are discovered only when everyday perspectives are rejected. Thus, whatever others might come to say, abstract art is part of the artistic mainstream.

Richard and Jung-Su disagree over whether

(A) makers of abstract art reject literal representation

(B) the fundamental requirement of art is that it represent

(C) musicians may reject literal representation

(D) abstract art will be seen as an aberration

(E) abstract art is representational

11. A person who knowingly brings about misfortune should be blamed for it. However, in some cases a person who unwittingly brings about misfortune should not be blamed for it. For example, a person should never be blamed for unwittingly bringing about misfortune if the person could not reasonably have foreseen it.

The principles above, if valid, most help to justify the reasoning in which one of the following?

(A) Although he would have realized it if he had thought about it, it did not occur to Riley that parking his car in the center lane of Main Street could lead to a traffic accident. So, if a traffic accident does result from Riley's parking his car in the center lane of Main Street, he should not be blamed for it.

(B) Oblicek had no idea that suggesting to her brother that he take out a loan to expand his business was likely to cause the business to go bankrupt, nor could she have reasonably foreseen this. So, if the loan does cause her brother's business to go bankrupt, Oblicek should not be blamed for it.

(C) Gougon had no reason to think that serving the hollandaise sauce would make his guests ill, but he was concerned that it might. Thus, if the hollandaise sauce does make Gougon's guests ill, Gougon should be blamed for it.

(D) When Dr. Fitzpatrick gave his patient the wrong medicine, he did not know that it would cause the patient to experience greatly increased blood pressure. So, if no one else knowingly did anything that contributed to the patient's increase in blood pressure, no one other than Dr. Fitzpatrick is to blame for it.

(E) Any reasonable person could have foreseen that dropping a lit cigarette in dry leaves would start a fire. Thus, even if Kapp did not realize this, she is to blame for starting a fire on Rodriguez's farm since she dropped a lit cigarette in dry leaves there.

GO ON TO THE NEXT PAGE.

12. Researcher: Research has shown that inhaling the scent of lavender has measurable physiological effects tending to reduce stress. It is known that intense stress can impair the immune system, making one more susceptible to illness. Therefore, it is likely that the incidence of illness among those who regularly inhale the scent of lavender is reduced by this practice.

Which one of the following is an assumption that the researcher's argument requires?

(A) Many, if not all, of the scents that have a tendency to reduce susceptibility to illness do so, at least in part, by reducing stress.

(B) Some people who regularly inhale the scent of lavender would otherwise be under enough stress to impair their immune systems.

(C) At least some people who use the scent of lavender to induce relaxation and reduce stress are no more susceptible to illness than average.

(D) In anyone for whom the scent of lavender reduces susceptibility to illness, it does so primarily by reducing stress.

(E) Reduced stress diminishes susceptibility to illness only for people who are under enough stress to impair their immune systems to at least some degree.

13. Government statistics show that the real (adjusted for inflation) average income for families has risen over the last five years. Therefore, since this year the Andersen family's income is average for families, the family's real income must have increased over the last five years.

The reasoning in the argument is most vulnerable to criticism on the grounds that the argument

(A) ambiguously uses the term "average" in two different senses

(B) fails to take into account inflation with respect to the Andersen family's income

(C) overlooks the possibility that most families' incomes are below average

(D) fails to consider the possibility that the Andersen family's real income was above average in the recent past

(E) presumes, without providing justification, that the government makes no errors in gathering accurate estimates of family income

14. Certain methods of creating high-quality counterfeit banknotes involve making accurate measurements of the images printed on genuine banknotes. Hence, if the production of high-quality counterfeit banknotes is to be prevented, some of the images on banknotes must be made very difficult or impossible to measure accurately.

The argument's conclusion can be properly drawn if which one of the following is assumed?

(A) Today's copying technology is sophisticated enough to replicate almost any paper product with great precision.

(B) Once the images printed on a banknote have been measured accurately, there is no further impediment to the banknote's being exactly replicated.

(C) Governments have better printing technology available to them than counterfeiters do.

(D) Few countries produce banknotes with images that are difficult for counterfeiters to measure accurately.

(E) New designs in banknotes generally lead to decreases in the amount of counterfeit currency in circulation.

15. Armstrong: For the treatment of a particular disease, Dr. Sullivan argues for using nutritional supplements rather than the pharmaceuticals that most doctors prescribe. But this is in his self-interest since he is paid to endorse a line of nutritional supplements. Thus, we should not use nutritional supplements in treating the disease.

Armstrong's argument is flawed in that it

(A) relies on two different meanings of the term "supplement" to draw a conclusion

(B) relies solely on an appeal to an authority whose trustworthiness should not necessarily be taken for granted

(C) appeals to people's emotions regarding the treatment of disease rather than to the efficacy of the two approaches to treatment

(D) criticizes Dr. Sullivan's motives for holding a position rather than addressing the position itself

(E) fails to justify its presumption that nutritional supplements cannot be used in conjunction with other treatments

GO ON TO THE NEXT PAGE.

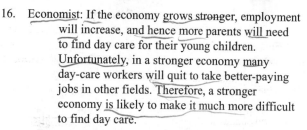

16. Economist: If the economy grows stronger, employment will increase, and hence more parents will need to find day care for their young children. Unfortunately, in a stronger economy many day-care workers will quit to take better-paying jobs in other fields. Therefore, a stronger economy is likely to make it much more difficult to find day care.

Which one of the following is an assumption the economist's argument requires?

(A) If the economy grows stronger, most of the new jobs that are created will be in fields that pay well.

(B) If the economy grows stronger, the number of new day-care workers will not be significantly greater than the number of day-care workers who move to better-paying jobs in other fields.

(C) If the economy grows stronger, the number of workers employed by day-care centers is likely to decrease.

(D) The shortage of day care for children is unlikely to worsen unless employment increases and many day-care center employees quit to take better-paying jobs in other fields.

(E) The total number of young children in day-care centers will decrease if the cost of day care increases significantly.

17. Ostrich farming requires far less acreage than cattle ranching requires, and ostriches reproduce much faster than cattle. Starting out in cattle ranching requires a large herd of cows, one bull, and at least two acres per cow. By contrast, two pairs of yearling ostriches and one acre of similar land are enough to begin ostrich farming. The start-up costs for ostrich farming are greater, but it can eventually bring in as much as five times what cattle ranching does.

Which one of the following is most strongly supported by the information above?

(A) Two pairs of yearling ostriches are more expensive than a herd of cows and a bull.

(B) Cattle ranching is not a good source of income.

(C) A cow consumes no more feed than an ostrich does.

(D) The average ostrich farm generates almost five times as much profit as the average cattle ranch.

(E) Ostrich farmers typically lose money during their first year.

18. For several centuries there have been hairless dogs in western Mexico and in coastal Peru. It is very unlikely that a trait as rare as hairlessness emerged on two separate occasions. Since the dogs have never existed in the wild, and the vast mountainous jungle separating these two regions would have made overland travel between them extremely difficult centuries ago, the dogs must have been transported from one of these regions to the other by boat, probably during trading expeditions.

Which one of the following is an assumption that the argument requires?

(A) Hairless dogs have never been found anywhere except in the regions of western Mexico and coastal Peru.

(B) Most of the trade goods that came into western Mexico centuries ago were transported by boat.

(C) Centuries ago, no one would have traveled between western Mexico and coastal Peru by boat except for the purposes of carrying out a trading expedition.

(D) If hairless dogs were at one time transported between western Mexico and coastal Peru by boat, they were traded in exchange for other goods.

(E) Centuries ago, it was easier to travel by boat between western Mexico and coastal Peru than to travel by an overland route.

19. Researchers working in Western Australia have discovered the oldest fragments of the Earth's early crust that have yet been identified: microdiamonds. These microscopic crystals measure only 50 microns across and were formed 4.2 billion years ago. This discovery sheds light on how long it took for the Earth's crust to form, since this date is only 300 million years after the formation of the Earth itself.

If the statements above are true, which one of the following must also be true?

(A) The Earth's crust took no longer than 300 million years to start to form.

(B) The Earth's crust first formed in the area that is now Western Australia.

(C) The Earth's crust took billions of years to form.

(D) Microdiamonds were the first components of the Earth's crust to form.

(E) All naturally occurring microdiamonds were formed at the time the Earth's crust was being formed.

GO ON TO THE NEXT PAGE.

20. The public square was an important tool of democracy in days past because it provided a forum for disparate citizens to discuss the important issues of the day. Today, a person with Internet access can discuss important issues with millions of people across the nation, allowing the Internet to play the role once played by the public square. Hence, we should ensure that Internet users have at least as much freedom of expression as did people speaking in the public square.

Which one of the following is an assumption required by the argument?

(A) People speaking in the public square of days past had complete freedom of expression.

(B) All citizens have the same level of access to the Internet.

(C) A public forum can lose effectiveness as a tool of democracy if participants cannot discuss issues freely.

(D) The Internet is more often used to discuss important issues than to discuss frivolous issues.

(E) Other than the Internet, no other public forum today is an important tool of democracy.

21. At a large elementary school researchers studied a small group of children who successfully completed an experimental program in which they learned to play chess. The study found that most of the children who completed the program soon showed a significant increase in achievement levels in all of their schoolwork. Thus, it is likely that the reasoning power and spatial intuition exercised in chess-playing also contribute to achievement in many other areas of intellectual activity.

Which one of the following, if true, most tends to undermine the argument?

(A) Some students who did not participate in the chess program had learned to play chess at home.

(B) Those children who began the program but who did not successfully complete it had lower preprogram levels of achievement than did those who eventually did successfully complete the program.

(C) Many of the children who completed the program subsequently sought membership on a school chess team that required a high grade average for membership.

(D) Some students who did not participate in the chess program participated instead in after-school study sessions that helped them reach much higher levels of achievement in the year after they attended the sessions.

(E) At least some of the students who did not successfully complete the program were nevertheless more talented chess players than some of the students who did complete the program.

GO ON TO THE NEXT PAGE.

22. On Wednesdays, Kate usually buys some guava juice. But the only place she can buy guava juice is the local health food store. It follows that she must sometimes shop at the local health food store on Wednesdays.

The argument above is most similar in its pattern of reasoning to which one of the following arguments?

(A) Only teachers at the Culinary Institute are allowed to use the institute's main kitchen. Most dinners at Cafe Delice are prepared in that kitchen. So at least some dinners at Cafe Delice must be prepared by Culinary Institute teachers.

(B) All dinners at Cafe Delice are prepared in the main kitchen of the Culinary Institute. But only teachers at the institute are allowed to use that kitchen. So the dinners at Cafe Delice must be prepared by Culinary Institute teachers.

(C) Most dinners at Cafe Delice are prepared in the main kitchen of the Culinary Institute. All the teachers at the institute are allowed to use that kitchen. So at least some dinners at Cafe Delice must be prepared by Culinary Institute teachers.

(D) Most teachers at the Culinary Institute are allowed to use the institute's main kitchen. Dinners at Cafe Delice are only prepared in that kitchen. So dinners at Cafe Delice must sometimes be prepared by Culinary Institute teachers.

(E) Only teachers at the Culinary Institute are allowed to use the main kitchen of the institute. Dinners at Cafe Delice are usually prepared by Culinary Institute teachers. So dinners at Cafe Delice must sometimes be prepared in the main kitchen of the Culinary Institute.

23. Editor: The city's previous recycling program, which featured pickup of recyclables every other week, was too costly. The city claims that its new program, which features weekly pickup, will be more cost effective, since the greater the volume of recyclables collected per year, the more revenue the city gains from selling the recyclables. But this is absurd. People will put out the same volume of recyclables overall; it will just be spread out over a greater number of pickups.

Which one of the following, if true, most weakens the editor's argument?

(A) The cost of collecting and disposing of general trash has been less than the cost of collecting and disposing of recyclables, and this is still likely to be the case under the new recycling program.

(B) Even if the volume of collected recyclables increases, that increase might not be enough to make the recycling program cost effective.

(C) Because the volume of recyclables people accumulate during a week is less than what they accumulate during two weeks, the city expects a recyclables pickup to take less time under the new program.

(D) A weekly schedule for recyclables pickup is substantially easier for people to follow and adhere to than is a schedule of pickups every other week.

(E) Because of the increase in the number of pickups under the new program, the amount charged by the contractor that collects the city's recyclables will increase significantly.

GO ON TO THE NEXT PAGE.

24. Professor: Many introductory undergraduate science courses are intended to be "proving grounds," that is, they are designed to be so demanding that only those students most committed to being science majors will receive passing grades in these courses. However, studies show that some of the students in these very demanding introductory courses who are least enthusiastic about science receive passing grades in these courses. Hence, designing introductory science courses to serve as proving grounds has not served its intended purpose.

Which one of the following is an assumption that the professor's argument requires?

(A) If some of the students who are most enthusiastic about science do not receive passing grades in introductory science courses, then designing these courses to serve as proving grounds has been unsuccessful.

(B) Science departments need a way to ensure that only those students most committed to being science majors will receive passing grades in introductory science courses.

(C) Some of the students in the very demanding introductory science courses who are most enthusiastic about science do not receive passing grades in those courses.

(D) None of the students in the very demanding introductory science courses who are least enthusiastic about science are among the students most committed to being science majors.

(E) Introductory science courses should not continue to be designed to serve as proving grounds if doing so has not served its intended purpose.

25. Many bird and reptile species use hissing as a threat device against potential predators. The way these species produce hissing sounds is similar enough that it is likely that this behavior developed in an early common ancestor. At the time this common ancestor would have lived, however, none of its potential predators would have yet acquired the anatomy necessary to hear hissing sounds.

Which one of the following, if true, most helps to resolve the apparent discrepancy in the information above?

(A) Like its potential predators, the common ancestor of bird and reptile species would have lacked the anatomy necessary to hear hissing sounds.

(B) The common ancestor of bird and reptile species would probably have employed multiple threat devices against potential predators.

(C) The production of a hissing sound would have increased the apparent body size of the common ancestor of bird and reptile species.

(D) The use of hissing as a threat device would have been less energetically costly than other threat behaviors available to the common ancestor of bird and reptile species.

(E) Unlike most modern bird and reptile species, the common ancestor of these species would have had few predators.

S T O P

IF YOU FINISH BEFORE TIME IS CALLED, YOU MAY CHECK YOUR WORK ON THIS SECTION ONLY.
DO NOT WORK ON ANY OTHER SECTION IN THE TEST.

Topic Code	Print Your Full Name Here		
134262	Last	First	M.I.

Date	Sign Your Name Here
/ /	

LSAC®

Scratch Paper
Do not write your essay in this space.

LSAT® Writing Sample Topic

Directions: The scenario presented below describes two choices, either one of which can be supported on the basis of the information give Your essay should consider both choices and argue for one over the other, based on the two specified criteria and the facts provided. Ther is no "right" or "wrong" choice: a reasonable argument can be made for either.

Yasmin Parsi is deciding whether to cast an unknown actor to star in her new studio film or to hire Jonathan Tauzen, an actor with m fans. Using the facts below, write an essay in which you argue for one choice over the other, based on the following two criteria:

- Parsi wants to have as much creative control over her film as possible.
- Parsi wants to make it as likely as possible that the studio will hire her to make another film in the future.

If a known star is not used, the studio will provide a minimal marketing budget and release the film in only a few markets. In the past the studio has given movies in limited release time to build an audience before deciding whether its investment was worthwhile. Though successful, Parsi's previous films were all independently produced with unknown actors. Under her current deal, the studio retains some control over the content of her film. The studio's history is to provide oversight in proportion to the amount of money it is contributing.

If Parsi hires Tauzen, the studio would provide extra funding to cover the cost of an established star. The studio would also provide a moderate publicity budget to allow for a wide release of the film. The studio has a history of abandoning movies in wide release if they do not quickly become popular. With a known actor there would be pressure from both the studio and the actor to make the actor's part more central to the film. Tauzen could be an effective ally if Parsi has other creative differences with the studio. Tauzen has a history of causing delays in filming. This has sometimes led to the films going over budget.

WP-W134

Scratch Paper
Do not write your essay in this space.

Directions:

1. Use the Answer Key on the next page to check your answers.

2. Use the Scoring Worksheet below to compute your raw score.

3. Use the Score Conversion Chart to convert your raw score into the 120–180 scale.

Scoring Worksheet

1. Enter the number of questions you answered correctly in each section.

Number
Correct

SECTION I .... 18 /27
SECTION II .... 15 /26
SECTION III .... 23 /23
SECTION IV .... 18 /25

2. Enter the sum here: _72_

This is your Raw Score.

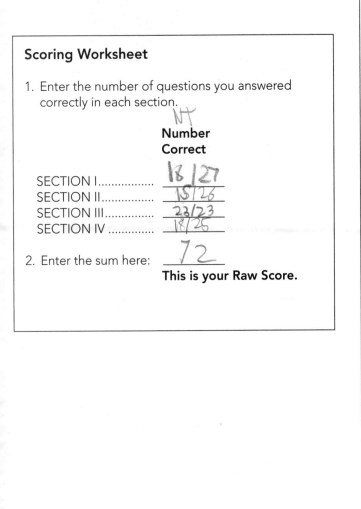

Conversion Chart
For Converting Raw Score to the 120–180 LSAT Scaled Score
LSAT Form 5LSN115

Reported Score	Raw Score Lowest	Raw Score Highest
180	99	101
179	98	98
178	97	97
177	96	96
176	95	95
175	94	94
174	93	93
173	92	92
172	91	91
171	90	90
170	89	89
169	87	88
168	86	86
167	84	85
166	83	83
165	82	82
164	80	81
163	78	79
162	77	77
161	75	76
160	73	74
159	72	72
158	70	71
157	68	69
156	66	67
155	65	65
154	63	64
153	61	62
152	59	60
151	58	58
150	56	57
149	54	55
148	53	53
147	51	52
146	49	50
145	48	48
144	46	47
143	44	45
142	43	43
141	41	42
140	40	40
139	38	39
138	37	37
137	35	36
136	34	34
135	33	33
134	31	32
133	30	30
132	28	29
131	27	27
130	26	26
129	25	25
128	23	24
127	22	22
126	21	21
125	20	20
124	19	19
123	17	18
122	16	16
121	*	*
120	0	15

*There is no raw score that will produce this scaled score for this form.

ANSWER KEY

SECTION I

1.	C	8.	B	15.	E	22.	C
2.	B	9.	B	16.	C	23.	D
3.	D	10.	C	17.	C	24.	B
4.	A	11.	B	18.	B	25.	A
5.	D	12.	D	19.	E	26.	B
6.	A	13.	D	20.	C	27.	E
7.	D	14.	B	21.	C		

SECTION II

1.	B	8.	E	15.	A	22.	A
2.	B	9.	B	16.	C	23.	E
3.	C	10.	B	17.	D	24.	D
4.	C	11.	A	18.	B	25.	D
5.	C	12.	B	19.	C	26.	E
6.	D	13.	D	20.	E		
7.	C	14.	E	21.	B		

SECTION III

1.	D	8.	C	15.	C	22.	A
2.	C	9.	D	16.	B	23.	B
3.	D	10.	A	17.	E		
4.	B	11.	C	18.	B		
5.	A	12.	E	19.	E		
6.	B	13.	C	20.	C		
7.	B	14.	A	21.	B		

SECTION IV

1.	C	8.	E	15.	D	22.	A
2.	B	9.	C	16.	B	23.	D
3.	D	10.	E	17.	A	24.	D
4.	B	11.	B	18.	E	25.	C
5.	C	12.	B	19.	A		
6.	D	13.	D	20.	C		
7.	C	14.	B	21.	C		

THE OFFICIAL LSAT
PREPTEST®

77

- PrepTest 77
- Form 5LSN116

DECEMBER 2015

SECTION I

Time—35 minutes

27 Questions

Directions: Each set of questions in this section is based on a single passage or a pair of passages. The questions are to be answered on the basis of what is stated or implied in the passage or pair of passages. For some of the questions, more than one of the choices could conceivably answer the question. However, you are to choose the best answer; that is, the response that most accurately and completely answers the question, and blacken the corresponding space on your answer sheet.

The Federal Theater Project (FTP) was established in the late 1930s by the United States government. Although it existed for only four years, at its peak the FTP employed an average of 10,000
(5) workers, operated 185 production units in 28 states, and entertained a weekly audience of nearly half a million people. One of the most important, though until recently little-studied, legacies of the program were its "Negro Units," which were dedicated to
(10) producing plays on African American subjects for primarily African American audiences. Hundreds of actors, directors, designers, technicians, and playwrights were employed by as many as eighteen of these units in cities spread throughout the United States. Defying
(15) the external forces of racism and bureaucracy, and overcoming internal artistic and personal differences, the people working in these units arguably came closer than any other group of African American theater artists had come before to founding a truly national
(20) black theater.

The creation of the FTP came on the heels of the Harlem Renaissance, a period of intense creativity and innovation within the African American arts community. Thus, by the time the FTP was founded,
(25) a diverse body of thought concerning the social function of art already existed within the African American community. The question of what kinds of plays the Negro Units should produce gave rise to vigorous, sometimes heated, debates: some producers
(30) favored folk dramas exploring rural roots and culture; others preferred urban realistic dramas depicting contemporary dilemmas for African Americans; and still others advocated adapting dramas written by white playwrights for performance by African
(35) American acting troupes. These debates were motivated in part by larger debates over whether black theater should attempt to blend into mainstream culture or capitalize on its difference from the cultural mainstream; whether it should aim for the African
(40) American or the white part of its audience; and whether it should endeavor to instruct or be content simply to entertain. These disagreements resulted in a wide range of productions reflecting the diverse views and interests of the African American community.
(45) Among them was *The Swing Mikado*, a musical that inverted the minstrel tradition by casting African American performers in an ironic adaptation of a white classic. Calling attention to the artifice of the performers' roles, this play challenged its audience to
(50) think about what it means to assume black roles both on and beyond the stage.

Although it did not have a long history, the FTP provided a lifeline for the theater during the Great Depression, a time when the performing arts in the
(55) United States faced an uncertain fate. This allowed the Negro Units to produce dramatic art that reflected the genuine diversity of African American artists and their audiences nationwide.

1. Which one of the following most accurately expresses the main point of the passage?

(A) The actors, directors, designers, and playwrights who worked in the Federal Theater Project's Negro Units have recently been rediscovered by theater historians, who now rank them among the most talented and influential stage performers and producers of their day.

(B) Of all the programs created under the auspices of the United States government, the Federal Theater Project has had the most lasting effect on the African American arts community in the United States.

(C) The Federal Theater Project's Negro Units are now being recognized for the pivotal role they played in creating what was perhaps the first truly national black theater in the United States, one reflective of the diversity of views and interests of the African American community.

(D) Although the Federal Theater Project's Negro Units produced a wide variety of plays in the late 1930s, they are best known today for their highly creative productions of folk dramas.

(E) By supporting the work of the Federal Theater Project's Negro Units in the late 1930s, the U.S. government provided much needed aid for the theater during the Great Depression, a time when the arts in general had an uncertain future.

GO ON TO THE NEXT PAGE.

2. According to the passage, the Federal Theater Project did all of the following EXCEPT:

(A) evolve over the course of several decades
(B) operate in cities throughout the United States
(C) produce plays about African American subjects
(D) employ designers and technicians
(E) entertain large audiences weekly

3. With which one of the following statements would the author be most likely to agree?

(A) Government funding for the FTP would probably have continued beyond the late 1930s if the plays produced in the program had been more popular.
(B) The artists of the Harlem Renaissance were more polarized in their views about the social function of art than were the people working in the Negro Units.
(C) Philosophical and aesthetic disagreements among the people working in the Negro Units contributed to the diversity of those units' dramatic legacy.
(D) African American theater artists working today have equaled if not surpassed the artistic contribution made in the 1930s by the people working in the Negro Units.
(E) The urban realistic dramas produced by the Negro Units were more popular with African American audiences than folk dramas were.

4. The author refers to the Harlem Renaissance at the beginning of the second paragraph primarily in order to

(A) give an example of a successful African American artistic movement that preceded the founding of the Negro Units
(B) emphasize the contribution made by African American artists to the overall political advancement of the African American community
(C) provide a historical explanation for why the work of the Negro Units fell into obscurity
(D) establish a historical context for important artistic debates that occurred within the Negro Units
(E) prove a point about the nature of the relationship between African American culture and mainstream U.S. culture in the 1930s

5. In referring to "a truly national black theater" (lines 19–20) the author most likely means

(A) a publicly funded performing arts center dedicated to the production of plays for African American audiences
(B) a broad-based dramatic-arts enterprise reflecting the diversity of views and tastes of African American artists and communities
(C) a federal government program established during the Great Depression to promote the dramatic arts in African American communities
(D) a canon of plays written by African American playwrights and endorsed by scholars
(E) a successful chain of black-owned playhouses spread throughout the United States

6. The passage provides the most support for inferring that the producers of the musical *The Swing Mikado* were among those who

(A) believed that playwrights should avoid controversial themes in their work
(B) opposed the idea that plays should instruct as well as entertain the audience
(C) favored folk dramas exploring rural roots and culture
(D) favored urban realistic dramas depicting contemporary dilemmas for African Americans
(E) advocated adapting dramas written by white playwrights for performance by African American troupes

7. Which one of the following statements, if true, most strengthens the author's claim that the African American artists working in the Negro Units came closer than any others before them to founding a truly national black theater?

(A) The majority of plays produced by black theater groups predating the Negro Units were from original scripts by African American playwrights.
(B) Before the Negro Units were founded, government funding for the dramatic arts in African American communities was almost nonexistent.
(C) Prior to the establishment of the Negro Units, the vast majority of dramas written by and for African Americans were produced and performed exclusively in large eastern cities.
(D) African American dramatic arts organizations founded prior to the Negro Units drew audiences of fewer than 100 people on average to any given production.
(E) Theater historians have had difficulty locating historical documents relating to the earliest activity of organized African American theater groups.

GO ON TO THE NEXT PAGE.

The following passage is adapted from an article published in 1993.

How severe should the punishment be for a corporate crime—e.g., a crime in which a corporation profits from knowingly and routinely selling harmful products to consumers? Some economists argue that
(5) the sole basis for determining the penalty should be the reckoning of cost and benefit: the penalty levied should exceed the profit that accrued to the corporation as a result of committing the crime. For example, if a corporation made a profit of $6 million from selling an
(10) unsafe product and the fine were, say, $7 million, these economists would feel that justice had been done.

In arguing thus, the economists hold that the fact that a community may find some crimes more abhorrent than others or wish to send a message about
(15) the importance of some values—such as, say, not endangering citizens' health by selling tainted food— should not be a factor in determining penalties. The law, the economists argue, should affect corporations' earnings rather than try to assess their morality.
(20) But this approach seems highly impractical if not impossible to follow. For the situation is complicated by the fact that an acceptable reckoning of cost and benefit needs to take into account estimated detection ratios—the estimated frequency at which those
(25) committing a given type of crime are caught. Courts must assume that not all corporate crimes are detected, and legal wisdom holds that penalties must be higher as detection ratios decrease. Otherwise, a corporation might calculate that since it has only, say, a 1-in-10
(30) chance of being caught committing a crime, even if the potential penalty is somewhat larger than the profit to be gained from violating the law it may still ultimately be more profitable to repeatedly commit the crime. A true reckoning of cost and benefit would therefore
(35) have to take estimated detection ratios into account, but this means that, in the above scenario, if the profit resulting from a crime were $6 million, the penalty would have to be not $7 million but at least $60 million, according to the economists' definition, to be just.
(40) The economists' approach requires that detection ratios be high enough for courts to ignore them (50 percent or more), but recent studies suggest that ratios are in fact closer to 10 percent. Given this, the astronomical penalties necessary to satisfy the full
(45) reckoning of cost and benefit might arguably put convicted corporations out of business and throw thousands of people out of work. Thus, some other criterion in addition to the reckoning of cost and benefit—such as the assignment of moral weight to
(50) particular crimes—is necessary so that penalties for corporate crimes will be practical as well as just.

8. Which one of the following most accurately captures the main point of the passage?

(A) Because not all corporate crimes are detected, courts must supplement the reckoning of cost and benefit by taking detection ratios into account when determining penalties for such crimes if the penalties are to be both practical and fair.

(B) The reckoning of cost and benefit as the sole basis for determining penalties for corporate crimes would be an appropriate means of assessing such penalties if it took estimated detection ratios into account.

(C) Because they argue that the reckoning of cost and benefit should be the sole basis for determining penalties for corporate crimes, economists do an injustice to communities that believe that the penalties must affect not only corporate earnings but corporate morality.

(D) Because it does not take detection ratios into account, the reckoning of cost and benefit as the sole basis for determining penalties for corporate crimes results in penalties that are not high enough both to satisfy community moral standards and to send a message about the importance of preventing corporate crime.

(E) Because the need to take detection ratios into account makes reckoning cost and benefit impractical as the sole basis for determining penalties for corporate crimes, another method of determining the penalties must be found to supplement such reckoning.

9. The primary purpose of the passage is to

(A) criticize courts for their leniency in punishing corporate crime

(B) describe some of the reasons corporations engage in corporate crime

(C) condemn corporations for failing to consider the moral implications of their actions

(D) argue against some economists' view of how to penalize corporate crime

(E) urge the implementation of a specific proposal for penalizing corporate crime

GO ON TO THE NEXT PAGE.

10. Suppose a corporation is convicted of a crime having a detection ratio of 1-in-10. Based on the passage, the author would be most likely to endorse which one of the following penalties?

(A) a fine exactly equal to the corporation's profit from committing the crime

(B) a fine slightly higher than the corporation's profit from committing the crime

(C) a fine enough higher than the corporation's profit from committing the crime to demonstrate community opinion of the crime without putting the corporation out of business

(D) a fine determined by taking the corporation's profit from committing the crime and raising it tenfold in order to reflect the detection ratio

(E) a fine high enough to put the corporation out of business

11. The author ascribes which one of the following views to the economists discussed in the passage?

(A) A community's moral judgment of certain corporate crimes is most reliable when the crime in question endangers the community as a whole.

(B) A community's moral judgment of certain corporate crimes is only occasionally useful in determining penalties for such crimes.

(C) A community's moral judgment of certain corporate crimes is often more severe than the penalties levied against such crimes.

(D) A community's moral judgment of certain corporate crimes is irrelevant to assessing the morality of corporations that commit the crimes.

(E) A community's moral judgment of certain corporate crimes is inappropriate in determining penalties for such crimes.

12. Which one of the following most accurately represents the organization of the passage?

(A) A question is raised; one answer to the question is summarized; an important aspect of this answer is presented; a flaw in the answer is identified; the need for an alternative answer is affirmed.

(B) A problem is posed; one solution to the problem is summarized; a view held by those who favor the solution is presented; a criticism of the solution is identified; the criticism is evaluated and rejected.

(C) A view is summarized; the ethics of those who hold the view are discussed; a flaw in the ethics of those holding the view is identified and described in detail; the view is rejected; an alternative view is offered.

(D) A question is raised; two answers to the question are identified and compared; an assumption underlying each answer is identified; the assumption of one answer is found to be incorrect and this answer is rejected.

(E) A problem is posed; the consequences of failing to solve the problem are described; one solution to the problem is suggested; an objection to this solution is described; the proposed solution is rejected.

13. With which one of the following statements would the economists discussed in the passage be most likely to agree?

(A) The possibility of a corporation's going out of business should not be a factor in determining the size of the penalty levied against the corporation for committing a crime.

(B) The community's opinion of the moral offensiveness of a corporate crime should not be a factor in assigning a moral weight to that crime.

(C) The moral offensiveness of a corporate crime should not be a factor in determining the penalty levied against the corporation unless it tends to increase the size of the penalty.

(D) The likelihood of a corporation's recommitting a particular crime should be the main factor in determining the size of the penalty levied against the corporation for committing the crime.

(E) The penalty levied against a corporation for a particular crime should increase in direct relation to the number of times the corporation has previously been convicted of the crime.

GO ON TO THE NEXT PAGE.

Passage A

During the 1990s, the study of history witnessed both a dramatic integration of the study of women's history into the historical mainstream and a transition from the subject of women to the issue of gender.
(5) Women as individuals receded into the background, and something more abstract called gender relations came to the fore. Since gender relations involved turning to an exploration of the social systems that underlay the relationships of men and women, the
(10) shift seemed to many historians to be a retreat from the effort to uncover the history of women per se. The new work took several forms: Articles about men evaluated the role of masculinity in shaping thought and action, and articles about women gave way to explorations of
(15) how an imagined domesticity, or separate sphere for women, shaped culture and politics.

This scholarship demonstrates the explanatory potential embedded in gender, but it also reveals why the topic "women" is now so often dismissed as too
(20) narrow and particular a category to illuminate historical processes. Where the study of the history of women is seen today as having celebratory content— its effort is to find our lost ancestors and restore them to a place in our memories—that of gender offers an
(25) analytic framework within which to analyze social and political structures.

And yet I am left to wonder what we have lost as we turn our attention to gender. I share the suspicion of many of my colleagues that gender obscures as
(30) much as it reveals: that in focusing on underlying structures, we overlook the particular ways in which individual women engaged their worlds.

Passage B

Part of the Roman emperor Augustus's response to the disorder and disharmony of the Triumviral Wars
(35) (32–30 B.C.E.) was to promote laws aimed at restoring old-fashioned Roman morality. Augustus presented the peace and stability of Rome as resting upon the integrity of the Roman family, and he paid particular attention to relocating women in this domestic context
(40) as wives and mothers. Among the laws passed were the marital laws of 19–18 B.C.E. and 9 C.E. that penalized adultery and rewarded bearers of legitimate children.

When Augustus thereby rooted Roman prosperity
(45) and peace in the Roman family, he drew particular attention to women as significant participants in the system: their good behavior was partly responsible for the health of the state. Thus in this period, the gender roles assigned to women were becoming at once more
(50) constrained but also more visible and more politicized. The success and significance of this familial language became clear in 2 B.C.E. when Augustus articulated his unusual position in the state by accepting the title *Pater Patriae*, "Father of the Fatherland."
(55) Within such a sociopolitical setting, it should occasion no surprise that Augustan-period artists drew

on the iconography of the household in imagining the empire. Images of women concisely expressed Augustus's imperial project, a control of domestic
(60) space made visible in an old-fashioned style making the present look like the idealized past.

14. Which one of the following is a central topic in each passage?

   (A) the decline of historical research on individual women
   (B) the role of gender in shaping politics and culture
   (C) the creation of an imagined domesticity in ancient Rome
   (D) the function of masculinity in history
   (E) the "celebratory" goals of women's history

15. The author of passage A would be most likely to agree with which one of the following statements regarding the type of historical analysis found in passage B?

   (A) It indicates that ancient conceptions of gender were radically different from our own modern ones.
   (B) It focuses on the Roman conception of femininity but neglects to take into account the equally important role of masculinity.
   (C) It fails to bring to light any substantive information about how particular Roman women lived during the reign of Augustus.
   (D) It demonstrates that domesticity played a larger role in the politics of ancient Rome than it has played in the politics of recent history.
   (E) It succeeds in revealing portions of Augustus's marital laws of which historians were not previously aware.

16. According to passage A, during the 1990s the focus in the study of women's history shifted to which one of the following?

   (A) investigating the social systems that shaped the interactions of men and women
   (B) bringing attention to and clarifying the previously ignored contributions of women to the social order
   (C) revealing the gender biases that distorted traditional historical scholarship
   (D) criticizing earlier generations of historians for their lack of attention to women
   (E) documenting shifts in the conception of domesticity as part of social interaction

GO ON TO THE NEXT PAGE.

17. Which one of the following most accurately describes the relationship between passage A and passage B?

(A) Passage A endorses a trend in the study of social history as that trend is reflected in passage B.

(B) Passage A criticizes passage B for failing to take all of the available evidence into account in passage B's analysis.

(C) Passage A offers an analysis that is similar to that in passage B in both the evidence used and the conclusions drawn.

(D) Passage A discusses the strengths and weaknesses of a trend in scholarship that is exemplified by passage B.

(E) Passage A advances an argument that is parallel in general terms to that in passage B, though different frames of reference are used.

18. The summary given in passage B (lines 36–43) most closely corresponds to which one of the following approaches to historical analysis described in passage A?

(A) seeking to uncover the history of women per se

(B) exploring how a concept of domesticity shapes culture and politics

(C) trying to rediscover and honor lost ancestors

(D) evaluating the role of masculinity in regulating thought and action

(E) arguing that gender analysis obscures as much as it reveals

19. The author of passage A would be most likely to agree with which one of the following statements about passage B?

(A) It demonstrates that the integration of women's history into the historical mainstream is far from complete.

(B) It indicates why historians of women have been justified in abandoning the effort to uncover the lives of individual women.

(C) It illustrates a current trend in historical scholarship toward increased attention to the political influence of women.

(D) It suggests that much recent historical scholarship focusing on women fails to recognize the significance of gender.

(E) It shows how the analytical tool of gender can be successfully used to shed light on politics and culture.

GO ON TO THE NEXT PAGE.

The French biologist Jean-Baptiste de Lamarck (1744–1829) outlined a theory of evolutionary change in 1809, 50 years before Darwin's *On the Origin of Species*. Lamarck's basic idea was that organisms
(5) change in adapting to their environment and then pass on to their offspring the new characteristics they have acquired. Since then, Lamarck has been ridiculed for presumably implying, for example, that giraffes developed their long necks by stretching, generation
(10) after generation, toward the leaves of trees. Most modern biologists are adamant that nothing of the sort occurs, ever. But the molecular immunologist Edward J. Steele is attempting to revive Lamarckism: he and his colleagues claim to have found evidence
(15) for a Lamarckian hereditary mechanism in the immune system.

The immune system is an evolutionary puzzle in its own right: How is it that our bodies can quickly respond to so many different kinds of attacks? Is all
(20) this information in the genes? If so, then how does our immune system defend against new diseases? Part of the answer comes from the fact that some immune system cells contain genes that mutate with unusual frequency. The most common type of mutation is a
(25) sort of genetic "typo" that occurs when a cell's DNA is transcribed into RNA, the molecule that helps to assemble proteins. These mutations allow the immune system to test out different defenses until it finds one that does the job.
(30) Steele hypothesizes that the altered RNA then reverts back into DNA. Indeed, such "reverse transcription" of RNA back into DNA has been observed frequently in other contexts. But the troublesome question for Lamarckians is this: Could
(35) this new DNA then be carried to the reproductive genes (in the sperm and egg cells), replace the original DNA there, and so be passed on to an organism's offspring? Steele and company believe this is possible, and they have devised an elegant, but speculative,
(40) story to describe how it might happen using known biological mechanisms. They believe a virus could carry the altered DNA to the reproductive cells and replace the DNA in those cells.

But even if the process Steele and his colleagues
(45) describe is possible, does it ever actually occur? Evolutionary mechanisms are never observed directly, so we must make do with circumstantial evidence. Steele and his colleagues claim to have found such evidence, namely a "signature" of past events that is
(50) "written all over" the genes that carry instructions for immune system responses. They claim that a distinct pattern of mutations concentrated in particular areas of these genes "strongly suggests" that, in the past, information has been transferred into DNA in the
(55) reproductive organs. Other biologists are not so easily swayed. They suggest there may be other, less radical explanations for the pattern of mutations that Steele cites.

20. Which one of the following most accurately states the main point of the passage?

(A) The long-derided Lamarckian theory that organisms can pass on acquired characteristics to their offspring has been proven correct by the discoveries of Steele and his colleagues regarding the immune system.

(B) Steele and his colleagues have devised an account of a mechanism by which acquired characteristics could be passed on to an organism's offspring, and they claim to have found evidence for the operation of this Lamarckian mechanism.

(C) Although Steele and his colleagues have succeeded in showing that changes that occur in the immune system can be passed on to offspring, it is unlikely that a similar mechanism operates elsewhere in the body.

(D) In contrast to the standard theory of evolution, the claims of Steele and his colleagues that organisms can pass on acquired characteristics to their offspring are highly speculative and rest on purely circumstantial evidence.

(E) By showing that RNA can revert back into DNA, Steele and his colleagues have removed the main obstacle to general acceptance of the Lamarckian hypothesis that organisms can pass on acquired characteristics to their offspring.

21. The author most likely calls a certain kind of mutation a "typo" (line 25) primarily in order to

(A) distinguish it from mutations that are adaptive
(B) characterize it as relatively inconsequential
(C) indicate that it is an instance of imperfect copying
(D) emphasize that it is easily overlooked
(E) suggest an analogy between scientific investigation and textual analysis

22. The passage most strongly suggests that the author has which one of the following attitudes toward the theory proposed by Steele and his colleagues?

(A) confidence in its truth
(B) indignation at its divergence from Darwinism
(C) distrust of its novelty
(D) doubt concerning its plausibility
(E) dismay at its lack of rigor

GO ON TO THE NEXT PAGE.

23. The passage is primarily concerned with

  (A)   offering a historical account of the development of an evolutionary theory
  (B)   describing the efforts of a modern biologist to vindicate a long-disregarded evolutionary theory
  (C)   answering a set of questions about the immune system in light of evolutionary theory
  (D)   evaluating the overall merits of an evolutionary theory that has been rejected by most modern biologists
  (E)   presenting a discredited evolutionary theory as a case study in the philosophy of science

24. What is the primary function of the last paragraph in the structure of the passage as a whole?

  (A)   to present various objections that have been raised against the neo-Lamarckian theory outlined in the preceding paragraphs
  (B)   to dismiss the neo-Lamarckian theory outlined in the preceding paragraphs as not being supported by evidence
  (C)   to explain how the neo-Lamarckian theory outlined in the preceding paragraphs could be revised to take new findings into account
  (D)   to suggest several possible directions for further research regarding the neo-Lamarckian theory outlined in the preceding paragraphs
  (E)   to indicate the nature of the evidence for the neo-Lamarckian theory outlined in the preceding paragraphs

25. The passage most strongly suggests that the author would agree with which one of the following statements?

  (A)   Contrary to the opinion of most modern biologists, certain acquired characteristics probably can be passed on from one generation to the next.
  (B)   Steele and his colleagues have not actually observed the process of reverse transcription in immune cells.
  (C)   The patterns of mutations concentrated in particular areas of genes that carry instructions for immune system responses indicate that the DNA in these genes has been altered by a virus.
  (D)   The passing on of acquired characteristics from one generation to the next, if it occurs at all, is probably confined to the immune system.
  (E)   Unless a hypothesis can be confirmed by direct observation, it should be regarded as speculation rather than as science.

26. Which one of the following, if true, would most strengthen the position attributed to Steele and his colleagues in the passage?

  (A)   Scientists have succeeded in altering the DNA in reproductive cells of laboratory mice by introducing a virus carrying new DNA.
  (B)   The patterns of mutations found in the genes that carry instructions for immune system responses are also found in genes in the nervous system.
  (C)   The process by which the immune system tests out the efficacy of cellular mutations is one of random trial and error.
  (D)   Fossil remains show that giraffes gradually evolved with increasingly long necks.
  (E)   It is known that birds can pass on acquired immunities to their gestating chicks via the yolk sacs in their eggs.

27. Suppose a scholar believes that the surviving text of a classical Greek play contains alterations introduced into the original text by a copyist from a later era. Which one of the following pieces of evidence bearing upon the authenticity of the surviving text is most analogous to the kind of evidence mentioned in the last paragraph of the passage?

  (A)   a copy of the original, unaltered text discovered in a manuscript independently known to date from the classical period
  (B)   a letter in which the copyist admits to having altered the original text in question
  (C)   an allegation by one of the copyist's contemporaries that the copyist altered the original text
  (D)   an account dating from the playwright's time of a performance of the play that quotes a version of the text that differs from the surviving version
  (E)   vocabulary in the surviving text that is typical of the later era and not found in other texts dating from the classical period

S T O P

IF YOU FINISH BEFORE TIME IS CALLED, YOU MAY CHECK YOUR WORK ON THIS SECTION ONLY.
DO NOT WORK ON ANY OTHER SECTION IN THE TEST.

SECTION II

Time—35 minutes

25 Questions

<u>Directions:</u> The questions in this section are based on the reasoning contained in brief statements or passages. For some questions, more than one of the choices could conceivably answer the question. However, you are to choose the <u>best</u> answer; that is, the response that most accurately and completely answers the question. You should not make assumptions that are by commonsense standards implausible, superfluous, or incompatible with the passage. After you have chosen the best answer, blacken the corresponding space on your answer sheet.

1. An electric utility has determined that a new power plant is needed and has decided to build either a natural gas-fired plant or a waste-to-energy plant that would serve as both a trash incinerator and a power plant. Surprisingly, although the waste-to-energy plant would produce roughly three times as much air pollution as the gas-fired plant, environmentalists have come out in unanimous support of this option.

   Which one of the following, if true, most helps to justify the environmentalists' position?

   (A) Modern gas-fired power plants produce significantly less pollution than gas-fired power plants that were built several decades ago.

   (B) In the area where the utility operates, both energy use and the volume of trash produced have increased substantially over the last several years.

   (C) The waste-to-energy plant would replace an existing trash incinerator that produces much more air pollution than the waste-to-energy plant would.

   (D) Most of the environmentalists believe that air pollution is the area's most serious environmental problem.

   (E) The vast majority of the air pollution in the area where the utility operates is produced by trucks and automobiles.

2. Anthropologist: One of the distinctive traits of humans is the ability to support a large brain with a small gut, which requires getting more calories from less food. It was likely the development of cooking that made this possible. After all, our ancestors developed large brains around the time that they began to control fire. And even today, people who choose to eat only raw food have difficulty getting enough calories.

   Which one of the following, if true, most strengthens the anthropologist's argument?

   (A) Cooked foods contain the same number of calories as raw foods.

   (B) Raw meat contains more calories than a similar quantity of raw vegetables.

   (C) The human body is able to extract a similar number of calories from cooked food and raw food.

   (D) The human body uses more calories to process raw food than it uses to process cooked food.

   (E) Domesticated plants and animals are richer in calories than their wild counterparts are.

GO ON TO THE NEXT PAGE.

3. The current sharp decline in commercial honeybee populations has been attributed to the same viral and bacterial infections, pesticide poisonings, and mite infestations that devastated bees in the past. Whichever of these adverse conditions is the immediate cause, it is highly likely that there is also a long-ignored underlying condition, and that is inbreeding. Decades of breeding practices meant to maximize pollinating efficiency have limited honeybees' genetic diversity.

Which one of the following is an assumption that is required by the argument?

(A) Commercial honeybees are more vulnerable to problems with inbreeding than wild honeybees are.

(B) The results of decades of breeding practices cannot be quickly undone.

(C) The genetic diversity of the honeybee population continues to decline.

(D) In the past, viral infections and mites have devastated genetically diverse honeybee populations.

(E) Lack of genetic diversity can make honeybees more vulnerable to adverse conditions.

4. The northern cardinal, a nonmigratory songbird, was rare in Nova Scotia in 1980; the province was considered to be beyond that bird's usual northern range. By 2000, however, field observations indicated that northern cardinals were quite common there. The average winter temperature rose slightly over that period, so warmer winters are probably responsible for the northern cardinal's proliferation in Nova Scotia.

Which one of the following, if true, most weakens the argument?

(A) Bird feeders, an important source of nutrition to wintering birds, became far more common in Nova Scotia after 1980.

(B) Because of their red plumage, northern cardinals are easier to spot than most other songbird species are.

(C) Some songbird species other than the northern cardinal also became more common between 1980 and 2000.

(D) According to field observations, the populations of migratory birds fluctuated less during the period from 1980 to 2000 than the populations of nonmigratory birds.

(E) Birds that prey on songbirds became more common in Nova Scotia between 1980 and 2000.

5. A person's personality is linked to that person's genes. And since a person's genes do not ordinarily change over time, it follows that a person's personality remains unchanged with the passing of time.

Which one of the following is most closely parallel in its reasoning to the flawed reasoning in the argument above?

(A) The way historians understand the First World War is related to what happened in that war. But what actually happened in that war cannot change. Therefore, historians' understanding of the war cannot change.

(B) Market forces are to some degree influenced by governmental actions. Hence, a change in the government's policies could result in a change in the economy.

(C) It is well known that some diseases have genetic causes. Therefore, it should be possible to prevent such diseases by manipulating the genes that cause them.

(D) Getting regular exercise over a long period contributes to the prevention of heart disease. Therefore, getting regular exercise over a short period contributes slightly to the prevention of heart disease.

(E) The levels of certain hormones control body temperature. Therefore, if one has a high fever, the levels of one's hormones must be elevated as well.

A = B
B → A

GO ON TO THE NEXT PAGE.

6. Political analyst: Several years ago, McFarlane, the military dictator, had Brooks, the former prime minister, arrested on charges of corruption. After years of negotiation, McFarlane has pardoned Brooks, and she has agreed to join his government. Almost all of McFarlane's supporters believe that Brooks is guilty of corruption. Moreover, almost all of McFarlane's opponents will oppose anyone who agrees to join his government. So Brooks will have few supporters in this country.

The political analyst's argument depends on the assumption that

(A) Brooks's joining McFarlane's government inappropriately gives that government a semblance of legitimacy

(B) there is less corruption in the country's government now than when Brooks was prime minister

(C) Brooks's political positions do not overlap with those of McFarlane

(D) most people in the country are either supporters or opponents of McFarlane

(E) the charges on which Brooks was arrested were unfounded

7. Amber—fossilized tree resin sold as a gemstone—is particularly valuable when it contains fossilized life forms. Forgers can create fake amber and, in an attempt to improve its value, often embed small, normal-appearing insects in it. Therefore, pieces that are sold as amber are far more likely to be fake if they contain normal-appearing insects than if they do not.

Which one of the following, if true, most strengthens the argument?

(A) Amber is often sold by small shops and street vendors that take few precautions to ensure authenticity.

(B) Pieces of amber that contain fossilized life forms are generally larger than plain pieces of amber.

(C) Amber that contains insects usually demands a higher price than does amber that contains small plants.

(D) It is very difficult to distinguish between genuine and fake amber without destroying some of it.

(E) Insects struggling to free themselves from tree resin are usually fossilized in awkward or grotesque positions.

8. Widespread use of the Internet has led to an increase in certain crimes such as information theft and to new crimes like hacking. This seems due, at least in part, to the impersonal nature of the Internet. People seem to feel more free to harm others through the Internet than in person, suggesting that people feel less morally constrained when they use the Internet. For this reason, steps should be taken to educate people about the ethical use of the Internet.

Which one of the following principles, if valid, most helps to justify the reasoning in the argument?

(A) Education about the ethical use of a tool increases one's sense of moral responsibility regarding its use.

(B) When new technologies emerge, society needs to formulate new ethical guidelines to cover the use of those technologies.

(C) The more educated that people are about the ethical usage of the Internet, the greater the amount of harm that they can do to others.

(D) People feel morally constrained from doing an action only if that action causes harm to others.

(E) People who harm others through impersonal means are no less culpable for their actions than are people who harm others in person.

9. Columnist: Video games are not works of art. No matter how rich the aesthetic experience produced by a video game might be, it is interactive: players make choices that affect the outcome of the game. For something to be a work of art, it must produce an aesthetic experience that is controlled by the artist or artists who created the work.

The conclusion of the columnist's argument can be properly drawn if which one of the following is assumed?

(A) Most video game creators do not intend their video games to be works of art.

(B) An aesthetic experience cannot be both interactive and controlled by the artist or artists who created the work.

(C) For something to be a work of art, it must produce a rich aesthetic experience.

(D) Typically, video game players do not themselves create video games.

(E) Players' choices that have no effect on the outcome of a video game are irrelevant to the aesthetic experience produced by that game.

GO ON TO THE NEXT PAGE.

10. One year ago, a municipality banned dishwasher detergents containing phosphates. Anecdotal evidence indicates that many residents continued to use detergents containing phosphates; they just purchased them from out-of-town stores. However, it is clear that some residents did switch to phosphate-free detergents, since phosphate pollution from the municipal wastewater treatment plant decreased significantly in the past year.

The answer to which one of the following questions would most help in evaluating the argument above?

(A) Why did many residents continue to use detergents containing phosphates?

(B) What pollutants, if any, are present in phosphate-free dishwashing detergents?

(C) Were any changes made in the past year to the way the municipality's wastewater treatment plant treats phosphates?

(D) Does most of the phosphate pollution in the municipality's waterways come from treated wastewater from the municipal treatment plant?

(E) Did municipal officials try to stop people from bringing detergents containing phosphates into the municipality?

11. Farmers who use genetically engineered plants on a large scale are at great financial risk because at any time a study could be published that would undermine what little confidence consumers have in genetically engineered foods. It is unwise for farmers to grow such crops. They do not fetch a high enough price to compensate for the risk.

Which one of the following most accurately expresses the conclusion of the argument as a whole?

(A) A farmer who grows genetically engineered crops on a large scale is taking a financial risk.

(B) It is not prudent for a farmer to grow genetically engineered crops.

(C) The price paid for genetically engineered crops does not compensate for the financial risk farmers incur by growing them.

(D) A study could come out at any time that would greatly undermine public confidence in genetically engineered foods.

(E) Consumers have very little confidence in genetically engineered foods.

12. When doctors vaccinate a patient, their intention is to expose him or her to a weakened form of a disease-causing pathogen and thus to make the patient better able to resist the pathogen and less likely to develop a severe form of that disease later.

Which one of the following best illustrates the principle that the passage illustrates?

(A) Some directors instruct actors not to rehearse their lines in the several days preceding the opening night of a play, so that the actors will not become so confident that they forget their lines out of inattentiveness.

(B) Some parents read their children fairy tales containing allegorical treatments of treachery and cruelty, with the intention of making them less emotionally vulnerable to these phenomena when they encounter them later in life.

(C) In some circumstances, firefighters use fire to fight fire by creating an intense explosion very close to an uncontrollable blaze that they wish to extinguish, thus momentarily depriving it of the oxygen it needs to continue burning.

(D) In some cases, a business will close down some of its operations, its intention being to position the company to be more profitable later even though this involves expenses in the current period.

(E) Some police departments energetically pursue those who commit minor crimes; in doing so they intend to provide examples to deter people who might be tempted to commit more-serious crimes.

GO ON TO THE NEXT PAGE.

13. Nations that have little interaction with one another have little knowledge of one another's needs and problems. Because both sympathy and justice depend largely on understanding the needs and problems of others, it follows that _____.

Which one of the following most logically completes the argument?

(A) nations that have knowledge of one another's needs and problems will treat each other with sympathy and justice

(B) without some interaction, nations are bound to find it difficult to extend sympathy and justice to one another

(C) almost all problems between nations stem from lack of sympathy and justice

(D) there is no way to eliminate conflict among nations

(E) only nations that have some interaction with one another have knowledge of one another's needs and problems

14. Activist: Medical conditions such as cancer and birth defects have been linked to pollutants in water. Organic pollutants such as dioxins, and inorganic pollutants such as mercury, are ingested by fish and move up the food chain to people, where they accumulate in tissue. Since most cancers and birth defects are incurable, we need to aim at their prevention. Clearly, the only effective way to reduce significantly their overall incidence is to halt industries known to produce these pollutants, given that such industries are unlikely to comply adequately with strict environmental regulations.

A flaw in the activist's reasoning is that it

(A) fails to consider the possibility that a significant number of occurrences of cancer and birth defects may be caused by preventable factors other than industrial pollutants

(B) does not consider the possibility that pollutants can cause harm to nonhuman species as well as to human beings

(C) takes for granted that certain effects can be produced independently by several different causes

(D) fails to consider whether industries may voluntarily decrease their output of pollutants

(E) fails to consider the possibility that chemicals now classified as pollutants have some beneficial effects not yet discovered

15. Political leader: In this political dispute, our side will benefit from showing a desire to compromise with the opposition. If the opposition responds positively, then a compromise will be reached. If they do not, then they will be held responsible for the failure to reach a compromise and our side will benefit.

The conclusion of the political leader's argument follows logically if which one of the following is assumed?

(A) The political leader's side has a desire to compromise with the opposition.

(B) The opposition is rarely willing to compromise with the political leader's side.

(C) The political leader's side will benefit if a compromise is reached.

(D) The opposition would benefit from showing a desire to compromise.

(E) The opposition will compromise if the political leader's side shows a desire to compromise.

16. Some people see no harm in promoting a folk remedy that in fact has no effect. But there is indeed harm: many people who are convinced to use an ineffective remedy continue with it for years rather than pursuing conventional treatments that would almost certainly help them.

Which one of the following principles, if valid, most helps to justify the reasoning in the argument?

(A) One should not promote a remedy if one believes that using that remedy will cause harm.

(B) It is harmful to interfere with someone doing something that is likely to benefit that person.

(C) To convince people of something for which one knows there is no evidence is to be dishonest.

(D) A person is responsible for harm he or she does to someone even if the harm was done unintentionally.

(E) A person who convinces someone to take a course of action is in part responsible for the consequences of that action.

GO ON TO THE NEXT PAGE.

17. The radio station claims that its new format is popular with listeners because more than three-quarters of the listeners who call in requests to the station say they are pleased with the format. This, however, is hardly conclusive. It would be like trying to determine whether a political candidate is popular with voters by interviewing only those people who have already decided to vote for the candidate.

The argument proceeds by

(A) concluding that an inference is flawed on the grounds that it is based on a survey conducted by a biased party

(B) referring to an inference that is clearly flawed in order to undermine an analogous inference

(C) questioning the legitimacy of an inference by proposing a more reasonable inference that could be drawn from the evidence

(D) providing a direct counterexample to a conclusion in order to show that the conclusion is false

(E) claiming that an inference leads to a contradiction in order to show that the inference is unreasonable

18. Historian: Those who claim that Shakespeare did not write the plays commonly attributed to him are motivated purely by snobbery. Shakespeare was the son of a glove maker, whereas every other person proposed as the true author of the plays was an aristocrat, and many of those who argue that one or another of these aristocrats wrote the plays are the aristocrats' descendants.

The reasoning in the historian's argument is most vulnerable to criticism on the grounds that the argument

(A) presumes, without providing justification, that a claim cannot be true if those who advance it are motivated by snobbery

(B) takes for granted that anyone who is motivated purely by snobbery cannot also be motivated by legitimate historical evidence

(C) fails to consider adequately the possible motives of those who claim that Shakespeare did write the plays commonly attributed to him

(D) fails to exclude the possibility that there might be legitimate evidence motivating those who reject Shakespeare's authorship

(E) makes use of an assumption that one would accept only if one has already accepted the truth of the conclusion

19. A recent study examined the daytime and nighttime activity patterns of two populations of tree-dwelling lemurs—the first living in a rain forest, where tree canopy cover is consistent year-round, and the second living in a deciduous forest, where many trees lose their leaves during the winter months. Both groups of lemurs were found to be more nocturnal during winter months than they were the rest of the year. However, the winter increase in nocturnal activity was significantly more pronounced for the population living in the deciduous forest than it was for the population living in the rain forest.

Which one of the following, if true, most helps to explain the difference between the two lemur populations with respect to winter activity patterns?

(A) For both lemur populations, the primary competitors for food resources are species active during daylight.

(B) The primary predators for both lemur populations are high-flying birds that rely on their eyesight to hunt prey during daylight.

(C) In both habitats, species of predatory snakes active during daylight are most active during winter months.

(D) The lemur population in the rain forest is twice the size of the population in the deciduous forest.

(E) The lemur population in the rain forest eats both plants and insects whereas the population in the deciduous forest eats only plants.

GO ON TO THE NEXT PAGE.

20. Critic: It is common to argue that there is a distinction between "literary" and "genre" fiction. The first should be interpreted, so this argument goes, while the second is merely a source of easy pleasure. But this is a specious distinction—not because every work should be interpreted, but because no work should be. When we evaluate a work principally for its themes and ideas, we cut ourselves off from the work's emotional impact.

Which one of the following most accurately describes the role played in the critic's argument by the claim that when we evaluate a work principally for its themes and ideas, we cut ourselves off from the work's emotional impact?

(A) It states the conclusion.
(B) It is offered as support for the conclusion.
(C) It attempts to spell out the practical implications of the critic's conclusion.
(D) It attempts to explain the nature of the distinction that the critic considers.
(E) It attempts to anticipate an objection to the critic's conclusion.

21. Principle: If one does not criticize a form of behavior in oneself or vow to stop it, then one should not criticize that form of behavior in another.

Application: If Shimada does not vow to stop being tardy himself, he should not criticize McFeney for tardiness.

Which one of the following, if true, justifies the above application of the principle?

(A) Both McFeney and Shimada are regularly tardy, but Shimada criticizes McFeney's tardiness without criticizing his own.
(B) McFeney is regularly tardy, but Shimada is almost never tardy.
(C) McFeney often criticizes Shimada for being tardy, but neither Shimada nor McFeney ever vows to cease being tardy.
(D) Shimada criticizes McFeney for regularly being tardy, but also criticizes himself for occasional tardiness.
(E) Neither McFeney nor Shimada is regularly tardy, but Shimada criticizes McFeney for tardiness nonetheless.

22. Everyone should have access to more than one newspaper, for there are at least two sides to every story. Since all sides of an important story should be covered, and no newspaper adequately covers all sides of every one of its stories, some important stories would not be adequately covered if there were only one newspaper.

Which one of the following most accurately describes a flaw in the reasoning of the argument?

(A) The argument confuses the inability to cover all sides of every story with the inability to cover all sides of any important story.
(B) The argument overlooks the possibility that two newspapers could provide the same incomplete coverage of the same important stories.
(C) A conclusion about what newspapers should do is inferred solely from statements about what newspapers in fact do.
(D) The argument takes for granted that everyone has access to all newspapers.
(E) The argument is concerned only with important stories and not with all stories.

23. Most of the mines that Moradco operates in the province of Velyena have never violated environmental regulations. Every one of the gold mines that Moradco operates throughout the world has at some time or another violated environmental regulations.

Which one of the following statements follows logically from the statements above?

(A) Moradco operates more mines in Velyena than any other company operates there.
(B) The total number of gold mines that Moradco operates is larger than the total number of mines it operates in Velyena.
(C) Most of the gold mines that Moradco operates are not located in Velyena.
(D) Most of the mines that Moradco operates in Velyena are not gold mines.
(E) Most of the mines that Moradco operates throughout the world are not gold mines.

GO ON TO THE NEXT PAGE.

24. Tariffs on particular products tend to protect the small percentage of the population that works in industries that make those products while hurting everyone else through higher costs. Polls show that in fact most people oppose such tariffs. So politicians would be more likely to be reelected if they voted against these tariffs.

Which one of the following is an assumption on which the argument relies?

(A)　Supporters of tariffs on particular products are not significantly more likely than opponents to base their vote for a politician on the politician's stand on this issue.

(B)　Politicians always vote according to what is most likely to get them reelected.

(C)　Politicians should support only general tariffs, since such tariffs would be more widely popular with voters than tariffs on particular products.

(D)　Politicians should never support measures that favor only a small percentage of the population.

(E)　People who would be hurt by tariffs generally know that they would be hurt by them.

25. Among small- to medium-sized marine mammals such as seals and dolphins, the longer an animal can stay submerged during a dive, the greater the depth the animal can reach. Dolphins can dive to greater depths than northern fur seals can, and elephant seals can stay submerged longer than Weddell seals can.

If the information above is accurate, then each of the following statements could be true EXCEPT:

(A)　Dolphins can dive to greater depths than Weddell seals can, but not to depths as great as elephant seals can.

(B)　Weddell seals can stay submerged longer than northern fur seals can, but dolphins can dive to greater depths than Weddell seals can.

(C)　Weddell seals can dive to greater depths than dolphins can and can stay submerged longer than northern fur seals can.

(D)　Northern fur seals can stay submerged longer than elephant seals can, but Weddell seals can dive to greater depths than dolphins can.

(E)　Northern fur seals can stay submerged longer than Weddell seals can, but elephant seals can dive to greater depths than northern fur seals can.

S T O P

IF YOU FINISH BEFORE TIME IS CALLED, YOU MAY CHECK YOUR WORK ON THIS SECTION ONLY.
DO NOT WORK ON ANY OTHER SECTION IN THE TEST.

SECTION III

Time—35 minutes

23 Questions

Directions: Each group of questions in this section is based on a set of conditions. In answering some of the questions, it may be useful to draw a rough diagram. Choose the response that most accurately and completely answers each question and blacken the corresponding space on your answer sheet.

Questions 1–5

Six entertainers—Robinson, Shahpari, Tigay, Wu, Yeaton, and Zane—are being scheduled for the six performances on the opening day of a community festival. Each entertainer will perform at one of six times—in the morning at 9:00 A.M., 10:00 A.M., or 11:00 A.M., or in the afternoon at 2:00 P.M., 3:00 P.M., or 4:00 P.M.—with no two entertainers performing at the same scheduled time. The order in which the entertainers perform is subject to the following constraints:

 Robinson must perform at some time before Zane.
 Yeaton's performance must be the next performance
  after Wu's.
 Tigay must perform in the afternoon.
 Zane must perform in the morning.

1. Which one of the following could be the order, from first to last, in which the entertainers are scheduled to perform?

(A) Robinson, Shahpari, Zane, Tigay, Wu, Yeaton
(B) Robinson, Wu, Yeaton, Zane, Shahpari, Tigay
(C) Robinson, Zane, Tigay, Shahpari, Wu, Yeaton
(D) Shahpari, Robinson, Zane, Wu, Tigay, Yeaton
(E) Wu, Yeaton, Zane, Shahpari, Tigay, Robinson

GO ON TO THE NEXT PAGE.

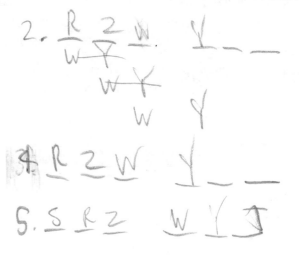

2. If Wu is scheduled to perform in the morning, then which one of the following could be true?

(A) Robinson is scheduled to perform at 10:00 A.M.
(B) Shahpari is scheduled to perform at 3:00 P.M.
(C) Tigay is scheduled to perform at 2:00 P.M.
(D) Yeaton is scheduled to perform at 3:00 P.M.
(E) Zane is scheduled to perform at 11:00 A.M.

3. Shahpari CANNOT be scheduled to perform at which one of the following times?

(A) 9:00 A.M.
(B) 10:00 A.M.
(C) 11:00 A.M.
(D) 2:00 P.M.
(E) 3:00 P.M.

4. What is the earliest time that Wu could be scheduled to perform?

(A) 9:00 A.M.
(B) 10:00 A.M.
(C) 11:00 A.M.
(D) 2:00 P.M.
(E) 3:00 P.M.

5. Which one of the following is a complete and accurate list of the entertainers who must be scheduled to perform in the afternoon?

(A) Tigay
(B) Tigay, Wu
(C) Tigay, Yeaton
(D) Tigay, Wu, Yeaton
(E) Tigay, Shahpari, Yeaton

GO ON TO THE NEXT PAGE.

Questions 6–12

Exactly six of eight ceramic bowls, each crafted by exactly one of eight potters—Larsen, Mills, Neiman, Olivera, Park, Reigel, Serra, and Vance—will be displayed in a row in positions consecutively numbered 1 through 6, one bowl per position. The display is subject to the following conditions:

    If Larsen's bowl is displayed, Mills's bowl cannot be displayed.

    Park's bowl can be displayed only if it is next to Olivera's bowl and next to Serra's bowl.

    Reigel's bowl can be displayed only in either position 1 or position 6.

    Serra's bowl cannot be displayed in either position 2 or position 4.

    Neiman's bowl can be displayed only in position 5.

6. Which one of the following could be the display of bowls, listed by potter's name, in order from position 1 through position 6?

(A)   Larsen, Mills, Serra, Park, Olivera, Reigel
(B)   Larsen, Neiman, Olivera, Park, Serra, Vance
(C)   Mills, Olivera, Park, Serra, Reigel, Vance
(D)   Reigel, Park, Serra, Olivera, Neiman, Mills
(E)   Serra, Park, Olivera, Vance, Larsen, Reigel

GO ON TO THE NEXT PAGE.

7. If Neiman's bowl and Park's bowl are both displayed, which one of the following is a potter whose bowl could be displayed in position 1?

(A)   Larsen
(B)   Park
(C)   Reigel
(D)   Serra
(E)   Vance

8. If Larsen's bowl is displayed in position 6 and Olivera's bowl is displayed in position 2, which one of the following must be true?

(A)   Mills's bowl is displayed in position 3.
(B)   Serra's bowl is displayed in position 1.
(C)   Serra's bowl is displayed in position 3.
(D)   Vance's bowl is displayed in position 1.
(E)   Vance's bowl is displayed in position 3.

9. If Park's bowl is displayed in position 4, then the bowl displayed in position 2 must be

(A)   Larsen's, Mills's, or Vance's
(B)   Larsen's, Neiman's, or Vance's
(C)   Larsen's, Serra's, or Vance's
(D)   Mills's, Reigel's, or Vance's
(E)   Mills's, Serra's, or Vance's

10. If Larsen's bowl is displayed in position 1 and Olivera's bowl is displayed in position 4, which one of the following is a potter whose bowl CANNOT be displayed?

(A)   Neiman
(B)   Park
(C)   Reigel
(D)   Serra
(E)   Vance

11. Which one of the following is a potter whose bowl must be displayed?

(A)   Neiman
(B)   Olivera
(C)   Park
(D)   Reigel
(E)   Vance

12. If Neiman's bowl, Park's bowl, and Reigel's bowl are all displayed, which one of the following must be true?

(A)   Neiman's bowl is displayed next to Reigel's bowl.
(B)   Neiman's bowl is displayed next to Vance's bowl.
(C)   Olivera's bowl is displayed next to Reigel's bowl.
(D)   Olivera's bowl is displayed next to Vance's bowl.
(E)   Serra's bowl is displayed next to Vance's bowl.

GO ON TO THE NEXT PAGE.

Questions 13–17

Four employees—Jackson, Larabee, Paulson, and Torillo—are to select from among four offices—W, X, Y, and Z. The order in which they select, from first to fourth, is to be decided by a random drawing. Each employee has ranked the offices from first (highest) to fourth (lowest) as follows:

    Jackson: Y, X, Z, W
    Larabee: X, Z, W, Y
    Paulson: Y, Z, X, W
    Torillo: X, Y, Z, W

The following restrictions must apply:

    Each employee selects an office that has not been selected previously.

    Each employee selects only one office.

    Each employee selects the office that he or she ranks highest among the unselected offices.

13.   Which one of the following is a possible matching of employees with the offices they select?

    (A)   Jackson: W; Larabee: Y; Paulson: X; Torillo: Z
    (B)   Jackson: Z; Larabee: X; Paulson: W; Torillo: Y
    (C)   Jackson: X; Larabee: W; Paulson: Z; Torillo: Y
    (D)   Jackson: Y; Larabee: W; Paulson: X; Torillo: Z
    (E)   Jackson: Y; Larabee: Z; Paulson: X; Torillo: W

GO ON TO THE NEXT PAGE.

14. Which one of the following must be true?

   (A)   At most one of the employees selects the office he or she ranks first.

   (B)   At most one of the employees selects the office he or she ranks second.

   (C)   At least one of the employees selects the office he or she ranks first.

   (D)   At least one of the employees selects the office he or she ranks second.

   (E)   At least one of the employees selects the office he or she ranks third.

15. Which one of the following could be true?

   (A)   Exactly two of the employees each selects the office he or she ranks third.

   (B)   Exactly two of the employees each selects the office he or she ranks fourth.

   (C)   Exactly three of the employees each selects the office he or she ranks second.

   (D)   Exactly three of the employees each selects the office he or she ranks third.

   (E)   Exactly three of the employees each selects the office he or she ranks fourth.

16. If Paulson selects office W, then which one of the following could be true?

   (A)   Exactly two of the employees each selects the office he or she ranks second.

   (B)   Exactly two of the employees each selects the office he or she ranks third.

   (C)   Exactly three of the employees each selects the office he or she ranks first.

   (D)   Jackson selects office X.

   (E)   Larabee selects office Z.

17. Which one of the following must be true?

   (A)   Jackson does not select office X.

   (B)   Larabee does not select office W.

   (C)   Larabee does not select office Z.

   (D)   Torillo does not select office X.

   (E)   Paulson does not select office X.

GO ON TO THE NEXT PAGE.

Questions 18–23

Exactly five volunteers—Haddad, Joslin, Kwon, Molina, and Nash—are being assigned to three community committees—X, Y, and Z. Each committee will have three volunteers assigned to it, with each volunteer on a committee holding exactly one of three positions—leader, secretary, or treasurer. The following conditions apply:

If Nash is assigned to a committee, Nash must be the leader for that committee.

Molina must be assigned to exactly one committee.

Kwon must be assigned to Y but cannot be assigned to Z.

Joslin must be the secretary for Y but cannot be assigned to X or Z.

18. Which one of the following could be the assignment of volunteers to Z?

(A) leader: Haddad; secretary: Molina; treasurer: Joslin

(B) leader: Joslin; secretary: Haddad; treasurer: Molina

(C) leader: Kwon; secretary: Haddad; treasurer: Molina

(D) leader: Molina; secretary: Nash; treasurer: Haddad

(E) leader: Nash; secretary: Molina; treasurer: Haddad

GO ON TO THE NEXT PAGE.

19. If Kwon is assigned to be treasurer for exactly two of the committees, then any of the following could be true EXCEPT:

   (A) Haddad is assigned to be leader for Y.
   (B) Haddad is assigned to be secretary for Z.
   (C) Haddad is assigned to be treasurer for X.
   (D) Molina is assigned to be treasurer for Z.
   (E) Nash is assigned to be leader for Y.

20. Each of the following must be true EXCEPT:

   (A) Haddad is assigned to X.
   (B) Haddad is assigned to Y.
   (C) Kwon is assigned to X.
   (D) Molina is assigned to Z.
   (E) Nash is assigned to X.

21. If Kwon is assigned to be leader for exactly one of the committees, then for which of the committees is the assignment of volunteers to positions fully determined?

   (A) X only
   (B) Y only
   (C) X and Y, but not Z
   (D) Y and Z, but not X
   (E) X, Y, and Z

22. The assignment of volunteers to committees and positions is fully determined if which one of the following is true?

   (A) Haddad is assigned to be leader for exactly one of the committees.
   (B) Haddad is assigned to be secretary for exactly two of the committees.
   (C) Haddad is assigned to be treasurer for all three of the committees.
   (D) Kwon is assigned to be treasurer for exactly two of the committees.
   (E) Nash is assigned to be leader for all three of the committees.

23. Which one of the following, if substituted for the condition that Molina must be assigned to exactly one committee, would have the same effect in determining the assignment of volunteers to committees?

   (A) Haddad must be assigned to more committees than Molina.
   (B) Joslin must be assigned to more committees than Molina.
   (C) Kwon must be assigned to more committees than Molina.
   (D) Molina must be assigned to more committees than Haddad.
   (E) Nash must be assigned to more committees than Molina.

S T O P

IF YOU FINISH BEFORE TIME IS CALLED, YOU MAY CHECK YOUR WORK ON THIS SECTION ONLY.
DO NOT WORK ON ANY OTHER SECTION IN THE TEST.

SECTION IV

Time—35 minutes

26 Questions

<u>Directions:</u> The questions in this section are based on the reasoning contained in brief statements or passages. For some questions, more than one of the choices could conceivably answer the question. However, you are to choose the <u>best</u> answer; that is, the response that most accurately and completely answers the question. You should not make assumptions that are by commonsense standards implausible, superfluous, or incompatible with the passage. After you have chosen the best answer, blacken the corresponding space on your answer sheet.

1. Pundit: Grenier will almost certainly not be elected as mayor. Although she says she believes in raising city employees' wages, it was only a few years ago that she was arguing that their wages should not be increased. Her claim that she has learned more about the issue since then—though sincere—will not matter to most voters, who will see her as insincere.

Which one of the following principles, if valid, most helps to justify the pundit's reasoning?

(A) Voters are unlikely to vote for a politician whom they perceive to be insincere.

(B) Voters are unlikely to notice whether a politician's stance on issues has changed over time.

(C) Voters are unlikely to be influenced by what a politician's views were in the past if the voters agree with the politician's current positions.

(D) Voters are likely to elect a politician who they believe understands their financial concerns.

(E) Voters are likely to question the sincerity of a politician who does not hold the same beliefs they do.

2. Albert: Swenson's popular book, which argues that sun exposure does not harm skin cells, is a model of poor scholarship. Nonetheless, it is valuable because it has stimulated new research on sun exposure.

Yvonne: You're kidding me! You might as well say that a virus is valuable because it stimulates epidemiologists.

The dialogue provides the most support for the claim that Albert and Yvonne disagree over whether

(A) sun exposure harms skin cells

(B) Swenson's book is a model of poor scholarship

(C) Swenson's book should be considered valuable

(D) Swenson's book has stimulated new research on sun exposure

(E) something that does not stimulate new research can have value

3. Researchers have found that the percentage of people who start new businesses is much higher in countries with high per capita income than in countries with moderate per capita income. This is to be expected since most entrepreneurs in high- and middle-income countries start businesses to take advantage of perceived business opportunities, and there are more such opportunities in high-income countries. Surprisingly, however, the researchers also found that the percentage of people who start businesses is even higher in low-income countries than in high-income ones.

Which one of the following, if true, would most help to explain the researchers' surprising finding?

(A) In both high- and low-income countries, well over half of new businesses expect to provide jobs for no more than one or two people.

(B) Many governments of high-income countries provide assistance to individuals who want to start businesses, but very few governments of low-income countries do so.

(C) The percentage of new businesses that fail within a few years of being founded is generally no higher in low-income countries than in high-income countries.

(D) In high-income countries, many entrepreneurs who start businesses to take advantage of perceived business opportunities soon discover that the opportunities were illusory.

(E) In low-income countries, most entrepreneurs start businesses because all other employment options are either absent or unsatisfactory.

GO ON TO THE NEXT PAGE.

4. Film director: It's inaccurate to say that filmgoers stayed away from my film because it received one or two negative reviews. My film had such a small audience during its opening weekend simply because it was competing with several other films that appeal to the same type of filmgoer that mine does, and the number of such viewers is relatively small.

Which one of the following, if true, most helps to support the film director's explanation?

(A) The film director's film received no positive reviews.

(B) Filmgoers seldom see more than one film in a weekend.

(C) The total number of filmgoers was larger than average on the weekend the film director's film opened.

(D) Each of the other films that the film director alludes to received one or two positive reviews.

(E) Most filmgoers are drawn to a variety of kinds of film.

5. Some scientific issues are so complex and counterintuitive that they cannot be well understood by readers of popular magazines. Nonetheless, stories about these difficult scientific issues are frequently the ones that these readers would find most fascinating. Unfortunately, this means that some of the scientific stories that would be most interesting to readers are usually not covered in popular magazines since _____.

The conclusion of the argument is strongly supported if which one of the following completes the passage?

(A) editors of popular magazines generally do not approve stories about issues that cannot be well understood by those magazines' readers

(B) popular magazines cannot stay in business unless they regularly publish stories that their readers find interesting

(C) highly complex and counterintuitive theories are increasingly common in almost all branches of science

(D) readers of popular magazines are generally unable to accurately assess their own understanding of complex scientific issues

(E) most readers of popular magazines are unwilling to seek out other sources in order to read about scientific issues that they find interesting

6. Letter to the editor: Your newspaper's advertisement claims that you provide coverage of the high school's most popular sports. Clearly this is false advertising. Of the school's students, 15 percent compete on the track team, while only 5 percent of the students play basketball. Hence, track is far more popular than basketball, yet track gets no coverage and basketball gets full-page coverage.

The reasoning in the letter to the editor is most vulnerable to the criticism that it

(A) infers a cause from a mere correlation

(B) bases its conclusion on a sample that is too small

(C) misinterprets a key word in the newspaper's advertisement

(D) employs as a premise the contention it purports to show

(E) criticizes the source of a claim rather than the claim itself

7. It is widely believed that the most environmentally sensible thing to do is to buy food from local farmers whenever it is available. But the distance that food travels turns out to be only a small part of its environmental impact. Certain foods can be produced with far less impact in some places rather than others. So, sometimes it is environmentally preferable to buy food that is not produced locally, rather than buy locally produced food.

The claim that the most environmentally sensible thing to do is to buy food from local farmers whenever it is available plays which one of the following roles in the argument?

(A) It is a principle upon which the reasoning in the argument is based.

(B) It is a general principle that is used to support a particular activity that falls under it.

(C) It is a general principle that is used to reject a particular activity that is not compatible with it.

(D) It is a view that is rejected by the argument.

(E) It is the conclusion of the argument.

GO ON TO THE NEXT PAGE.

8. Technology is radically improving the quality of life in some communities, and not only by direct application of innovations. After all, the design, production, testing, and marketing of new technology has itself become a growing industry that is turning around the fortunes of once-ailing communities. The companies involved create jobs, add to the tax base, and contribute to an upbeat spirit of renewal.

Which one of the following most accurately expresses the conclusion drawn by the argument as a whole?

(A) The direct application of innovations is not the only way in which technology is radically improving the quality of life in some communities.

(B) The design, production, testing, and marketing of new technology has itself become a growing industry that is turning around the fortunes of once-ailing communities.

(C) Companies involved in the design, production, testing, and marketing of new technology create jobs, add to the tax base, and contribute to an upbeat spirit of renewal.

(D) Either the creation or the direct application of technological innovations is radically improving the quality of life in most communities.

(E) The only ways in which technology is radically improving the quality of life in some communities are by creating jobs, adding to the tax base, and contributing to an upbeat spirit of renewal.

9. Joshi is clearly letting campaign contributions influence his vote in city council. His campaign for re-election has received more financial support from property developers than any other city councilor's has. And more than any other councilor's, his voting record favors the interests of property developers.

The reasoning in the argument is most vulnerable to criticism on the grounds that the argument

(A) takes for granted that because certain events occurred sequentially, the earlier events caused the later events

(B) confuses one thing's being necessary for another to occur with its being sufficient to make it occur

(C) makes a moral judgment when only a factual judgment can be justified

(D) presumes that one thing is the cause of another when it could easily be an effect of it

(E) has a conclusion that is simply a restatement of one of the argument's stated premises

10. Columnist: Some people argue that the government should not take over failing private-sector banks because the government does not know how to manage financial institutions. However, rather than managing a bank's day-to-day operations, the government would just need to select the bank's senior management. Most politicians have never been military professionals, yet they appoint the top military officials entrusted with defending the country—at least as great a responsibility as managing a bank.

The columnist's statements, if true, provide reason for rejecting which one of the following?

(A) Commanding a branch of the military requires greater knowledge than running a bank does.

(B) Politicians do an adequate job of appointing the top military officials entrusted with defending the country.

(C) Politicians are not capable of managing a bank's day-to-day operations.

(D) Banks that are owned by the government cannot be well managed.

(E) The government should not take over private-sector banks that are financially sound.

GO ON TO THE NEXT PAGE.

11. Polls have shown that a higher percentage of graduating university students are against proposals to reduce government social services than are students entering their first year at a university. These polls lead us to the conclusion that people with a university education are more likely to favor retaining or increasing the present level of government social services than are members of the overall population.

Which one of the following, if true, most seriously weakens the argument?

(A) The polls of graduating university students were designed to avoid overrepresenting any single academic discipline.

(B) The political views of people with a university education are to a large degree influenced by their professors, and university professors are usually against reducing government social services.

(C) Polls of retired persons who have not graduated from a university show a higher percentage of persons in favor of reducing government social services than do polls of retired persons who have graduated from a university.

(D) Polls of those who graduated from a university more than five years before being polled show a higher percentage of people in favor of reducing government social services than do polls of the overall population.

(E) In the polls cited, graduating university students were more likely to express strong opinions about the question of reducing government social services than were students entering a university.

12. Several movie critics have claimed that this movie will inspire people to act in socially irresponsible ways, yet this claim relies entirely on survey data that have turned out to be deeply flawed. Thus these critics have made a claim that is not only untrue but also potentially harmful to the moviemakers' reputations.

The argument is flawed in that it

(A) infers that a claim is false merely on the grounds that no satisfactory evidence for it has been offered

(B) fails to consider that a pejorative claim that is true can be more harmful to a person's reputation than a false claim

(C) relies on a sample that is likely to be unrepresentative

(D) attacks the persons making an argument rather than attacking the substance of the argument

(E) fails to consider that, even if an argument's conclusion is false, some of the evidence used to justify that conclusion may nonetheless be true

13. Most people who are skilled banjo players are also skilled guitar players. But most people who are skilled guitar players are not skilled banjo players.

If the statements above are true, which one of the following must also be true?

(A) There are more people who are skilled at playing both the guitar and the banjo than there are people who are skilled at playing only one of the two instruments.

(B) A person trying to learn how to play the guitar is more likely to succeed in doing so than is a person trying to learn how to play the banjo.

(C) Playing the guitar takes more skill than playing the banjo does.

(D) There are more people who are skilled at playing the guitar than there are people who are skilled at playing the banjo.

(E) There are more people who are skilled at playing the banjo than there are people who are skilled at playing the guitar.

14. Obviously, entrepreneurial ability is needed to start a successful company. Yet many entrepreneurs who succeed in starting a company fail later for lack of managerial skills. For instance, they do not adequately analyze market trends and, consequently, they fail in managing company growth. Hence, the lack of managerial skills and the lack of entrepreneurial ability can each inhibit the development of successful companies.

The proposition that certain entrepreneurs fail in managing company growth plays which one of the following roles in the argument above?

(A) It is the main conclusion drawn in the argument.

(B) It is presented as an example of the phenomenon the argument seeks to explain.

(C) It is meant as an aside and is not supposed to provide evidence in support of the argument's conclusion.

(D) It is a premise that is intended to support the argument's main conclusion directly.

(E) It is an example that is offered in support of a premise that is intended to support the argument's main conclusion directly.

GO ON TO THE NEXT PAGE.

15. Outsiders in any field often believe that they can bring in fresh, useful solutions that have been overlooked by insiders. But in fact, attempts at creativity that are not grounded in relevant experience are futile. Problems can be solved only by people who really understand them, and no one gains such understanding without experience.

Which one of the following is most strongly supported by the information above?

(A) The more experience a person has in a field, the more creatively that person can solve problems in the field.

(B) Those people who are experienced in a field rarely overlook creative solutions.

(C) Creative solutions in a field always come from people with experience in that field.

(D) The experience required for effective problem-solving in a field does not vary depending on the field's complexity.

(E) Outsiders should be properly trained in a field before being given responsibility in that field.

16. Researcher: Dinosaurs lack turbinates—nasal cavity bone structures in warm-blooded species that minimize water loss during breathing. According to some paleobiologists, this implies that all dinosaurs were cold-blooded. These paleobiologists must be mistaken, however, for fossil records show that some dinosaur species lived in Australia and Alaska, where temperatures drop below freezing. Only warm-blooded animals could survive such temperatures.

Which one of the following most accurately describes the role played in the researcher's argument by the claim that only warm-blooded animals could survive temperatures below freezing?

(A) It is presented as a potential counterexample to the argument's main conclusion.

(B) It is a premise offered in support of the argument's main conclusion.

(C) It is presented as counterevidence to the paleobiologists' assertion that dinosaurs lack turbinates.

(D) It is the argument's main conclusion.

(E) It is an intermediate conclusion for which the claim that some dinosaur species lived in Australia and Alaska is offered as support.

17. Principle: The government should not prevent someone from expressing a true belief unless expressing it would be harmful to people generally.

Application: The government was wrong to prevent Calista from publicly expressing her belief that there is evidence that cancer rates have increased slightly over the last two decades and that this increase was due partly to excessive use of cell phones.

Which one of the following, if true, would most help to justify the above application of the principle?

(A) The government has conducted extensive research to determine whether there is any causal link between use of cell phones and cancer.

(B) Several studies have found evidence that use of cell phones has been partially responsible for the increase in cancer rates over the last two decades, and it would benefit people to know this.

(C) Calista firmly believes that knowing about the causes of the increase in cancer rates over the last two decades would greatly benefit people generally.

(D) Unless there is strong evidence of a link between use of a product and disease, the suggestion that use of the product causes disease is usually harmful to people.

(E) Most people would reduce their use of cell phones if they were convinced that they were using them enough to increase their risk of developing cancer.

GO ON TO THE NEXT PAGE.

18. Psychologist: Phonemic awareness, or the knowledge that spoken language can be broken into component sounds, is essential for learning to read an alphabetic language. But one also needs to learn how sounds are symbolically represented by means of letters; otherwise, phonemic awareness will not translate into the ability to read an alphabetic language. Yet many children who are taught by the whole-language method, which emphasizes the ways words sound, learn to read alphabetic languages.

Which one of the following can be properly inferred from the psychologist's statements?

(A) The whole-language method invariably succeeds in teaching awareness of how spoken language can be broken into component sounds.

(B) When the whole-language method succeeds in teaching someone how to represent sounds by means of letters, that person acquires the ability to read an alphabetic language.

(C) Those unable to read an alphabetic language lack both phonemic awareness and the knowledge of how sounds are symbolically represented.

(D) Some children who are taught by the whole-language method are not prevented from learning how sounds are represented by means of letters.

(E) The whole-language method succeeds in teaching many children how to represent sounds symbolically by means of letters.

19. Studies have shown that pedestrians are struck by cars when crossing streets in crosswalks more often than they are struck when crossing outside of crosswalks. This is because crosswalks give many pedestrians an overly strong sense of security that oncoming cars will follow the signals, and these pedestrians are less likely to look both ways before crossing the street.

Which one of the following, if true, most undermines the explanation proposed above?

(A) The overwhelming majority of pedestrians in high-traffic areas cross streets in crosswalks.

(B) The number of pedestrians struck by cars has increased in recent years.

(C) Pedestrians tend to underestimate the chances that the signals at a crosswalk will malfunction.

(D) Drivers are generally most alert to pedestrians who are in or near crosswalks.

(E) Measures intended to promote safety tend to make people less cautious.

20. Selena claims to have psychic powers. So if we find out whether Selena's claim is true, we will thereby determine whether it is possible to have psychic powers.

The conclusion drawn above follows logically if which one of the following is assumed?

(A) No one else has yet been found to have psychic powers.

(B) If it is possible to have psychic powers, then Selena has them.

(C) It is possible to determine whether Selena has psychic powers.

(D) If Selena's claim turns out to be false, we will not know whether it is possible to have psychic powers.

(E) We will not be able to determine whether it is possible to have psychic powers unless we find out whether Selena's claim is true.

21. In a recent study, researchers collected current prices for the 300 most common pharmaceutical drugs from the leading wholesalers specializing in bulk sales. It was found that these prices average 60 to 80 percent below the suggested wholesale prices listed for the same drugs in the current annual edition of a widely used, independently published pharmaceutical price guidebook.

Each of the following, if true, would help to explain the situation described above EXCEPT:

(A) A price war wherein pharmaceutical drug wholesalers tried to undercut each others' prices began shortly before the study was conducted.

(B) Suggested wholesale prices for the most common pharmaceutical drugs tend to be less than those for less common pharmaceutical drugs.

(C) Wholesale prices for pharmaceutical drugs often fluctuate dramatically from one month to the next.

(D) Wholesale prices suggested by the independently published pharmaceutical price guidebook are calculated to allow every pharmaceutical wholesaler to make substantial profits.

(E) The prices suggested by the independently published pharmaceutical price guidebook are for sales of relatively small quantities of pharmaceutical drugs to individual doctors.

GO ON TO THE NEXT PAGE.

22. Theorist: Hatred and anger, grief and despair, love and joy are pairs of emotions that consist of the same core feeling and are distinguishable from each other only in terms of the social conditions that cause them and the behavior they in turn cause. So even if the meaning of a given piece of music is the emotion it elicits, this can mean only that music produces the core of a given emotion, for music is merely sound and, therefore, by itself creates neither social conditions nor human behavior.

The claim that music is merely sound plays which one of the following roles in the theorist's argument?

(A) It is a generalization a particular instance of which is cited by the argument in order to undermine the viewpoint that the argument is attacking.

(B) It is a portion of the conclusion drawn in the argument.

(C) It is a claim that is offered as partial support for the argument's conclusion.

(D) It is a generalization the truth of which is claimed to be necessary to establish the conclusion of the argument.

(E) It is a hypothesis that must be rejected, according to the argument, because it is inconsistent with certain evidence.

23. For a computer to be intelligent, it must possess at least one of three qualities: creativity, self-awareness, or the ability to learn from its mistakes. Because the AR3000 is not creative or self-aware, it must have the ability to learn from its mistakes if it is intelligent.

Which one of the following arguments is most similar in its reasoning to the argument above?

(A) Every vaccine is either an attenuated-virus vaccine, a dead-virus vaccine, or a pure DNA vaccine. Vaccine X cannot fall into the last two categories, because it contains living viral cells. Therefore, vaccine X must be an attenuated-virus vaccine.

(B) Every commonly used vaccine is either a dead-virus vaccine, an attenuated-virus vaccine, or a pure DNA vaccine. Vaccine X is not a dead- or attenuated-virus vaccine. Therefore, if it is a commonly used vaccine, it must be a pure DNA vaccine.

(C) Every vaccine is either a dead-virus vaccine, an attenuated-virus vaccine, or a pure DNA vaccine. Thus, if vaccine X is not a dead- or attenuated-virus vaccine, it must be a pure DNA vaccine.

(D) Every commonly used vaccine is either a dead-virus vaccine, an attenuated-virus vaccine, or a pure DNA vaccine. Vaccine X stimulates the production of killer T cells in the immune system, unlike any pure DNA vaccine. Therefore, if it is not a dead-virus vaccine, then it must be an attenuated-virus vaccine.

(E) Every commonly used vaccine is either a dead-virus vaccine, an attenuated-virus vaccine, or a pure DNA vaccine. Because vaccine X is not an attenuated-virus vaccine, it must be a pure DNA vaccine if it is not a dead-virus vaccine.

GO ON TO THE NEXT PAGE.

24. Mallotech portrays itself to the public as a socially responsible company, but critics charge that employees in many of its factories work in unsanitary conditions. Unless these critics are mistaken, then, Mallotech is not accurately portraying itself to the public.

The argument's conclusion follows logically if which one of the following is assumed?

(A) A socially responsible company would never lie about whether its employees are working in unsanitary conditions.

(B) No company that conceals information from the public is socially responsible.

(C) Many employees in Mallotech's factories work in unsanitary conditions.

(D) A socially responsible company would not have employees working in unsanitary conditions.

(E) Every company that is well managed is socially responsible.

25. Many conceptual categories are parts of dichotomous (distinct and mutually exclusive) pairs: good or bad, right or wrong, rational or irrational, etc. However, advances in scientific understanding have shown some long-held dichotomies to be untenable. Some life forms have characteristics of both animals and plants; also, matter can be converted into energy and vice versa. Therefore, dichotomous classifications into mutually exclusive categories should generally be abandoned.

Which one of the following exhibits flawed reasoning most similar to that in the argument above?

(A) Review by outside consultants has shown that this company should replace all of its computers with more powerful models. Therefore, not all of this company's computers are powerful enough.

(B) Recent clinical trials have shown that some antianxiety drugs are addictive and can have life-threatening side effects. Therefore, the use of drugs for the treatment of anxiety should be discontinued.

(C) Current highway safety data clearly demonstrate that all intoxicated drivers are dangerous. So we should get intoxicated drivers off the roads.

(D) The longer fruit is kept, the more likely it is to become rotten. While these peaches seem to be fine, they have been kept for a rather long time. So it is best to throw them away now before they begin to rot.

(E) This budget is based on the assumption that revenue will increase for the next two years. However, revenue figures for past years show that assumption to be untenable. Therefore, this budget should be replaced by a more realistic one.

26. All oceangoing ships carry seawater ballast tanks whose weight improves stability. To maintain the ship's proper stability, water must be pumped out of these tanks when cargo is loaded and into them when cargo is unloaded. As a result, sea creatures often get into the tanks and are then inadvertently deposited into new habitats, where they can wreak ecological havoc. One viable way of addressing this problem would be to empty and then immediately refill the tanks in midocean, since midocean creatures and coastal sea creatures usually cannot survive in one another's habitats.

Which one of the following is an assumption the argument requires?

(A) Emptying and refilling an oceangoing ship's ballast tanks in midocean would ensure at least that no sea creatures capable of disturbing the ecology in a new habitat are pumped into the tanks.

(B) An oceangoing ship's ballast tanks could be emptied and refilled in midocean only in conditions of calm air and flat seas.

(C) Sea creatures have rarely, if ever, wreaked ecological havoc in a new habitat, unless they have been able to survive in that habitat after having been deposited there by oceangoing ships.

(D) Currently, seawater is pumped into or out of the ballast tanks of oceangoing ships to maintain proper stability only when unloading or loading cargo.

(E) There are at least some oceangoing ships whose stability could be adequately maintained while emptying and refilling their ballast tanks in midocean.

S T O P

IF YOU FINISH BEFORE TIME IS CALLED, YOU MAY CHECK YOUR WORK ON THIS SECTION ONLY.
DO NOT WORK ON ANY OTHER SECTION IN THE TEST.

Wait for the supervisor's instructions before you open the page to the topic.
Please print and sign your name and write the date in the designated spaces below.
Time: 35 Minutes

General Directions

ill have 35 minutes in which to plan and write an essay on the topic inside. Read the topic and the accompanying directions carefully. ill probably find it best to spend a few minutes considering the topic and organizing your thoughts before you begin writing. In your essay, re to develop your ideas fully, leaving time, if possible, to review what you have written. **Do not write on a topic other than the one ified. Writing on a topic of your own choice is not acceptable.**

ecial knowledge is required or expected for this writing exercise. Law schools are interested in the reasoning, clarity, organization, age usage, and writing mechanics displayed in your essay. How well you write is more important than how much you write.

ne your essay to the blocked, lined area on the front and back of the separate Writing Sample Response Sheet. Only that area will be duced for law schools. Be sure that your writing is legible.

Both this topic sheet and your response sheet must be turned in to the testing staff before you leave the room.

Topic Code	Print Your Full Name Here		
140365	Last	First	M.I.

Date	Sign Your Name Here
/ /	

LSAC®

Scratch Paper
Do not write your essay in this space.

LSAT® Writing Sample Topic

Directions: The scenario presented below describes two choices, either one of which can be supported on the basis of the information give Your essay should consider both choices and argue for one over the other, based on the two specified criteria and the facts provided. Ther is no "right" or "wrong" choice: a reasonable argument can be made for either.

A university has limited funds for developing new online degree programs. It must decide whether to contract with an educational software firm for a generic course delivery software package or to develop its own customized software. Using the facts given below, write an essay in which you argue for one choice over the other based on the following two criteria:

- The university wants to provide the best possible educational resources and experience for online students.
- The university wants to most efficiently use its limited funds for developing online programs.

Using an existing generic software package would allow quick introduction of some online courses. The best generic software would require upgrading the university's computer hardware. Most of the university's courses were not designed to be delivered online. The softwa vendor would provide training for users. Some faculty and staff have experience with online courses that use generic course delivery softwa The software vendor would provide maintenance and upgrades for the software. The cost for use of a generic course delivery software package would be a fixed annual licensing fee set by the vendor. Later changing to a different software package would require a complete overhaul of the course delivery system.

Developing its own course delivery software would require the university to invest heavily in expanding its current software developm capability. Newly developed software requires lengthy testing. Expanded software development capability might benefit the university as a whole. Customized software could be designed for the university's existing hardware and to accommodate most of the university's existing courses without significant adjustment. Support for and upgrades to the software would require the university to maintain an expanded permanent software development staff. The university would control the budget and costs for the development and maintenance of its own software.

WP-X

Scratch Paper
Do not write your essay in this space.

Writing Sample Response Sheet

DO NOT WRITE
IN THIS SPACE

Begin your essay in the lined area below.
Continue on the back if you need more space.

COMPUTING YOUR SCORE

Directions:

1. Use the Answer Key on the next page to check your answers.

2. Use the Scoring Worksheet below to compute your raw score.

3. Use the Score Conversion Chart to convert your raw score into the 120–180 scale.

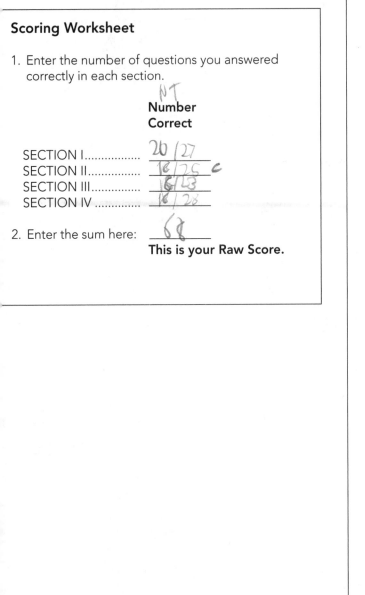

Scoring Worksheet

1. Enter the number of questions you answered correctly in each section.

Number Correct

SECTION I .... 20 / 27

SECTION II .... 18 / 25 c

SECTION III .... 16 / 23

SECTION IV .... 18 / 28

2. Enter the sum here: 68

This is your Raw Score.

Conversion Chart
For Converting Raw Score to the 120–180 LSAT Scaled Score
LSAT Form 5LSN116

Reported Score	Raw Score Lowest	Raw Score Highest
180	99	101
179	98	98
178	97	97
177	*	*
176	96	96
175	95	95
174	94	94
173	93	93
172	92	92
171	91	91
170	89	90
169	88	88
168	87	87
167	85	86
166	84	84
165	82	83
164	81	81
163	79	80
162	77	78
161	76	76
160	74	75
159	72	73
158	70	71
157	69	69
156	67	68
155	65	66
154	63	64
153	62	62
152	60	61
151	58	59
150	57	57
149	55	56
148	53	54
147	52	52
146	50	51
145	48	49
144	47	47
143	45	46
142	44	44
141	42	43
140	41	41
139	39	40
138	38	38
137	36	37
136	35	35
135	33	34
134	32	32
133	31	31
132	29	30
131	28	28
130	27	27
129	26	26
128	25	25
127	24	24
126	22	23
125	21	21
124	20	20
123	19	19
122	18	18
121	17	17
120	0	16

*There is no raw score that will produce this scaled score for this form.

ANSWER KEY

SECTION I

1.	C	8.	E	15.	C	22.	D
2.	A	9.	D	16.	A	23.	B
3.	C	10.	C	17.	D	24.	E
4.	D	11.	E	18.	B	25.	B
5.	B	12.	A	19.	E	26.	A
6.	E	13.	A	20.	B	27.	E
7.	C	14.	B	21.	C		

SECTION II

1.	C	8.	A	15.	C	22.	A
2.	D	9.	B	16.	B	23.	D
3.	E	10.	C	17.	B	24.	A
4.	A	11.	B	18.	D	25.	D
5.	A	12.	B	19.	B		
6.	D	13.	B	20.	B		
7.	E	14.	A	21.	A		

SECTION III

1.	A	8.	C	15.	A	22.	C
2.	B	9.	A	16.	E	23.	C
3.	D	10.	B	17.	E		
4.	C	11.	B	18.	E		
5.	C	12.	A	19.	C		
6.	E	13.	B	20.	B		
7.	D	14.	C	21.	B		

SECTION IV

1.	A	8.	A	15.	C	22.	C
2.	C	9.	D	16.	B	23.	B
3.	E	10.	D	17.	B	24.	D
4.	B	11.	D	18.	D	25.	B
5.	A	12.	A	19.	A	26.	E
6.	C	13.	D	20.	B		
7.	D	14.	E	21.	B		

THE OFFICIAL LSAT
PREPTEST®

78

- PrepTest 78
- Form 7LSN122

JUNE 2016

SECTION I

Time—35 minutes

25 Questions

Directions: The questions in this section are based on the reasoning contained in brief statements or passages. For some questions, more than one of the choices could conceivably answer the question. However, you are to choose the best answer; that is, the response that most accurately and completely answers the question. You should not make assumptions that are by commonsense standards implausible, superfluous, or incompatible with the passage. After you have chosen the best answer, blacken the corresponding space on your answer sheet.

1. Grecia: The survey that we are conducting needs to track employment status by age, so respondents should be asked to indicate their age.

   Hidalgo: We don't need results that provide employment status figures for every single age. So we should instead ask respondents merely to identify the age range that they fall into.

   Which one of the following principles, if valid, most justifies Hidalgo's stance?

   (A) Surveys gathering information for a specific purpose should not collect more detailed personal information than is necessary to achieve the purpose.

   (B) Survey respondents should not be asked a particular question if they are unlikely to answer accurately.

   (C) Sensitive personal information should be gathered only if a secure means of storing that information is available.

   (D) Surveys should be allowed to gather any information that might be needed to meet their purposes.

   (E) Surveys should gather detailed personal information only if survey respondents are first told about how that information will be used.

2. In 1893, an excavation led by Wilhelm Dörpfeld uncovered an ancient city he believed to be Troy, the site of the war described in Homer's epic poem the *Iliad*. But that belief cannot be correct. In the *Iliad*, the Trojan War lasted ten years, but a city as small as the one uncovered by Dörpfeld's team could not have withstood a siege lasting ten years.

   Which one of the following is an assumption required by the argument?

   (A) In 1893, scholars knew of no other ancient city that could have been Troy.

   (B) The *Iliad* does not provide any clues about the specific location of Troy.

   (C) Dörpfeld's team found no evidence in the city they excavated that a siege had occurred there.

   (D) The city excavated by Dörpfeld's team had many features that scholars of the time believed Troy had.

   (E) The *Iliad* accurately represents the duration of the Trojan War.

3. Flynn: Allowing people to collect large damage awards when they successfully sue corporations that produce dangerous products clearly benefits consumers, since the possibility of large awards gives corporations a strong incentive to reduce safety risks associated with their products.

   Garcia: Without sensible limits, damage awards can be so high that corporations are destroyed. As a result, employees lose their jobs and the productivity of the corporation is lost. This harms the economy and thus harms consumers.

   Garcia responds to Flynn's argument by

   (A) arguing that the policy supported in Flynn's argument could have undesirable consequences

   (B) providing evidence that undermines one of the premises of Flynn's argument

   (C) comparing Flynn's argument to an obviously flawed argument that has the same logical structure

   (D) contending that Flynn's argument could be used to support a policy that is inconsistent with the policy that Flynn advocates

   (E) providing an alternative explanation for a situation described in Flynn's argument

GO ON TO THE NEXT PAGE.

4. Monroe: Our organization's project has been a failure. Our stated goal was to reduce as much as possible the number of homes in the community that lack electricity. Now, at the project's conclusion, approximately 2,000 homes are still without electricity.

Wilkerson: But before the project began, over 5,000 homes in the community had no electricity. Surely bringing electricity to around 3,000 homes counts as a success for the project.

Monroe and Wilkerson disagree over the truth of which one of the following?

(A) Approximately 2,000 homes in the community are still without electricity.
(B) Before the organization's project began, over 5,000 homes in the community had no electricity.
(C) The organization's project must be considered a failure if any home in the community has no electricity.
(D) The stated goal of the project was to reduce as much as possible the number of homes in the community that lack electricity.
(E) Leaving approximately 2,000 homes in the community without electricity at the conclusion of the project counts as a failure for the project.

5. Researchers asked 100 fifty-year-olds and 100 twenty-year-olds whether they gave blood. Because nearly twice as many fifty-year-olds as twenty-year-olds reported that they sometimes gave blood, the researchers concluded that, on average, fifty-year-olds are more altruistic than twenty-year-olds. But there is reason for skepticism. Many people hesitate to admit that their behavior does not conform to societal expectations.

The reasoning above calls into question a conclusion drawn from statistical data by

(A) showing that the data are based on an unrepresentative sample
(B) offering an alternative explanation of some of the data
(C) showing that one cannot directly observe altruism
(D) criticizing the motives of the researchers
(E) offering a specific counterexample

6. Mario: I see that the only rug store in Glendale has gone out of business. Evidently there's little demand for rugs in Glendale. So if you're planning to open a new business there, rugs would be one product to avoid.

Renate: It's true that the store is gone, but its closing had little to do with the product it sold. All this means is that the market for rugs in Glendale is now wide open.

The dialogue provides the most support for the claim that Mario and Renate disagree over whether

(A) the rug store in Glendale sold rugs of inferior quality
(B) it is a good idea to open a rug store in Glendale
(C) it is possible to determine the market for rugs in Glendale
(D) any other stores have gone out of business in Glendale
(E) rug stores can close because of insufficient demand for rugs

7. Editorialist: The city council is considering increasing the amount of air traffic allowed at the airport beyond its original design capacity. Several council members say that this increase would not decrease safety as it would be accompanied by the purchase of the latest safety technology. But in fact it would decrease safety. Numerous studies conducted 30 years ago show that safety was reduced at every airport where the permitted level of traffic was increased beyond the airport's original design capacity, even when those airports made use of the latest safety technology.

Which one of the following most accurately describes a flaw in the editorialist's argument?

(A) The argument draws a conclusion on the basis of a general statement that has in turn been inferred from a very limited number of particular instances.
(B) The argument fails to consider the possibility that whether an airport can allow more air traffic than it was originally designed for without reducing safety depends largely on what the latest technology is.
(C) The argument fails to consider the possibility that the city council members who support the increase are aware of the studies that were conducted 30 years ago.
(D) The argument confuses an absence of evidence for the claim that the airport can safely permit air traffic in excess of its original design capacity with the existence of evidence against this claim.
(E) The argument fails to consider that a slight increase in safety risks might be acceptable if it yields overriding benefits of another kind.

8. Philosopher: It has been argued that because particular moral codes differ between cultures, morality must be entirely a product of culture and cannot be grounded in some universal human nature. This argument is flawed. Research suggests that certain moral attitudes, such as disapproval of unfairness and cruelty, are shared across all cultures. And just as certain universal tastes like sweetness and saltiness can, in different cultural contexts, provide the basis for many different cuisines, _____.

Which one of the following most logically completes the argument?

(A)   moral codes tend to be based in the specific contexts in which they arise
(B)   the moral codes of most cultures resemble each other in many respects
(C)   a variety of moral codes can be based in shared moral attitudes
(D)   it is possible to understand the basis of the moral codes of different cultures
(E)   moral attitudes can be adapted to suit the moral codes of many different cultures

9. In a recent field study of prairie plants, the more plant species a prairie plot had, the more vigorously the plants grew and the better the soil retained nutrients. Thus, having more plant species improves a prairie's ability to support plant life.

The argument is most vulnerable to criticism on the grounds that it

(A)   infers of two correlated phenomena, X and Y, that X causes Y without considering whether Y causes X
(B)   fails to describe the mechanism by which productivity is supposedly increased
(C)   takes for granted that the characteristics of one prairie plot could reveal something about the characteristics of other prairie plots
(D)   bases a general conclusion on data that is likely to be unrepresentative
(E)   takes an increase in number to indicate an increase in proportion

10. Anthropologist: In an experiment, two groups of undergraduates were taught how to create one of the types of stone tools that the Neanderthals made in prehistoric times. One group was taught using both demonstrations and elaborate verbal explanations, whereas the other group learned by silent example alone. The two groups showed a significant difference neither in the speed with which they acquired the toolmaking skills nor in the level of proficiency they reached. This shows that Neanderthals could just as well have created their sophisticated tools even if they had no language.

Which one of the following, if true, most weakens the anthropologist's argument?

(A)   Apart from the sophistication of their stone tools, there is a great deal of evidence suggesting that Neanderthals possessed some form of language.
(B)   The students who were taught with verbal explanations were allowed to discuss the toolmaking techniques among themselves, whereas the students who learned by silent example were not.
(C)   The tools that the undergraduates were taught to make were much simpler and easier to make than most types of tools created by Neanderthals.
(D)   The instructor who taught the group of students who learned by silent example alone was much less proficient at making the stone tools than was the instructor who taught the other group of students.
(E)   The tools created by Neanderthals were much less sophisticated than the tools created by anatomically modern humans who almost certainly possessed language and lived at the same time as the Neanderthals.

GO ON TO THE NEXT PAGE.

11. Modest amounts of exercise can produce a dramatic improvement in cardiovascular health. One should exercise most days of the week, but one need only do the equivalent of half an hour of brisk walking on those days to obtain cardiovascular health benefits. More vigorous exercise is more effective, but a strenuous workout is not absolutely necessary.

Which one of the following is most strongly supported by the statements above?

(A) Having a strenuous workout most days of the week can produce a dramatic improvement in cardiovascular health.

(B) Doing the equivalent of an hour of brisk walking two or three times a week generally produces dramatic improvements in cardiovascular health.

(C) It is possible to obtain at least as great an improvement in cardiovascular health from doing the equivalent of half an hour of brisk walking most days of the week as from having a strenuous workout most days of the week.

(D) Aside from exercise, there is no way of improving one's cardiovascular health.

(E) To obtain a dramatic improvement in one's cardiovascular health, one must exercise strenuously at least occasionally.

12. Sartore is a better movie reviewer than Kelly. A movie review should help readers determine whether or not they are apt to enjoy the movie, and a person who is likely to enjoy a particular movie is much more likely to realize this by reading a review by Sartore than a review by Kelly, even though Sartore is more likely to give a movie an unfavorable review than a favorable one.

Which one of the following, if true, most strengthens the argument?

(A) Sartore has technical knowledge of film, whereas Kelly is merely a fan.

(B) Most of Kelly's movie reviews are unfavorable to the movie being reviewed.

(C) One who is apt not to enjoy a particular movie is more likely to realize this by reading a review by Sartore than a review by Kelly.

(D) Reading a movie review by Sartore will usually help one to enjoy the movie more than one otherwise would have.

(E) Most of the movies that Sartore reviews are also reviewed by Kelly.

13. Specially bred aquarium fish with brilliant coloration and unusual body shapes may be popular with connoisseurs, but they are inferior to ordinary fish. Hampered by their elaborate tails or strangely shaped fins, the specially bred fish cannot reach food as quickly as can the ordinary fish that compete with them for food, and so they are often underfed. Also, they do not breed true; most offspring of the specially bred fish lack the elaborate tails and brilliant coloration of their parents.

Which one of the following is most strongly supported by the information above?

(A) Specially bred aquarium fish must receive special care if they are to survive.

(B) Connoisseurs are not interested in dull-colored, simply shaped fish.

(C) Most specially bred aquarium fish are purchased by connoisseurs.

(D) Ordinary fish tend not to have elaborate tails or strangely shaped fins.

(E) Strangely shaped fins and elaborate tails interfere with a fish's ability to reproduce.

14. Ethicist: The general principle—if one ought to do something then one can do it—does not always hold true. This may be seen by considering an example. Suppose someone promises to meet a friend at a certain time, but—because of an unforeseen traffic jam—it is impossible to do so.

Which one of the following is an assumption required by the ethicist's argument?

(A) If a person failed to do something she or he ought to have done, then that person failed to do something that she or he promised to do.

(B) Only an event like an unforeseen traffic jam could excuse a person from the obligation to keep a promise.

(C) If there is something that a person ought not do, then it is something that that person is capable of not doing.

(D) The obligation created by a promise is not relieved by the fact that the promise cannot be kept.

(E) If an event like an unforeseen traffic jam interferes with someone's keeping a promise, then that person should not have made the promise to begin with.

GO ON TO THE NEXT PAGE.

15. The production of leather and fur for clothing is labor intensive, which means that these materials have tended to be expensive. But as fashion has moved away from these materials, their prices have dropped, while prices of some materials that require less labor in their production and are more fashionable have risen.

The situation described above conforms most closely to which one of the following generalizations?

(A) The price of any manufactured good depends more on how fashionable that good is than on the materials it is made from.

(B) It is more important for the materials used in the manufacture of clothing to be fashionable than it is for them to be practical.

(C) Materials that require relatively little labor in their production tend to be fashionable.

(D) The appearance of a manufactured good is the only thing that determines whether it is fashionable.

(E) Cultural trends tend to be an important determinant of the prices of materials used in manufacturing.

16. In most of this forest, the expected outbreak of tree-eating tussock moths should not be countered. After all, the moth is beneficial where suppression of forest fires, for example, has left the forest unnaturally crowded with immature trees, and _____.

The conclusion of the argument is most strongly supported if which one of the following completes the passage?

(A) more than half of the forest is unnaturally crowded with immature trees

(B) mature trees are usually the first to be eaten by tussock moths

(C) usually a higher proportion of mature trees than of immature ones are destroyed in forest fires

(D) the expected outbreak of tussock moths will almost certainly occur if no attempt is made to counter it

(E) there are no completely effective countermeasures against the moth

17. In order to relieve traffic congestion, the city of Gastner built a new highway linking several of the city's suburbs to the downtown area. However, the average commute time for workers in downtown Gastner increased after the new highway opened.

Which one of the following, if true, most helps to explain the increase in average commute time?

(A) Most people who work in the downtown area of Gastner commute from one of the city's suburbs.

(B) The location of the new highway is most convenient for people who commute to and from Gastner's largest suburbs.

(C) Shortly after the new highway was opened, several suburban roads connecting to the new highway were upgraded with new stoplights.

(D) At the same time the new highway was being built, road repair work was being done on important streets leading to downtown Gastner.

(E) In Gastner's downtown area, traffic on the roads near the new highway became more congested after the new highway was opened.

18. Office worker: I have two equally important projects that remain undone. The first one is late already, and if I devote time to finishing it, then I won't have time to finish the second one before its deadline. Admittedly, there's no guarantee that I can finish the second project on time even if I devote all of my time to it, but I should nonetheless devote all of my time to the second one.

Which one of the following principles, if valid, most helps to justify the office worker's reasoning?

(A) It is better to focus one's time on a single project than to split one's time between two projects.

(B) It is better to finish one of two projects than to risk failing to finish both projects.

(C) It is better to first finish those projects that must be done than to interrupt them with projects that are merely optional.

(D) It is better not to worry about having failed to finish a project on time than to allow such worry to interfere with finishing a competing project on time.

(E) It is better to attempt to finish a project on time than to attempt to finish a late project that does not have higher priority.

GO ON TO THE NEXT PAGE.

19. Science teacher: An abstract knowledge of science is very seldom useful for the decisions that adults typically make in their daily lives. But the skills taught in secondary school should be useful for making such decisions. Therefore, secondary school science courses should teach students to evaluate science-based arguments regarding practical issues, such as health and public policy, instead of or perhaps in addition to teaching more abstract aspects of science.

Which one of the following is an assumption the science teacher's argument requires?

(A) Secondary schools should teach only those skills that are the most useful for the decisions that adults typically make in their daily lives.

(B) Teaching secondary school students the more abstract aspects of science is at least as important as teaching them to evaluate science-based arguments regarding practical issues.

(C) Adults who have an abstract knowledge of science are no better at evaluating science-based arguments regarding practical issues than are adults who have no knowledge of science at all.

(D) No secondary school science courses currently teach students how to evaluate science-based arguments regarding practical issues.

(E) The ability to evaluate science-based arguments regarding practical issues is sometimes useful in making the decisions that adults typically make in their daily lives.

20. Lyle: Admittedly, modernizing the language of premodern plays lessens their aesthetic quality, but such modernizing remains valuable for teaching history, since it makes the plays accessible to students who would otherwise never enjoy them.

Carl: But such modernizing prevents students from understanding fully what the plays said to premodern audiences. Thus, modernizing plays is of no use for teaching history, because students cannot gain deep knowledge of the past from modernized plays.

Which one of the following most accurately expresses a point of disagreement between Lyle and Carl?

(A) whether modernizing the language of premodern plays results in plays that have different pedagogical value than the originals

(B) whether the loss in aesthetic quality that results from modernizing the language of premodern plays lessens the plays' usefulness for teaching history

(C) whether the highest form of aesthetic enjoyment of premodern plays comes from seeing them as they were originally performed

(D) whether increasing the accessibility of premodern plays through modernizing their language is valuable for teaching history

(E) whether using plays with modernized language to teach history requires that there be some loss in the aesthetic quality of the plays

GO ON TO THE NEXT PAGE.

21. Most kinds of soil contain clay, and virtually every kind of soil contains either sand or organic material, or both. Therefore, there must be some kinds of soil that contain both clay and sand and some that contain both clay and organic material.

The pattern of flawed reasoning in which one of the following arguments is most parallel to that in the argument above?

(A) Most pharmacies sell cosmetics. Virtually every pharmacy sells shampoo or toothpaste, or both. Therefore, if there are pharmacies that sell both cosmetics and toothpaste, there must also be some that sell both cosmetics and shampoo.

(B) Undoubtedly, most pharmacies sell cosmetics, for almost all pharmacies sell either shampoo or toothpaste, or both, and there are some pharmacies that sell both cosmetics and shampoo and some that sell both cosmetics and toothpaste.

(C) Most pharmacies sell cosmetics. Nearly all pharmacies sell shampoo or toothpaste, or both. Therefore, unless there are some pharmacies that sell both cosmetics and toothpaste, there must be some that sell both cosmetics and shampoo.

(D) Virtually every pharmacy that sells shampoo also sells toothpaste. Most pharmacies sell cosmetics. Therefore, there must be some pharmacies that sell both cosmetics and toothpaste and some that sell both cosmetics and shampoo.

(E) Nearly all pharmacies sell either shampoo or toothpaste, or both. Therefore, since most pharmacies sell cosmetics, there must be some pharmacies that sell both cosmetics and toothpaste and some that sell both cosmetics and shampoo.

22. In 2005, an environmental group conducted a study measuring the levels of toxic chemicals in the bodies of eleven volunteers. Scientifically valid inferences could not be drawn from the study because of the small sample size, but the results were interesting nonetheless. Among the subjects tested, younger subjects showed much lower levels of PCBs—toxic chemicals that were banned in the 1970s. This proves that the regulation banning PCBs was effective in reducing human exposure to those chemicals.

The reasoning in the argument is most vulnerable to criticism on the grounds that the argument

(A) takes an inconsistent stance regarding the status of the inferences that can be drawn from the study

(B) overlooks the possibility that two or more chemicals produce the same effects

(C) concludes that a generalization has been proven true merely on the grounds that it has not been proven false

(D) takes something to be the cause of a reduction when it could have been an effect of that reduction

(E) does not consider the possibility that PCBs have detrimental effects on human health several years after exposure

GO ON TO THE NEXT PAGE.

23. A spy fails by being caught, and it is normally only through being caught that spies reveal their methods. The successful spy is never caught. So the available data are skewed: One can learn a lot about what makes a spy fail but very little about what makes a spy succeed.

Which one of the following arguments is most similar in its reasoning to the argument above?

(A) Of those who participated in the marathon, some succeeded and others failed. But those who did not participate at all neither succeeded nor failed, since both success and failure require participation.

(B) People who are aware of their motives can articulate them. But unconscious motives are usually impossible to acknowledge. So people are more likely to hear about other people's conscious motives than their unconscious ones.

(C) It is unclear whether the company's venture succeeded, because the criteria for its success are undefined. But if the venture had had a measurable goal, then it would have been possible to judge its success.

(D) A teacher is someone who teaches. In addition, there are people who teach but are not called teachers. So while the number of those called teachers is large, the number of those who teach is even larger.

(E) Because someone intervened in the conflict, the effects of that intervention can be discerned. But since no one can investigate what does not happen, it is impossible to discern what would have happened had someone not intervened.

24. Families with underage children make up much of the population, but because only adults can vote, lawmakers in democracies pay too little attention to the interests of these families. To remedy this, parents should be given additional votes to cast on behalf of their underage children. Families with underage children would thus receive fair representation.

The argument requires assuming which one of the following principles?

(A) The amount of attention that lawmakers give to a group's interests should be directly proportional to the number of voters in that group.

(B) Parents should not be given responsibility for making a decision on their child's behalf unless their child is not mature enough to decide wisely.

(C) The parents of underage children should always consider the best interests of their children when they vote.

(D) It is not fair for lawmakers to favor the interests of people who have the vote over the interests of people who do not have the vote.

(E) A group of people can be fairly represented in a democracy even if some members of that group can vote on behalf of others in that group.

25. Critic: The *Gazette-Standard* newspaper recently increased its editorial staff to avoid factual errors. But this clearly is not working. Compared to its biggest competitor, the *Gazette-Standard* currently runs significantly more corrections acknowledging factual errors.

Which one of the following, if true, most seriously weakens the critic's argument?

(A) The *Gazette-Standard* pays its editorial staff lower salaries than its biggest competitor pays its editorial staff.

(B) The *Gazette-Standard* has been in business considerably longer than has its biggest competitor.

(C) The *Gazette-Standard* more actively follows up reader complaints about errors in the paper than does its biggest competitor.

(D) The *Gazette-Standard*'s articles are each checked by more editors than are the articles of its biggest competitor.

(E) The increase in the *Gazette-Standard*'s editorial staff has been offset by a decrease in the reporting staff at the newspaper.

S T O P

IF YOU FINISH BEFORE TIME IS CALLED, YOU MAY CHECK YOUR WORK ON THIS SECTION ONLY.
DO NOT WORK ON ANY OTHER SECTION IN THE TEST.

SECTION II

Time—35 minutes

23 Questions

Directions: Each group of questions in this section is based on a set of conditions. In answering some of the questions, it may be useful to draw a rough diagram. Choose the response that most accurately and completely answers each question and blacken the corresponding space on your answer sheet.

Questions 1–5

Seven workers—Quinn, Ruiz, Smith, Taylor, Verma, Wells, and Xue—are being considered for a special project. Exactly three of the workers will be selected to be project members, and exactly one of these project members will be the project leader. The selection is subject to the following constraints:

Quinn or Ruiz can be a project member only if leading the project.

If Smith is a project member, Taylor must also be.

If Wells is a project member, neither Ruiz nor Verma can be.

1. Which one of the following is an acceptable selection for the project?

(A) Ruiz (leader), Taylor, Wells
(B) Verma (leader), Quinn, Taylor
(C) Verma (leader), Smith, Taylor
(D) Verma (leader), Smith, Xue
(E) Xue (leader), Verma, Wells

GO ON TO THE NEXT PAGE.

2. If Taylor is the project leader and Wells is a project member, then the third project member must be either

(A) Quinn or Smith
(B) Quinn or Xue
(C) Ruiz or Verma
(D) Smith or Xue
(E) Verma or Xue

3. Verma could be the project leader if which one of the following is true?

(A) Neither Quinn nor Smith is selected.
(B) Neither Ruiz nor Taylor is selected.
(C) Neither Smith nor Taylor is selected.
(D) Neither Smith nor Xue is selected.
(E) Neither Taylor nor Wells is selected.

4. If Taylor is not a project member, which one of the following workers must be a project member?

(A) Quinn
(B) Ruiz
(C) Verma
(D) Wells
(E) Xue

5. The selection for the project is completely determined if which one of the following is true?

(A) Neither Quinn nor Smith is selected.
(B) Neither Quinn nor Taylor is selected.
(C) Neither Quinn nor Xue is selected.
(D) Neither Ruiz nor Wells is selected.
(E) Neither Ruiz nor Verma is selected.

GO ON TO THE NEXT PAGE.

Questions 6–11

Four students will be assigned to a history project in which they will search archives from the years 1921, 1922, 1923, and 1924. Each of the four years will have exactly one student assigned to it. Six students—Louis, Mollie, Onyx, Ryan, Tiffany, and Yoshio—are available for this project. The following conditions apply:

Only Louis or Tiffany can be assigned to 1923.

If Mollie is assigned to the project, then she must be assigned to either 1921 or 1922.

If Tiffany is assigned to the project, then Ryan must be assigned to the project.

If Ryan is assigned to the project, then Onyx must be assigned to the year immediately prior to Ryan's.

6. Which one of the following could be an accurate assignment of students, in order from the earliest year to the latest?

(A)   Louis, Onyx, Ryan, Yoshio
(B)   Mollie, Yoshio, Tiffany, Onyx
(C)   Onyx, Ryan, Louis, Tiffany
(D)   Tiffany, Onyx, Louis, Ryan
(E)   Yoshio, Onyx, Louis, Mollie

GO ON TO THE NEXT PAGE.

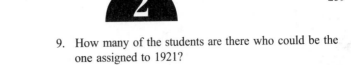

7. Mollie must be assigned to 1922 if which one of the following is true?

(A) Louis is assigned to 1924.
(B) Onyx is assigned to 1921.
(C) Onyx is assigned to 1924.
(D) Tiffany is assigned to 1923.
(E) Yoshio is assigned to 1921.

8. If both Ryan and Yoshio are assigned to the project, which one of the following could be true?

(A) Louis is assigned to 1923.
(B) Mollie is assigned to 1921.
(C) Onyx is assigned to 1922.
(D) Tiffany is assigned to 1924.
(E) Yoshio is assigned to 1922.

9. How many of the students are there who could be the one assigned to 1921?

(A) six
(B) five
(C) four
(D) three
(E) two

10. If Yoshio is not assigned to the project, which one of the following could be true?

(A) Louis is not assigned to the project.
(B) Ryan is not assigned to the project.
(C) Tiffany is not assigned to the project.
(D) Onyx is assigned to 1922.
(E) Louis is assigned to 1924.

11. Which one of the following students CANNOT be assigned to 1922?

(A) Louis
(B) Mollie
(C) Onyx
(D) Ryan
(E) Yoshio

GO ON TO THE NEXT PAGE.

Questions 12–17

During the weeklong grand opening of a new antique shop, the antique dealer will auction exactly one antique per day for six consecutive days—June 1st through June 6th. The antiques to be auctioned are: a harmonica, a lamp, a mirror, a sundial, a table, and a vase. The following conditions apply:

The sundial is not auctioned on June 1st.

If the harmonica is auctioned on an earlier date than the lamp, then the mirror is also auctioned on an earlier date than the lamp.

The sundial is auctioned on an earlier date than the mirror and also on an earlier date than the vase.

The table is auctioned on an earlier date than the harmonica or on an earlier date than the vase, but not both.

12. Which one of the following could be an accurate list of the six antiques, in the order in which they are auctioned, from June 1st through June 6th?

(A)   harmonica, table, sundial, lamp, vase, mirror
(B)   lamp, harmonica, sundial, mirror, vase, table
(C)   harmonica, sundial, table, mirror, lamp, vase
(D)   sundial, mirror, harmonica, table, vase, lamp
(E)   vase, sundial, lamp, harmonica, table, mirror

GO ON TO THE NEXT PAGE.

h.
l.
m.
s.
t.
v.

$\overline{1}\ \overline{2}\ \overline{3}\ \overline{4}\ \overline{5}\ \overline{6}$
8

h_l → m_l   h,m _l

s_m, s_v   s_m,v

t_h / t_v

13. $\underline{v}\ \underline{t}\ \underline{l}\ \underline{h}\ \underline{s}$ ✓
    $\underline{h}\ \underline{t}\ \underline{l}\ \underline{s}\ \underline{m}\ \underline{v}$
    $\underline{l}\ \underline{s}\ \underline{m}\ \underline{t}\ \underline{h}$ ✓

14. $\underline{l}\ \underline{s}\ \underline{m}\ \underline{v}\ \underline{t}\ \underline{h}$ ✓

    t_h

15. $\underline{h}\ \underline{s}\ \underline{l}\ \underline{t}\ \underline{m}\ \underline{v}$
    $\underline{h}\ \underline{t}\ \underline{l}\ \underline{s}\ \underline{m}\ \underline{v}$
    $\underline{h}\ \underline{t}\ \underline{s}\ \underline{t}\ \underline{m}\ \underline{v}$
    $\underline{}\ \underline{l}\ \underline{h}\ \underline{t}\ \underline{m}\ \underline{v}$
    $\underline{h}\ \underline{l}\ \underline{t}\ \underline{s}\ \underline{m}\ \underline{v}$
    $\underline{}\ \underline{}\ \underline{s}\ \underline{m}\ \underline{v}\ \underline{}$
    $\underline{}\ \underline{m}\ \underline{}\ \underline{}\ \underline{}$
    ✓ $\underline{h}\ \underline{t}\ \underline{s}\ \underline{v}\ \underline{m}\ \underline{l}$
    ✓ $\underline{h}\ \underline{s}\ \underline{t}\ \underline{v}\ \underline{m}\ \underline{l}$

13. Which one of the following could be true?

(A) The table is auctioned on June 2nd and the lamp is auctioned on June 3rd.
(B) The sundial is auctioned on June 2nd and the vase is auctioned on June 3rd.
(C) The mirror is auctioned on June 3rd and the sundial is auctioned on June 4th.
(D) The vase is auctioned on June 4th and the sundial is auctioned on June 5th.
(E) The sundial is auctioned on June 4th and the table is auctioned on June 5th.

14. If the table is auctioned on a date that is later than both the date on which the mirror is auctioned and the date on which the vase is auctioned, then which one of the following could be true?

(A) The harmonica is auctioned on an earlier date than the table.
(B) The table is auctioned on an earlier date than the lamp.
(C) The table is auctioned on an earlier date than the sundial.
(D) The mirror is auctioned on an earlier date than the vase.
(E) The sundial is auctioned on an earlier date than the lamp.

15. Which one of the following CANNOT be the antique auctioned on the day immediately preceding the day on which the vase is auctioned?

(A) the harmonica
(B) the lamp
(C) the mirror
(D) the sundial
(E) the table

16. Which one of the following could be true?

(A) The mirror is auctioned on June 2nd.
(B) The lamp is auctioned on June 2nd.
(C) The vase is auctioned on June 2nd.
(D) The lamp is auctioned on June 3rd.
(E) The mirror is auctioned on June 5th.

17. Which one of the following could be true?

(A) The sundial is auctioned on June 5th.
(B) The sundial is auctioned on June 4th.
(C) The lamp is auctioned on June 5th and the mirror is auctioned on June 6th.
(D) The table is auctioned on June 3rd and the lamp is auctioned on June 4th.
(E) The harmonica is auctioned on June 2nd and the vase is auctioned on June 3rd.

GO ON TO THE NEXT PAGE.

Questions 18–23

A chorus director is planning to audition exactly six singers: Kammer, Lugo, Trillo, Waite, Yoshida, and Zinn. Kammer's audition and Lugo's audition will be recorded; the other four will not be. The six auditions are to take place one after the other on a single day, in accordance with the following conditions:

The fourth audition cannot be recorded.
The fifth audition must be recorded.
Waite's audition must take place earlier than the two recorded auditions.
Kammer's audition must take place earlier than Trillo's audition.
Zinn's audition must take place earlier than Yoshida's audition.

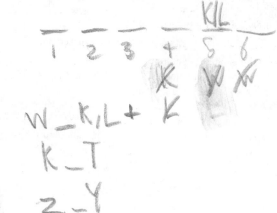

18. Which one of the following could be the order of the auditions, from first to last?

(A)   Kammer, Trillo, Zinn, Waite, Lugo, Yoshida
(B)   Waite, Kammer, Yoshida, Zinn, Lugo, Trillo
(C)   Waite, Lugo, Kammer, Trillo, Zinn, Yoshida
(D)   Waite, Zinn, Kammer, Trillo, Lugo, Yoshida
(E)   Zinn, Yoshida, Waite, Lugo, Kammer, Trillo

GO ON TO THE NEXT PAGE.

19. Which one of the following CANNOT be the second audition?

(A) Kammer's audition
(B) Lugo's audition
(C) Trillo's audition
(D) Waite's audition
(E) Zinn's audition

20. Which one of the following could be the sixth audition?

(A) Kammer's audition
(B) Lugo's audition
(C) Trillo's audition
(D) Waite's audition
(E) Zinn's audition

21. If Kammer's audition is immediately before Yoshida's, which one of the following could be true?

(A) Kammer's audition is second.
(B) Trillo's audition is fourth.
(C) Waite's audition is third.
(D) Yoshida's audition is sixth.
(E) Zinn's audition is second.

22. Yoshida's audition could be

(A) fifth
(B) fourth
(C) third
(D) second
(E) first

23. Which one of the following, if substituted for the condition that Waite's audition must take place earlier than the two recorded auditions, would have the same effect in determining the order of the auditions?

(A) Zinn's audition is the only one that can take place earlier than Waite's.
(B) Waite's audition must take place either immediately before or immediately after Zinn's.
(C) Waite's audition must take place earlier than Lugo's.
(D) Waite's audition must be either first or second.
(E) The first audition cannot be recorded.

S T O P

IF YOU FINISH BEFORE TIME IS CALLED, YOU MAY CHECK YOUR WORK ON THIS SECTION ONLY.
DO NOT WORK ON ANY OTHER SECTION IN THE TEST.

SECTION III

Time—35 minutes

26 Questions

Directions: The questions in this section are based on the reasoning contained in brief statements or passages. For some questions, more than one of the choices could conceivably answer the question. However, you are to choose the best answer; that is, the response that most accurately and completely answers the question. You should not make assumptions that are by commonsense standards implausible, superfluous, or incompatible with the passage. After you have chosen the best answer, blacken the corresponding space on your answer sheet.

1. A nonprofit organization concerned with a social issue sent out a fund-raising letter to 5,000 people. The letter was accompanied by a survey soliciting recipients' opinions. Of the 300 respondents, 283 indicated in the survey that they agreed with the organization's position on the social issue. This suggests that most of the 5,000 people to whom the letter was sent agreed with that position.

   The argument is most vulnerable to criticism on which one of the following grounds?

   (A) It draws a conclusion about a population from observations of a subgroup that is quite likely to be unrepresentative of that population in certain relevant respects.
   (B) It takes for granted that most individuals do not vary significantly in the opinions they would express on a given issue if surveyed regarding that issue on different occasions.
   (C) It relies on the accuracy of a survey made under conditions in which it is probable that most of the responses to that survey did not correctly reflect the opinions of the respondents.
   (D) It uses evidence about an opinion held by the majority of a population in an attempt to justify a conclusion regarding the opinion of a small part of that population.
   (E) It takes for granted that the fund-raising letter had some influence on the opinions of most of the people who received it.

2. An unstable climate was probably a major cause of the fall of the Roman empire. Tree-ring analysis shows that Europe's climate underwent extreme fluctuations between 250 A.D. and 550 A.D., a period that encompasses Rome's decline and fall. This highly variable climate surely hurt food production, which made the empire harder to rule and defend.

   Which one of the following, if true, most strengthens the argument?

   (A) Political failures within the Roman empire during its last years led to conflicts that hampered agricultural production.
   (B) The areas of the Roman empire that had the greatest climatic instability between 250 A.D. and 550 A.D. did not experience unusual levels of unrest during that period.
   (C) Poor farming practices led to depleted soil in many parts of Europe during the last years of the Roman empire.
   (D) During periods when the Roman empire was thriving, Europe consistently experienced weather that was favorable for agriculture.
   (E) Total food production in Europe was likely greater in the years around 550 A.D. than in the years around 250 A.D.

3. Sales manager: Having spent my entire career in sales, most of that time as a sales manager for a large computer company, I know that natural superstar salespeople are rare. But many salespeople can perform like superstars if they have a good manager. Therefore, companies should _____.

   Which one of the following most logically completes the sales manager's argument?

   (A) devote more effort to training than to evaluating salespeople
   (B) devote more effort to finding good managers than to finding natural superstar salespeople
   (C) keep to a minimum the number of salespeople for which a manager is responsible
   (D) promote more natural superstar salespeople to management positions
   (E) reward superstar performance more than superstar talent

GO ON TO THE NEXT PAGE.

4. According to economists, people's tendency to purchase a given commodity is inversely proportional to its price. When new techniques produced cheaper steel, more steel was purchased. Nevertheless, once machine-produced lace became available, at much lower prices than the handcrafted variety, lace no longer served to advertise its wearers' wealth and the lace market collapsed. Obviously, then, there are exceptions to the economists' general rule.

The claim that more steel was purchased when it could be manufactured more cheaply plays which one of the following roles in the argument?

(A) It is described as inadequate evidence for the falsity of the argument's conclusion.

(B) It is described as an exception to a generalization for which the argument offers evidence.

(C) It is used to illustrate the generalization that, according to the argument, does not hold in all cases.

(D) It is the evidence that, according to the argument, led economists to embrace a false hypothesis.

(E) It is cited as one of several reasons for modifying a general assumption made by economists.

5. Resident: Data indicates that 30 percent of the houses in our town have inadequate site drainage and 30 percent have structural defects that could make them unsafe. Hence, at least 60 percent of our town's houses have some kind of problem that threatens their integrity.

The reasoning in the resident's argument is flawed in that the argument overlooks the possibility that

(A) the town has a relatively small number of houses

(B) inadequate site drainage can make a house unsafe

(C) structural defects are often easier to fix than inadequate site drainage

(D) many houses in the town have neither inadequate site drainage nor structural defects that could make them unsafe

(E) some of the houses that have structural defects that could make them unsafe also have inadequate site drainage

6. The decisions that one makes can profoundly affect one's life years later. So one should not regret the missed opportunities of youth, for had one decided instead to seize one of these opportunities, one would not have some of the close personal relationships one currently has. And everyone deeply cherishes their close personal relationships.

Which one of the following principles, if valid, most helps to justify the reasoning in the argument?

(A) One should not regret making a decision unless a different decision would have resulted in one having a greater number of close personal relationships.

(B) One should not regret making a decision if it helped to bring about something that one cherishes.

(C) One should not regret making a decision that had little effect on one's life.

(D) People who regret the missed opportunities of youth should cherish their close personal relationships more deeply.

(E) People with few close personal relationships should cherish the ones they have.

7. The Kuna, a people native to several Panamanian islands, generally have a low incidence of high blood pressure. But Kuna who have moved to the Panamanian mainland do not have a low incidence of high blood pressure. Kuna who live on the islands, unlike those who live on the mainland, typically drink several cups of cocoa a day. This cocoa is minimally processed and thus high in flavonoids.

Of the following, which one is most strongly supported by the information above?

(A) Foods high in flavonoids are not readily available on the Panamanian mainland.

(B) Kuna who live on the islands drink cocoa because they believe that it is beneficial to their health.

(C) The Kuna have a genetic predisposition to low blood pressure.

(D) Kuna who live on the Panamanian mainland generally have higher blood pressure than other people who live on the mainland.

(E) Drinking several cups of flavonoid-rich cocoa per day tends to prevent high blood pressure.

GO ON TO THE NEXT PAGE.

8. Numerous studies suggest that when scientific evidence is presented in a trial, jurors regard that evidence as more credible than they would if they had encountered the same evidence outside of the courtroom context. Legal theorists have hypothesized that this effect is primarily due to the fact that judges prescreen scientific evidence and allow only credible scientific evidence to be presented in the courtroom.

Which one of the following would be most useful to know in order to evaluate the legal theorists' hypothesis?

(A) whether jurors typically know that judges have appraised the scientific evidence presented at trial

(B) whether jurors' reactions to scientific evidence presented at trial are influenced by other members of the jury

(C) how jurors determine the credibility of an expert witness who is presenting scientific evidence in a trial

(D) whether jurors typically draw upon their own scientific knowledge when weighing scientific evidence presented at trial

(E) how jurors respond to situations in which different expert witnesses give conflicting assessments of scientific evidence

9. Organized word-of-mouth marketing campaigns are driven by product boosters who extol a product to friends and acquaintances. A study found that these campaigns are more successful when the product booster openly admits to being part of an organized marketing campaign. This is surprising because one of the purported advantages of word-of-mouth campaigns is that consumers take a less skeptical stance toward word-of-mouth messages than toward mass-media advertisements.

Which one of the following, if true, most helps to explain the surprising finding?

(A) Word-of-mouth marketing campaigns are generally used for specialty products that are not well suited to being marketed through mass-media advertisements.

(B) Those who tend to be the most receptive to mass-media marketing campaigns are also the least likely to be influenced by knowledge of a product booster's affiliation.

(C) Most people who work as product boosters in word-of-mouth marketing campaigns have themselves been recruited through a word-of-mouth process.

(D) Most word-of-mouth marketing campaigns cost far less than marketing campaigns that rely on mass-media advertisements.

(E) When a word-of-mouth product booster admits his or her affiliation, it fosters a more relaxed and in-depth discussion of the marketed product.

10. Consultant: If Whalley sticks with her current platform in the upcoming election, then she will lose to her opponent by a few percentage points among voters under 50, while beating him by a bigger percentage among voters 50 and over. Therefore, sticking with her current platform will allow her to win the election.

The consultant's conclusion follows logically if which one of the following is assumed?

(A) There is no change Whalley could make to her platform that would win over more voters under 50 than it would lose voters 50 and over.

(B) The issues that most concern voters under 50 are different from those that most concern voters 50 and over.

(C) If Whalley changes her platform, her opponent will not change his platform in response.

(D) There will be more voters in the election who are 50 and over than there will be voters under 50.

(E) Whalley would change her platform if she thought it would give her a better chance to win.

11. From 1880 to 2000 Britain's economy grew fivefold, but emissions of carbon dioxide, a greenhouse gas, were the same on a per capita basis in Britain in 2000 as they were in 1880.

The claims made above are incompatible with which one of the following generalizations?

(A) A decrease in per capita emissions of carbon dioxide never occurs during a period of economic growth.

(B) Countries whose economies are growing slowly or not at all usually cannot afford to enact laws restricting carbon dioxide emissions.

(C) Economic growth initially leads to increased per capita emissions of greenhouse gases, but eventually new technologies are developed that tend to reduce these emissions.

(D) As the world's population grows, emissions of greenhouse gases will increase proportionately.

(E) Economic growth always increases household income and consumption, which inevitably increases per capita emissions of carbon dioxide.

GO ON TO THE NEXT PAGE.

12. Advertisement: When you need a will, consulting a lawyer is much more expensive than using do-it-yourself software. And you get a valid will either way. However, when you're ill, you aren't satisfied with simply getting some valid prescription or other; what you pay your doctor for is the doctor's expert advice concerning your particular illness. Similarly, what you pay a lawyer for is to tailor your will to your particular circumstances. Clearly, when you need a will, a lawyer's expert advice is always worth paying for.

Which one of the following is an assumption required by the argument presented in the advertisement?

(A) A lawyer's knowledge and level of expertise is at least as complex as that of a doctor.

(B) Do-it-yourself software cannot tailor a person's will to meet that person's particular circumstances as well as a lawyer can.

(C) Many people who prepare their wills using do-it-yourself software are not satisfied with the results.

(D) In the majority of cases, valid wills do not adequately meet the needs of the persons for whom the wills were prepared.

(E) There is some way for an ill person to get a valid prescription without first consulting a doctor.

13. Pollution is a problem wherever there are people who are indifferent to their environment, and nature's balance is harmed wherever there is pollution. So wherever there are people who are indifferent to their environment, nature's balance is harmed.

The reasoning in which one of the following arguments is most similar to that in the argument above?

(A) Any dessert with chocolate is high in calories, and any dessert high in calories is fattening. So any dessert with chocolate is fattening.

(B) Every dessert with chocolate is high in calories, and every fattening dessert is also high in calories. So any dessert with chocolate is fattening.

(C) Any dessert that is high in calories has chocolate in it, and any dessert that is high in calories is fattening. So every dessert with chocolate is fattening.

(D) Every dessert with chocolate is high in calories, and every dessert that is high in calories is fattening. So every fattening dessert has chocolate in it.

(E) Any dessert with chocolate is high in calories, and many desserts that are high in calories are fattening. So many desserts with chocolate are fattening.

14. Seventeenth-century proponents of the philosophical school of thought known as mechanism produced numerous arguments that sought to use the principles of mechanism to establish the superiority of monarchies over all other systems of government. This proliferation of arguments has been construed as evidence that the principles of mechanism themselves are in tension with democracy. But it is more likely that the principles of mechanism support democracy and that the arguments multiplied because none of them worked.

The claim that the proliferation of arguments has been construed as evidence that the principles of mechanism themselves are in tension with democracy plays which one of the following roles in the argument?

(A) It states a principle that the argument seeks to establish.

(B) It describes a general phenomenon that the argument seeks to explain.

(C) It introduces a hypothesis that the argument challenges.

(D) It provides evidence in support of the conclusion of the argument.

(E) It expresses the conclusion of the argument.

15. A good manager must understand people and be able to defuse tense situations. But anyone who is able to defuse tense situations must understand people. Since Ishiko is able to defuse tense situations, she must be a good manager.

The reasoning in the argument is flawed in that it

(A) confuses a quality that shows an understanding of people with a quality that is necessary for understanding people

(B) confuses a quality that usually correlates with being a good manager with a quality that results from being a good manager

(C) confuses qualities necessary for being a good manager with qualities that guarantee being a good manager

(D) overlooks the possibility that different managers defuse tense situations in different ways

(E) takes for granted that because all good managers have a certain quality, Ishiko must have that quality

GO ON TO THE NEXT PAGE.

16. Babblers, a bird species, live in large cooperative groups. Each member attempts to defend the group by sounding a loud barklike call when it spots a predator, inciting the others to bark too. Babblers, however, are extremely well camouflaged and could usually feed safely, unnoticed by predators. These predators, indeed, generally become aware of the presence of babblers only because of their shrill barks, which continue long after most members of the group have been able to take cover and which signal the group's approximate location to the predators.

Which one of the following, if true, would most help to explain the babblers' strange behavior?

(A) Babblers fly much faster than the predators that prey upon them.

(B) Babblers' predators are generally intimidated by large numbers of babblers.

(C) There is more than one type of predator that preys upon babblers.

(D) Babblers' predators have very good eyesight but relatively weak hearing.

(E) Animals that live in close proximity to babblers are also preyed upon by the predators that prey upon babblers.

17. Photographs show an area of Europa, a moon of Jupiter, where the icy surface appears to have buckled as a result of turbulent water moving underneath. This photographic evidence indicates that there is a warm sea beneath Europa's icy surface. The presence of such a sea is thought by scientists to be a primary factor in the early development of life, so there is reason to believe that there may be life on Europa.

The claim that there is a warm sea beneath Europa's icy surface figures in the argument in which one of the following ways?

(A) It is a subsidiary conclusion used by the argument to support its overall conclusion.

(B) It is the overall conclusion of the argument.

(C) It is used to discredit a theory that the argument disputes.

(D) It is the only consideration presented in support of the argument's overall conclusion.

(E) It is presented as support for a subsidiary conclusion drawn in the argument.

18. For consumers, the most enjoyable emotional experience garnered from shopping is feeling lucky. Retailers use this fact to their advantage, but too often they resort to using advertised price cuts to promote their wares. Promotions of this sort might make bargain-minded consumers feel lucky, but they cut into profit margins and undermine customer loyalty.

Which one of the following most accurately describes the overall conclusion drawn in the argument?

(A) Feeling lucky is the most enjoyable emotional experience garnered from shopping.

(B) Retailers take advantage of the fact that shoppers enjoy feeling lucky.

(C) Advertised price cuts are overused as a means of gaining retail sales.

(D) Using advertised price cuts to promote retail products reduces profit margins and undermines customer loyalty.

(E) Making consumers feel lucky is usually not a good formula for retail success.

19. Jurist: To ensure that a legal system remains just, it is important to guarantee that lawbreaking does not give lawbreakers an unfair advantage over law abiders. Thus, notwithstanding any other goals that criminal punishment may serve, it should certainly attempt to ensure that criminal wrongdoing remains profitless.

The jurist's claim that it is important to guarantee that lawbreaking does not give lawbreakers an unfair advantage over law abiders functions in the argument in which one of the following ways?

(A) It states a condition that, if fulfilled, will ensure that a legal system remains just.

(B) It expresses a principle that is offered as support for the conclusion.

(C) It is a conclusion for which the only support offered is the claim that the legal system serves multiple goals.

(D) It is a premise presented as support for the claim that the most important goal of criminal punishment is to ensure that criminal wrongdoing remains profitless.

(E) It is presented as refuting an argument that criminal punishment has goals other than guaranteeing that lawbreaking remains profitless.

GO ON TO THE NEXT PAGE.

20. The company president says that significant procedural changes were made before either she or Yeung was told about them. But, according to Grimes, the contract requires that either the company president or any lawyer in the company's legal department be told about proposed procedural changes before they are made. Thus, unless what Grimes or the company president said is incorrect, the contract was violated.

The argument's conclusion can be properly inferred if which one of the following is assumed?

(A) Yeung is a lawyer in the company's legal department.

(B) Neither Grimes nor Yeung was told about the procedural changes until after they were made.

(C) No lawyer in the company's legal department was told about the procedural changes until after they were made.

(D) If the company's president was told about the procedural changes before they were made, then the contract was not violated.

(E) If no lawyer in the company's legal department was told about the procedural changes before they were made, then the contract was violated.

21. Journalist: People whose diets contain a relatively large amount of iron are significantly more likely to develop Parkinson's disease than are those whose diets contain less of this mineral. Limiting one's intake of meats, seafood, and other foods rich in iron should thus reduce one's chances of contracting this disease.

Which one of the following, if true, most strengthens the journalist's reasoning?

(A) Most people who have a genetic predisposition to Parkinson's disease have no more iron in their diets than people without the predisposition.

(B) Many of the vegetables regularly consumed by vegetarians who do not contract Parkinson's disease are as rich in iron as meat and seafood.

(C) Children and adolescents require a much larger amount of iron in their diets than do mature adults.

(D) The iron in some foods is much less easily absorbed by the body than the iron contained in other foods.

(E) The amounts of iron-rich foods consumed by people starts to decline beginning at age 50.

22. Riverdale's Modern Party Chairperson: Maples, the Modern Party candidate, would be a better mayor than his opponent, Tannett, who is a member of the Traditionalist Party. Every member of the Modern Party is better qualified to be mayor than is any member of the Traditionalist Party.

If the statements of Riverdale's Modern Party Chairperson are true, each of the following could be true EXCEPT:

(A) Maples has the least seniority of any member of Riverdale's Modern Party and was recently ousted from the Traditionalist Party.

(B) Tannett would be a better mayor than would any other member of Riverdale's Traditionalist Party.

(C) Few residents of Riverdale believe that Maples would be a better mayor than Tannett.

(D) Of all the members of Riverdale's Modern Party, Maples would be the worst mayor.

(E) Tannett is better qualified to be mayor than is Riverdale's Modern Party Chairperson.

GO ON TO THE NEXT PAGE.

23. Businessperson: Because the parking area directly in front of the building was closed for maintenance today, I was late to my meeting. If the maintenance had been done on a different day, I would have gotten to the meeting on time. After finding out that I could not park in that area it took me 15 minutes to find an available parking space, making me a few minutes late.

The answer to which one of the following questions would be most useful to know in order to evaluate the reasoning in the businessperson's argument?

(A) What were the reasons for performing maintenance on the parking area directly in front of the building on that particular day?

(B) Were any other of the meeting attendees also late to the meeting because they had difficulty finding parking?

(C) What are the parking patterns in the building's vicinity on days when the parking area in front of the building is open?

(D) Does the businessperson have a tendency to be late to meetings?

(E) Was it particularly important that the businessperson not be late to this meeting?

24. For a work to be rightly thought of as world literature, it must be received and interpreted within the writer's own national tradition and within external national traditions. A work counts as being interpreted within a national tradition if authors from that tradition use the work in at least one of three ways: as a positive model for the development of their own tradition, as a negative case of a decadent tendency that must be consciously avoided, or as an image of radical otherness that prompts refinement of the home tradition.

The statements above, if true, most strongly support which one of the following?

(A) A work of literature cannot be well received within an external national tradition if it is not well received within the writer's own national tradition.

(B) A work of world literature offers more to readers within external national traditions than it offers to readers within the writer's national tradition.

(C) A work should not be thought of as world literature if it is more meaningful to readers from the writer's national tradition than it is to readers from external national traditions.

(D) A work of world literature is always influenced by works outside of the writer's national tradition.

(E) A work is not part of world literature if it affects the development of only one national tradition.

GO ON TO THE NEXT PAGE.

25. At Morris University this semester, most of the sociology majors are taking Introduction to Social Psychology, but most of the psychology majors are not. Hence, there must be more sociology majors than psychology majors enrolled in the class.

The flawed pattern of reasoning in the argument above is most similar to that in which one of the following?

(A) Most of the paintings on display at the Metro Art Museum are from the twentieth century, but most of the paintings the Metro Art Museum owns are from the nineteenth century. It follows that the museum owns few if any of the twentieth-century paintings it displays.

(B) In an opinion poll of Silver Falls residents, more said they were in favor of increased spending on roads than said they were in favor of increased spending on parks. So most Silver Falls residents must be in favor of spending more on roads but opposed to spending more on parks.

(C) In the San Felipe city arboretum, most of the trees are of local rather than exotic species. Therefore, in the San Felipe area, there must be more trees of local species than of exotic species.

(D) Most of the vegetables available at the Valley Food Co-op are organic, but most of the vegetables available at the Jumbo Supermarket are not. Thus, more organic vegetables are available at Valley Food than are available at Jumbo.

(E) The Acme Realty website has photos of most of the houses, but of fewer than half of the condominiums, that Acme is offering for sale. So Acme must have more houses than condominiums for sale.

26. Film director: Although the production costs of my latest film are very high, there is little risk that the film studio will not recover these costs. Even if the film is unpopular, much of the money is being spent to develop innovative special-effects technology that could be used in future films.

Which one of the following, if true, most seriously weakens the argument?

(A) Because the film studio owns the new technology, the studio will be able to control its use in any future films.

(B) Films that introduce innovative special-effects technologies generally draw large audiences of people who are curious about the new effects.

(C) The production costs of this film are so high that, even if the film is popular, it is unlikely that the film's ticket sales will offset those costs.

(D) In the past, many innovative special-effects technologies were abandoned after the films for which they were developed proved to be unpopular.

(E) The use of the new special-effects technology would lower the production costs of other films that use it.

S T O P

IF YOU FINISH BEFORE TIME IS CALLED, YOU MAY CHECK YOUR WORK ON THIS SECTION ONLY.
DO NOT WORK ON ANY OTHER SECTION IN THE TEST.

SECTION IV

Time—35 minutes

27 Questions

<u>Directions</u>: Each set of questions in this section is based on a single passage or a pair of passages. The questions are to be answered on the basis of what is <u>stated</u> or <u>implied</u> in the passage or pair of passages. For some of the questions, more than one of the choices could conceivably answer the question. However, you are to choose the <u>best</u> answer; that is, the response that most accurately and completely answers the question, and blacken the corresponding space on your answer sheet.

Passage A

Jury nullification occurs when the jury acquits the defendant in a criminal case in disregard of the judge's instructions and contrary to the jury's findings of fact. Sometimes a jury's nullification decision is based on
(5) mercy for the defendant, sometimes on dislike for the victim. Juries have also sometimes nullified when the defendant engaged in civil disobedience and the jurors agreed with the actions. While instances of jury nullification are probably few, the problems created
(10) by the jury's power to nullify are great.

First, we do not know how the power is used. Because juries are not required to and typically do not explain their verdicts, it is impossible to say how often nullification occurs. This means that we also do not
(15) know how often juries use this power for evil ends rather than for good ones.

Second, juries often have insufficient evidence to make a reasoned nullification decision. Evidence that might inform such a decision, such as a defendant's
(20) past brushes with the law, usually is not admitted at trial because it is irrelevant to the technical question of guilt or innocence.

Third, jurors are not legislators. We have an elected legislature to pass laws and elected or
(25) appointed judges to interpret them. The jury is unelected, is unaccountable, and has no obligation to think through the effect an acquittal will have on others.

Reasonable people can disagree on the proper
(30) reach of the criminal laws. Nevertheless, the place for them to disagree is in public, where the reasons for revisions of the laws can be scrutinized and debated.

Passage B

Police and prosecutors have discretion to decide which violations of the law to pursue and which to
(35) overlook. Even with such discretion, however, these officials can sometimes be overzealous. In such cases, the jury can act as a safety valve and use its own discretion to decide, for example, that a case is too trivial or the circumstances too extenuating for the
(40) case to result in a conviction.

When a jury nullifies because it does not believe a law should be applied to a particular defendant, the jury can also be viewed as assisting the legislature. Legislatures create <u>general laws</u> both because they
(45) cannot foresee every variation that may arise, and because legislators often have competing views about what should be included in legislation and so must settle for broad language if any laws are to be passed.

Similarly, when a jury nullifies because it
(50) believes a law is unjust, it also performs a useful function vis-à-vis the legislature, namely indicating to the legislature that there may be a problem with the law in question.

It may happen that a jury will be persuaded to
(55) nullify by factors they should ignore, but such instances of nullification are likely to be uncommon. For a jury to agree to nullify means that the case for nullification must be so compelling that all twelve of the jurors, despite their different backgrounds and
(60) perspectives, nevertheless agree that nullification is the appropriate course of action.

1. The author of passage B suggests that some laws justify the use of jury nullification because they are too

   (A) complicated
   (B) antiquated
   (C) permissive
   (D) intrusive
   (E) general

2. The authors of the passages differ in their attitudes towards juries in that the author of passage B is

   (A) less trusting with regard to the motivations behind juries' nullification decisions
   (B) less skeptical of the capacity of juries to understand the laws they are expected to apply
   (C) more concerned about the fact that juries rarely provide the reasoning behind their verdicts
   (D) more confident in the ability of juries to exercise the power to nullify in a just manner
   (E) more disappointed in the failure of juries to use the power to nullify to effect social change

GO ON TO THE NEXT PAGE.

3. Based on what can be inferred from their titles, the relationship between the documents in which one of the following pairs is most analogous to the relationship between passage A and passage B?

(A) "Cameras in the Courtroom: A Perversion of Justice?"
"The Pros and Cons of Televising Courtroom Proceedings"

(B) "Cameras in the Courtroom: Three Central Issues in the Debate"
"The Unexpected Benefits of Permitting Cameras in Court"

(C) "The Inherent Dangers of Permitting Cameras in Court"
"How Televising Courtroom Proceedings Can Assist the Law"

(D) "The Troublesome History of Cameras in the Courtroom"
"The Laudable Motives Behind Televised Courtroom Proceedings"

(E) "Why Cameras Should Be Banned from the Courtroom"
"The Inevitability of Televised Courtroom Proceedings"

4. The authors of the passages would be most likely to disagree over whether

(A) juries should be more forthcoming about the reasoning behind their verdicts

(B) laws are subject to scrutiny and debate by reasonable people

(C) it is likely that elected officials are more biased in their decision making than jurors are

(D) it is within the purview of juries not only to apply the law but to interpret it

(E) police and prosecutors should have less discretion to decide which violations of the law to pursue

5. Which one of the following is a criticism that the author of passage A would be likely to offer regarding the suggestion in passage B that juries are justified in nullifying when they view a case as too trivial to result in a conviction?

(A) Prosecutors rarely bring cases to trial that they regard as trivial.

(B) Prosecutors are unlikely to present a case in a manner that makes it appear trivial to a jury.

(C) The members of a jury are unlikely to be in accord in their evaluation of a case's seriousness.

(D) Jurors may not have sufficient expertise to evaluate the strengths and weaknesses of a case.

(E) Jurors may not be aware of all the reasons why a case was brought against a defendant.

6. Which one of the following most accurately characterizes the relationship between the two passages?

(A) Passage A offers a critique of a power possessed by juries, while passage B argues in support of that power.

(B) Passage A denounces a judicial custom, while passage B proposes improvements to that custom.

(C) Passage A surveys a range of evidence about jury behavior, while passage B suggests a hypothesis to explain that behavior.

(D) Passage A argues that a problem facing legal systems is intractable, while passage B presents a solution to that problem.

(E) Passage A raises a question concerning a legal procedure, while passage B attempts to answer that question.

GO ON TO THE NEXT PAGE.

Most sociohistorical interpretations of art view a body of work as the production of a class, generally a dominant or governing class, imposing its ideals. For example, Richard Taruskin writes in his *Oxford*
(5) *History of Western Music* that one of the defining characteristics of "high art" is that "it is produced by and for political and social elites." What Taruskin and others fail to clarify, however, is that there are two different ways that art, historically, was "produced
(10) by and for political and social elites."

The first way was for a member of the elite to engage a well-known artist to produce something for display. For instance, if one commissions a famous architect to design one's house, that may reflect great
(15) credit on one's taste, even if one finds the house impossible to live in. The second way was to create, or to have created, a work that expressed and mirrored one's ideals and way of life, like Raphael's frescoes in the Vatican apartments commissioned by Pope Julius II.

(20) Sociohistorical critics like Taruskin prefer to deal with art produced the second way, because it enables them to construct a subtle analysis of the way such art embodied the ideology of the elite, whatever the identity of the artist. For this kind of analysis to work,
(25) however, it must be the case that the elite had a recognizable identity and displayed some kind of consensus about the world and the way life was to be lived, and it must also be the case that we can eliminate the possibility that artists subverted the
(30) ideals of the patron for their own reasons.

Historically, the two social classes able to commission art were the aristocratic, or governing class, and the well-to-do middle class, what used to be called the bourgeoisie. The taste of the aristocracy and
(35) the upper middle class has not always been apt to produce an art that endures. In his characterization of nineteenth-century English culture, cultural critic Matthew Arnold identified the aristocracy as Barbarians, interested largely in fox hunting and
(40) gaming, and the middle class as Philistines, obsessed with respectability. As a result, the more talented artists sometimes had to find a place in the margins of the establishment—engaged by a rich patron with eccentric tastes, for example.

(45) Moreover, a great deal of art that went against the grain of elite values was paid for by the establishment unwillingly and with misgivings. Because some of this art endured, the sociohistorical critic, like Taruskin, must engage in an analogue of Freudian analysis, and
(50) claim that in hidden ways such art embodied the ideals of the elite, who were unaware that those ideals are revealed by work of which they overtly disapproved.

7. Which one of the following most accurately expresses the main point of the passage?

(A)   Historically, art was primarily commissioned by the governing classes and the well-to-do middle classes, despite the fact that this arrangement was not apt to produce art that endures.

(B)   Sociohistorical interpretations of art that claim that art merely reflects the ideals and values of the elite classes are overly simplistic.

(C)   Historically, patrons of the arts have generally been more interested in what being a patron would do for their reputation than in influencing the development of the arts.

(D)   Sociohistorical critics must engage in a form of Freudian analysis to justify, in light of apparently conflicting evidence, the claim that works of art embody the ideals of the elite.

(E)   There have historically been two distinct ways in which members of the elite classes have had art produced for them.

8. In using the phrase "something for display" (lines 12–13), the author most probably means art that

(A)   allowed the patron to make a political statement to the world

(B)   could be used to attract customers to the patron's business

(C)   was meant to create an impression that reflected positively on the patron

(D)   was representative of the artist's broader body of work at the time

(E)   provided the patron with personal satisfaction

9. It can be inferred from the passage that the attitude of Matthew Arnold toward the aristocratic and middle classes can best be described as one of

(A)   respect
(B)   empathy
(C)   indifference
(D)   disappointment
(E)   scorn

GO ON TO THE NEXT PAGE.

10. The passage raises all of the following as complications for the sociohistorical interpretation of art EXCEPT:

(A) artists who subverted the ideals of patrons for reasons of their own

(B) patrons who had eccentric tastes not reflective of the ideals of the elite classes

(C) patrons whose taste was unlikely to produce art that endured

(D) patrons who bought artwork solely for the purpose of reselling that artwork for a profit

(E) patrons who unwillingly bought artwork that conflicted with their values

11. The passage suggests that Taruskin's position commits him to which one of the following views?

(A) The most talented artists throughout history have been those whose work embodied the ideology of the elite in hidden ways.

(B) The most successful artists working today are those whose work reflects the ideology of the elite.

(C) If it endures, high art that appears to undermine the ideology of the elite actually supports that ideology in some way.

(D) Typically, art that reflects the ideology of the elite is produced by artists who are themselves members of the aristocratic or middle classes.

(E) The most talented artists throughout history have been those whose work subverted the ideology of the elite in subtle ways.

12. The primary function of the third paragraph is to

(A) reject a possible response to the argument made in the first paragraph

(B) identify assumptions relied upon by a type of analysis referred to in the first paragraph

(C) present an argument that weakens the argument made in the second paragraph

(D) offer additional evidence for the conclusion reached in the second paragraph

(E) draw a definitive conclusion from the claims made in the second paragraph

13. The author mentions "Raphael's frescoes in the Vatican apartments" (lines 18–19) for which one of the following reasons?

(A) to provide an example that illustrates the understanding of elitism in art favored by sociohistorical critics

(B) to illustrate the influence of religion on the historical development of art

(C) to present an example of the most common type of relationship between a patron and an artist

(D) to show how an artist can subvert the ideals of the patron

(E) to show that there are cases of artist/patron relationships that do not fit the pattern preferred by sociohistorical critics

14. The passage suggests that Matthew Arnold would be most likely to identify which one of the following as the primary reason why, historically, people in the middle class became patrons of the arts?

(A) a belief in the importance of the arts to society as a whole

(B) a dislike for the kind of art typically sponsored by the aristocracy

(C) a belief that patronage would ultimately prove profitable

(D) a realization that patronage ensures the production of high-quality art

(E) a desire to establish a reputation as a patron of the arts

GO ON TO THE NEXT PAGE.

Hundreds of clay tablets marked in cuneiform have been found in excavations of the Sumerian city of Uruk (in present-day Iraq). Though the tablets date from roughly 3000 B.C., the writing on them uses
(5) relatively few pictographs; instead, numerous abstract symbols are used. The sign for "sheep," for example, is not an image of a sheep, but rather a circled cross, while the sign for "metal" is a crescent with five lines. Because of its early date, this seemingly sudden
(10) appearance of such abstract writing has long puzzled researchers. At the same time, among prepottery clay artifacts found at archaeological sites along the Jordan and nearby rivers are thousands of small, hand-modeled tokens of fired clay, some dating to before
(15) 4000 B.C. Often ignored by archaeologists—some concluded without evidence that they were amulets or game pieces—the tokens are identified by Denise Schmandt-Besserat in her book *Before Writing* (1992) as overlooked predecessors to the written word.
(20) The earliest of the tokens were simple in form— small cones, spheres, and pyramids—and they were often inscribed. In 1966, a hollow tablet containing several of these tokens was discovered, and more than 100 additional tablets, which are now recognized as
(25) sealed envelopes of clay, have since been found. Later envelopes are also inscribed with impressions of tokens in the outer clay, signaling exactly what each envelope contained. Noting that these inscriptions are clearly traceable to later, known inscriptions of farm
(30) products, Schmandt-Besserat theorizes that the envelopes contained official records of villagers' contributions to temple-based grain and livestock pools. After 4000 B.C., hundreds of new token forms developed, as a rise in industry boosted the token
(35) system. Many forms are figurative, such as bowls or jars with handles, suggesting that villagers' crafts were becoming more diversified and sophisticated.
The token system, essentially a system of three-dimensional nouns, was replaced in about 3100 B.C.
(40) by a system of marks on clay tablets. A few centuries later, this latter system was to display the first use of numerals, where simple marks coded the concepts of one, two, and so forth. The eventual evolution of this system into mature writing, Schmandt-Besserat
(45) suggests, can be seen in the following example: At first it took two ovoid tokens to record two jars of oil. A little later, it took two markings on a clay tablet to achieve this—one mark, using the outline of the old token, to record the customary unit measure for oil,
(50) the jarful, and a second mark to convey the numeral: two oil jars. Eventually, it took three signs on the tablet, one for the numeral 2, one for the standard jarful, and a new symbol that denoted oil itself. With three such signs, an abstract and flexible written form
(55) had arrived.

15. Which one of the following most accurately expresses the main point of the passage?

(A) Based on her analysis of inscription-bearing clay envelopes containing tokens dating to roughly 4000 B.C., Schmandt-Besserat concludes that this system of tokens eventually evolved into an abstract written language.

(B) The discovery of clay tablets bearing inscriptions representing the tokens they contain confirms the belief of Schmandt-Besserat that these tokens served to designate the products given by villagers to their temples.

(C) Inscription-bearing clay envelopes containing tokens discovered in modern Iraq have provided Schmandt-Besserat with the evidence required to resolve the puzzlement of archaeologists over the sudden appearance of sophisticated crafts.

(D) The inscriptions found on clay envelopes containing small clay tokens have enabled Schmandt-Besserat to formulate a more detailed picture of the way in which a simple system of three-dimensional nouns evolved into modern languages.

(E) The discovery of inscription-bearing clay envelopes containing small tokens confirms Schmandt-Besserat's hypothesis that a language becomes increasingly abstract as the arts and crafts of the people who use the language become more abstract.

16. With which one of the following statements about the society in which the clay tokens were used would Schmandt-Besserat be most likely to agree?

(A) Society members' trade and other economic activities were managed by a strong centralized governmental authority.

(B) Religious rituals were probably less important to the society's members than agriculture and trade were.

(C) Society members regarded whatever was produced by any individual as the common property of all.

(D) The society eventually came to regard the clay tokens as redundant.

(E) Without a readily available supply of raw clay, the society could not have developed a system of representation that used tokens.

GO ON TO THE NEXT PAGE.

17. The passage states that the writing on clay tablets found in Uruk

(A) was not deciphered by archaeologists until 1992
(B) used relatively few pictographic symbols
(C) eventually evolved into a more abstract and flexible linguistic system
(D) transcribed a language that was commonly spoken along the Jordan and nearby rivers
(E) transcribed a language that was much older than archaeologists would have expected

18. According to the passage, the token system

(A) was eventually abandoned because it was not capable of representing quantity and other abstractions
(B) came to designate a broad range of objects as the crafts of the people who used it became more diverse and sophisticated
(C) could be understood only because some tokens were inscribed with symbols known to represent agricultural products
(D) was originally thought by most archaeologists to have had a primarily religious function
(E) became physically unwieldy and cumbersome as its users' agricultural products became more diverse

19. By characterizing certain cuneiform inscriptions on the clay tablets found in Uruk as "abstract" (line 10) the author most likely means that

(A) the meaning of the inscriptions is obscure and hard for linguists to decipher
(B) the inscriptions are meant to represent intangible concepts
(C) the inscriptions do not resemble what they designate
(D) the inscriptions refer to general categories rather than specific things
(E) the terms represented by the inscriptions were more ceremonial in nature than most daily speech was

20. It can be inferred from the discussion of clay tokens in the second paragraph that

(A) there were many tokens that designated more than one type of item
(B) nonagricultural goods and products came to be preferred as contributions to temple-based pools
(C) some later tokens were less abstract than some earlier ones
(D) the storage and transportation of liquids were among the most important tasks performed by the token system's users
(E) the token system was as abstract and flexible as later written languages

21. With which one of the following statements regarding the sign for "sheep" (line 6) would the author of the passage be most likely to agree?

(A) It could have been replaced without loss of significance by any other sign that was not already being used for something else.
(B) The sign gets its meaning in a radically different way from the way in which the cuneiform sign for "metal" gets its meaning.
(C) The way in which it represents its meaning resulted from the fact that sheep are an agricultural commodity rather than a product of human industry.
(D) The way in which it represents its meaning was not the subject of scientific scrutiny prior to that given it by Schmandt-Besserat.
(E) The abstract nature of the sign reveals a great deal about the political life of the people who used the language expressed by cuneiform writing.

22. Which one of the following, if true, would most call into question Schmandt-Besserat's theory mentioned in lines 28–33?

(A) The more than 100 clay envelopes discovered at archaeological sites along the Jordan come in many different dimensions, thicknesses, and styles of composition.
(B) It was customary for villagers who performed services for another person to receive in return a record of a promise of agricultural products or crafted objects as compensation.
(C) The tablets marked in cuneiform dating after 3000 B.C. do not seem to function as records of villagers' contributions to a temple-based pool of goods.
(D) There is no archaeological evidence suggesting that the tokens in use from about 4000 B.C. to 3100 B.C. were necessarily meant to be placed in clay envelopes.
(E) Villagers were required not only to contribute goods to central pools but also to contribute labor, which was regularly accounted for.

GO ON TO THE NEXT PAGE.

By 1970 it was well established that ultraviolet light from the sun contributes to skin cancer. Fortunately, much of the sun's most damaging ultraviolet radiation is screened out by a thin, diffuse
(5) layer of ozone—a toxic form of oxygen—in the stratosphere, 10 to 25 miles above the earth's surface.

During the 1970s, however, public policy makers worldwide were alerted to the fragility of the ozone layer through the pioneering research and advocacy of
(10) two Nobel Prize-winning scientists, Mario Molina and F. Sherwood Rowland. In the absence of pollutants, stratospheric ozone concentrations should remain stable over time, with natural production and destruction of the gas in rough equilibrium. Molina
(15) and Rowland showed how manufactured chlorofluorocarbons (CFCs)—highly volatile chemicals, millions of tons of which had been used each year in products such as aerosol sprays and refrigerants—chemically attack and deplete the ozone
(20) layer, diminishing its effectiveness as a shield against ultraviolet radiation. Studying two freon gases—types of CFCs—they observed that, when released into the lower atmosphere (troposphere), these gases slowly diffuse upward into the stratosphere. There, subjected
(25) to massive ultraviolet radiation, they break down into their constituent elements, including chlorine. The resulting increase in the concentration of chlorine in the stratosphere is devastating to the ozone layer. Chlorine and ozone chemically react in a way that
(30) both destroys the ozone and regenerates the chlorine atoms. As a result of this chemical reaction, each chlorine atom could destroy as many as 100,000 ozone molecules before becoming inactive.

In 1974 the two scientists estimated that the
(35) atmosphere contained the accumulation of five years of global CFC production. This meant that, given the rate of diffusion and breakdown of CFCs in the atmosphere, the depletion of the ozone layer would continue for years, if not decades, even if the
(40) production and use of CFCs were to cease immediately. Recognizing this as a pressing environmental threat, Molina and Rowland became public advocates for a prompt and proportionate public policy response. As a result, Molina was invited to
(45) testify before the U.S. Congress and was later appointed to the U.S. National Science Foundation Committee on Fluorocarbon Technology Assessment.

Predictably, the work of Molina and Rowland and their advocacy of dramatic policy changes were
(50) subjected to attacks by critics, especially scientists with ties to the CFC industry. However, over time their views were corroborated, especially by the discovery of a hole in the ozone layer over Antarctica, and this led to the development of an international agreement
(55) (the Montreal Protocol of 1987) to ban the production of ozone-depleting gases. In North America, CFCs were banned in the late 1970s, leading to a transformation in packaging for consumer spray products and the development of more
(60) environmentally friendly refrigerant chemicals.

23. The information in the passage most helps to answer which one of the following questions?

(A) What laboratory experiments were conducted by Molina or Rowland in their research on CFCs?

(B) What was the estimated concentration of CFCs in the atmosphere in 1987?

(C) In what year did Molina testify before the U.S. Congress?

(D) Does any chemical that does not contain chlorine contribute to the destruction of ozone molecules?

(E) Which constituent element of CFCs is most damaging to ozone?

24. Which one of the following, if true, would most strengthen the conclusions of Molina and Rowland concerning the long-term effects of CFCs in the stratosphere?

(A) The hole in the ozone layer over Antarctica continued to grow for years after CFC emissions had almost ceased.

(B) Other manufactured chemicals have been found to diffuse upward into the stratosphere when released into the troposphere.

(C) Ozone has been shown to react more violently with chlorine than with many other chemicals.

(D) Many scientists who in the 1970s were highly critical of the research methods of Molina and Rowland have come to accept the soundness of their methods.

(E) Current CFC levels in the troposphere suggest that not all nations currently abide by the Montreal Protocol.

25. Which one of the following statements is most strongly supported by the information in the passage?

(A) Little or no ozone destruction occurs naturally in the stratosphere unless chlorine is present.

(B) Skin cancers occur primarily because of excessive absorption of ultraviolet light.

(C) Few chemicals besides CFCs can result in the release of chlorine in the upper atmosphere.

(D) Regulating the use of CFCs contributes indirectly to lowering the incidence of skin cancer.

(E) The upward flow of CFCs into the stratosphere occurs mainly in Antarctica.

GO ON TO THE NEXT PAGE.

26. Based on the passage, the information yielded by which one of the following experiments would be most useful in determining whether a particular chemical could replace CFCs without damaging the ozone layer?

    (A) testing to see whether the chemical is capable of reacting with forms of oxygen other than ozone

    (B) testing to see whether the chemical, when released into the lower atmosphere, would react with other chemicals commonly found there

    (C) testing the chemical to determine whether it would chemically react with chlorine

    (D) testing to see what chemical properties the chemical or its constituent elements share with chlorine

    (E) testing the chemical to see if it would break down into its components when subjected to ultraviolet radiation

27. Which one of the following statements is most strongly supported by the information in the passage?

    (A) No refrigerant chemicals other than CFCs had been discovered when Molina and Rowland suggested that CFC production cease.

    (B) Refrigerant chemicals developed as substitutes for CFCs after 1987 release fewer chlorine atoms into the stratosphere than CFCs do.

    (C) CFCs were originally used in refrigeration components because they provided the most energy-efficient means of refrigeration.

    (D) The Montreal Protocol led to the cessation of CFC production in North America.

    (E) Some of the refrigerant chemicals being manufactured today contain chemicals known to be environmentally damaging.

S T O P

IF YOU FINISH BEFORE TIME IS CALLED, YOU MAY CHECK YOUR WORK ON THIS SECTION ONLY.
DO NOT WORK ON ANY OTHER SECTION IN THE TEST.

FIRST NAME (Print)

MI

TEST CENTER NO.

SIGNATURE

M M D D Y Y
TEST DATE

LSAC ACCOUNT NO.

TOPIC CODE

Writing Sample Response Sheet

DO NOT WRITE IN THIS SPACE

Begin your essay in the lined area below.
Continue on the back if you need more space.

Wait for the supervisor's instructions before you open the page to the topic.
Please print and sign your name and write the date in the designated spaces below.

Time: 35 Minutes

General Directions

ill have 35 minutes in which to plan and write an essay on the topic inside. Read the topic and the accompanying directions carefully.
ill probably find it best to spend a few minutes considering the topic and organizing your thoughts before you begin writing. In your essay,
re to develop your ideas fully, leaving time, if possible, to review what you have written. **Do not write on a topic other than the one**
fied. Writing on a topic of your own choice is not acceptable.

ecial knowledge is required or expected for this writing exercise. Law schools are interested in the reasoning, clarity, organization,
age usage, and writing mechanics displayed in your essay. How well you write is more important than how much you write.

he your essay to the blocked, lined area on the front and back of the separate Writing Sample Response Sheet. Only that area will be
duced for law schools. Be sure that your writing is legible.

Both this topic sheet and your response sheet must be turned in to the testing staff
before you leave the room.

Topic Code	Print Your Full Name Here		
144171	Last	First	M.I.

Date	Sign Your Name Here
/ /	

Scratch Paper
Do not write your essay in this space.

LSAT® Writing Sample Topic

Directions: The scenario presented below describes two choices, either one of which can be supported on the basis of the information giv[en]. Your essay should consider both choices and argue for one over the other, based on the two specified criteria and the facts provided. The[re] is no "right" or "wrong" choice: a reasonable argument can be made for either.

An archaeological team has found the site of an ancient marketplace buried by centuries of accumulated soil. The team is deciding whether to excavate the site or scan its structures and artifacts from the surface with electronic instruments. Using the facts below, write an essay in which you argue for one option over the other based on the following two criteria:

- The structures and artifacts located on the site should be preserved from damage and theft.
- Information obtained from the site should be used to inform the country's people about their land's ancient history.

If the site is excavated, transportable artifacts and structures would be shipped to various museums in the country. The museums grant researchers access to their collections. Roughly a third of the country's population visits the museums at least once during their lifetim[e]. The excavation tools and techniques used would pose some risk to delicate structures and artifacts. The country has the resources to keep [the] site guarded and secure during the excavation.

If the site is electronically scanned, its artifacts and structures would remain in their original context, untouched. The scans would yi[eld] digital graphical reconstructions of the structures and artifacts. The scans would not yield conclusive information concerning the materials w[ith] which the structures and artifacts were made. The scanned information would be posted on the Internet for public access. Eighty percent o[f the] country's people have Internet access. The country's national museum has expressed interest in using the scans to reconstruct the structu[re] and layout of the site for exhibit. It is not possible to fully guarantee the security of the site after the scanning is complete. The country has [a] few instances of looting at its other historically important sites.

WP-AA1

Scratch Paper
Do not write your essay in this space.

COMPUTING YOUR SCORE

Directions:

1. Use the Answer Key on the next page to check your answers.

2. Use the Scoring Worksheet below to compute your raw score.

3. Use the Score Conversion Chart to convert your raw score into the 120–180 scale.

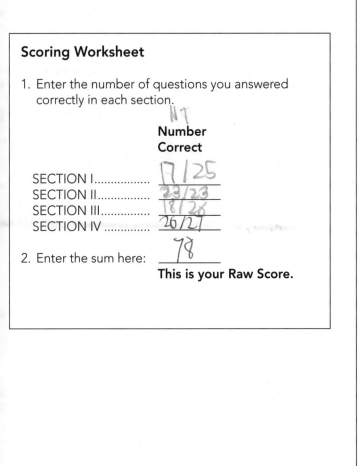

Scoring Worksheet

1. Enter the number of questions you answered correctly in each section.

Number
Correct

SECTION I.................. 17 / 25
SECTION II................ 23 / 23
SECTION III.............. 18 / 28
SECTION IV .... 26 / 27

2. Enter the sum here: 78

This is your Raw Score.

Conversion Chart
For Converting Raw Score to the 120–180 LSAT Scaled Score
LSAT Form 7LSN122

Reported Score	Raw Score Lowest	Raw Score Highest
180	100	101
179	99	99
178	98	98
177	97	97
176	*	*
175	96	96
174	95	95
173	94	94
172	93	93
171	92	92
170	90	91
169	89	89
168	87	88
167	86	86
166	84	85
165	83	83
164	81	82
163	79	80
162	77	78
161	75	76
160	73	74
159	71	72
158	69	70
157	67	68
156	65	66
155	64	64
154	62	63
153	60	61
152	58	59
151	56	57
150	54	55
149	53	53
148	51	52
147	49	50
146	48	48
145	46	47
144	44	45
143	43	43
142	41	42
141	40	40
140	39	39
139	37	38
138	36	36
137	35	35
136	33	34
135	32	32
134	31	31
133	30	30
132	29	29
131	28	28
130	27	27
129	26	26
128	25	25
127	24	24
126	23	23
125	22	22
124	21	21
123	20	20
122	19	19
121	18	18
120	0	17

*There is no raw score that will produce this scaled score for this form.

ANSWER KEY

SECTION I

1.	A	8.	C	15.	E	22.	A
2.	E	9.	A	16.	A	23.	B
3.	A	10.	C	17.	E	24.	E
4.	E	11.	A	18.	E	25.	C
5.	B	12.	C	19.	E		
6.	B	13.	D	20.	D		
7.	B	14.	D	21.	E		

SECTION II

1.	C	8.	A	15.	A	22.	B
2.	D	9.	D	16.	E	23.	A
3.	A	10.	E	17.	B		
4.	E	11.	A	18.	D		
5.	B	12.	C	19.	C		
6.	C	13.	B	20.	C		
7.	E	14.	D	21.	E		

SECTION III

1.	A	8.	A	15.	C	22.	E
2.	D	9.	E	16.	B	23.	C
3.	B	10.	D	17.	A	24.	E
4.	C	11.	E	18.	C	25.	D
5.	E	12.	B	19.	B	26.	D
6.	B	13.	A	20.	C		
7.	E	14.	C	21.	A		

SECTION IV

1.	E	8.	C	15.	A	22.	B
2.	D	9.	E	16.	D	23.	E
3.	C	10.	D	17.	B	24.	A
4.	D	11.	C	18.	B	25.	D
5.	E	12.	B	19.	C	26.	D
6.	A	13.	A	20.	C	27.	B
7.	B	14.	E	21.	A		

THE OFFICIAL LSAT
PREPTEST®

79

- PrepTest 79
- Form 6LSN120

SEPTEMBER 2016

SECTION I

Time—35 minutes

26 Questions

Directions: The questions in this section are based on the reasoning contained in brief statements or passages. For some questions, more than one of the choices could conceivably answer the question. However, you are to choose the best answer; that is, the response that most accurately and completely answers the question. You should not make assumptions that are by commonsense standards implausible, superfluous, or incompatible with the passage. After you have chosen the best answer, blacken the corresponding space on your answer sheet.

1. After a major toll highway introduced a system of electronic toll paying, delays at all of its interchanges declined significantly. Travel time per car trip decreased by an average of 10 percent. Tailpipe pollution for each trip decreased commensurately. Despite this, the total air pollution from vehicles on that highway did not decrease measurably.

   Which one of the following, if true, most helps to resolve the apparent discrepancy in the information above?

   (A) The highway began charging higher tolls when it switched to electronic toll paying.
   (B) Even after the switch to electronic toll paying, there were sometimes long delays at the highway's interchanges.
   (C) The prospect of faster, more convenient travel induced more drivers to use the highway.
   (D) Travel time on the highway for car trips under 30 kilometers (18.6 miles) did not decrease appreciably.
   (E) Some drivers did not switch to the electronic system but instead continued to use cash to pay their tolls at toll booths.

2. A lack of trust in one's neighbors leads to their lack of respect for the law. A new study provides compelling evidence for this. Neighborhoods in which people routinely lock their doors have higher burglary rates than neighborhoods in which people do not routinely lock their doors.

   The reasoning in the argument is flawed in that the argument

   (A) treats something that is merely sufficient to produce a result as if it were necessary to produce that result
   (B) draws a moral conclusion from evidence that could only support a factual conclusion
   (C) bases its conclusion on data that are contradictory
   (D) asserts in a premise what it is trying to establish in its conclusion
   (E) treats what could be the effect of something as if it were the cause of that thing

3. In recent decades, government efforts to fight counterfeiting have been extremely successful, especially efforts to remove counterfeit bills from circulation. Yet counterfeiters are not finding it at all difficult to get away with passing counterfeit bills to merchants and even banks.

   Which one of the following, if true, most helps to resolve the apparent discrepancy in the information above?

   (A) Government information campaigns that teach merchants and bank tellers how to detect counterfeit bills are more effective than ever.
   (B) Governments are continually developing new currency designs with features that are difficult for criminals to counterfeit.
   (C) Counterfeiters are generally unaware that the percentage of fake bills in circulation is the lowest it has ever been.
   (D) Government success in removing counterfeit bills from circulation has caused merchants and bank tellers to become lax in checking for counterfeit bills.
   (E) Governments are spending larger and larger sums of money in their efforts to remove counterfeit bills from circulation.

GO ON TO THE NEXT PAGE.

4. If a civilization as technologically advanced as human civilization existed on another planet and that planet were within 50 light years of Earth, that civilization would have found evidence of intelligent life on Earth and could have easily contacted us. Scientists can thus rule out the possibility of finding a civilization as technologically advanced as our own within 50 light years of Earth.

Which one of the following is an assumption required by the argument?

(A) Scientists who are searching for evidence of extraterrestrial life forms generally focus their search on evidence of technologically advanced life forms.

(B) There is no reason to doubt the possibility that there are technologically advanced civilizations on planets more than 50 light years from Earth.

(C) If scientists received a message from a technologically advanced civilization on another planet, they would be able to decipher it fully.

(D) A technologically advanced civilization on another planet would want to communicate with intelligent life that it detected on Earth.

(E) Intelligent life forms on other planets would be able to recognize all signs of intelligent life on Earth.

5. Recently, many traffic lights and street markings were temporarily removed from a heavily traveled street in a major metropolitan area. Given that this street experiences significant volumes of automobile traffic, the number of accidents on the street was expected to increase. However, even though the street experienced no reduction in traffic, the number of accidents was greatly reduced.

Which one of the following, if true, most helps to resolve the apparent conflict described above?

(A) People often disregard traffic lights and street markings.

(B) The lack of traffic lights and street markings caused drivers to drive more cautiously.

(C) Most drivers were not aware that traffic lights and street markings had been removed.

(D) Traffic lights and street markings are intended to have benefits in addition to those related to safety.

(E) Drivers were given advance notice that the traffic lights and street markings would be removed.

6. Some have argued that body size influences mating decisions throughout all societies. Their argument rests largely on self-reports of university-age students and on analyses of personal advertisements in newspapers for dating partners.

The reasoning in the argument described above is most vulnerable to criticism on the grounds that the argument

(A) concludes that one kind of event causes another kind of event without ruling out the possibility that both kinds of events are the result of a third kind of event

(B) bases a conclusion on a sample that may be unrepresentative of the population about which the conclusion is drawn

(C) concludes that an effect has only one cause in the face of evidence that the effect has multiple causes

(D) uses a claim that applies only to entire societies to draw a conclusion about individual persons

(E) draws a universal conclusion on the basis of a very small number of individual cases

7. Journalist: The new mayor is undeniably bold. His assertions are made with utter certainty and confidence. While these kinds of assertions may make him popular with the public, they also demonstrate that he is not an introspective person.

Which one of the following is an assumption required by the journalist's argument?

(A) Introspective people do not make assertions with utter certainty and confidence.

(B) Politicians who make assertions with utter certainty and confidence are popular with the public.

(C) People who are bold make public assertions with utter certainty and confidence.

(D) People whose assertions are uncertain and lack confidence are introspective.

(E) Politicians who are not bold are unpopular with the public.

GO ON TO THE NEXT PAGE.

8. While studying a large colony of macaque monkeys, scientists interacting with baby monkeys under a week old found that the babies would imitate some, but not all, of the scientists' actions. The babies readily smacked their lips and stuck out their tongues when the scientists did, but stared impassively when the scientists opened and closed their mouths or made hand gestures. Of these four kinds of actions, only lip smacking and sticking out the tongue are used by adult macaques when interacting with babies.

The statements above, if true, most strongly support which one of the following?

(A) Baby macaques under a week old are natural mimics of whatever they see.

(B) Baby macaques under a week old cannot imitate hand gestures because they do not yet control the necessary muscles.

(C) Adult macaques use lip smacking and sticking out the tongue to entertain infant macaques.

(D) Baby macaques under a week old mistake the scientists interacting with them for adult macaques.

(E) Baby macaques under a week old only imitate human gestures also used by adult macaques.

9. Some scientists believe that small humanoid skeletons found on an Indonesian island are the remains of human beings with a growth disorder. It is more likely that they represent a distinct human species that became smaller over time due to environmental pressure. These skeletons do not fit the pattern of known growth disorders. And evidence suggests that certain fox and mouse species on the island have evolved into smaller versions of their common counterparts.

Which one of the following most accurately expresses the conclusion drawn in the argument?

(A) Some scientists believe that the humanoid skeletons are the remains of human beings with a growth disorder.

(B) It is more likely that the humanoid skeletons represent a distinct human species than that they are the remains of human beings with a growth disorder.

(C) The humanoid skeletons do not fit the pattern of known growth disorders.

(D) Certain fox and mouse species on an Indonesian island have evolved into smaller versions of their common counterparts.

(E) Environmental pressure can cause species living on islands to become smaller over time.

10. The more sunlight our planet reflects back into space, the cooler the global atmosphere tends to become. Snow and ice reflect much more sunlight back into space than do ocean water or land without snow cover. Therefore, the greater the area of Earth's surface that is covered with snow and ice, the cooler, on average, the global atmosphere is likely to become.

Which one of the following, if true, would most strengthen the argument?

(A) Low atmospheric temperatures are required for the formation of clouds that result in snow.

(B) Other factors besides the reflectivity of ice and snow affect the cooling of Earth's atmosphere.

(C) Ocean water and land heated by sunlight in turn warm Earth's atmosphere.

(D) The atmosphere derives most of its heat from the passage of sunlight through it.

(E) Lighter-colored soil reflects more sunlight back into space than does darker-colored soil.

11. Nick: The Pincus family and their construction company have supported our university financially for decades. The university should not give the contract for building its new library to the family's main competitor. Doing so would be disloyal to a friend of the university.

Pedro: Accepting a donation does not oblige the university to give the donor any special privileges. If it did, then it wouldn't really be a charitable contribution. We should award the contract to whatever company makes the most competitive bid.

The dialogue provides the most support for the claim that Nick and Pedro disagree over whether

(A) loyalty should sometimes be a consideration in making business decisions

(B) the Pincus family and their construction company donated money for the purpose of acquiring special privileges from the university

(C) the acceptance of donations places a university under a special obligation to the donor

(D) the university should be more grateful to donors with a long history of financial support than to new donors

(E) the Pincus family's construction company did not make the most competitive bid

GO ON TO THE NEXT PAGE.

12. Ampicillin and other modern antibiotics kill a much wider variety of bacteria than penicillin does. They also carry higher profit margins, so drug companies now have an incentive to stop manufacturing the older, less profitable antibiotics. This could cause a penicillin shortage, forcing doctors to use the much more powerful new antibiotics in cases where they might otherwise be unnecessary. Thus, these newer antibiotics are likely to result in an outbreak of diseases caused by drug-resistant bacteria, since _____.

The conclusion of the argument is most strongly supported if which one of the following completes the passage?

(A) drug-resistant bacteria flourish in the absence of competition from a wide variety of other bacteria

(B) older antibiotics like penicillin have been widely used for many decades

(C) a shortage of penicillin would drive up its price and profit margin

(D) treatment of diseases with the powerful new antibiotics is much more expensive than treatment with the older ones

(E) most bacteria that are resistant to penicillin are not resistant to ampicillin and other modern antibiotics

13. Weingarten claims that keeping animals in zoos is unethical. He points out that it involves placing animals in unnatural environments merely for the sake of human amusement. However, since Weingarten sees nothing wrong with owning pets, and keeping pets surely involves placing an animal in an unnatural environment merely for human amusement, his claim should be rejected.

The reasoning in the argument is flawed in that the argument

(A) takes for granted that Weingarten owns one or more pets

(B) inappropriately generalizes from a particular case

(C) misrepresents the conclusion of the opposing argument

(D) takes a necessary condition for a practice's being unethical as a sufficient condition for its being so

(E) rejects a claim merely on the grounds that its proponent holds another view inconsistent with it

14. Activist: President Zagel should resign, because she is unable to govern effectively given the widespread belief that she rigged the election.

President Zagel: Over the last decade, scandals have forced two presidents of this country to resign. If I were to resign, the rest of the world would see us as a country whose political system is hopelessly unstable. That would be unacceptable, so I must remain in office.

Which one of the following principles, if valid, most helps to justify the activist's argument in the face of President Zagel's argument?

(A) A country whose election procedures are resistant to illegitimate manipulation will eventually become politically stable.

(B) The leader of a country should resign if doing so is likely to improve that country's international reputation for political stability.

(C) If a president is involved in a scandal that is more serious than scandals that have forced previous leaders to resign, then that president should resign.

(D) If it can be conclusively proven that an officeholder rigged an election, then that officeholder should be removed from office.

(E) It is more important for a country to have a leader who can govern effectively than it is to be viewed by other countries as having a stable political system.

15. A popular book argues that people who are successful in business have, without exception, benefited from a lot of luck on their way to success. But this is ridiculous. Anyone who has studied successful people knows that success requires a lot of hard work.

The argument commits which one of the following errors of reasoning?

(A) It mistakes the claim that something is required for a purpose for the claim that it is sufficient for that purpose.

(B) It accepts a view as authoritative without establishing the authority of the source of the view.

(C) It takes for granted in a premise what it is trying to prove in its conclusion.

(D) It treats an effect of something as the cause of that thing.

(E) It attacks the source of an argument rather than attacking the substance of that argument.

GO ON TO THE NEXT PAGE.

16. University president: When a faculty member's falsification of research was uncovered, the media treated it as evidence of the university's low standards, even though in truth it was a mere case of dishonesty. But since vigilance with respect to academic standards is always necessary, it's good that standards have become a topic of discussion.

Which one of the following conforms most closely to the principle illustrated above?

(A) The latest government scandal was caused primarily by a lack of oversight, which in turn led to corruption. Since no amount of oversight can eliminate all corruption, it is important that the problems with oversight are not the only topic of discussion.

(B) The latest government scandal has been attributed to lack of oversight, although the true cause of the scandal was simple corruption. Nonetheless, this discussion of oversight is welcome, because oversight is important in its own right.

(C) The latest government scandal has been attributed to both lack of oversight and corruption. As a result, these important concerns are now being discussed. So, despite the harm that it caused, it is good that the scandal occurred.

(D) The latest government scandal has been analyzed as a case of simple corruption, although corruption had little to do with it. Because the true cause of the scandal was lack of oversight, attributing the cause of the scandal to simple corruption is harmful.

(E) The latest government scandal has been analyzed as a case of simple corruption, with no mention of the role played by lack of oversight. Nonetheless, the focus on corruption is welcome, because corruption played the largest role in the scandal.

17. Politician: Over the next decade, our city will be replacing all of its street signs with signs that are designed for improved readability. But since no one is complaining about the current signs, installing the new ones is a colossal waste of time and money.

Which one of the following would be most useful to know in evaluating the politician's argument?

(A) What features of the new street signs improve the readability of the signs?

(B) Are the new street signs considerably more expensive to manufacture than the current street signs were?

(C) What percentage of its street signs does the city replace annually in the course of ordinary maintenance?

(D) Do any other cities plan to replace their street signs with signs designed for improved readability?

(E) Were experts consulted when the new street signs were designed?

18. A large survey of scientists found that almost all accept Wang's Law, and almost all know the results of the Brown-Eisler Experiment. But those results together with Wang's Law contradict the Minsk Hypothesis. Therefore, most of the scientists surveyed reject the Minsk Hypothesis.

The argument requires assuming which one of the following?

(A) The scientists surveyed are generally aware that the results of the Brown-Eisler Experiment together with Wang's Law contradict the Minsk Hypothesis.

(B) The scientists in the survey who know the results of the Brown-Eisler Experiment are exactly the same ones who accept Wang's Law.

(C) Almost all of the scientists surveyed are familiar with the way in which the results of the Brown-Eisler Experiment were obtained.

(D) The sample is large enough to be representative of scientists in the field.

(E) Wang's Law has in fact been shown to be true.

GO ON TO THE NEXT PAGE.

1

19. Any literary translation is a compromise between two goals that cannot be entirely reconciled: faithfulness to the meaning of the text and faithfulness to the original author's style. Thus, even the most skillful translation will be at best a flawed approximation of the original work.

Which one of the following principles, if valid, most helps to justify the reasoning in the argument above?

(A) A translation of a literary work should be entirely faithful to neither the meaning of the text nor the original author's style.

(B) If a literary translation is flawed as an approximation of the original work, it cannot be regarded as a successful compromise between faithfulness to the meaning of the text and faithfulness to the original author's style.

(C) The most skillful literary translation of a work will not necessarily be the most balanced compromise between faithfulness to the meaning of the text and faithfulness to the original author's style.

(D) Any translation that is not entirely faithful to both the meaning of the text and the original author's style will be at best a flawed approximation of that work.

(E) Not even the most skillful literary translation could be faithful to both the literal meaning of the text and the original author's style.

20. Sociologist: Television, telephones, and other electronic media encourage imprecise, uncritical thinking. Yet critical thinking is the only adequate protection against political demagogues, who seek to exploit people by presenting emotionally loaded language as an objective description of reality.

If the sociologist's statements are true, then each of the following statements could be true EXCEPT:

(A) There are no political demagogues in some highly technological societies.

(B) Political demagogues are not the only ones who seek to exploit people by presenting emotionally loaded language as an objective description of reality.

(C) Highly emotional people are more easily exploited than less emotional people.

(D) The mere presence of an orderly system of government in a society provides adequate protection against political demagogues.

(E) The mere presence of electronic communications technology in a society provides adequate protection against the erosion of media freedoms.

21. People with higher-than-average blood levels of a normal dietary by-product called homocysteine are twice as likely to be diagnosed with Alzheimer's disease as are those with average or below-average homocysteine levels. Thus, it is likely that the risk of developing Alzheimer's disease could be reduced by including in one's diet large amounts of B vitamins and folic acid, which convert homocysteine into substances known to have no relation to Alzheimer's disease.

Which one of the following, if true, most seriously weakens the argument?

(A) Many Alzheimer's patients have normal homocysteine levels.

(B) The substances into which homocysteine is converted can sometimes have harmful effects unrelated to Alzheimer's disease.

(C) B vitamins and folic acid are not metabolized by the body very efficiently when taken in the form of vitamin-mineral supplements.

(D) People whose relatives contracted Alzheimer's disease are much more likely to develop Alzheimer's than those whose relatives did not.

(E) Alzheimer's disease tends to increase the levels of homocysteine in the blood.

22. Consumer advocate: Economists reason that price gouging—increasing the price of goods when no alternative seller is available—is efficient because it allocates goods to people whose willingness to pay more shows that they really need those goods. But willingness to pay is not proportional to need. In the real world, some people simply cannot pay as much as others. As a result, a price increase will allocate goods to the people with the most money, not to those with the most need.

Which one of the following most accurately describes the role played in the consumer advocate's argument by the claim that willingness to pay is not proportional to need?

(A) It disputes one explanation in order to make way for an alternative explanation.

(B) It is the overall conclusion of the argument.

(C) It is a component of reasoning disputed in the argument.

(D) It is a general principle whose validity the argument questions.

(E) It denies a claim that the argument takes to be assumed in the reasoning that it rejects.

GO ON TO THE NEXT PAGE.

23. Zoologist: Plants preferentially absorb heavy nitrogen from rainwater. Heavy nitrogen consequently becomes concentrated in the tissues of herbivores, and animals that eat meat in turn exhibit even higher concentrations of heavy nitrogen in their bodily tissues. We compared bone samples from European cave bears of the Ice Age with blood samples from present-day bears fed meat-enriched diets, and the levels of heavy nitrogen present in these samples were identical. Thus, the prehistoric European cave bears were not exclusively herbivores.

Which one of the following, if true, would most strengthen the zoologist's argument?

(A) Plants can also absorb heavy nitrogen from a variety of sources other than rainwater.

(B) The rate at which heavy nitrogen accumulated in the blood of Ice Age herbivores can be inferred from samples of their bones.

(C) The same number of samples was taken from present-day bears as was taken from Ice Age cave bears.

(D) Bone samples from present-day bears fed meat-enriched diets exhibit the same levels of heavy nitrogen as do their blood samples.

(E) The level of heavy nitrogen in the bones of any bear fed a meat-enriched diet is the same as that in the bones of any other meat-eating bear.

24. Biologist: Some computer scientists imagine that all that is required for making an artificial intelligence is to create a computer program that encapsulates the information contained in the human genome. They are mistaken. The operation of the human brain is governed by the interactions of proteins whose structures are encoded in the human genome.

Which one of the following is an assumption required by the biologist's argument?

(A) The functions of the human brain are governed by processes that cannot be simulated by a computer.

(B) The interactions of the proteins that govern the operation of the human brain are not determined by the information contained in the human genome.

(C) The only way to create an artificial intelligence is to model it on the operation of the human brain.

(D) The amount of information contained in the human genome is too large to be easily encapsulated by a computer program.

(E) It is much more difficult to write a program that encapsulates the interactions of proteins than to write a program that encapsulates the information contained in the human genome.

GO ON TO THE NEXT PAGE.

25. Some advertisers offer certain consumers home computers free of charge. Advertisements play continuously on the computers' screens whenever they are in use. As consumers use the computers to browse the Internet, information about their browsing patterns is sent to the advertisers, enabling them to transmit to each consumer advertising that accurately reflects his or her individual interests. The advertisers can afford to offer the computers for free because of the increased sales that result from this precise targeting of individual consumers.

Which one of the following is most strongly supported by the information above?

(A) At least some consumers who use a computer offered free of charge by advertisers for browsing the Internet spend more money on purchases from those advertisers than they would if they did not use such a computer to browse the Internet.

(B) No advertisers could offer promotions that give away computers free of charge if consumers never used those computers to browse the Internet.

(C) There are at least some consumers who browse the Internet using computers offered free of charge by the advertisers and who, if they did not use those computers to browse the Internet, would spend little if any money on purchases from those advertisers.

(D) The advertisers would not be able to offer the computers absolutely free of charge if advertisements that accurately reflected the interests of the computers' users did not play continuously across the computers' screens whenever they were in use.

(E) Consumers who use a computer offered free of charge by the advertisers can sometimes choose to abstain from having information about their browsing patterns sent to the advertisers.

26. Some eloquent speakers impress their audiences with the vividness and clarity of the messages conveyed. Speakers who resort to obscenity, however, are not genuinely eloquent, so none of these speakers impress their audiences.

The flawed reasoning in which one of the following is most similar to that in the argument above?

(A) A culture without myths will also lack fundamental moral certainties. Thus, this culture must lack fundamental moral certainties, since it is devoid of myth.

(B) There are authors who write one page a day and produce one book per year. Serious authors, however, do not write one page per day, so some authors who write one book a year are not serious.

(C) Cities that are centers of commerce are always centers of industry as well. It follows that some centers of commerce are small cities, since there are centers of industry that are not small cities.

(D) Most farmers like living in rural areas. Since Carla is not a farmer, she probably would not enjoy living in the country.

(E) Sculptors sometimes produce significant works of art. But musicians are not sculptors. Hence, musicians never produce significant works of art.

S T O P

IF YOU FINISH BEFORE TIME IS CALLED, YOU MAY CHECK YOUR WORK ON THIS SECTION ONLY.
DO NOT WORK ON ANY OTHER SECTION IN THE TEST.

SECTION II

Time—35 minutes

27 Questions

<u>Directions</u>: Each set of questions in this section is based on a single passage or a pair of passages. The questions are to be answered on the basis of what is <u>stated</u> or <u>implied</u> in the passage or pair of passages. For some of the questions, more than one of the choices could conceivably answer the question. However, you are to choose the <u>best</u> answer; that is, the response that most accurately and completely answers the question, and blacken the corresponding space on your answer sheet.

Passage A

Muscle memory is a puzzling phenomenon. Most bodybuilders have experienced this phenomenon, yet virtually no discussions of it have appeared in scientific publications. Bodybuilders who start training
(5) again after a period of inactivity find that gaining muscle size seems easier the second time around— even if starting from the same place. With so many athletes observing muscle memory, some plausible explanation must exist.
(10) One potential explanation of muscle memory involves the neurons (nerve cells) that stimulate your muscles, telling the muscle fibers to contract. It is well established that during weight lifting, only a small percentage of neurons for the working muscles
(15) are recruited. The more weight you lift, the more neurons are involved and the more muscle fibers are stimulated. But even when attempting your maximum weight, you don't recruit all the fibers in your working muscles. Now it could be that one way your body
(20) adapts to the demands of consistent training is by gradually increasing the percentage of muscle fibers that are stimulated by neurons during maximal lifts. When you're making a comeback, this ability to recruit more muscle fibers may remain intact. If so,
(25) your muscles would start with a greater capacity to develop force. Although you may think you're starting from the same place, this greater strength would enable faster progress.

Then again, it's also possible that the ease of
(30) retraining has nothing to do with your muscles: it could all be in your head. The first time you trained, you didn't know how much you could lift. So you increased weight cautiously. When retraining, you already know you can handle increasing weight
(35) because you've done it before. So you are likely to add weight more rapidly. These more rapid weight increases produce quicker gains in strength and size.

Passage B

Pumping up is easier for people who have been buff before, and now scientists think they know
(40) why—muscles retain one aspect of their former fitness even as they wither from lack of use.

Because muscle cells are huge, more than one nucleus is needed for making the large amounts of the proteins that give muscles their strength. Previous
(45) research has demonstrated that with exercise, muscle cells get even bigger by merging with stem cells that are nested between them. The muscle cells incorporate the nuclei that previously belonged to the stem cells. Researchers had thought that when muscles atrophy,
(50) the extra cell nuclei are killed by a cell death program called apoptosis.

In a recent study, researchers regularly stimulated the leg muscles of mice over a two-week period, during which time the muscle cells gained nuclei and
(55) increased in size. The researchers then let the muscles rest. As the muscles atrophied, the cells deflated to about 40 percent of their bulked-up size, but the number of nuclei in the cells did not change. Since the extra nuclei don't die, they could be poised to make
(60) muscle proteins again, providing a type of muscle memory at the cellular level.

1. Both passages seek an answer to which one of the following questions?

(A) Why are explanations in the field of exercise physiology so inconclusive?

(B) What is the best way for bodybuilders to begin training again after a period of inactivity?

(C) Why is building muscle easier for people who have done so in the past?

(D) Is muscle memory a purely psychological phenomenon?

(E) Is there a psychological basis for the increases in muscle size and strength that result from exercise?

2. Passage B, but not passage A, seeks to achieve its purpose by

(A) questioning the reality of an alleged phenomenon

(B) discussing the results of a recent scientific experiment

(C) appealing to the reader's personal experience

(D) considering the psychological factors involved in bodybuilding

(E) speculating about the cause of an observed phenomenon

GO ON TO THE NEXT PAGE.

3. Passage B, unlike passage A, suggests that the phenomenon of muscle memory might be due to

(A) muscle cells' ability to merge with stem cells
(B) the body's ability to adapt to consistent training
(C) psychological factors
(D) a cell death program known as apoptosis
(E) the neurons that stimulate muscles

4. It can be inferred from the passages that the author of passage A

(A) is more certain than the author of passage B about the existence of muscle memory
(B) probably agrees with the author of passage B about the explanation for muscle memory
(C) was probably not aware of the scientific research that is described in passage B
(D) probably disagrees with the author of passage B about how muscle cells' nuclei affect muscle strength
(E) tends to be more skeptical than the author of passage B about conclusions drawn about one species on the basis of experiments involving another species

5. Given the style and tone of each passage, which one of the following is most likely to correctly describe the expected audience of each passage?

(A) Passage A: skeptics of the phenomenon under discussion
Passage B: people with personal experience of the phenomenon under discussion
(B) Passage A: scientific researchers
Passage B: athletic trainers and coaches
(C) Passage A: athletes who work with a trainer
Passage B: people who pursue a fitness program on their own
(D) Passage A: bodybuilders
Passage B: a general audience
(E) Passage A: sports psychologists
Passage B: exercise physiologists

6. The author of passage B would be most likely to hold which one of the following views about the characterization of muscle memory offered in the first sentence of passage A?

(A) It confirms that bodybuilders' experiences should not be accepted at face value.
(B) It reflects a dichotomy between athletes' experience and processes occurring at the cellular level of their muscles.
(C) It would not be accepted by most athletes who have started retraining after a period of inactivity.
(D) It is less apt now in light of recent research than it was before that research was conducted.
(E) It stems from a fundamental misunderstanding of the principles of exercise psychology.

7. Which one of the following is explicitly mentioned in passage B but not in passage A?

(A) the condition of a person's muscles when that person begins retraining
(B) muscles' adaptation to exercise
(C) the percentage of muscle fibers used in a working muscle
(D) the prevalence of discussions of muscle memory in scientific publications
(E) the large amounts of protein responsible for muscles' strength

GO ON TO THE NEXT PAGE.

Best known for her work with lacquer,
Eileen Gray (1878–1976) had a fascinating and
multifaceted artistic career: she became a designer of
ornaments, furniture, interiors, and eventually homes.
(5)　Though her attention shifted from smaller objects to
the very large, she always focused on details, even
details that were forever hidden. In Paris she studied
the Japanese tradition of lacquer, employing wood
surfaces—e.g., bowls, screens, furniture—for the
(10)　application of the clear, hard-drying liquid. It is a
time-consuming craft, then little known in Europe, that
superimposes layer upon layer, sometimes involving
twenty layers or more. The tradition of lacquer fit well
with her artistic sensibilities, as Gray eschewed the
(15)　flowing, leafy lines of the Art Nouveau movement that
had flourished in Paris, preferring the austere beauty
of straight lines and simple forms juxtaposed.
　　　In addition to requiring painstaking layering, the
wood used in lacquer work must be lacquered on both
(20)　sides to prevent warping. This tension between
aesthetic demands and structural requirements, which
invests Gray's work in lacquer with an architectural
quality, is critical but not always apparent: a folding
screen or door panel reveals more of the artist's work
(25)　than does a flat panel, which hides one side. In Gray's
early work she produced flat panels; later she made
door panels and even unfolded the panels into screens.
In a screen she made for the lobby of an apartment,
she fully realizes the implications of this expansion
(30)　from two to three dimensions: the screen juts out from
a wall, and that wall visually disintegrates into panels
of lacquered bricks on the screen. The screen thus
becomes a painting, a piece of furniture, and an
architectural element all at once. She subsequently
(35)　became heavily invested in the design of furniture,
often tailoring pieces to fit a particular interior
environment. She often used modern materials, such as
tubular steel, to create furniture and environments that,
though visually austere, meet their occupants' needs.
(40)　　　Gray's work in both lacquer and interior design
prefigures her work as an architect. She did not believe
that one should divorce the structural design of the
exterior from the design of the interior. She designed
the interior elements of a house together with the
(45)　more permanent structures, as an integrated whole.
Architecture for her was like work in lacquer: it
could only be achieved from the inside out. But in
architecture we discover the hidden layers; in fact we
inhabit them. We find storage cabinets in the recesses
(50)　of a staircase, desks that are also cabinets, and tables
that are set on pivots to serve different functions in
different contexts. One such table can be positioned
either outside, on a balcony, or inside the house.
Gray placed a carpet underneath it in each location,
(55)　as though to underscore that there is no important
distinction between exterior and interior.

8. Which one of the following most accurately summarizes
the main point of the passage?

(A)　Eileen Gray's artistic career, which ranged from
interior to exterior design, was greatly
influenced by her early work in lacquer, which
molded her aesthetic sensibilities and caused
her to develop independence as an artist, yet
prevented her from garnering acclaim by
critics of contemporary art.

(B)　Eileen Gray's artistic career, ranging from the
design of ornaments and interiors to
architectural design, was exemplified by her
work in lacquer, from which she derived an
aesthetic that downplayed the distinctions
between interior and exterior and sought
integral wholeness in a work of art.

(C)　Eileen Gray, a multifaceted artist whose designs
ranged from ornaments to houses, is best
known for her use of modern materials such
as tubular steel in the design of furniture and
houses, which, while informed by an austerity
of line, create humanistic environments that
meet their occupants' needs.

(D)　Although Eileen Gray's artistic endeavors
ranged from the design of ornaments and
interiors to architectural design, her distinctive
style, which is characterized by a sense of the
hidden, is evident in all her work, making it
readily identifiable.

(E)　The fact that Eileen Gray's artistic career
evolved from the design of ornaments and
furniture to architecture ultimately derives
from her eventual dissatisfaction with
Japanese traditional art and its emphasis on
integral wholeness.

9. Which one of the following comes closest to
exemplifying the characteristics of Gray's work as
described in the passage?

(A)　an upholstered sofa with tasseled fringes and
curved, wooden arms

(B)　a coffee table decorated with intricate carvings
of birds, trees, and grasses that are painted in
bright colors

(C)　a thin, stainless steel vase intended to resemble
the ornate flowers it will hold

(D)　a round, wooden picture frame inlaid with glass
beads, pearls, and gracefully cut pieces of
colorful shells

(E)　a metal chair whose simple shape is adapted to
fit the human form

GO ON TO THE NEXT PAGE.

10. The passage provides information that most strongly supports which one of the following assertions?

(A) Gray's reputation rests primarily on the range of styles and media in which she worked, rather than on her work in any particular medium.

(B) Gray personally constructed most of the interior furnishings that she designed.

(C) In Paris in Gray's time, wood was generally considered an inappropriate medium for visual art.

(D) Few of Gray's works in lacquer were intended for public viewing.

(E) Much of Gray's later work was functional as well as ornamental.

11. Information in the passage most helps to answer which one of the following questions?

(A) When did the tradition of lacquer first become known in Europe?

(B) What types of wood are usually considered best for use in traditional Japanese lacquer work?

(C) Were the artistic motifs of traditional lacquer work similar to those that were typical of Art Nouveau?

(D) Did Gray allow the style of her architecture to be informed by the landscape that surrounded the building site?

(E) What is a material that Gray used both structurally for its superior strength and decoratively for its visual interaction with another material?

12. Which one of the following most accurately characterizes the author's attitude toward Gray's artistic accomplishments?

(A) appreciation of the fact that her aesthetic philosophy, as well as the materials she used and the range of her work, sets her work apart from that of many of her contemporaries

(B) admiration for her artistic independence and refusal to conform to contemporary art trends even though such refusal positioned her on the periphery of the art world

(C) appreciation for the interpretation of Japanese tradition in her work, by which she made a unique contribution to modern architectural design while remaining faithful to Japanese architectural traditions

(D) admiration for the rapid development in her career, from the production of smaller works, such as ornaments, to large structures, like houses, that ensured her reputation as an avant-garde artist

(E) appreciation for her help in revolutionizing the field of structural design through her use of traditional materials and modern materials in her furniture creations and architectural work

13. The passage most strongly suggests that which one of the following principles was used by Gray in her work?

(A) Traditional lacquering techniques can be applied to nontraditional materials, such as brick and steel, with artistically effective results.

(B) The nature and placement of a dwelling's interior features can be essential factors in determining the overall structural design of the dwelling.

(C) Traditional ornamental techniques that are usually applied to small items are especially suitable for use on large structural elements of buildings.

(D) Excellent artistic effects can be achieved through the juxtaposition of visually austere elements with gracefully ornate elements of design.

(E) The superficial visual aspects of a building's decor can give evidence of the materials that have been used in its basic, unseen structural components.

14. The passage most strongly suggests that the author would agree with which one of the following statements about Gray's architectural work?

(A) It was considered by other architects of her time to be iconoclastic and inconsistent with sound principles of structural design.

(B) Her involvement in it was marked by a radical shift in her attitude toward the relation between the expressive and functional aspects of her work.

(C) The public is less knowledgeable about it than about at least some of her other work.

(D) It has been less controversial among recent critics and scholars than has at least some of her work in interior design.

(E) Unlike her work in lacquer, it was not influenced by an established tradition of Asian art.

GO ON TO THE NEXT PAGE.

It is generally accepted that woodland clearings were utilized by Mesolithic human populations (populations in Europe roughly 7,000 to 12,000 years ago) for food procurement. Whether there was

(5) deliberate removal of tree cover to attract grazing animals or whether naturally created clearings just afforded opportunistic hunting, the common view is that clearings had an economic use. The archaeological evidence for this, however, is at best circumstantial.

(10) Some locales where the presence of clearings has been demonstrated in the paleoecological record of vegetation have also yielded human artifacts from around the same time, but the two kinds of evidence are never securely linked. Furthermore, artifactual

(15) evidence that preparation of animals for human consumption took place within or near such clearings is generally lacking.

Most of the evidence invoked in favor of the resource-procurement model for clearings comes from

(20) ethnography rather than archaeology, and principally from the recognition that some recent premodern populations used fire to increase grazing areas. But while some ethnographic evidence has been used to bolster the resource-procurement model, other

(25) ethnographic evidence may suggest a different vision, a noneconomic one, of why clearings may have been deliberately created and/or used.

Geographer Yi-Fu Tuan argues that right up through the modern era, human behavior has been

(30) driven by fear of the wilderness. While we might be tempted to see this kind of anxiety as a product of modern urban life, it is clear that such fears are also manifest in preliterate and nonurban societies. If we apply this insight to the Mesolithic era, our view of the

(35) purpose and use of woodland clearings may change.

We have recently become aware of the importance of woodland paths in prehistory. The fact that Mesolithic human populations moved around the landscape is not a new idea. However, the fact that

(40) they may have done so along prescribed pathways has only recently come to the fore. I propose that one of the primary motivators in establishing paths may have been fear of the wooded surroundings—whether fear of harm from wildlife or spirits, or of simply

(45) getting lost.

From this view an alternative hypothesis may be developed. First, paths become established and acquire a measure of long-term permanence. Then this permanence leads to concentration of activity in some

(50) areas (near the paths) rather than others (away from the paths). This allows us to legitimately consider wilderness as a motivating concept in the Mesolithic, and may force us to consider environment as more than "backdrop." And finally, it may lead us to

(55) explain some clearings as purely social phenomena, since where paths meet, wider clearings emerge as corners are cut and intersections become convenient spots for resting.

15. Which one of the following most accurately states the main idea of the passage?

(A) Though fear of the wilderness is commonly thought to be a modern urban phenomenon, archaeological evidence suggests that the concept of wilderness may go as far back as the Mesolithic period.

(B) Though the resource-procurement model for Mesolithic woodland clearings is widely accepted, the available evidence provides comparable support for an alternative, noneconomic model.

(C) Though ethnographic evidence appears to support the resource-procurement model for woodland clearings, archaeological evidence suggests that clearings were used for multiple purposes by Mesolithic human populations.

(D) Evidence of woodland clearings from the paleoecological record of plant types may lend support to the hypothesis that Mesolithic human populations moved around the landscape via established paths.

(E) Ethnography provides clear and unambiguous insight into the purpose and use of woodland clearings during the Mesolithic period.

16. According to the resource-procurement model for clearings, Mesolithic human populations engaged in which one of the following practices?

(A) They traveled on preestablished pathways.
(B) They hunted animals that grazed in clearings.
(C) They grazed domesticated animals in clearings.
(D) They used clearings as resting sites.
(E) They planted crops in clearings.

17. Which one of the following is most clearly an example of the kind of evidence that would lend support to the author's proposal in the next-to-last paragraph?

(A) Mesolithic artwork that appears to depict woodland paths and clearings
(B) the ubiquity of paths and roads in areas densely settled by humans
(C) maps showing pathways used by certain recent premodern human populations
(D) survey results showing that modern urban dwellers experience heightened anxiety in wilderness areas
(E) rituals performed by certain recent premodern populations for the purpose of protection in the forest

GO ON TO THE NEXT PAGE.

18. The author suggests that which one of the following may have been true of Mesolithic human populations?

   (A)   They were the first people to use fire to increase grazing areas.
   (B)   They were the first people to travel in prescribed pathways.
   (C)   They worshipped nature.
   (D)   They possessed a concept of wilderness.
   (E)   They had a complex economic system.

19. In the third paragraph, the author mentions Yi-Fu Tuan's argument primarily in order to

   (A)   render doubtful the hypothesis about clearings that the author seeks to challenge
   (B)   exemplify the kind of argument about clearings that the author seeks to challenge
   (C)   give credit to the scholar who developed the hypothesis about clearings that the author favors
   (D)   lay the groundwork for the hypothesis about clearings that the author outlines
   (E)   point out the similarity between Tuan's view about clearings and the author's view

20. It can be inferred that the author would be more likely to endorse the resource-procurement model for clearings if this model were supported by which one of the following kinds of evidence?

   (A)   artifactual evidence that it was near or within clearings that Mesolithic human populations processed animals for human consumption
   (B)   ethnographic evidence that certain recent premodern populations used clearings for resource procurement
   (C)   experimental evidence that the creation of clearings is an effective means of attracting grazing animals
   (D)   paleoecological evidence that the majority of woodland clearings during the Mesolithic period were the result of wildfires
   (E)   statistical evidence that there was a significant increase in the number of woodland clearings during the Mesolithic period

21. Which one of the following comes closest to capturing what the phrase "purely social phenomena" means in line 55?

   (A)   phenomena that arise as by-products of a society's noneconomic practices
   (B)   phenomena that are universal and unique to human societies
   (C)   phenomena that serve the purpose of strengthening ties between a society's members
   (D)   phenomena that are intentionally created by human actions to produce a social benefit
   (E)   phenomena that reveal information about a society's cultural and economic development

22. Which one of the following arguments is most closely analogous to the author's argument in the second paragraph?

   (A)   The prosecution's case against the defendant rests almost entirely on circumstantial evidence. The defense, in contrast, has provided direct evidence that establishes that the defendant could not have committed the crime in question.
   (B)   The prosecution maintains that the physical evidence presented establishes the defendant's guilt. However, that same physical evidence can be interpreted in such a way that it instead establishes the defendant's innocence.
   (C)   The prosecution's case against the defendant rests entirely on circumstantial evidence. This suggests that there is no direct evidence to support the charge against the defendant.
   (D)   The prosecution's primary witness against the defendant is known to be untrustworthy. The defense, in contrast, has provided a parade of witnesses whose reputations are beyond reproach.
   (E)   The prosecution's case against the defendant rests almost entirely on circumstantial evidence. However, there is other circumstantial evidence that suggests that the defendant is innocent.

GO ON TO THE NEXT PAGE.

A remedy that courts sometimes use in disputes involving a breach of contract is simply to compel the participants in the contract to do precisely what they have agreed to do. Specific performance, as this

(5) approach is called, can be used as an alternative to monetary damages—that is, to requiring the one who has violated the agreement to pay a specified amount of money in compensation for the loss that is incurred or the wrong that is suffered. But while there are some

(10) cases for which specific performance can be a better alternative than monetary damages, there are many instances in which it is clearly not a suitable remedy.

Whether or not specific performance is an appropriate remedy in a case depends on the particular

(15) characteristics of that case. It is often the only reasonable remedy when monetary damages could not adequately compensate the one who has been harmed by the breach of contract. For example, a contract may provide for one party to sell some item of personal

(20) property that is unique or of such subjective importance to the buyer that there is no way to assign an accurate financial measure of the buyer's loss in not possessing the item. When the promised seller in such a case refuses to complete the sale, the best remedy would be

(25) to order that the contract be fulfilled exactly according to its terms.

Nevertheless, in many cases monetary payment can adequately compensate for the refusal to fulfill the terms of a contract, and thus the court commonly need

(30) not consider ordering specific performance. In fact, in some types of cases, court-enforced performance of the contract would actually be detrimental to those involved in the dispute and thus should be avoided. This most often occurs when a contract calls for a

(35) service to be performed and the one who has previously agreed to perform the service now refuses to do so— especially if a contract has been broken through someone's refusal to undertake employment as promised. The most compelling reasons against

(40) enforcement of contracts in such cases have to do with the kind of coercion that enforcement would necessitate. Forcing someone to perform a service in association with, and especially under the direction of, another who has become an antagonist can, at the very

(45) least, heighten dissatisfaction and intensify psychological friction. Even if a court had the resources necessary to ensure that such a contract would be enforced according to its terms, it would often do better to avoid imposing such uncomfortable

(50) conditions. Awarding monetary compensation where possible in such cases permits the court to steer clear of entanglement in troublesome aspects of the disputed relationship while still providing relief to the wronged party.

23. Based on the information in the passage, which one of the following is most clearly an example of a court's ordering specific performance?

(A) A publishing house is ordered by a court to return a manuscript to a writer after it has broken its contract for publication of the manuscript, and the contract has subsequently been nullified.

(B) A systems analyst who refuses to work for a certain company as she has contracted to do is ordered by a court to assume her contracted duties with the company, and the company is ordered to pay her the contracted salary.

(C) A building contractor who has received the full payment specified in his contract with a developer for the construction of a new mall but fails to complete the project is ordered to transfer all of the funds to a new contractor who will complete the construction.

(D) A dealer in rare antique furniture is ordered to return a contracted buyer's down payment for a chair after an expert appraiser has informed the buyer and the court that the chair's authenticity is questionable.

(E) An engineer who has agreed to work for a certain company but no longer intends to do so is ordered to pay the company for the losses it will incur as a result of the breach of agreement, but the company is not ordered to compensate the engineer.

24. Based on the passage, the author would be most likely to agree with which one of the following statements regarding cases in which someone is deemed by the court to have failed to undertake employment as contracted?

(A) Often specific performance in such cases can help the courts avoid problematic involvement in difficult aspects of the cases.

(B) While specific performance costs the court less to enforce than monetary damages, the savings should be weighed against the former's negative psychological repercussions.

(C) Enforcement of specific performance by the courts in such cases would often be less than fully successful.

(D) If the person who failed to fulfill the contract also refuses to pay monetary damages, specific performance should be imposed instead.

(E) Specific performance is more often considered by the courts in such cases than in other cases involving someone's refusal to perform services.

GO ON TO THE NEXT PAGE.

25. The main purpose of the passage is to

   (A)   predict the consequences of following a policy whereby a particular legal remedy becomes the standard approach

   (B)   argue for the implementation of a set of standards for the use of a new legal measure

   (C)   explain the differences among a group of interrelated legal procedures

   (D)   generate a set of guidelines for the evaluation of evidence in a particular type of legal dispute

   (E)   identify some criteria for the application of two different legal remedies

26. The passage most strongly suggests that the author would agree with which one of the following statements?

   (A)   Courts should examine the suitability of assessing monetary damages in breach-of-contract cases before they consider ordering specific performance.

   (B)   Specific performance is usually the most appropriate remedy for violations of contracts to sell personal property.

   (C)   In general, coercive court-ordered remedies in contract violation cases are unfair and should be avoided.

   (D)   Specific performance is successful at resolving disputes only when the objective value of the personal property contracted for sale is reasonably low.

   (E)   To provide fair enforcement of contracts, legal systems should offer disputing parties the option to use any of a number of resolution methods.

 27. Which one of the following would, if true, most strengthen the author's position with regard to remedies in employment contract cases?

   (A)   Court-ordered compensation in employment cases is often nearly impossible to enforce.

   (B)   All types of court-ordered remedies for contract violations entail coercion of one or more of the parties involved in the dispute.

   (C)   Most people who are sued for violating their agreement to undertake employment have adequate financial resources to compensate their would-be employers.

   (D)   The legal issues involved in employment contract disputes are for the most part very different from the legal issues involved in other disputes over contracts for performance of services.

   (E)   The rights of potential employees often override the monetary considerations involved in employment contract disputes.

S T O P

IF YOU FINISH BEFORE TIME IS CALLED, YOU MAY CHECK YOUR WORK ON THIS SECTION ONLY. DO NOT WORK ON ANY OTHER SECTION IN THE TEST.

SECTION III
Time—35 minutes

23 Questions

Directions: Each group of questions in this section is based on a set of conditions. In answering some of the questions, it may be useful to draw a rough diagram. Choose the response that most accurately and completely answers each question and blacken the corresponding space on your answer sheet.

Questions 1–5

In one week—Monday through Friday—a library's bookmobile will visit five of the following six neighborhoods—Hidden Hills, Lakeville, Nottingham, Oldtown, Park Plaza, and Sunnyside. Exactly one neighborhood will be visited on each of the five days, and none of the neighborhoods will be visited on more than one day. The bookmobile's schedule must conform to the following conditions:

Hidden Hills is visited, but not on Friday.
If Oldtown is visited, then it is visited on the day immediately before Hidden Hills is visited.
If Lakeville is visited, then it is visited on Wednesday.
Nottingham and Sunnyside are both visited, but not on consecutive days.

1. The five neighborhoods visited by the bookmobile, listed in order from Monday through Friday, could be

(A) Nottingham, Lakeville, Oldtown, Hidden Hills, and Sunnyside
(B) Nottingham, Oldtown, Hidden Hills, Sunnyside, and Park Plaza
(C) Oldtown, Hidden Hills, Lakeville, Nottingham, and Sunnyside
(D) Sunnyside, Oldtown, Lakeville, Hidden Hills, and Nottingham
(E) Sunnyside, Park Plaza, Nottingham, Oldtown, and Hidden Hills

GO ON TO THE NEXT PAGE.

2. Which one of the following neighborhoods CANNOT be visited on Thursday?

(A) Hidden Hills
(B) Nottingham
(C) Oldtown
(D) Park Plaza
(E) Sunnyside

3. If Hidden Hills is visited on Monday, which one of the following must be true?

(A) Lakeville is visited on Wednesday.
(B) Nottingham is visited on Tuesday.
(C) Park Plaza is visited on Thursday.
(D) Sunnyside is visited on Tuesday.
(E) Sunnyside is visited on Friday.

4. If Hidden Hills is visited on Wednesday, which one of the following must be true?

(A) Nottingham is visited on Monday.
(B) Oldtown is visited on Tuesday.
(C) Park Plaza is visited on Friday.
(D) Sunnyside is visited on Monday.
(E) Sunnyside is visited on Thursday.

5. If Nottingham is visited on Thursday, which one of the following must be true?

(A) Hidden Hills is visited on Wednesday.
(B) Lakeville is visited on Wednesday.
(C) Oldtown is visited on Monday.
(D) Park Plaza is visited on Friday.
(E) Sunnyside is visited on Tuesday.

GO ON TO THE NEXT PAGE.

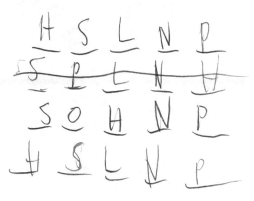

Questions 6–12

Six park rangers—Jefferson, Koguchi, Larson, Mendez, Olsen, and Pruitt—are each to be assigned to monitor one of three areas—area 1, area 2, and area 3—in a national park. At least one ranger, but no more than three, is assigned to each area. The assignment must conform to the following conditions:

Mendez is assigned to area 3.
Neither Olsen nor Pruitt is assigned to area 1.
Larson is assigned to the same area as either Koguchi or Mendez but not to the same area as both.
If Olsen is assigned to area 2, then Jefferson is assigned to the same area as Koguchi; otherwise, Jefferson is assigned to a different area than Koguchi.

6. Which one of the following is a permissible assignment of rangers to park areas?

(A) area 1: Jefferson, Koguchi
area 2: Larson, Olsen
area 3: Mendez, Pruitt

(B) area 1: Koguchi, Larson
area 2: Olsen, Pruitt
area 3: Jefferson, Mendez

(C) area 1: Koguchi, Pruitt
area 2: Jefferson
area 3: Larson, Mendez, Olsen

(D) area 1: Jefferson, Koguchi, Larson
area 2: Mendez, Olsen
area 3: Pruitt

(E) area 1: Jefferson, Koguchi, Larson
area 2: Olsen, Pruitt
area 3: Mendez

GO ON TO THE NEXT PAGE.

7. If Olsen is the sole ranger assigned to area 2, then which one of the following could be the complete assignment of rangers to area 3?

   (A)   Mendez
   (B)   Larson, Mendez
   (C)   Mendez, Pruitt
   (D)   Jefferson, Koguchi, Mendez
   (E)   Jefferson, Mendez, Pruitt

8. If exactly one ranger is assigned to area 1, then which one of the following must be true?

   (A)   Jefferson is assigned to area 1.
   (B)   Koguchi is assigned to area 2.
   (C)   Larson is assigned to area 3.
   (D)   Olsen is assigned to area 3.
   (E)   Pruitt is assigned to area 2.

9. Which one of the following rangers CANNOT be assigned to area 3?

   (A)   Pruitt
   (B)   Olsen
   (C)   Larson
   (D)   Koguchi
   (E)   Jefferson

10. If Koguchi is assigned to area 2, then which one of the following could be true?

   (A)   Jefferson is assigned to area 2.
   (B)   Jefferson is assigned to area 3.
   (C)   Larson is assigned to area 1.
   (D)   Olsen is assigned to area 2.
   (E)   Pruitt is assigned to area 3.

11. If Larson and Olsen are assigned to the same area, then which one of the following could be true?

   (A)   Jefferson is assigned to area 3.
   (B)   Koguchi is assigned to area 2.
   (C)   Larson is assigned to area 1.
   (D)   Olsen is assigned to area 2.
   (E)   Pruitt is assigned to area 3.

12. If Jefferson is assigned to area 2, then which one of the following must be true?

   (A)   Koguchi is assigned to area 1.
   (B)   Larson is assigned to area 1.
   (C)   Olsen is assigned to area 2.
   (D)   Pruitt is assigned to area 2.
   (E)   Pruitt is assigned to area 3.

GO ON TO THE NEXT PAGE.

Questions 13–17

An economics department is assigning six teaching assistants—Ramos, Smith, Taj, Vogel, Yi, and Zane—to three courses—Labor, Markets, and Pricing. Each assistant will be assigned to exactly one course, and each course will have at least one assistant assigned to it. The assignment of assistants to courses is subject to the following conditions:

Markets must have exactly two assistants assigned to it.
Smith and Taj must be assigned to the same course as each other.
Vogel and Yi cannot be assigned to the same course as each other.
Yi and Zane must both be assigned to Pricing if either one of them is.

13. Which one of the following could be the complete assignment of assistants to Pricing?

(A) Ramos, Yi, and Zane
(B) Smith, Taj, and Yi
(C) Smith, Taj, Yi, and Zane
(D) Taj, Yi, and Zane
(E) Vogel, Yi, and Zane

GO ON TO THE NEXT PAGE.

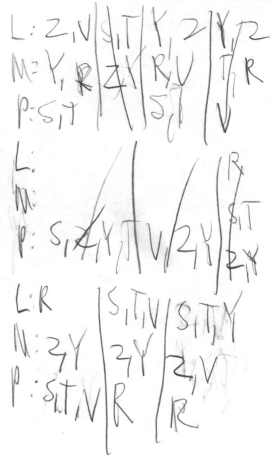

14. Which one of the following CANNOT be the complete assignment of assistants to Labor?

 (A) Ramos, Vogel
 (B) Ramos, Zane
 (C) Smith, Taj
 (D) Vogel, Zane
 (E) Yi, Zane

15. Which one of the following could be true?

 (A) Ramos and Vogel are both assigned to Markets.
 (B) Ramos and Taj are both assigned to Markets.
 (C) Smith and Vogel are both assigned to Markets.
 (D) Smith and Zane are both assigned to Pricing.
 (E) Vogel and Zane are both assigned to Pricing.

16. If Vogel is assigned to the same course as Zane, which one of the following CANNOT be true?

 (A) Ramos is assigned to Labor.
 (B) Smith is assigned to Labor.
 (C) Taj is assigned to Markets.
 (D) Ramos is assigned to Pricing.
 (E) Smith is assigned to Pricing.

17. If no other assistant is assigned to the same course as Ramos, which one of the following must be true?

 (A) Taj is assigned to Labor.
 (B) Vogel is assigned to Labor.
 (C) Yi is assigned to Markets.
 (D) Zane is assigned to Markets.
 (E) Smith is assigned to Pricing.

GO ON TO THE NEXT PAGE.

Questions 18–23

There are exactly six computers—P, Q, R, S, T, and U—
on a small network. Exactly one of those computers was
infected by a virus from outside the network, and that virus
was then transmitted between computers on the network.
Each computer received the virus exactly once. The following
pieces of information concerning the spread of the virus have
been established:

  No computer transmitted the virus to more than two other
   computers on the network.
  S transmitted the virus to exactly one other computer on
   the network.
  The computer that transmitted the virus to R also
   transmitted it to S.
  Either R or T transmitted the virus to Q.
  Either T or U transmitted the virus to P.

18. One possible route of the virus from the first computer
    in the network infected to Q is

    (A) from R to P to T to Q
    (B) from T to S to R to Q
    (C) from T to S to U to Q
    (D) from U to P to R to Q
    (E) from U to T to P to R to Q

GO ON TO THE NEXT PAGE.

P
Q
R
S
T
U

Q to R to S to T
P to S   T
P to R to S to T
    U to S to T
U to P to S to T

19. Which one of the following could be the computer that was infected from outside the network?

    (A)   P
    (B)   Q
    (C)   R
    (D)   S
    (E)   T

20. If T did not transmit the virus to any other computer on the network, which one of the following must be true?

    (A)   P transmitted the virus to S.
    (B)   Q transmitted the virus to R.
    (C)   U transmitted the virus to S.
    (D)   P did not transmit the virus to any other computer on the network.
    (E)   R did not transmit the virus to any other computer on the network.

21. Any of the following computers could have transmitted the virus to two other computers on the network EXCEPT:

    (A)   P
    (B)   Q
    (C)   R
    (D)   T
    (E)   U

22. The spread of the virus among the computers is completely determined if which one of the following is true?

    (A)   R transmitted the virus to Q.
    (B)   T transmitted the virus to Q.
    (C)   T transmitted the virus to S.
    (D)   U transmitted the virus to P.
    (E)   U transmitted the virus to R.

23. If P is the only computer that transmitted the virus to two other computers on the network, which one of the following must be true?

    (A)   S transmitted the virus to T.
    (B)   T transmitted the virus to P.
    (C)   Q did not transmit the virus to any other computer on the network.
    (D)   R did not transmit the virus to any other computer on the network.
    (E)   U did not transmit the virus to any other computer on the network.

S T O P

IF YOU FINISH BEFORE TIME IS CALLED, YOU MAY CHECK YOUR WORK ON THIS SECTION ONLY.
DO NOT WORK ON ANY OTHER SECTION IN THE TEST.

SECTION IV

Time—35 minutes

25 Questions

Directions: The questions in this section are based on the reasoning contained in brief statements or passages. For some questions, more than one of the choices could conceivably answer the question. However, you are to choose the best answer; that is, the response that most accurately and completely answers the question. You should not make assumptions that are by commonsense standards implausible, superfluous, or incompatible with the passage. After you have chosen the best answer, blacken the corresponding space on your answer sheet.

1. Cool weather typically weakens muscle power in cold-blooded creatures. In the veiled chameleon, a cold-blooded animal, the speed at which the animal can retract its tongue declines dramatically as the temperature falls. However, the speed at which this chameleon can extend its tongue does not decline much as the temperature falls.

Which one of the following, if true, most helps to resolve the apparent discrepancy in the information above?

(A) Most cold-blooded animals are much more active in warmer weather than in cooler weather.

(B) Many cold-blooded animals, including the veiled chameleon, have tongues that can extend quite a distance.

(C) Veiled chameleons are found in a wide range of habitats, including ones with wide variations in temperature and ones with moderate climates.

(D) In the veiled chameleon, tongue retraction is powered by muscles, whereas tongue extension is driven by energy stored in a rubber band-like sheath.

(E) Compared with the muscles in the tongues of most cold-blooded animals, the retraction muscles in the veiled chameleon's tongue are considerably stronger.

2. Acme's bank loan must be immediately repaid in full if Acme's earnings fall below $1 million per year. If Acme has to repay the entire loan immediately, it will have to declare bankruptcy. Acme had seemed safe from bankruptcy, having reported annual earnings of well over $1 million in each year it has had the bank loan. However, Acme has now admitted overstating its earnings for last year, so it will have to declare bankruptcy.

The argument requires the assumption that

(A) Acme's earnings for last year, when accurately stated, are below $1 million

(B) Acme has other debts besides the bank loan

(C) last year is not the only year for which Acme overstated earnings

(D) Acme's earnings for the current year will fall below $1 million

(E) Acme would be able to avoid bankruptcy if it did not have to repay the bank loan

3. Hospital patients generally have lower infection rates and require shorter hospital stays if they are housed in private rooms rather than semiprivate rooms. Yet in Woodville's hospital, which has only semiprivate rooms, infection rates and length of stays are typically the same as in several nearby hospitals where most of the rooms are private, even though patients served by these hospitals are very similar to those served by Woodville's hospital.

Which one of the following, if true, most helps to resolve the apparent conflict in the information above?

(A) Many of the doctors who routinely treat patients in Woodville's hospital also routinely treat patients in one or more of the nearby hospitals.

(B) Most of the nearby hospitals were built within the last 10 years, whereas Woodville's hospital was built about 50 years ago.

(C) Infection is more likely to be spread where people come into close contact with one another than where they do not.

(D) Woodville's hospital has a policy of housing one patient per room in semiprivate rooms whenever possible.

(E) Woodville's hospital is located in its central business district, whereas most of the nearby hospitals are located outside their municipalities' business districts.

GO ON TO THE NEXT PAGE.

4. Economist: Unemployment will soon decrease. If total government spending significantly increases next year, the economy will be stimulated in the short term and unemployment will decrease. If, on the other hand, total government spending significantly decreases next year, businesses will retain more of their earnings in the short term and employ more workers, thereby decreasing unemployment.

The conclusion drawn by the economist is properly inferred if which one of the following is assumed?

(A) Either total government spending will significantly decrease next year or else total government spending will significantly increase next year.

(B) Government officials are currently implementing policies that are intended to reduce unemployment.

(C) If there is a significantly increased demand for workers, then there will be a significant decrease in unemployment.

(D) A significant increase in total government spending will slow the economy in the long run.

(E) If the economy is not stimulated and businesses do not retain more of their earnings, then unemployment will not decrease.

5. Marisa: Existing zoning regulations must be loosened; in some places the restrictions on development are now so prohibitive as to reduce the property values of undeveloped areas significantly.

Tyne: I disagree. Though it is true that the recent increase in the stringency of zoning regulations could be seen by developers as merely an activists' ploy to restrict development further, the value of natural, undisturbed areas can only be better preserved by such regulatory protection.

Tyne's response to Marisa suggests that Tyne has misinterpreted which one of the following words in Marisa's remarks?

(A) regulations
(B) development
(C) prohibitive
(D) values
(E) significantly

6. Scientist: Laboratory animals have access to ample food, and they get relatively little exercise. These factors can skew the results of research using animals, since such studies often rely on the assumption that the animal subjects are healthy. For instance, animal studies that purport to show that extreme caloric restriction can extend lifespans take for granted that their subjects were not overfed to begin with.

The scientist's argument requires assuming which one of the following?

(A) Laboratory animals are healthy if they are fed a carefully restricted diet and get plenty of exercise.

(B) Laboratory conditions that provide animals with ample food but relatively little exercise can be unhealthy for the animals.

(C) It is not unusual for animals outside of laboratory settings to have access to ample food and get relatively little exercise.

(D) Some animal studies take into consideration the differences between the living conditions of laboratory animals and those of other animals.

(E) When provided with unlimited food over a long period of time, animals show little day-to-day variation in their eating habits.

7. Trade negotiator: Increasing economic prosperity in a country tends to bring political freedom to its inhabitants. Therefore, it is wrong for any country to adopt trade policies that are likely to seriously hinder growth in the prosperity of any other country.

Which one of the following principles, if valid, would most help to justify the trade negotiator's reasoning?

(A) Every country should adopt at least some policies that encourage the development of political freedom in other countries.

(B) Both economic prosperity and political freedom can contribute to the overall well-being of any country's inhabitants.

(C) The primary reason that any country seeks economic prosperity is to foster political freedom in that country.

(D) A country should not do anything that might hinder the growth of political freedom in any other country.

(E) It is wrong for any country to adopt trade policies that might diminish the prosperity of its inhabitants.

GO ON TO THE NEXT PAGE.

8. Whenever an artist endowed with both a high level of artistic skill and a high degree of creativity combines these two abilities in the process of creating an artwork, the resulting product is a great work of art. Moreover, no work of art can be great unless both of these elements are combined in its execution. Thus, great works of art are necessarily rare.

Which one of the following is an assumption required by the argument?

(A) Not every artist possesses a high level of artistic skill.

(B) A high degree of creativity and a high level of artistic skill are seldom combined in the creation of a work of art.

(C) An artist endowed with a high degree of creativity and a high level of artistic skill will necessarily produce great works of art.

(D) Few artists are endowed with a high degree of creativity.

(E) Anyone endowed with both a high level of artistic skill and a high degree of creativity will produce only a few great works of art.

9. Cereal advertisement: Fitness experts say that regular exercise is the most effective way to become physically fit, and studies have shown that adults who eat cereal every day exercise more regularly than adults who do not eat cereal. So by eating Fantastic Flakes every morning, you too will be on the most effective path to physical fitness.

The argumentation in the advertisement is flawed in that it

(A) infers a cause from a mere correlation

(B) presumes, without providing justification, that Fantastic Flakes are more nutritious than other cereals

(C) infers that a given factor is the sole predictor of a result merely on the grounds that the factor has been shown to contribute to that result

(D) draws a conclusion about all adults from a sample that is too small to be representative

(E) infers that some members of a group have a particular characteristic merely from the fact that the group as a whole has it

10. Journalist: Some critics argue that as the entertainment value of news reporting increases, the caliber of that reporting decreases. Yet the greatest journalists have been the most entertaining. So these critics are mistaken.

The journalist's conclusion is properly drawn if which one of the following is assumed?

(A) The news reporting of the greatest journalists has been of the highest caliber.

(B) The greatest journalists have been entertainers who report the news.

(C) Journalistic greatness involves producing news that is very valuable in some sense.

(D) Entertainment and news are not mutually exclusive categories.

(E) The worst journalists have been more entertaining than informative.

11. Linguist: Three of the four subfamilies of the so-called "Austronesian" languages are found only among indigenous peoples in Taiwan, whereas the fourth is found on islands over a huge area stretching from Madagascar to the eastern Pacific Ocean. Since these subfamilies all originated in the same language, which must have been originally spoken in a single geographic location, these facts suggest that Taiwan is the homeland where Austronesian languages have been spoken longest and, hence, that Austronesian-speaking peoples originated in Taiwan and later migrated to other islands.

Which one of the following most accurately expresses the overall conclusion drawn in the linguist's argument?

(A) The Austronesian family of languages has four subfamilies, three of which are found only among indigenous peoples in Taiwan.

(B) Wherever most subfamilies of the Austronesian family of languages have been spoken longest is probably the homeland where Austronesian languages originated.

(C) Taiwan is probably the homeland where Austronesian languages have been spoken longest.

(D) Austronesian-speaking peoples originated in the homeland where Austronesian languages have been spoken longest.

(E) Austronesian-speaking peoples probably originated in Taiwan and later migrated to other islands.

GO ON TO THE NEXT PAGE.

12. West: Of our company's three quality control inspectors, Haynes is clearly the worst. Of the appliances that were returned to us last year because of quality control defects, half were inspected by Haynes.

Young: But Haynes inspects significantly more than half the appliances we sell each year.

Young responds to West's argument by

(A) contending that the argument presupposes what it is trying to prove

(B) questioning the relevance of West's conclusion

(C) disputing the accuracy of one of the argument's stated premises

(D) arguing for a less extreme version of West's conclusion

(E) denying one of the argument's presuppositions

13. While playing a game with a ball, both Emma and John carelessly ignored the danger their game posed to nearby objects. An errant throw by John struck and broke a neighbor's window. Because his throw broke the window, John, but not Emma, should be required to perform chores for the neighbor as compensation for the damage.

Which one of the following conforms most closely to the principle illustrated above?

(A) While looking after her neighbor's pets, Laura left the door to her neighbor's house unlocked. Fortunately, nothing bad happened as a result. But her neighbor should not trust Laura to look after her pets in the future.

(B) Gerald hired Linda and Seung to move his furniture to a new residence. Linda and Seung carefully followed Gerald's instructions, but not all of the furniture fit in the moving truck. Gerald should still be required to pay Linda and Seung for the work they did.

(C) Terry and Chris were racing their cars on a public street. Chris lost control of his car and struck a parked car. Chris, but not Terry, should be required to pay to repair the damage.

(D) Alexis and Juan rented a boat for the afternoon. Because of improper use by the previous renter, the boat's engine malfunctioned during their excursion. The boat's owner should be required to refund Alexis's and Juan's rental fees.

(E) Susan and Leland disregarded posted warnings in order to skate on a frozen pond. When the ice broke, Susan's ankle was injured. Susan cannot hold the pond's owners responsible for her injuries.

14. Psychology researchers observed that parents feel emotion while singing to their infants. The researchers hypothesized that this emotion noticeably affects the sound of the singing. To test this hypothesis the parents were recorded while singing to their infants and while singing with no infant present. They were instructed to make the two renditions as similar as possible. These recordings were then played for psychologists who had not observed the recordings being made. For 80 percent of the recordings, these psychologists were able to correctly identify, by listening alone, which recordings were of parents singing to their children. The researchers concluded that their hypothesis was correct.

Which one of the following, if true, would most strengthen the researchers' reasoning?

(A) A separate study by the same researchers found that parents feel more emotion when singing to their own children than when singing to other children.

(B) Some, but not all, of the parents in the study realized that their song renditions were being recorded.

(C) Parents displayed little emotion when singing with no child or adult present.

(D) When a person feels emotion, that emotion provokes involuntary physiological responses that affect the vocal cords and lungs.

(E) Most of the parents who participated in the study believed that the emotion they felt while singing to their infants affected their singing.

GO ON TO THE NEXT PAGE.

15. Many scholars claim that Shakespeare's portrayal of Richard III was extremely inaccurate, arguing that he derived that portrayal from propagandists opposed to Richard III. But these claims are irrelevant for appreciating Shakespeare's work. The character of Richard III as portrayed in Shakespeare's drama is fascinating and illuminating both aesthetically and morally, regardless of its relation to historical fact.

Which one of the following principles, if valid, most helps to justify the reasoning in the argument above?

(A)   In historical drama, the aesthetic value of the work is not necessarily undermined by historical inaccuracies.
(B)   In dealing with real people, dramatists should reflect their lives accurately.
(C)   Shakespeare's historical importance puts him beyond the scope of all literary criticism.
(D)   History is always told by propagandists from the winning side.
(E)   Historical inaccuracies should be corrected only when they impugn the reputations of good people.

16. Voter: Our prime minister is evidently seeking a job at an international organization. Anyone seeking a job at an international organization would surely spend a lot of time traveling abroad, and our prime minister has spent more days abroad than at home so far this year.

Which one of the following arguments is most similar in its flawed reasoning to the voter's argument?

(A)   Kao must be a golfer. Kao is planning to run for office, and most people who run for office play golf.
(B)   Franklin will lose the coming election. The opposing candidate has better policy ideas and brings more relevant experience to the job.
(C)   Ramirez is evidently able to control the traffic signals. Just now, as Ramirez approached the curb, the traffic signal changed from red to green.
(D)   Thompson must be negotiating a personal loan. Thompson was at the bank yesterday, and people who are negotiating a personal loan go to the bank to meet with a loan agent.
(E)   McKinsey must have committed a crime at some point. After all, despite extensive background checks no one has been able to show that McKinsey has never committed a crime.

17. It is pointless to debate the truth of the law of noncontradiction, a fundamental logical principle according to which two statements that contradict each other cannot both be true. For a debate to be productive, participants must hold some basic principles in common. But the principles held in common in a debate over the law of noncontradiction would be much less certain than that law, so it matters little whether the law of noncontradiction can be defended on the basis of those principles.

Which one of the following most accurately expresses the overall conclusion drawn in the argument?

(A)   It is pointless to debate the truth of the law of noncontradiction.
(B)   Statements that contradict each other cannot both be true.
(C)   The participants in a productive debate must hold at least some basic principles in common.
(D)   The law of noncontradiction is a principle that the participants in a productive debate must hold in common.
(E)   Any principles that could be used to defend the law of noncontradiction are less certain than it is.

18. Pundit: For many high school graduates, attending a university would be of no help in getting a corporate job. The attributes corporations value most in potential employees are initiative, flexibility, and the ability to solve practical problems. Many new high school graduates have these attributes already.

The pundit's argument is most vulnerable to criticism on the grounds that it

(A)   fails to establish that university graduates do not have initiative, flexibility, and the ability to solve practical problems
(B)   overlooks the possibility that corporations may require an attribute that potential employees can obtain only by attending a university
(C)   provides no justification for the presumption that corporations only hire employees who have initiative, flexibility, and the ability to solve practical problems
(D)   takes for granted that the only reason that high school graduates go on to attend university is to improve their job prospects
(E)   takes for granted that initiative, flexibility, and the ability to solve practical problems are attributes that can be acquired through study

GO ON TO THE NEXT PAGE.

19. Archaeologist: Neanderthals, a human-like species living 60,000 years ago, probably preserved meat by smoking it. Burnt lichen and grass have been found in many Neanderthal fireplaces. A fire of lichen and grass produces a lot of smoke but does not produce nearly as much heat or light as a wood fire.

Which one of the following, if true, would most weaken the archaeologist's argument?

(A) In close proximity to the fireplaces with lichen and grass are other fireplaces that, evidence suggests, burned material that produced more heat than smoke.

(B) In the region containing the Neanderthal fireplaces in which lichen and grass were burnt, no plants that could be burned more effectively to produce heat or light were available 60,000 years ago.

(C) Some of the fireplaces containing burnt lichen are in regions in which lichen is not believed to have been plentiful and so would have had to have been brought in from some distance.

(D) There is clear evidence that at least some groups of Neanderthals living more recently than 60,000 years ago developed methods of preserving meat other than smoking it.

(E) The ability to preserve meat through smoking would have made the Neanderthal humans less vulnerable to poor periods of hunting.

20. Edgar: Some of the pumps supplying water to our region have been ordered shut down in order to protect a species of small fish. But it is absurd to inconvenience thousands of people for the sake of something so inconsequential.

Rafaela: You're missing the point. The threat to that fish species is a sign of a very serious threat to our water supply.

The dialogue provides the most support for the claim that Edgar and Rafaela disagree over whether

(A) shutting down the pumps will actually inconvenience a large number of people

(B) the survival of the fish species is the only reason for shutting down the pumps

(C) species of small fish are inconsequential

(D) the order to shut down the pumps was legal

(E) shutting down the pumps will be sufficient to protect the fish species

21. Only engineering is capable of analyzing the nature of a machine in terms of the successful working of the whole; physics and chemistry determine the material conditions necessary for this success, but cannot express the notion of purpose. Similarly, only physiology can analyze the nature of an organism in terms of organs' roles in the body's healthy functioning. Physics and chemistry cannot ascertain by themselves any of these operational principles.

Which one of the following is an assumption required by the analogy?

(A) The functioning of the human organism is machine-like in nature.

(B) Physics and chemistry determine the material conditions required for good physiological functioning.

(C) The notion of purpose used by engineers to judge the success of machinery has an analog in organisms.

(D) Physiology as a science is largely independent of physics and chemistry.

(E) Biological processes are irreducible to mechanical or chemical processes.

GO ON TO THE NEXT PAGE.

22. After a hepadnavirus inserts itself into a chromosome of an animal, fragments of the virus are passed on to all of that animal's descendants. A hepadnavirus fragment is present in a chromosome of the zebra finch and in precisely the same location in a corresponding chromosome of the dark-eyed junco. The fact that these two bird species diverged from each other about 25 million years ago therefore means that the hepadnavirus is at least 25 million years old.

Which one of the following, if true, most strengthens the argument?

(A) Viruses can affect the evolution of an organism and can thereby influence the likelihood of their diverging into two species.

(B) The chromosomes of the zebra finch and the dark-eyed junco contain fragments of no virus other than the hepadnavirus.

(C) When a virus inserts itself into an animal's chromosome, the insertion occurs at a random spot.

(D) Many bird species other than the zebra finch and the dark-eyed junco contain fragments of the hepadnavirus.

(E) The presence of a hepadnavirus in an animal species does not affect the likelihood of that species' survival.

23. The diet of *Heliothis subflexa* caterpillars consists entirely of fruit from plants of the genus *Physalis*. These fruit do not contain linolenic acid, which is necessary to the growth and maturation of many insects other than *H. subflexa*. Linolenic acid in an insect's diet is also necessary for the production of a chemical called volicitin. While most caterpillar species have volicitin in their saliva, *H. subflexa* does not.

Which one of the following can be properly inferred from the statements above?

(A) *H. subflexa* caterpillars synthesize linolenic acid within their bodies.

(B) Most species of caterpillar have sources of linolenic acid in their diets.

(C) Any caterpillar that has linolenic acid in its diet has volicitin in its saliva.

(D) A food source containing linolenic acid would be poisonous to *H. subflexa* caterpillars.

(E) No caterpillars other than *H. subflexa* eat fruit from plants of the genus *Physalis*.

GO ON TO THE NEXT PAGE.

24. Politician: Democracy requires that there be no restrictions on the ability of citizens to share their ideas freely, without fear of reprisal. Therefore the right to have private conversations, unmonitored by the government, is essential to democracy. For a government to monitor conversations on the Internet would thus be a setback for democracy.

Which one of the following most accurately describes the role played in the argument by the claim that democracy depends on the ability of citizens to share their ideas freely, without fear of reprisal?

(A) It is a claim for which no support is provided, and which is used to support only the argument's main conclusion.

(B) It is a claim for which no support is provided, and which is used to support a claim that is itself used to support the argument's main conclusion.

(C) It is a claim for which support is provided, and which is in turn used to support the argument's main conclusion.

(D) It is the argument's main conclusion and is inferred from two other statements in the argument, one of which is used to support the other.

(E) It is the argument's main conclusion and is inferred from two other statements in the argument, neither of which is used to support the other.

25. One way to compare chess-playing programs is to compare how they perform with fixed time limits per move. Given any two computers with which a chess-playing program is compatible, and given fixed time limits per move, such a program will have a better chance of winning on the faster computer. This is simply because the program will be able to examine more possible moves in the time allotted per move.

Which one of the following is most strongly supported by the information above?

(A) If one chess-playing program can examine more possible moves than a different chess-playing program run on the same computer under the same time constraints per move, the former program will have a better chance of winning than the latter.

(B) How fast a given computer is has no effect on which chess-playing computer programs can run on that computer.

(C) In general, the more moves a given chess-playing program is able to examine under given time constraints per move, the better the chances that program will win.

(D) If two different chess-playing programs are running on two different computers under the same time constraints per move, the program running on the faster computer will be able to examine more possible moves in the time allotted.

(E) If a chess-playing program is run on two different computers and is allotted more time to examine possible moves when running on the slow computer than when running on the fast computer, it will have an equal chance of winning on either computer.

S T O P

IF YOU FINISH BEFORE TIME IS CALLED, YOU MAY CHECK YOUR WORK ON THIS SECTION ONLY.
DO NOT WORK ON ANY OTHER SECTION IN THE TEST.

Acknowledgment is made to the following sources from which material has been adapted for use in this test booklet:

Paul Clerkin and Beth McLendon, "Eileen Gray" in *Irish Architecture Online*. ©1997 by Archéire.

Paul Davies, John G. Robb, and Dave Ladbrook, "Woodland Clearance in the Mesolithic: The Social Aspects" in *Antiquity*. ©2005 by *Antiquity* Publications, Ltd.

David Lewis, Letter in *The Law of Non-Contradiction*. Graham Priest, J.C. Beall, and Bradley Armour-Garb, eds. ©2004 by Oxford University Press.

Sandra Prior, "Does Muscle Memory Occur?" in EzineArticles.com. ©2007 by EzineArticles.com. http://ezinearticles.com/?Does-Muscle-Memory-Occur?&id=759493.

Tina Hesman Saey, "Muscles Can Remember Past Glory" in *ScienceNews*. ©2010 by Society for Science & the Public.

Topic Code	Print Your Full Name Here		
133273	Last	First	M.I.

Date	Sign Your Name Here
/ /	

LSAC®

Scratch Paper
Do not write your essay in this space.

LSAT® Writing Sample Topic

Directions: The scenario presented below describes two choices, either one of which can be supported on the basis of the information giv
Your essay should consider both choices and argue for one over the other, based on the two specified criteria and the facts provided. The
is no "right" or "wrong" choice: a reasonable argument can be made for either.

Stonewall Construction is deciding which of two upcoming construction projects to bid on—resurfacing Hilltop Road or expanding
Carlene Boulevard. Since Stonewall cannot fulfill both contracts at the same time and bids constitute binding commitments, Stonewall can
bid on one of them. Using the facts below, write an essay in which you argue for bidding on one project over the other based on the followi
two criteria:

- Stonewall wants to enhance its reputation among potential clients.
- Stonewall wants to increase its capacity to take on bigger projects.

The Hilltop Road resurfacing is a small project. The potential profit is relatively low. With Stonewall's experience and resources, it is
almost certain to win the contract, and it is highly likely to finish on time and within budget. Stonewall has an established reputation for
finishing projects on time and within budget. Stonewall has specialized in small projects. Construction firms specializing in small projects fin
increasingly difficult over time to win contracts for bigger projects. If the project is completed under budget, Stonewall will keep the extra mo
If it is over budget, Stonewall must cover the additional costs. Stonewall will use any extra money to purchase additional heavy equipment.

The Carlene Boulevard expansion is a large project. The potential profit is much higher. It involves kinds of work Stonewall has not d
before and would require it to expand its operation. Because of the overall nature of this project Stonewall believes it has a good chance of
winning the contract. It is uncertain whether Stonewall can finish the project on time and within budget. Even if Stonewall exceeds time and
budget constraints, it will gain valuable experience. If the project goes over budget, Stonewall will lose money.

WP-W

Scratch Paper
Do not write your essay in this space.

$$\begin{array}{cccccc}
0 & 0 & 0 & 0 & 0 & 0 \\
1 & 1 & 1 & 1 & 1 & 1 \\
2 & 2 & 2 & 2 & 2 & 2 \\
3 & 3 & 3 & 3 & 3 & 3 \\
4 & 4 & 4 & 4 & 4 & 4 \\
5 & 5 & 5 & 5 & 5 & 5 \\
6 & 6 & 6 & 6 & 6 & 6 \\
7 & 7 & 7 & 7 & 7 & 7 \\
8 & 8 & 8 & 8 & 8 & 8 \\
9 & 9 & 9 & 9 & 9 & 9 \\
\end{array}$$

LSAC ACCOUNT NO.

TOPIC CODE

Writing Sample Response Sheet

DO NOT WRITE
IN THIS SPACE

Begin your essay in the lined area below.
Continue on the back if you need more space.

COMPUTING YOUR SCORE

Directions:

1. Use the Answer Key on the next page to check your answers.

2. Use the Scoring Worksheet below to compute your raw score.

3. Use the Score Conversion Chart to convert your raw score into the 120–180 scale.

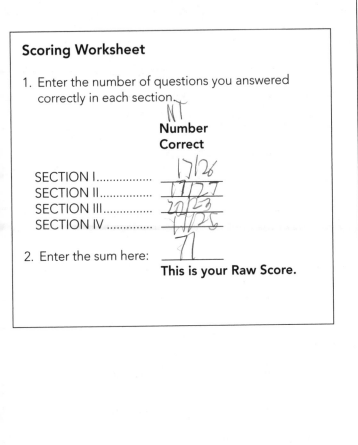

Scoring Worksheet

1. Enter the number of questions you answered correctly in each section.

	Number Correct
SECTION I	17/26
SECTION II	17/27
SECTION III	20/23
SECTION IV	17/25

2. Enter the sum here: 71

This is your Raw Score.

Conversion Chart
For Converting Raw Score to the 120–180 LSAT Scaled Score
LSAT Form 6LSN120

Reported Score	Raw Score Lowest	Raw Score Highest
180	99	101
179	98	98
178	97	97
177	96	96
176	*	*
175	95	95
174	94	94
173	93	93
172	92	92
171	91	91
170	89	90
169	88	88
168	87	87
167	85	86
166	84	84
165	83	83
164	81	82
163	79	80
162	78	78
161	76	77
160	74	75
159	72	73
158	71	71
157	69	70
156	67	68
155	65	66
154	63	64
153	61	62
152	59	60
151	58	58
150	56	57
149	54	55
148	52	53
147	50	51
146	49	49
145	47	48
144	45	46
143	44	44
142	42	43
141	41	41
140	39	40
139	38	38
138	36	37
137	35	35
136	33	34
135	32	32
134	31	31
133	29	30
132	28	28
131	27	27
130	26	26
129	25	25
128	24	24
127	23	23
126	22	22
125	21	21
124	20	20
123	19	19
122	18	18
121	*	*
120	0	17

*There is no raw score that will produce this scaled score for this form.

ANSWER KEY

SECTION I

1.	C	8.	E	15.	A	22.	E
2.	E	9.	B	16.	B	23.	D
3.	D	10.	C	17.	C	24.	B
4.	D	11.	C	18.	A	25.	A
5.	B	12.	A	19.	D	26.	E
6.	B	13.	E	20.	D		
7.	A	14.	E	21.	E		

SECTION II

1.	C	8.	B	15.	B	22.	E
2.	B	9.	E	16.	B	23.	B
3.	A	10.	E	17.	E	24.	C
4.	C	11.	C	18.	D	25.	E
5.	D	12.	A	19.	D	26.	A
6.	D	13.	B	20.	A	27.	C
7.	E	14.	C	21.	A		

SECTION III

1.	B	8.	D	15.	A	22.	C
2.	C	9.	D	16.	C	23.	C
3.	A	10.	E	17.	D		
4.	B	11.	B	18.	D		
5.	D	12.	A	19.	E		
6.	E	13.	A	20.	A		
7.	C	14.	B	21.	C		

SECTION IV

1.	D	8.	B	15.	A	22.	C
2.	A	9.	A	16.	D	23.	B
3.	D	10.	A	17.	A	24.	B
4.	A	11.	E	18.	B	25.	C
5.	D	12.	E	19.	B		
6.	B	13.	C	20.	B		
7.	D	14.	D	21.	C		

THE OFFICIAL LSAT
PREPTEST®

80

- PrepTest 80
- Form 6LSN121

DECEMBER 2016

1

SECTION I

Time—35 minutes

25 Questions

Directions: The questions in this section are based on the reasoning contained in brief statements or passages. For some questions, more than one of the choices could conceivably answer the question. However, you are to choose the best answer; that is, the response that most accurately and completely answers the question. You should not make assumptions that are by commonsense standards implausible, superfluous, or incompatible with the passage. After you have chosen the best answer, blacken the corresponding space on your answer sheet.

1. In a recent study of dust-mite allergy sufferers, one group slept on mite-proof bedding, while a control group slept on bedding that was not mite-proof. The group using mite-proof bedding had a 69 percent reduction in the dust-mite allergen in their mattresses, whereas there was no significant reduction in the control group. However, even though bedding is the main source of exposure to dust mites, no symptom reduction was reported in either group.

   Which one of the following, if true, most helps to resolve the apparent conflict in the statements above?

   (A) Dust-mite allergens in bedding tend to irritate many allergy sufferers' nasal passages more than do the same allergens in other locations, such as carpets.
   (B) When people report their own allergy symptoms, they tend to exaggerate the severity of those symptoms.
   (C) The medical community does not fully understand how dust-mite allergens cause allergy.
   (D) For dust-mite allergy sufferers to get relief from their allergies, dust-mite allergens must be reduced by 90 to 95 percent.
   (E) All of the participants in the study were told that one group in the study would be sleeping on mite-proof bedding.

2. Five years ago, the hair dryer produced by the Wilson Appliance Company accounted for 50 percent of all sales of hair dryers nationwide. Currently, however, Wilson Appliance's product makes up only 25 percent of such sales. Because of this decline, and because the average net income that Wilson receives per hair dryer sold has not changed over the last 5 years, the company's net income from sales of the product must be only half of what it was 5 years ago.

   The reasoning in the argument is flawed because the argument

   (A) mistakes a decline in the market share of Wilson Appliance's hair dryer for a decline in the total sales of that product
   (B) does not provide specific information about the profits hair dryers generate for the companies that produce them
   (C) fails to discuss sales figures for Wilson Appliance's products other than its hair dryers
   (D) overlooks the possibility that the retail price of Wilson Appliance's hair dryer may have increased over the past 5 years
   (E) provides no independent evidence that Wilson Appliance's hair dryer is one of the company's least profitable products

GO ON TO THE NEXT PAGE.

3. Whether or not one can rightfully call a person's faithfulness a virtue depends in part on the object of that person's faithfulness. Virtues are by definition praiseworthy, which is why no one considers resentment virtuous, even though it is in fact a kind of faithfulness—faithfulness to hatreds or animosities.

Which one of the following most accurately expresses the overall conclusion drawn in the argument?

(A) The object of a person's faithfulness partially determines whether or not that faithfulness is virtuous.

(B) Virtuous behavior is praiseworthy by definition.

(C) Behavior that emerges from hatred or animosity cannot be called virtuous.

(D) Faithfulness and resentment are obviously different, despite some similarities.

(E) Resentment should not be considered a virtuous emotion.

4. Columnist: A government-owned water utility has received approval to collect an additional charge on water bills and to use that additional revenue to build a dam. A member of the legislature has proposed not building the dam but instead spending the extra money from water bills to build new roads. That proposal is unacceptable.

Which one of the following principles, if valid, most helps to justify the columnist's judgment that the legislator's proposal is unacceptable?

(A) Customers of a utility have a right to know how the money they pay to the utility will be used.

(B) Money designated for projects that benefit an entire community should not be used for projects that benefit only some members of a community.

(C) An additional charge on water bills should not be used to fund a project that most of the utility's customers disapprove of.

(D) An additional charge on water bills should not be imposed unless it is approved by the legislature.

(E) A water utility should not collect an additional charge unless the money collected is used for water-related expenditures.

5. During its caterpillar stage, the leopard magpie moth feeds on a plant called the Natal grass cycad and by so doing laces its body with macrozamin, a toxin that makes the moth highly unpalatable to would-be predators. Since the Natal grass cycad is now endangered and facing extinction, the leopard magpie moth is also in danger of extinction.

Which one of the following is an assumption required by the argument?

(A) Feeding on the Natal grass cycad is the only means by which the leopard magpie moth can make itself highly unpalatable to predators.

(B) The leopard magpie moth does not have the speed or the agility to escape from any of its potential predators.

(C) Potential predators of the leopard magpie moth cannot determine from appearance alone whether a moth's body is laced with macrozamin.

(D) Leopard magpie moths are not able to locate Natal grass cycads unless those plants are abundant.

(E) None of the potential predators of the leopard magpie moth have developed a tolerance to macrozamin.

GO ON TO THE NEXT PAGE.

6. Citizen: Our government has a large budget surplus, which our leaders wish to use to pay down the national debt. This makes no sense. Because of underfunding, our military is inadequate, the infrastructures of our cities are decaying, and our highways are in disrepair. If homeowners used all their money to pay off their mortgages early, while refusing to pay for upkeep of their homes, this would not make them better off financially. The same goes for the country as a whole.

Which one of the following most accurately expresses the conclusion drawn in the citizen's argument?

(A) Homeowners should not pay off their mortgages early if they must neglect upkeep of their homes in order to do so.

(B) It does not make sense for the government to use the budget surplus to pay down the national debt.

(C) A homeowner's personal financial situation is analogous in relevant ways to the financial situation of a country's government.

(D) Because of underfunding, the government does not maintain adequate standards in the services it provides.

(E) Government leaders want to use the country's large budget surplus to pay down the national debt.

7. Peraski: Although driving gas-guzzling automobiles produces a greater level of pollution than driving smaller cars, those of us who drive smaller cars when we could use a bicycle cannot speak out against the use of gas guzzlers. We would be revealing our hypocrisy.

Jackson: I acknowledge I could do better in this area. But, it would be worse not to speak out against greater sources of pollution just because I am being hypocritical.

The dialogue provides the most support for the claim that Peraski and Jackson disagree over whether

(A) driving a gas-guzzling automobile produces a greater level of pollution than driving a smaller car

(B) speaking out against the use of gas guzzlers despite driving in situations in which one could use a bicycle reveals hypocrisy

(C) driving even a small car when one could use a bicycle contributes to the level of pollution

(D) one should speak out against polluting even if doing so reveals one's own hypocrisy

(E) there is no moral difference between driving a gas guzzler and driving a smaller car

8. For a species of large abalone shellfish to develop from a species of smaller ones, they must spend less energy on finding food and avoiding predators, and more on competition in mating. So it is surprising that the fossil record shows that a species of large abalones developed from a smaller one only after otters, which prey on abalones, began to dominate the waters in which the abalones lived.

Which one of the following, if true, most helps to resolve the apparent discrepancy in the information above?

(A) Otters and abalones also compete for the same types of food and so are drawn to the same waters.

(B) The fossils that were studied showed the development of only one of the two species of large abalones known to exist.

(C) Otters also prey on the abalones' competitors for food and so indirectly make it easier for abalones to get food.

(D) Small abalone species tend to reproduce more rapidly than larger abalone species.

(E) Otters have a preference for large abalones over small ones and so prefer waters in which large abalones are found.

9. Some managers think that the best way to maximize employee performance is to institute stiff competition among employees. However, in situations where one competitor is perceived to be clearly superior, other competitors become anxious and doubt their own ability to perform. Thus, stiff competition can undermine the result it was intended to achieve.

The conclusion of the argument can be properly drawn if which one of the following is assumed?

(A) Those who are perceived to be clearly superior almost always win.

(B) The winner of a competition is often the competitor who exerts the most effort.

(C) When competitors perceive the competition as winnable, their overall performance generally improves.

(D) Doubting one's own ability to perform can decrease one's overall performance.

(E) Competitors who work to undermine the confidence of other participants often do better in competitions.

GO ON TO THE NEXT PAGE.

1

10. Creating a database of all the plant species in the scientific record has proved to be no easy task. For centuries, botanists have been collecting and naming plants without realizing that many were in fact already named. And by using DNA analysis, botanists have shown that varieties of plants long thought to belong to the same species actually belong to different species.

Of the following claims, which one can most justifiably be rejected on the basis of the statements above?

(A) Most of the duplicates and omissions among plant names in the scientific record have yet to be cleared up.

(B) An accurate database of all the plant species in the scientific record can serve as an aid to botanists in their work.

(C) Duplicates and omissions in the scientific record also occur in fields other than botany.

(D) Botanists have no techniques for determining whether distinct plant species have been given distinct names.

(E) A person who consults the scientific record looking under only one of a plant's names may miss available information about that plant.

11. A year ago several regional hospitals attempted to reduce the number of patient injuries resulting from staff errors by implementing a plan to systematically record all such errors. The incidence of these injuries has substantially decreased at these hospitals since then. Clearly, the knowledge that their errors were being carefully monitored made the hospitals' staffs much more meticulous in carrying out their patient-care duties.

Which one of the following, if true, most strengthens the argument?

(A) Before the plan was implemented the hospitals already had a policy of thoroughly investigating any staff error that causes life-threatening injury to a patient.

(B) The incidence of patient injuries at a regional hospital that did not participate in the plan also decreased over the year in question.

(C) The plan did not call for the recording of staff errors that could have caused patient injuries but did not.

(D) The decrease in the incidence of the injuries did not begin at any hospital until the staff there became aware that the records were being closely analyzed.

(E) Under the plan, the hospitals' staff members who were found to have made errors that caused injuries to patients received only reprimands for their first errors.

12. In a national park located on an island, a herd of moose was increasing in number and threatening to destroy species of native plants. Wolves were introduced to the island to reduce the herd and thereby prevent destruction of the vegetation. Although the wolves prospered, the moose herd continued to grow.

Which one of the following, if true, most helps to explain the failure of the strategy involving wolves?

(A) The presence of wolves in an area tends to discourage other predators from moving into the area.

(B) Attempts to control moose populations in other national parks by introducing predators have also been unsuccessful.

(C) Wolves often kill moose weakened by diseases that probably would have spread to other moose.

(D) Healthy moose generally consume more vegetation than do those that are diseased or injured.

(E) Moose that are too old to breed are just as likely to die of natural causes as of attack by wolves.

13. If the purpose of laws is to contribute to people's happiness, we have a basis for criticizing existing laws as well as proposing new laws. Hence, if that is not the purpose, then we have no basis for the evaluation of existing laws, from which we must conclude that existing laws acquire legitimacy simply because they are the laws.

The reasoning in the argument is flawed in that the argument

(A) takes a sufficient condition for a state of affairs to be a necessary condition for it

(B) infers a causal relationship from the mere presence of a correlation

(C) trades on the use of a term in one sense in a premise and in a different sense in the conclusion

(D) draws a conclusion about how the world actually is on the basis of claims about how it should be

(E) infers that because a set of things has a certain property, each member of that set has the property

GO ON TO THE NEXT PAGE.

A - B
B - A

14. In order for life to exist on the recently discovered planet P23, there must be water on the planet's surface. But there is no water on P23's surface, so there is no life on planet P23.

The pattern of reasoning in the argument above is most similar to that in which one of the following arguments?

(A)   A company must have efficient employees to be successful. And if a company's employees are knowledgeable and hardworking, then they are probably efficient. Thus, in order for a company to be successful, it must have knowledgeable and hardworking employees.

(B)   The fact that the suspect was flustered when questioned by the police might be a result of the suspect's surprise at being questioned. But if it is, the probability that the suspect is guilty is very low. Thus, the fact that the suspect was flustered is not necessarily a sign that the suspect is guilty.

(C)   Oil companies are not buying new drilling equipment. But if they were planning on increasing their drilling, they would be buying new drilling equipment. Thus, oil companies are not planning on increasing their drilling.

(D)   The price of real estate in a particular town is increasing. And if the town's economy were improving, the price of real estate there would increase. Thus, the town's economy is improving.

(E)   The exports of a particular nation have recently decreased. But whenever that nation's exports decrease, its trade deficit increases. Thus, the nation's trade deficit has recently increased.

15. Sanchez: The sixteen new computers that the school purchased were not as expensive as many people assume. So it isn't true that too much was spent on computers.

Merriweather: It isn't that the school paid more for each computer than it was worth, but that the computers that were purchased were much more elaborate than they needed to be.

The dialogue provides the most support for the claim that Sanchez and Merriweather disagree over whether the school

(A)   needed sixteen new computers
(B)   purchased more computers than it should have
(C)   spent more in purchasing the sixteen computers than it should have
(D)   paid more for each computer than it was worth
(E)   has been harshly criticized for purchasing the sixteen computers

16. Airport administrator: According to the latest figures, less than 1 commercial flight in 2 million strays off course while landing, a number low enough to allow runways to be built closer together without a significant increase in risk. Opponents of closer runways claim that the number is closer to 1 in 20,000, but this figure is based on a partial review of air traffic control tapes and so is relatively unreliable compared to the other figure, which is based on a thorough study of the flight reports required of pilots for all commercial flights.

Which one of the following most accurately describes a flaw in the airport administrator's argument?

(A)   The argument presumes, without providing justification, that building runways closer together will encourage pilots to be more cautious while landing.

(B)   The argument overlooks the fact that those who make mistakes are often unreliable sources of information about those mistakes.

(C)   The argument questions the integrity of those who are opposed to allowing runways to be built closer together.

(D)   The argument presumes, without providing justification, that the air traffic control tapes studied do not provide accurate information concerning specific flights.

(E)   The argument infers from a lack of conclusive evidence supporting the higher number's accuracy that it must be inaccurate.

GO ON TO THE NEXT PAGE.

17. In deep temperate lakes, water temperatures vary according to depth. In winter, the coldest water is at the top; in summer, at the bottom. The changes in temperature distribution, or "turnover," occur in fall and late winter. Lake trout will be found, as a rule, in the coldest water. So, if anglers seek lake trout in deep temperate lakes while these lakes are partially iced over in late winter, they will do best to eschew the lake trout's summer haunts and fish instead in a shallow bay or close to the surface off a rocky point.

Which one of the following is an assumption on which the argument depends?

(A) The ease with which lake trout can be caught by anglers varies with the time of year and the water temperature.

(B) Cold water is denser, and therefore heavier, than relatively warmer water.

(C) Lake trout are found exclusively in deep temperate lakes.

(D) Lake trout do not alter their feeding habits from one part of the year to another.

(E) In deep temperate lakes that have ice residues on the surface, late-winter "turnover" has not yet occurred.

18. Liang: Watching movies in which violence is portrayed as an appropriate way to resolve problems increases levels of aggression in viewers. Therefore, children's access to these movies should be restricted.

Sarah: Watching a drama whose characters are violent allows the audience to vicariously experience the emotions associated with aggression and thus be purged of them. Hence, the access by mature audiences to such forms of entertainment should not be restricted.

The dialogue provides the most support for inferring that Liang and Sarah agree with each other that

(A) people who experience an emotion vicariously are likely to purge themselves of that emotion

(B) the members of a mature audience are unlikely to believe that violence is sometimes an appropriate way to resolve problems

(C) if violence in certain movies causes violence in viewers, access to those movies should be restricted

(D) the effects of dramatic depictions of violence on audiences are at least partially understood

(E) children are more likely than adults to be attracted to dramas involving characters who behave violently

19. Politician: Of the candidates running, Thompson is the best person to lead this nation. For one thing, Thompson opposes higher taxes whereas the other candidates support them. Many would agree that anyone who opposes higher taxes will make a better leader than someone who supports them.

Which one of the following, if true, casts the most doubt on the politician's argument?

(A) Opposing higher taxes is not a factor contributing to good leadership.

(B) Being opposed to higher taxes is not a sufficient condition for good leadership.

(C) Thompson has questionable opinions concerning important issues other than taxes.

(D) All of the past leaders who supported higher taxes performed their jobs adequately.

(E) All of the past leaders who supported higher taxes were hardworking.

20. Patterson: Bone flutes dating to the Upper Paleolithic are the earliest evidence for music. Thus it is likely that music first arose during this period.

Garza: But the Upper Paleolithic is exceptional for the intensive use of bone, which typically survives well in archaeological contexts, unlike other materials commonly used for musical instruments, such as wood.

Garza responds to Patterson by doing which one of the following?

(A) arguing that the body of evidence to which Patterson appeals is insufficient for Patterson's purposes

(B) offering evidence to challenge the truth of the premise of Patterson's argument

(C) presenting a counterexample to the general conclusion drawn in Patterson's argument

(D) presenting an argument analogous to Patterson's argument to reveal a potential flaw in Patterson's reasoning

(E) using Patterson's evidence to draw a conclusion inconsistent with the conclusion drawn in Patterson's argument

GO ON TO THE NEXT PAGE.

21. No occupation should be subject to a licensing requirement unless incompetence in the performance of tasks normally carried out within that occupation poses a plausible threat to human health or safety.

The principle stated above, if valid, most helps to justify the reasoning in which one of the following arguments?

(A) Because some of the duties that police officers carry out have no connection to human health or safety, police officers should not be subject to a licensing requirement.

(B) Because there are no realistic circumstances in which poor work by an interior designer poses a danger to human beings, interior designers should not be subject to a licensing requirement.

(C) Because hospital administrators routinely make decisions that affect the health of hundreds of people, hospital administrators should be subject to a licensing requirement.

(D) Because hair stylists regularly use substances that can pose a threat to human health if handled improperly, hair stylists should be subject to a licensing requirement.

(E) Because tattoo artists who do not maintain strict sanitation pose a serious threat to human health, tattoo artists should be subject to a licensing requirement.

22. Most of the new cars that Regis Motors sold last year were purchased by residents of Blomenville. Regis Motors sold more new cars last year than it did in any previous year. Still, most new cars purchased by Blomenville residents last year were not purchased from Regis Motors.

If the statements above are true, which one of the following must also be true?

(A) Regis Motors sold more new cars to residents of Blomenville last year than they had in any previous year.

(B) The total number of new cars purchased by residents of Blomenville was greater last year than it was in any previous year.

(C) A car retailer other than Regis Motors sold the most new cars to residents of Blomenville last year.

(D) The number of new cars purchased last year by residents of Blomenville is greater than the number of new cars sold by Regis Motors.

(E) Regis Motors' share of the new car market in Blomenville last year increased over its share the year before.

23. Editorial: Teenagers tend to wake up around 8:00 A.M., the time when they stop releasing melatonin, and are sleepy if made to wake up earlier. Since sleepiness can impair driving ability, car accidents involving teenagers driving to school could be reduced if the school day began later than 8:00 A.M. Indeed, when the schedule for Granville's high school was changed so that school began at 8:30 A.M. rather than earlier, the overall number of car accidents involving teenage drivers in Granville declined.

Which one of the following, if true, provides the most support for the argument in the editorial?

(A) Teenagers start releasing melatonin later at night and stop releasing it later in the morning than do young children.

(B) Sleepy teenagers are tardy for school more frequently than teenagers who are well rested when the school day begins.

(C) Teenagers who work at jobs during the day spend more time driving than do teenagers who attend high school during the day.

(D) Many of the car accidents involving teenage drivers in Granville occurred in the evening rather than in the morning.

(E) Car accidents involving teenage drivers rose in the region surrounding Granville during the time they declined in Granville.

GO ON TO THE NEXT PAGE.

24. Lucinda will soon be attending National University as an engineering major. At National University, most residents of Western Hall are engineering majors. Therefore, Lucinda will probably live in Western Hall.

Which one of the following arguments exhibits a flawed pattern of reasoning most similar to that exhibited by the argument above?

(A) A major shopping mall is now being constructed in our city. Most cities with major shopping malls are regional economic hubs. Therefore, our city will probably become a regional economic hub.

(B) Cities that are regional economic hubs generally experience tremendous economic growth at some point. Our city is a regional economic hub that has never experienced tremendous economic growth. Thus it will probably experience tremendous economic growth in the future.

(C) Cities that are regional economic hubs always have excellent transportation systems. It is widely agreed that our city's transportation system is inadequate. Therefore, our city will probably never become a regional economic hub.

(D) A major shopping mall was built in our city ten years ago, and our city has experienced tremendous economic growth since then. Therefore, most cities in which major shopping malls are built will experience tremendous economic growth shortly afterward.

(E) Most cities that are regional economic hubs contain major shopping malls. A major shopping mall is now being constructed in our city. Therefore, our city will probably become a regional economic hub.

25. Oceanographer: To substantially reduce the amount of carbon dioxide in Earth's atmosphere, carbon dioxide should be captured and pumped deep into the oceans, where it would dissolve. The cool, dense water in ocean depths takes centuries to mix with the warmer water near the surface, so any carbon dioxide pumped deep into oceans would be trapped there for centuries.

Which one of the following is an assumption that the oceanographer's argument requires?

(A) Carbon dioxide will dissolve much more thoroughly if it is pumped into cold water than it will if it is pumped into warmer water.

(B) Evaporation of warmer ocean water near an ocean's surface does not generally release into the atmosphere large amounts of the carbon dioxide dissolved in the evaporating water.

(C) Carbon dioxide dissolved in cool, dense water in ocean depths will not escape back into Earth's atmosphere a long time before the water in which that carbon dioxide is dissolved mixes with warmer water near the surface.

(D) It is the density of the water in the ocean depths that plays the main role in the trapping of the carbon dioxide.

(E) Carbon dioxide should be pumped into ocean depths to reduce the amount of carbon dioxide in the atmosphere only if the carbon dioxide pumped into ocean depths would be trapped there for hundreds of years.

S T O P

IF YOU FINISH BEFORE TIME IS CALLED, YOU MAY CHECK YOUR WORK ON THIS SECTION ONLY. DO NOT WORK ON ANY OTHER SECTION IN THE TEST.

SECTION II

Time—35 minutes

27 Questions

Directions: Each set of questions in this section is based on a single passage or a pair of passages. The questions are to be answered on the basis of what is stated or implied in the passage or pair of passages. For some of the questions, more than one of the choices could conceivably answer the question. However, you are to choose the best answer; that is, the response that most accurately and completely answers the question, and blacken the corresponding space on your answer sheet.

The following passage is adapted from a journal article.

To understand John Rawls's theory of justice, one first needs to grasp what he was reacting against. The dominant approach in pre-Rawls political philosophy was utilitarianism, which emphasized
(5) maximizing the fulfillment of people's preferences. At first sight, utilitarianism seems plausible—what else should we do but try to achieve the most satisfaction possible for the greatest number of people?—but the theory has some odd consequences. Suppose executing
(10) an innocent person will appease a mob, and that doing so will therefore increase total satisfaction. Incredibly, a utilitarian would have to endorse the execution. Rawls accordingly complains that, in the utilitarian view, there is no reason "why the violation of the
(15) liberty of a few might not be made right by the greater good shared by many."

If we reject utilitarianism and its view about the aim of the good life, how can we know what justice requires? Rawls offers an ingenious answer. He asserts
(20) that even if people do not agree on the aim of the good life, they can accept a fair procedure for settling what the principles of justice should be. This is key to Rawls's theory: Whatever arises from a fair procedure is just.

(25) But what is a fair procedure? Rawls again has a clever approach, beginning with his famous veil of ignorance. Suppose five children have to divide a cake among themselves. One child cuts the cake but does not know who will get which shares. The child is
(30) likely to divide the cake into equal shares to avoid the possibility of receiving the smallest share, an arrangement that the others will also admit to be fair. By denying the child information that would bias the result, a fair outcome can be achieved.

(35) Rawls generalizes the point of this example of the veil of ignorance. His thought experiment features a situation, which he calls the original position, in which people are self-interested but do not know their own station in life, abilities, tastes, or even gender. Under
(40) the limits of this ignorance, individuals motivated by self-interest endeavor to arrive at a solution in which they will not lose, because nobody loses. The result will be a just arrangement.

Rawls thinks that people, regardless of their plan
(45) of life, want certain "primary goods." These include rights and liberties, powers and opportunities, and income and wealth. Without these primary goods, people cannot accomplish their goals, whatever they may be. Hence, any individual in the original position
(50) will agree that everyone should get at least a minimum amount of these primary goods. Unfortunately, this is an inherently redistributionist idea, since the primary goods are not natural properties of human beings. If someone lacks a primary good, it must be provided,
(55) at the expense of others if necessary.

1. According to the passage, Rawls uses which one of the following devices to explain his theory?

 (A) a thought experiment
 (B) a process of elimination
 (C) an empirical study of social institutions
 (D) a deduction from a few basic principles
 (E) a consideration of the meaning of words

2. The purpose of the question in lines 6–8 is to

 (A) point out an implausible feature of utilitarianism
 (B) characterize utilitarianism as internally contradictory
 (C) establish that utilitarianism must be true
 (D) suggest the intuitive appeal of utilitarianism
 (E) inquire into ways of supplementing utilitarianism

3. The author's primary purpose in the passage is to

 (A) show why a once-dominant theory was abandoned
 (B) describe the novel way in which a theory addresses a problem
 (C) sketch the historical development of a celebrated theory
 (D) debate the pros and cons of a complex theory
 (E) argue for the truth of a controversial theory

GO ON TO THE NEXT PAGE.

4. With which one of the following statements would both Rawls and the author of the passage be most likely to agree?

(A) There are situations in which it is permissible to treat the fulfillment of one person's preferences as more important than the fulfillment of the majority's preferences.

(B) Unless individuals set aside their own self-interest, they cannot make fair judgments about the distribution of goods.

(C) If an individual lacks a good, society must sometimes provide that good, even if this means taking it from others.

(D) Most people agree about which of the primary goods is the most valuable.

(E) It is fair to sacrifice the individual's interests if doing so will maximize the satisfaction of the majority.

5. The author's stance toward Rawls's theory is most accurately described as one of

(A) scholarly neutrality with respect both to its objectives and its development

(B) disdain for its pretensions camouflaged by declarations of respect for its author

(C) sympathy with its recommendations tempered with skepticism about its cogency

(D) enthusiasm for its aims mingled with doubts about its practicality

(E) admiration for its ingenuity coupled with misgivings about some of its implications

6. Which one of the following would, if true, most call into question the claim in lines 49–51 of the passage?

(A) Most people value the fulfillment of their own preferences over the fulfillment of the preferences of strangers.

(B) It is impossible in practice for people to be ignorant of their stations in life, abilities, and tastes.

(C) Some people would be willing to risk a complete loss of one primary good for the chance of obtaining an enormous amount of another primary good.

(D) Few people believe that they would be satisfied with only a minimum amount of primary goods.

(E) People tend to overestimate the resources available for distribution and to underestimate their own needs.

GO ON TO THE NEXT PAGE.

This passage was adapted from an article written by three economists.

Roughly 40 percent of the African American population of the Southern United States left the South between 1915 and 1960, primarily for the industrial cities of the North. While there was some African
(5) American migration to the North during the nineteenth century, most accounts point to 1915 as the start of what historians call the Great Migration. There were at least three catalysts of the Great Migration. First, World War I increased labor demand in the industrial
(10) North. Second, the war in Europe cut off immigration, which led many Northern employers to send labor agents to recruit African American labor in the South. Finally, a boll weevil infestation ruined cotton crops and reduced labor demand in much of the South in
(15) the 1910s and 1920s.

In short, the Great Migration began in 1915 and not earlier, because it was only then that the North–South income gap became large enough to start such a large-scale migration. Less clear, however, is
(20) why migration continued, and even accelerated, in subsequent decades, at the same time that North–South income differences were narrowing.

We propose that once started, migration develops momentum over time as current migration reduces the
(25) difficulty and cost of future migration. Economists have typically assumed that people migrate if their expected earnings in the destination exceed those of the origin enough to outweigh the difficulties and one-time costs of migration. Previous research
(30) suggests that the difficulties and costs arise from several sources. First, the uncertainty that potential migrants face concerning housing and labor-market conditions in the destination presents a significant hindrance. Second, there is the simple cost in terms of
(35) time and money of physically moving from the origin to the destination. Third, new migrants must familiarize themselves with local labor- and housing-market institutions once they arrive; they must find housing and work, and they must often
(40) adapt to a new culture or language.

Empirical studies show that during the Great Migration, information was passed through letters that were often read by dozens of people and through conversation when migrants made trips back to their
(45) home communities. Thus early migrants provided information about labor- and housing-market conditions to friends and relatives who had not yet made the trip. First-time African American migrants often traveled with earlier migrants returning to the
(50) North after a visit to the South, which reduced physical costs. Additionally, previous migrants reduced new migrants' cost of adapting to a new locale and culture by providing them with temporary housing, food, and even credit. Previous migrants
(55) also provided a cultural cushion for later migrants, so that they did not have to struggle as hard with their new surroundings.

7. Which one of the following most accurately expresses the main point of the passage?

(A) Approximately 40 percent of the African American population left the Southern U.S. between 1915 and 1960—an event historians refer to as the Great Migration.

(B) The Great Migration was triggered by an increased labor demand in the North due to the onset of World War I and a reduced labor demand in the South due to a boll weevil infestation.

(C) Because earlier migrants helped defray the financial costs of migration for later migrants, African American migration to the North accelerated at a time when income differences were narrowing.

(D) In migration movements, earlier migrants reduce the physical costs of moving and provide a cultural and linguistic cushion for later migrants.

(E) Although the Great Migration was initially triggered by the income differential between the North and South, other factors must be cited in order to explain its duration over several decades.

8. According to the passage, the Great Migration did not start earlier than 1915 because

(A) the income gap between the North and South was not large enough to induce people to migrate

(B) the cost of living in the North was prohibitively high before World War I

(C) industrial jobs in the North required specialized training unavailable in the South

(D) previous migration had yet to develop sufficient momentum to induce further migration

(E) agricultural jobs in the South paid very well before the boll weevil infestation

9. The third and fourth paragraphs of the passage function primarily to

(A) cast doubt upon a historical explanation presented in the first paragraph

(B) survey the repercussions of a historical event described in the first two paragraphs

(C) derive a historical model from evidence presented in the first two paragraphs

(D) answer a question raised in the second paragraph about a historical event

(E) provide additional evidence for historical claims made in the first paragraph

GO ON TO THE NEXT PAGE.

10. The authors of the passage would be most likely to agree with which one of the following statements?

(A) Expected financial gains alone may not be a reliable indicator of the likelihood that an individual will migrate.

(B) A complete explanation of the Great Migration must begin with an account of what triggered nineteenth-century migrations to the North.

(C) The Great Migration is not parallel in its broadest patterns to most other known migration movements.

(D) Most large-scale migrations can be adequately explained in terms of the movement of people from lower- to higher-income regions.

(E) Large-scale migrations generally did not occur until the early twentieth century, when significant interregional income differences arose as a result of rapid industrialization.

11. The primary purpose of the last sentence of the second paragraph is to

(A) indicate why previous research on the Great Migration has been misguided

(B) extend the authors' explanation of the causes of the Great Migration to include later events

(C) challenge the traditional view that Northern wages were higher than Southern wages prior to 1915

(D) present a fact about the Great Migration that the authors seek to explain

(E) suggest that the Great Migration cannot be explained

12. The passage provides the most support for which one of the following statements?

(A) The highest-paying agricultural jobs in the South prior to 1915 did not pay more than the lowest-paying manufacturing jobs in the North.

(B) The overall cost of migrating from the South to the North in the twentieth century was lower for the earliest migrants because there were more of the highest-paying jobs available for them to choose from.

(C) The North–South income gap increased around 1915 because of the increase in demand for labor in the North and the decrease in demand for labor in the South.

(D) The average wages in the South, though dramatically lower than the average wages in the North, held roughly steady for all workers during the 1910s and 1920s.

(E) Most migrants in the Great Migration made at least one trip back to the South to provide help and information to other people who were considering migrating as well.

13. Which one of the following, if true, would provide the most support for the authors' analysis of the Great Migration?

(A) The average amount of time it took new migrants to find employment in the North grew at a steady rate between 1915 and 1960.

(B) In general, communities of African Americans in the North consisted largely of individuals who shared a common geographic place of origin in the South.

(C) Housing prices in the North fluctuated between high and low extremes from 1915 to 1960, while housing prices in the South remained relatively constant.

(D) To maintain a steady rate of recruitment after World War I, Northern employers had to send more and more labor agents to recruit employees in the South.

(E) There was a large-scale reverse migration of African Americans back to Southern locations later in the twentieth century.

GO ON TO THE NEXT PAGE.

Passage A

Insider-trading law makes it a crime to make stock transactions, or help others make stock transactions, based on information you have ahead of the general public because of your special position
(5) within a company.

However, trading based on information you have that everyone else doesn't—isn't this part of the very definition of a functioning stock market? The entire field of stock brokering is based on people gaining
(10) knowledge that others don't have and then using it to profit themselves or their clients. If you analyze a stock, decide that it is overvalued, and sell it, you are taking advantage of knowledge that many others don't have. That doesn't make you a criminal; it means
(15) you've done your homework.

Stock markets work best when all the relevant information about a company is spread as widely as possible, as quickly as possible. Stock prices represent a constantly shifting amalgamation of everyone's
(20) information about and evaluations of a company's value. It helps when those who have accurate information about changing circumstances are permitted to act so that stock prices reflect them.

Someone selling a stock because they know
(25) something will happen soon that will lower the stock's value helps spread the knowledge that the price ought to be dropping. Such actions help ensure that stock prices do reflect a more accurate assessment of all the relevant facts. That's good for everyone in the
(30) stock market.

When contemplating insider-trading law, it helps to consider a far more widespread practice: "insider nontrading"—stock sales or purchases that would have been made, but aren't because of inside knowledge.
(35) This is certainly happening every day, and rightfully so. No one would think to lock someone up for it.

Passage B

One of the basic principles of the stock market is transparency. In a transparent market, information that influences trading decisions is available to all
(40) participants at the same time. Success in the market can then be gained only by skill in analyzing the information and making good investing decisions. In a transparent stock market, everyone has the same chance of making a good investment, and success is
(45) based on individual merit and skill.

In insider-trading situations, some people make investment decisions based on information that other people don't have. People who don't have access to the inside information can't make similarly informed
(50) investment decisions. That unfairly compromises the market: people with inside information can make informed trade decisions far before everyone else, making it difficult or impossible for other people to earn money in the stock market.
(55) This, in turn, causes a loss of investor confidence and could ultimately destroy the market. People invest in the stock market because they believe they can make money. The whole point of capital investments

is to make good investing decisions and make money
(60) over time. If investors believe they can't make money, they won't invest. Undermining investor confidence would thus deny companies access to the funds they need to grow and be successful, and it could ultimately lead to widespread financial repercussions.

14. Both passages are primarily concerned with answering which one of the following questions?

(A) How is insider trading defined?
(B) Should there be severer penalties for insider trading?
(C) Why do investors engage in insider trading?
(D) Is insider trading harmful to the stock market?
(E) What is the best means of regulating insider trading?

15. In their attitudes toward stock trades based on inside information, the author of passage A and the author of passage B, respectively, may be most accurately described as

(A) positive and neutral
(B) positive and negative
(C) neutral and negative
(D) neutral and neutral
(E) negative and negative

16. The authors would be most likely to agree that

(A) insider trading tends to undermine investor confidence in the stock market
(B) all information should be available to all market participants at the same time
(C) it is appropriate for investors to seek to gain an advantage by superior stock analysis
(D) insider nontrading should be regulated to the same extent as insider trading
(E) insider trading is the best means for disseminating information possessed by insiders

GO ON TO THE NEXT PAGE.

17. Which one of the following laws would conform most
    closely to the position articulated by the author of
    passage A but not that articulated by the author of
    passage B?

    (A)   a law that prohibits trading based on
           information that is not shared by everyone
    (B)   a law that permits trading based on information
           gained from analysis of a stock but prohibits
           trading based on information obtained from
           one's position within a company
    (C)   a law that prohibits trading that could
           reasonably be expected to undermine investors'
           confidence in the stock market
    (D)   a law that legalizes selling based on inside
           information that a stock's price ought to be
           dropping but prohibits buying based on inside
           information that it should be rising
    (E)   a law that legalizes trading based on inside
           information, as long as that information is not
           acquired by theft or other unlawful means

18. Passage A, unlike passage B, seeks to advance its
    argument by

    (A)   applying general principles to particular examples
    (B)   pointing out similarities between a controversial
           activity and uncontroversial ones
    (C)   describing the consequences that would result
           from allowing an activity
    (D)   showing how a specific activity relates to a
           larger context
    (E)   examining the motivations of an activity's
           participants

19. The passages' references to the analysis of information
    about stocks (lines 11–14, lines 40–42) are related in
    which one of the following ways?

    (A)   Passage A presents it as unnecessary, since
           all relevant information is already reflected
           in stock prices, whereas passage B presents
           it as necessary for making sound investment
           decisions.
    (B)   Passage A uses it as an example of an activity
           that compensates for the market's lack of
           transparency, whereas passage B uses it as an
           example of an activity whose viability is
           conditional upon the transparency of the market.
    (C)   Passage A presents it as an activity that gives
           some investors an unfair advantage over
           others, whereas passage B presents it as an
           activity that increases the transparency of
           the market.
    (D)   Passage A presents it as comparable to the
           acquisition of inside information, whereas
           passage B contrasts it with the acquisition
           of inside information.
    (E)   Passage A treats it as an option available only
           to brokers and other stock-market professionals,
           whereas passage B treats it as an option
           available to ordinary investors as well.

GO ON TO THE NEXT PAGE.

There are some basic conceptual problems hovering about the widespread use of brain scans as pictures of mental activity. As applied to medical diagnosis (for example, in diagnosing a brain tumor),
(5) a brain scan is similar in principle to an X-ray: it is a way of seeing inside the body. Its value is straightforward and indubitable. However, the use of neuroimaging in psychology is a fundamentally different kind of enterprise. It is a research method the
(10) validity of which depends on a premise: that the mind can be analyzed into separate and distinct modules, or components, and further that these modules are instantiated in localized brain regions. This premise is known as the modular theory of mind.

(15) It may in fact be that neither mental activity, nor the physical processes that constitute it, are decomposable into independent modules. Psychologist William Uttal contends that rather than distinct entities, the various mental processes are likely to be
(20) properties of a more general mental activity that is distributed throughout the brain. It cannot be said, for instance, that the amygdala is the seat of emotion and the prefrontal cortex is the seat of reason, as the popular press sometimes claims. For when I get angry,
(25) I generally do so for a reason. To cleanly separate emotion from reason-giving makes a hash of human experience.

But if this critique of the modular theory of mind is valid, how can one account for the fact that brain
(30) scans do, in fact, reveal well-defined areas that "light up" in response to various cognitive tasks? In the case of functional magnetic resonance imaging (fMRI), what you are seeing when you look at a brain scan is actually the result of a subtraction. The fMRI is
(35) usually interpreted as a map of the rate of oxygen use in different parts of the brain, which stands as a measure of metabolic activity. But what it actually depicts is the differential rate of oxygen use: one first takes a baseline measurement in the control condition,
(40) then a second measurement while the subject is performing some cognitive task. The baseline measurement is then subtracted from the on-task measurement. The reasoning, seemingly plausible, is that whatever remains after the subtraction represents
(45) the metabolic activity associated solely with the cognitive task in question.

One immediately obvious (but usually unremarked) problem is that this method obscures the fact that the entire brain is active in both conditions.
(50) A false impression of neat functional localization is given by differential brain scans that subtract out all the distributed brain functions. This subtractive method produces striking images of the brain at work. But isn't the modular theory of mind ultimately
(55) attractive in part because it is illustrated so well by the products of the subtractive method?

20. Which one of the following most accurately states the main point of the passage?

(A) In spite of troubling conceptual problems surrounding brain scan technology, its use in psychological research on mental activity has grown rapidly.

(B) The use of brain scans to depict mental activity relies on both a questionable premise and a misleading methodological approach.

(C) Contrary to what is usually asserted in the popular press, reason and emotion are probably not located in the prefrontal cortex and the amygdala, respectively.

(D) Although the fMRI is usually interpreted as a measure of metabolic activity in the brain, this interpretation is misguided and therefore leads to false results.

(E) The modular theory of mind has gained wide currency precisely because it is illustrated effectively by the images produced by the subtractive method.

21. According to the modular theory of mind, as described in the passage, mental activity

(A) consists of distinct components in localized areas of the brain

(B) requires at least some metabolic activity in all parts of the brain

(C) involves physical processes over which people have only limited control

(D) is localized in the amygdala and the prefrontal cortex

(E) generally involves some sort of reason-giving

22. The author of the passage would be most likely to agree with which one of the following statements regarding the subtractive method?

(A) Because the subtractive method masks distributed brain functions, empirical results derived using the method are invalid for medical applications.

(B) The subtractive method results in images that strongly support Uttal's view that mental processes are simply properties of a more general mental activity.

(C) Brain scans of individuals experiencing anger that were produced using the subtractive method show that emotions are not actually seated in the amygdala.

(D) The subtractive method seems to strongly support the modular theory of mind because it creates an illusion that brain functions are localized.

(E) The view that the subtractive method depicts differential rates of oxygen use in the brain is based on a fundamental misconception of the method.

GO ON TO THE NEXT PAGE.

23. A central function of the final paragraph of the passage is to

(A) — criticize the research results described in the third paragraph on the grounds that they are incompatible with the basic premise described in the first paragraph

(B) suggest that the position articulated in the first paragraph needs to be modified to accommodate the results outlined in the third paragraph

(C) contend that the research method detailed in the third paragraph relies upon an outdated theoretical model described in the second paragraph

(D) argue that the empirical research outlined in the third paragraph points to the inadequacy of the competing views described in the first two paragraphs

(E) show why the type of empirical evidence discussed in the third paragraph does not defeat the argument presented in the second paragraph

24. The author draws an analogy between brain scans and X-rays primarily in order to

(A) contrast a valid use of brain scans with one of more doubtful value

(B) suggest that new technology can influence the popularity of a scientific theory

(C) point to evidence that brain scans are less precise than other available technologies

(D) argue that X-ray images undermine a theory that brain scans are often used to support

(E) show how brain scan technology evolved from older technologies such as X-rays

25. According to the passage, psychologist William Uttal contends that the various mental processes are likely to be

(A) independent modules that are based in different areas of the brain

(B) essentially an amalgamation of emotion and reason

(C) generally uniform in their rates of oxygen use

(D) detectable using brain scans enhanced by means of the subtractive method

(E) features of a general mental activity that is spread throughout the brain

26. Which one of the following statements is most strongly supported by the passage?

(A) Although there are important exceptions, most cognition does in fact depend on independent modules located in specific regions of the brain.

(B) The modular theory of mind holds that regions of the brain that are not engaged in a specific cognitive task have a rate of oxygen use that is close to zero.

(C) During the performance of certain cognitive tasks, the areas of the brain that are most metabolically active show a rate of oxygen use that is higher than that of the rest of the brain.

(D) The baseline measurements of oxygen use taken for use in the subtractive method show that some regions of the brain have high metabolic activity at all times.

(E) When a brain scan subject experiences anger, the subtractive method shows several regions of the brain as "lit up" with metabolic activity.

27. Which one of the following is most analogous to the manner in which fMRI scans of brain activity are typically interpreted, as described in the last two paragraphs?

(A) One particular district in the city voted for the new mayor by an unusually large margin, so the mayor could not have won without that district.

(B) A store launched a yearlong advertising campaign and had an increase in shoppers only during the summer, so the advertisements affected only the summer shoppers.

(C) Much more of the water supply is used by agricultural customers than by residential customers, so it is the agricultural sector that is impacted most severely when droughts occur.

(D) Internet traffic is highest during the evening hours, so most Internet traffic during these peak hours originates in homes rather than in office buildings.

(E) The cheetah is the world's fastest land animal only for short distances, so most cheetahs cannot outrun another land animal over long distances.

S T O P

IF YOU FINISH BEFORE TIME IS CALLED, YOU MAY CHECK YOUR WORK ON THIS SECTION ONLY.
DO NOT WORK ON ANY OTHER SECTION IN THE TEST.

SECTION III

Time—35 minutes

23 Questions

Directions: Each group of questions in this section is based on a set of conditions. In answering some of the questions, it may be useful to draw a rough diagram. Choose the response that most accurately and completely answers each question and blacken the corresponding space on your answer sheet.

Questions 1–5

A teacher will assign each of five students—Juana, Kelly, Lateefah, Mei, and Olga—to exactly one of two research teams, the green team and the red team. One team will have two members, and the other will have three members. One member of each team will be designated as facilitator. The assignment must satisfy the following conditions:

Juana is assigned to a different team than Olga is.
Lateefah is assigned to the green team.
Kelly is not a facilitator.
Olga is a facilitator.

1. Which one of the following could be an accurate listing of the members and facilitators of the two research teams?

(A) green team: Juana, Lateefah, Olga (facilitator)
red team: Kelly, Mei (facilitator)
(B) green team: Kelly, Lateefah (facilitator), Olga
red team: Juana, Mei (facilitator)
(C) green team: Kelly, Lateefah, Olga (facilitator)
red team: Juana (facilitator), Mei
(D) green team: Kelly, Mei, Olga (facilitator)
red team: Juana (facilitator), Lateefah
(E) green team: Lateefah, Olga (facilitator)
red team: Juana, Kelly (facilitator), Mei

GO ON TO THE NEXT PAGE.

2. Which one of the following must be true?

   (A)   Juana is assigned to the red team.
   (B)   Lateefah is a facilitator.
   (C)   Olga is assigned to the green team.
   (D)   Juana and Mei are not both facilitators.
   (E)   Neither Juana nor Kelly is a facilitator.

3. Which one of the following must be false?

   (A)   Lateefah is a facilitator, and she is assigned to
         the same team as Kelly is.
   (B)   Mei is a facilitator, and she is assigned to the
         same team as Kelly is.
   (C)   Olga is a facilitator, and she is assigned to the
         same team as Mei is.
   (D)   Lateefah is a facilitator, and she is assigned to a
         different team than Juana is.
   (E)   Mei is a facilitator, and she is assigned to a
         different team than Olga is.

4. If Lateefah is a facilitator, then which one of the
   following could be true?

   (A)   Juana and Kelly are both assigned to the
         red team.
   (B)   Juana and Mei are both assigned to the
         red team.
   (C)   Lateefah and Olga are both assigned to the
         green team.
   (D)   Mei and Olga are both assigned to the
         green team.
   (E)   Mei and Olga are both assigned to the red team.

5. If Mei is assigned to the green team, then which one of
   the following must be true?

   (A)   Juana is assigned to the green team.
   (B)   Kelly is assigned to the red team.
   (C)   Olga is assigned to the green team.
   (D)   Lateefah is a facilitator.
   (E)   Mei is a facilitator.

g - L, M, O
r - K, J

GO ON TO THE NEXT PAGE.

Questions 6–11

An author is planning to write a mystery novel consisting of seven chapters, chapter 1 through chapter 7. Each of seven different clues—R, S, T, U, W, X, and Z—is to be mentioned exactly <u>once</u>, one clue per chapter. The order in which the clues are mentioned is subject to the following constraints:

T cannot be mentioned in chapter 1.

T must be mentioned before W, and there must be exactly two chapters separating the mention of T from the mention of W.

S and Z cannot be mentioned in adjacent chapters.

W and X cannot be mentioned in adjacent chapters.

U and X must be mentioned in adjacent chapters.

6. Which one of the following could be the order in which the clues are mentioned, from the first chapter through the seventh?

(A)   S, T, Z, X, U, W, R
(B)   T, X, U, W, S, R, Z
(C)   U, S, X, T, Z, R, W
(D)   X, U, T, Z, R, W, S
(E)   Z, R, T, U, X, W, S

GO ON TO THE NEXT PAGE.

7. If X is mentioned in chapter 1, which one of the following could be true?

   (A)   R is mentioned in chapter 3.
   (B)   R is mentioned in chapter 7.
   (C)   S is mentioned in chapter 2.
   (D)   W is mentioned in chapter 5.
   (E)   Z is mentioned in chapter 3.

8. If U is mentioned in chapter 3, which one of the following could be true?

   (A)   R is mentioned in chapter 1.
   (B)   R is mentioned in chapter 5.
   (C)   S is mentioned in chapter 7.
   (D)   W is mentioned in chapter 6.
   (E)   X is mentioned in chapter 4.

9. If Z is mentioned in chapter 7, which one of the following could be true?

   (A)   R is mentioned in chapter 3.
   (B)   S is mentioned in chapter 3.
   (C)   T is mentioned in chapter 4.
   (D)   U is mentioned in chapter 1.
   (E)   X is mentioned in chapter 5.

10. Which one of the following could be true?

   (A)   R is mentioned in chapter 7.
   (B)   T is mentioned in chapter 5.
   (C)   U is mentioned in chapter 7.
   (D)   W is mentioned in chapter 3.
   (E)   X is mentioned in chapter 6.

11. Which one of the following, if substituted for the constraint that T cannot be mentioned in chapter 1, would have the same effect in determining the order in which the clues are mentioned?

   (A)   U cannot be mentioned in chapter 2.
   (B)   W cannot be mentioned in chapter 4.
   (C)   X cannot be mentioned in chapter 6.
   (D)   U must be mentioned in an earlier chapter than T.
   (E)   X must be mentioned in an earlier chapter than W.

GO ON TO THE NEXT PAGE.

Questions 12–18

At an upcoming exhibition, four art students—Franz, Greene, Hidalgo, and Isaacs—will each display exactly two paintings—an oil and a watercolor. Exactly two paintings will be displayed on each of the walls of the exhibition room—walls 1, 2, 3, and 4—with one painting in the upper position and one in the lower position. The following conditions will apply:

No wall has only watercolors displayed on it.

No wall has the work of only one student displayed on it.

No wall has both a painting by Franz and a painting by Isaacs displayed on it.

Greene's watercolor is displayed in the upper position of the wall on which Franz's oil is displayed.

Isaacs's oil is displayed in the lower position of wall 4.

12. Which one of the following could be an accurate list of the paintings displayed in the <u>lower</u> position on walls 1 through 4, listed in that order?

(A) Franz's oil, Franz's watercolor, Greene's oil, Isaacs's oil

(B) Franz's oil, Hidalgo's watercolor, Isaacs's watercolor, Isaacs's oil

(C) Greene's oil, Franz's oil, Isaacs's oil, Hidalgo's oil

(D) Hidalgo's oil, Greene's oil, Greene's watercolor, Isaacs's oil

(E) Hidalgo's watercolor, Franz's oil, Greene's oil, Isaacs's oil

GO ON TO THE NEXT PAGE.

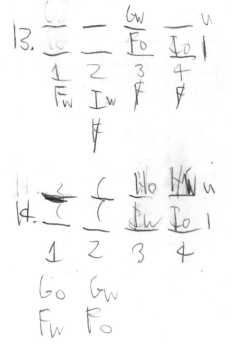

13. If Isaacs's watercolor is displayed on wall 2 and Franz's oil is displayed on wall 3, which one of the following must be displayed on wall 1?

(A) Franz's watercolor
(B) Greene's oil
(C) Greene's watercolor
(D) Hidalgo's oil
(E) Hidalgo's watercolor

14. If Hidalgo's oil is displayed on wall 2, which one of the following could also be displayed on wall 2?

(A) Franz's oil
(B) Greene's watercolor
(C) Greene's oil
(D) Hidalgo's watercolor
(E) Isaacs's watercolor

15. If Greene's oil is displayed on the same wall as Franz's watercolor, which one of the following must be true?

(A) Greene's oil is displayed in an upper position.
(B) Hidalgo's watercolor is displayed on the same wall as Isaacs's watercolor.
(C) Hidalgo's oil is displayed in an upper position.
(D) Hidalgo's oil is displayed on the same wall as Isaacs's watercolor.
(E) Isaacs's watercolor is displayed in a lower position.

16. If Franz's oil is displayed on wall 1, which one of the following could be true?

(A) Franz's watercolor is displayed on wall 4.
(B) Greene's oil is displayed on wall 2.
(C) Greene's watercolor is displayed on wall 2.
(D) Hidalgo's watercolor is displayed on wall 3.
(E) Isaacs's oil is displayed on wall 1.

17. Which one of the following could be true?

(A) Both of Franz's paintings and both of Greene's paintings are displayed in lower positions.
(B) Both of Franz's paintings and both of Greene's paintings are displayed in upper positions.
(C) Both of Franz's paintings and both of Hidalgo's paintings are displayed in upper positions.
(D) Both of Greene's paintings and both of Hidalgo's paintings are displayed in lower positions.
(E) Both of Greene's paintings and both of Hidalgo's paintings are displayed in upper positions.

18. Which one of the following CANNOT be true?

(A) Franz's watercolor is displayed on the same wall as Greene's oil.
(B) Franz's watercolor is displayed on the same wall as Hidalgo's oil.
(C) Greene's oil is displayed in an upper position.
(D) Hidalgo's watercolor is displayed in a lower position.
(E) Isaacs's watercolor is displayed on the same wall as Hidalgo's oil.

GO ON TO THE NEXT PAGE.

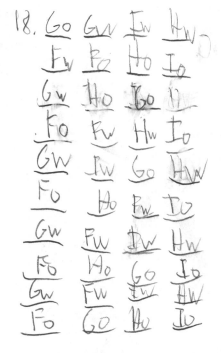

Questions 19–23

Three real estate companies—RealProp, Southco, and Trustcorp—are considering trading buildings with one another. Each building they own is categorized as either class 1, class 2, or class 3, depending on its approximate value:

RealProp owns the Garza Tower (class 1), the Yates House (class 3), and the Zimmer House (class 3).

Southco owns the Flores Tower (class 1) and the Lynch Building (class 2).

Trustcorp owns the King Building, the Meyer Building, and the Ortiz Building, all of which are class 2.

Each trade must be of exactly <u>one</u> of the following <u>three</u> kinds:

Trading one building for one other building of the same class

Trading one class 1 building for two class 2 buildings

Trading one class 2 building for two class 3 buildings

R
S
T

1 2 3

R: GT(1), YH(3), ZH(3)

S: FT(1) LB(2)

T: KB(2), MB(2), OB(2)

19. Which one of the following could be the buildings owned by the three companies after only one trade is made?

(A) RealProp: the Flores Tower and the Garza Tower
Southco: the Lynch Building, the Yates House, and the Zimmer House
Trustcorp: the King Building, the Meyer Building, and the Ortiz Building

(B) RealProp: the Garza Tower, the King Building, and the Ortiz Building
Southco: the Flores Tower and the Lynch Building
Trustcorp: the Meyer Building, the Yates House, and the Zimmer House

(C) RealProp: the Garza Tower and the Lynch Building
Southco: the Flores Tower, the Yates House, and the Zimmer House
Trustcorp: the King Building, the Meyer Building, and the Ortiz Building

(D) RealProp: the Garza Tower, the Meyer Building, and the Yates House
Southco: the Flores Tower and the Lynch Building
Trustcorp: the King Building, the Ortiz Building, and the Zimmer House

(E) RealProp: the Garza Tower, the Yates House, and the Zimmer House
Southco: the Lynch Building and the Ortiz Building
Trustcorp: the Flores Tower, the King Building, and the Meyer Building

GO ON TO THE NEXT PAGE.

20. Which one of the following CANNOT be true, no matter how many trades are made?

   (A) The buildings owned by RealProp are the Flores Tower and the Garza Tower.
   (B) The buildings owned by Southco are the Flores Tower and the Meyer Building.
   (C) The buildings owned by Southco are the Garza Tower and the Lynch Building.
   (D) The buildings owned by Trustcorp are the Flores Tower and the Ortiz Building.
   (E) The buildings owned by Trustcorp are the Garza Tower and the Meyer Building.

21. If RealProp owns only class 2 buildings after some number of trades, which one of the following must be true?

   (A) Trustcorp owns a class 1 building.
   (B) Trustcorp owns the Meyer Building.
   (C) Southco owns a class 2 Building.
   (D) Southco owns both of the class 3 buildings.
   (E) Southco owns the Flores Tower.

22. If Trustcorp owns no class 2 buildings after some number of trades, which one of the following must be true?

   (A) RealProp owns a class 1 building.
   (B) Southco owns only class 2 buildings.
   (C) Southco has made at least one trade with Trustcorp.
   (D) Trustcorp owns the Garza Tower.
   (E) Trustcorp owns the Zimmer House.

23. Which one of the following CANNOT be true, no matter how many trades are made?

   (A) The buildings owned by RealProp are the Lynch Building, the Meyer Building, and the Ortiz Building.
   (B) The buildings owned by Southco are the Garza Tower and the Meyer Building.
   (C) The buildings owned by Southco are the King Building, the Meyer Building, and the Ortiz Building.
   (D) The buildings owned by Trustcorp are the Flores Tower and the Yates House.
   (E) The buildings owned by Trustcorp are the Garza Tower and the Lynch Building.

S T O P

IF YOU FINISH BEFORE TIME IS CALLED, YOU MAY CHECK YOUR WORK ON THIS SECTION ONLY.
DO NOT WORK ON ANY OTHER SECTION IN THE TEST.

SECTION IV

Time—35 minutes

26 Questions

Directions: The questions in this section are based on the reasoning contained in brief statements or passages. For some questions, more than one of the choices could conceivably answer the question. However, you are to choose the best answer; that is, the response that most accurately and completely answers the question. You should not make assumptions that are by commonsense standards implausible, superfluous, or incompatible with the passage. After you have chosen the best answer, blacken the corresponding space on your answer sheet.

1. Community organizer: Before last year's community cleanup, only 77 of the local residents signed up to participate, but then well over 100 actually participated. This year, 85 residents have signed up to participate. Since our community cleanup will be a success if we have at least 100 participants, we can be confident that this year's cleanup will be a success.

The reasoning in the community organizer's argument is most vulnerable to criticism on the grounds that the argument

(A) generalizes about the outcome of an event based on a single observation of a similar situation
(B) takes for granted that people who participated in last year's cleanup will participate this year
(C) confuses a condition that is required for an outcome with one that is sufficient for that outcome
(D) overlooks the possibility that the cleanup will attract participants who are not residents in the community
(E) defines a term in such a way as to ensure that whatever the outcome, it will be considered a positive outcome

2. Bell: Commentators in the media are wrong to criticize the policies Klein implemented. Although her policies are unpopular, they avoided an impending catastrophe. Klein is just the person we need making important decisions in the future.

Soltan: Klein's policies have been effective, but politics matters. In the future, important decisions will need to be made, and she will not have the political support to make them. So she should step down.

Bell and Soltan disagree with each other about which one of the following?

(A) Klein's policies have been effective.
(B) Klein's policies are unpopular.
(C) Klein should step down.
(D) There are important decisions to be made in the future.
(E) Klein's policies were implemented in the face of an impending catastrophe.

3. Psychologist: In our study, participants who were offered the opportunity to purchase a coffee mug were not willing to pay more than $5. If, however, they were given a very similar mug and asked immediately afterwards how much they would be willing to sell it for, most of them held out for more than $5.

Which one of the following, if true, most helps to resolve the apparent discrepancy described above?

(A) A person's assessment of the value of an object depends on his or her evaluation of the inherent properties of the object.
(B) People are usually unable to judge the value of an object when they have possessed it for a long period of time.
(C) The amount a person is willing to spend on an object is determined by the amount that object sold for in the past.
(D) People tend to value an object that they do not own less than they value a very similar object that they already own.
(E) People are more likely to undervalue objects they have been given than objects they have purchased.

GO ON TO THE NEXT PAGE.

4. Ecologist: Before finding a mate, male starlings decorate their nests with fragments of aromatic plants rich in compounds known to kill parasitic insects. Since these parasites are potentially harmful to nestlings, some researchers have hypothesized that the function of these decorations is nestling protection. However, males cease to incorporate such greenery once egg laying starts, which suggests instead that the function of the decorations is to attract females.

Which one of the following, if true, most strengthens the support for the ecologist's conclusion?

(A) Adult starlings are able to defend themselves against parasitic insects.

(B) Male starlings do not decorate their nests in areas with unusually small populations of parasitic insects.

(C) Nestlings grow faster in nests that incorporate aromatic plants than in nests that do not.

(D) Male starlings tend to decorate their nests with a greater number of aromatic plants when a caged female is positioned adjacent to the nest.

(E) The compounds in the aromatic plants used by the male starlings to decorate their nests are harmless to nestlings.

5. A commission has been formed to report on the nation's preparedness for a major natural disaster. The commission's report will not be effective unless the commission speaks with a unified voice. Since individual members of the commission have repeatedly expressed their own opinions about disaster preparedness in the news media well in advance of completion of the report, it will not be effective.

The conclusion of the argument follows logically if which one of the following is assumed?

(A) Commission members who have expressed their opinions about disaster preparedness in the news media have also emphasized their commitment to producing an effective report.

(B) News organizations should not provide a platform for members of the commission to express their opinions about disaster preparedness if doing so will undermine the effectiveness of the commission's report.

(C) The commission will be able to speak with a uniform voice only if individual members' opinions about disaster preparedness are not made public before the report is completed.

(D) If commission members had not expressed their opinions about disaster preparedness in the news media before the report was completed, there would have been much public speculation about what those views were.

(E) The commission's report will not be effective if some of the commission members already had opinions about the nation's disaster preparedness even before the commission was formed.

6. Engineer: Wide roads free of obstructions have been shown to encourage drivers to take more risks. Likewise, a technical fix to slow or reverse global warming by blocking out a portion of the sun's rays would encourage more carbon dioxide emissions, which might cause more global warming in the future.

The engineer's argument can most reasonably be interpreted as invoking which one of the following principles?

(A) Conditions that create a feeling of security also encourage risk taking.

(B) Problems created by humans require human-created solutions.

(C) Technical fixes are inevitably temporary.

(D) Technical fixes cannot discourage risk-taking behavior.

(E) The longer a problem goes unresolved, the worse it becomes.

7. Although some animals exhibit a mild skin reaction to urushiol, an oil produced by plants such as poison oak and poison ivy, it appears that only humans develop painful rashes from touching it. In fact, wood rats even use branches from the poison oak plant to build their nests. Therefore, urushiol probably did not evolve in these plants as a chemical defense.

Which one of the following, if true, adds the most support for the conclusion of the argument?

(A) Wood rats build their nests using dead, brittle branches, not live ones.

(B) A number of different animals use poison oak and poison ivy as food sources.

(C) It is common for plants to defend themselves by producing chemical substances.

(D) In approximately 85 percent of the human population, very small amounts of urushiol can cause a rash.

(E) Poison oak and poison ivy grow particularly well in places where humans have altered natural forest ecosystems.

GO ON TO THE NEXT PAGE.

8. Politician: Some cities have reversed the decay of aging urban areas by providing tax incentives and zoning variances that encourage renovation and revitalization in selected areas. But such legislation should not be commended. Its principal beneficiaries have turned out to be well-to-do professionals who could afford the cost of restoring deteriorating buildings; the long-term residents these programs were intended to help now face displacement due to increased rent and taxes.

Which one of the following principles, if valid, most helps to justify the politician's criticism?

(A) Evaluation of legislation should take into account actual results, not intentions alone.
(B) The wealthier members of a community should not have undue influence on its governance.
(C) A community's tax laws and zoning regulations should apply equally to all individuals within selected areas.
(D) Legislation that is not to anyone's benefit should not be commended.
(E) Laws that give advantage to the well-to-do can also benefit society as a whole.

9. Pundit: It is good to have national leaders voted out of office after a few years. The reason is that reforms are generally undertaken early in a new government. If leaders do not act quickly to solve a problem and it becomes an issue later, then they must either deny that there is a problem or deny that anything could have been done about it; otherwise, they will have to admit responsibility for the persistence of the problem.

Which one of the following most accurately expresses the main conclusion of the pundit's argument?

(A) If national leaders who fail to solve problems are voted out of office after a few years, new leaders will be more motivated to solve problems.
(B) National leaders who stay in power too long tend to deny responsibility for problems that they could have dealt with earlier.
(C) National leaders are most likely to undertake reforms early in a new government.
(D) National leaders who immediately respond to problems upon taking office should be given enough time to succeed at solving them.
(E) National leaders should be removed from office every few years by the voting in of new leaders.

10. Farmer: Agricultural techniques such as crop rotation that do not use commercial products may solve agricultural problems at least as well as any technique, such as pesticide application, that does use such products. Nonetheless, no private for-profit corporation will sponsor research that is unlikely to lead to marketable products. Thus, for the most part, only government-sponsored research investigates agricultural techniques that do not use commercial products.

Which one of the following, if true, most strengthens the farmer's argument?

(A) The government sponsors at least some investigations of agricultural techniques that are considered likely to solve agricultural problems and do not use commercial products.
(B) For almost any agricultural problem, there is at least one agricultural technique that does not use commercial products but that would solve that agricultural problem.
(C) Investigations of agricultural techniques are rarely sponsored by individuals or by any entity other than private for-profit corporations or the government.
(D) Most if not all investigations of agricultural techniques that use commercial products are sponsored by private for-profit corporations.
(E) Most if not all government-sponsored agricultural research investigates agricultural techniques that do not use commercial products.

GO ON TO THE NEXT PAGE.

11. University spokesperson: Most of the students surveyed at the university said they would prefer that the current food vendor be replaced with a different food vendor next year. Several vendors have publicly expressed interest in working for the university. For a variety of reasons, however, the only alternative to the current vendor is Hall Dining Services, which served as the university's food vendor up until this past year. Since, other things being equal, the preferences of the majority of students should be adhered to, we should rehire Hall Dining next year.

The spokesperson's argument is most vulnerable to criticism on the grounds that it

(A) overlooks the possibility that the students surveyed were unaware that only Hall Dining Services could be hired if the current vendor were not hired

(B) relies on a sample that is likely to be unrepresentative

(C) overlooks the possibility that student preference is not the only factor to be considered when it comes to deciding which food vendor the university should hire

(D) overlooks the possibility that there is disagreement among students concerning the issue of food vendors

(E) argues that a certain action ought to be undertaken merely on the grounds that it would be popular

12. On average, cats fed canned cat food eat fewer ounces of food per day than do cats fed dry cat food; the canned food contains more calories per ounce than does the dry food. Nonetheless, feeding a cat canned cat food typically costs more per day than does feeding it dry cat food.

Which one of the following is most strongly supported by the information above?

(A) On average, cats fed canned cat food eat more calories per day than do cats fed dry cat food.

(B) Typically, cats are fed either canned cat food or dry cat food, or both.

(C) How much it costs to feed a cat a given kind of food depends only on how many calories per ounce that food contains.

(D) On average, it costs no less to feed a cat that eats fewer ounces of food per day than it does to feed a cat that eats more ounces of food per day.

(E) Canned cat food typically costs more per ounce than does dry cat food.

13. The Frauenkirche in Dresden, a historic church destroyed by bombing in World War II, has been reconstructed to serve as a place for church services and cultural events. The foundation doing the reconstruction took extraordinary care to return the church to its original form. It is a puzzle, then, why the foundation chose not to rebuild the eighteenth-century baroque organ originally designed for the church and instead built a modern organ, even though a donor had offered to pay the full cost of rebuilding the original.

Which one of the following, if true, would most help to resolve the puzzle described above?

(A) An eighteenth-century baroque organ cannot adequately produce much of the organ music now played in church services and concerts.

(B) The organ originally designed for the church had some features that modern organs lack.

(C) The donation for rebuilding the original eighteenth-century baroque organ was designated for that purpose alone.

(D) By the time the church was destroyed in World War II, the eighteenth-century baroque organ had been modified several times.

(E) In the eighteenth century, the organ played an important role in church services at the Frauenkirche.

14. Principle: A government should reduce taxes on imports if doing so would financially benefit many consumers in its domestic economy. There is a notable exception, however: it should never reduce import taxes if one or more of its domestic industries would be significantly harmed by the added competition.

Conclusion: The government should not reduce taxes on textile imports.

Which one of the following is a statement from which the conclusion can be properly drawn using the principle?

(A) Reducing taxes on textile imports would not financially benefit many consumers in the domestic economy.

(B) Reducing taxes on textile imports would financially benefit some consumers in the domestic economy but would not benefit the domestic textile industry.

(C) The domestic textile industry faces significant competition in many of its export markets.

(D) The domestic textile industry and consumers in the domestic economy would benefit less from reductions in taxes on textile imports than they would from other measures.

(E) The added competition produced by any reduction of taxes on imports would significantly harm the domestic textile industry.

15. Global warming has contributed to a rise in global sea level not only because it causes glaciers and ice sheets to melt, but also simply because when water is heated its volume increases. But this rise in global sea level is less than it otherwise would be, since over the years artificial reservoirs have been built all around the world that collectively contain a great deal of water that would otherwise reach the sea.

Which one of the following can most reasonably be concluded on the basis of the information above?

(A) The exact magnitude of the rise in global sea level is in dispute.

(B) Rises in global sea level that occurred before the world's reservoirs were built are difficult to explain.

(C) Little is known about the contribution of global warming to the rise in global sea level.

(D) The amount of water in the world's reservoirs is about equal to the amount of water that results from the melting of glaciers and ice sheets.

(E) The amount of water that results from the melting of glaciers and ice sheets cannot be determined by looking at the rise in global sea level alone.

16. Last year, a software company held a contest to generate ideas for their new logo. According to the rules, everyone who entered the contest would receive several prizes, including a T-shirt with the company's new logo. Juan has a T-shirt with the company's new logo, so he must have entered the contest.

The reasoning in the argument is flawed in that the argument

(A) infers a causal relationship when the evidence only supports a correlation

(B) takes a condition that is sufficient for a particular outcome as one that is necessary for that outcome

(C) infers that every member of a group has a feature in common on the grounds that the group as a whole has that feature

(D) has a premise that presupposes the truth of the conclusion

(E) constructs a generalization on the basis of a single instance

17. When expert witnesses give testimony, jurors often do not understand the technical information and thereby are in no position to evaluate such testimony. Although expert witnesses on opposite sides often make conflicting claims, the expert witnesses on both sides frequently seem competent, leaving the jury unable to assess the reliability of their testimonies.

The statements above, if true, most strongly support which one of the following?

(A) There should be limits placed on how much technical information can be considered by both sides in preparing a legal case.

(B) Jury decisions in cases involving expert witness testimonies are not always determined by the reliability of those testimonies.

(C) Jurors who understand the technical information presented in a case can usually assess its legal implications accurately.

(D) Jury members should generally be selected on the basis of their technical expertise.

(E) Expert witnesses who testify on opposite sides in legal cases are likely to agree in their evaluations of technical claims.

18. Tax reformer: The proposed tax reform legislation is being criticized by political groups on the right for being too specific and by political groups on the left for being too vague. Since one and the same statement cannot be both too specific and too vague, the criticisms just go to show that the legislation is framed just as it should be.

Which one of the following is an assumption on which the argument depends?

(A) It is rare for political groups both on the right and on the left to criticize a particular tax reform proposal.

(B) Even an overly specific or vague tax reform proposal can be implemented in a way that produces beneficial results.

(C) The proposed legislation has not been criticized by any group that does not identify itself with the political right or the political left.

(D) The proposed legislation as it is framed was not meant to satisfy either political groups on the right or political groups on the left.

(E) The proposed legislation is not made up of a set of statements some of which are overly specific and some of which are overly vague.

GO ON TO THE NEXT PAGE.

19. Employee: The company I work for has installed website filtering software that blocks access to non-work-related websites. It claims that being able to visit such sites distracts us, keeping us from doing our best work. But offices that have windows or are nicely decorated can be highly distracting too, and no one claims that people do their best work in an undecorated, windowless room.

Which one of the following arguments is most similar in its reasoning to the employee's argument?

(A) Some people advocate moderation in all things. But different people react differently to certain substances, so what counts as a moderate amount of, say, caffeine for you might be too much for me. So to talk about moderation is to fail to take into account people's basic biological differences.

(B) Activists are calling for an electronic device to be banned, for research has shown that prolonged exposure to the device while it is in use causes cancer in laboratory animals. But most chemicals probably cause cancer when administered in very high doses, yet no one would argue that we should ban all these chemicals for that reason.

(C) Acme expects that approximately 1,000 of its employees will retire over the next year. No one would claim that Acme does not need a work force as large as its present one. So Acme will need to hire approximately 1,000 people over the next year.

(D) In many creative writing classes, aspiring writers are told that if the characters they create are not engaging, their novels and stories will not sell. But this does not mean that engaging characters guarantee a sale— publishers and agents often reject manuscripts that emphasize character to the exclusion of other elements.

(E) In the movie industry, a film's success is judged in terms of its profit relative to its cost. This is misguided, because under this criterion an expensive movie that sells just as many tickets as a lower-budget movie would be less successful than the lower-budget movie, which is clearly counterintuitive.

20. At Tromen University this semester, some students taking French Literature 205 are also taking Biology 218. Every student taking Biology 218 at Tromen is a biology major. Therefore, some of the students taking French Literature 205 are not French-literature majors.

The conclusion drawn above follows logically if which one of the following is assumed to be true at Tromen University?

(A) French Literature 205 is a required course for French-literature majors.

(B) Only biology majors are allowed to take Biology 218.

(C) There are more biology majors than there are French-literature majors.

(D) There are more French-literature majors than there are biology majors.

(E) It is not possible to major in both biology and French literature.

21. Critic: To be a literary classic a book must reveal something significant about the human condition. Furthermore, nothing that is unworthy of serious study reveals anything significant about the human condition.

If the critic's statements are true, which one of the following must also be true?

(A) Any book worthy of serious study is a literary classic.

(B) A book is a literary classic only if it is worthy of serious study.

(C) There are no literary classics worthy of serious study.

(D) Some books worthy of serious study do not reveal anything significant about the human condition.

(E) Some books that reveal something significant about the human condition are not literary classics.

GO ON TO THE NEXT PAGE.

22. Scientists once believed that the oversized head, long hind legs, and tiny forelimbs that characterized *Tyrannosaurus rex* developed in order to accommodate the great size and weight of this prehistoric predator. However, this belief must now be abandoned. The nearly complete skeleton of an earlier dinosaur has recently been discovered. This specimen had the characteristic *T. rex* features but was one-fifth the size and one-hundredth the weight.

The answer to which one of the following questions would most help in evaluating the argument?

(A) Was the ratio of the head size of the recently discovered dinosaur to its body size the same as that for *T. rex*?

(B) At what stage in its life did the recently discovered dinosaur die?

(C) Was *T. rex* the largest and heaviest prehistoric predator?

(D) Was the species to which the recently discovered dinosaur belonged related to *T. rex*?

(E) Did the recently discovered dinosaur prey on species as large as those that *T. rex* preyed on?

23. YXK is currently the television network with the highest overall number of viewers. Among YXK's programs, *Bliss* has the highest numbers of viewers. So *Bliss* currently has more viewers than any other program on television.

The flawed reasoning exhibited by the argument above is most similar to that exhibited by which one of the following?

(A) Soccer players suffer more leg injuries, on average, than any other athletes at this university. Linda Wilson has suffered more leg injuries than any other soccer player at this university. Thus, Linda Wilson is the athlete at this university who has suffered the most leg injuries.

(B) Teachers at our school have won more teaching awards, on average, than teachers at any other school in this city. Janna Patel is the teacher who has won the most awards in the city. So Janna Patel is the best teacher at our school.

(C) The Olson Motor Company manufactures the three best-selling automobile models in the country. The Decade is the Olson Motor Company's best-selling model. Thus, the Decade is the best-selling model in the country.

(D) In this city the highest-paid police officer earns more than the highest-paid firefighter, and the lowest-paid police officer earns more than the lowest-paid firefighter. So in this city police officers earn more, on average, than firefighters do.

(E) *Falling Fast* is the film that is currently earning the most at the box office in the country. The most successful film in the country is typically the one that is showing in the most theaters. So *Falling Fast* is probably the film that is currently showing in the most theaters.

GO ON TO THE NEXT PAGE.

24. A contract between two parties is valid only if one party accepts a legitimate offer from the other; an offer is not legitimate if someone in the position of the party to whom it was made would reasonably believe the offer to be made in jest.

The principle stated above, if valid, most helps to justify the reasoning in which one of the following arguments?

(A) Joe made a legitimate offer to buy Sandy's car and Sandy has not rejected the offer. Thus, there was a valid contract.

(B) Kenta accepted Gus's offer to buy a shipment of goods, but Gus, unknown to Kenta, made the offer in jest. Thus, the contract was not valid.

(C) Frank's offer to buy Mindy's business from her was legitimate. Thus, if Mindy is a reasonable person, she will accept the offer.

(D) Hai's offer to sell artworks to Lea was made in such a way that no one in Lea's position would have reasonably believed it to be made in jest. Thus, if Lea accepts the offer, they have a valid contract.

(E) The only offer that Sal made to Veronica was not a legitimate one. Thus, regardless of whether Sal made the offer in jest, there is no valid contract between them.

25. Scientist: A small group of islands near Australia is inhabited by several species of iguana; closely related species also exist in the Americas, but nowhere else. The islands in question formed long after the fragmentation of Gondwana, the ancient supercontinent that included present-day South America and Australia. Thus, these species' progenitors must have rafted on floating debris across the Pacific Ocean from the Americas.

Which one of the following, if true, most weakens the scientist's argument?

(A) A number of animal species that inhabit the islands are not found in the Americas.

(B) Genetic analysis indicates that the iguana species on the islands are different in several respects from those found in the Americas.

(C) Documented cases of iguanas rafting long distances between land masses are uncommon.

(D) Fossils of iguana species closely related to those that inhabit the islands have been found in Australia.

(E) The lineages of numerous plant and animal species found in Australia or in South America date back to a period prior to the fragmentation of Gondwana.

26. A recent archaeological find in what was once the ancient kingdom of Macedonia contains the remains of the largest tomb ever found in the region. It must be the tomb of Alexander the Great since he was the greatest Macedonian in history, and so would have had the largest tomb. After all, he conquered an empire that stretched from Greece to much of Asia, though it collapsed after his death.

The reasoning in the argument is most vulnerable to criticism on the grounds that the argument

(A) takes for granted that greatness can be attained only by military conquest

(B) takes for granted that the largest tomb found so far must be the largest that was built

(C) does not show how the recently discovered tomb compares with other tombs from the same period that have been found in other regions

(D) fails to evaluate the significance of the fact that Alexander's empire did not survive his death

(E) takes for granted that archaeologists can determine the size of the tomb from its remains

S T O P

IF YOU FINISH BEFORE TIME IS CALLED, YOU MAY CHECK YOUR WORK ON THIS SECTION ONLY.
DO NOT WORK ON ANY OTHER SECTION IN THE TEST.

Acknowledgment is made to the following sources from which material has been adapted for use in this test booklet:

Dachary Carey, "What's Wrong With Insider Trading?" ©2009 by Life123, Inc.

William J. Carrington, Enrica Detragiache, and Tara Vishwanath, "Migration with Endogenous Moving Costs" in *The Economic Review.* ©1996 by American Economic Association.

"Carrots Dressed as Sticks: An Experiment on Economic Incentives" in *The Economist.* ©2010 by The Economist Newspaper Limited.

Matthew B. Crawford, "The Limits of Neuro-Talk." ©2008 by The New Atlantis.

Brian Doherty, "Free Samuel Waksal" in *Reason Magazine.* ©2002 by Reason Magazine.

David Gordon, "Going off the Rawls" in *The American Conservative.* ©2008 by The American Conservative. http://www.amconmag.com/print.html?Id=AmConservative-2008jul2.

Topic Code	Print Your Full Name Here		
146379	Last	First	M.I.

Date	Sign Your Name Here
/ /	

LSAC®

Scratch Paper
Do not write your essay in this space.

LSAT® Writing Sample Topic

Directions: The scenario presented below describes two choices, either one of which can be supported on the basis of the information giv‌ Your essay should consider both choices and argue for one over the other, based on the two specified criteria and the facts provided. The‌ is no "right" or "wrong" choice: a reasonable argument can be made for either.

Tony, a beer brewer, is deciding whether to start a production brewery—a brewery that brews, packages, and distributes specialty b‌ to be sold at other locations—or to start a brewpub—a full-service restaurant that serves specialty beer brewed on-site. Using the facts bel‌ write an essay in which you argue for one option over the other based on the following two criteria:

- Tony wants to develop a reputation among beer critics and connoisseurs for producing high-quality beer.
- Tony wants to be able to devote time and resources to the development of new beer offerings.

A production brewery would be able to distribute its products to a large geographic area. In order to get the brewery's beers to be‌ carried in stores or offered at bars, Tony would need to put time into sales and marketing. There are already a large number of breweries t‌ distribute to the area. A production brewery's products are likely to be reviewed by beer critics. A production brewery would initially need to‌ focus on a small number of core offerings. If these proved to be popular, Tony would be able to introduce a series of experimental, limited-edition beer offerings.

A brewpub would draw most of its customers from the local area, which has few brewpubs. Tony would need to oversee the day-to-‌ operations of the restaurant side of the business. Tony might be able to eventually hire a restaurant manager. Many customers at brewpub‌ are interested primarily in the food. Brewpubs are more likely to be reviewed by restaurant critics rather than beer critics. Beer connoisseur‌ enthusiastically seek out brewpubs, and share information about brewpubs on social media. Tony would interact directly with customers at‌ brewpub. Brewpubs brew batches of beer in relatively small volumes and can rotate their offerings relatively quickly.

WPAA

Scratch Paper
Do not write your essay in this space.

FIRST
NAME
(Print)

LAST 4 DIGITS OF SOCIAL
SECURITY/SOCIAL
INSURANCE NO.

MI

TEST
CENTER NO.

SIGNATURE

M   M   D   D   Y   Y
TEST DATE

LSAC ACCOUNT NO.

TOPIC CODE

Writing Sample Response Sheet

DO NOT WRITE
IN THIS SPACE

**Begin your essay in the lined area below.
Continue on the back if you need more space.**

COMPUTING YOUR SCORE

Directions:

1. Use the Answer Key on the next page to check your answers.

2. Use the Scoring Worksheet below to compute your raw score.

3. Use the Score Conversion Chart to convert your raw score into the 120–180 scale.

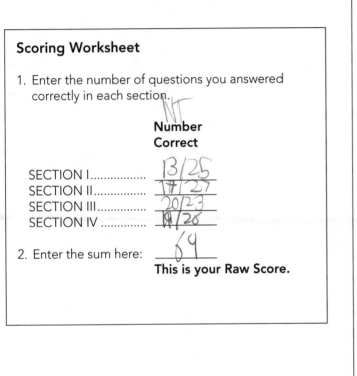

Scoring Worksheet

1. Enter the number of questions you answered correctly in each section.

   Number Correct

   SECTION I................. 13/25
   SECTION II................ 17/27
   SECTION III............... 20/23
   SECTION IV 19/26

2. Enter the sum here: _____ 59
   This is your Raw Score.

Conversion Chart
For Converting Raw Score to the 120–180 LSAT Scaled Score
LSAT Form 6LSN121

Reported Score	Raw Score Lowest	Raw Score Highest
180	100	101
179	99	99
178	98	98
177	97	97
176	*	*
175	96	96
174	95	95
173	94	94
172	93	93
171	92	92
170	90	91
169	89	89
168	87	88
167	86	86
166	84	85
165	83	83
164	81	82
163	79	80
162	77	78
161	76	76
160	74	75
159	72	73
158	70	71
157	68	69
156	66	67
155	64	65
154	62	63
153	61	61
152	59	60
151	57	58
150	55	56
149	53	54
148	51	52
147	50	50
146	48	49
145	46	47
144	44	45
143	43	43
142	41	42
141	40	40
140	38	39
139	37	37
138	35	36
137	34	34
136	33	33
135	32	32
134	30	31
133	29	29
132	28	28
131	27	27
130	26	26
129	25	25
128	24	24
127	23	23
126	22	22
125	*	*
124	21	21
123	20	20
122	18	19
121	*	*
120	0	17

*There is no raw score that will produce this scaled score for this form.

ANSWER KEY

SECTION I

1.	D	8.	C	15.	C	22.	D
2.	A	9.	D	16.	B	23.	E
3.	A	10.	D	17.	E	24.	E
4.	E	11.	D	18.	D	25.	C
5.	A	12.	C	19.	A		
6.	B	13.	A	20.	A		
7.	D	14.	C	21.	B		

SECTION II

1.	A	8.	A	15.	B	22.	D
2.	D	9.	D	16.	C	23.	E
3.	B	10.	A	17.	E	24.	A
4.	A	11.	D	18.	B	25.	E
5.	E	12.	C	19.	D	26.	C
6.	C	13.	B	20.	B	27.	B
7.	E	14.	D	21.	A		

SECTION III

1.	C	8.	B	15.	D	22.	E
2.	D	9.	D	16.	B	23.	D
3.	D	10.	A	17.	E		
4.	E	11.	B	18.	D		
5.	B	12.	A	19.	C		
6.	D	13.	A	20.	A		
7.	E	14.	E	21.	A		

SECTION IV

1.	A	8.	A	15.	E	22.	B
2.	C	9.	E	16.	B	23.	A
3.	D	10.	C	17.	B	24.	E
4.	D	11.	A	18.	E	25.	D
5.	C	12.	E	19.	B	26.	B
6.	A	13.	A	20.	E		
7.	B	14.	E	21.	B		

THE OFFICIAL LSAT
PREPTEST®

81

- PrepTest 81
- Form 8LSN127

JUNE 2017

SECTION I

Time—35 minutes

27 Questions

Directions: Each set of questions in this section is based on a single passage or a pair of passages. The questions are to be answered on the basis of what is stated or implied in the passage or pair of passages. For some of the questions, more than one of the choices could conceivably answer the question. However, you are to choose the best answer; that is, the response that most accurately and completely answers the question, and blacken the corresponding space on your answer sheet.

This passage was adapted from an article published in 2003.

For two decades, Wynton Marsalis complemented his extraordinary gifts as a jazz trumpeter with persuasive advocacy of the importance of jazz history and jazz masters. At his peak, Marsalis ruled the jazz
(5) universe, enjoying virtually unqualified admiration as a musician and unsurpassed influence as the music's leading promoter and definer. But after drawing increasing fire from critics and fellow musicians alike for his neotraditionalism, the biggest name in jazz
(10) faces an uncertain future, as does jazz itself.
In 1999, to mark the end of the century, Marsalis issued a total of fifteen new CDs. In the following two years he did not release a single collection of new music. In fact, after two decades with Columbia
(15) Records—the prestigious label historically associated with Duke Ellington, Thelonious Monk, and Miles Davis—Marsalis has no record contract with any company. Over the past few years Columbia has drastically reduced its roster of active jazz musicians,
(20) shifting its emphasis to reissues of old recordings. Atlantic Records folded its jazz catalog into the operations of its parent company, Warner Music, and essentially gave up on developing new artists.
For this grim state of affairs in jazz, Marsalis,
(25) the public face of the music and the evident master of its destiny, has been accused of being at least partly culpable. Critics charge that, by leading jazz into the realm of unbending classicism and by sanctifying a canon of their own choosing, Marsalis and his
(30) adherents have codified the music into a stifling orthodoxy and inhibited the innovative impulses that have always advanced jazz. As a former executive with Columbia noted, "For many people, Marsalis has come to embody some retro ideology that is not really
(35) of the moment—it's more museumlike in nature, a look back."
Indeed, in seeking to elevate the public perception of jazz and to encourage young practitioners to pay attention to the music's traditions, Marsalis put great
(40) emphasis on its past masters. Still, he never advocated mere revivalism, and he has demonstrated in his compositions how traditional elements can be alluded to, recombined, and reinvented in the name of individualistic expression, taking the nature of that
(45) tradition and trying to push it forward. However, record executives came away with a different message: if the artists of the past are so great and enduring, why continue investing so much in young talent? So they

shifted their attention to repackaging their catalogs of
(50) vintage recordings.
Where the young talent saw role models and their critics saw idolatry, the record companies saw brand names—the ultimate prize of marketing. For long-established record companies with vast archives of
(55) historic recordings, the economics were irresistible: it is far more profitable to wrap new covers around albums paid for generations ago than it is to find, record, and promote new artists.

1. Which one of the following most accurately expresses the main point of the passage?

    (A) Although he was once heralded as the leading promoter and definer of jazz, Wynton Marsalis's recent turn toward traditional elements in his music has made record companies reluctant to contract with him.

    (B) Contrary to critics who accuse him of narrow neotraditionalism that stifles the evolution of jazz, Wynton Marsalis plays jazz that is new and innovative and his emphasis on past masters has widened the audience for jazz.

    (C) Though Wynton Marsalis enjoyed great success for two decades, the shift in focus by record companies to re-releasing traditional recordings has caused him to move away from the traditionalism that initially fueled his success.

    (D) By emphasizing appreciation of traditional jazz, Wynton Marsalis has unintentionally led major record companies to shun developing new talent in favor of re-releasing vintage jazz recordings.

    (E) Despite widespread acknowledgement of his musical gifts, Wynton Marsalis has come under increasing criticism for what many regard as excessive traditionalism.

GO ON TO THE NEXT PAGE.

2. By stating that many people consider Marsalis to embody a "retro ideology," the former executive quoted at the end of the third paragraph most likely means that they believe that Marsalis

(A)   revived a discredited set of ideas
(B)   merely recombined other people's ideas
(C)   overemphasized strict adherence to tradition
(D)   reinvented and reinterpreted traditional forms
(E)   seized on a set of inauthentic musical ideas

3. The author would most likely be less negative about the state of affairs in jazz if

(A)   critics were to soften their outspoken indictment of what they view as Marsalis's neotraditionalism
(B)   Marsalis were to continue focusing on releasing new music that was informed by traditional jazz
(C)   Marsalis were to speak out against those who describe his adherence to tradition as unbending
(D)   record companies were to emphasize developing new artists while reissuing old recordings
(E)   young jazz musicians were to favor a respect for tradition over impulsive innovation

4. Which one of the following describes a situation most analogous to the situation facing Marsalis, as described in the passage?

(A)   A town council's successful plan to slow the pace of housing development on its remaining rural lands has the unintended consequence of forcing housing prices to rise significantly faster than in neighboring towns.
(B)   A well-known seed research firm aggressively markets new hybrid tomatoes designed to taste like older traditional varieties, but as a result, sales of traditional varieties skyrocket while hybrid sales decline.
(C)   A producer of wool fabrics finds that business has increased substantially since synthetic-fabric producers have begun marketing fabrics that most consumers find less attractive than wool fabric.
(D)   A firm that has been selling and promoting herbal medicines for several decades finds that sales are slumping because of increasing competition from upstart herbal products companies.
(E)   A campaign to save an endangered fish species in a chain of lakes backfires when a ban on fishing in those lakes allows a predatory fish species to thrive and diminish stocks of the endangered species.

5. According to the passage, Marsalis encouraged young jazz musicians to

(A)   restrain their revolutionary, innovative impulses
(B)   learn to compose as well as perform jazz
(C)   play sessions with older musicians
(D)   ignore the prevailing public perceptions of jazz
(E)   stay in touch with the traditions of jazz

6. The author would be most likely to agree with which one of the following?

(A)   Ironically, record companies have embraced a kind of classicism that is more rigid than that attributed to Marsalis by critics.
(B)   Contrary to what critics charged, Marsalis energetically promoted new artists.
(C)   Understandably, Marsalis's fellow musicians have been more vocal in their displeasure with his views than have music critics.
(D)   Surprisingly, most of today's young artists take issue with critics' increasingly negative views of Marsalis's neotraditionalism.
(E)   In saturating the market with fifteen new collections of music in 1999, Marsalis made himself especially vulnerable to criticism.

7. The passage provides information sufficient to answer which one of the following questions?

(A)   In the two years after 1999, did Marsalis compose any new music?
(B)   Are Marsalis's fans drawn mainly from younger or from older jazz lovers?
(C)   Has Marsalis ever released a CD consisting of only jazz standards?
(D)   Why did Marsalis have no recording contract at the time the passage was written?
(E)   What is a factor that contributed to the shift by record companies toward reissuing vintage jazz recordings?

GO ON TO THE NEXT PAGE.

Common sense suggests that we know our own thoughts directly, but that we infer the thoughts of other people. The former process is noninferential and infallible, while the latter is based on others' behavior
(5) and can always be wrong. But this assumption is challenged by experiments in psychology demonstrating that in certain circumstances young children tend to misdescribe their own thoughts regarding simple phenomena while nonetheless
(10) correctly describing those phenomena. It seems that these children have the same thoughts that adults have regarding the phenomena but are much less capable of identifying these thoughts. Some psychologists argue that this indicates that one's awareness of one's own
(15) thoughts is every bit as inferential as one's awareness of another person's thoughts. According to their interpretation of the experiments, thoughts are unobservable entities that, among other things, help to explain why we act as we do. It follows from this that
(20) we are wrong to think of ourselves as having noninferential and infallible access to our own thoughts.

Recognizing an obligation to explain why we cling so tenaciously to an illusory belief in noninferential and infallible knowledge of our own thoughts, these
(25) psychologists suggest that this illusion is analogous to what happens to us when we become experts in a particular area. Greater expertise appears to change not only our knowledge of the area as a whole, but our very perception of entities in that area. It appears to us
(30) that we become able to see and to grasp these entities and their relations directly, whereas before we could only make inferences about them. For instance, chess experts claim the ability to see without calculation whether a position is weak or strong.
(35) From a psychological perspective, we become so expert in making incredibly fast introspective inferences about our thinking that we fail to notice that we are making them. This failure leads naturally to the supposition that there is no way for us to be wrong in
(40) our identification of what we ourselves think because we believe we are perceiving it directly.

In claiming that we have only inferential access to our thoughts, the psychologists come perilously close to claiming that we base our inferences about what we
(45) ourselves are thinking solely on observations of our own external behavior. But, in fact, their arguments do not commit them to this claim; the psychologists suggest that we are somehow able to base our inferences about what we are thinking on internal
(50) cognitive activity that is not itself thought— e.g., fleeting and instantaneous sensations and emotions. The frequent occurrence of such internal activities explains why we develop the capacity to make quick and reliable inferences. Their internality
(55) makes it impossible for anyone else to make an inference based on them that contradicts our own. Thus, they are crucial in creating the illusion of noninferentiality and infallibility.

8. Which one of the following most accurately expresses the main point of the passage?

(A) Only experts within a given domain have noninferential and infallible access to their own thoughts; other people must infer their own thoughts as they do others' thoughts.

(B) In opposition to the common belief that thoughts are directly perceived, some psychologists argue that people infer what their own thoughts are.

(C) In response to the common belief that thoughts are directly perceived, some psychologists claim that this belief is an illusion resulting from our inability to make quick and reliable inferences.

(D) Some psychologists have recently attributed children's failure to give an accurate description of their own thoughts to their lack of expertise.

(E) Some psychologists hold that people are able to make inferences about what they are thinking that are based solely on observing their own external behavior.

9. Which one of the following, if true, would most call into question the psychologists' interpretation of the experiments with children (lines 10–16)?

(A) Some children who took part in the experiments were no less capable than some adults at identifying their own thoughts.

(B) Experiments with older children found that they were as accurate as adults in identifying their thoughts.

(C) The limited language skills possessed by young children make it difficult for them to accurately communicate their thoughts.

(D) Most young children cannot be expected to know the difference between direct and indirect access to one's thoughts.

(E) The psychologists who conducted the experiments with children were concerned with psychological issues other than the nature of people's access to their own thoughts.

GO ON TO THE NEXT PAGE.

10. Based on the passage, the author is most likely to believe which one of the following about the view that "we base our inferences about what we ourselves are thinking solely on observations of our own external behavior" (lines 44–46)?

(A) It constitutes a denial of the possibility of scientifically studying thinking processes.

(B) It has often been misunderstood by psychologists.

(C) It was the prevailing view until undermined by recent psychology experiments.

(D) It seems to contradict common sense but is basically sound.

(E) It is not considered to be an intellectually defensible position.

11. Which one of the following is most closely analogous to the explanation in the passage of how persons fail to notice that they are making inferences about their thoughts?

(A) An anthropologist cannot describe his own culture accurately because he has become too familiar with its workings and therefore takes them for granted.

(B) Science is limited with regard to studying the human mind because science necessarily depends on human reasoning.

(C) As they develop, children become increasingly comfortable with formal abstraction and therefore become vulnerable to failures to learn from concrete experiences.

(D) Judges are barred from trying cases involving their family members because of a potential conflict of interest.

(E) A ship's commander must delegate certain duties and decisions to other officers on her ship because she is too busy to attend to those duties and decisions.

12. According to the passage, one's gaining greater expertise in a field appears to result in

(A) an altered way of expressing one's judgments about issues in that field

(B) a more detail-oriented approach to questions in that field

(C) an increased tendency to ignore one's own errors in judgment within that field

(D) a substantively different way of understanding relations within that field

(E) a reduced reliance on sensations and emotions when inferring one's thoughts regarding that field

13. According to the psychologists cited in the passage, the illusion of direct knowledge of our own thoughts arises from the fact that

(A) we ignore the feedback that we receive regarding the inaccuracy of the inferences we make about our thought processes

(B) knowledge of our own thoughts is usually unmediated due to our expertise, and we simply overlook instances where this is not the case

(C) we are unaware of the inferential processes that allow us to become aware of our thoughts

(D) our inferences regarding our own thoughts are generally extremely accurate, as are our perceptions of the world

(E) our inferences regarding our own thoughts are sometimes clouded and uncertain, as are our perceptions of the world

14. It can most reasonably be inferred that the choice of children as the subjects of the psychology experiments discussed in the passage was advantageous to the experimenters for which one of the following reasons?

(A) Experiments involving children are more likely to give interesting results because children are more creative than adults.

(B) Adults are more likely than children to give inaccurate reports of their thought processes.

(C) Since adults are infallible in their access to their own thoughts, only the thought processes of children shed light on the nature of inference.

(D) Mental processes are sometimes easier to study in children because children are more likely than adults to make certain cognitive errors.

(E) Children are less experienced than adults in inferring the thoughts of others from observations of their behavior.

GO ON TO THE NEXT PAGE.

This passage is based on an article written in 1995.

Dowsing is the practice of detecting resources or objects beneath the ground by passing handheld, inert tools such as forked sticks, pendulums, or metal rods over a terrain. For example, dowsers typically
(5) determine prospective water-well drilling locations by walking with a horizontally held forked tree branch until it becomes vertical, claiming the branch is pulled to this position. The distance to the water from the surface and the potential well's flow rate are then
(10) determined by holding the branch horizontally again and either walking in place or backwards while the branch is pulled vertical again. The number of paces indicates the distance to the water, and the strength of the pull felt by the dowser correlates with the potential
(15) well's flow rate.

Those skeptical of dowsing's efficacy point to the crudeness of its methods as a self-evident reason to question it. They assert that dowsers' use of inert tools indicates that the dowsers themselves actually make
(20) subconscious determinations concerning the likely location of groundwater using clues derived from surface conditions; the tools' movements merely reflect the dowsers' subconscious thoughts. Further, skeptics say, numerous studies show that while a few
(25) dowsers have demonstrated considerable and consistent success, the success rate for dowsers generally is notably inconsistent. Finally, skeptics note, dowsing to locate groundwater is largely confined to areas where groundwater is expected to
(30) be ubiquitous, making it statistically unlikely that a dowsed well will be completely dry.

Proponents of dowsing point out that it involves a number of distinct techniques and contend that each of these techniques should be evaluated separately. They
(35) also note that numerous dowsing studies have been influenced by a lack of care in selecting the study population; dowsers are largely self-proclaimed and self-certified, and verifiably successful dowsers are not well represented in the typical study. Proponents
(40) claim that successful dowsers may be sensitive to minute changes in Earth's electromagnetic field associated with variations in subsurface conditions. They also claim that these dowsers have higher success rates than geologists and hydrologists who
(45) use scientific tools such as electromagnetic sensors or seismic readings to locate groundwater.

The last two claims were corroborated during a recent and extensive study that utilized teams of the most successful dowsers, geologists, and hydrologists
(50) to locate reliable water supplies in various arid countries. Efforts were concentrated on finding groundwater in narrow, tilted fracture zones in bedrock underlying surface sediments. The teams were unfamiliar with the areas targeted, and they agreed
(55) that no surface clues existed that could assist in pinpointing the locations of fracture zones. The dowsers consistently made significantly more accurate predictions regarding drill sites, and on request even located a dry fracture zone, suggesting that dowsers
(60) can detect variations in subsurface conditions.

15. Which one of the following most accurately describes the primary purpose of the second paragraph?

(A) to add detail to the description presented in the first paragraph

(B) to offer two perspectives that are synthesized into a new perspective presented in the final paragraph

(C) to present arguments against which the third paragraph presents counterarguments

(D) to explore in detail the ramifications of one claim made in the first paragraph

(E) to clarify the issues on both sides in a dispute that the third paragraph attempts to resolve

16. According to the passage, dowsing's skeptics acknowledge which one of the following?

(A) A few dowsers have shown considerable and consistent success.

(B) Dowsing techniques are generally rejected by scientists.

(C) Successful dowsers are not well represented in the typical study of dowsing's efficacy.

(D) Successful dowsers may be sensitive to minute changes in Earth's electromagnetic field.

(E) Each dowsing technique should be evaluated separately.

17. The reasoning in which one of the following is most analogous to an argument explicitly attributed to dowsing's skeptics in the passage?

(A) Some weather analysts claim that no one can forecast the weather a week ahead with better than 40 percent accuracy, but some computer models have been known to perform with more accuracy than that.

(B) Some people claim to have seen ghosts, but very few of these people can adduce even the smallest piece of credible evidence to support their claims.

(C) Some musicians perform so well that their performances have been said to express a pure, innate talent, but such performances are in fact due to years of very intense practice.

(D) Some people claim to be able to sense where the area's good fishing spots are, but the lakes in the area are so loaded with fish it would be difficult not to pick a good spot.

(E) Some people have memories of participating in historical events in which they did not actually participate, but this does not prove that they have been reincarnated.

GO ON TO THE NEXT PAGE.

18. The author of the passage would be most likely to agree with which one of the following statements about the results of the groundwater-locating study discussed in the final paragraph?

(A) The results suggest that geologists and hydrologists would likely be of little service to any groundwater-locating effort.

(B) The results leave open the possibility that dowsers can sense minute changes in Earth's electromagnetic field.

(C) The results prove conclusively that dowsing is the most dependable technique for finding water in arid countries.

(D) The results demonstrate that dowsers are most successful in their efforts to locate groundwater when they use tools that are typically employed by geologists and hydrologists.

(E) The results do not help to refute skeptics' arguments, because the results provide evidence for dowsing's efficacy in only one type of terrain.

19. The passage provides information most helpful in answering which one of the following questions?

(A) When was dowsing first employed as a means of locating groundwater?

(B) Is the success of dowsers affected by rainstorms that may have saturated the ground in the area being dowsed?

(C) What proportion of successful dowsers use forked sticks in locating groundwater?

(D) Is dowsing ever utilized to try to locate anything other than water?

(E) What are some of the specific surface clues that can indicate the presence of groundwater?

20. The passage provides the most support for inferring which one of the following statements?

(A) Narrow, tilted fracture zones in underlying bedrock are more likely to be found in arid regions than in other regions.

(B) There are no reliable studies indicating that dowsers are consistently able to locate subsurface resources other than groundwater.

(C) A dowser attempting to locate a dry fracture zone would not use the same tools as a dowser attempting to locate groundwater.

(D) Geologists and hydrologists participating in the groundwater-locating study described in the final paragraph could not locate a dry fracture zone upon request.

(E) The groundwater-locating study described in the final paragraph was not a typical dowsing study.

GO ON TO THE NEXT PAGE.

Passage A

Why do some trial court judges oppose conducting independent research to help them make decisions? One of their objections is that it distorts the adversarial system by requiring an active judicial role and
(5) undermining the importance of evidence presented by the opposing parties. Another fear is that judges lack the wherewithal to conduct first-rate research and may wind up using outlier or discredited scientific materials.
(10) While these concerns have some merit, they do not justify an absolute prohibition of the practice. First, there are reasons to sacrifice adversarial values in the scientific evidence context. The adversarial system is particularly ill-suited to handling specialized
(15) knowledge. The two parties prescreen and compensate expert witnesses, which virtually ensures conflicting and partisan testimony. At the same time, scientific facts are general truths not confined to the immediate cases. Because scientific admissibility decisions can
(20) exert considerable influence over future cases, erroneous decisions detract from the legitimacy of the system. Independent research could help judges avoid such errors.

Second, a trial provides a structure that guides
(25) any potential independent research, reducing the possibility of a judge's reaching outlandish results. Independent research supplements, rather than replaces, the parties' presentation of the evidence, so the parties always frame the debate.

Passage B

(30) Regardless of what trial courts may do, appellate courts should resist the temptation to conduct their own independent research of scientific literature.

As a general rule, appellate courts do not hear live testimony. Thus these courts lack some of the
(35) critical tools available at the trial level for arriving at a determination of the facts: live testimony and cross-examination. Experts practicing in the field may have knowledge and experience beyond what is reflected in the available scientific literature. And
(40) adverse parties can test the credibility and reliability of proffered literature by subjecting the expert witness to the greatest legal engine ever invented for the discovery of truth—cross-examination. The trial judge may even participate in the process by questioning
(45) live witnesses. However, these events can only occur at the trial level.

Literature considered for the first time at the appellate level is not subject to live comment by practicing experts and cannot be tested in the crucible
(50) of the adversarial system. Thus one of the core criticisms against the use of such sources by appellate courts is that doing so usurps the trial court's fact-finding function. Internet sources, in particular, have come under criticism for their potential unreliability.

(55) When an appellate court goes outside the record to determine case facts, it ignores its function as a court of review, and it substitutes its own questionable research results for evidence that should have been

tested in the trial court. This criticism applies with
(60) full force to the use of outside-the-record texts and treatises, regardless of the medium in which they are found.

21. Which one of the following principles underlies the arguments in both passages?

 (A) It is more appropriate for trial judges to conduct independent research than for appellate judges to do so.
 (B) Judges should conduct independent research in order to determine what evidence parties to a trial should be allowed to present.
 (C) Independent research by judges should not supersede evidence presented by the opposing parties in a trial.
 (D) Judges' questioning of witnesses should be informed by the judges' own independent research.
 (E) Both trial and appellate judges should conduct research based on standard, reliable sources.

22. It can be inferred that each author would agree that if judges conduct independent research, that research

 (A) should be constrained by the structure of a trial
 (B) is typically confined to standard, reliable sources
 (C) replaces, rather than supplements, party-presented evidence
 (D) should be conducted at the trial level but not at the appellate level
 (E) usurps the trial court's fact-finding function

23. Which one of the following phrases is used by the author of passage B to express a concern that is most closely related to the concern expressed by the author of passage A using the phrase "lack the wherewithal" (line 7)?

 (A) experience beyond what is reflected (lines 38–39)
 (B) may even participate in the process (line 44)
 (C) subject to live comment (line 48)
 (D) questionable research results (lines 57–58)
 (E) outside-the-record texts (line 60)

GO ON TO THE NEXT PAGE.

24. Given the statements about cross-examination in lines 39–43, the author of passage B would be most likely to take issue with which one of the following claims by the author of passage A?

(A) An absolute prohibition of independent research by trial judges is not justified.
(B) The adversarial system is particularly ill-suited to handling specialized knowledge.
(C) Scientific admissibility decisions exert considerable influence over future cases.
(D) Erroneous decisions can be readily exposed by third parties.
(E) A trial provides a structure that guides any potential independent research.

25. Which one of the following words as used in passage B comes closest to having the same reference as the word "crucible" in line 49?

(A) temptation (line 31)
(B) credibility (line 40)
(C) engine (line 42)
(D) function (line 53)
(E) medium (line 61)

26. It can be inferred, based on their titles, that the relationship between which one of the following pairs of documents is most analogous to the relationship between passage A and passage B, respectively?

(A) "Negative Effects of Salt Consumption"
"Unhealthy Amounts of Salt in the Diet"
(B) "Salt Can Be Beneficial for Some People"
"People with High Blood Pressure Should Avoid Salt"
(C) "Debunking the Alleged Danger Posed by Salt"
"Inconclusive Research Results on the Health Effects of Salt Consumption"
(D) "Substitutes for Dietary Salt"
"Salt Substitutes Come Under Fire"
(E) "The Health Effects of Salt Consumption"
"Salt Deficiency in a Sample Population"

27. The stances of the authors of passage A and passage B, respectively, toward independent research on the part of trial judges are most accurately described as

(A) resigned acceptance and implicit disapproval
(B) cautious ambivalence and strict neutrality
(C) reasoned skepticism and veiled antipathy
(D) qualified approval and explicit noncommitment
(E) forceful advocacy and tentative opposition

S T O P

IF YOU FINISH BEFORE TIME IS CALLED, YOU MAY CHECK YOUR WORK ON THIS SECTION ONLY.
DO NOT WORK ON ANY OTHER SECTION IN THE TEST.

SECTION II

Time—35 minutes

26 Questions

<u>Directions:</u> The questions in this section are based on the reasoning contained in brief statements or passages. For some questions, more than one of the choices could conceivably answer the question. However, you are to choose the <u>best</u> answer; that is, the response that most accurately and completely answers the question. You should not make assumptions that are by commonsense standards implausible, superfluous, or incompatible with the passage. After you have chosen the best answer, blacken the corresponding space on your answer sheet.

1. For the first few weeks after birth, the dunnart has such poor control over its respiratory muscles that it cannot use them to breathe. Instead, this tiny marsupial breathes through its thin skin, which gradually thickens as the dunnart matures inside its mother's pouch. The dunnart is unique among warm-blooded animals, the rest of which need thick skin throughout their lives to maintain body temperature and reduce water loss.

    Which one of the following, if true, most helps explain how newborn dunnarts manage to survive despite their thin skins?

    (A)   The dunnart's respiratory muscles begin to develop a few days after birth.
    (B)   The dunnart's body temperature is higher than that of many other warm-blooded animals.
    (C)   Adult dunnarts experience more heat and water loss through their skin than other adult marsupials do.
    (D)   Its mother's pouch keeps a newborn dunnart warm and reduces water loss through its skin.
    (E)   Some dunnarts live where daytime temperatures are high and the climate is dry.

2. Successful stand-up comedians are able to keep the attention of a large audience for a few hours, in such a way that the audience remembers long afterwards what the comedian said. And in their routines, many comedians make interesting points about serious topics. Unsurprisingly, humor is the means through which comedians are able to accomplish all of this. University professors hope to achieve much the same in their lectures. Thus, _____.

    Which one of the following most logically completes the argument?

    (A)   stand-up comedians and university professors have the same skill set
    (B)   incorporating humor into lectures can help professors to achieve the goals they have for those lectures
    (C)   university professors can achieve the goals they have for their lectures only if they incorporate humor into them
    (D)   there is no reason to suppose that a lecture lasting several hours cannot hold an audience's attention
    (E)   university professors should treat even the most serious topics in a humorous way

3. Reviewer: Almost all books that offer management advice are written from the perspective of the CEO. But most managers aren't CEOs and don't have the same perspective as CEOs. So the advice in management books is of limited use for most managers.

    The conclusion of the reviewer's argument can be properly drawn if which one of the following is assumed?

    (A)   Advice books rarely take the perspective of their intended audience.
    (B)   Most people who read management advice books aspire to be CEOs.
    (C)   Almost all CEOs have experience as lower level managers.
    (D)   Advice is of limited use unless it is offered from the perspective of the recipient.
    (E)   Most managers prefer to read books that they think will be useful to them in their work.

4. The mayor has been accused of taking a bribe based on the fact that a consultant that does business with the city paid for improvements to the mayor's vacation house. In his own defense, the mayor has said that he paid every bill for those improvements that was presented to him.

    Which one of the following, if true, most undermines the mayor's defense?

    (A)   Authorities are investigating the consultant for taking bribes from officials of other cities.
    (B)   The mayor was aware that many of the bills were being presented to the consultant rather than to the mayor.
    (C)   The building contractor in charge of the improvements to the mayor's house had done business with the city in the past.
    (D)   The improvements to the mayor's house were done with expensive materials and involved thousands of hours of labor.
    (E)   The amount of money that the city paid the consultant over the last year greatly exceeded the cost of the improvements to the mayor's house.

GO ON TO THE NEXT PAGE.

5. Archaeologist: The earliest evidence of controlled fire use in Europe dates to just 400,000 years ago. This casts doubt on the commonly held view that, because of Europe's cold winter climate, mastery of fire was a necessary prerequisite for humans' migration there.

Which one of the following is an assumption required by the argument?

(A) The humans who first mastered fire used it for heat but not for cooking.

(B) The climate in Europe was significantly colder 400,000 years ago than it is today.

(C) Prior to 400,000 years ago, humans occasionally took advantage of naturally occurring fires.

(D) Humans would not have mastered fire were it not for the need for heat in a cold climate.

(E) There were humans inhabiting Europe prior to 400,000 years ago.

6. Astronomer: This country's space agency is currently building a new space telescope that is, unfortunately, way over budget. Some people argue that the project should be canceled. But that would be a mistake. If we cancel it now, all the money that has already been spent—which is more than the additional cost required to complete the project—would be wasted.

Which one of the following principles, if valid, would most help to justify the astronomer's argument?

(A) A government agency should not cancel a partially completed project unless the amount of money already spent on the project is small relative to the agency's overall budget.

(B) If more than half of the total cost of a project has already been spent, then the project should be completed.

(C) If it becomes clear that the total cost of a project will be more than twice the amount originally budgeted, then the project should be canceled.

(D) One should not commit additional funding to a project just because one has spent considerable money on it in the past.

(E) In determining which scientific projects to fund, governments should give priority to the projects that are most likely to lead to important new discoveries.

7. Naturalist: Different nonhuman primate species exhibit many contrasts in behavior. If a zookeeper leaves a screwdriver within reach of a chimpanzee, the animal is likely to examine and play with it for a time, and then move on to something else. In the same circumstances, an orangutan is likely to pretend to ignore the tool at first; later, in the zookeeper's absence, the orangutan may use the screwdriver to try to dismantle its cage.

Which one of the following is most strongly supported by the naturalist's statements?

(A) Orangutans are the most intelligent of nonhuman primates.

(B) Orangutans have better memories than chimpanzees have.

(C) Some nonhuman primates are capable of deception.

(D) Orangutans dislike being caged more than chimpanzees do.

(E) Not all nonhuman primates understand tool use.

8. Manager: The only employees who should receive bonuses this year are those who were exceptionally productive over the past year. Liang is an excellent account executive, but she works in a corporate division that has failed to meet its productivity goals for the year. Thus Liang should not receive a bonus this year.

The reasoning in the manager's argument is flawed in that the argument

(A) fails to take into account the possibility that the standards by which productivity is judged might vary across different divisions of a corporation

(B) overlooks the possibility that a corporation as a whole can have a profitable year even though one division of the corporation does not

(C) fails to justify its use of one group's performance as the basis for a conclusion about a wholly different group

(D) reaches a conclusion about the performance of one member of a group merely on the basis of the performance of the group as a whole

(E) takes for granted that an employee who has an unproductive year will not be exceptionally productive in subsequent years

GO ON TO THE NEXT PAGE.

9. Even though she thought the informant was untrustworthy, the journalist promised not to reveal his identity so long as the information he provided did not turn out to be false. However, she will publicly reveal the informant's identity if she is ordered to do so by a judge or her editor. After all, the information concerns safety violations at the power plant. Thus, the journalist will surely reveal the informant's identity even if the information is accurate.

The conclusion of the argument follows logically if which one of the following is assumed?

(A) The information that the informant provided is known to be false.

(B) The journalist's editor will not order her to reveal the informant's identity unless the information is accurate and concerns public safety.

(C) If the information concerns safety at the power plant, a judge will order the journalist to reveal her informant's identity.

(D) The truth of the information provided by the informant can be verified only if the informant's identity is publicly revealed.

(E) The informant understood, at the time the journalist promised him confidentiality, that she would break this promise if ordered to do so by a judge.

10. One who has borrowed an item from someone and promised to return it by a certain date should do so if it would not be difficult to return it on time and the person from whom one has borrowed it has not given permission to return the item late.

The principle stated above most helps to justify the reasoning in which one of the following arguments?

(A) Christopher told Sumi that the book she borrowed from him need not be returned by Friday. Thus, it would be wrong for Sumi to return the book earlier than Friday.

(B) Nick promised Wanda that he would return the bicycle he borrowed from her by tomorrow. Thus, if Wanda did not give Nick permission to return it late, he ought to return it by tomorrow even if doing so is difficult.

(C) Val should return Ted's car to him today, because although he told her that she could return it late, she promised that she would return it today and it would not be difficult for her to do so.

(D) Yesenia borrowed Mike's computer, and he has just requested that she return it to him by tomorrow. Although Yesenia has not promised to return it by tomorrow, she should return it by then since it would not be difficult for her to do so.

(E) Oliver borrowed Madeline's guitar from her yesterday and promised to bring it back today. So, since it would be easy for Oliver to return the guitar today, and Madeline has not given him permission to return it late, he should return it today.

11. Human skin gives off an array of gaseous substances, including carbon dioxide and lactic acid, both of which attract mosquitoes. However, neither of these two substances, whether alone or combined with one another, will attract mosquitoes as much as a bare human arm will, even in complete darkness, where a mosquito has no visual cues. Therefore, some other gaseous substance given off by human skin also attracts mosquitoes.

The reasoning in the argument requires which one of the following assumptions?

(A) Mosquitoes do not communicate with one another.

(B) Mosquitoes are not attracted to humans by body heat.

(C) Human skin gives off gaseous substances in greater amounts during the day than during the night.

(D) Mosquitoes are no more successful in finding a bare human arm in darkness than in light.

(E) Human skin never gives off any gaseous substances that repel mosquitoes.

12. A 1955 analysis of paint samples from an Italian painting found evidence of cobalt, suggesting the use of cobalt blue, a pigment not used in Europe before 1804. The painting was thus deemed to have been produced sometime after 1804. A 2009 analysis also found cobalt, but that analysis suggested that the painting might have been produced before 1804.

Which one of the following, if true, most helps to resolve the apparent discrepancy in the information above?

(A) The 2009 analysis revealed that cobalt was located only in the topmost paint layer, which was possibly applied to conceal damage to original paint layers.

(B) The 2009 analysis used sophisticated scientific equipment that can detect much smaller amounts of cobalt than could the equipment used for the 1955 analysis.

(C) The 2009 analysis took more samples from the painting than the 1955 analysis did, though those samples were smaller.

(D) Many experts, based on the style and the subject matter of the painting, have dated the painting to the 1700s.

(E) New information that came to light in the 1990s suggested that cobalt blue was used only rarely in Italy in the years immediately following 1804.

GO ON TO THE NEXT PAGE.

13. A six-month public health campaign sought to limit the spread of influenza by encouraging people to take precautions such as washing their hands frequently and avoiding public places when they experience influenza symptoms. Since the incidence of influenza was much lower during those months than experts had predicted, the public evidently heeded the campaign.

Which one of the following, if true, most strengthens the argument?

(A) The incidence of food-borne illnesses, which can be effectively controlled by frequent hand washing, was markedly lower than usual during the six-month period.

(B) During the six-month period, the incidence of the common cold, which has many of the same symptoms as influenza, was about the same as usual.

(C) There were fewer large public gatherings than usual during the six-month period.

(D) Independently of the public health campaign, the news media spread the message that one's risk of contracting influenza can be lessened by frequent hand washing.

(E) In a survey completed before the campaign began, many people admitted that they should do more to limit the spread of influenza.

14. A study at a company found that most meetings showed diminishing returns after 30 minutes, and little could be expected after 60 minutes. Moreover, the most productive meetings were those for which a clear time frame was established. For a meeting at the company to achieve maximum productivity, then, it needs to have a clear time frame and be no more than 30 minutes long.

Which one of the following most accurately expresses the conclusion drawn in the argument?

(A) In general, a meeting at the company that is no more than 30 minutes long and has a clear time frame will achieve maximum productivity.

(B) Most meetings at the company show diminishing returns after 30 minutes, according to a study.

(C) A meeting at the company will be maximally productive only if it has a clear time frame and lasts no more than 30 minutes.

(D) According to a study, meetings at the company were the most productive when they had clear time frames.

(E) A study of meetings at the company says that little productivity should be expected after the 60-minute mark.

15. Nutritionist: Most fad diets prescribe a single narrow range of nutrients for everyone. But because different foods contain nutrients that are helpful for treating or preventing different health problems, dietary needs vary widely from person to person. However, everyone should eat plenty of fruits and vegetables, which protect against a wide range of health problems.

Which one of the following is most strongly supported by the nutritionist's statements?

(A) Most fad diets require that everyone following them eat plenty of fruits and vegetables.

(B) Fruits and vegetables are the only foods that contain enough different nutrients to protect against a wide range of health problems.

(C) Any two people have different health problems and thus different dietary needs.

(D) Most fad diets fail to satisfy the dietary needs of some people.

(E) There are very few if any nutrients that are contained in every food other than fruits and vegetables.

GO ON TO THE NEXT PAGE.

16. The caffeine in coffee stimulates the production of irritating acid in the stomach. But darker roasts of coffee, produced by roasting the coffee beans longer, contain more N-methylpyridinium (NMP) than lighter roasts, and NMP tends to suppress production of acid in the stomach. Therefore if you drink caffeinated coffee, darker roasts will irritate your stomach less than lighter roasts.

The answer to which one of the following questions most helps in evaluating the argument?

(A) Does extending the roasting time of coffee beans increase the amount of caffeine present in the brewed coffee?

(B) Does a reduction in acid production in the stomach have an adverse effect on stomach function?

(C) Would coffee drinkers who drink caffeinated coffee increase their coffee consumption if the coffee they drank contained less caffeine?

(D) Do some coffee drinkers who switch from lighter to darker roasts of coffee increase their daily coffee consumption?

(E) Do lighter roasts of coffee have any important health benefits that darker roasts of coffee lack?

17. Film historians often find it difficult to determine typical audience members' responses to particular films, especially those from the early twentieth century. Box office figures help little, for they indicate only a film's financial success or failure; they do not show what audiences found funny, or frightening, or moving. These historians also find that newspaper and magazine reviews fail to provide much insight.

Which one of the following is most strongly supported by the statements above?

(A) Newspaper and magazine reviews of films are usually written in advance of a film's general release.

(B) Typical audience members' responses to films from the latter part of the twentieth century are easy to determine.

(C) The box office success of a film does not depend on its viewers finding it funny, frightening, or moving.

(D) Film historians do not believe that film reviews in newspapers and magazines reveal typical film audience members' views.

(E) Films from the early part of the twentieth century were not usually reviewed in newspapers or magazines.

18. The consensus among astronomers, based upon observations of the surfaces of pulsars, is that pulsars are spinning balls of neutrons compressed into a sphere some 10 kilometers in diameter with a mass roughly equal to that of our sun. However, their observed properties are also consistent with some pulsars actually being filled with quarks, the building blocks of neutrons. Because the core of a quark-filled pulsar, unlike a neutron-filled one, would have an overall positive charge, it would attract a layer of negatively charged particles that could support a crust of neutrons.

The statement that the core of a quark-filled pulsar would have an overall positive charge plays which one of the following roles in the argument above?

(A) It helps explain how pulsars could have neutrons on their surface even if they were not entirely made up of neutrons.

(B) It forms part of a challenge to the claim that some pulsars may be made up of quarks.

(C) It helps explain why some pulsars would not be readily recognized as such by astronomers.

(D) It presents a new finding that challenges the consensus view of the structure of pulsars.

(E) It points out a problem with the view that pulsars have a mass roughly equal to that of our sun.

GO ON TO THE NEXT PAGE.

19. Analyst: Any new natural-gas-powered electrical generation station needs to be located close to a natural-gas pipeline, a large body of water for cooling, and transmission lines. It also must be situated in a region where residents will not oppose construction. Our country has an extensive system of transmission lines, but our natural-gas pipelines run in the vicinity of only three of our large bodies of water, and residents would oppose any significant construction projects near these bodies of water.

The analyst's statements, if true, most strongly support which one of the following statements about the analyst's country?

(A) Future electrical needs will have to be met by alternatives to natural-gas-powered generation.
(B) If a new natural-gas-powered electrical station is built in a region, many residents will move away from that region.
(C) No site would be suitable for constructing a natural-gas-powered electrical station unless the existing system of natural-gas pipelines is expanded.
(D) There currently is no natural-gas-powered electrical generation station near any of the three largest bodies of water.
(E) Many residents who would oppose the construction of a new natural-gas-powered electrical station in their region would not oppose the construction of new transmission lines there.

20. Voting records regularly show that people over 65 vote in the highest percentages while young adults are least likely to vote. This indicates that citizens are becoming increasingly disconnected from the political system with each passing generation.

The argument's reasoning is questionable in that the argument

(A) compares an early stage of one generation to a later stage of another
(B) fails to take into account the relative sizes of the generations compared
(C) provides evidence for a phenomenon without providing an explanation of the phenomenon
(D) confuses the cause of an effect with the effect itself
(E) overlooks the possibility that voting patterns among age groups will change in the future

21. A local marsh would need to be drained before the proposed office complex could be built. Such marshes often play crucial roles in purifying groundwater and there has been no scientific assessment of the marsh's role in maintaining the quality of the city's well water. The city should therefore block the proposed office complex pending such an assessment.

The principle underlying the argument above is most similar to the principle underlying which one of the following arguments?

(A) A new highway cannot be built in the lake district unless an environmental impact assessment is first carried out. An environmental impact assessment would cost more than the projected economic benefit of the highway. The proposal for a new highway in the lake district should therefore be rejected.
(B) Defective products can cost an appliance manufacturer millions of dollars because of product recalls and lawsuits. Yova Corporation's new line of appliances has not yet been thoroughly tested for defects. Thus, Yova should not bring its new line to market at this time.
(C) A laboratory safety check of a portable grill requires a week of uninterrupted testing. The new portable grill has been at the testing lab for a week, but the testing could not begin until the paperwork arrived three days later. Therefore, no report on the results of the safety check should be released at this time.
(D) Building the new highway along the proposed northern route would inevitably damage an adjoining wilderness area. The highway would also cause environmental damage if it follows the proposed southern route, but it would not harm any wilderness areas. Thus, if the highway is built, it should be built on the southern route.
(E) Building a light rail line to serve the downtown core could involve cost overruns and expensive delays, but traffic congestion will become intolerable within ten years without a light rail line. A light rail line should therefore be built.

GO ON TO THE NEXT PAGE.

22. In a recent study, one group of participants watched video recordings of themselves running on treadmills, and a second group watched recordings of other people running on treadmills. When contacted later, participants in the first group reported exercising, on average, 1 hour longer each day than did the other participants. This shows that watching a recording of yourself exercising can motivate you to exercise more.

Which one of the following, if true, most weakens the argument?

(A) In another study, people who watched recordings of themselves lifting weights exercised for more time each day than did people who watched recordings of themselves running.

(B) Another study's members exhibited an increased willingness to give to charity after hearing stories in which people with whom they identified did so.

(C) Participants who were already highly motivated to exercise did not report exercising for any longer each day than they had before the study.

(D) In studies of identical twins, participants who observed their twin reading overreported by a significant amount how much time they themselves spent reading in the days that followed.

(E) A third group of participants who watched recordings of themselves sitting on couches afterwards reported being sedentary for more time each day than did the other participants.

23. Environmentalist: Efforts to attain an overall reduction in carbon use by convincing people to focus on their personal use of fossil fuels cannot achieve that goal. Even if most people changed their behavior, changes in personal use of fossil fuels cannot produce the needed reductions in carbon use. Only government policies can produce change on the required scale.

The environmentalist's argument requires assuming which one of the following?

(A) Convincing most people to focus on their personal use of fossil fuels would not lead to their successfully pressuring the government into implementing policies that reduce carbon use.

(B) The calculations needed to determine how best to minimize one's personal use of fossil fuels are too difficult for individuals to carry out on their own.

(C) Efforts to convince people to focus on reducing their personal use of fossil fuels have been made only by those who are not currently involved in framing government policy.

(D) It is easier to convince the government to change its policies on carbon use than to convince people to reduce their personal use of fossil fuels.

(E) People who are concerned about environmental issues are more likely to support political candidates who support environmental issues.

GO ON TO THE NEXT PAGE.

24. There are only two plausible views about where the aesthetic value of a painting lies: either in its purely formal qualities or in what the painting means. But there exists no compelling general account of how a painting could derive its value from its purely formal characteristics. Therefore, the aesthetic value of a painting lies in what it means.

The pattern of questionable reasoning in the argument above is most similar to that in which one of the following?

(A) This cardiac patient could be treated with surgery or angioplasty, among other methods. But his weak condition would make recovery from surgery a very long process. Therefore, the doctors ought to perform angioplasty.

(B) Should the company be outbid on the new project, it will either have to lay off workers or find new business. But it does not expect to find new business in the foreseeable future. Therefore, it must be expecting to win the bid on the new project.

(C) History is driven primarily by economic forces or primarily by political forces. But no historian has shown convincingly that history is driven mainly by economic forces. Therefore, it is driven primarily by political forces.

(D) Some analysts are forecasting that if the economy expands, the inflation rate will rise or the unemployment rate will fall. But the unemployment rate promises to remain stable. Therefore, the inflation rate will not change either.

(E) If the party does not change its policies, it will lose heavily in the next election. But if it changes its policies, some people who support those policies will be upset and will sit out the next election. Therefore, it is impossible for the party to win in the next election.

25. Substantial economic growth must be preceded by technological innovations that expanding industries incorporate into their production or distribution procedures. Since a worldwide ban on the use of fossil fuels would surely produce many technological innovations, it is obvious that such a ban would be followed by an economic boom rather than by the economic depression forecast by the critics of such a ban.

Which one of the following most accurately describes a flaw in the argument's reasoning?

(A) The argument assumes the truth of the conclusion for which it purports to be providing evidence.

(B) The argument attempts to establish the falsehood of a proposition by criticizing the reasoning of those who assert its truth.

(C) The argument attempts to establish a conclusion on the basis of stronger evidence than the conclusion requires.

(D) The argument confuses a necessary condition for a phenomenon with a sufficient condition for that phenomenon.

(E) The argument presumes, without providing warrant, that because certain conditions only sometimes precede a certain phenomenon, these conditions always bring about the phenomenon.

26. Winston: The rules for awarding Nobel Prizes stipulate that no more than three people can share the same prize. Nobel Prizes in scientific disciplines are generally given in recognition of particular scientific results, however, and many important results are the work of four or more scientists.

Sanjay: Those rules also stipulate that prize winners must be living, but some highly influential scientists died before their work was fully appreciated.

The dialogue most strongly supports the claim that Winston and Sanjay agree that

(A) the rules that govern the awarding of Nobel Prizes should be changed so that prizes can be awarded to deceased persons

(B) the rules that govern the awarding of Nobel Prizes in scientific disciplines should be different from the rules for other Nobel Prizes

(C) Nobel Prizes in scientific disciplines should not be given in recognition of particular scientific results

(D) the evaluation of individual achievement in science is a highly subjective matter

(E) Nobel Prizes are inaccurate indicators of scientists' contributions to their disciplines

S T O P

IF YOU FINISH BEFORE TIME IS CALLED, YOU MAY CHECK YOUR WORK ON THIS SECTION ONLY.
DO NOT WORK ON ANY OTHER SECTION IN THE TEST.

SECTION III

Time—35 minutes

25 Questions

<u>Directions:</u> The questions in this section are based on the reasoning contained in brief statements or passages. For some questions, more than one of the choices could conceivably answer the question. However, you are to choose the <u>best</u> answer; that is, the response that most accurately and completely answers the question. You should not make assumptions that are by commonsense standards implausible, superfluous, or incompatible with the passage. After you have chosen the best answer, blacken the corresponding space on your answer sheet.

1. Joe: All vampire stories are based on an absurd set of premises. Since, according to such stories, every victim of a vampire becomes a vampire, and vampires have existed since ancient times and are immortal, vampires would by now have almost completely eliminated their prey.

    Maria: In most of the vampire stories I am familiar with, vampires turn only a few of their victims into vampires. The rest are permanently dead.

    Joe and Maria <u>disagree over the truth of which one of</u> the following?

    (A) Vampires are always depicted in vampire stories as immortal.
    (B) Vampires are always depicted in vampire stories as having existed since ancient times.
    (C) No vampire stories are incoherent.
    (D) No vampire stories depict the vampire population as being very large.
    (E) In all vampire stories, every victim of a vampire becomes a vampire.

2. A company decided to scan all of its salespersons' important work that existed only in paper form into a central computer database that could be easily accessed using portable computers, thereby saving salespersons the effort of lugging their paper files all over the country. The project was a dismal failure, <u>however;</u> salespersons rarely accessed the database and continued to rely on many paper files, <u>which</u> they had refused to turn over to the staff responsible for creating the database.

    Which one of the following, if true, <u>most helps to account for the failure</u> described above?

    (A) Some of the salespersons gave huge paper files to the staff responsible for creating the database while other salespersons gave them much smaller files.
    (B) Most of the salespersons already had portable computers before the new database was created.
    (C) The papers that the salespersons found most important all contained personal information about employees of client companies, which the salespersons did not want in a central database.
    (D) All of the salespersons were required to attend a series of training sessions for the new database software even though many of them found the software easy to use even without training.
    (E) The number of staff required to create the database turned out to be larger than anticipated, and the company had to pay overtime wages to some of them.

GO ON TO THE NEXT PAGE.

3. Politician: The legal right to free speech does not protect all speech. For example, it is illegal to shout "Fire!" in a crowded mall if the only intent is to play a practical joke; the government may ban publication of information about military operations and the identity of undercover agents; and extortion threats and conspiratorial agreements are also criminal acts. The criminalization of these forms of speech is justified, since, although they are very different from each other, they are all likely to lead directly to serious harm.

In the statements above, the politician argues that

(A) it is legitimate to prohibit some forms of speech on the grounds that they are likely to lead directly to serious harm

(B) a form of speech can be restricted only if it is certain that it would lead directly to serious harm

(C) in all but a few cases, restricting speech eventually leads directly to serious harm

(D) any form of speech may, one way or another, lead directly to serious harm

(E) all but one of several possible reasons for restricting freedom of speech are unjustified

4. Art critic: Nowadays, museum visitors seldom pause to look at a work of art for even a full minute. They look, perhaps take a snapshot, and move on. This tells us something about how our relationship to art has changed over time. People have become less willing to engage with works of art than they once were.

The art critic's argument depends on the assumption that

(A) museum visitors today generally look at more pieces of art during each museum visit than museum visitors looked at in the past

(B) the ease with which museum visitors can take snapshots of art contributes to the speed with which they move through art museums

(C) visitors would enjoy their museum experiences more if they took more time with individual works of art

(D) museum visitors who take snapshots of works of art rarely look at the pictures afterward

(E) the amount of time spent looking at a work of art is a reliable measure of engagement with that work

5. Heavy tapestry fabrics are appropriate only for use in applications that will not need to be laundered frequently. These applications do not include any types of clothing—such as skirts or even jackets—but instead include swags and balloon valances, which are types of window treatments.

Which one of the following statements is most supported by the information above?

(A) If a fabric is not a heavy tapestry fabric, then it is not appropriate for use in swags.

(B) Heavy tapestry fabrics should not be used unless swags or balloon valances are being made.

(C) If heavy tapestry fabrics are appropriate for a particular application, then that application must be a window treatment.

(D) If a fabric is appropriate for use in a skirt or jacket, then that fabric is not a heavy tapestry fabric.

(E) Heavy tapestry fabrics are sometimes appropriate for use in types of clothing other than skirts and jackets.

6. The construction of new apartments in Brewsterville increased the supply of available housing there. Ordinarily, increasing the supply of available housing leads to lower rents for existing apartments. But in Brewsterville, rents for existing apartments rose.

Which one of the following, if true, most helps to explain the discrepancy described above?

(A) Fewer new apartments were constructed than originally planned.

(B) The new apartments were much more desirable than the existing apartments.

(C) Rents in some areas close to Brewsterville dropped as a result of the construction of the new apartments.

(D) A sizeable number of people moved out of the existing apartments while the new apartments were being constructed.

(E) The new apartments were constructed at the outset of a trend of increasing numbers of people seeking residence in Brewsterville.

GO ON TO THE NEXT PAGE.

3 -386-

7. Politicians often advocate increased overall economic productivity while ignoring its drawbacks. For example, attempting to increase the productivity of a corporation means attempting to increase its profitability, which typically leads to a reduction in the number of workers employed by that corporation. Thus, attempting to increase productivity in the economy as a whole may benefit business owners, but will increase the number of unemployed workers.

The reasoning in the argument is most vulnerable to criticism on the grounds that the argument

(A) presumes, without providing justification, that increased unemployment is sufficient reason to abandon increased productivity as an economic goal

(B) fails to justify its presumption that attempting to increase productivity in the economy as a whole would produce results similar to those produced by attempting to increase productivity in a single corporation

(C) unfairly criticizes politicians in general on the basis of the actions of a few who are unwilling to consider the drawbacks of attempting to increase productivity

(D) fails to justify its presumption that attempting to increase productivity in the economy as a whole is always more important than the interests of workers or business owners

(E) fails to address all potential drawbacks and benefits of attempting to increase productivity at a single corporation

8. A good movie reviewer should be able to give favorable reviews of movies that are not to his or her taste. Because movie reviewers have seen so many movies, their tastes are very different from and usually better informed than those of most moviegoers. Yet the function of movie reviewers, as opposed to film critics, is to help people determine which movies they might enjoy seeing, not to help them better appreciate movies.

Which one of the following most accurately expresses the overall conclusion drawn in the argument?

(A) Movie reviewers' tastes in movies are very different from and usually better informed than those of most moviegoers.

(B) If a movie reviewer is good, he or she should be able to give favorable reviews of movies that are not to his or her taste.

(C) The function of a movie reviewer is different from that of a film critic.

(D) Movie reviewers see many more movies than most moviegoers see.

(E) The role of movie reviewers is to help people determine which movies they might enjoy seeing, not to help people better appreciate movies.

9. The brain area that enables one to distinguish the different sounds made by a piano tends to be larger in a highly skilled musician than in someone who has rarely, if ever, played a musical instrument. This shows that practicing on, and playing, a musical instrument actually alters brain structure.

Which one of the following most accurately describes a flaw in the argument?

(A) The argument presumes, without providing justification, that what is true about the brain structures of highly skilled pianists is also true of the brain structures of other highly skilled musicians.

(B) The argument fails to address the possibility that people who become highly skilled musicians do so, in part, because of the size of a certain area of their brains.

(C) The argument draws a conclusion about a broad range of phenomena from evidence concerning a much narrower range of phenomena.

(D) The argument fails to address the possibility that a certain area of the brain is smaller in people who have listened to a lot of music but who have never learned to play a musical instrument than it is in people who have learned to play a musical instrument.

(E) The argument presumes, without providing justification, that highly skilled musicians practice more than other musicians.

GO ON TO THE NEXT PAGE.

10. Researcher: Overhearing only one side of a cell-phone conversation diverts listeners' attention from whatever they are doing. Hearing only part of a conversation leaves listeners constantly trying to guess what the unheard talker has just said. Listeners' attention is also diverted because cell-phone talkers speak abnormally loudly.

The researcher's statements, if true, most strongly support which one of the following?

(A) The risk that a driver will cause an accident is increased when the driver is talking on a cell phone.

(B) When a driver hears a passenger in the driver's vehicle talking on a cell phone, that detracts from the driver's performance.

(C) Overhearing one side of a conversation on a traditional telephone does not divert listeners' attention from tasks at hand.

(D) People who overhear one side of a cell-phone conversation inevitably lose track of their thoughts.

(E) Conversing on a cell phone requires making more guesses about what one's conversational partner means than other forms of conversation do.

11. A new treatment for muscle pain that looked very promising was tested in three separate studies. Although the results were positive, it turned out that all three studies had critical methodological flaws. So the treatment is probably not actually effective.

The flawed nature of the argument above can most effectively be demonstrated by noting that, by parallel reasoning, we could conclude that

(A) since the judges in a baking contest did not have uniform criteria for selecting a winner, the cake that won is probably a bad one

(B) since some people who fish seldom catch any fish, they probably have some reason for fishing other than catching fish

(C) since some foods have very little nutritional value, people who include those foods in their diets are probably malnourished

(D) since all scarves are at least somewhat decorative, it is likely that when scarves were first adopted, they were purely decorative

(E) since all members of the city council have a financial stake in the city's development, any development proposal they make is likely to be motivated purely by self-interest

12. If future improvements to computer simulations of automobile crashes enable computers to provide as much reliable information about the effectiveness of automobile safety features as is provided by actual test crashes, then manufacturers will use far fewer actual test crashes. For the costs of designing and running computer simulations are much lower than those of actual test crashes.

Which one of the following, if true, most strongly supports the argument?

(A) Apart from information about safety features, actual test crashes provide very little information of importance to automobile manufacturers.

(B) It is highly likely that within the next 20 years computer simulations of automobile crashes will be able to provide a greater amount of reliable information about the effectiveness of automobile safety features than can be provided by actual test crashes.

(C) If computer simulations will soon be able to provide more information about the effectiveness of automobile safety features, automobile manufacturers will soon be able to produce safer cars.

(D) The cost per automobile of testing and designing safety features is decreasing and will continue to decrease for the foreseeable future.

(E) For years, the aviation industry has been successfully using computer simulations of airplane crashes to test the effectiveness of safety features of airplane designs.

GO ON TO THE NEXT PAGE.

13. Legislator: My colleague says we should reject this act because it would deter investment. But because in the past she voted for legislation that inhibited investment, this surely is not the real reason she opposes the act. Since she has not revealed her real reason, it must not be very persuasive. So we should vote to approve the act.

The reasoning in the legislator's argument is most vulnerable to the criticism that the argument

(A)   treats a personal character trait as if it were evidence of the professional viewpoint of the person having that trait

(B)   fails to address the grounds on which the colleague claims the act should be rejected

(C)   presumes, without providing justification, that the colleague's opposition to the act is the minority position in the legislature

(D)   presumes, without providing justification, that voters will oppose legislation that deters investment

(E)   fails to consider that the colleague's opposition to the act may be a response to constituents' wishes

14. A new computer system will not significantly increase an organization's efficiency unless the computer system requires the organization's employees to adopt new, more productive ways of working. The Ministry of Transportation is having a new computer system custom built to fit the ministry's existing ways of working, so _____.

Which one of the following most logically completes the argument?

(A)   the new computer system will not increase the efficiency of the Ministry of Transportation to any appreciable degree

(B)   it is likely that the new computer system will not function correctly when it is first installed

(C)   the leaders of the Ministry of Transportation must not be concerned with the productivity of the ministry's employees

(D)   the new computer system will be worthwhile if it automates many processes that are currently performed manually

(E)   it will be easy for employees of the Ministry of Transportation to learn to use the new computer system

15. Columnist: Many car manufacturers trumpet their cars' fuel economy under normal driving conditions. For all three of the cars I have owned, I have been unable to get even close to the fuel economy that manufacturers advertise for cars of those makes. So manufacturers probably inflate those numbers.

The reasoning in the columnist's argument is most vulnerable to criticism on the grounds that the argument

(A)   draws a conclusion on the basis of a sample that is too small

(B)   presumes, without providing justification, that driving conditions are the same in every geographical region

(C)   overlooks the possibility that the source of a cited claim may be biased and hence unreliable

(D)   presumes, without providing justification, that car manufacturers knowingly market cars that fail to meet minimum fuel efficiency standards

(E)   uses the term "fuel economy" in two different senses

16. Tenants who do not have to pay their own electricity bills do not have a financial incentive to conserve electricity. Thus, if more landlords install individual electricity meters on tenant dwellings so that tenants can be billed for their own use, energy will be conserved as a result.

Which one of the following, if true, most weakens the argument?

(A)   Tenants who do not have to pay their own electricity bills generally must compensate by paying more rent.

(B)   Many initiatives have been implemented to educate people about how much money they can save through energy conservation.

(C)   Landlords who pay for their tenants' electricity have a strong incentive to make sure that the appliances they provide for their tenants are energy efficient.

(D)   Some tenant dwellings can only support individual electricity meters if the dwellings are rewired, which would be prohibitively expensive.

(E)   Some people conserve energy for reasons that are not related to cost savings.

GO ON TO THE NEXT PAGE.

17. The position that punishment should be proportional to how serious the offense is but that repeat offenders should receive harsher punishments than first-time offenders is unsustainable. It implies that considerations as remote as what an offender did years ago are relevant to the seriousness of an offense. If such remote considerations were relevant, almost every other consideration would be too. But this would make determining the seriousness of an offense so difficult that it would be impossible to apply the proportionality principle.

The statement that considerations as remote as what an offender did years ago are relevant to the seriousness of an offense plays which one of the following roles in the argument?

(A) It is a statement the argument provides grounds to accept and from which the overall conclusion is inferred.

(B) It is a statement inferred from a position the argument seeks to defend.

(C) It is the overall conclusion in favor of which the argument offers evidence.

(D) It is an allegedly untenable consequence of a view rejected in the argument's overall conclusion.

(E) It is a premise offered in support of an intermediate conclusion of the argument.

18. Blogger: Traditionally, newspapers have taken objectivity to be an essential of good journalism. However, today's newer media are more inclined to try to create a stir with openly partisan reporting. This contrast in journalistic standards is best understood in terms of differing business strategies. The newer media outlets need to differentiate themselves in a crowded marketplace. The standard of objectivity developed primarily among newspapers with no serious rivals, so the most important objective was to avoid offending potential readers.

Which one of the following is an assumption required by the blogger's argument?

(A) Journalists at traditional newspapers are just as partisan as journalists who work for newer media outlets.

(B) People prefer objective reporting to partisan reporting that merely reinforces their own partisan leanings.

(C) The newer media outlets are increasing in popularity at the expense of traditional newspapers.

(D) Newspapers have regarded objective reporting as less likely to offend people than openly partisan reporting.

(E) There can be no basis for taking objectivity to be an essential journalistic standard.

19. Any government practice that might facilitate the abuse of power should not be undertaken except in cases in which there is a compelling reason to do so. The keeping of government secrets is one such practice. Though government officials are sometimes justified in keeping secrets, too often they keep secrets for insubstantial reasons, and in so doing they wind up enabling abuses of power. When government officials conceal from the public the very fact that they are keeping a secret, this practice opens up even greater opportunity for abuse.

Which one of the following can be properly inferred from the statements above?

(A) In most cases in which government officials conceal information from the public, they are not justified in doing so.

(B) In those cases in which government officials have a compelling reason to keep a secret, doing so does not facilitate an abuse of power.

(C) A government official who justifiably keeps a secret should not conceal its existence without having a compelling reason to do so.

(D) Government officials who conceal information without a compelling reason are thereby guilty of an abuse of power.

(E) Government officials should keep information secret only if doing so does not make it easier for those officials to abuse their power.

GO ON TO THE NEXT PAGE.

20. According to a theory embraced by some contemporary musicians, music is simply a series of sounds, bereft of meaning. But these musicians, because they understand that their theory is radically nonconformist, encourage audience acceptance by prefacing their performances with explanations of their intentions. Thus, even their own music fails to conform to their theory.

Which one of the following, if assumed, enables the argument's conclusion to be properly drawn?

(A) The human ability to think symbolically and to invest anything with meaning makes it very difficult to create music that has no meaning.

(B) It will be possible for musicians to create music that means nothing only when listeners are able to accept such a theory of music.

(C) The fact that music is distinguishable from a random series of sounds only when it has meaning makes music with meaning more appealing to audiences than music without meaning.

(D) Music that opposes current popular conceptions of music is less likely to be enjoyed by audiences than is music that accords with such conceptions.

(E) Musicians whose music has no meaning do not preface their performances with explanations of their intentions.

21. Evolution does not always optimize survival of an organism. Male moose evolved giant antlers as a way of fighting other males for mates, giving those with the largest antlers an evolutionary advantage. But those antlers also make it harder to escape predators, since they can easily get tangled in trees. All male moose would be better off with antlers half the current size: they would all be less vulnerable to predators, and those with the largest antlers would maintain their relative advantage.

Which one of the following is a technique of reasoning used in the argument?

(A) citing an example to cast doubt on a competing argument

(B) employing an analogy in order to dispute a generalization

(C) challenging a general claim by presenting a counterexample

(D) disputing the relevance of an example thought to support an opposing view

(E) undermining a claim by showing that it is self-contradictory

22. Biologist: When bacteria of a particular species are placed in a test tube that has different areas lit with different colors of light, the bacteria move only into the areas lit with a particular shade of red. The bacteria contain chlorophyll, a chemical that allows them to produce energy more effectively from this color of light than from any other. This suggests that the bacteria detect this color of light by monitoring how much energy their chlorophyll is producing.

Which one of the following, if true, most weakens the biologist's argument?

(A) If the chlorophyll is removed from the bacteria, but the bacteria are otherwise unharmed, they no longer show any tendency to move into the areas lit with the particular shade of red.

(B) The bacteria show little tendency to move into areas containing light in colors other than the particular shade of red, even if their chlorophyll can produce some energy from light in those colors.

(C) The areas of the test tube lit with the particular shade of red favored by the bacteria are no warmer, on average, than areas lit with other colors.

(D) The bacteria show no tendency to move into areas lit with blue even when those areas are lit so brightly that the bacteria's chlorophyll produces as much energy in those areas as it does in the red areas.

(E) There are species of bacteria that do not contain chlorophyll but do move into areas lit with particular colors when placed in a test tube lit with different colors in different places.

GO ON TO THE NEXT PAGE.

23. If a piece of legislation is the result of negotiation and compromise between competing interest groups, it will not satisfy any of those groups. So, we can see that the recently enacted trade agreement represents a series of compromises among the various interest groups that are concerned with it, because all of those groups are clearly unhappy with it.

Which one of the following most accurately describes a logical flaw in the argument?

(A) It draws a conclusion that is merely a disguised restatement of one of its premises.

(B) It concludes that a condition is necessary for a certain result merely from the claim that the condition leads to that result.

(C) It relies on understanding a key term in a quite different way in the conclusion from the way that term is understood in the premises.

(D) It takes for granted that no piece of legislation can ever satisfy all competing interest groups.

(E) It bases a conclusion about a particular case on a general principle that concerns a different kind of case.

24. After a nuclear power plant accident, researchers found radioactive isotopes of iodine, tellurium, and cesium—but no heavy isotopes—in the atmosphere downwind. This material came either from spent fuel rods or from the plant's core. Spent fuel rods never contain significant quantities of tellurium isotopes. Radioactive material ejected into the atmosphere directly from the core would include heavy isotopes. After the accident, steam, which may have been in contact with the core, was released from the plant. The core contains iodine, tellurium, and cesium isotopes, which are easily dissolved by steam.

Of the following statements, which one is most strongly supported by the information above?

(A) Radioactive material ejected into the environment directly from a nuclear power plant's core would not include tellurium isotopes.

(B) The radioactive material detected by the researchers was carried into the atmosphere by the steam that was released from the plant.

(C) The nuclear power plant's spent fuel rods were not damaged.

(D) The researchers found some radioactive material from spent fuel rods as well as some material that was ejected into the atmosphere directly from the plant's core.

(E) Spent fuel rods do not contain heavy isotopes in significant quantities.

25. If ecology and the physical sciences were evaluated by the same criteria, ecology would fail to be a successful science because it cannot be captured by a set of simple laws. But ecology is a successful science, although of a different sort from the physical sciences. Therefore, it clearly is not being evaluated by means of the criteria used to evaluate the physical sciences.

Which one of the following arguments is most similar in its reasoning to the argument above?

(A) If sales taxes are increased, then either the price of woodchips will go up and the consumer will have to pay more for them, or the woodchip industry will disappear. But the market cannot bear an increase in the price of woodchips, so the woodchip industry will disappear.

(B) If this gallery could borrow some of Matisse's early works, then, together with its own permanent collection of Matisse, the gallery could have the largest exhibition of Matisse ever. But there is no demand for larger exhibitions of Matisse's work. Therefore, no gallery will be inclined to lend their early Matisses to this gallery.

(C) If cars of the future are made of lighter and stronger materials, then the number of fatalities due to driving accidents will be drastically reduced. It is obvious that cars will be made of lighter and stronger materials in the future. Therefore, the number of fatalities due to driving accidents will be drastically reduced.

(D) If physicists attempted research in the social sciences, they would probably be as successful in those areas as researchers who restrict their concentration to the social sciences. However, physicists rarely attempt social science research. Therefore, physicists are not among the most successful researchers in the social sciences.

(E) If any economic theory were an adequate description of the principles according to which economies operate, then it would be possible to make accurate economic forecasts. But accurate economic forecasts cannot be made. Therefore, no economic theory is an adequate description of the principles according to which economies operate.

S T O P

IF YOU FINISH BEFORE TIME IS CALLED, YOU MAY CHECK YOUR WORK ON THIS SECTION ONLY.
DO NOT WORK ON ANY OTHER SECTION IN THE TEST.

SECTION IV

Time—35 minutes

23 Questions

Directions: Each group of questions in this section is based on a set of conditions. In answering some of the questions, it may be useful to draw a rough diagram. Choose the response that most accurately and completely answers each question and blacken the corresponding space on your answer sheet.

Questions 1–6

A new magazine is assigning photo essays to be featured in its first five monthly issues, one essay per issue. Three of the essays will have a rural theme and two will have an urban theme. Each essay will be assigned to a different one of five photographers: Fetter, Gonzalez, Howland, Jordt, and Kim. The assignment of photographers and themes to issues is subject to the following constraints:

The essay featured in the first issue must have a rural theme.
Kim's essay must be featured in the issue immediately preceding the issue in which Fetter's essay is featured.
Fetter's essay cannot have the same type of theme as Kim's.
Gonzalez's essay must be featured in the third issue.
Jordt's essay must have an urban theme.

1. Which one of the following is an acceptable assignment of photographers to issues, listed in order from the first issue to the fifth?

(A) Fetter, Jordt, Gonzalez, Kim, Howland
(B) Gonzalez, Kim, Fetter, Jordt, Howland
(C) Howland, Kim, Gonzalez, Fetter, Jordt
(D) Jordt, Howland, Gonzalez, Kim, Fetter
(E) Kim, Fetter, Gonzalez, Jordt, Howland

GO ON TO THE NEXT PAGE.

2. Which one of the following could be true?

(A) Fetter's essay is featured in the issue immediately preceding the issue in which Jordt's essay is featured.

(B) Gonzalez's essay is featured in the issue immediately preceding the issue in which Howland's essay is featured.

(C) Howland's essay is featured in the issue immediately preceding the issue in which Kim's essay is featured.

(D) Jordt's essay is featured in the issue immediately preceding the issue in which Kim's essay is featured.

(E) Kim's essay is featured in the issue immediately preceding the issue in which Gonzalez's essay is featured.

3. If the essay featured in the fourth issue has an urban theme, then any of the following could be true EXCEPT:

(A) Fetter's essay is featured in the second issue.
(B) Fetter's essay is featured in the fifth issue.
(C) Howland's essay is featured in the fourth issue.
(D) Howland's essay is featured in the fifth issue.
(E) Jordt's essay is featured in the fourth issue.

4. Which one of the following must be true?

(A) The essay featured in the third issue has an urban theme.
(B) The essay featured in the fifth issue has a rural theme.
(C) Fetter's essay has an urban theme.
(D) Gonzalez's essay has a rural theme.
(E) Kim's essay has a rural theme.

5. Any of the following could be featured in the fourth issue EXCEPT:

(A) an essay by Fetter that has a rural theme
(B) an essay by Howland that has a rural theme
(C) an essay by Kim that has a rural theme
(D) an essay by Jordt that has an urban theme
(E) an essay by Kim that has an urban theme

6. Which one of the following, if substituted for the constraint that Fetter's essay cannot have the same type of theme as Kim's, would have the same effect in determining the assignment of photographers and themes to issues?

(A) Howland's essay must have a rural theme.
(B) Gonzalez's essay and Howland's essay must both have a rural theme.
(C) Fetter's essay cannot have the same type of theme as Jordt's.
(D) Jordt's essay must be featured in an issue immediately following an issue whose essay has a rural theme.
(E) Kim's essay must have the same type of theme as Gonzalez's essay or Howland's essay, but not both.

GO ON TO THE NEXT PAGE.

Questions 7–11

A concert organizer is planning the order in which exactly seven musicians—Lowe, Miller, Nadel, Otero, Parker, Sen, and Thomas—will perform. The musicians will perform consecutively, one at a time. The order of the performances is constrained by the following conditions:

Lowe must perform earlier than Nadel.

Miller must perform earlier than Thomas.

There must be exactly one performance between the performances of Lowe and Otero, whether or not Lowe performs earlier than Otero.

There must be exactly one performance between the performances of Miller and Parker, whether or not Miller performs earlier than Parker.

Parker must perform either first or seventh.

7. Which one of the following could be true?
   (A) Miller performs fourth.
   (B) Nadel performs first.
   (C) Otero performs fifth.
   (D) Sen performs seventh.
   (E) Thomas performs second.

GO ON TO THE NEXT PAGE.

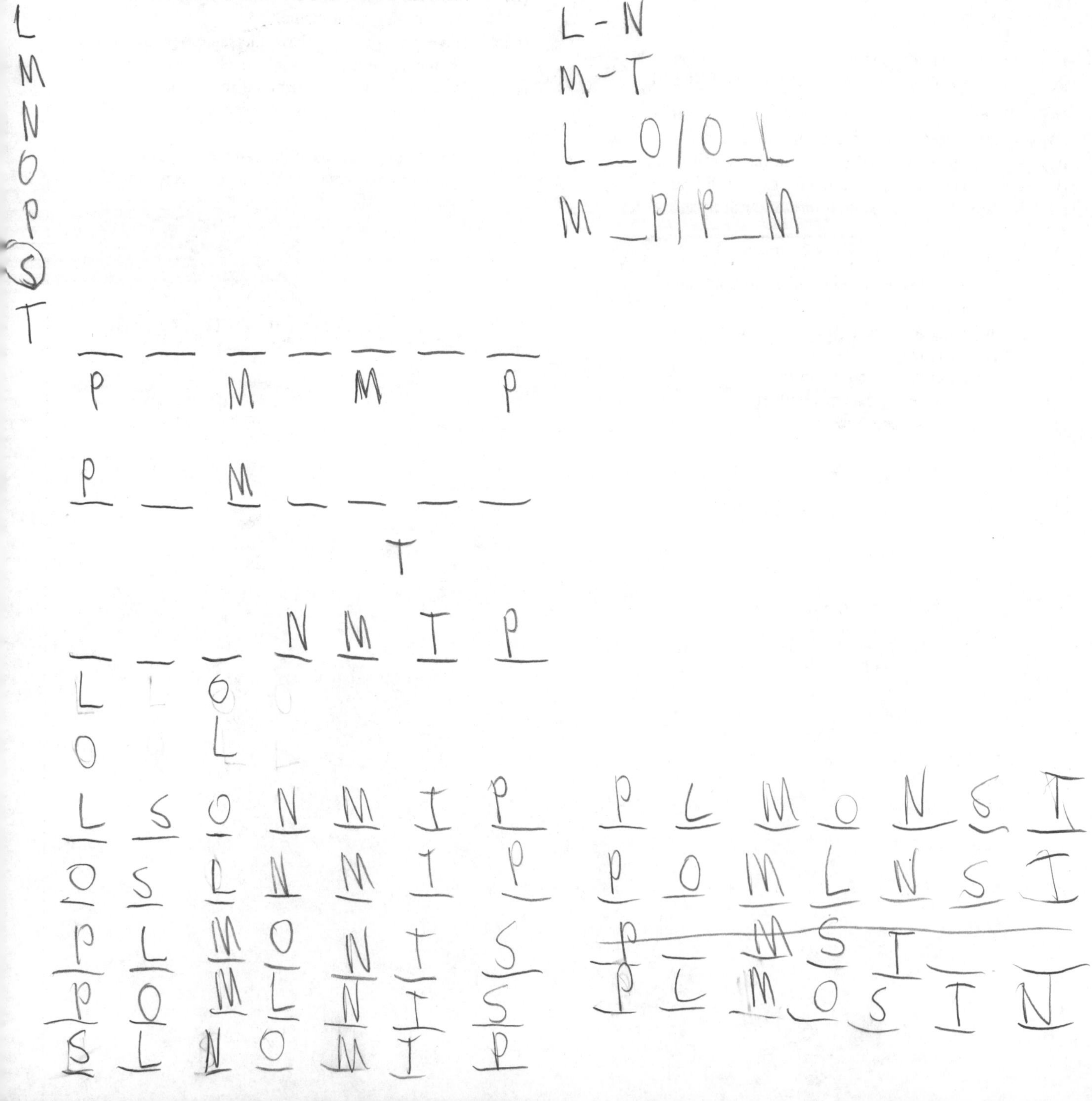

[Handwritten work:]

L-N
M-T
L_O/O_L
M_P/P_M

L M N O P S T

[handwritten diagrams of orderings]

P _ M _ M _ P
P _ M _ _ _ _
      T
_ _ _ N M T P
L   L   O
        L
L S O N M T P
O S L N M T P
P L M O N T S
P O M L N T S
S L N O M T P

P L M O N S T
P O M L N S T
P _ M S T
P L M O S T N

8. If Otero performs earlier than Miller, then the fifth performer could be any of the following EXCEPT:

    (A) Lowe
    (B) Miller
    (C) Nadel
    (D) Sen
    (E) Thomas

9. Which one of the following CANNOT be the third performer?

    (A) Lowe
    (B) Miller
    (C) Nadel
    (D) Otero
    (E) Sen

10. If Sen performs immediately before Thomas, which one of the following CANNOT be true?

    (A) Lowe performs second.
    (B) Lowe performs fourth.
    (C) Sen performs fifth.
    (D) Thomas performs fifth.
    (E) Thomas performs seventh.

11. The order in which the musicians perform is completely determined if which one of the following is true?

    (A) Lowe performs fourth.
    (B) Miller performs fifth.
    (C) Nadel performs fourth.
    (D) Otero performs third.
    (E) Sen performs first.

GO ON TO THE NEXT PAGE.

Questions 12–16

The operators of an outdoor amusement center are designing an obstacle course that will consist of a sequence of six separate obstacles: a rope bridge, a spinning platform, a tunnel, a vaulting apparatus, a wall, and a zipline. The obstacles will be placed in order from start to finish (first to sixth), in accordance with the following constraints:

The spinning platform must be the third or fourth obstacle.
The wall must be placed just before the zipline.
The rope bridge cannot be placed just before or just after the vaulting apparatus.

12. Which one of the following is an acceptable sequence of obstacles in the obstacle course, in order from first to sixth?

(A) rope bridge, tunnel, spinning platform, wall, vaulting apparatus, zipline

(B) tunnel, rope bridge, vaulting apparatus, spinning platform, wall, zipline

(C) tunnel, rope bridge, wall, zipline, spinning platform, vaulting apparatus

(D) vaulting apparatus, tunnel, spinning platform, rope bridge, wall, zipline

(E) wall, zipline, spinning platform, vaulting apparatus, rope bridge, tunnel

GO ON TO THE NEXT PAGE.

13. If the tunnel is the first obstacle, which one of the following must be true?

(A) The rope bridge is the second obstacle.
(B) The rope bridge is the fourth obstacle.
(C) The spinning platform is the third obstacle.
(D) The wall is the fourth obstacle.
(E) The zipline is the sixth obstacle.

14. Which one of the following is a complete and accurate list of the positions in which the tunnel could be placed?

(A) first, second, fifth
(B) first, second, fifth, sixth
(C) first, second, third, fourth, sixth
(D) first, second, third, fifth, sixth
(E) first, second, third, fourth, fifth, sixth

15. If the rope bridge is the second obstacle, which one of the following must be true?

(A) The spinning platform is the fourth obstacle.
(B) The tunnel is the first obstacle.
(C) The vaulting apparatus is the sixth obstacle.
(D) The wall is the fourth obstacle.
(E) The zipline is the sixth obstacle.

16. If the rope bridge and the vaulting apparatus are both earlier in the sequence than the tunnel, which one of the following must be true?

(A) The spinning platform is the fourth obstacle.
(B) The tunnel is the fifth obstacle.
(C) The vaulting apparatus is the fifth obstacle.
(D) The wall is the first obstacle.
(E) The zipline is the third obstacle.

GO ON TO THE NEXT PAGE.

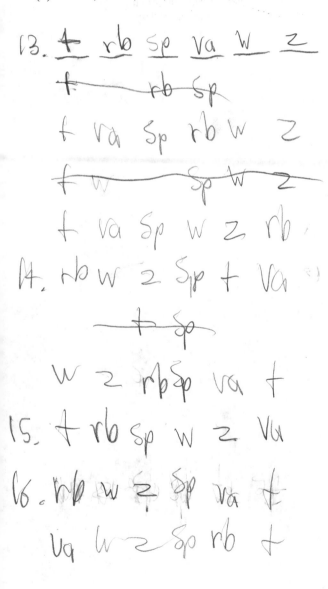

Questions 17–23

A company is sending its four product managers—Fan, Gleeson, Haley, and Ibañez—to visit three cities—Manila, Sydney, and Tokyo. Each manager will visit at least one of the cities, and each city will be visited by exactly two of the managers. The managers will be assigned to visit the cities according to the following conditions:

    Ibañez must visit exactly two of the cities.
    Fan and Haley cannot visit the same city as each other.
    If Manila is visited by Gleeson, then Tokyo must be
     visited by Haley.
    Gleeson cannot visit Sydney.

17. Which one of the following could be the assignment of managers to cities?

(A)   Manila: Fan and Gleeson
       Sydney: Haley and Ibañez
       Tokyo: Gleeson and Haley

(B)   Manila: Fan and Ibañez
       Sydney: Gleeson and Haley
       Tokyo: Haley and Ibañez

(C)   Manila: Gleeson and Haley
       Sydney: Fan and Ibañez
       Tokyo: Haley and Ibañez

(D)   Manila: Gleeson and Haley
       Sydney: Haley and Ibañez
       Tokyo: Fan and Ibañez

(E)   Manila: Gleeson and Ibañez
       Sydney: Haley and Ibañez
       Tokyo: Fan and Haley

GO ON TO THE NEXT PAGE.

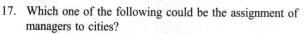

[Handwritten work in left margin:]

F
G
H
I

M : S
S :
T :

I̶ I
F̶/H̶

M: G — T: H

S: G̶

[Handwritten work right/center:]

18. M: I | G, I
    S: I | I, F
    T: G, H | F, G | G, H
        X   X   ✓

19. M: G, F | H, I | F, F | H, I
    S: F, | I, F | H, I | H, I
    T: H, I | H, G | G, H | F, G
        X   ✓   ✓   ✓

20. M: F, H | I, F
    S: I, G | H, G
    T: G, I | I, G
       X   X 22.

21. M: G, H | G, I | H, I | F, G | H, F
    S: I, F | F | F | H, I | H, I
    T: H, I | I, H | I, G | I, F | I, G
      ✓   X   X   X   ✓

18. Which one of the following, if true, completely determines the assignment of managers to cities?

    (A)   Fan visits exactly two of the cities.
    (B)   Gleeson visits exactly two of the cities.
    (C)   Haley visits exactly two of the cities.
    (D)   Fan and Gleeson visit Tokyo.
    (E)   Gleeson and Haley visit Tokyo.

19. Which one of the following must be true?

    (A)   Fan visits Sydney.
    (B)   Gleeson visits Tokyo.
    (C)   Haley visits Tokyo.
    (D)   Ibañez visits Sydney.
    (E)   Ibañez visits Tokyo.

20. Which one of the following could be true?

    (A)   Fan and Ibañez visit Manila.
    (B)   Gleeson and Ibañez visit Tokyo.
    (C)   Ibañez visits Manila and Tokyo.
    (D)   Fan visits all three of the cities.
    (E)   Haley visits all three of the cities.

21. If one of the cities is visited by both Gleeson and Haley, which one of the following must be true?

    (A)   Fan visits Manila.
    (B)   Fan visits Sydney.
    (C)   Gleeson visits Manila.
    (D)   Haley visits Tokyo.
    (E)   Ibañez visits Tokyo.

22. If Ibañez visits Tokyo, which one of the following could be true?

    (A)   Fan and Gleeson visit Manila.
    (B)   Gleeson and Ibañez visit Manila.
    (C)   Haley and Ibañez visit Manila.
    (D)   Fan visits Manila and Tokyo.
    (E)   Haley visits Manila and Sydney.

23. Which one of the following, if substituted for the condition that Fan and Haley cannot visit the same city as each other, would have the same effect in determining the assignment of managers to cities?

    (A)   Gleeson and Ibañez cannot visit the same city as each other.
    (B)   If Sydney is visited by Fan, then Tokyo must be visited by Haley.
    (C)   Tokyo must be visited by either Fan or Haley, but cannot be visited by both.
    (D)   Any city that Fan does not visit must be visited by Haley.
    (E)   Any city that Ibañez does not visit must be visited by Gleeson.

S T O P

IF YOU FINISH BEFORE TIME IS CALLED, YOU MAY CHECK YOUR WORK ON THIS SECTION ONLY.
DO NOT WORK ON ANY OTHER SECTION IN THE TEST.

Acknowledgment is made to the following sources from which material has been adapted for use in this test booklet:

Mirko Bagaric, "Double Punishment and Punishing Character" in *Criminal Justice Ethics*. ©2000 by Institute for Criminal Justice Ethics.

Daniel Ben-Ami, "Delving into the Mind of the Technocrat" in *spiked* website. ©2000–2012 by *spiked*. http://www.spiked-online.com/index.php/site/reviewofbooks_article/12149.

Hans-Dieter Betz, "Unconventional Water Detection: Field Test of the Dowsing Technique in Dry Zones: Part 1" in *Journal of Scientific Exploration*. ©1998 by Society for Scientific Exploration.

Edward K. Cheng, "Should Judges Do Independent Research on Scientific Issues?" in *Judicature*. ©2006 by American Judicature Society.

Alison Gopnik, "How We Know Our Minds: The Illusion of First-Person Knowledge of Intentionality." ©1993 by Cambridge University Press.

David Hajdu, "Wynton's Blues." ©March 2003 by the Atlantic Monthly.

Sharon Keller and Donald Cimics, "Appellate Courts Should Resist the Temptation to Conduct Their Own Independent Research on Scientific Issues" in *Judicature*. ©2006 by American Judicature Society.

Wait for the supervisor's instructions before you open the page to the topic.
Please print and sign your name and write the date in the designated spaces below.

Time: 35 Minutes

General Directions

ll have 35 minutes in which to plan and write an essay on the topic inside. Read the topic and the accompanying directions carefully.
ll probably find it best to spend a few minutes considering the topic and organizing your thoughts before you begin writing. In your essay,
e to develop your ideas fully, leaving time, if possible, to review what you have written. **Do not write on a topic other than the one**
ied. Writing on a topic of your own choice is not acceptable.

cial knowledge is required or expected for this writing exercise. Law schools are interested in the reasoning, clarity, organization,
ge usage, and writing mechanics displayed in your essay. How well you write is more important than how much you write.

e your essay to the blocked, lined area on the front and back of the separate Writing Sample Response Sheet. Only that area will be
uced for law schools. Be sure that your writing is legible.

Both this topic sheet and your response sheet must be turned in to the testing staff
before you leave the room.

Topic Code	Print Your Full Name Here		
149186	Last	First	M.I.

Date	Sign Your Name Here
/ /	

LSAC®

Scratch Paper
Do not write your essay in this space.

LSAT® Writing Sample Topic

Directions: The scenario presented below describes two choices, either one of which can be supported on the basis of the information give
Your essay should consider both choices and argue for one over the other, based on the two specified criteria and the facts provided. Ther
is no "right" or "wrong" choice: a reasonable argument can be made for either.

A city councilor in a medium-sized city is deciding whether to support or oppose a proposal that would combine a decrease in the city
sales tax with the transformation of a portion of a highway in the councilor's district into a toll road. Using the facts below, write an essay in
which you argue for one option over the other based on the following two criteria:

- The councilor wants the district to be an attractive shopping destination for people coming in from the suburbs.
- The councilor wants the continued support of voters in the district.

Currently, the city's sales tax is slightly higher than that of the surrounding suburbs. The sales tax applies only to goods that are not
deemed essential. Most of the goods bought by non-locals are subject to the tax. The highway is the most popular route into the city. Altern
routes generally run at a third of the speed, except during rush hour when the highway slows to a crawl. The stretch of highway targeted by
the proposal lies entirely within the councilor's district. Shopping districts have developed at most of the exits along this stretch. Most of the
employees of these retail businesses live in the councilor's district.

Institution of the proposal is not expected to change the total revenue collected by the city. The sales tax would be decreased to sligh
less than that of the surrounding suburbs. The stretch of highway would be the first toll road in the metropolitan area. Polls show that the
majority of residents in the councilor's district believe it would be unfair to have to pay a toll. In other cities, dissatisfaction with tolls has falle
after they have been imposed. Traffic is expected to move more quickly during rush hour if a toll is imposed.

WPAA

Scratch Paper
Do not write your essay in this space.

Writing Sample Response Sheet

DO NOT WRITE IN THIS SPACE

Begin your essay in the lined area below.
Continue on the back if you need more space.

COMPUTING YOUR SCORE

Directions:

. Use the Answer Key on the next page to check your answers.

. Use the Scoring Worksheet below to compute your raw score.

. Use the Score Conversion Chart to convert your raw score into the 120–180 scale.

Scoring Worksheet

1. Enter the number of questions you answered correctly in each section.

NT

Number Correct

SECTION I................. 20/27
SECTION II............... 19/26
SECTION III............. 17/23
SECTION IV 23/23

2. Enter the sum here: 79

This is your Raw Score.

Conversion Chart
For Converting Raw Score to the 120–180 LSAT Scaled Score
LSAT Form 8LSN127

Reported Score	Raw Score Lowest	Raw Score Highest
180	100	101
179	*	*
178	99	99
177	98	98
176	97	97
175	*	*
174	96	96
173	95	95
172	94	94
171	93	93
170	92	92
169	91	91
168	89	90
167	88	88
166	86	87
165	85	85
164	83	84
163	81	82
162	79	80
161	77	78
160	75	76
159	73	74
158	71	72
157	69	70
156	67	68
155	65	66
154	63	64
153	61	62
152	59	60
151	57	58
150	55	56
149	53	54
148	51	52
147	50	50
146	48	49
145	46	47
144	44	45
143	43	43
142	41	42
141	40	40
140	38	39
139	37	37
138	35	36
137	34	34
136	33	33
135	32	32
134	31	31
133	30	30
132	29	29
131	28	28
130	27	27
129	26	26
128	25	25
127	*	*
126	24	24
125	23	23
124	22	22
123	*	*
122	21	21
121	20	20
120	0	19

*There is no raw score that will produce this scaled score for this form.

ANSWER KEY

SECTION I

1.	D	8.	B	15.	C	22.	A
2.	C	9.	C	16.	A	23.	D
3.	D	10.	E	17.	D	24.	B
4.	B	11.	A	18.	B	25.	C
5.	E	12.	D	19.	D	26.	B
6.	A	13.	C	20.	E	27.	D
7.	E	14.	D	21.	C		

SECTION II

1.	D	8.	D	15.	D	22.	D
2.	B	9.	C	16.	A	23.	A
3.	D	10.	E	17.	D	24.	C
4.	B	11.	B	18.	A	25.	D
5.	E	12.	A	19.	C	26.	E
6.	B	13.	A	20.	A		
7.	C	14.	C	21.	B		

SECTION III

1.	E	8.	B	15.	A	22.	D
2.	C	9.	B	16.	C	23.	B
3.	A	10.	B	17.	D	24.	B
4.	E	11.	A	18.	D	25.	E
5.	D	12.	A	19.	C		
6.	E	13.	B	20.	E		
7.	B	14.	A	21.	C		

SECTION IV

1.	E	8.	A	15.	B	22.	A
2.	B	9.	E	16.	A	23.	E
3.	C	10.	D	17.	C		
4.	D	11.	E	18.	B		
5.	A	12.	D	19.	D		
6.	B	13.	C	20.	A		
7.	D	14.	B	21.	D		

LSAT® PREP TOOLS

The Official LSAT SuperPrep II™

SuperPrep II contains everything you need to prepare for the LSAT—a guide to all three LSAT question types, three actual LSATs, explanations for all questions in the three practice tests, answer keys, writing samples, and score-conversion tables, plus invaluable test-taking instructions to help with pacing and timing. SuperPrep has long been our most comprehensive LSAT preparation book, and SuperPrep II is even better. The practice tests in SuperPrep II are PrepTest 62 (December 2010 LSAT), PrepTest 63 (June 2011 LSAT), and one test that has never before been disclosed.

With this book you can

- Practice on genuine LSAT questions
- Review explanations for right and wrong answers
- Target specific categories for intensive review
- Simulate actual LSAT conditions

LSAC sets the standard for LSAT prep—and SuperPrep II raises the bar!

Available at your favorite bookseller.

LSAC.org

General Directions for the LSAT Answer Sheet

This portion of the test consists of five multiple-choice sections, each with a time limit of 35 minutes. The supervisor will tell you when to begin and end each section. If you finish a section before time is called, you may check your work on that section **only**; do not turn to any other section of the test book and do not work on any other section either in the test book or on the answer sheet.

There are several different types of questions on the test, and each question type has its own directions. **Be sure you understand the directions for each question type before attempting to answer any questions in that section.**

Not everyone will finish all the questions in the time allowed. Do not hurry, but work steadily and as quickly as you can without sacrificing accuracy. You are advised to use your time effectively. If a question seems too difficult, go on to the next one and return to the difficult question after completing the section. **MARK THE BEST ANSWER YOU CAN FOR EVERY QUESTION. NO DEDUCTIONS WILL BE MADE FOR WRONG ANSWERS. YOUR SCORE WILL BE BASED ONLY ON THE NUMBER OF QUESTIONS YOU ANSWER CORRECTLY.**

ALL YOUR ANSWERS MUST BE MARKED ON THE ANSWER SHEET. Answer spaces for each question are lettered to correspond with the letters of the potential answers to each question in the test book. After you have decided which of the answers is correct, blacken the corresponding space on the answer sheet. **BE SURE THAT EACH MARK IS BLACK AND COMPLETELY FILLS THE ANSWER SPACE.** Give only one answer to each question. If you change an answer, be sure that all previous marks are **erased completely.** Since the answer sheet is machine scored, incomplete erasures may be interpreted as intended answers. **ANSWERS RECORDED IN THE TEST BOOK WILL NOT BE SCORED.**

There may be more question numbers on this answer sheet than there are questions in a section. Do not be concerned, but be certain that the section and number of the question you are answering matches the answer sheet section and question number. Additional answer spaces in any answer sheet section should be left blank. Begin your next section in the number one answer space for that section.

LSAC takes various steps to ensure that answer sheets are returned from test centers in a timely manner for processing. In the unlikely event that an answer sheet is not received, LSAC will permit the examinee either to retest at no additional fee or to receive a refund of his or her LSAT fee. **THESE REMEDIES ARE THE ONLY REMEDIES AVAILABLE IN THE UNLIKELY EVENT THAT AN ANSWER SHEET IS NOT RECEIVED BY LSAC.**

HOW DID YOU PREPARE FOR THE LSAT?
(Select all that apply.)

Responses to this item are voluntary and will be used for statistical research purposes only.

○ By using Khan Academy's official LSAT practice material.
○ By taking the free sample questions and/or free sample LSAT available on LSAC's website.
○ By working through official LSAT *PrepTest* and/or other LSAC test prep products.
○ By using LSAT prep books or software **not** published by LSAC.
○ By attending a commercial test preparation or coaching course.
○ By attending a test preparation or coaching course offered through an undergraduate institution.
○ Self study.
○ Other preparation.
○ No preparation.

CERTIFYING STATEMENT

Please write the following statement. Sign and date.

I certify that I am the examinee whose name appears on this answer sheet and that I am here to take the LSAT for the sole purpose of being considered for admission to law school. I further certify that I will neither assist nor receive assistance from any other candidate, and I agree not to copy, retain, or transmit examination questions in any form or discuss them with any other person.

_____
_____
_____
_____
_____
_____
_____
_____
_____

SIGNATURE: _____   TODAY'S DATE: ___/___/___
                                                                   MONTH DAY YEAR

DO NOT WRITE IN THIS BOX.

FOR LSAC USE ONLY   ●

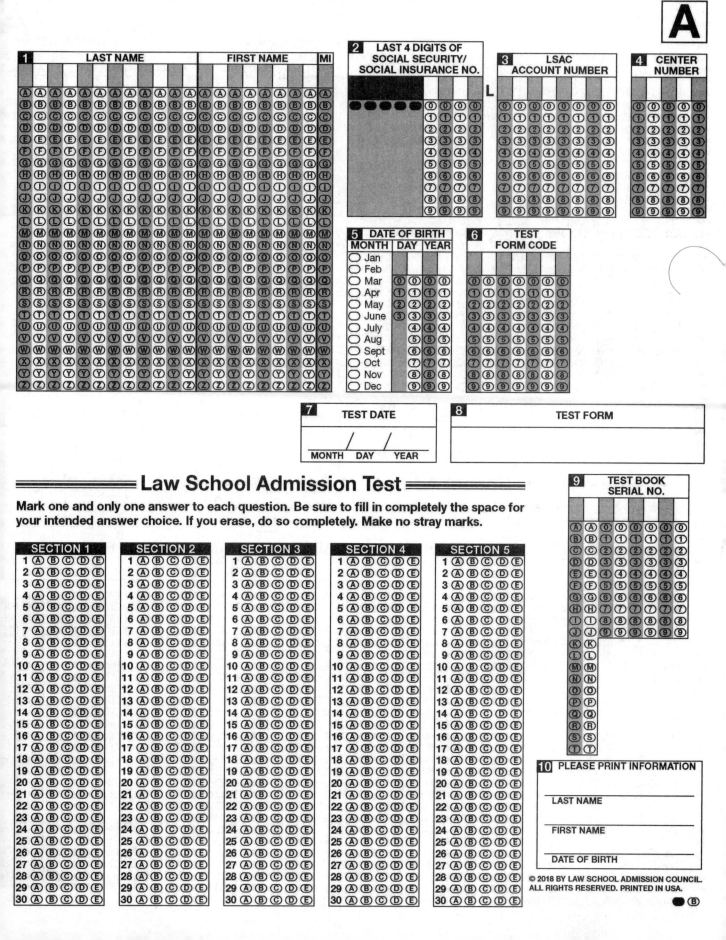

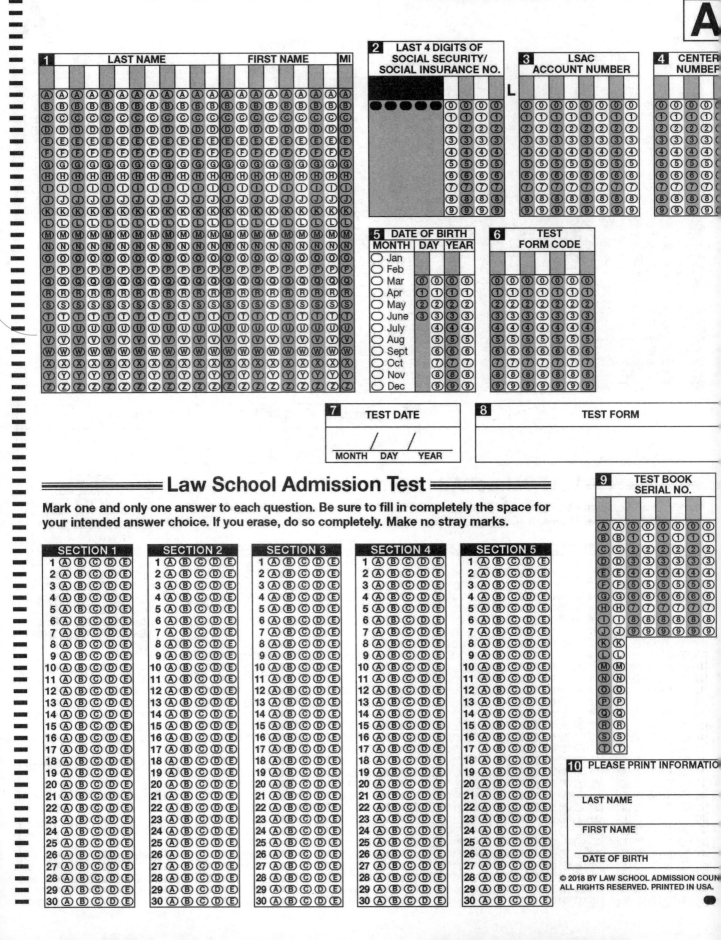

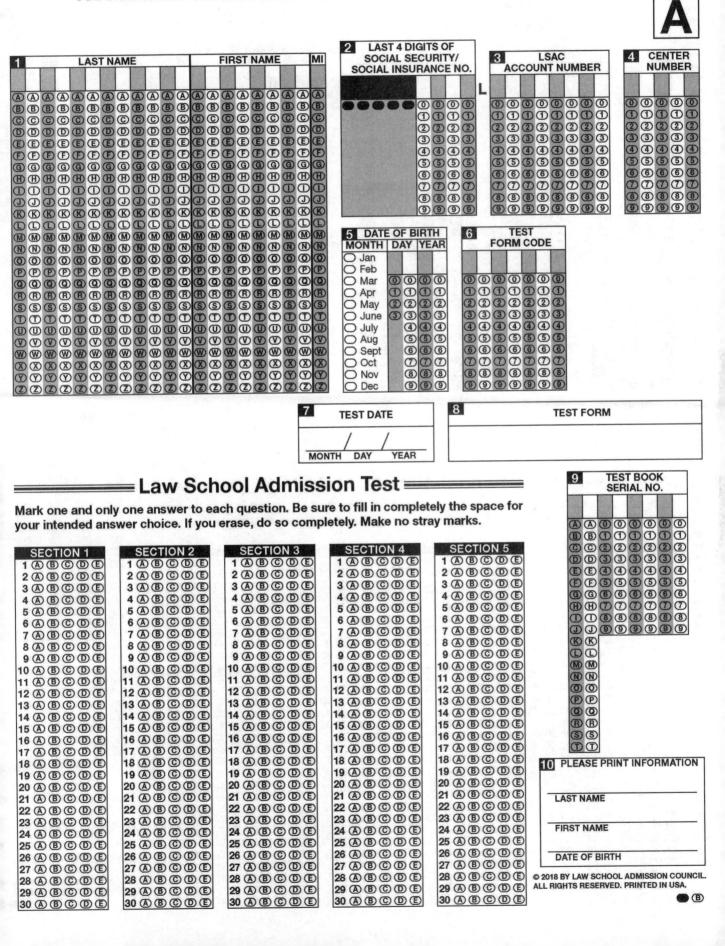

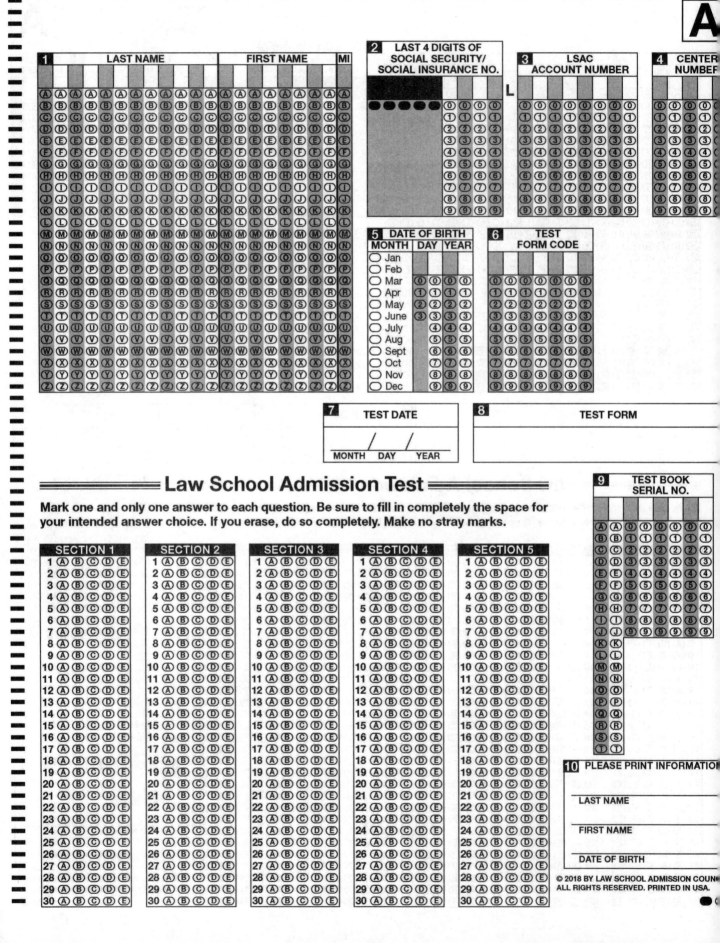

SCANTRON. EliteView™ EM-295665-4:654321

INSTRUCTIONS FOR COMPLETING THE BIOGRAPHICAL AREA ARE ON THE BACK COVER OF YOUR TEST BOOKLET.
USE ONLY A NO. 2 OR HB PENCIL TO COMPLETE THIS ANSWER SHEET. DO NOT USE INK.

A

1 LAST NAME / FIRST NAME / MI

2 LAST 4 DIGITS OF SOCIAL SECURITY/ SOCIAL INSURANCE NO.

3 LSAC ACCOUNT NUMBER

4 CENTER NUMBER

5 DATE OF BIRTH

MONTH	DAY	YEAR
Jan		
Feb		
Mar		
Apr		
May		
June		
July		
Aug		
Sept		
Oct		
Nov		
Dec		

6 TEST FORM CODE

7 TEST DATE

/ /

MONTH   DAY   YEAR

8 TEST FORM

═══ Law School Admission Test ═══

Mark one and only one answer to each question. Be sure to fill in completely the space for your intended answer choice. If you erase, do so completely. Make no stray marks.

9 TEST BOOK SERIAL NO.

SECTION 1	SECTION 2	SECTION 3	SECTION 4	SECTION 5
1 A B C D E	1 A B C D E	1 A B C D E	1 A B C D E	1 A B C D E
2 A B C D E	2 A B C D E	2 A B C D E	2 A B C D E	2 A B C D E
3 A B C D E	3 A B C D E	3 A B C D E	3 A B C D E	3 A B C D E
4 A B C D E	4 A B C D E	4 A B C D E	4 A B C D E	4 A B C D E
5 A B C D E	5 A B C D E	5 A B C D E	5 A B C D E	5 A B C D E
6 A B C D E	6 A B C D E	6 A B C D E	6 A B C D E	6 A B C D E
7 A B C D E	7 A B C D E	7 A B C D E	7 A B C D E	7 A B C D E
8 A B C D E	8 A B C D E	8 A B C D E	8 A B C D E	8 A B C D E
9 A B C D E	9 A B C D E	9 A B C D E	9 A B C D E	9 A B C D E
10 A B C D E	10 A B C D E	10 A B C D E	10 A B C D E	10 A B C D E
11 A B C D E	11 A B C D E	11 A B C D E	11 A B C D E	11 A B C D E
12 A B C D E	12 A B C D E	12 A B C D E	12 A B C D E	12 A B C D E
13 A B C D E	13 A B C D E	13 A B C D E	13 A B C D E	13 A B C D E
14 A B C D E	14 A B C D E	14 A B C D E	14 A B C D E	14 A B C D E
15 A B C D E	15 A B C D E	15 A B C D E	15 A B C D E	15 A B C D E
16 A B C D E	16 A B C D E	16 A B C D E	16 A B C D E	16 A B C D E
17 A B C D E	17 A B C D E	17 A B C D E	17 A B C D E	17 A B C D E
18 A B C D E	18 A B C D E	18 A B C D E	18 A B C D E	18 A B C D E
19 A B C D E	19 A B C D E	19 A B C D E	19 A B C D E	19 A B C D E
20 A B C D E	20 A B C D E	20 A B C D E	20 A B C D E	20 A B C D E
21 A B C D E	21 A B C D E	21 A B C D E	21 A B C D E	21 A B C D E
22 A B C D E	22 A B C D E	22 A B C D E	22 A B C D E	22 A B C D E
23 A B C D E	23 A B C D E	23 A B C D E	23 A B C D E	23 A B C D E
24 A B C D E	24 A B C D E	24 A B C D E	24 A B C D E	24 A B C D E
25 A B C D E	25 A B C D E	25 A B C D E	25 A B C D E	25 A B C D E
26 A B C D E	26 A B C D E	26 A B C D E	26 A B C D E	26 A B C D E
27 A B C D E	27 A B C D E	27 A B C D E	27 A B C D E	27 A B C D E
28 A B C D E	28 A B C D E	28 A B C D E	28 A B C D E	28 A B C D E
29 A B C D E	29 A B C D E	29 A B C D E	29 A B C D E	29 A B C D E
30 A B C D E	30 A B C D E	30 A B C D E	30 A B C D E	30 A B C D E

10 PLEASE PRINT INFORMATION

LAST NAME

FIRST NAME

DATE OF BIRTH

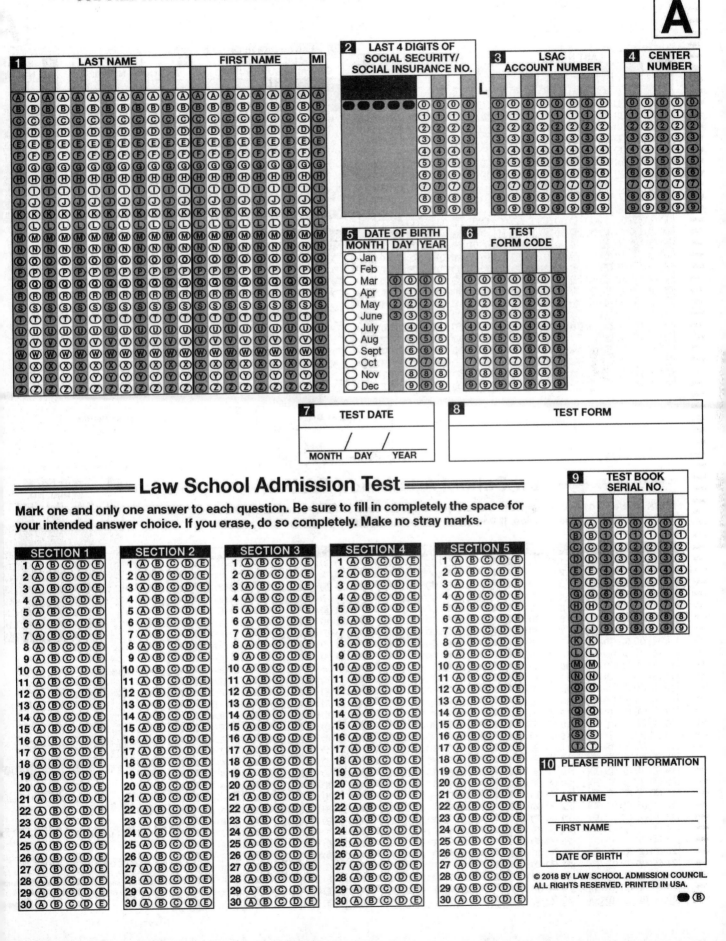

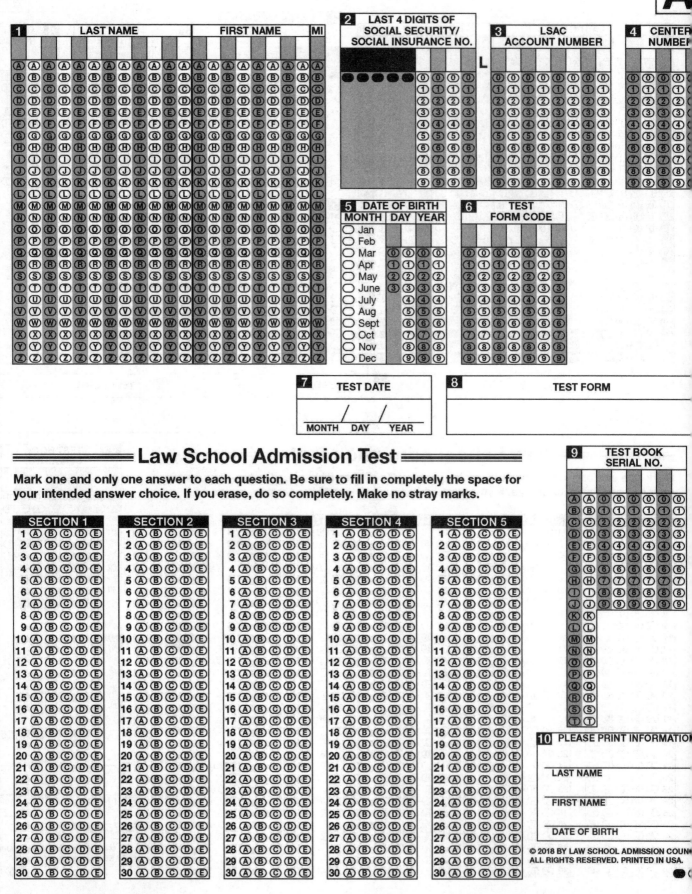

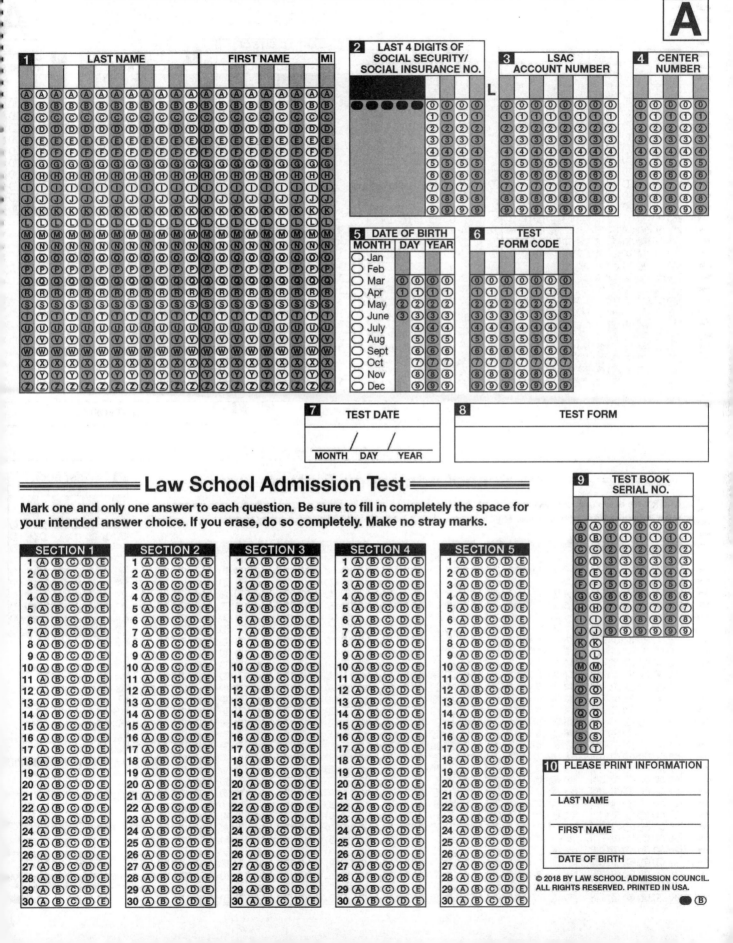

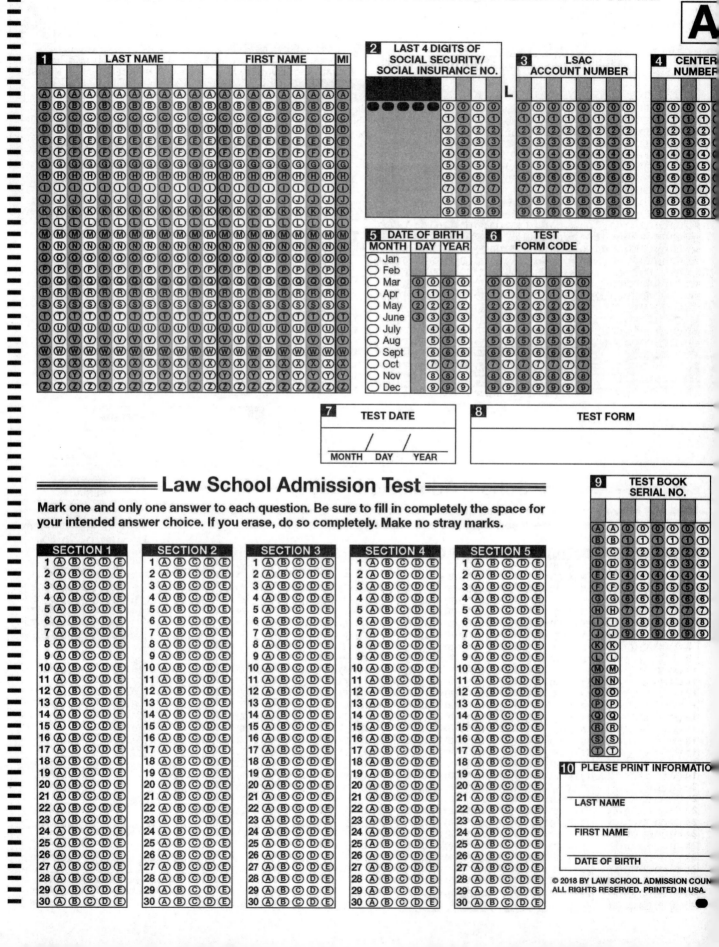

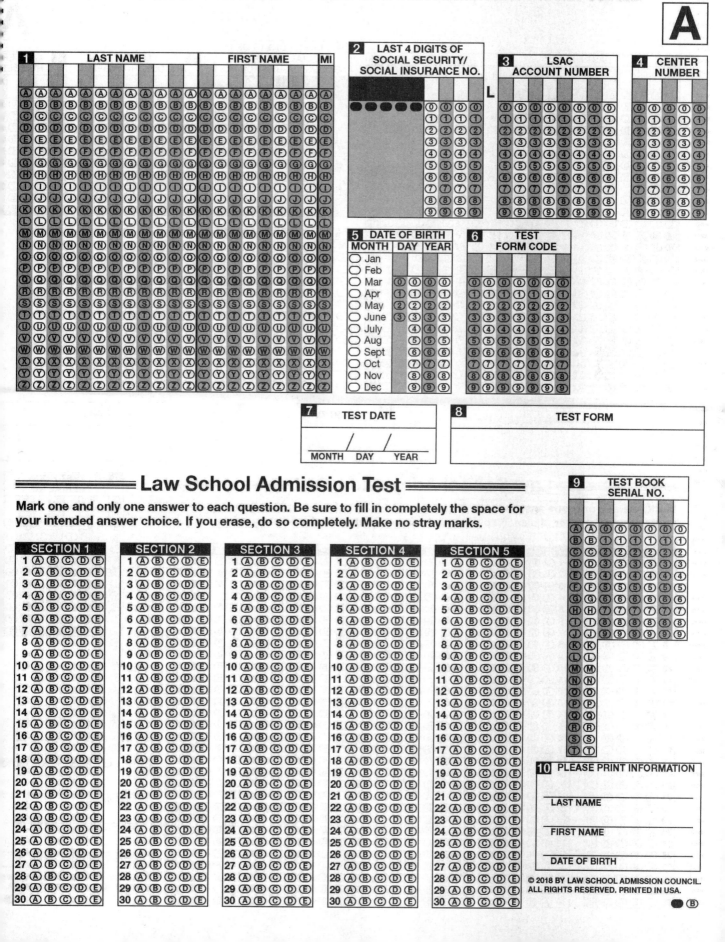

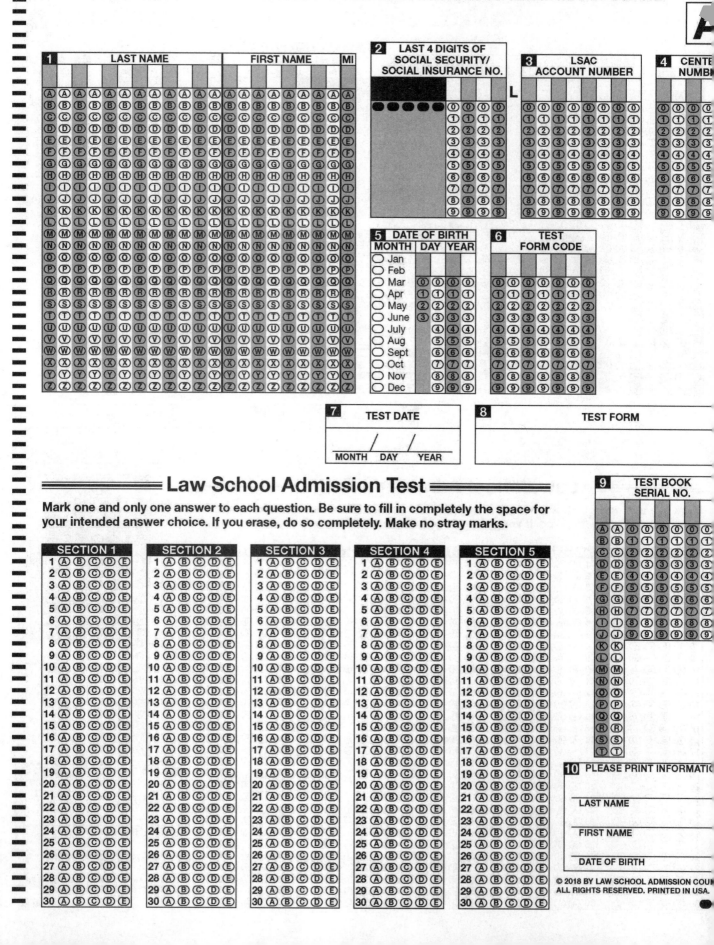

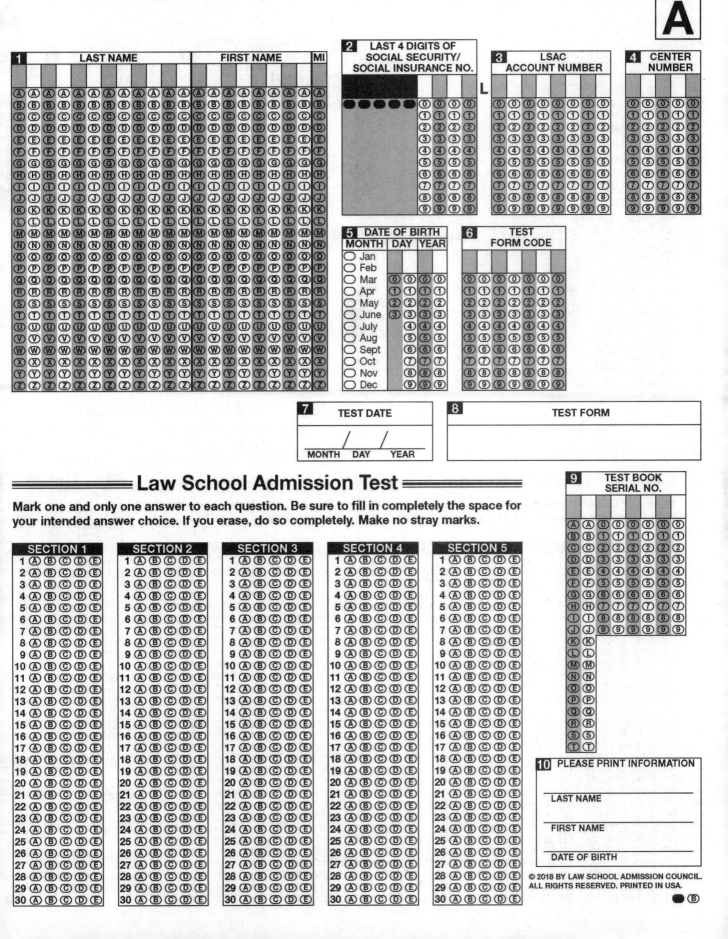

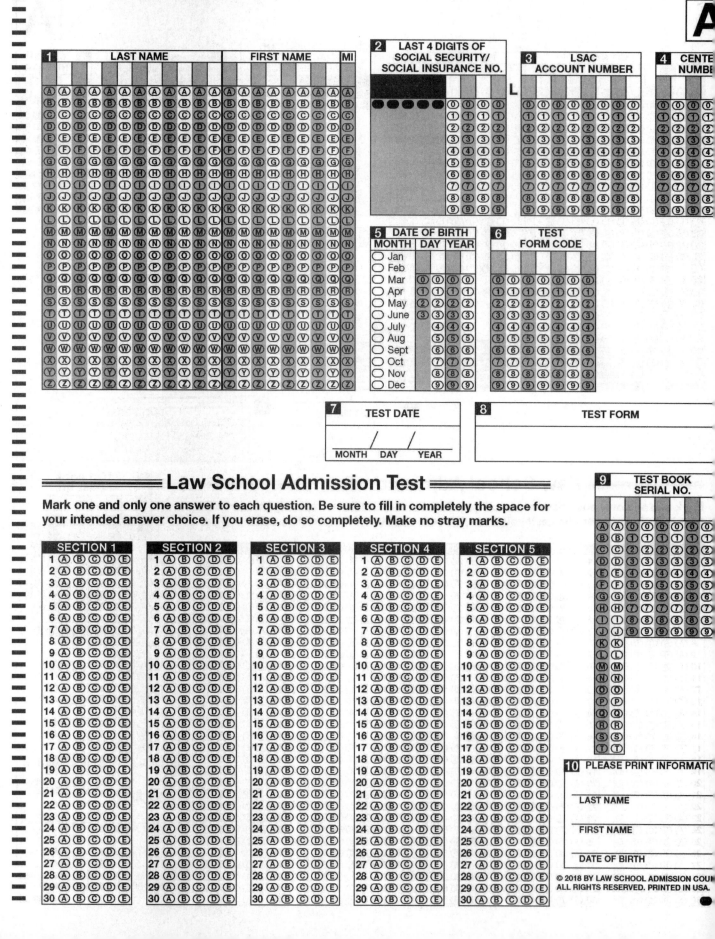

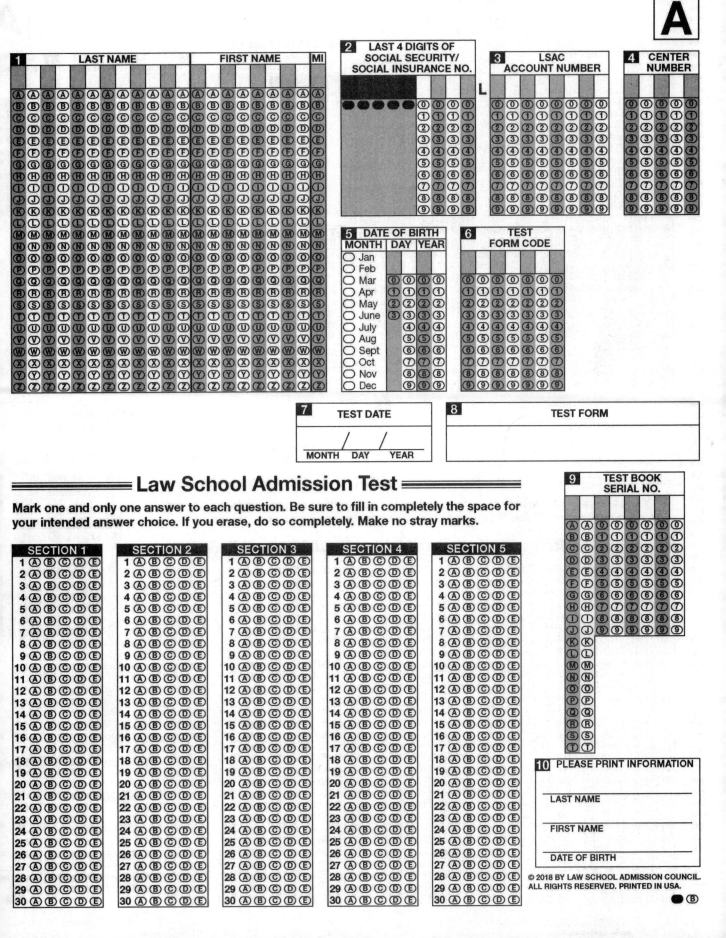

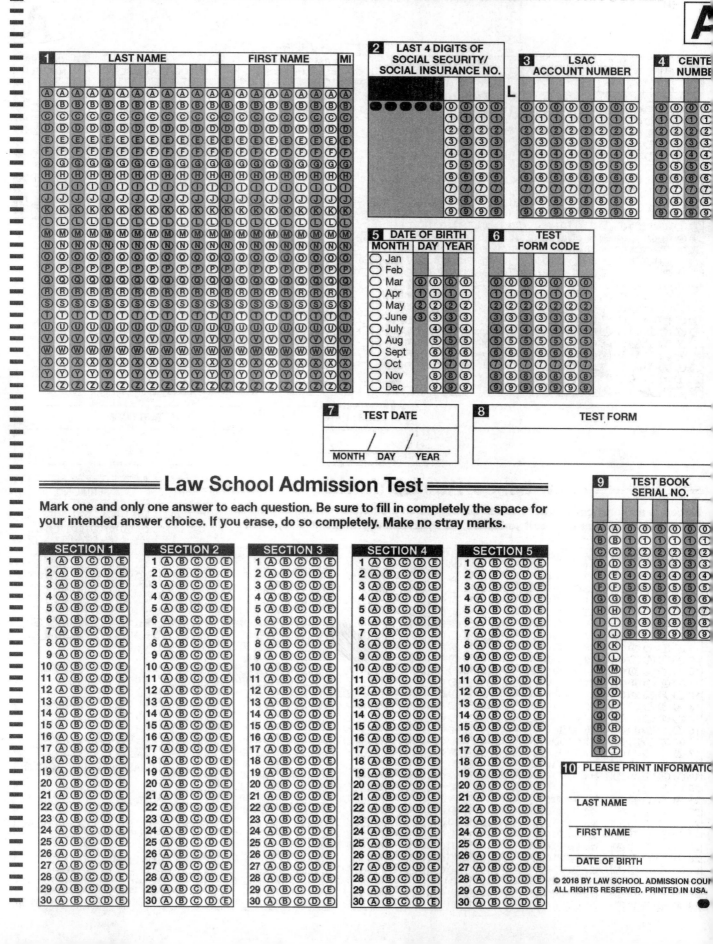